K. Hicks
Finance

W9-AUQ-358

Case Problems in Finance

Case Problems in Finance

Edited by

J. KEITH BUTTERS
*Thomas D. Casserly, Jr., Professor
of Business Administration*

WILLIAM E. FRUHAN, JR.
Professor of Business Administration

DAVID W. MULLINS, JR.
Associate Professor of Business Administration

THOMAS R. PIPER
Professor of Business Administration

*All of the
Graduate School of Business Administration
Harvard University*

 1981   Eighth edition

RICHARD D. IRWIN, INC.   *Homewood, Illinois   60430*
Irwin-Dorsey Limited   *Georgetown, Ontario   L7G 4B3*

© RICHARD D. IRWIN, INC., 1949, 1953, 1959, 1962, 1969,
1972, 1975, and 1981

All rights reserved. No part of this publication may be
reproduced, stored in a retrieval system, or transmitted,
in any form or by any means, electronic, mechanical,
photocopying, recording, or otherwise, without the prior
written permission of the publisher. The copyright on
all cases in this book unless otherwise noted is held by
the President and Fellows of Harvard College, and they
are published herein by express permission.

Case material of the Harvard Graduate School of
Business Administration is made possible by the
cooperation of business firms who may wish to remain
anonymous by having names, quantities, and other
identifying details disguised while basic relationships
are maintained. Cases are prepared as the basis for
class discussion rather than to illustrate either effective
or ineffective handling of administrative situations.

ISBN 0-256-02500-2
Library of Congress Catalog Card No. 80–84592

Printed in the United States of America

2 3 4 5 6 7 8 9 0 H 8 7 6 5 4 3 2 1

Acknowledgments

To the businessmen who contributed the material for the cases in this volume we express our sincere gratitude. In the development of these cases they gave liberally of their time, and in most instances, they made available to us facts about their businesses normally held confidential.

We wish to acknowledge our debt to Pearson Hunt, Charles M. Williams, James T. S. Porterfield, Leonard C. R. Langer, Robert F. Vandell, Alan B. Coleman, Frank L. Tucker, James E. Walter, Erich A. Helfert, and Victor L. Andrews, whose names have appeared as editors of the first four editions of this book. Their influence on the organization and objectives of the current edition will be obvious to anyone who has used the early editions of *Case Problems in Finance.*

Cases in this edition, or prior versions of these cases, were written or supervised by 19 members, or former members, of the faculty of the Harvard University Graduate School of Business Administration. Two cases were written or coauthored by James T. S. Porterfield and John G. McDonald, members of the faculty of the Stanford University Graduate School of Business. Most of the cases appearing for the first time in this edition were written by one of the editors of this volume.

In addition to the editors of earlier editions of this volume we wish to thank M. Edgar Barrett, Lee Bodenhamer, Dwight B. Crane, Robert R. Glauber, John H. McArthur, John G. McDonald, Ronald W. Moore, Powell Niland, William A. Sahlman, William W. Sihler, Lawrence E. Thompson, Richard F. Vancil, and Harold E. Wyman for permission to use cases for which they are responsible as author or supervisor. We also wish to express our appreciation to the Stanford University Graduate School of Business for permission to reprint Chem-Cal Corporation and the Midwest Communications, Inc., cases in this volume.

We also wish to extend our thanks to the many instructors and research assistants of the Harvard University Graduate School of Business Administration and to Thomas Schiff of the Stanford University Graduate School of Business who wrote or assisted in the writing of many of the cases in this volume under the supervision of senior faculty members.

Most of all we should like to express our special appreciation to Rita D. Colella and Hedwig E. Pocius for their invaluable assistance in the preparation of this volume. Their care in putting the manuscript into proper form for submission to the publisher has contributed importantly to its quality. Ms. Pocius has also taken primary responsibility for handling communications with the publisher and for reviewing the galley and page proofs as the volume has been processed for publication.

The editors assume full responsibility for the contents of this edition, but they are keenly aware of their obligation to their predecessors and associates.

Graduate School of Business Administration
Harvard University

J. Keith Butters
William E. Fruhan, Jr.
David W. Mullins, Jr.
Thomas R. Piper

Contents

Dividend Policy

PART III: INVESTMENT DECISIONS, MERGERS, AND ACQUISITIONS

Investment Decisions

Mergers and Acquisitions

PART IV: COMPREHENSIVE OVERVIEW

Comprehensive Cases

APPENDIXES

INDEX

Introduction

Many readers may be meeting the case method of instruction for the first time. More often than not the experience is a frustrating one, for cases typically end at the critical point—in the words of some, "just when they seem to be getting some place." At that point the reader is left to make her/his own way. It may be helpful, therefore, to know from the outset what case problems are and what advantages we believe can be gained from their use.

The heart of the case method of instruction is the use of problems to train the student to discover, and then to fix in her/his mind, *ways of thinking that are productive in the subject area*. Appropriate use of theory and the acquisition of factual material and procedural skills are also important goals, but the main objective is an ability to handle different types of managerial problems intelligently.

The word *decisional* is sometimes used to contrast the case method with *expository* teaching. The reader will find, for example, that most of the cases in this book are essentially descriptions of actual business situations. The facts are those which were known to some executive; in total they present an immediate financial problem which that person had to decide. Some cases emphasize the preliminaries of decision making—the difficulty of isolating and defining the crucial problem or of determining whether enough information is at hand to make an intelligent decision. The great majority of cases, however, are "issue" cases; these present reasonable alternative courses of action which might have been followed in the given situation. Sufficient information is given for the reader to place himself or herself in the executive's position. From this vantage point the student is challenged to analyze the problem and to decide upon the course of action to be taken.

The cases themselves depict a wide variety of financial problems and business situations. Reference to the Table of Contents will show that problems have been drawn from most of the major areas covered in financial courses. Cases have been selected from a wide variety of industries and from different time periods. Cases are also included which illustrate different phases in the life cycle of business firms and problems of cyclical decline as well as of prosperity.

Twenty-four of the 47 cases and notes in this edition are new. Of these 24 cases and notes, 18 are completely new cases, 4 are completely new notes, and 2 are updates of cases from the Seventh Edition. These changes result in the inclusion of more cases in which inflation is a major consideration. A number of the new cases also involves national settings other than the United States.

Three new notes discuss specific aspects of capital market theory. The note on the theory of optimal capital structure presents a concrete, numerical example of the determination of optimal debt ratios. The note on the capital asset pricing model (CAPM) is a concise description of the basic tenets of the theory and illustrates its application to the task of estimating the cost of equity capital. In the note on financial leverage and CAPM, the impact of financial leverage on betas and costs of equity is explored. The objective of these notes is to facilitate the application of these concepts with simple, concrete presentations. Many of the cases provide opportunities for the application of these techniques to managerial problems. More extensive treatment of underlying theory, its derivation, extensions and limitations, is presented in several recent finance texts.

Inevitably, some instructors will find that some of their favorite cases have been omitted in this edition. The editors share this feeling. If an instructor is especially eager to continue to use one or more of the cases dropped from the Seventh Edition, they can be ordered separately from the Intercollegiate Case Clearing House, Soldiers Field Post Office, Boston, Massachusetts 02163.

No major changes have been made in the basic structure of the book. The effort rather has been to improve its overall quality by weeding out old, outdated cases and substituting more timely material. In our judgment, Part I of the Seventh Edition consisted of well-tested cases that provided a very teachable sequence of material offering a good opportunity for drill on fundamental techniques of analysis. Several of the cases, however, had been impaired by the fact that they were badly dated. They have been replaced by two new cases. Hampton Machine Tool Company provides a useful drill in the fundamentals of financial forecasting, particularly including emphasis on the interlocking character of consistently constructed forecasts. It replaces the Sprague Machine Tool Company case. Carrefour, S.A. replaces the old Koehring Company case and relates trade credit strategy and corporate strategy. Lastly, "The Case of the Unidentified Industries" has been revised and incorporated in a note and programmed text on "Assessing the Financial Health of a Firm."

Part II of the book has been changed substantially. The three new technical notes on capital market theory represent a major addition. Revisions in several of the cases from the Seventh Edition and the inclusion of a new case, Communications Satellite Corporation, provide interesting opportunities to apply the theory to actual situations. Five other new cases have been added to this section. Two of them, Georgia Power Company and Systems Engineering Laboratories, Inc., explore the rapid shifts in the appetite of the public bond market for debt of various ratings. Chinon, S.A. raises the issue of estimating the adequacy of financial reserves for a highly cyclical company. The Digi Terminal case provides an opportunity to discuss bankruptcy and reorganization. And the case on Consolidated Edison's dividend decision in 1974 replaces the old Winn-Dixie Stores case.

The section on investment decisions, mergers, and acquisitions has been expanded to include three new cases on industry and competitive analysis, as well as a case on capital budgeting in a multinational context. We have also decided with some regret to replace an old favorite, Economy Shipping Company, with two new cases, Evaluation of Investment Alternatives and Pressco, Inc. A new acquisition case, Kennecott Copper Corporation, has been included to allow students to use modern financial theory to value an acquisition.

All of these cases are designed to provide a basis for class discussion; as such they are not intended to present either correct or incorrect illustrations of the solution of management problems. It need hardly be added that the discussion which they provoke will move along more realistic lines if students also have a standard finance text or reference book available and use it freely for background information not provided by this casebook. In addition, students will need to acquire proficiency in a number of analytical techniques useful in handling the quantitative aspects of cases.

Case problems confront students with the necessity of making decisions, and this is perhaps their greatest value. The student cannot stop with an understanding of the facts and a listing of items that deserve consideration. Mastery of these matters is merely the jumping-off point for class discussion. To be effective, the student must actually think the problem through to a decision, explain her/his analysis to her/his classmates, and defend it against their ideas. The need to choose among balanced alternatives and to discuss the decision intelligently is a great force in learning. It helps to provide that elusive quality of judgment that is often missed when learning is restricted to memorization of fact and views which others have codified.

Since the cases present business situations that pose debatable alternatives of action, they contain problems which can be narrowed but not settled by the usual techniques of financial analysis. Judgment must enter into the process of decision making, and therefore unanimous agreement as to the best decision is neither an expected nor a desired result of class meetings. This end result also contributes to the initial frustration of many students who have been working with scientific and technical problems; in the beginning phases of study in these areas a mechanistic approach can usually be counted on to yield a single "right" conclusion.

In developing a logical approach toward case problems, the reader should not overlook intangible human factors. The choice between financial alternatives in many, if not all, of the cases depends in part upon the principal's disposition for risk taking and other matters of judgment and taste.

In some instances, work with cases may require more of the student's time than would normal textbook reading assignments; however, the satisfaction of handling problems that bridge the gap between classroom study and business action, and the zest of independent thinking are usually adequate recompense for any extra time employed.

Part I

financing current operations

ASSESSING THE FINANCIAL HEALTH OF A FIRM

∧∧

An assessment of the long-term financial health of a company is an important task for outsiders considering the extension of credit and for insiders in their formulation of strategy. History abounds with examples of firms that embarked upon overly ambitious programs and subsequently discovered that their portfolio of programs could not be financed on acceptable terms. The outcome frequently was the abandonment of programs in midstream at considerable financial and organizational cost to the company, its vendors, its employees, and/or its creditors.

A necessary first step in the evaluation of a firm's financial health is the development of a comprehensive series of questions. It is possible to calculate a multitude of ratios, but unless they relate to specific questions and concerns, their usefulness will be minimal. Furthermore, unless one starts with a clear understanding of the right questions, one's analysis will inevitably be determined by whatever information is readily available.

The following represents some of the questions that seem important in assessing the future financial health of a company. The key issue is whether or not the company's goals, strategy, investment requirements, and financing capabilities are in balance.

1. Will the company need to raise additional finance over the next year/ over the next three to five years to carry out strategically important programs? *What are management's goals for the company? How does it*

3

plan to reach these goals? What investments must be made in working capital and in plant and equipment to support the programs? Will the company be a generator of excess cash, or will it be a consumer of cash? How important is its future access to finance from outsiders?

   a. Does the company have a seasonal financing need? If so, how large is it and what will be the perceptions of suppliers of finance at the time of the need?

   b. Might the company have a cyclical financing need? If so, how large might it be and what will be the perceptions of suppliers of finance at the time of the need?

   c. Does the company have a long-term need for additional finance? If so, how large is it and what will be the perceptions of suppliers of finance at the time of the need?

2. Is the company profitable? (Future profitability is one of the keys to raising finance.)

   a. What are the underlying financial accounting practices? For example, are all subsidiaries consolidated? What lives have been assumed for depreciation purposes?

   b. What is the trend in profitability? Is the improvement due to:
      (1) Short-lived supply shortages?
      (2) Opportunistic changes in financial accounting?
      (3) Cyclical factors?
      (4) Curtailment of strategically important expenses?

   c. Is the return on equity high/low/average due to:
      (1) Its operating margins?
      (2) Its asset utilization?
      (3) Its financing mix?

   d. Is the level of profitability sustainable, *given the outlook for the market and for competitive and regulatory pressures?*

   e. Are the earnings available to corporate or are they blocked in other countries?

3. Are there any "hidden" problems?

   a. Suspiciously large levels and/or buildups of accounts receivable or inventories relative to sales, *given the competitive and operating characteristics of the business?* What is the historical trend in collection period, inventory stockturn? Do the absolute levels seem reasonable?

   b. Unconsolidated subsidiaries with high debt levels?

   c. Large contingent liabilities or unfunded pension liabilities or uncompleted contracts?

   d. Lease commitments not shown on balance sheet?

4. How soundly is the company financed, given its riskiness *and* its future need for additional finance?

   a. What is the maturity structure of the company's debt? Is it faced with large debt repayments in the near future?

SOURCES OF DOWNWARD PRESSURE ON ABOVE-MARKET RETURNS

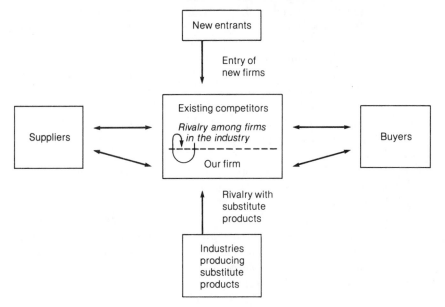

b.   How current is the company in the payment of its suppliers?
c.   What is the foreign exchange exposure of the company?
d.   Is the company close to its borrowing limit in terms of restrictive covenants?
e.   Is the company within its capacity to service the debt?
   (1)   Will it service the debt by paying the interest and principal out of internal cash flow?
   (2)   Will it service existing debt by selling new debt?
5. Does the company have assured access on acceptable terms to external sources of funds in amounts needed to meet its seasonal/cyclical/long-term needs?
   a.   Can the company raise equity funds?
      (1)   Is there a market for the shares?
      (2)   How many shares could be sold?
      (3)   At what price could the shares be sold?
      (4)   To whom would new shares be sold?
      (5)   Would management be willing to sell equity?
         (a)   Concern about control?
         (b)   Concern about impact on earnings per share and dividends per share?
   b.   Can the company raise long-term debt?
      (1)   Who are the possible suppliers?

(2)   What are their criteria for lending?

(3)   How well does the company meet these criteria?

(4)   How much additional long-term debt can the company raise? On what conditions? At what price? How quickly?

c.   Can the company raise short-term debt?

d.   How well will the financing plan work if adversity strikes?

e.   Does the company have assets that could be sold to raise funds? How quickly could they be sold?

6.   Are the company's goals, product-market choices and strategies, investment requirements, financing needs, and financing capabilities in balance?

7.   Will the company's goals, strategies, investment requirements, financing needs, and financing capabilities remain in balance if the firm is struck by adversity?

a.   What are the main regulatory, competitive, and operating risks? What combination of them might reasonably be expected to occur?

b.   How would management respond in strategic and operating terms?

c.   What would the implications be for future financing needs? For future financial performance?

d.   Will it be possible to raise the finance needed on acceptable terms, given the perceptions of suppliers of finance and of the firm's strategic, competitive, and financial performance?

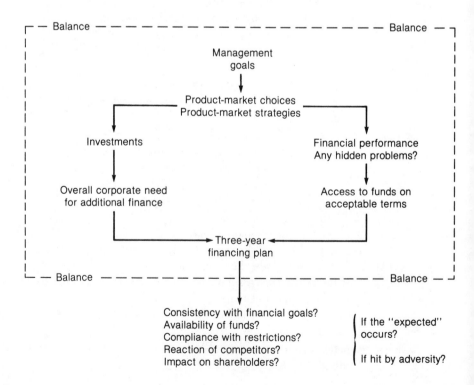

Clearly, many of the questions go beyond the information contained in the published financial statements of a company. Many require an understanding of (1) future industry economics and structure, (2) the competitive and operating characteristics of the business, (3) the long-term goals and plans of management, (4) the lending criteria of various segments of the capital markets, and (5) the soundness of management. Analysis of the published financial statements and the footnotes to the statements is only *one part* of a complete analysis of the future financial health of a company.

It is also clear that the evaluation of a firm's "financial health" can vary substantially, depending on the perspective of the individual asking the question. A bank or supplier considering the extension of seasonal credit may consider a company a very safe bet; whereas a long-term lender—dependent on the health and profitability of the company over a 15-year period—may be very nervous.

The remainder of this note is designed to provide familiarity with the financial ratios that can be useful in answering some of the questions suggested in the preceding framework. Financial statements for 1973 and 1977 are provided in Exhibit 1 for a hypothetical company (Electromagnetics, Inc.), and a series of questions is asked. On the basis of your analysis, has the financial condition of the company changed during the four-year period? What are the most significant changes, as indicated by the financial ratios?

Financial ratios and financial analysis

The two basic sources of financial data for a business entity are the income statement and the balance sheet, and their accompanying footnotes. The income statement summarizes revenues and expenses over a period of time; for example, for the year ended December 31, 1977. The balance sheet is a list of what the business owns (its assets), what it owes (its liabilities), and what has been invested by the owners (owners' equity) at a specific point in time; for example, *at* December 31, 1977.

From the numbers found on the income statement and the balance sheet, one can calculate the following types of financial ratios:

1. Profitability ratios.
2. Activity ratios.
3. Leverage ratios.
4. Liquidity ratios.

I. HOW PROFITABLE IS THE COMPANY—PROFITABILITY RATIOS

One measure of the profitability of a business is its "profit as a percentage of sales" (Net profit after taxes/Net sales). The information necessary to determine a company's profit as a percentage of sales can be found in the company's _____.

a. Electromagnetics' profit as a percentage of sales for 1977 (see Exhibit 1) was $_____ divided by $_____, or _____%.

b. This represented an *increase/decrease* from _____% in 1973.

c. The improvement in profitability resulted from an *increase/decrease* in cost of goods sold as a percentage of sales and from an *increase/decrease* in operating expenses as a percentage of sales. The only adverse factor was the increase in the _____.

Managements and investors often are more interested in the return earned on the funds invested than in the level of profits as a percentage of sales. Companies operating in businesses requiring very little investment in assets often have low profit margins but earn very attractive returns on invested funds. Conversely, there are numerous examples of companies in very capital-intensive businesses that earn miserably low returns on invested funds, despite seemingly attractive profit margins.

Therefore, it is useful to examine both the level of and the trend in the company's operating profits as a percentage of total assets. To increase the comparability across companies within the same industry, it is useful to use profit before taxes and before any interest charges. (This figure is also called "earnings before interest and taxes," or "EBIT.") This allows the analyst to focus on the profitability of operations, without any distortion due to tax factors and/or the method by which the company has financed itself.

d. Electromagnetics had a total of $_____ invested in assets at year-end 1977 and earned before interest and taxes $_____ during 1977. Its operating profit as a percentage of total assets (Profit before taxes + Interest charges/ Total assets) in 1977 was _____%, which represented an *increase/ decrease* from the _____% earned in 1973.

e. From the viewpoint of the shareholders, an equally important figure is the company's return on equity. Return on equity is calculated by dividing profit after tax by the owners' equity (Profit after taxes/Owners' equity). It indicates how profitably the company is utilizing shareholders' funds.

f. Electromagnetics had $_____ of owners' equity and earned $_____ after taxes in 1977. Its return on equity was _____%, an *improvement/deterioration* from the _____% earned in 1973.

II. ARE THERE ANY "HIDDEN" PROBLEMS—ACTIVITY RATIOS

The second basic type of financial ratio is the activity ratio. Activity ratios indicate how well a company employs its assets. Ineffective utilization of assets results in the need for more finance, unnecessary interest costs, and a correspondingly lower return on capital employed. Furthermore, low activity ratios and/or a deterioration in the activity ratios may indicate uncollectible accounts receivables or obsolete inventory or equipment.

"Total asset turnover" measures the effectiveness of the company in utilizing its total assets and is calculated by dividing total assets into sales (Net sales/ Total assets).

a. Total asset turnover for Electromagnetics in 1977 can be calculated by dividing $_____$ into $_____$. The turnover had *improved/deteriorated* from $\_\_\_\_\_$ times in 1973 to $\_\_\_\_\_$ times in 1977.

It is useful to examine the turnover ratios for each type of asset, as the use of total assets may hide important problems in one of the specific asset categories. One important category is accounts receivables. The "average collection period" measures the number of days that the company must wait on average between the time of sale and the time when it is paid. The "average collection period" is calculated in two steps. First, divide annual credit sales by 365 days to determine average sales per day (Net sales/365 days). Then, divide the accounts receivable by the average sales per day to determine the number of days of sales that are still unpaid (Accounts receivable/Average sales per day).

b. Electromagnetics had $_____$ invested in accounts receivables at year-end 1977. Its average sales per day were $_____$ during 1977 and its average collection period was $\_\_\_\_\_$ days. This represented an *improvement/ deterioration* from the average collection period of $\_\_\_\_\_$ days in 1973.

c. A third activity ratio is the "inventory turnover ratio," which indicates the effectiveness with which the company is employing inventory. Since inventory is recorded on the balance sheet at cost (not at its sales value), it is advisable to use cost of goods sold as the measure of activity. The "inventory turnover" figure is calculated by dividing cost of goods sold by inventory (Cost of goods sold/Inventories).

Electromagnetics apparently needed $_____$ of inventory at year-end 1977 to support its operations during 1977. Its activity during 1977, as measured by the cost of goods sold, was $_____$. It therefore had an inventory turnover of $\_\_\_\_\_$ times. This represented an *improvement/deterioration* from $\_\_\_\_\_$ times in 1973.

d. A fourth and final activity ratio is the "fixed asset turnover ratio" (Net sales/Net fixed assets) which measures the effectiveness of the company in utilizing its plant and equipment.

Electromagnetics had net fixed assets of $_____$ and sales of $_____$ in 1977. Its fixed asset turnover ratio in 1977 was $\_\_\_\_\_$ times, an *improvement/deterioration* from $\_\_\_\_\_$ times in 1973.

e. To this point, we have discussed three measures of profitability. They are (1) $_____$, (2) $_____$, and (3) $_____$.

We have also discussed four activity ratios which measure the effectiveness with which the company is utilizing its assets. They are (1) $_____$, (2) $_____$, (3) $_____$, and (4) $_____$.

f. The improvement in Electromagnetics' operating profits as a percentage of total assets between 1973 and 1977 was primarily due to $_____$
$_____$.

III. HOW SOUNDLY IS THE COMPANY FINANCED— LEVERAGE RATIOS

The third basic type of financial ratio is the leverage ratio. The various leverage ratios measure the relationship of funds supplied by creditors and the funds supplied by the owners. The use of borrowed funds by profitable companies will improve the return on equity. However, it increases the riskiness of the business and, if used in excessive amounts, can result in financial embarrassment.

a. One leverage ratio—"the debt ratio"—measures the total funds provided by creditors as a percentage of total assets (Total debt/Total assets). Total debt includes both current and long-term liabilities.

The total debt of Electromagnetics as of December 31, 1977, was $_____, or _____% of total assets. This represented an *increase/decrease* from _____% as of December 31, 1973.

b. The ability of Electromagnetics to meet its interest payments can be estimated by relating its earnings before interest and taxes to its interest payments (Earnings before interest and taxes/Interest charges). This ratio is called the "times interest earned ratio."

Electromagnetics' earnings before interest and taxes (EBIT) was $_____ in 1977 and its interest charges were $_____. Its times interest earned was _____ times. This represented an *improvement/deterioration* from the 1973 level of _____ times.

c. A similar ratio to the "times interest earned ratio" is "fixed charge coverage." This ratio recognizes that lease payments under long-term contracts are usually as mandatory as interest and principal payments on debt. The ratio is calculated as follows:

$$\frac{\text{EBIT} + \text{Lease payments}}{\text{Interest charges} + \text{Lease payments}}$$

Electromagnetics had annual lease payments of $760. Its fixed charge coverage in 1977 was _____ times.

d. A fourth and final leverage ratio is the "number of days of payables." This ratio measures the average number of days that the company is taking to pay its suppliers of raw materials. It is calculated by dividing annual purchases by 365 days to determine average purchases per day (Annual purchases/365 days). Accounts payable are then divided by average purchases per day (Accounts payable/Average purchases per day) to determine the number of days of purchases that are still unpaid.

It is often difficult to determine the purchases of a firm. Instead, the income statement shows cost of goods sold—a figure that includes not only raw materials but also labor and overhead. Thus, it often is only possible to gain a rough idea as to whether or not a firm is becoming more or less dependent on its suppliers for finance. This can be done by relating accounts payable to cost of goods sold (Accounts payable/Cost of goods sold) and following this ratio over time.

Electromagnetics owed its suppliers $_____ at year-end 1977. This represented _____% of cost of goods sold and was an *increase/decrease* from the _____% at year-end 1973. The company appears to be *more/less* prompt in paying its suppliers in 1977 than it was in 1973.

e. The improvement in Electromagnetics' profitability, as measured by its return on equity, from 5.8% in 1973 to 16% in 1977 resulted from the combined impact of _____

and _____

_____.

f. The financial riskiness of Electromagnetics *increased/decreased* between 1973 and 1977.

IV. HOW LIQUID IS THE COMPANY—LIQUIDITY RATIOS

The fourth type of financial ratio is the liquidity ratio. These ratios measure a company's ability to meet financial obligations as they become current. The "current ratio," defined as current assets divided by current liabilities (Current assets/Current liabilities), considers current assets as being much more readily and assuredly convertible into cash. It relates these fairly liquid assets to the claims that are due within one year—the current liabilities.

a. Electromagnetics held $_____ of current assets at year-end 1977 and owned $_____ to creditors due to be paid within one year. Its current ratio was _____, an *improvement/deterioration* from the ratio of _____ at year-end 1973.

b. The "quick ratio" or "acid test" is similar to the current ratio but excludes inventories from the current assets (Current assets − inventories/Current liabilities). Inventories are excluded as they often are difficult to convert into cash—at least at book value—if the company is struck by adversity.

The "quick ratio" for Electromagnetics at year-end 1977 was _____, an *improvement/deterioration* from the ratio of ——— at year-end 1973.

CASE OF THE UNIDENTIFIED INDUSTRIES

The preceding exercise suggested a series of questions that may be helpful in assessing the future financial health of a company. It also described several ratios that are useful in answering some of the questions, especially if the historical trend in these ratios is examined.

However, it is also important to compare the actual, absolute value with some standard to determine whether or not the company is performing well. Unfortunately, there is no single current ratio or inventory turnover or debt ratio, and so forth, that is appropriate to all industries; and even within a specific industry, ratios may vary significantly among companies. The operating and competitive characteristics of the company's industry greatly influence its investment in the various types of assets, the riskiness of these investments, and the financial structure of its balance sheet.

Try to match the five following types of companies with their corresponding balance sheets and financial ratios, as shown in Exhibit 2.

1. Electric utility.
2. Japanese trading company.
3. Retail jewelry chain.
4. Automobile manufacturer.
5. Supermarket chain.

In doing the exercise, it may be helpful to first consider the operating and competitive characteristics of the industry and their implications for (a) the collection period, (b) inventory turnover, (c) the amount of plant and equipment, and (d) the appropriate financial structure. Then identify which one of the five sets of balance sheets and financial ratios best matches your expectations.

Exhibit 1

ASSESSING THE FINANCIAL HEALTH OF A FIRM
ELECTROMAGNETICS, INC.
STATEMENT OF CONSOLIDATED EARNINGS

	1973	1977
Net sales...	$44,991	$70,100
Cost of goods sold...................................	23,715	33,504
Gross profit...	21,276	36,596
Operating expenses...................................	19,078	28,238
Interest expenses....................................	1,041	1,418
Income before taxes..................................	1,157	6,940
Federal income taxes.................................	82	3,200
Net income..	$ 1,075	$ 3,740

CONSOLIDATED BALANCE SHEETS, AT DECEMBER 31

ASSETS	1973	1977
Cash...	$ 639	$ 1,079
Accounts receivable..................................	11,936	18,145
Inventories...	14,672	24,162
Total current assets...............................	27,247	43,386
Net fixed assets.....................................	6,518	7,706
Total assets......................................	$33,765	$51,092

LIABILITIES AND STOCKHOLDERS' EQUITY

	1973	1977
Notes payable—banks.................................	$ 8,480	$ 2,719
Accounts payable.....................................	2,154	6,528
Accrued expenses and taxes...........................	1,660	7,482
Total current liabilities..........................	12,294	16,729
Long-term debt......................................	3,088	11,230
Stockholders' equity.................................	18,383	23,133
Total liabilities and stockholders' equity.........	$33,765	$51,092

Exhibit 2

ASSESSING THE FINANCIAL HEALTH OF A FIRM
DATA FOR UNIDENTIFIED INDUSTRIES

	A	B	C	D	E
BALANCE SHEET PERCENTAGES					
Cash and marketable....................	15.4%	7.6%	.5%	2.7%	7.2%
Receivables...........................	15.6	2.2	3.8	19.0	60.3
Inventories...........................	26.5	41.4	2.2	55.8	8.7
Other current assets....................	2.0	4.7	2.6	1.1	7.3
Property and equipment (net)............	29.6	42.9	90.0	21.4	4.3
Other assets..........................	10.9	1.2	0.9	—	12.2
Total assets.....................	100.0%	100.0%	100.0%	100.0%	100.0%
Notes payable.........................	—	2.3%	3.1%	4.9%	50.8%
Accounts payable......................	15.1%	33.3	2.6	8.0	15.2
Accrued taxes.........................	3.9	4.0	1.4	6.6	0.5
Other current liabilities.................	11.5	—	2.6	5.0	5.2
Long-term debt.......................	5.8	6.7	43.3	11.4	22.7
Other liabilities.......................	4.3	3.2	1.8	—	1.3
Owners' equity.......................	59.4	50.5	45.2	64.1	4.3
Total liabilities and owners' equity.....	100.0%	100.0%	100.0%	100.0%	100.0%

SELECTED RATIOS					
Net profits/net sales....................	.04	.02	.15	.04	.01
Net profits/total assets..................	.06	.09	.05	.12	.01
Net profits/owners' equity..............	.10	.19	.11	.12	.13
Net sales/total assets...................	1.65	6.06	.32	1.94	2.07
Receivables collection period (days).......	33	1	44	61	106
Inventory turnover.....................	5.2 x	11 x	—	2.4 x	23.2 x
Total debt/total assets..................	.41	.50	.55	.36	.96
Long-term debt/owners' equity...........	.10	.13	.96	.18	5.25
Current assets/current liabilities..........	1.62	1.41	.93	4.02	1.02
Quick ratio..........................	1.08	.37	.64	.93	.90
Average price/earnings ratio..............	10.5	12.0	7.5	16.0	15.0

Exhibit 3

ASSESSING THE FINANCIAL HEALTH OF A FIRM
SUMMARY OF FINANCIAL RATIOS

Ratio	Formula	Indication
Profitability ratios		
Profit as a percent of sales	$\dfrac{\text{Profit after taxes}}{\text{Sales}}$	Profit margin on sales
Return on total assets	$\dfrac{\text{Earnings before interest} + \text{Taxes}}{\text{Total assets}}$	Return on total investment
Return on net worth	$\dfrac{\text{Profit after taxes}}{\text{Owners' equity}}$	Return on owners' investment
Activity ratios		
Fixed assets ratio	$\dfrac{\text{Sales}}{\text{Fixed assets}}$	Turnover on plant and equipment
Total asset turnover	$\dfrac{\text{Sales}}{\text{Total assets}}$	Turnover on all assets
Inventory turnover	$\dfrac{\text{Cost of goods sold}}{\text{Inventories}}$	Level of inventory
Average collection period	$\dfrac{\text{Accounts receivable}}{\text{Sales per day}}$	Length of time between making a sale and receiving cash for it
Leverage ratios		
Debt ratio	$\dfrac{\text{Total debt}}{\text{Total assets}}$	Level of funds provided by creditors
Times interest earned	$\dfrac{\text{Earnings before interest} + \text{Taxes}}{\text{Interest charges}}$	Ability to meet current debt obligation
Fixed charge coverage	$\dfrac{\text{Earnings before taxes} + \text{Interest} + \text{Lease charges obligation}}{\text{Interest charge} + \text{Lease obligations}}$	Ability to meet current debt and lease obligation
Days payable	$\dfrac{\text{Accounts payable}}{\text{Purchases per day}}$	Level of financing by suppliers
Liquidity ratios		
Current ratio	$\dfrac{\text{Current assets}}{\text{Current liabilities}}$	Short-term solvency
Quick ratio	$\dfrac{\text{Current assets} - \text{Inventories}}{\text{Current liabilities}}$	Very short-term solvency

BROWNING LUMBER COMPANY

∧∧

After a rapid growth in its business during recent years, the Browning Lumber Company in the spring of 1972 anticipated a further substantial increase in sales. Despite good profits, which were largely retained in the business, the company had experienced a shortage of cash and had found it necessary to increase its borrowing from the Suburban National Bank to $99,000 in the spring of 1972. The maximum loan that Suburban National would make to any one borrower was $100,000, and Browning had been able to stay within this limit in the spring of 1972 only by relying very heavily on trade credit. Mr. Roger Browning, proprietor of the Browning Lumber Company, was therefore actively looking elsewhere for a new banking relationship where he would be able to negotiate a larger loan.

Mr. Browning had recently been introduced by a personal friend to Mr. George Dodge, an officer of a much larger bank, the Northrup National Bank. The two men had tentatively discussed the possibility that the Northrup bank might extend a line of credit to Browning Lumber up to a maximum amount of $200,000. Mr. Browning thought that a loan of this size would more than meet his foreseeable needs, but he was eager for the flexibility that a line of credit of this size would provide. Subsequent to this discussion Mr. Dodge had arranged for the credit department of the Northrup National Bank to investigate Mr. Browning and his company.

The Browning Lumber Company had been founded in 1962 as a partnership by Mr. Browning and his brother-in-law, Mr. Henry Stark. In 1969 Mr. Browning bought out Mr. Stark's interest for $50,000 and continued the business as a sole proprietorship. Mr. Stark had taken a note for $50,000, to be paid off in 1970, in order to give Mr. Browning time to arrange for the financing necessary to make the payment of $50,000 to him. The major portion of the funds needed for this payment were raised by a mortgage of $30,000 on the company's buildings. This mortgage, negotiated in late 1969, carried an interest rate of 8%, and was repayable in quarterly installments at the rate of $3,000 a year over the next ten years.

The business was located in a growing suburb of a large city in the southern section of the Midwest. The company owned land with access to a railroad siding, and two large storage buildings had been erected on this land. The company's operations were limited to the wholesale distribution of lumber products in the local area. Typical products included plywood, moldings, and sash and door products. Quantity discounts and credit terms of net 30 days on open account were usually offered to customers.

Sales volume had been built up largely on the basis of successful price competition made possible by careful control of operating expenses and by quantity purchases of materials at substantial discounts. Much of the moldings and sash and door products, which constituted significant items of sales, were used for repair work. About 55% of total sales were made in the six months from March through August. No sales representatives were employed, orders being taken exclusively over the telephone. Annual sales of $314,000 in 1967 and $476,000 in 1968 gave profits of $40,000 and $49,000, respectively.[1] Comparative operating statements for the years 1969 through 1971 and for three months ending March 31, 1972, are given in Exhibit 1.

Mr. Browning was an energetic man, 39 years of age, who worked long hours on the job, not only handling management matters but also performing part of the clerical work. He was helped by an assistant who, in the words of the investigator of the Northrup National Bank, "has been doing and can do about everything that Mr. Browning does in the organization." Other employees numbered 12 in early 1972, 10 who worked in the yard and drove trucks and 2 who assisted in the office.

As a part of its customary investigation of prospective borrowers, the Northrup National Bank sent inquiries concerning Mr. Browning to a number of firms that had business dealings with him. The manager of one of his large suppliers, the Barker Company, wrote in answer:

> The conservative operation of his business appeals to us. He has not wasted his money in disproportionate plant investment. His operating expenses are as low as they could possibly be. He has personal control over every feature of his business, and he possesses sound judgment and a willingness to work harder than anyone I have ever known. This, with a good personality, gives him an excellent turnover; and from my personal experience in watching him work, I know that he keeps close check on his own credits.

All the other trade letters received by the bank bore out the statements quoted above.

In addition to the ownership of his lumber business, which was his major source of income, Mr. Browning held jointly with his wife an equity in their home. The house cost $35,000 to build in 1963 and was mortgaged for $28,-000. He also held a $30,000 life insurance policy, payable to Mrs. Browning. Mrs. Browning owned independently a half interest in a house worth about $30,000. Otherwise, they had no sizable personal investments.

---

[1] The profits figures for 1967 and 1968 are not comparable with those shown in Exhibit 1 for 1969–71. The 1967 and 1968 figures do not reflect the payment of salaries to either Mr. Browning or Mr. Stark. Their remuneration would constitute a "drawing by proprietors" rather than an operating expense. When Mr. Stark withdrew from the business in 1968, the employee who took his place was paid a salary which is shown in Exhibit 1 as a component of the "operating expense" account, not as a drawing by a proprietor.

The bank gave particular attention to the debt position and current ratio of the business. It noted the ready market for the company's products at all times and the fact that sales prospects were favorable. The bank's investigator reported: ". . . Sales are expected to reach $1,600,000 in 1972 and may exceed this level if prices of lumber should rise substantially in the near future." On the other hand, it was recognized that a general economic downturn or a return to the very tight credit conditions of 1969–70 with the resultant shortage of funds for residential mortgages might slow down the rate of increase in sales. Browning Lumber's sales, however, were protected to some degree from fluctuations in new housing construction because of the relatively high proportion of its repair business. Projections beyond 1972 were difficult to make, but the prospects appeared good for a continued growth in the volume of Browning Lumber's business over the foreseeable future.

The bank also noted the rapid increase in Browning Lumber's accounts and notes payable in the recent past, especially in the spring of 1972. The usual terms of purchase in the trade provided for a discount of 2% for payments made within 10 days of the invoice date. Accounts were due in 30 days at the invoice price but suppliers ordinarily did not object if payments lagged somewhat behind the due date. During the last two years Mr. Browning had taken very few purchase discounts because of the shortage of funds arising from his purchase of Mr. Stark's interest in the business and the additional investments in working capital associated with the company's increasing sales volume. Trade credit was seriously extended in the spring of 1972 as Mr. Browning strove to hold his bank borrowing within the $100,000 ceiling imposed by the Suburban National Bank.

Comparative balance sheets as of December 31, 1969–71, are presented in Exhibit 2. A detailed balance sheet drawn up for the bank as of March 31, 1972, and the change in proprietorship for the first quarter of 1972 appear as Exhibits 3 and 4.

The tentative discussions between Mr. Dodge and Mr. Browning had been in terms of a revolving, unsecured 90-day note not to exceed $200,000 in amount. The specific details of the loan had not been worked out, but Mr. Dodge had explained that the loan agreement would involve the standard covenants applying to such a loan. He cited as illustrative provisions the requirement that restrictions on additional borrowing would be imposed, that net working capital would have to be maintained at an agreed level, that additional investments in fixed assets could be made only with the prior approval of the bank, and that limitations would be placed on withdrawals of funds from the business by Mr. Browning. Interest would be set on a floating rate basis at 3 percentage points above the lowest rate charged by the bank on short-term loans. Mr. Dodge indicated that the initial rate to be paid would be approximately 10% under conditions in effect in early 1972. Both men also understood that Mr. Browning would sever his relationship with the Suburban National Bank if he entered into a loan agreement with the Northrup National Bank.

In addition to working out arrangements for increased bank credit, a second issue of concern to Mr. Browning was whether he should continue to operate as a proprietorship or whether it would be better for him to incorporate his business. As a proprietorship he paid taxes on the full amount earned by the business, the item shown as "net profit before taxes" in Exhibit 1. As explained in Exhibit 1, this figure was computed without any allowance for a salary for Mr. Browning. As the business became increasingly profitable, Mr. Browning was subject to increasingly severe individual income taxes.

Mr. Browning understood that if he were to incorporate his business he would be able to deduct a reasonable salary in computing his net profits subject to the corporation income tax. The salary so deducted would be taxable to him as an individual. Profits retained in the business would not be subject to the individual income tax if the business were incorporated. On the other hand, any dividends paid to Mr. Browning would be taxed twice, first as income to the corporation and then as personal income to the stockholder.

Exhibit 5 summarizes briefly the tax rates applicable to individuals and to corporations as of 1972.

Exhibit 1

BROWNING LUMBER COMPANY

OPERATING STATEMENTS FOR THE YEARS ENDING DECEMBER 31, 1969
THROUGH 1971 AND FOR THE THREE MONTHS
ENDING MARCH 31, 1972

(In thousands)

	1969	1970	1971	First Quarter 1972
Net sales (after discounts)	$733	$869	$1,163	$310*
Cost of goods sold:				
Beginning inventory	$ 79	$103	$ 141	$180
Purchases	552	658	881	285
	$631	$761	$1,022	$465
Ending inventory	103	141	180	240
Cost of goods sold	$528	$620	$ 842	$225
Gross profit	$205	$249	$ 321	$ 85
Operating expenses†	160	194	249	68
Net profit before taxes†	$ 45	$ 55	$ 72	$ 17
Drawings by proprietor	$ 29	$ 37	$ 49	$ 12

* In the first quarter of 1971 sales were $252,000 and net profit was $13,000.
† No allowance for a salary for Mr. Browning is included in either of these items. For a discussion of the tax treatment of a proprietorship see the text and Exhibit 5.

Exhibit 2

BROWNING LUMBER COMPANY

COMPARATIVE BALANCE SHEETS AS OF DECEMBER 31, 1969–71

(In thousands)

	1969	1970	1971
ASSETS			
Cash	$ 26	$ 21	$ 18
Accounts receivable—net	74	96	137
Inventory	103	141	180
Total current assets	$203	$258	$335
Property—net	56	61	65
Total assets	$259	$319	$400
LIABILITIES AND NET WORTH			
Notes payable—bank	...	$ 61	$ 91
Notes payable—Mr. Stark	$ 50	...	...
Notes payable—trade	...	...	...
Accounts payable	52	83	110
Accrued expenses	10	13	17
Long-term debt—current portion	3	3	3
Total current liabilities	$115	$160	$221
Long-term debt	27	24	21
Total liabilities	$142	$184	$242
Net worth	117	135	158
Total liabilities and net worth	$259	$319	$400

Exhibit 3

BROWNING LUMBER COMPANY

BALANCE SHEET AS OF MARCH 31, 1972

(In thousands)

ASSETS

Cash..		$ 15
Accounts receivable...............................	$152	
Less reserve.....................................	3	
Accounts receivable—net..........................		149
Inventory...		240
Total current assets............................		$404
Land, buildings, and equipment......................	$ 75	
Less: Accumulated depreciation.....................	21	
Land, buildings, and equipment—net.................		54
Trucks and automobile..............................	$ 22	
Less: Accumulated depreciation.....................	10	
Trucks and automobile—net........................		12
Total assets...................................		$470

LIABILITIES AND NET WORTH

Notes payable—bank...............................	$ 99
Notes payable—trade..............................	68
Accounts payable—trade............................	102
Accrued expenses.................................	15
Long-term debt—current portion.....................	3
Total current liabilities...........................	$287
Long-term debt...................................	20
Total liabilities.................................	$307
Net worth..	163
Total liabilities and net worth.....................	$470

Exhibit 4

BROWNING LUMBER COMPANY

CHANGE IN PROPRIETORSHIP, FIRST QUARTER, 1972

(In thousands)

Proprietorship, December 31, 1971.....................		$158
Net profit, first quarter............................	$17	
Drawings by proprietor............................	12*	
Balance...		5
Proprietorship (net worth), March 31, 1972.............		$163

* Drawings to cover living expenses and provision for payment of income taxes.

Exhibit 5

BROWNING LUMBER COMPANY

SUMMARY OF TAX RATES APPLICABLE TO A PROPRIETORSHIP AND TO A CORPORATION

Tax Rates Applicable to Individuals and Proprietorships

As noted in the text of the case the income of a sole proprietorship or a partnership is taxable to the owner(s) rather than to the business as such. Thus, the income of the Browning Lumber Company would be taxable in its entirety to Mr. Browning. It is probably reasonable to assume that the taxable income attributable to Mr. Browning from his company would be approximately equal to the amount shown as "net profit before taxes" in Exhibit 1. Since the case indicates that Mr. Browning and his wife have little or no income from sources other than his business, the figures shown in Exhibit 1 can be assumed to be Mr. Browning's sole (or principal) source of taxable income. In interpreting the following table, it should be recognized that the tax brackets and tax rates shown refer to "taxable income" in the legal sense. Mr. Browning, of course, would be entitled to any deductions and personal exemptions authorized by the Internal Revenue Code. Since Mr. Browning is married, he presumably would file a joint tax return and benefit from the lower rates applicable to married couples. The following table presents the tax brackets and corresponding tax liabilities applying to individual taxpayers filing joint returns for the tax brackets in which Mr. Browning's income might fall:

Taxable Income	Tax	Rate on Excess*
$ 20,000	$ 4,380	32%
24,000	5,660	36
28,000	7,100	39
32,000	8,660	42
36,000	10,340	45
40,000	12,140	48
44,000	14,060	50
52,000	18,060	53
64,000	24,420	55
76,000	31,020	58
88,000	37,980	60
100,000	45,180	62
120,000	57,580	64
140,000	70,380	66
160,000	83,580	68
180,000	97,180	69
200,000	110,980	70

Tax Rates Applicable to a Corporation

If the Browning Lumber Company were incorporated, Mr. Browning could, of course, deduct as an expense a reasonable salary for himself. This salary would then be taxable to him as personal income. Since Mr. Browning and his wife had little or no income other than his salary, he would not be subject to the top brackets of the individual income tax on his salary. If, for example, he paid himself a salary of $32,000 of which $28,000 was taxable, after deducting personal exemptions and other allowable deductions, his personal tax liability would be $7,100, as shown in the preceding tabulation.

The corporation income tax rates to which the Browning Lumber Company would be subject are as follows:

Taxable Income	Tax
$25,000 or less	22% of taxable income
Over $25,000	$5,500 plus 48% of taxable income in excess of $25,000

In 1972, after the deduction of a reasonable allowance for a salary, a large fraction of the income of Browning Lumber Company, if organized as a corporation, would be subject to the 22% tax rate.

Any dividends paid by the company would of course be taxable as ordinary income to its stockholders.

---

* The current tax law provides a "maximum tax on earned income." The top *marginal* tax rate under this provision applicable to an individual's *earned* taxable income is limited to 50%. A taxpayer engaged in a business where both services and capital are material income-producing factors may treat a reasonable amount (not more than 30% of his share of the net profits) as earned income. The provision with respect to the maximum tax supersedes those in the general schedule of tax rates.

It is unlikely that the "maximum tax" would have any bearing on Mr. Browning in the foreseeable future.

SUNSHINE TOY COMPANY

In early January, 1973, Mr. William Kincaid, president and part owner of Sunshine Toy Company, was considering a proposal to adopt level monthly production for the coming year. In the past, the company's production schedules had always been highly seasonal, reflecting the seasonality of sales. Mr. Kincaid was aware that a marked improvement in production efficiency could result from level production, but he was uncertain what the impact on other phases of the business might be.

Sunshine Toy Company was a manufacturer of plastic toys for children. Its product groups included billiard sets, automobiles, trucks, construction equipment, guns, rockets, spaceships and satellites, musical instruments, animals, and cartoon figures. Under most of the product categories, the company produced a wide range of designs, colors, and sizes. Dollar sales of a particular product item had sometimes varied by 30–35% from one year to the next.

The manufacture of plastic toys was a highly competitive business. The industry was populated by a large number of companies, many of which were short on capital and management talent. Since capital requirements were not large, and the technology was relatively simple, it was easy for new competitors to enter the industry. On the other hand, design and price competition was fierce, resulting in short product lives and a relatively high rate of company failures. A company was sometimes able to steal a march on the competition by designing a popular new toy, often of the fad variety. Such items generally commanded very high margins until competitors were able to offer a similar product. For example, Sunshine's introduction of moon rocket launcher sets in 1967 had contributed importantly to that year's profits. However, in 1968 eleven competitors had marketed a similar product, and the factory price of the Sunshine offering had plummeted. In recent years, competitive pressures on smaller firms had been intensified by the rise of a number of large, national toy manufacturers, which had comparatively ample financial resources to employ in elaborate product development and advertising programs.

Sunshine Toy Company had been founded in 1955 by Mr. Joseph Richardson after his release from naval service. Before the Korean War, Mr. Richardson had been employed as production manager by a large manufacturer of plastic toys. Mr. Richardson and his former assistant, Mr. William Kincaid,

23

established Sunshine Toy Company with their savings in 1955. Originally a partnership, the firm had been incorporated in 1956, with Mr. Richardson taking 75% of the capital stock and Mr. Kincaid, 25%. The latter served as production manager, and Mr. Richardson, as president, was responsible for overall direction of the company's affairs. After a series of illnesses, Mr. Richardson's health had broken down in 1970 and he had been forced to retire from active participation in the business. Mr. Kincaid had assumed the presidency at that time. In 1971, he had hired Mr. James Hardy, a recent graduate of a prominent eastern technical institute, as production manager. Mr. Hardy had worked during summers in the plastics plant of a large diversified chemical company and thus had a basic familiarity with plastics production processes.

Sunshine Toy Company had experienced relatively rapid growth since its founding and had enjoyed profitable operations each year since 1959. Sales were $3 million in 1972, and on the strength of a number of promising new products, were projected at $3.6 million for 1973. Net profits had reached $86,000 in 1972 and were estimated at $108,000 in 1973, under seasonal production, after taxes of 50%. Exhibits 1 and 2 present the latest financial statements for the company. The cost of goods sold had averaged 80% of sales in the past and was expected to maintain approximately that proportion in 1973 under seasonal production. In keeping with the company's experience, operating expenses were considered likely to be incurred evenly throughout each month of 1973 under either seasonal or level production.

Expanding operations had resulted in a somewhat strained working capital position for Sunshine Toy Company. The year-end cash balance of $140,000 in 1972 was regarded as the minimum necessary for the operations of the business. The company had periodically borrowed from its bank of account, Hood Trust Company, on an unsecured line of credit. A loan of $294,000 was outstanding at the end of 1972. Mr. Kincaid had been assured that the bank would be willing to extend a credit line of up to $850,000 in 1973, with the understanding that the loan would be completely repaid and "off the books" for at least a 30-day period during the year. Interest would be charged at a rate of 8%, and any advances in excess of $850,000 would be subject to further negotiations.

The company's sales were highly seasonal. Over 80% of annual dollar volume usually was sold during August–November. Exhibit 3 shows sales by months for 1972 and projected monthly sales for 1973. Sales were made principally to large variety store chains and toy brokers. Although the company quoted terms of net 30 days, most customers took 60 days to pay. Collection experience had been excellent, however.

The company's production processes were not complex. Plastic molding powder, the principal raw material, was processed by injection molding presses and formed into the shapes desired. The plastic shapes were next painted at "merry-go-round" painting machines. The final steps in the process were assembly of the toy sets and packaging in cardboard cartons or plastic bags. Typically, all runs begun were completed on the same day so that there was virtually no work in process at the end of the day. Purchases on net 30-day terms were made weekly in amounts necessary for estimated production in the forthcoming week. Total purchases in 1973 were forecast at $1,080,000. It was the company's policy to retire trade debt promptly as it came due.

Mr. Hardy, the production manager, believed the company would be able to hold capital expenditures during the coming year to an amount equal to depreciation, though he had cautioned that 1973's projected volume would approach the full capacity of Sunshine's equipment.

The company's practice was to produce in response to customer orders. This meant only a small fraction of capacity was needed to meet demand for the first seven months of the year. Ordinarily, not more than 25–30% of manufacturing capacity was used at any one time during this period. The first sizable orders for Christmas business arrived around the middle of August. For the rest of the year, the work force was greatly expanded and put on overtime, and all equipment was utilized 16 hours a day. In 1972, overtime premiums had amounted to $66,000. Shipments were made whenever possible on the day that an order was produced. Hence, production and sales amounts in each month tended to be equal.

As in the past, pro forma balance sheets and income statements based on an assumption of seasonal production had been prepared for 1973 and presented to Mr. Kincaid for his examination. These appear in Exhibits 4 and 5.

Having experienced a selling season at Sunshine, Mr. Hardy was deeply impressed by the many problems that arose from the company's method of scheduling production. Overtime premiums reduced profits. Seasonal expansion and contraction of the work force resulted in recruiting difficulties and high training and quality control costs. Machinery stood idle for seven and a half months, then was subjected to heavy use. Accelerated production schedules during the peak season resulted in frequent setup changes on the machinery. Seemingly unavoidable confusion in scheduling runs resulted. Short runs and frequent setup changes caused inefficiencies in assembly and packaging as workers encountered difficulty relearning their operations.

For these reasons, Mr. Hardy had urged upon Mr. Kincaid adoption of a policy of level monthly production in 1973. He pointed out that estimates of sales volume had usually proved to be reliable in the past. Purchase terms would not be affected by the rescheduling of purchases. The elimination of overtime wage premiums would result in substantial savings, estimated at $80,000 in 1973. Moreover, Mr. Hardy firmly believed that significant additional direct labor savings, amounting to about $94,000 would result from orderly production. A portion of the savings would be offset, however, by higher storage and handling costs estimated at $40,000 annually. Mr. Kincaid speculated upon the effect that level production might have on the company's funds requirements in 1973. He assumed that except for profits and fluctuations in the levels of inventories, accounts receivable, and accounts payable, funds inflows and outflows would be approximately in balance. To simplify the problem, Mr. Kincaid decided to assume that gross margin percentages would not vary significantly by months under either method of production; that is, cost of goods sold would be 80% of sales in each of the 12 months under seasonal production and would be 75.2% of sales in each of the 12 months under level production. The increased storage and handling costs of $40,000 would be included in operating expenses.

Exhibit 1

SUNSHINE TOY COMPANY

CONDENSED INCOME STATEMENTS, 1970–72

(In thousands)

	1970	1971	1972
Net sales......................	$2,079	$2,380	$2,973
Cost of goods sold..............	1,628	1,961	2,387
Gross profit...................	$ 451	$ 419	$ 586
Operating expenses..............	304	376	416
Profit before taxes..............	$ 147	$ 43	$ 170
Federal income taxes............	71	16	84
Net profit.....................	$ 76	$ 27	$ 86

Exhibit 2

SUNSHINE TOY COMPANY

BALANCE SHEET, DECEMBER 31, 1972

(In thousands)

ASSETS

Cash...	$ 140
Accounts receivable..............................	1,051
Inventory..	212
Total current assets...........................	$1,403
Plant and equipment, net.........................	428
Total assets...................................	$1,831

LIABILITIES

Accounts payable................................	$ 102
Notes payable—bank..............................	294
Accrued taxes.....................................	60*
Current portion—long-term debt.....................	40
Total current liabilities.......................	$ 496
Long-term debt...................................	160
Shareholders' equity..............................	1,175
Total liabilities..............................	$1,831

* Taxes payable on 1972 income are due in equal installments on March 15 and June 15, 1973.

Exhibit 3

SUNSHINE TOY COMPANY

MONTHLY SALES, 1972

(In thousands)

January	$28	July	$ 39
February	35	August	469
March	39	September	556
April	36	October	648
May	35	November	711
June	38	December	340

PROJECTED MONTHLY SALES, 1973

(In thousands)

January	$43	July	$ 58
February	50	August	583
March	58	September	662
April	50	October	770
May	50	November	823
June	50	December	403

Exhibit 4

SUNSHINE TOY COMPANY

Pro Forma Balance Sheets, 1973 (Seasonal Production)

(In thousands)

ASSETS	Actual Dec. 31, 1972	Jan. 31, 1973	Feb. 28, 1973	Mar. 31, 1973	Apr. 30, 1973	May 31, 1973	June 30, 1973	July 31, 1973	Aug. 31, 1973	Sept. 30, 1973	Oct. 31, 1973	Nov. 30, 1973	Dec. 31, 1973
Cash (a)	$ 140	$ 392	$ 652	$ 579	$ 524	$ 500	$ 397	$ 361	$ 140	$ 140	$ 140	$ 140	$ 140
Accounts receivable (b)	1,051	383	93	108	108	100	100	108	641	1,245	1,432	1,593	1,226
Inventory (c)	212	212	212	212	212	212	212	212	212	212	212	212	212
Total current assets	$1,403	$ 987	$ 957	$ 899	$ 844	$ 812	$ 709	$ 681	$ 993	$1,597	$1,784	$1,945	$1,578
Net plant and equipment (d)	428	428	428	428	428	428	428	428	428	428	428	428	428
Total assets	$1,831	$1,415	$1,385	$1,327	$1,272	$1,240	$1,137	$1,109	$1,421	$2,025	$2,212	$2,373	$2,006
LIABILITIES AND NET WORTH													
Accounts payable (e)	$ 102	$ 13	$ 15	$ 17	$ 15	$ 15	$ 15	$ 17	$ 175	$ 199	$ 231	$ 247	$ 121
Notes payable—bank (f)	294	0	0	0	0	0	0	0	80	591	634	657	418
Accrued taxes (g)	60	44	28	(17)	(54)	(70)	(137)	(152)	(115)	(91)	(35)	26	24
Current portion—long-term debt	40	40	40	40	40	40	40	40	40	40	40	40	40
Total current liabilities	$ 496	$ 97	$ 83	$ 40	$ 1	$ (15)	$ (82)	$ (95)	$ 180	$ 739	$ 870	$ 970	$ 603
Long-term debt (h)	160	160	160	160	160	160	140	140	140	140	140	140	120
Shareholders' equity (i)	1,175	1,158	1,142	1,127	1,111	1,095	1,079	1,064	1,101	1,146	1,202	1,263	1,283
Total liabilities and net worth	$1,831	$1,415	$1,385	$1,327	$1,272	$1,240	$1,137	$1,109	$1,421	$2,025	$2,212	$2,373	$2,006

(a) Assumes maintenance of minimum $140,000 balance and includes excess cash in months when company is out of debt.

(b) Assumes 60-day collection period.

(c) Assumes inventories maintained at December 31, 1972 level for all of 1973.

(d) Assumes equipment purchases equal to depreciation expense.

(e) Assumed equal to 30% of the current month's sales and relates to material purchases of $1,080,000 for year as against sales of $3,600,000 for year as against purchases of $1,080,000 for year as against sales of $3,600,000. This represents a 30-day payment period. Since inventories are level, purchases will follow seasonal production and sales pattern.

(f) Plug figure.

(g) Taxes payable on 1972 income are due in equal installments on March 15 and June 15, 1973. On April 15, June 15, September 15, and December 15, 1973, payments of 25% each of the estimated tax for 1973 are due. In estimating its tax liability for 1973, the company had the option of using the prior year's tax liability ($84,000) for its estimate and making any adjusting tax payment in 1974. Alternatively, the company could estimate its 1973 tax liability directly. Sunshine planned to use its prior year's tax liability as its estimate and to pay $21,000 in April, June, September, and December, 1973.

(h) To be repaid at rate of $20,000 each June and December.

(i) Adjusted for net profit from current month's operations, as per attached pro forma income statements.

Exhibit 5

SUNSHINE TOY COMPANY

PRO FORMA INCOME STATEMENTS, 1973 (SEASONAL PRODUCTION)

(In thousands)

	January	February	March	April	May	June	July	August	September	October	November	December	Total
Net sales	$ 43	$ 50	$ 58	$ 50	$ 50	$ 50	$ 58	$583	$662	$770	$823	$403	$3,600
Cost of goods sold (a)	34	40	46	40	40	40	46	467	530	616	659	322	2,880
Gross profit	$ 9	$ 10	$ 12	$ 10	$ 10	$ 10	$ 12	$116	$132	$154	$164	$ 81	$ 720
Operating expenses (b)	42	42	42	42	42	42	42	42	42	42	42	42	504
Profit (loss) before taxes	$(33)	$(32)	$(30)	$(32)	$(32)	$(32)	$(30)	$ 74	$ 90	$112	$122	$ 39	$ 216
Federal income taxes (c)	(16)	(16)	(15)	(16)	(16)	(16)	(15)	37	45	56	61	19	108
Net profit	$(17)	$(16)	$(15)	$(16)	$(16)	$(16)	$(15)	$ 37	$ 45	$ 56	$ 61	$ 20	$ 108

(a) Assumes cost of goods sold equal to 80% sales.
(b) Assumed to be same for each month throughout the year.
(c) Parentheses show tax credits from operating losses, and reduce accrued taxes shown on balance sheet.

CUTRITE SHEARS, INC.

^^

On April 28, 1970, Mr. Hamilton, Senior Loan Officer at the Fulton National Bank of New York, was reviewing the credit file of Cutrite Shears, Inc. in preparation for a luncheon meeting with the company's president and treasurer. Mr. Schultz, treasurer of Cutrite, had recently informed Mr. Hamilton that the company would be unable to liquidate its outstanding seasonal loan as initially anticipated. Mr. Hamilton, while agreeing to extend the outstanding $500,000 loan, had suggested that he would like to stop by and discuss the company's recent progress when he was next in the vicinity of Savannah, Georgia, where Cutrite's home plant and offices were located.

Cutrite Shears, Inc. manufactured a complete line of household scissors and shears. Its quality lines were distributed through jobbers to specialty, hardware, and department stores, located throughout the country. Its cheaper products were sold directly to large variety chains. Although competition, particularly from companies in foreign countries, was severe, Cutrite had made profits in each year since 1934. Sales and profits had grown fairly steadily, if not dramatically, throughout the postwar period.

Fulton National Bank had been actively soliciting the Cutrite account for several years prior to early 1969. Mr. Hamilton, after several unsuccessful calls, finally convinced the officers of Cutrite that association with a large New York bank offered several advantages not to be found with local banks. Mr. Hamilton was particularly pleased with the success of his efforts because Cutrite historically held fairly sizable deposit balances in its principal banks.

The company had sufficient capital to cover its permanent requirements over the immediate foreseeable future. Its short-term borrowings from banks were typically confined to the period July through December of each year, when additional working capital was needed to support a seasonal sales peak. As a matter of policy the company attempted to produce at an even rate throughout the year, and this accounted in good part for the sizable need for seasonal funds.

In June, 1969, Mr. Schultz arranged a line of credit of $1,200,000 with the Fulton National Bank to cover requirements for the fall. At the time, Mr. Schultz anticipated that the loan would be completely paid off by December, 1969. He gave Mr. Hamilton a pro forma estimate of the company's fund requirements over the forthcoming 12-month period to support his request.

(These estimates are shown in Exhibits 1 and 2.) In addition to the above requirements, the forecast showed a need for a new loan of approximately $600,-000 by June, 1970. Mr. Schultz attributed this increase in fund requirements (no funds were needed in June, 1969) to a plant modernization program. He explained that the program, requiring expenditures of $2,000,000, was approximately half completed and would be finished by August, 1969. Efficiencies resulting from the modernization program, once completed, were expected to save about $300,000 per year before taxes in manufacturing costs.

Mr. Schultz called Mr. Hamilton in early September, 1969 to let him know that the company would require $150,000 more than had been initially requested to cover peak seasonal needs. Mr. Schultz explained that the principal reason for the larger requirements was higher expenditures for modernization than had initially been estimated. Mr. Hamilton informed Mr. Schultz that the bank would be happy to accommodate the additional loan requirements.

In January, 1970, Mr. Schultz again contacted Mr. Hamilton. Mr. Schultz noted that sales had slackened considerably since his previous call. He attributed this decline largely to the economic recession then in progress, not to any special conditions affecting his company or the shear industry. Slackening in sales demand, however, had created a need for additional short-term borrowing. Mr. Schultz believed that additional funds would be required until the company could adjust to the new economic conditions. He envisioned that this adjustment probably would not occur until mid-April, 1970, or thereabouts. Once more, Mr. Hamilton agreed to extend the necessary loan funds to Cutrite.

In early April, 1970, Mr. Schultz telephoned Mr. Hamilton a third time to inform him that Cutrite would probably not be able to repay its outstanding short-term loan of $500,000 before the seasonal upturn in fund requirements in June. Mr. Schultz explained that a further sales decline, occasioned by the recession, was largely responsible for the company's inability to liquidate the loan as anticipated. Mr. Hamilton, in reply, noted that the bank preferred seasonal loans to be "off the books" for at least two months of the year, but saw no reason why he would not be willing to renew Cutrite's outstanding loan. He nevertheless thought it advisable to explore whether or not the inability to repay the seasonal loan in 1970 might be caused by a permanent change in the nature of the company's loan needs, such as might be occasioned by the modernization program. He consequently suggested a meeting for April 29 to discuss the company's recent progress.

In preparing for this meeting, Mr. Hamilton examined carefully the various profit and loss statements and balance sheets that Mr. Schultz had submitted to the bank over the course of the last nine months. (These data are shown in Exhibits 3 and 4.) He hoped this analysis might uncover the reasons for Cutrite's inability to repay its loan in accordance with original estimates.

Exhibit 1

CUTRITE SHEARS, INC.

PRO FORMA BALANCE SHEETS BY MONTHS, FISCAL 1970

(In thousands)

	Actual June 30, 1969	1969						1970					
		July 31	Aug. 31	Sept. 30	Oct. 31	Nov. 30	Dec. 31	Jan. 31	Feb. 28	March 31	April 30	May 31	June 30
ASSETS													
Cash	$ 864	$ 400	$ 400	$ 400	$ 400	$ 400	$ 404	$ 894	$ 1,084	$ 759	$ 699	$ 539	$ 400
Accounts receivable*	697	950	1,250	1,550	2,050	2,050	1,750	1,250	1,050	950	800	650	700
Inventories (see below)	2,711	2,800	2,780	2,640	2,260	2,000	1,860	1,960	2,060	2,220	2,440	2,720	2,940
Total current assets	$ 4,272	$ 4,150	$ 4,430	$ 4,590	$ 4,710	$ 4,450	$ 4,014	$ 4,104	$ 4,194	$ 3,929	$ 3,939	$ 3,909	$ 4,040
Net plant	8,215	8,715	9,215	9,215	9,215	9,215	9,215	9,215	9,215	9,215	9,215	9,215	9,215
Total assets	$12,487	$12,865	$13,645	$13,805	$13,925	$13,665	$13,229	$13,319	$13,409	$13,144	$13,154	$13,124	$13,255
LIABILITIES AND NET WORTH													
Bank loans payable	$ 0	$ 327	$ 926	$ 1,151	$ 861	$ 271	$ 0	$ 0	$ 0	$ 0	$ 0	$ 0	$ 636
Accounts payable—trade†	288	249	260	260	260	260	260	260	260	260	260	260	260
Taxes payable‡	0	45	130	40	245	410	320	365	410	220	225	210	0
Miscellaneous other	90	90	90	90	90	90	90	90	90	90	90	90	90
Total current liabilities	$ 378	$ 711	$ 1,406	$ 1,541	$ 1,456	$ 1,031	$ 670	$ 715	$ 760	$ 570	$ 575	$ 560	$ 986
Mortgage at 6%	4,000	4,000	4,000	4,000	4,000	4,000	3,900	3,900	3,900	3,900	3,900	3,900	3,800
Common stock	4,000	4,000	4,000	4,000	4,000	4,000	4,000	4,000	4,000	4,000	4,000	4,000	4,000
Earned surplus	4,109	4,154	4,239	4,264	4,634	4,634	4,659	4,704	4,749	4,674	4,679	4,664	4,469
Total liabilities and net worth	$12,487	$12,865	$13,645	$13,805	$13,925	$13,665	$13,229	$13,319	$13,409	$13,144	$13,154	$13,124	$13,255

1969   1970

Inventory Subsidiary Data (FIFO)	July	Aug.	Sept.	Oct.	Nov.	Dec.	Jan.	Feb.	March	April	May	June
Raw Materials												
Opening balances	$ 271	$ 260	$ 260	$ 260	$ 260	$ 260	$ 260	$ 260	$ 260	$ 260	$ 260	$ 260
Plus purchases	249	260	260	260	260	260	260	260	260	260	260	260
Less transfers to work-in-process	260	260	260	260	260	260	260	260	260	260	260	260
Closing balance	$ 260	$ 260	$ 260	$ 260	$ 260	$ 260	$ 260	$ 260	$ 260	$ 260	$ 260	$ 260
Work-in-Process												
Opening balance	$1,040	$1,040	$1,040	$1,040	$1,040	$1,040	$1,040	$1,040	$1,040	$1,040	$1,040	$1,040
Plus raw material additions	260	260	260	260	260	260	260	260	260	260	260	260
Plus labor additions	260	260	260	260	260	260	260	260	260	260	260	260
Transfers to finished goods	520	520	520	520	520	520	520	520	520	520	520	520
Closing balance	$1,040	$1,040	$1,040	$1,040	$1,040	$1,040	$1,040	$1,040	$1,040	$1,040	$1,040	$1,040
Finished Goods												
Opening balance	$1,400	$1,500	$1,480	$1,340	$ 960	$ 700	$ 560	$ 660	$ 760	$ 920	$1,140	$1,420
Plus additions from work-in-process	520	520	520	520	520	520	520	520	520	520	520	520
Less cost of goods sold	420	540	660	900	780	660	420	420	360	300	240	300
Closing balance	$1,500	$1,480	$1,340	$ 960	$ 700	$ 560	$ 660	$ 760	$ 920	$1,140	$1,420	$1,640
Total closing inventory	$2,800	$2,780	$2,640	$2,260	$2,000	$1,860	$1,960	$2,060	$2,220	$2,440	$2,720	$2,940

* Assumes collections lag sales by 45 days.
† Assumes 30-day payment period, in accordance with trade terms.
‡ Estimated taxes are paid in four equal installments of $215,000 each in September, December, March, and June based on pro forma earnings calculated the previous June.

Exhibit 2

CUTRITE SHEARS, INC.

PRO FORMA INCOME STATEMENTS BY MONTHS—FISCAL YEAR ENDING JUNE 30, 1970

(In thousands)

	Actual Year Ended June 30, 1969	July	Aug.	Sept.	Oct.	Nov.	Dec.	Jan.	Feb.	March	April	May	June	Pro Forma, Year Ending June 30, 1970
		1969						1970						
Sales	$10,079	$700	$900	$1,100	$1,500	$1,300	$1,100	$700	$700	$600	$500	$400	$500	$10,000
Less cost of goods sold: Materials and labor at 60% of sales	6,184	420	540	660	900	780	660	420	420	360	300	240	300	6,000
Overhead (includes depreciation of $50 per month)	1,191	100	100	100	100	100	100	100	100	100	100	100	100	1,200
Total costs	$7,375	$520	$640	$760	$1,000	$880	$760	$520	$520	$460	$400	$340	$400	$7,200
Gross profit	2,704	180	260	340	500	420	340	180	180	140	100	60	100	2,800
Selling and administrative expenses	1,033	90	90	90	90	90	90	90	90	90	90	90	90	1,080
Profit before taxes	$1,671	$90	$170	$250	$410	$330	$250	$90	$90	$50	$10	$(30)	$10	$1,720
Taxes at 50%	837	45	85	125	205	165	125	45	45	25	5	(15)	5	860
Profits after taxes	$834	$45	$85	$125	$205	$165	$125	$45	$45	$25	$5	$(15)	$5	$860
Dividends	500			100			100			100			200	500
Retained earnings	$334	$45	$85	$25	$205	$165	$25	$45	$45	$(75)	$5	$(15)	$(195)	$360
Cumulative retained earnings	...	45	130	155	360	525	550	595	640	565	570	555	360	360

Exhibit 3

CUTRITE SHEARS, INC.

ACTUAL INCOME STATEMENTS BY MONTHS, JULY 1969–MARCH 1970

(In thousands)

| | 1969 | | | | | | 1970 | | |
	July	*Aug.*	*Sept.*	*Oct.*	*Nov.*	*Dec.*	*Jan.*	*Feb.*	*March*
Sales	$692	$871	$1,030	$1,360	$1,128	$936	$588	$581	$ 501
Less cost of goods sold:									
Materials and labor	436	549	652	816	677	562	353	366	321
Overhead (includes depreciation of $50 per month)	99	97	114	104	101	96	98	125*	108*
Total costs	$535	$646	$ 766	$ 920	$ 778	$658	$451	$491	$ 429
Gross profit	157	225	264	440	350	278	137	90	72
Selling and administrative expenses	91	93	98	93	92	90	87	86	86
Profit before tax	$ 66	$132	$ 166	$ 347	$ 258	$188	$ 50	$ 4	$ (14)
Taxes at 50%	33	66	83	174	129	94	25	2	(7)
Profits after tax	$ 33	$ 66	$ 83	$ 174	$ 129	$ 94	$ 25	$ 2	$ (7)
Dividends			100			100			100
Retained earnings	$ 33	$ 66	$ (17)	$ 174	$ 129	$ (6)	$ 25	$ 2	$(107)
Cumulative retained earnings	33	99	82	256	385	379	404	406	299

* Includes special costs for laying off personnel.

Exhibit 4

CUTRITE SHEARS, INC.

ACTUAL BALANCE SHEETS BY MONTHS, JUNE 30, 1969–MARCH 31, 1970

(In thousands)

	1969							1970		
	June 30	July 31	Aug. 31	Sept. 30	Oct. 31	Nov. 30	Dec. 31	Jan. 31	Feb. 28	March 31
ASSETS										
Cash.................	$ 864	$ 474	$ 345	$ 388	$ 387	$ 432	$ 367	$ 533	$ 514	$ 385
Accounts receivable........	697	949	1,219	1,470	1,890	1,848	1,864	1,324	1,060	882
Inventories.............	2,711	2,802	2,777	2,663	2,401	2,242	2,174	2,316	2,398	2,466
Total current assets...	$ 4,272	$ 4,225	$ 4,341	$ 4,521	$ 4,678	$ 4,522	$ 4,405	$ 4,173	$ 3,972	$ 3,733
Net plant...........	8,215	8,730	9,255	9,314	9,317	9,312	9,326	9,312	9,301	9,287
Total assets.........	$12,487	$12,955	$13,596	$13,835	$13,995	$13,834	$13,731	$13,485	$13,273	$13,020
LIABILITIES AND NET WORTH										
Bank loans payable.........	$ 0	$ 424	$ 924	$ 1,300	$ 1,099	$ 699	$ 875	$ 575	$ 375	$ 500
Accounts payable—trade......	288	264	259	282	293	279	229	234	220	172
Taxes payable.........	0	33	99	(33)	141	270	149	174	176	(46)
Miscellaneous other........	90	92	106	95	97	92	90	89	87	86
Total current liabilities..	$ 378	$ 813	$ 1,388	$ 1,644	$ 1,630	$ 1,340	$ 1,343	$ 1,072	$ 858	$ 712
Mortgage at 6%.........	4,000	4,000	4,000	4,000	4,000	4,000	3,900	3,900	3,900	3,900
Common stock.........	4,000	4,000	4,000	4,000	4,000	4,000	4,000	4,000	4,000	4,000
Earned surplus..........	4,109	4,142	4,208	4,191	4,365	4,494	4,488	4,513	4,515	4,408
Total liabilities and net worth.....	$12,487	$12,955	$13,596	$13,835	$13,995	$13,834	$13,731	$13,485	$13,273	$13,020

	1969						1970		
Inventory Subsidiary Data (FIFO)	July	Aug.	Sept.	Oct.	Nov.	Dec.	Jan.	Feb.	March
Raw Materials									
Opening balance	$ 271	$ 272	$ 253	$ 254	$ 265	$ 275	$ 260	$ 255	$ 252
Plus purchases	263	260	280	290	268	230	231	218	173
Less transfers to work-in-process	262	279	279	279	258	245	236	221	201
Closing balance	$ 272	$ 253	$ 254	$ 265	$ 275	$ 260	$ 255	$ 252	$ 224
Work-in-Process									
Opening balance	$1,040	$1,047	$1,069	$1,077	$1,078	$1,049	$1,015	$ 987	$ 929
Plus raw material additions	262	279	279	279	258	245	236	221	201
Plus labor additions	264	264	258	264	250	264	264	230	216
Transfers to finished goods	519	521	529	542	537	543	528	509	500
Closing balance	$1,047	$1,069	$1,077	$1,078	$1,049	$1,015	$ 987	$ 929	$ 846
Finished Goods									
Opening balance	$1,400	$1,483	$1,455	$1,332	$1,058	$ 918	$ 899	$1,074	$1,217
Plus additions from work-in-process	519	521	529	542	537	543	528	509	500
Less cost of goods sold	436	549	652	816	677	562	353	366	321
Closing balance	$1,483	$1,455	$1,332	$1,058	$ 918	$ 899	$1,074	$1,217	$1,396
Total inventory	$2,802	$2,777	$2,663	$2,401	$2,242	$2,174	$2,316	$2,398	$2,466

HAMPTON MACHINE TOOL COMPANY

On September 14, 1979, Mr. Jerry Eckwood, vice president of the St. Louis National Bank, was considering a loan request from a customer located in a nearby city. The company, Hampton Machine Tool Company, had requested renewal of an existing $1 million loan originally due to be repaid on September 30. In addition to the renewal of the existing loan, Hampton was asking for an additional loan of $350,000 for planned equipment purchases in October. Under the terms of the company's request, both loans, totaling $1.35 million, would be repayable at the end of 1979.

Since its establishment in 1915, Hampton Machine Tool Company had successfully weathered the severe cyclical fluctuations characteristic of the machine tool manufacturing business. In the most recent cycle, Hampton had experienced record production and profitability during the mid- and late-1960s. Because Hampton's major customers included the military aircraft manufacturers and automobile manufacturers in the St. Louis area, the company's success in the 1960s reflected a strong automobile market and the heavy defense spending associated with the Vietnam War. Hampton rode the 1960s boom into the early 1970s. Hampton, along with the rest of the capital goods industry, experienced a severe decline in sales and profitability in the mid-1970s. Precipitous declines in the production of automobiles in St. Louis facilities reflected the Arab oil embargo, subsequent increases in the price of gasoline, and the 1974–75 recession. Massive reductions in defense spending in the post-Vietnam War period had a severe adverse impact on Hampton's other major customer segment, military aircraft manufacturers. Hampton's sales had bottomed out in the mid-1970s, and the several years prior to 1978 had seen a steady rebuilding of sales. Hampton's recovery was due primarily to three factors. First, military aircraft sales had increased substantially reflecting both an expanding export market and a more benign domestic market. Secondly, though the automobile manufacturers in the area were not expanding, this segment of Hampton's market had at least stabilized. Finally, the adverse economic conditions in the mid-1970s had taken their toll in the regional capital goods industry. Consequently, Hampton's market share increased as many thinly capitalized competitors had been forced out of the industry. Hampton's recovery had suffered a mild setback as 1978 sales were far below capacity. However, with a substantial backlog of firm sales orders, Hampton entered 1979 expecting its first year of capacity sales since 1972.

Hampton's conservative financial policies had contributed to its survival and success in the volatile capital goods industry. The company had traditionally maintained a strong working capital position as a buffer against economic uncertainty. As a result, the company had no debt on its balance sheet during the ten years prior to December 1978. In a meeting in early December 1978, Mr. Benjamin G. Cowins, president of Hampton, requested the initial loan of $1 million to facilitate purchasing the stock of several dissident shareholders. While Hampton had some cash in excess of that required for normal operations, excess cash was not sufficient to effect the stock redemption. Therefore, Mr. Cowins had asked Mr. Eckwood for a loan from the St. Louis National Bank. The loan of $1 million was to be taken down at the end of December 1978. Hampton would make monthly interest payments at an interest rate of $1\frac{1}{2}\%$ per month (approximately 18% on an annual basis) on the principal which would be due at the end of September 1979. In support of his request, Mr. Cowins had submitted a forecast of monthly shipments for 1979 (see Exhibit 1), a balance sheet dated November 30, 1978 (presented in the first column of Exhibit 2), and documentation of Hampton's backlog of sales orders. Mr. Eckwood felt at the time that the documentation provided by Mr. Cowins was sufficient to support favorable action on the request. Furthermore, Hampton had traditionally kept its ample cash balances on deposit at the St. Louis National Bank, and the bank's management knew Mr. Cowins well. Mr. Cowins, then 58 years old, had succeeded his father-in-law as president of Hampton in 1963. He was widely respected in the business community as an energetic and successful executive. In mid-December 1978, Mr. Eckwood had approved the loan to Hampton.

Hampton took down the loan at the end of December 1978. The proceeds of the loan plus $2 million in excess cash were used immediately to repurchase 75,000 shares of Hampton's $10 par value stock from several dissident shareholders at an aggregate cost of $3 million.

After the loan was made, Mr. Cowins regularly sent the bank profit and loss statements and balance sheets documenting Hampton's financial condition. In preparing his analysis of Mr. Cowins' request, Mr. Eckwood focused on the documents presented in Exhibits 1, 2, and 3. In examining Hampton's financial statements, Mr. Eckwood recalled that Hampton's selling terms were 30 days net. Occasionally a customer placing a large order would make an advance payment to help Hampton finance the construction of the machines ordered. Because Hampton's products were largely made to order, the construction period involved five to six months for some of the larger, more complex types of machines. Upon completion and shipment of orders against which advances had been paid, Hampton deducted the amount of the advance from the amount billed to the customer. Also, Mr. Eckwood understood that the company purchased its materials on terms of net 30 days.

In a letter to Mr. Eckwood, Mr. Cowins had made his request for the extension of the existing Hampton note until the end of the year plus an additional loan of $350,000 to finance equipment purchases. The additional loan would be needed by the end of October and would be payable at the end of the year with monthly interest payments remaining 1½% of principal. In his letter, Mr. Cowins commented at some length on the company's financial condition, the reasons for the shortfall of actual from projected 1979 shipments, and Hampton's substantial backlog of firm sales orders. In addition, Mr. Cowins stated that he expected to be able to repay both loans in full by December 31, 1979. Mr. Cowins' letter is presented in full as Exhibit 4. Although Hampton would not need the additional $350,000 loan until the end of October, the maturity date of the existing note was fast approaching. Therefore, Mr. Eckwood needed to decide upon a response to Mr. Cowins' request.

Exhibit 1

HAMPTON MACHINE TOOL COMPANY
SHIPMENTS AT SELLING PRICE
(Dollar figures in thousands)

		As Forecast December 1978	Actual	As Forecast September 1979
1979	January........	$1,302	$ 861	
	February.......	1,872	672	
	March.........	1,635	1,866	
	April..........	1,053	1,566	
	May...........	1,293	873	
	June...........	1,479	1,620	
	July...........	1,488	723	
	August........	1,797	507	
	Eight-months total...	$11,919	$8,688	
	September......	1,299		$2,163
	October........	1,347		1,505
	November......	1,311		1,604
	December......	2,298		2,265

Exhibit 2

HAMPTON MACHINE TOOL COMPANY
BALANCE SHEETS
(Dollar figures in thousands)

	11/30/78	12/31/78	3/31/79	6/30/79	7/31/79	8/31/79
Cash..................................	$2,379	$ 491	$ 485	$1,152	$1,678	$1,559
Accounts receivable, net.............	1,245	1,863	1,971	1,893	1,269	684
Inventories...........................	2,601	2,478	3,474	3,276	3,624	4,764
Total current assets............	$6,225	$4,832	$5,930	$6,321	$6,571	$7,007
Gross fixed assets...................	$4,010	$4,010	$4,010	$4,010	$4,010	$4,010
Accumulated depreciation...........	2,998	3,010	3,020	3,030	3,040	3,050
Net fixed assets.....................	$1,012	$1,000	$ 990	$ 980	$ 970	$ 960
Prepaid expenses....................	62	40	39	24	24	42
Total assets....................	$7,299	$5,872	$6,959	$7,325	$7,565	$8,009
Notes payable, bank..................	—	$1,000	$1,000	$1,000	$1,000	$1,000
Accounts payable....................	$ 348	371	681	399	621	948
Accruals.............................	420	777	849	537	444	411
Taxes payable*......................	150	74	373	535	588	660
Customer advance payments.........	840	1,040	1,040	1,566	1,566	1,566
Total current liabilities........	$1,758	$3,262	$3,943	$4,037	$4,219	$4,585
Common stock ($10 par value).......	$1,178	$ 428	$ 428	$ 428	$ 428	$ 428
Surplus..............................	4,363	2,182	2,588	2,860	2,918	2,996
Net worth.......................	$5,541	$2,610	$3,016	$3,288	$3,346	$3,424
Total liabilities and net worth....	$7,299	$5,872	$6,959	$7,325	$7,565	$8,009

*Tax payments in 1979 include: $75,000 due March 15 on underpayment of 1978 taxes and four equal payments of $181,000 due on the 15th of April, June, September, and December for estimated 1979 tax liability with any underpayment of 1979 taxes due March 15, 1980.

Exhibit 3

HAMPTON MACHINE TOOL COMPANY
INCOME STATEMENTS
(Dollar figures in thousands)

	Fiscal Year Ending 12/31/78	Dec. 1978	1979 Jan.	Feb.	Mar.	Apr.	May	June	July	Aug.	Eight Months Ending 8/31/79
Net sales	$7,854	$1,551	$861	$672	$1,866	$1,566	$873	$1,620	$723	$507	$8,688
Cost of sales*	5,052	1,122	474	369	1,362	1,137	567	1,197	510	276	5,892
Gross profit	$2,802	$ 429	$387	$303	$ 504	$ 429	$306	$ 423	$213	$231	$2,796
Selling and administration expenses	1,296	248	103	61	205	172	96	130	87	66	920
Interest expense	—	—	15	15	15	15	15	15	15	15	120
Net income before taxes	$1,506	$ 181	$269	$227	$ 284	$ 242	$195	$ 278	$111	$150	$1,756
Income taxes	723	87	129	109	136	116	94	133	53	72	842
Net income	$ 783	$ 94	$140	$118	$ 148	$ 126	$101	$ 145	$ 58	$ 78	$ 914
Dividends	$ 50	$ 25	—	—	—	—	—	$ 100	—	—	$ 100

*Includes depreciation charges of $150,000 in 1978, $12,000 in December 1978, and $10,000 per month in 1979.

Exhibit 4

HAMPTON MACHINE TOOL COMPANY
EAST ST. LOUIS, ILLINOIS

September 12, 1979

Mr. Jerry Eckwood
Vice President
St. Louis National Bank
St. Louis, Missouri

Dear Mr. Eckwood:

I enclose the company's August 31 financial statements. While these statements show our cash balance as $1,559,000, you will note we have an obligation to a customer for cash advances of $1,566,000, and we expect to ship this order over the next three months. With respect to our note for $1,000,000 due September 30, we request that you renew it until the end of 1979. We also wish to borrow an additional $350,000 to be available at the end of October to be repaid by the end of the year with interest at the rate of 1½% per month on the principal. This additional loan is required to purchase certain needed equipment. At the end of the year, as you can see for yourself, we expect to be able to have enough cash on hand to retire our obligations in full.

For the past month or more we have been producing at capacity and expect to continue at this rate through the end of the year and beyond. On August 31, our backlog of unfilled orders amounted to about $16,500,000—approximately 90% of annual capacity. I should stress that these are firm orders from respected customers.

Despite our backlog, our shipment schedule has been upset, particularly the last several months, because we have had to wait on our suppliers for shipment of electronic control mechanisms. On August 31, we had seven machines with an accumulated cost of about $1,320,000 completed except for the installation of these electronic components. The components were finally received last week and will enable us to complete a number of machines in the next few weeks. After this imminent reduction in work in progress of about $1,320,000, the remainder of our work in progress inventories will probably remain stable for the foreseeable future because of our capacity rate of production.

We bought raw materials beyond our immediate needs in July and August to be assured of completing our orders scheduled to be shipped by the end of the year. We have accumulated about $420,000 worth of scarcer components above our normal raw materials inventories. The extra $420,000 will be used up by the end of the year, bringing our raw materials inventories back to normal levels for capacity production. Because we bought ahead this way, we expect to cut raw materials purchases to about $600,000 a month in each of the four remaining months of 1979.

Our finished goods inventories are, of course, negligible at all times since we ship machines within a day of completion.

Our revised shipment estimates are as follows:

(At Selling Prices)

September.........	$2,163,000
October...........	1,505,000
November.........	1,604,000
December.........	2,265,000
	$7,537,000

The shipment estimates include the $2,100,000 order for the General Aircraft Corporation. We are now scheduled to ship against this order as follows: September, $840,000; October, $840,000; November, $420,000. Since we obtained a $1,566,000 advance from General Aircraft on this order, we will be due nothing on these shipments until their $1,566,000 credit with us is exhausted.

You will note the decline in our accrued expenses. As I mentioned to you last month when you visited us, we have been paying off commissions due to our three principal salesmen (who are also large stockholders in the company). Last year when we needed funds

Exhibit 4—Continued

to redeem part of our capital stock, these men agreed to defer their commissions until the funds could be more easily spared. In August, we paid off the last of these back commissions. This has been the principal cause of the decline in accruals, which, like prepaid expenses, normally does not change much from month to month. Assuming accruals will stay about the same as on August 31, our monthly outlay for all expenses other than interest and raw materials purchases should be around $400,000 per month.

Due to poor economic conditions and our desire to conserve cash, we have spent very little on new equipment in the last several years, and this has contributed somewhat to the difficulties we have had in maintaining production at a capacity rate this year. We feel that we should not further postpone replacing certain essential equipment if we are to avoid a possible major breakdown at an inconvenient time. Therefore, we think it necessary to purchase additional equipment costing $350,000 in October to maintain production efficiency. The proceeds from the additional loan we have requested will be used at the end of October to pay for this equipment. This equipment has an estimated life of eight years, an estimated net salvage value of zero, and the $350,000 purchase price will be depreciated on a straight-line basis.

Our tax people tell us that the equipment will qualify for a 10% investment tax credit (ITC). However, the tax savings of $35,000 will not affect our scheduled tax payments this year. We are scheduled to pay $181,000 in taxes on September 15 and to make another payment of the same amount on December 15. As I understand it, the ITC savings of $35,000 will reduce both our tax liability and the taxes payable on our balance sheet as well as increase reported earnings. However, the cash flow impact of this savings will not be felt until March 1980 when we make our final settlement with the government on 1979 taxes.

Despite temporary bottlenecks which reduced shipments, our profits for the year to date have been quite satisfactory. With raw materials and components supply assured and the efficiency provided by the new equipment we plan to purchase, we feel confident we can meet our shipment forecasts for the rest of the year. Furthermore, the business which we expect to ship in the next four months is on our books on profitable terms. While our profit, as you know, varies with the item involved, our engineering estimates indicate that we expect to earn a profit before taxes and interest of about 23% of sales on these shipments. Even after taking into account our tax rate of 48% and the interest we must pay on our notes, 1979 looks like a very good year. Because of these good results and in view of our conservative dividend policy during the last several years of economic uncertainty, we plan to pay a dividend to our stockholders. Our dividend disbursements in 1979 have continued to be quite modest, and we want to be sure that those stockholders who stood by us last December have no cause to regret their action. Under the circumstances, we feel that a dividend of $150,000 payable in December is the least we can do in view of our high earnings and our stockholders' patient support.

If there is anything further you need to know, please do not hesitate to write or phone.

Sincerely yours,
(*Signed*) B. G. Cowins

Benjamin G. Cowins
President

SCIENCE TECHNOLOGY COMPANY

^^

Early in April, 1974, Bill Watson, president of Science Technology Company (STC), was reviewing a "Five-Year Capital and Financing Plan" prepared for the company by Mr. Finson, STC's chief financial officer. Mr. Finson intended to discuss the Plan at a forthcoming board meeting. Presumably if the Plan and the premises on which it was drawn were endorsed by the board it would greatly influence the financial policies and indeed the total development of the firm in the coming years.

Mr. Watson had spent much of his 30 years at STC in various engineering and sales positions. His appointment as president in 1973 had followed several years of very disappointing performance by the company—years that had impaired STC's financial strength significantly. He knew that other members of the board would be keenly interested in his comments on the Plan, especially as indications of his willingness to relax the stringent controls imposed in 1973.

After some study, Mr. Watson identified several questions as important for his further consideration and resolution. Among these were the following:

1. In view of the uneven growth in sales, inventory and receivables, and earnings in the past, was Mr. Finson's use of averages for his projections a valid and useful approach?
2. What were the implications of forecasting that both volume and dollar sales would increase at 10% per year? More specifically, Mr. Watson wondered what impact inflation would have on STC and whether it should be factored into the financial forecasts.
3. What corporate sales and profit performance would be required over the next 3–5 years to secure financing and to allow STC to "go public"?
4. What should STC do?

Science Technology Company

STC was founded in 1915 and for the first 30 years of its existence pioneered the design, manufacture, and use of electronic measuring instruments. Its major product categories included: instruments and systems for testing electronic circuits and components; equipment for measuring and analyzing noise and vibration; audiometric devices for dealing with speech and hearing problems; and computer-controlled systems for testing high-frequency integrated circuitry.

Until World War II the company faced very little serious competition and it successfully pursued a policy of self-financed, controlled growth. In many ways, STC was as much a family as a business in its first 50 years. The 40-hour week and profit sharing were both introduced in 1919. During the Great Depression of the 1930's, the company retained its entire work force. Moreover, when one of the banks used by the company failed in 1932, the directors voted to give employees cash to make up for their lost deposits. The directors reasoned that workers banked there because the company did, and that STC thus had some responsibility for their loss.

Management's belief in a primary responsibility to both employees and existing customers was reflected in a 1942 advertisement headlined, "We Don't Want to Grow Too Large." Operationally, this policy was implemented in decisions such as abandoning development of the oscilloscope, which was first developed as a commercial product in STC's laboratories. By 1974, the oscilloscope was an instrument with an annual market of several hundred million dollars.

The competitive situation changed dramatically during the 1950's. The explosive growth of the electronics industry encouraged the entry of a number of new firms eager to participate in large government contracts. STC, with its policy of self-financing all growth, watched its sales growth slip from 10% per year during 1945–55, to only 8% per year during 1965–72—well below the 20–25% annual growth rate of its prime competitor, Hewlett-Packard Company. The company also experienced a steady decline in its profitability, as price competition heightened.

STC RETURN ON NET WORTH

1935–45	1946–55	1956–65	1966–69
12%	11%	9%	6%

It was apparent to management by 1969 that STC had not been keeping up with the dynamic electronics industry and that substantial changes were needed to convert it from a sedate, if not stodgy, company to an active, growing company responsive to the opportunities arising from new technology and new markets. For many in management, job security seemed assured and their interest was in establishing an exciting track record that might one day be converted into a high multiple for the stock.

Efforts to revitalize the company proceeded on two fronts. Research and development had always been a central part of STC's strategy. Approximately one third of its sales at any point in time were from products introduced within the most recent three years. Beginning in 1968, however, expenditures on research and development were increased from 9–10% of sales to 14% as STC began the development of its own minicomputer. It was felt that the minicomputer project was consistent both with the trend toward computer-linked, electronic testing systems and with management's interest in converting the image of the company.

Two acquisitions were also made in 1969–70 to position STC in several embryonic but potentially high growth areas. Both involved the application of sophisticated electronic measuring systems in areas requiring substantial customer education and custom design.

The results of the crash catch-up program were extremely mixed. By 1974 STC had positioned itself in a mix of growth areas and cash generating areas that would provide:

1. A satisfactory overall corporate growth rate of at least 10% per year (in constant dollars), in line with the company's past experience (see Exhibit 1).
2. Reasonable market and product diversification.
3. A balance of products in terms of their product-life cycles.
4. Challenging career opportunities for the engineering staff.
5. Concentration on a limited number of product-markets in which STC's expertise and competitive prospects should enable it to maintain a strong market position.

The company also strengthened its sales and distribution system to improve both geographic coverage and field servicing. By 1974 there were 10 sales engineering offices in North America, staffed by 45 sales engineers all of whom held degrees in electrical engineering or had equivalent technical experience. European operations, which accounted for 18% of total sales, were conducted through manufacturers' representatives.

Unfortunately, the catch-up program placed heavy financing pressures on STC. The company's control systems were inadequate and management lost control of operations. Profitability fell sharply and the company operated at a cumulative deficit of $0.2 million during the period 1969–73. (See Exhibit 1.) This low profitability, when combined with a 75% increase in sales, created a substantial financing need (see Exhibit 2). In addition, the cash acquisition of Acoustical Controls Company for $1.9 million in 1970 further strained STC's financial position.

Management had no alternative to meeting these needs with additional debt financing. One of the basic tenets of the company since its founding was the policy that the stock would be owned solely by the employees. Departing employees were not allowed to retain their stockholdings, but first were required to offer the shares back to the company at their then book value.[1] During the period 1963–72, stock repurchases by the company (net of stock sales to employees) had totaled $3 million. Beginning in 1973, however, STC ceased all stock repurchases in an effort to conserve cash.

---

[1] With no public market for the stock, the book value seemed the least controversial measure of the stock's value and in 1974 was accepted without question by the employee-stockholders. At year-end 1973 book value per share was $51.

The outstanding debt of STC rose from $400,000 in 1962 to $3 million in 1969 to $12 million by year-end 1973. Of the $12 million, $3 million represented a long-term mortgage bond secured by all of the company's real estate and the remainder represented short-term bank debt at a cost of 2½% over the prime rate and secured by all remaining assets.

It seemed clear to Mr. Watson that STC was approaching the prudent limit of debt financing in relation to its equity. Furthermore, the sale of stock seemed unattractive in 1974, both as a matter of policy and from the standpoint of market timing. The stock prices of small, publicly-traded electronics companies had been under substantial selling pressure in recent months. Price-earnings ratios had plummeted from 15–20 times in 1973 to only 6–7 times in early 1974. While Hewlett-Packard Company still commanded a multiple of 40 times, its sales and earnings record was far superior to that of STC. (See Exhibit 3).

Mr. Watson was therefore encouraged by Mr. Finson's projections of reasonable sales growth financed without new equity issues. (See Exhibit 4.)

Exhibit 1

SCIENCE TECHNOLOGY COMPANY

CONSOLIDATED INCOME STATEMENTS, 1969–73

(Dollar figures in thousands)

	1969	1970	1971	1972	1973
Net sales	$25,780	$26,451	$29,411	$33,350	$44,991
Cost of goods sold	13,212	13,173	15,117	18,745	23,715
Gross profit	$12,568	$13,278	$14,294	$14,605	$21,276
Research and development expenses	3,239	3,777	4,271	4,870	4,195
Selling, administrative, and general expenses	8,156	8,929	9,140	11,814	14,783
Interest expense	294	366	311	494	1,041
Other expenses	140	143	141	93	100
Profit before taxes	$ 739	$ 63	$ 431	$(2,666)	$ 1,157
Taxes	434	18	187	(839)*	82*
Profit after taxes	$ 305	$ 45	$ 244	$(1,827)†	$ 1,075
Earnings per common share (in dollars)	$ 0.94	$ 0.14	$ 0.75	$ (5.65)†	$ 3.30

SELECTED FINANCIAL RATIOS

% of Sales:					
Cost of goods sold	51.2%	49.8%	51.4%	56.2%	52.7%
Research and development	12.6	14.3	14.5	14.6	9.3
Selling, administrative, and general	31.6	33.8	31.1	35.3	32.8
Interest	1.1	1.4	1.1	1.5	2.3
Profit after taxes	1.2	0.2	0.8	—	2.4

* The tax figures reflect tax loss carrybacks and carryforwards.
† The deficit in 1972 resulted in part from delays in production. Substantial shipments scheduled for 1972 were actually made in 1973. However, all of the expenditures programmed for 1972 were made in that year.

Exhibit 2

SCIENCE TECHNOLOGY COMPANY

CONSOLIDATED BALANCE SHEETS AT DECEMBER 31, 1969–73

(Dollar figures in thousands)

	1969	1970	1971	1972	1973
Cash	$ 858	$ 1,304	$ 1,217	$ 436	$ 639
Accounts receivable	5,019	5,422	7,711	10,129	11,936
Inventories—at lower of cost					
(first-in, first-out) or market*	9,400	10,396	9,833	12,820	13,918
Other	43	66	—	905	754
Total current assets	$15,320	$17,188	$18,761	$24,290	$27,247
Net fixed assets	5,923	5,744	5,289	5,129	4,991
Patents and trademarks	330	288	245	203	166
Goodwill	457	904	911	911	931
Other	603	842	742	642	430
Total assets	$22,633	$24,966	$25,948	$31,175	$33,765
Notes payable—banks	$ —	$ 1,110	$ 984	$ 6,346	$ 8,480
Accounts payable	1,140	1,012	1,580	4,349	3,154
Accrued expenses	441	540	622	711	1,614
Accrued payroll	339	282	659	400	610
Other	644	537	483	29	436
Total current liabilities	$ 2,564	$ 3,481	$ 4,328	$11,835	$14,294
Long-term debt†	3,133	4,236	4,360	4,032	3,088
Other liabilities	111	132	26	—	—
Shareowners' equity	16,825	17,117	17,234	15,308	16,383
Total liabilities and net worth	$22,633	$24,966	$25,948	$31,175	$33,765

SELECTED FINANCIAL RATIOS

% of Sales:

Accounts receivable	19.5%	20.5%	26.2%	30.4%	26.5%
Inventories	36.5	39.3	33.4	38.4	30.9
Net fixed assets	23.0	21.7	18.0	15.4	11.1
Accounts payable	4.4	3.8	5.4	13.0	7.0
Notes payable, long-term					
debt, and equity	77.4	84.9	76.8	77.0	62.1

*A number of manufacturing items are expensed as period costs, rather than being included in inventory. Inventories would be higher by $3.4 million at year-end 1973 if they fully absorbed all manufacturing costs.
†To be repaid in semi-annual payments of $175,000.

Exhibit 3

SCIENCE TECHNOLOGY COMPANY
FINANCIAL INFORMATION ON PRIMARY COMPETITORS

	Fluke	Teradyne	Hewlett-Packard	STC
Size ($ millions):				
1973 Sales.............................	$26.3	$40.7	$661	$45.0
1973 Assets............................	$17.7	$31.4	$580	$33.8
Five-Year Growth:				
Sales.................................	+171%	+347%	+146%	+96%
Net income...........................	+592%	+454%	+143%	+79%
Earnings per share.....................	+546%	+313%	+128%	+82%
Profitability—1973:				
Cost of goods sold as % of sales...........	52%	} 57%	44%	53%
Research and development as % of sales....	9%		9%	9%
Selling, general, and administrative				
expenses as % of sales.................	25%	23%	31%	33%
Earnings before interest and taxes				
as % of sales........................	13%	20%	15%	5%
Net income as % of sales.................	6.8%	8.8%	7.7%	2.4%
Return on equity.......................	18%	20%	15%	4%
Return on capital.......................	15%	16%	11%	4%
Financial condition—in 1973:				
Current ratio...........................	2.2	2.0	1.8	1.9
Acid ratio.............................	1.2	1.2	.9	.9
Total liabilities as % of total assets.........	42%	42%	40%	51%
Bank and long-term debt as % of equity....	25%	32%	35%	71%
EBIT ÷ Interest expense..................	26x	16x	20x	2x
Per share data—1973:				
Market price...........................	$14–37	$12–27	$71–101	N/A
Earnings per share.....................	$ 1.81	$ 1.24	$ 1.89	$ 3.30
Dividends per share....................	$ 0	$ 0	$ 0.20	$ 0
Earnings multiple......................	8–20	10–22	38–53	N/A

Exhibit 4

SCIENCE TECHNOLOGY COMPANY

FIVE-YEAR CAPITAL AND FINANCING PLAN: 1974–78,

(Prepared by Mr. Finson, chief financial officer)

Permanent *new* capital requirements for STC depend almost entirely on sales growth, retained profits, and the efficiency with which corporate assets are employed. Our growth has been strong—15% per year compounded since 1969. Our net profits after taxes since 1969 have ranged from a deficit in 1972 to 2.4% of sales in 1973. Profits have not increased our equity rapidly enough to keep up with requirements, resulting in the necessary increase of $8.4 million in debt.

At the end of 1973 total assets were $33.8 million, or 75% of sales. The company has improved its asset turnover ratio in recent years as utilization of plant and equipment moved toward full capacity. Further improvement is anticipated as the new inventory control system comes on stream. I have used 69% of sales as a reasonable target for total assets—a figure that if anything seems high in relation to the asset turnover ratios of our competitors.

	Percent of Sales		
	STC's Range 1969-1973	STC 1973	Competitors 1973
Accounts receivable...............	20%–30%	27%	25%–31%
Inventories (FIFO)...............	31 –39	31	24 –29
Net fixed assets...................	11 –23	11	15 –26
Other assets.....................	5 – 8	5	4 – 6
Total assets.....................	75 –94	75	67 –88

The accompanying table shows a 5-year projection of shipments at a 10% growth rate per year compounded, a 3.0% profit margin on sales, and the forecasted improvement in the turnover of total assets. The projections are based on the forecasts prepared by the divisional managers, with active consultation with International Consultants, Inc., earlier this year. The figures are in constant dollars; that is, both volume and dollar sales are projected to increase at a 10% annual rate. The 10% volume growth is probably somewhat on the low side, as a number of our markets have very promising prospects.

From 1974 to 1978 shipments are projected to grow from $50 million to $74 million, and net profit from $1.4 million to $2.2 million. By 1978 total debt will be 39% of total capital—an improvement from the present 41% level and in line with our target level of 40%.

Earnings per share grow from $4.30 in 1974 to $6.75 and the possible market price of the stock, if the company goes public in 1978, reaches $74 (assuming a multiple of 11 times).

FINANCIAL PROJECTIONS, 1974–78

(Dollar figures in millions)

	1974	1975	1976	1977	1978	Assumptions
Net sales.....................	$50	$55	$61	$67	$74	+10% per year
Gross profit..................	24.1	26.6	29.5	32.4	35.9	48% of sales
Research and development expenses...................	4.8	5.2	5.8	6.4	7.0	$9\frac{1}{2}\%$ of sales
Selling, administrative, and general expenses.............	15.5	17.1	18.9	20.8	22.9	31% of sales
Interest expense...............	1.0	1.1	1.3	1.4	1.6	10% rate
Profit before tax..............	$ 2.8	$ 3.2	$ 3.5	$ 3.8	$ 4.4	
Taxes.......................	1.4	1.6	1.8	1.9	2.2	
Profit after tax...............	$ 1.4	$ 1.6	$ 1.7	$ 1.9	$ 2.2	

Exhibit 4—Continued

ASSETS

Current assets..................	$29.0	$31.9	$35.4	$38.9	$42.9	58% of sales
Fixed assets..................	5.0	5.5	6.0	6.6	7.2	increase with sales
Other........................	0.5	0.6	0.6	0.7	0.7	1% of sales
Total assets..............	$34.5	$38.0	$42.0	$46.2	$50.8	

LIABILITIES AND NET WORTH

Accounts payable..............	$ 4.1	$ 4.5	$ 5.0	$ 5.5	$ 6.0	60 days
Accrued expenses..............	1.5	1.7	1.8	2.0	2.2	3% of sales
Accrued payroll................	0.5	0.6	0.6	0.7	0.7	1% of sales
Income taxes payable...........	0.9	0.4	0.6	0.5	0.7	
Total current liabilities.....	$ 7.0	$ 7.2	$ 8.0	$ 8.7	$ 9.6	
Debt (plug figure)..............	9.7	11.4	12.9	14.5	16.0	
Equity........................	17.8	19.4	21.1	23.0	25.2	
Total liabilities and net worth................	$34.5	$38.0	$42.0	$46.2	$50.8	

It is extremely interesting to note the relationship to net profit of additional debt financing requirements, earnings per share, and market price per share.

Net Profit as % Sales	5-Year Cumulative Profit ($ millions)	Net Worth 1978	Total Debt Needed	Total Capital	Debt as % of Total Capital	Earnings per Share 1978	Stock Price 1978
2%............	$ 6.1	$22.5	$18.7	$41.2	45%	$4.54	$ 50
3%............	8.8	25.2	16.0	41.2	39%	6.75	74
4%............	12.3	28.7	12.5	41.2	30%	9.08	100

Obviously, the higher the profit rate, the lower the need for additional debt financing and the higher the earnings per share. This demonstrates the importance of the programs to reduce manufacturing costs by adopting assembly line techniques and to control expenditures on research. The 5% increase in product prices and sharp reduction in research expenditures in 1973 contributed to the improved operating results, and continuing review will be essential if inflation remains at a high rate.

The stock prices per share are based purely on 11 times earnings, and assume that STC goes public in 1978. It seems likely that the price-earnings ratio will be influenced by the growth rate of sales and earnings. The following table, based on a profit margin of 3% and an asset-to-sales ratio of .69, considers the implications for stock price of different levels of sales growth. While no one knows with certainty the price-earnings ratio at which a stock will sell five years hence, the table does suggest the importance of maintaining a strong sales pattern.

Annual Sales Growth	Earnings per Share 1974	Earnings per Share 1978	Annual % Increase in Earnings per Share	Price/ Earnings Ratio 1978	Stock Price 1978	Debt as % of Total Capital
0%.........	$4.30	$5.06	4%	8	$ 40	11%
10...........	4.30	6.75	12	11	74	39
15...........	4.30	8.28	18	14	116	46

The implications for the stock are clear. Continued strong sales growth should help the price of the stock substantially. With almost 45% of the stock scheduled to be held by retired employees by 1978, it is important that both a source of liquidity and an attractive price be provided for them. By far the best possible operation is to generate profit at a rate sufficient to sustain strong internal growth while lowering our level of debt to total capital.

AMERICAN MOTORS CORPORATION

During the fall of 1973, Mr. Alan Foster, treasurer of American Motors Corporation, was preparing recommendations to the Executive Committee regarding the company's large holdings of marketable securities. Three years of sharply improved profitability had resulted in the accumulation of over $100 million of excess cash. While the riskiness of automobile manufacturing seemed to warrant the maintenance of financial reserves, Mr. Foster questioned the need for such a high level. American Motors had a number of strategically important investment opportunities, several of which would have to be deferred for lack of funds. All excess cash not needed to ensure the company's solvency was needed to finance these major capital expenditures.

American Motors had been incorporated as Nash Motors Corporation in 1916 and, with the exception of a period during World War II, had been engaged in the manufacture and sale of passenger vehicles continuously. The company, with a 3% share of market, was dwarfed by GM, Ford, and Chrysler, which had market shares of 45%, 25%, and 14%, respectively. Imports accounted for the remaining sales. American Motors also produced utility and recreational vehicles, and military and special purpose vehicles.

The auto industry[1]

The auto industry was subject to cyclical fluctuations in sales. For most buyers, the purchase of a car represented a major expenditure which could be, and often was, deferred in times of adversity. Year-to-year swings in industry sales of 10–15% were not unusual. In addition, within any year there was a pronounced seasonal pattern with sales strong at the start of the model year in October and again in the spring.

Market shares of the four major producers varied quite widely, which tended to magnify the underlying cyclical changes inherent in the industry. (See Exhibit 1.) Consumer tastes often changed quickly and dramatically, and cars that sold well one year might miss totally the next. The Ford Falcon, for example, sold 482,000 units in 1961 and slid downhill thereafter to a level of only 110,000 units in 1967. The Chevrolet Corvair took an even steeper dive. Sales in 1965 were a respectable 209,000 units. By 1967, after Ralph

---

[1] Based in part on "Tiny American Motors Struggles to Survive as a Separate Concern," *The Wall Street Journal*, July 12, 1971, pp. 1, 13.

Nader's claims of the dangerous qualities of earlier Corvairs, sales fell to fewer than 25,000 units.

The volatility of consumer tastes, together with a long lead time for design and with heavy tooling and development expenditures, resulted in substantial risks for the auto manufacturers. Roughly three years were required from the initial design stage until the new model first reached the dealers' showrooms. Millions of dollars had to be invested in tooling and engineering long before any inkling of consumer reaction to the new product filtered in. As early as one year before delivery date, 40% of the new model costs was irretrievably sunk and the other 60% was largely committed unless the project was scrapped. The amounts of capital involved could be substantial. Ford, for example, spent $40 million on the development and tooling for the Mustang. And an estimated $250 million was invested in tooling, development, and plant capacity for the ill-fated Edsel before the car was ever unveiled.

Competition in the industry was largely on the basis of product design, price, promotion, and intensive distribution. Both to conserve space and to assure adequacy of dealer inventories, manufacturers normally shipped cars as soon as they rolled off the assembly line. Sales were made on a cash basis but dealer financing was available from commercial banks and the manufac- turer's own captive finance company. In addition to financial support, the companies also spent millions of dollars on advertising to maintain brand loyalty and to get potential buyers into the showrooms.

American Motors

The ability of a small producer to survive in the auto industry was a sub- ject of almost continuous debate by industry observers. American Motors had lived under clouds of speculation about its viability and future ever since Nash-Kelvinator Corporation merged with Hudson Motor Car Company in 1954. The merged enterprise stumbled along with 2% or less of the U.S. auto market for the first four years of its existence, posting deficits each year. In fact, the only time the rumors ever really went away was during the small-car boom in the late 1950's after American Motors gambled everything on its ability to make and sell cheap, economical small cars. The gamble paid off handsomely.

Tiny AMC plunged into the small car market a year before its Big Three rivals, set low but reasonably profitable prices on its Ramblers, and roared off to its most profitable years, tripling its share of all cars sold to over 6%.

But the rumors started to swirl again in the early 1960's when the small- car boom began to fade. A number of importers were driven out of the market through the enormous economic and marketing clout of GM, Ford, and Chrys- ler, who then turned around and made their compacts bigger. AMC was left with the tough choice of sticking with its successful compact cars and battling for sales in a shrinking market, or augmenting its line with new, bigger cars to compete against the Big Three.

AMC chose the multicar approach, bringing out sporty cars to compete against Ford's successful Mustang and intermediate-sized cars to battle Chevelles, Fairlanes, and Belvederes. But the proliferation of models did not succeed. AMC's original sporty car, the Marlin, flopped and was killed after only three years. Its intermediates—the Rebel, now called Matador, and Ambassador—never caught fire. So AMC's share of all car sales shrank to under 3% again, plunging the auto maker into the red. Between 1967 and 1970, the company lost a total of $115 million. (See Exhibit 2.)

By 1971 many industry observers were forecasting imminent doom. Demand for small cars, which first showed up with a resurgence of imported-car sales in the mid-1960's, was growing even faster than expected. But AMC's marketing strategies were not panning out and its market share declined to only 2.5% in early 1971. Increasingly, the company was forced to turn to General Motors for help. To get emergency financing for some of its dealers, AMC worked out a special arrangement with General Motors Acceptance Corporation. (Unlike the Big Three, AMC did not have a captive finance subsidiary and its dealers were dependent upon banks and finance companies to finance their inventories.) To augment its limited research budget, AMC turned to GM for technical help to meet the goverment's new, more stringent standards on auto exhaust emissions. And to bolster its shrunken dealer network, AMC worked out a plan to sign up Pontiac and Oldsmobile dealers to also handle AMC cars in key markets.

Many marketing men in Detroit believed that AMC was floundering in the midst of the small-car boom because it had elected to continue selling many sizes of cars rather than revert to its successful one-car formula of the late 1950's. "AMC's big mistake was to toss aside the idea of one car, of selling to its strength," commented an official at a rival company. "The cost of proliferation has killed them. The costs of manufacturing and developing cars are very high and spread over too few car sales at American Motors."

Mr. Chapin, president of American Motors, agreed that competing in several markets, rather than just one, was difficult. But he stoutly defended AMC's basic multicar strategy as the only way a company its size could survive in the fiercely competitive, high cost auto industry. "We have an inherent structure as an automobile company where you have certain levels of fixed costs, and you have to get units to support it."

The results of the period 1971–73 seemed to substantiate the soundness of Mr. Chapin's strategy. They also attested to the powerful competitive advantage gained by AMC by the devaluation of the U.S. dollar. In 1971 American Motor's Gremlin was selling for about $150 more than the Volkswagen Beetle. By late 1973 it sold for $500 less, and in the meantime its price had gone up a couple of hundred dollars. AMC's sales rose 64%, from $1.1 billion in 1970 to over $1.7 billion in 1973. More importantly, the increased sales pushed AMC well beyond the $1.3 billion sales level at which it covered its fixed operating costs of approximately $260 million. Pre-tax earnings rebounded strongly from a deficit of $56 million in 1970 to a profit of $76 million in 1973.

Expansion plans and financial policies

Management of American Motors was committed to a strategy of capitalizing more fully on the scale economies inherent in the industry by expanding its domestic car sales from 380,000 units in 1973 to 500,000 units by 1977. (Exhibit 3 indicates the extent of potential scale economies.) Though the industry was heading into rough times as energy shortages cut into sales, management believed that the shift toward small cars that conserved on gas would allow AMC to increase its market share. It was also hoped that AMC's passenger car business, which accounted for two thirds of the company's sales in 1973, would decline to a 50% share by 1977 as the company moved into related businesses by acquisition.

Continued expansion within the auto and utility-trailer markets would require capital expenditures of $100 million per year during 1974–75, and could place the company under unexpected and substantial additional financing pressures. However, with renewed profitability, $100 million of marketable securities, and bank credit lines totaling $70 million, management felt confident that "We have the financial muscle to provide the products and facilities to meet these objectives." (See Exhibit 4 for a summary of AMC's financial condition.)

Mr. Foster questioned, however, the extent to which the holdings of liquid assets should be used to finance acquisitions or the expansion of either plant capacity or the dealer system. An important characteristic of the auto industry was that all the major manufacturers maintained large liquid balances (cash and marketable securities) to provide for operations and protect against wide fluctuations in funds needs. (Exhibit 5 provides financial information on the four auto manufacturers.) In line with industry practice, AMC had funded its peak seasonal and cyclical funds requirements internally insofar as possible rather than borrow such amounts externally as they were required. To give just one example of what this meant, the annual retooling and model change-over resulted in a period of weeks each summer during which there were no cash receipts from auto sales and sharply increased payments to suppliers and outside contractors. The cash deficit during this one short period often ranged up to $40 million. In addition to its seasonal need, the company also had significant cyclical financing pressures. (Exhibit 6 shows AMC's pattern of funds flows on an annual basis for the period 1963–73.) The cyclicality was reflected in a beta for the company's stock of 1.0 in spite of the absence of financial leverage. Clearly, any decision to reduce the level of marketable securities could only be made after first determining the magnitude of AMC's liquidity needs and reviewing alternative methods of meeting this need.

The market return and the risk-free rate of interest were estimated at 14% and 6%, respectively, in the fall of 1973.

Exhibit 1

AMERICAN MOTORS CORPORATION

MARKET SHARE—U.S. AUTO SALES BY CALENDAR YEAR

(Units in thousands)

	GM		Ford		Chrysler		AMC		Foreign		
	Units	%	Units	%	Units	%	Units	%	Units	%	Total
1972	4,824	44.2	2,668	24.5	1,518	13.9	312	2.9	1,586	14.5	10,908
1971	4,654	45.6	2,377	23.3	1,388	13.6	257	2.5	1,533	15.0	10,209
1970	3,333	39.8	2,216	26.4	1,350	16.1	254	3.0	1,231	14.7	8,384
1969	4,420	46.8	2,291	24.3	1,428	15.1	240	2.5	1,062	11.3	9,441
1968	4,395	46.7	2,228	23.7	1,528	16.3	259	2.8	986	10.5	9,396
1967	4,139	49.5	1,851	22.2	1,341	16.1	238	2.8	781	9.4	8,350
1966	4,336	48.2	2,349	26.1	1,387	15.4	266	3.0	658	7.3	8,996
1965	4,663	50.2	2,372	25.5	1,366	14.7	325	3.5	569	6.1	9,295
1964	3,959	49.3	2,097	26.1	1,114	13.9	379	4.7	481	6.0	8,030
1963	3,857	51.5	1,880	25.1	935	12.5	428	5.7	386	5.2	7,486
1962	3,599	52.5	1,825	26.6	667	9.7	423	6.2	339	5.0	6,853
1961	2,724	47.2	1,670	28.9	632	10.9	371	6.4	379	6.6	5,776

Exhibit 2

AMERICAN MOTORS CORPORATION

OPERATING HIGHLIGHTS, FISCAL YEARS 1963–73

(In millions)

	1963	1964	1965	1966	1967	1968*	1969	1970†	1971	1972	1973
Operating Results											
Net sales	$1,144	$1,022	$ 998	$ 876	$ 778	$ 766	$ 747	$1,098	$1,240	$1,413	$1,739
Profit before tax	75	42	7	(31)	(71)	10	7	(56)	11	31	76
Taxes	37	16	2	(15)	0	6	2	0	6	15	31
Profit after tax and before extraordinary items	$ 38	$ 26	$ 5	$ (16)	$ (71)	$ 4	$ 5	$ (56)	$ 5	$ 16	$ 45
Shareholder Information											
Earnings per share	$ 2.01	$ 1.38	$ 0.27	$(0.82)	$(3.70)	$ 0.17	$ 0.26	$(2.28)	$ 0.22	$ 0.64	$ 1.65
Dividends per share	1.00	1.15	0.875	0	0	0	0	0	0	0	0
Stock price range	16–23	14–18	7–15	6–14	7–16	10–16	8–14	6–12	6–9	7–11	7–10
Price-earnings ratio	8–11	10–13	27–56			60–90	31–54		27–41	10–17	4–6
Financial Condition											
Current ratio	1.7	1.7	1.5	1.3	1.2	1.5	1.7	1.3	1.4	1.6	1.7
Long-term debt as % of capital	0	0	0	0	0	0	15%	18%	17%	22%	16%

* Reflects sale of the Kelvinator division.
† Reflects acquisition of Kaiser-Jeep Corporation, which contributed $390 million to sales in 1970.

Exhibit 3

AMERICAN MOTORS CORPORATION

SCALE ECONOMIES

I. In Car Production

Annual Production of a Model	Relative Unit Cost
50,000 units	120
100,000	110–115
200,000	103–105
400,000	100
800,000	99+

II. In Advertising

	1972 National Advertising Budgets	Advertising Cost per Car Sold
Ford	$115 million	$43
GM	111	23
Chrysler	63	42
American Motors	18	58
VW	28	N.A.
Toyota	17	N.A.

Exhibit 4

AMERICAN MOTORS CORPORATION

BALANCE SHEETS—YEARS ENDED SEPTEMBER 30

(In millions)

	1963	1964	1965	1966	1967	1968	1969	1970	1971	1972	1973
ASSETS											
Cash	$48	$29	$29	$17	$12	$8	$8	$11	$18	$101	$110
Marketable securities	48	16	6	3	9	51	62	12			
Receivables	53	59	70	68	64	72	56	106	123	105	108
Inventories	127	124	151	136	122	94	108	202	172	166	201
Prepaid expenses	4	5	9	7	4	3	3	5	6	7	9
Returnable federal taxes				23	10				5		23
Total current assets	$280	$233	$265	$254	$221	$228	$237	$336	$324	$379	$450
Investments and other assets	54	62	51	55	19	15	21	33	33	42	68
Property, plant, and equipment	192	221	252	274	264	219	239	330	330	333	379
Less: Accumulated depreciation	86	95	111	123	126	113	120	162	171	180	191
Net property, plant, and equipment	$106	$126	$141	$151	$138	$106	$119	$168	$159	$153	$188
Unamortized debt expense							8	8	7		
Goodwill								2	2	2	7
Total assets	$440	$421	$457	$460	$378	$349	$385	$547	$525	$576	$713
LIABILITIES AND NET WORTH											
Short-term debt	$91	$86	$52	$73	$66	$23	$91	$30	$25	$25	$184
Accounts payable			85	90	82	85		169	148	149	
Current portion of long-term debt								3	5	1	1
Income taxes	27	9	3	3	3	3	6	6	5	6	17
Accrued expenses	43	43	41	35	35	39	42	51	51	50	69
Total current liabilities	$161	$138	$181	$201	$186	$150	$139	$259	$234	$231	$271
Long-term debt							35	45	43	68	64
Other liabilities	6	4	6	2	11	8	7	39	34	33	34
Minority interest			3	2	2						
Stockholder equity	273	279	267	255	179	191	204	204	214	244	344
Total liabilities and net worth	$440	$421	$457	$460	$378	$349	$385	$547	$525	$576	$713

Note: The following restrictions and covenants were in effect under the various debt issues and credit lines outstanding at September 30, 1973: (1) Consolidated working capital must exceed $100 million; (2) Dividends may only be paid out of cumulative earnings subsequent to 9/30/72 in excess of $11 million; (3) The company may not create, guarantee or assume any new Funded Debt unless immediately thereafter consolidated net tangible assets exceed 200% of the total funded debt; (4) Sinking fund payments commence in 1978 and gradually increase from $2.1 million in 1978 to $4.5 million in 1991.

Exhibit 5

AMERICAN MOTORS CORPORATION

FINANCIAL COMPARISONS—AMC, GM, FORD, CHRYSLER

(Dollar figures in millions except per share data)

	AMC	GM	Ford	Chrysler
1972 Operating Results				
Sales..............................	$1,413	$30,435	$20,194	$ 9,759
Net income........................	16	2,163	870	220
% Sales...........................	1.1%	7.1%	4.3%	2.3%
Earnings per share.................	.64	7.51	8.52	4.27
Dividends per share................	0	4.45	2.68	.90
Stock price range..................	7–11	71–85	61–80	28–42
Financial Position—Year-End 1972				
Cash and marketable securities.......	$ 101	$ 2,947	$ 1,469	$ 711
Total assets.......................	576	18,273	11,634	5,497
Long-term debt as % of capital......	22%	6%	15%	24%
Cash and marketable securities as % of total assets....................	18%	16%	13%	13%

Exhibit 6

AMERICAN MOTORS CORPORATION

Annual Funds Flow Analysis, 1963–73

(In millions)

	1963	1964	1965	1966	1967	1968	1969	1970	1971	1972	1973
Sources of Funds											
Net income (loss) before extraordinary items	$38	$26	$5	$(16)	$(71)	$4	$5	$(56)	$5	$16	$45
Depreciation and amortization	30	45	44	48	53	42	35	44	37	37	35
Funds from operations	$68	$71	$49	$32	$(18)	$46	$40	$(12)	$42	$53	$80
Tax credit from loss carryforward or carryback				4		19			5	14	41
Special credit (charges) to net income					(5)	(11)	8				
Decrease in receivables				2	4	28	16			18	
Decrease in inventories		3		15	14	11			30	6	
Decrease in other current assets					16					4	
Increase in accounts payable	16			5		3	6	78		1	35
Increase in other current liabilities	24					4	6	12			30
Total sources	$108	$74	$49	$58	$11	$100	$76	$78	$77	$96	$186
Uses of Funds											
Cash dividends	$19	$22	$17	$	$	$	$	$	$	$	$
Additions to property, plant, and equipment	47	65	59	58	40	10	48	93	28	31	70
Increase in receivables	3	6	11					50	17		3
Increase in inventories	31		27				14	94			35
Increase in other current assets		1	4	21	8	8		2	6	1	25
Decrease in accounts payable		5	1						21		
Decrease in other current liabilities		18	8	6		1			1		
Other uses (sources)		10	(16)	9	(17)		15	(16)	4	2	30
Total uses	$100	$127	$111	$94	$31	$19	$77	$223	$77	$34	$163
Financing (need) surplus	$8	$(53)	$(62)	$(36)	$(20)	$81	$(1)	$(145)	$0	$62	$23
Financed by:											
Cash and marketable securities (decrease)	$8	$(51)	$(10)	$(15)	$1	$38	$11	$(47)	$(5)	$83	$9
Short-term debt (increase)			(52)	(21)	7	43	23	(33)	3	4	25
Long-term debt (increase)							(35)	(10)	2	(25)	3
Sale of investment					(28)						
Issuance of common stock		(2)						(55)			(14)
	$8	$(53)	$(62)	$(36)	$(20)	$81	$(1)	$(145)	$0	$62	$23
Sales	$1,144	$1,022	$998	$876	$778	$766	$747	$1,098	$1,240	$1,413	$1,739

ALLEN DISTRIBUTION COMPANY

On June 16, 1967, Mr. William McConnell of the mid-Atlantic office of the Allen Distribution Company was considering whether his company should extend a credit limit of $1,000 to the Morse Photo Company of Harrisburg, Pennsylvania. Mr. McConnell had recently transferred from his job as credit representative in one of the company's western branch offices to become credit manager of the mid-Atlantic branch office, where he assumed full responsibility for initiating and supervising the branch's credit policies. When he assumed this position, Mr. McConnell had asked the five credit representatives who had been handling the branch's accounts on their own to submit to him for review a few borderline credit accounts waiting the establishment of credit limits. Mr. McConnell believed that his decision and method of analysis might prove helpful in setting the tone of future operations in the credit department. Therefore, he planned to write out his analysis and decision so that it could be circulated.

The Allen Distribution Company, a subsidiary of the Allen Electric Company, one of the nation's largest manufacturers of electrical appliances and lighting equipment, was a national wholesale distributor of the parent company's products. Merchandise sold by the Allen Distribution Company ranged from refrigerators and television sets to electric light bulbs. Its competition included other nationally known wholesalers and small regional wholesalers of the Allen line as well as wholesalers of a number of competing product lines.

The parent company sold goods to the Allen Distribution Company on the same terms as to independent wholesalers. Allen Distribution in turn usually sold its merchandise at the wholesale prices and on the terms suggested by the parent company, as did most other wholesalers of the Allen line. However, Allen Distribution maintained the right to set its own prices, and occasionally, when price competition developed in local areas, prices were reduced for short periods.

Since wholesale prices for competing products tended to be uniform, the intense competition for retail outlets and intermediary wholesale houses handling the Allen line caused the company to give major attention to the services offered these customers, including cooperative advertising, store displays, inventory control, and credit arrangements. However, the slight differences in the quality of services rendered by the large wholesalers of Allen products were not fully appreciated by customers, and sales often depended more on the personal relationships developed between the customer and company salesmen. For this reason, Allen Distribution's salesmen tended to concentrate on maintaining current accounts and on expanding sales by securing outlets carrying competing product lines where brand differentials could be emphasized.

These salesmen were paid a straight commission of 1% for net sales in their territory. An additional 1% commission was given salesmen on net sales to new accounts during the first year. Salesmen were not held responsible for bad debt losses resulting from their sales efforts, although they sometimes helped in collecting overdue receivables.

Sales during the first four months of 1967 for the entire company, as well as the mid-Atlantic branch, had decreased 2% in comparison with the similar period in 1966 even though the number of customers serviced remained relatively unchanged. In late May, 1967, the president of Allen Distribution had called together the branch managers and announced an intensified sales campaign for new outlets to offset the sales decline. Sales quotas by branch and by salesmen were established, and a prize system was devised to reward sales personnel for successful efforts. Mr. McConnell knew that the mid-Atlantic branch manager was actively supporting the program and that he wanted the branch to make a good showing.

The mid-Atlantic branch office of Allen Distribution had net sales of $78 million in 1966. A percentage analysis of the branch's 1966 income statement is shown below:

Net sales.......................	100.0%	
Cost of merchandise..............	92.0	(All costs variable)
Gross profit.....................	8.0%	
Operating and other expenses:		
Warehouse.....................	4.1	(Variable portion: 1.2% of sales)
Selling.......................	1.4	(Variable portion: 1.1% of sales)
Administrative................	1.1	(Variable portion: 0.1% of sales)
Bad debt loss.................	0.13	
Interest expense..............	0.27	
Total.....................	7.0%	
Net profit before taxes..........	1.0%	

Mr. McConnell found that throughout 1966 the branch's outstanding receivables had averaged $5.6 million, of which approximately $150,000 represented overdue amounts. The active accounts, numbering 15,000, were turning over approximately every 25 days. Twelve people were employed in the credit department, and its operating expenses (included in the administrative expenses above) were $150,000 per year. This did not include bad debt losses, which were 0.13% of sales in 1966 and had averaged 0.14% of sales in recent years. These bad debt losses derived principally from the marginal accounts and were, therefore, approximately 1.4% of sales to the marginal accounts.

In Mr. McConnell's belief, a credit department should have little difficulty in approving good accounts and rejecting the bad ones. The real core of the credit department's operation rested in the evaluation of marginal accounts. Although Mr. McConnell had not made a study of the branch's operation, it was his opinion that the good accounts covered Allen Distribution's total operating and overhead costs, whereas the selection and handling of marginal accounts made the difference between profit and loss. Furthermore, Mr. McConnell believed that the purpose of a credit department was not to minimize credit losses but rather to maximize profits. He thought it was significant to recognize that an increase in sales volume for Allen Distribution usually meant increased sales for the parent company.

In evaluating a marginal account, Mr. McConnell considered the cost of handling the account, the current and potential profitability of the account, and the inherent risks. Although Mr. McConnell did not know how much more it cost a credit department to maintain a marginal account, he knew the credit department spent at least twice as much time maintaining credit files and collecting overdue amounts on marginal accounts as on good accounts. He estimated that 20% of the branch's accounts, representing nearly 10% of sales, were marginal firms. Nevertheless, collections from these companies tended to be on the average only 5 to 10 days slower than collections from good accounts. Mr. McConnell had not determined an appropriate basis for distributing these costs to marginal firms, but he thought they should bear a substantial portion of the credit department's operating expenses. He also believed that the 7% interest charge on bank loans, which roughly paralleled the size of the accounts receivable balance, was a cost factor chargeable to his department. Although Mr. McConnell was not certain how it might apply, he knew that management of the parent company expected new investments to promise returns of 20% or more (before taxes) before the investment was considered acceptable.

Although Mr. McConnell hesitated to define a good account in specific terms, he generally considered that companies with a two-to-one current ratio and with an equity investment greater than outstanding debt fitted into this category. He also examined, when appropriate, acid test ratios, net working capital, inventory turnover, and other balance sheet and income statement relationships, but found it difficult to establish rules to cover every situation. Unsatisfactory credit requests were also difficult to define in terms of specific ratios. With experience, a good credit analyst was able to handle good and bad accounts in a routine manner. Real judgment, however, was required to select from the marginal applications those worthy of credit. In evaluating a marginal account, Mr. McConnell thought the principal's character, although difficult to ascertain, was as important as the company's financial status. In an analysis of a credit application, two factors were considered important: (1) the risk of losing all or part of the outstanding receivable balance through bankruptcy; and (2) the cost of having to carry the amount due beyond the net period. Since the credit department screened almost 1,000 new requests for credit annually, Mr. McConnell knew that the evaluative procedures would have to be streamlined.

Mr. McConnell thought that the most difficult aspect of his new job would be translating any changes in credit policy into appropriate action by the credit representatives. Consequently, he planned to analyze a few selected marginal accounts so he might set forth the reasons for accepting or rejecting the accounts as a step toward establishing new credit standards. The Morse Photo Company was the first situation he had decided to review.

A credit file on the Morse Photo Company had been established on the basis of the following memorandum, dated May 16, 1967, from the company's Harrisburg salesman:

> Have sold Mr. Anthony W. Morse, president of Morse Photo Company, 280 Carlisle Avenue, Harrisburg, Pennsylvania, on the idea of switching from Oliver Electric Company's flash bulbs to ours. Sales would be $5,000 a year on current volume, and the Morse company is a real grower. Tony Morse is a terrific salesman and should sell a whale of a lot of bulbs for us. He wants $1,000 worth (net cost to him) of bulbs as a starter.

Photographic flash bulbs were not a major product item and for statistical purposes were grouped with electric lighting equipment, which accounted for 25% of Allen Distribution's sales volume. These electrical lighting supplies normally carried gross margins of 7% to 10% for Allen Distribution, but photo bulbs, one of the highest profit items sold by the company, had a gross margin of 17% after cash discounts. In addition, the parent company earned a "contribution" profit margin of 20% (before taxes) on its sales of photo bulbs.

The Morse Photo Company was similar to a number of Allen Distribution's customers. Almost half of Allen Distribution's 15,000 credit accounts purchased only lighting supplies from the company. Many of these accounts were small wholesale houses or regional chain stores whose annual purchases were in the $5,000 to $20,000 range.

Largely in order to control the retail price, photo bulbs were sold only on a consignment basis, but the practice had possible financial significance. Although a supply of bulbs was delivered to a customer, Allen Distribution remained the owner until the bulbs were sold by the consignee and, hence, was entitled to recover its bulbs at any time from the consignee's stock. To insure recovery, segregation of inventory was agreed to by the customer. This meant that his stock of Allen bulbs should be plainly marked and physically separated from the remainder of his inventory.

After a sale of bulbs, the consignee was supposed to keep the resulting receivables or cash separate from its other accounts or funds until payment was made to Allen Distribution. Therefore, if the prescribed procedures were followed, it was possible to identify, as Allen Distribution's, the total value of a consignment, either in inventory, receivables, or cash. Thus, in the event of liquidation, no other creditor could make claim against these items.

Owing to the inconvenience of keeping separate stocks, accounts, and funds, the safeguards associated with these consignment shipments were not often observed in practice. Allen Distribution made little effort to verify whether a separate inventory was actually maintained by its photo bulb customers. Nevertheless, it was believed that the company might have some protection in recovering consigned merchandise in the event of a customer's bankruptcy, since the bulbs carried the Allen brand name. More significantly, Allen Distribution made no effort to enforce segregation of funds after bulb sales were made by the customer. In consequence, it stood in the same general position as other creditors from the time the bulbs were sold by the consignee until remittance was made. Mr. McConnell, therefore, concluded that the consignment method afforded little financial protection in practice and appraised these accounts in the same way as open accounts.

At each month's end, the consignee inventoried the bulb supply and made payment in the amount of actual sales, less its 25% trade discount. Credit terms were 5% 10 E. O. M. All photo bulb consignees were on a one-year contract basis, whereby the customer agreed to sell Allen bulbs exclusively, and Allen Distribution agreed to supply the customer's needs up to a predetermined limit ($1,000 in the case of Morse Photo Company), provided payments were made within terms.

In the credit file Mr. McConnell found a credit report containing balance sheets and income statements of the Morse Photo Company (Exhibit 1) and four letters in reply to credit inquiries sent out by a branch credit representative (Exhibit 2).

Exhibit 1

ASSOCIATED CREDIT AGENCY REPORT, MAY 27, 1967

Company:	Morse Photo Company, 280 Carlisle Avenue, Harrisburg, Pennsylvania.
Rating:	Limited (unchanged from previous report).
Business:	Commercial developing and photographic finishing. Also does a small volume of wholesaling films and camera supplies. Its distribution includes about 300 drug and periodical stores within a 130-mile radius of Harrisburg.
Management:	Anthony W. Morse, president and principal stockholder.
History:	Business started as proprietorship in May, 1961, with limited capital. On November 12, 1962, present owner purchased the assets but did not assume the liabilities for a reported $11,000; $2,000 was derived from savings and the balance was financed through a bank loan. On April 30, 1965, the proprietorship was succeeded by the present corporation, which corporation took over assets and assumed liabilities of the predecessor business.
Sales terms:	2% 10 days, net 30.
Employees:	Twelve individuals of which three are salesmen.

Exhibit 1—Continued
BALANCE SHEETS FOR THE PERIOD ENDED APRIL 30, 1966, AND 1967
(Figured in even dollars)

ASSETS	April 30, 1966	April 30, 1967
Cash	$ 320	$ 439
Accounts receivable, net	11,503	16,201
Inventory at cost	12,712	12,681
Total current assets	$ 24,535	$ 29,321
Fixed assets:		
Cost	$ 58,331	$ 93,574
Depreciation	12,573	21,492
Net	$ 45,758	$ 72,082
Other assets	2,839	9,641
Total assets	$ 73,132	$111,044

LIABILITIES		
Accounts payable	$ 9,953	$ 22,311
Note payable—bank	5,136	9,360
Notes payable—other	9,127	15,158
Income tax	198	373
Other tax	3,123	2,546
Interest payable	...	96
Payroll payable	...	1,514
Total current liabilities	$ 27,537	$ 51,358
Other liabilities:		
Notes payable—officers	2,648	2,648
Notes payable—bank	764	...
Notes payable—other	...	810
Bond payable	...	14,000
Total liabilities	$ 30,949	$ 68,816
Net worth:		
Preferred stock	$ 10,000	$ 10,000
Common stock	32,100	32,100
Earned surplus	83	128
Total net worth	$ 42,183	$ 42,228
Total liabilities and net worth	$ 73,132	$111,044

Exhibit 1—Continued

INCOME STATEMENT FOR FISCAL YEARS 1966 AND 1967
(Figured in even dollars)

	April 30, 1966	April 30, 1967
Net sales	$162,898	$269,461
Less cost of goods sold:		
Material	$ 58,453	$ 88,079
Wages	33,963	65,263
Other	28,841	44,049
Total cost of goods sold	$121,257	$197,391
Gross profit	$ 41,641	$ 72,070
Administrative and selling expense:		
Officers' salaries	$ 12,000	$ 22,000
Office salaries	5,733	10,000
Sales commissions	...	3,568
Depreciation	7,848	10,071
Other	15,779	25,613
Total administrative and selling expense	$ 41,360	$ 71,252
Net earnings before tax	$ 281	$ 818
Income tax	198	373
Earnings	$ 83	$ 445
Dividends	nil	400
Earnings transferred to surplus	$ 83	$ 45

Analysis of Financial Statements:

This seven-year old concern has expanded rapidly since its founding. This has been accomplished by expanding from a local territory to a radius of 130 miles and by giving 24-hour service to its customers. In order to accomplish this, there has been a substantial increase in fixed assets and approximately a 60% increase during the last year under review. This has been made possible in part by acquiring the Meade Photo Company in September, 1966. While the net earnings transferred to surplus have been small, there has been an increase in capital. During 1965 an 8% preferred stock issue of $10,000 was made, and in 1967 bonds were issued for $14,000. In connection with the acquisition of the Meade Photo Company for $24,000, $7,000 was borrowed from the Harrisburg Fidelity and Trust Company and the seller was given a chattel mortgage for $17,000, payable $180 a week. In addition Meade receives a payment of 10% of the net sales which are transacted from their former customers for a period of five years. During the year more equipment was purchased with money obtained in the form of notes from the bank. The amount due the bank is made up of five installment notes, secured by various pieces of equipment. Other notes payable consist of $5,500 payable to a large film manufacturer; $8,500 payable to Meade Photo; and the balance to others. Notes payable after one year are due to Meade Photo. Mr. Morse, the president, estimates that sales during the fiscal year, 1968, will be $320,000.

Exhibit 1—Concluded

CREDIT RECORD, MAY 15, 1967

High Credit	Owes Currently	Past Due	Terms	Payments
3,000	0	0	Net 30	Prompt
2,693	0	0	2% 10 E.O.M.	Prompt
2,740	245	127	Net 30	Slow 8 months
582	0	0	2% 10	Prompt to slow 60 days
108	108	108	Net 10	Slow
2,518	2,518	0	Net 30	Prompt
582	61	0	2% 10	Prompt
9,308	8,854	4,601	2% 10, net 30	Slow 30 to 60 days
5,000	4,800	4,800	2% 10 E.O.M.	Slow 90 to 120 days
4,492	3,452	3,452	2% 10 E.O.M.	Slow 90 to 120 days
167	0	0	Net 30	Slow 60 days
118	118	118	Net 15	Slow 60 to 90 days

Exhibit 2

ALLEN DISTRIBUTION COMPANY

LETTER FROM THE HARRISBURG FIDELITY AND TRUST COMPANY

Allen Distribution Company   June 6, 1967
Philadelphia, Pennsylvania

Attention: Credit Manager

GENTLEMEN:

Morse Photo Company has maintained a satisfactory account with us for a number of years and such accommodation as we have extended them is cared for as agreed. It is our feeling that they are entitled to their reasonable trade requirements.

Yours very truly,

(*Signed*) GEORGE GRUBB
Assistant Vice-President
Harrisburg Fidelity and Trust Company

LETTER FROM A LARGE FILM MANUFACTURER

Allen Distribution Company   June 5, 1967
Philadelphia, Pennsylvania

Attention: Credit Manager

GENTLEMEN:

Re: Morse Photo Company

With reference to your inquiry regarding the above account, we wish to advise that we have been doing business with them since 1961.

Recently we have had a fair amount of trouble with them because of overexpansion in relation to their net worth. In the past, customer's promises for payment could not be depended upon, although there has been a decided improvement in the last six months. Around the first of the year we had to take notes totaling $7,500 for the past-due accounts. At the present time $2,500 is still outstanding, but the notes are not in default. In April, we extended them $2,700 worth of credit, $2,600 of which was under the term

Exhibit 2—Continued

⅓ payable every ten days. The last payment was not received until June 1, whereas it was due May 22. At the present time the concern owes us outside of the notes $115 of which $76.70 represents the April charge which is past due in our books.

To sum the whole thing up we are willing to extend credit up to $5,000 but must watch the account carefully.

Yours very truly.

(*Signed*) ALFRED WHITTIER
Credit Manager

LETTER FROM A LARGE CHEMICAL COMPANY

Allen Distribution Company   June 7, 1967
Philadelphia, Pennsylvania

Attention: Credit Manager

GENTLEMEN:

The following summary is the information you requested with respect to Morse Photo Company:

How Long Sold—May, 1965
Last Sale—June, 1967
Highest Credit—$700
Amount Owing—$700
Past Due—0
Terms—2% 10 days
Amount Secured—None
Manner of Payment—Previous sales C.O.D.

This is a trial order on restricted credit terms. Future policy will be determined by payment record.

Yours very truly,

(*Signed*) ARNOLD HEAD
Credit Manager

LETTER FROM OLIVER ELECTRIC COMPANY

Allen Distribution Company   June 9, 1967
Philadelphia, Pennsylvania

Attention: Credit Manager

GENTLEMEN:

Re: Morse Photo Company
How Long Sold—July, 1962
Date of Last Sale—April, 1967
High Credit—$1,600
Amount Owing—$630
Past Due—$630
Terms—2% 10 End of the Month

Other comments:

We would suggest watching this account carefully. It has been up to nine months slow with us.

Yours very truly,

(*Signed*) J. E. STEWART
Credit Manager

THE O. M. SCOTT & SONS COMPANY

∧∧

Between 1955 and 1961, management of The O. M. Scott & Sons Company launched a number of new programs aimed at maintaining and increasing the company's past success and growth. Largely in response to these activities, Scott's field sales force grew from 6 to 150 men, several entirely new and expanded production facilities went on stream, and the number of products in the company's product line tripled. Sales increased from about $10 million to $43 million. In late 1961, company officials were preparing to review the results of all these changes to ascertain how, if at all, Scott's plans and financial policies should be changed.

The O. M. Scott & Sons Company commenced operations in 1868, when it began processing the country's first clean, weed-free grass seed. Scott's early business came from a small but rapidly growing local market in central Ohio. Later, however, the company went through several stages in its growth. At about the turn of the century the company turned from supplying its local market to selling grass and other farm seeds over a wider geographic area by mail. As its success with its mail-order business increased, the company began to advertise extensively and in 1927 added a free magazine called *Lawn Care*, which has been widely distributed ever since. In all of these early promotional activities, the company sought to sell the Scott name and products as well as the idea of improved care of lawns. In the 1920's a special lawn fertilizer developed for home use was added to the company's product line. During the 1930's the company began to distribute its products on a small scale through selected retail stores and garden centers. Sales and profits grew steadily throughout these years. Scott continued to grow along these same general lines until 1945, by which time sales reached $2.7 million and net profits after taxes were about $30,000.

Over the decade immediately following the war, pioneering research by Scott led to the development and introduction of a wide range of new chemical weed and garden pest controls and special-purpose lawn fertilizers. In addition, the company's grass seed lines were upgraded and supplemented. Largely in response to the success of this research, sales increased to $11.4 million and profits to over $210,000 in fiscal 1955.

By 1955, however, despite the company's impressive postwar record of growth in sales and profits, management was convinced that neither Scott nor its competitors had begun to develop and tap the potential inherent in the national lawn care market. In Scott's own case this failure to develop and tap the national market was attributed to the fact that Scott's customers could not buy its products easily where and when they expected to find them. The company's distribution system had not evolved adequately in response to developing market opportunities, and in many instances the company's dealers either were poorly stocked or were not the right kind of dealer for the company's products.

Thus began a new stage in Scott's development. Early in 1955 the company launched a program to build a national field sales organization with the objective of increasing the number, quality, and performance of its distributors so as to capitalize more fully on the success of its product research and development efforts. When this program started, the company had six field salesmen. By 1960 Scott had a field sales force of 150 men serving almost 10,000 retail dealers across the country. These dealers were mainly department stores and small hardware stores and garden supply centers. The company's salesmen spent most of their time training the dealers how to do a better selling job with Scott products and were paid a salary plus a bonus based on factory shipments to dealers.

Scott's product development program continued apace with the buildup in the direct selling force so that by the end of the 1950's the company was engaged in the purchase, processing, and sale of grass seed, and the manufacture and sale of fertilizers, weed and pest control products, mechanical spreaders, and electric lawn mowers. In 1959 sales increased to $30.6 million and profits to $1.5 million. A large proportion of these sales comprised new products that had been developed and patented by the company within the past few years.

Reviewing the company's progress again in early 1959, management was still not satisfied that the company was marketing its products as effectively as possible. For one thing, it was estimated that an annual market potential of at least $100 million existed for Scott products. Another important consideration was that several nationally known chemical firms had either begun or were expected to begin competing against Scott in certain lines. These facts led management to conclude that the most effective way for Scott to preserve its preeminent market position would be to push for immediate further market penetration. If successful, such a strategy would enable Scott to eclipse competition as completely as possible before its competitors could establish a firm market position against the company. In this context an annual growth rate in sales and profits of up to 25% was thought to be a reasonable goal for the company over the next few years.

Apart from the need to continue strengthening the company's field sales force and dealer organization, management thought in early 1959 that the most important factor standing in the way of further rapid growth and market penetration was the inability of the typical Scott dealer to carry an adequate inventory of Scott products. Because of the highly seasonal character of sales at retail of the company's products, it was essential that dealers have enough inventory on hand to meet local sales peaks when they came. Experience showed that in many parts of the country a large percentage of dealer sales were made on a few weekends each season. Failure to supply this demand when it materialized most often resulted in a sale lost to a competitor, although sometimes a customer simply postponed buying anything. The problem of assuring adequate dealer inventories had become more of a problem in recent years. The effectiveness of Scott's product development program meant that the dealer was expected to carry many more products than in the past. In addition, Scott had shifted its marketing emphasis from selling individual products to one of selling complete lawn and garden programs. And in order to sell a full lawn maintenance program it was necessary that the dealer carry the complete Scott line and have it on hand when needed by the consumer.

Because of their small size and often weak working capital position, most of Scott's dealers could not realistically be expected to increase their inventory investment in Scott products. This meant that any desired buildup in dealer inventory levels would have to be financed in some way by Scott itself. In the past the company had extended generous seasonal datings to its dealers, as was industry practice. As a normal pattern, winter and early spring shipments became due at the end of April or May, depending on the geographical area. Shipments during the summer months were due in October or November. The purpose of these seasonal datings was to enable and encourage as many dealers as possible to be well stocked in advance of seasonal sales peaks. Anticipation at the rate of 0.6% a month was offered on payments made in advance of these seasonal dates, although few dealers availed themselves of this opportunity. With purchases made outside the two main selling seasons, dealers were expected to pay on the tenth of the second month following shipment.

The company's past experience with seasonal datings suggested certain changes in the event Scott proceeded to finance a higher level of dealer inventories. Because of the seasonal nature of the business and the fact that most dealers were thinly capitalized, payment was not often received by Scott until the merchandise involved was sold, irrespective of the terms of sale. This meant that many dealers were continually asking for credit extensions. Another problem inherent in the seasonal dating policy was that Scott retained little or no effective security interest in the goods involved. A final problem was that in the past Scott had followed a policy of not selling to dealers that could not be relied upon to maintain prices at reasonable levels. It was thought that widespread selling at discount prices would undermine the company and the market image it was trying to project. Thus, in any decision to expand dealer inventories, management hoped to contrive a procedure whereby Scott would retain the right to reclaim goods from third parties in the event any of its dealers began selling at wholesale to a discounter.

After considerable study it was decided to continue the traditional seasonal dating plan and to introduce a new trust receipt plan as well. This combination was thought to fulfill all of the requirements outlined in the previous paragraph. As the particular trust receipt plan adopted by Scott worked, a trust receipt dealer was required to sign a trust receipt that provided for (1) immediate transfer to the dealer of title to any Scott products shipped in response to a dealer order, (2) retention of a security interest by Scott in merchandise so shipped until sold by the dealer acting in his capacity as a retailer, and (3) segregation of a sufficient proportion of the funds received from such sales to provide for payment to Scott as billed. Among other things, these provisions made it possible for Scott to move in and reclaim any inventory held by third parties that had been sold by a trust receipt dealer acting illegally as a wholesaler. Exhibit 5 shows the trust receipt form used by Scott. In addition to obtaining the trust receipt from its dealers, the company also was required to file a statement of trust receipt financing with the secretary of state in each state where a trust receipt plan dealer was domiciled. Such a statement is shown in Exhibit 6. Dealers using the trust receipt plan were charged an extra 3% on the cost of purchases from Scott. They also had to place all purchase orders directly through Scott's field salesmen, inasmuch as these account executives were held responsible by the company for controlling dealer inventories in connection with the trust receipt plan.

This last-mentioned role of Scott's sales force was absolutely central to the proper functioning of the trust receipt plan. Apart from simply policing the level and character of dealer inventories, the account executives also periodically inventoried the trust receipt dealers so that Scott could bill the dealers for merchandise sold. During the two peak retail selling seasons these physical inventories were taken once a month, and even oftener in the case of large dealers. In the off seasons the inspections occurred much less frequently. In any event, the terms of payment associated with the trust receipt plan required that the dealer pay Scott within 10 days of receipt of an invoice from the company for goods sold since the last physical inventory date.

After introduction of the two payment plans in 1960, about half of Scott's sales were by seasonal dating and half by trust receipt. The trust receipt dealers were for the most part local garden centers and hardware stores, whereas the seasonal dating dealers were the larger chain garden centers and department stores. The company's overall collection experience with both plans was that about 75% of receivables were collected in the month due, another 16% in the following month, an additional 6% in the next month after that, and the balance thereafter.

The rapid growth in outstanding receivables resulting from the trust receipt program was financed largely by a combination of subordinated notes, a revolving line of bank credit, and increased use of supplier credit arising out of special deferred payment terms extended by the company's chemical suppliers. The company also retained almost all of its earnings each year as had been its policy in the past.

At the end of fiscal 1961 Scott and its subsidiaries had $16.2 million of long-term debt outstanding, of which $12 million comprised renewable five-year subordinated notes of the parent company held by four insurance companies and a trustee and $4.2 million was publicly held bonds owed by Scotts Chemical Plant, Inc., a wholly owned subsidiary. The key terms associated with the $12 million of subordinated notes are summarized in the footnotes to Exhibits 1 and 2. The governing loan indenture limited the unconsolidated parent company's maximum outstanding debt at any time to an amount not greater than three times what was termed the company's "equity working capital" as of the preceding March 31. What was meant by equity working capital and the calculation of maximum allowed debt are shown in Exhibit 7. The note indenture restricted outstanding subordinated notes to only 60% of maximum allowed debt as determined by the above equity working capital formula. The agreement also required that Scott be out of bank debt for 60 consecutive days each year and that the company earn before taxes 1½ times its fixed financial charges including interest on funded and unfunded debt, amortization of debt discount, and rentals on leased properties.

In addition to the long-term debt just described, Scott also had a $12.5 million line of credit at the end of fiscal 1961 with a group of seven commercial banks. The purpose of this line was to provide for seasonal funds needs, and in recent years the maximum line had been used at some point during each year. An informal understanding covering this seasonal financing arrangement required that Scott maintain average compensating balances with the banks involved of 15% of the line of credit.

As far as accounts payable were concerned, Scott had negotiated an arrangement with its principal chemical suppliers whereby the company settled with these suppliers just once or twice a year. It had been possible to negotiate these favorable terms because the suppliers were persuaded that it was in their best interests to help Scott develop and expand the home lawn market. Generally, no interest or other charges were levied on these amounts.

As fiscal 1961 drew to a close, management was generally pleased with what appeared to have been the results of the trust receipt program, although final figures for the year just ending were not yet available. Company sales had increased from $31 million in 1959 to over $43 million in 1961. At this level of operations the company's break-even point was estimated at between $27.5 million and $30 million.

By the end of 1961, when company officials were reviewing the results of fiscal 1961 and preparing plans for the 1962 selling season, the audited statements shown in Exhibits 1 and 2 were available, as well as the unaudited and unconsolidated quarterly statements in Exhibits 3 and 4. In addition, on the basis of a physical inventory taken by the company's sales force, combined standard and trust receipt plan dealer inventories were estimated to be at a level of about $28 million at the end of calendar 1961. This compared with roughly $17 million at the end of 1960. On the basis of these and other data, Scott's sales department estimated that in terms of cost of sales, dealer sales in fiscal 1961 reached an all-time high of over $30 million. The recent record of earnings, dividends, and market price range is shown in Exhibit 8.

It was against this background that company officials began their review and evaluation of recent operations and current financial position. They were particularly anxious to formulate any indicated changes in company plans and financial policies before the new production and selling seasons were upon the company.

Exhibit 1

THE O. M. SCOTT & SONS COMPANY AND SUBSIDIARY COMPANIES

CONSOLIDATED BALANCE SHEETS AS OF SEPTEMBER 30, 1957–61

(Dollar amounts in thousands)

	1957	1958	1959	1960(a)	1961(e)
Cash	$ 533.9	$ 1,232.0	$ 1,736.4	$ 2,328.7	$ 1,454.3
Accounts receivable	2,640.0	4,686.5	5,788.4	15,749.7	21,500.5(f)
Inventories	2,340.3	3,379.8	6,993.2	3,914.3	5,590.5
Total current assets	$5,514.2	$ 9,298.3	$14,518.0	$21,992.7	$28,545.3
Land, buildings, equipment	$2,253.5	$ 2,439.5	$ 7,364.6	$ 8,003.4	$ 8,370.2
Less: Accumulated depreciation	544.0	650.0	1,211.3	1,687.1	2,247.1
Net fixed assets	$1,709.5	$ 1,789.5	$ 6,153.3	$ 6,316.3	$ 6,123.1
Investment in and advances to affiliates	1,165.6	28.9	232.3	462.0	133.6
Other assets	488.5	376.6	837.5	1,132.0	937.8
Total assets	$8,877.8	$11,493.3	$21,741.1	$29,903.0	$35,739.8
Accounts payable	$1,540.8	$ 2,134.6	$ 4,140.2	$ 2,791.0	$ 6,239.2
Notes payable—banks	300.0	.....	1,000.0	.....	.....
Accrued taxes, interest, and other expenses	674.3	1,437.7	1,900.7	1,941.2	1,207.7
Current sinking fund requirements	77.0	173.9	324.3	382.5	512.5
Total current liabilities	$2,592.1	$ 3,746.2	$ 7,365.2	$ 5,114.7	$ 7,959.4
Long-term debt:					
Of parent company (c) (b)	2,186.7	2,059.7	1,777.2	9,000.0	12,000.0
Of subsidiary (c) (b)	.....	.....	5,162.6	4,649.5	4,170.4
Total liabilities (d)	$4,778.8	$ 5,805.9	$14,305.0	$18,764.2	$24,129.8
Preferred stock (i)	1,757.2	2,432.2	2,392.5	2,347.5	2,254.3
Common stock and surplus	2,341.8	3,255.2	5,043.6	8,791.3 (b) (g)	9,355.7
Total liabilities and net worth	$8,877.8	$11,493.3	$21,741.1	$29,903.0	$35,739.8

See notes beginning p. 79.

Exhibit 2

THE O. M. SCOTT & SONS COMPANY AND SUBSIDIARY COMPANIES

CONSOLIDATED INCOME STATEMENTS FOR THE YEARS
ENDING SEPTEMBER 30, 1957–61

(Dollar amounts in thousands)

	1957	1958	1959	1960(a)	1961(e)
Net sales (b) (g)	$18,675.9	$23,400.2	$30,563.7	$38,396.4	$43,140.1
Cost of sales and operating expenses:					
Cost of products sold including processing, warehousing, delivery and merchandising (including lease rentals)	$15,500.9	$18,914.7	$24,119.5	$30,416.8(d)	$34,331.7
General and administrative, research and development expenses	1,817.2	2,134.1	2,499.3	2,853.6	3,850.7
Depreciation and amortization	263.2	185.9	377.6	584.2	589.6
Interest charges	199.8	212.7	410.6	881.6	1,131.5
Total cost of sales	$17,781.1	$21,447.4	$27,407.0	$34,736.2	$39,903.5
Earnings before taxes on income	$ 894.8	$ 1,952.7	$ 3,156.7	$ 3,660.2	$ 3,236.6
Federal and state taxes on income	443.5	1,051.6	1,671.2	1,875.2	1,665.9
Net income after taxes	$ 451.3	$ 901.1	$ 1,485.5	$ 1,785.0	$ 1,570.7

See notes following.

Exhibits 1 and 2—Continued

THE O. M. SCOTT & SONS COMPANY

NOTES TO FINANCIAL STATEMENTS

a) *1960 Auditor's Statement*

The Board of Directors
The O. M. Scott & Sons Company

We have examined the statement of consolidated financial position of The O. M. Scott & Sons Company and its subsidiaries as of September 30, 1960, the related consolidated statements of operations, capital surplus and retained earnings for the fiscal year then ended, and accompanying notes to financial statements. Our examination was made in accordance with generally accepted auditing standards, and accordingly included such tests of the accounting records and such other auditing procedures as we considered necessary in the circumstances.

In our opinion, the accompanying statements, together with the explanatory notes, present fairly the consolidated financial position of The O. M. Scott & Sons Company and its subsidiaries at September 30, 1960, and the results of their operations for the year then ended, in conformity with generally accepted accounting principles, except as described in note (*b*), applied on a basis consistent with that of the preceding year.

PEAT, MARWICK, MITCHELL & CO.

Columbus, Ohio
November 23, 1960

Exhibits 1 and 2—Continued

b) Sales

For several years the company has followed a prebilling system to obtain more efficient and economical control of production through the medium of unappropriated inventory. Under this system, the invoicing of customers predates shipment. Consequently, both fiscal 1960 and 1959 sales stated in the operating statement include firm orders received, billed, and costed-out in late September which were shipped early in the immediately following October. Prior to September 30, 1960, the amounts involved were not significant, but toward the end of that month shipment was delayed by the company to facilitate the taking of physical inventories at storage warehouses as of the month end. The result of the foregoing is to include an additional amount of approximately $343,000 in net earnings for the year 1960. In management's opinion, the earnings on these sales are properly earnings of the year 1960.

c) Long-Term Debt

All long-term obligations of the parent company at September 30, 1959, were retired prior to December 31, 1959.

In fiscal 1960, the parent company sold five-year subordinated promissory notes, principally to certain insurance companies, at the principal amount of $9 million, maturing October 13, 1964. The notes bear interest to October 10, 1960, at $6\frac{1}{2}\%$ per annum and thereafter to maturity at (a) 6% per annum, or (b) the New York prime commercial rate plus $1\frac{1}{2}\%$, whichever is higher.

The loan agreement provides, among other things, that (a) payment of principal and interest on the notes is subordinated to repayment of bank loans due within one year, (b) new or additional notes may be sold on October 28th of each future year, and (c) any holder of the notes may, before October 15th of each year, require payment by October 10th of the immediately ensuing year of all or part of the notes held.*

All holders of the notes at September 30, 1960, surrendered the notes then held in exchange for new notes having exactly the same terms but maturing October 28, 1965, at an interest rate of 6% per annum to October 10, 1961. Interest after October 10, 1961, accrues at the rate determinable under the provisions of the loan agreement.

Long-term obligations of subsidiary outstanding on September 30, 1960:

20-year $5\frac{3}{4}\%$ first mortgage bonds due March 15, 1977	$1,026,000
18-year 6% secured sinking fund debentures due Feb. 1, 1977	2,840,500
10-year 6% sinking fund notes due March 15, 1967	178,000
10-year 6% subordinated debentures due Dec. 15, 1967	950,000
	$4,994,500
Less: Current sinking fund provision	345,000
	$4,649,500

---

* Such payments were to be made in four equal annual installments beginning on October 10 of the immediately ensuing year.

Exhibits 1 and 2—Continued

The above obligations of a subsidiary are secured by property mortgages, and/or assignment of lease rentals payable by the parent company.

d) Long-Term Leases

The main production, warehousing, and office facilities used by the company are leased from affiliated interests not consolidated, namely, the company's Pension and Profit Sharing Trusts, and also from a consolidated subsidiary, Scotts Chemical Plant, Inc. These leases, all having over 10 years to run, required minimum annual rentals in fiscal 1960 of $872,577. This represented less than 17% of net taxable profit before deduction for rentals, depreciation, and expenses based on net profits. It is anticipated that in fiscal 1961, the fixed rentals under these leases will approximate the same amount.

e) 1961 Auditor's Statement

Board of Directors
The O. M. Scott & Sons Company
Marysville, Ohio

We have examined the statement of consolidated financial position of The O. M. Scott & Sons Company and its subsidiaries as of September 30, 1961, and the related statements of consolidated operations, capital surplus, and retained earnings for the year then ended. Our examination was made in accordance with generally accepted auditing standards, and accordingly included such tests of the accounting records and such other auditing procedures as we considered necessary in the circumstances.

In our opinion, the accompanying statements of financial position, operations, capital surplus, and retained earnings present fairly the consolidated financial position of The O. M. Scott & Sons Company and its subsidiaries at September 30, 1961, and the consolidated results of their operations for the year then ended, in conformity with generally accepted accounting principles which, except for the changes (in which we concur) referred to in Notes (*f*) and (*g*), have been applied on a basis consistent with that of the preceding year.

ERNST & ERNST

Dayton, Ohio
January 6, 1962

f) Accounts Receivable

Accounts receivable are stated net after reserve of $740,000 for dealer adjustments, allowances, and doubtful accounts.

In 1959 the company adopted a plan of deferred payments for certain retail dealers. Accounts receivable include $16,033,093 for shipments under this plan which are secured by trust receipts executed by the dealers. The trust receipt arrangements provide for (1) immediate transfer to the dealers of title to the merchandise shipped in response to the dealers' orders, (2) retention by the company of a security interest in the merchandise until sold by the dealers, and (3) payment by the dealers to the company as the merchandise

Exhibits 1 and 2—Continued

is sold at retail. The dealers, whether trust receipt or other, do not have the right to return any part of merchandise ordered by them and delivered in salable condition, but they may tender merchandise in full or part payment of their accounts in the event of termination by the company of their dealerships. To provide for possible adjustments and allowances in the liquidation of dealer accounts receivable, the company has provided an increase in reserve by a charge to net earnings of the current year of $150,000 and a charge to retained earnings at October 1, 1960, of $530,000.

g) *Sales*

In the financial statements for the year ended September 30, 1960, attention was directed to the company's policy of including in the operating statement firm orders received, billed, and costed out in late September which were shipped early in the immediately following October. During 1961, this policy was discontinued. In order to reflect this change in policy prebilled sales at September 30, 1960, together with related costs and expenses included in operations of the year then ended, have been carried forward and included in the operating statement for the year ended September 30, 1961, with a resulting charge to retained earnings at October 1, 1960, of $429,600. This change in accounting principle did not have a material effect on net earnings for the year ended September 30, 1961.

h) *Long-Term Debt: Five-Year Subordinated Promissory Notes*

The notes bear interest to October 10, 1961, at 6% per annum and thereafter to maturity at a rate which is the higher of (*a*) 6% per annum, or (*b*) the New York prime commercial rate plus 1½%. The loan agreement provides, among other things, that (*a*) payment of principal and interest on the notes is subordinated to repayment of bank loans due within one year, and (*b*) elections may be exercised annually by the holders to (1) exchange the notes currently held for new notes having a maturity extended by one year, (2) purchase additional notes if offered for sale by the company, or (3) require payment of all or part of the notes held, such payments to be made in four equal annual installments beginning on October 10 of the immediately ensuing year.

All holders of the notes at September 30, 1961, except for $1 million, surrendered the notes then held in exchange for new notes having exactly the same terms but maturing October 28, 1966, at an interest rate of 6% per annum to October 10, 1962. Subsequent to September 30, 1961, arrangements have been made for the note for $1 million not exchanged to mature September 1, 1962, and to issue a note for $1 million to another lender maturing October 28, 1966.

Exhibits 1 and 2—Continued

Obligations of Subsidiaries:

5¾% first mortgage bonds, due March 15, 1977	$ 964,000	
6% sinking fund notes, due March 15, 1967	147,500	
6% subordinated debentures, due December 15, 1967	819,000	
6% secured sinking fund debentures due February 1, 1977	2,620,500	
	$4,551,000	
Less classified as current liability...	414,000	$4,137,000
Real estate mortgage notes ($252 payable monthly for interest at 6% per annum and amortization of principal)	$ 34,383	
Less classified as current liabilities..	1,000	33,383
		$4,170,383

The above long-term obligations of subsidiaries are secured by mortgages on property, plant, and equipment, and/or assignment of lease rentals payable by the parent company.

i) Preferred Stock

Preferred stock is 5% cumulative, $100 par value.

Exhibit 3

THE O. M. SCOTT & SONS COMPANY

UNCONSOLIDATED QUARTERLY BALANCE SHEETS OF PARENT COMPANY FOR
FISCAL YEAR 1961*

(Dollar amounts in thousands)

	12/31/60	3/31/61	6/30/61	9/30/61
Cash	$ 1,810	$ 2,140	$ 1,760	$ 2,070
Accounts receivable:				
Standard plan	$ 1,500	$ 6,540	$ 3,110	$ 4,400
Trust receipt plan	8,660	15,880	11,890	16,830
Total receivables	$10,160	$22,420	$15,000	$21,230
Inventories:				
Finished goods	$ 7,390	$ 5,850	$ 6,420	$ 4,040
Raw materials and supplies	2,380	2,520	1,890	1,460
Total inventories	$ 9,770	$ 8,370	$ 8,310	$ 5,500
Total current assets	$21,740	$32,930	$25,070	$28,800
Land, buildings, equipment	$ 2,130	$ 2,190	$ 2,270	$ 2,290
Less: Accumulated depreciation	800	830	870	910
Net fixed assets	$ 1,330	$ 1,360	$ 1,400	$ 1,380
Other assets	$ 1,990	$ 1,730	$ 1,720	$ 1,240
Total assets	$25,060	$36,020	$28,190	$31,420
Accounts payable	$ 1,390	$ 3,680	$ 3,150	$ 7,040
Notes payable—bank	6,250	12,000	5,750	—
Accrued taxes, interest, and other expenses	(390)	950	110	1,170
Total current liabilities	$ 7,250	$16,630	$ 9,010	$ 8,210
Subordinated promissory notes	9,000	9,000	9,000	12,000
Total liabilities	$16,250	$25,630	$18,010	$20,210
Net worth:				
Preferred stock	2,380	2,380	2,350	2,250
Common stock and surplus	6,430	8,010	7,830	8,960
Total liabilities and net worth	$25,060	$36,020	$28,190	$31,420

* Excluding items relating to certain nonoperating subsidiaries. Unaudited and unpublished. For these reason Exhibit 3 does not correspond exactly with Exhibit 1. In particular, the cash account in Exhibit 3 is not consisten with that in Exhibit 1.

Exhibit 4

THE O. M. SCOTT & SONS COMPANY

UNCONSOLIDATED QUARTERLY INCOME STATEMENTS OF PARENT COMPANY
FOR THE YEAR ENDING SEPTEMBER 30, 1961*

(Dollar amounts in thousands)

	Quarter Ending 12/31/60	Quarter Ending 3/31/61	Quarter Ending 6/30/61	Quarter Ending 9/30/61	Year
Net sales..........................	$ 1,300	$15,780	$9,570	$14,740	$41,390
Cost of sales and operating expenses:					
Cost of products sold including processing, depreciation, warehousing, delivery and merchandising.........	$ 3,250	$11,730	$8,670	$10,790	$34,440
General and administrative, research and development expenses...........	660	800	940	1,000	3,400
Interest charges.....................	150	240	260	200	850
Total cost of sales...............	$ 4,060	$12,770	$9,870	$11,990	$38,690
Earnings (losses) before taxes on income............................	$(2,760)	$ 3,010	$ (300)	$ 2,750	$ 2,700
Federal taxes on income...............	(1,440)	1,570	(160)	1,390	1,360
Net income (loss) after taxes...........	$(1,320)	$ 1,440	$ (140)	$ 1,360	$ 1,340

* Excluding items relating to the operations of certain nonoperating subsidiaries. Unaudited and unpublished.

Exhibit 5

THE O. M. SCOTT & SONS COMPANY

TRUST RECEIPT

The undersigned Dealer, as Trustee, and Entruster agree to engage in Trust Receipt financing of the acquisition by Trustees of seed, fertilizer, weed controls, pest controls, applicators, mowers and other lawn and garden products, all bearing the brands and trade marks of The O. M. Scott & Sons Company. Entruster will direct said company to deliver said products from time to time as ordered by Dealer.

   a) Dealer agrees to hold said products in trust for the sole purpose of making sales to consumers, functioning as a retailer and not as a wholesaler.

   b) Dealer agrees to hold a sufficient proportion of the funds received from such sales for payment to Entruster as billed.

   c) Either party may terminate this Trust Receipt on notice. In such event Dealer will surrender to Entruster his complete stock of The O. M. Scott & Sons Company products, proceeds thereof to be credited to Dealer.*

Official Business Name
of Dealer as Trustee:

Accepted at Marysville, Ohio

_____ , 19__

- Street & No._____
City_____Zone____State_____

THE O. M. SCOTT & SONS COMPANY
(Entruster)

Authorized
Signature_____.
Date_____Title_____

President

* This statement differs from the statement quoted in footnote (*f*) to Exhibits 1 and 2. Presumably the statement in Exhibit 5 is correct.

Exhibit 6

THE O. M. SCOTT & SONS COMPANY

STATEMENT OF TRUST RECEIPT FINANCING

The Entruster, The O. M. Scott & Sons Company, whose chief place of business is at Marysville, Ohio, and who has no place of business within this state, is or expects to be engaged in financing under trust receipt transactions, the acquisition by the Trustee whose name and chief place of business within this state is:

of seed, fertilizers, weed controls, pest controls, applicators, mowers and other lawn and garden products, all bearing the brands and trade marks of The O. M. Scott & Sons Company.

Entruster: The O. M. Scott & Sons Company   Date_____, 19__
                                               For the Trustee   (Dealer)
By :_____   By :_____
                    President

Exhibit 7

THE O. M. SCOTT & SONS COMPANY

EXAMPLE SHOWING CALCULATION OF EQUITY WORKING CAPITAL AND MAXIMUM ALLOWED DEBT OF PARENT COMPANY FOR THE TWELVE MONTHS FOLLOWING MARCH 31, 1961*

(Dollar amounts in millions)

Calculation of equity working capital:

Current assets...		$32.9
Current liabilities...	$16.6	
Long-term debt..	9.0	
Total debt..	$25.6	25.6
Equity working capital......................................		$ 7.3

Calculation of maximum allowed parent company debt:

300% of equity working capital...............................	$21.9
Actual parent borrowings—March 31, 1961......................	21.0
Available debt capacity......................................	$ .9

Calculation of maximum allowed subordinated debt of parent:

60% of maximum allowed total debt ($21.9 million × 60%)........	$13.1

* Calculations based on figures taken from Exhibit 3.

Exhibit 8

THE O. M. SCOTT & SONS COMPANY

RECORD OF EARNINGS, DIVIDENDS, AND MARKET PRICE RANGE,
1958–61

Fiscal Year	Earnings per Share	Dividends per Share	Market Price Range*
1958	$0.69	10% stk.	6⅛– 1½
1959	1.15	10% stk.	32⅞– 6⅛
1960	1.21	10% stk.	51 –31⅞
1961	0.99	10¢ + 5% stk.	58¾–30

* Calendar year; bid prices. Closing prices September 29 and December 29, 1961 were $49 and $32¼ respectively. Stock first sold publicly in 1958 and has traded over-the-counter since then. The company had about 4,100 common shareholders in 1961.

CARREFOUR, S.A.

^^^

In mid-1972, the top management of Carrefour, S.A. faced several important policy decisions. They centered around the speed and direction of future growth and how that growth ought to be financed.

Company background

Carrefour began operations with a single 650-square-meter supermarket in Annecy, France, in the summer of 1960. This store tested the response of retail-food customers to the idea of one-stop,[1] self-service shopping with discount prices. The store proved to be popular; after considerable study, the firm's founders decided to test their retailing formula with additional products such as clothing, sporting equipment, auto accessories, and consumer electronics. In 1963, Carrefour thus opened the first hypermarket[2] in France at a location just outside of Paris. The store covered 2,500 square meters, sold both food and non-food products at discount prices, and provided parking for 450 cars.

The Carrefour hypermarket was accepted enthusiastically by French consumers, and the company began to grow rapidly. Between 1965 and 1971, Carrefour's sales grew at an annual rate exceeding 50% (Exhibit 1); nonfood items accounted for about 40% of total volume. The growth in corporate assets kept pace with the growth in sales (Exhibit 2).

As the company's revenue increased, so did the size of its stores. Starting in 1970, new stores called "commercial centers" were opened with selling areas as large as 25,000 square meters.

By the end of 1971, Carrefour had built and was operating 16 *wholly owned* stores; had an equity interest in five stores operated as *joint ventures;* and had *franchise* agreements with seven additional stores. Plans were under way to open 15 new stores under one of these three operating arrangements in 1972 (Exhibit 3).

---

[1] In France, as in most of Europe, retail distribution in 1960 was a highly fragmented activity. Small shopkeepers accounted for almost all sales of both food and nonfood products, and product lines in individual stores were very narrow. Food shopping was essentially a daily activity, and visits to four entirely separate shops were required in order to purchase baked goods, dairy products, meat products, and vegetables.

[2] A hypermarket was defined as a store with a selling area of 2,500 square meters or more. (One square meter equals approximately ten square feet.)

Carrefour's strategy was to build its stores outside of towns in locations where (1) highways provided easy access and (2) land could be acquired[3] very inexpensively. The company favored inexpensive construction in combination with low-cost land, which gave Carrefour a total investment per square meter of selling space in a fully equipped store equal to about one third that of traditional supermarkets and department stores.

Carrefour also followed a strategy of decentralized management. Each store manager was a profit center with almost complete freedom in decision-making. One Carrefour store manager (paid 12,000F per month versus 2,500F two years earlier when he was a store manager in a smaller competing supermarket chain) made the following comments:

> My previous job was demoralizing. It took a month to get authorization to buy something for the store which cost 14F. Now I am free to make all of my own decisions. I can hire 10 people, buy a new refrigeration unit, or hire a band for a parking lot festival.[4]

Factors favoring growth

The high degree of consumer acceptance which fueled Carrefour's growth at 50% per year stemmed in large measure from factors like convenience and price. Almost any product purchased more than once a year could be bought at a Carrefour store. The company even operated discount gasoline outlets at many stores. Indeed, Carrefour operated five of the ten largest volume gasoline stations in France.

While convenience was undoubtedly a strong factor in Carrefour's growth, so was price. Gross margins on food and nonfood items differed somewhat, but Carrefour operated on an average gross margin of about 15% (Exhibit 1). The gross margins (and, by implication, the prices) of retailers in traditional outlets averaged 5 to 10 percentage points more than Carrefour's.

Obstacles to growth

Convenience and price favored the growth of discount retail stores in France. Nonetheless, these firms suffered from obstacles not met by most rapidly growing businesses. First, for many years the nation's distribution system had lagged behind most other sectors of the economy in adopting modern techniques. When an economic rationalization of this sector started to occur, its results were especially severe for many small shopkeepers. As shown below, 40% or almost 80,000 of the 203,600 small retail shops in operation in 1961 had disappeared by 1971. These small shopkeepers represented a significant political force in France, and their problems could not be easily ignored.[5]

---

[3] In a few situations where large plots of land were not available for purchase within a market area, Carrefour leased land.

[4] *Les Informations*, January 11, 1971, p. 25.

[5] Groups of shopkeepers often staged protest demonstrations at public appearances of high government officials and at new hypermarkets. In May 1970, Carrefour's largest store was totally destroyed by a fire which did not appear to be accidental.

NUMBER OF RETAIL STORES IN OPERATION 1961–1971

	1961	1967	1969	1971
Grocery and dairy stores (selling area less than 400 m²)	149,100	111,900	96,480	85,090
Chain stores and cooperatives (selling area less than 400 m²)	35,000	31,980	29,295	26,050
Drug stores	19,500	14,280	14,280	13,710
Totals	203,600	158,160	140,055	124,850

Source: *Points de Vente*, March 1972, p. 125.

One way of addressing the problem of the small merchant was to slow down the growth of hypermarkets; another was to ease the financial burdens of those merchants forced out of business. Each of these solutions was used to some extent to reduce the size of the problem caused by the growth of hypermarkets in France. In an effort to slow the growth of hypermarkets, national and local governments in almost every country in Europe made it difficult to obtain construction permits[6] to build large new retail stores. Local merchants would generally lobby vigorously against the issuance of new construction permits in their market areas. This prompted some discount retailers to offer plans for large commercial centers in which space could be leased to as many as 40 independent shopkeepers. This type of plan allowed small merchants to set up specialty stores and boutiques, and usually generated some measure of local merchant support for the issuance of permits.

While specialty stores in commercial centers eliminated financial hardships for a few small merchants, this idea hardly represented a complete solution. In an attempt to attack the problem more broadly, the French National Assembly passed legislation in mid-1972 to tax retail stores in order to provide pensions for small shopkeepers who were unable to continue in business. The tax was to be paid by all retail merchants; the heaviest burden was to be borne by operators of large stores built after 1962. For Carrefour, the tax (based on 1971 operations) would have amounted to roughly 3 million francs.[7]

Joint ventures and franchises

The ability to get construction permits had a major impact on corporate growth potential for a retail discount chain. Through the late 1960s and early 1970s, Carrefour's rapid growth was made possible by the fact that the firm had been able to get two new construction permits each year. As more firms entered the discount retail field, however, the competition for permits became more difficult as many firms and individuals vied for authorization to build in attractive

---

[6] Permits were usually issued for a store of a specific size to be built in a specific location for a specific firm or individual. Once a permit was issued, it could not be sold, but the building itself, once constructed, could be sold to another firm or individual.

[7] An equivalent volume of sales generated in small shops built prior to 1962 would have generated a tax liability of about 500,000 francs.

locations. In the late 1960s, to achieve a more rapid pace of expansion than the firm could achieve if it were limited to two new stores per year, Carrefour offered to share its retailing know-how, trademark, and consumer goodwill with potential partners both in France and elsewhere in Europe. Carrefour offered its expertise in exchange for either an ownership interest in stores under construction or franchise fees. In joint ventures, Carrefour purchased an ownership interest ranging from 10% to 50% (Exhibit 3). Under franchising, Carrefour received a fee of 0.2% of total store sales, and Carrefour's central buying office for nonfood products (SAMOD) received a fee equal to 1% of the store's sales of nonfood items.[8]

Between 1969 and 1971, Carrefour was quite successful in adding selling area under the Carrefour name by means of joint ventures and franchises (Exhibit 4). Success in the area of joint ventures was evidenced by Carrefour's investments and advances to affiliates which had grown to almost 19 million francs (Exhibit 2). Joint venture stores which had been in operation long enough to permit evaluation of their profitability (e.g., SOGARA) were as profitable[9] as wholly owned Carrefour stores (Exhibit 5). However, they seemed to take a little longer than wholly owned stores to reach that position.

Competition

Carrefour's early success in discount retail distribution naturally attracted considerable competition. While Carrefour was, by far, the hypermarket leader in France in terms of selling space, other firms were becoming important factors in the business:

LEADING FRENCH HYPERMARKET CHAINS (6/30/72)

Trade Name	Owner Group	Number of Stores Operated under Trade Name	Total Selling Area of Stores (000's of m²)
Carrefour...............	Carrefour	28	250
Mammoth...............	Paridoc	28	153
Escale*.................	Au Printemps	13	83
Radar..................	Docks Remois	9	44
Rond-Point.............		8	27
Euromarché*............	G.S.R.P.	7	32
Auchan................		5	47
Record................		5	23
Geant Casino..........	Casino	4	36
Delta.................		4	24

* In mid-1972, Au Printemps and Euromarché concluded an agreement according to which all of Au Printemps stores would be operated under the Euromarché trade name. This consolidation was believed to represent an effort by Au Printemps to compete more effectively in the future with Carrefour.

Source: *Enterprise*, July 1972, p. 63; September 15, 1972, p. 78.

---

[8] SAMOD received a similar fee from the firm's wholly owned stores as well for performing the purchasing function on nonfood products.

[9] Carrefour did not consolidate the results of joint ventures and other affiliates for financial reporting purposes. The only income from these ventures included in Exhibit 1, for example, arose from dividends as shown in Exhibit 5.

By 1970, the combined building activity of all hypermarket operators was adding about 250,000 square meters per year of new selling space (Exhibit 6). Some industry analysts[10] suggested that consumer needs for stores of this size in France would be satisfied when total hypermarket selling area reached 2.2 million square meters. About one half this amount was in place by June 30, 1972.

Outside of France, Carrefour's management saw a need for hypermarkets which was as great as the need in France. However, existing large retailers outside of France appeared to be somewhat stronger financially than the competition which Carrefour had faced in France (Exhibit 7).

---

[10] *Enterprise*, September 15, 1972, p. 75.

Exhibit 1

CARREFOUR, S.A.

CARREFOUR, S.A. INCOME STATEMENT DATA, 1965–1971

(Millions of francs except per share data)

		1965	1966	1967	1968	1969	1970	1971
1	Revenues (all taxes included)	156	220	339	524	1,025	1,445	2,234
2	Less: value added tax	3	5	7	11	147	195	298
3	Revenues (net of value added tax)	153	215	332	513	878	1,250	1,936
4	Starting inventory	6	6	14	17	34	65	72
5	Plus: purchases	133	194	291	454	782	1,063	1,670
6	Less: ending inventory	6	14	17	30	65	72	107
7	Cost of goods sold	133	186	288	441	751	1,056	1,635
8	Gross margin	20	29	44	72	127	194	301
9	Salaries	8	11	16	26	56	82	119
10	Depreciation and amortization	2	5	4	8	15	19	32
11	Other expenses	3	7	11	17	26	41	61
12	Operating profit	7	6	13	21	30	52	89
13	Nonoperating gains (losses)	(1)	0	1	1	4	(5)	1
14	Investment provision	—	—	—	—	(4)	(7)	(10)
15	Profit before tax	6	6	14	22	30	40	80
16	Income tax	3	3	7	12	14	17	36
17	Profit after tax	3	3	7	10	16	23	44
	Allocation of profit after tax							
18	To: shareholders' equity	3	2	5	3	3	3	4
19	To: employee profit sharing*	—	—	—	4	7	10	20
20	To: dividends	—	1	2	3	6	10	20
	Income statement statistics							
21	Gross profit margin	13.1%	13.5%	13.3%	14.0%	14.4%	15.5%	15.5%
22	Profit/sales (net of VAT)	2.0%	1.4%	2.1%	2.0%	1.8%	1.8%	2.3%
23	Profit/equity	27.0%	22.0%	43.0%	26.0%	18.0%	23.0%	39.0%
24	Earnings per share (francs)	8.6	8.6	20	22	27	39	75
25	Dividends per share (francs)	—	2	4	7	11	18	34
26	Book value per share (francs)	33	40	48	84	151	168	191
27	Market value per share (francs)	—	—	—	—	—	1,040	1,980
28	Price earnings ratio	—	—	—	—	—	27	27
29	Dividend yield	—	—	—	—	—	1.7%	1.7%
30	Dividend payout ratio	0	33.0%	29.0%	30.0%	38.0%	43.0%	45.0%

* According to French law, large firms must share with employees a portion of profits after tax in excess of 5% of net worth. The amount shared is earned by employees in one year (line 19, above), becomes a tax deductible expense to the firm in the second year (included in line 9, above), and becomes the basis for a duplicate tax deduction (line 14, above) in the second year if the firm continues to make fixed asset investments equal to the charge. This legislation makes it possible for a firm to share profits with employees, yet incur no real aftertax cost (except for a potential one-year lag between profit-sharing payments and tax recovery) since the burden falls entirely on the government via a reduction in corporate income taxes.

Exhibit 2

CARREFOUR, S.A.
CARREFOUR, S.A. BALANCE SHEET DATA, 1965–1971
(Millions of francs)

	1965	1966	1967	1968	1969	1970	1971
1 Intangible assets	—	—	—	—	4	1	1
2 Land	5	8	8	14	20	25	28
3 Buildings and equipment	11	22	26	50	82	136	202
4 Other fixed assets	6	9	14	21	38	52	49
5 Total fixed assets	22	39	48	85	140	213	279
6 Less: depreciation	5	8	12	10	22	35	63
7 Net fixed assets	17	31	36	75	118	178	216
8 Investments and advances to affiliates	2	3	4	5	10	12	19
9 Inventory	6	14	17	30	65	72	107
10 Accounts receivable	—	—	1	2	2	3	4
11 Other current assets	1	9	19	58	50	75	124
12 Cash	9	5	8	18	51	116	151
13 Total current assets	16	28	45	108	168	266	386
14 Total assets	35	62	85	188	300	457	622
15 Shareholders' equity	11	14	17	39	89	98	112
16 Special provisions	—	—	—	—	—	1	1
17 Long-term debt	3	9	14	26	25	64	64
18 Accounts payable	—	—	—	—	48	61	77
19 Trade notes (noninterest bearing)	16	33	39	100	79	147	244
20 Other current liabilities	5	6	15	23	59	86	124
21 Total current liabilities	21	39	54	123	186	294	445
22 Total liabilities	35	62	85	188	300	457	622
Balance sheet statistics							
23 Current ratio	.76	.72	.83	.88	.90	.90	.87
24 Total debt/shareholders' equity	2.2	3.4	4.0	3.8	2.4	3.7	4.6
25 Net working capital (millions of francs)	(5)	(11)	(9)	(15)	(18)	(28)	(59)
26 Number of shares outstanding (000's)*†	347	347	347	462	588	588	588

*Over the course of its growth, Carrefour sold equity for the company's own account to groups outside the families of the founders on only two occasions. In early 1968, the firm sold approximately 75,000 shares at 145 francs per share to 40 employees at all levels in the firm (including store floorwalkers). In late 1969, the firm sold privately approximately 120,000 shares at 342 francs per share. About 50,000 of these shares were sold to the Banque Pour L'expansion Industrielle, which later offered them to the public (along with approximately 70,000 shares supplied by the founders), when Carrefour's stock was first introduced for trading on the Paris Bourse in June 1970. At 12/31/71, the company had granted employee stock options covering 4,880 shares to 244 employees.

† All case data adjusted for stock splits and stock dividends

Exhibit 3

CARREFOUR, S.A.
CARREFOUR NEW STORE OPENING DATA, 1960–1972

Country and City	Affiliate Name	Carrefour Ownership Interest (%)	Opening Date	Selling Surface (000's m²)	Parking Spaces (000's)
holly owned stores:					
France: Annecy............		100	6/60	.7	.1
Annecy............		100	5/63	.8	.1
Paris (region)......		100	6/63	5.5	1.0
Lyon.............		100	3/64	2.5	.2
Chalon-sur Saône..		100	5/65	1.0	.2
Lyon.............		100	10/66	11.5	2.0
Chartres.........		100	10/67	5.5	.7
Annecy...........		100	4/68	4.3	.7
Dijon............		100	9/68	9.0	1.5
Paris (region).....		100	10/68	9.1	2.4
Chambéry.........		100	5/69	4.6	.8
Grenoble.........		100	8/69	7.1	1.5
Paris (region).....		100	3/70	7.6	1.8
Marseille.........		100	9/70	21.3	4.0
Orléans...........		100	4/71	14.0	1.5
Melun...........		100	6/71	15.0	3.6
Meaux...........		100	10/72	11.3	3.0
Lyon.............		100	11/72	6.0	1.9
				136.8	27.0
int venture stores:					
France: Bayonne..........	SOGARA	49.9	3/67	3.2	.9
Bordeaux.........	SOGARA	49.9	10/69	16.2	1.8
Toulouse.........	SOGARA	49.9	3/72	25.0	4.0
LeMans..........	SOGRAMO	n.a.	6/72	7.5	1.0
Angers...........	SOGRAMO	n.a.	6/72	8.2	1.1
Nantes...........	SOGRAMO	n.a.	11/72	13.8	1.4
Charleville........	Ardennais	14.6	3/70	7.7	1.2
Belgium: Mons............	Ditrimas	49.9	11/69	7.6	1.0
Liège.............	Ditrimas	49.9	9/72	17.3	2.0
Switzerland: Lausanne.........	Hypermarche S.A.	30	4/70	6.3	1.0
Berne...........	Hypermarche S.A.	30	3/72	9.2	1.1
U.K.: Cardiff...........	Hypermarket Ltd.	10	9/72	5.5	1.0
				127.5	17.5
anchise stores:					
France: Paris (region)......	Bouriez	0	9/69	7.5	1.3
Strasbourg........	Bouriez	0	11/70	12.7	1.5
Lille..............	Bouriez	0	5/71	9.4	1.3
Nancy...........	Bouriez	0	10/71	8.7	1.5
Béthune..........	Bouriez	0	5/72	8.4	1.2
Lens.............	Bouriez	0	9/72	8.2	2.0
Colmar...........	Bouriez	0	12/72	6.6	1.0
Caen.............	Promodes	0	2/70	9.4	3.0
Alençon..........	Promodes	0	8/72	3.8	.9
Paris (region).....	Promodes	0	11/72	8.7	1.6
Valenciennes......	Promodes	0	10/72	8.6	1.4
Bourges..........	Dock de Nevers	0	3/69	7.5	1.1
Nevers..........	Dock de Nevers	0	10/69	7.1	1.2
				106.6	19.0

n.a. = not available.

Exhibit 4

CARREFOUR, S.A.

STORE SELLING AREA OPERATED UNDER THE CARREFOUR NAME, 1960–1972

	1960–1963	1964	1965	1966	1967	1968	1969	1970	1971	1972
	New Selling Area Opened Each Year (m² in 000's)									
Wholly owned stores.........	6.9	2.5	1.0	11.5	5.5	22.4	11.7	28.9	29.0	17.3
Joint venture stores...........					3.2		23.8	14.0		86.5
Franchise stores..............							22.1	22.1	18.1	44.3
Total................	6.9	2.5	1.0	11.5	8.7	22.4	57.6	65.0	47.1	148.1
	Cumulative Selling Area Operating under Carrefour Name (m² in 000's)									
Wholly owned stores.........	6.9	9.4	10.4	21.9	27.4	49.8	61.5	90.4	119.4	136.7
Joint venture stores...........					3.2	3.2	27.0	41.0	41.0	127.5
Franchise stores..............							22.1	44.2	62.3	106.6
Total................	6.9	9.4	10.4	21.9	30.6	53.0	110.6	175.6	222.7	370.8
	Percent of Cumulative Selling Area under Each Form of Operation									
Wholly owned stores.........	100	100	100	100	90	94	56	52	54	37
Joint venture stores...........					10	6	24	23	18	34
Franchise stores..............							20	25	28	29
Total................	100	100	100	100	100	100	100	100	100	100

Exhibit 5

CARREFOUR, S.A.

OWNERSHIP, PROFITABILITY, AND INVESTMENT DATA FOR CARREFOUR AFFILIATES, 1969–1971

Affiliate Name	Year	Carrefour Ownership (%)	Revenue (millions of francs)†	Profit after Tax (000's of francs)†	Dividends to Carrefour (000's of francs)†	Investments and Advances (millions of francs)*†
SAMOD	1969	92	5	417	174	
	1970	92	13	607	221	
	1971	90	17	1,089	221	1.8
SOGARA	1969	49.9	97	219	0	
	1970	49.9	257	3,930	150	
	1971	49.9	304	7,710	500	5.0
Ardennais	1969					
	1970					
	1971	14.6	58	175	0	.8
Ditrimas	1970	49.9	42	8	0	
	1971	49.9	45	19	0	2.6
Hypermarche S.A.	1969	30	n.a.	n.a.	0	
	1970	30	n.a.	n.a.	0	
	1971	30	n.a.	n.a.	0	4.8
Italmare		50				2.2
Hypermarket Ltd.		10				1.3
Pelaza		68				
Other Affiliates		—				.2
						18.7

n.a. = Not available.

* At cost; does not include equity in earnings retained in affiliate.

† All values expressed in French francs.

Exhibit 6

CARREFOUR, S.A.

NUMBER AND SIZE OF HYPERMARKETS CONSTRUCTED IN FRANCE, 1963–1972

Number of Hypermarkets Constructed

Store Type	1963–1966	1967	1968	1969	1970	1971	6 mos. 1972
Independent..........................	3	3	6	16	11	7	8
Chain................................	1	2	8	19	21	10	14
Department stores.....................	—	2	—	7	5	4	5
Cooperatives and others...............	—	1	2	3	5	8	5
Total for year...................	4	8	16	45	42	29	32
Cumulative total...............	4	12	28	73	115	144	176

Hypermarket Selling Space Constructed (m^2 in thousands)

Selling space constructed in year.........	19	42	77	270	258	155	207
Cumulative selling space constructed.....	19	61	138	408	666	821	1,028

Carrefour Hypermarket Selling Space Constructed (m^2 in thousands)

Wholly owned........................	17	8	22	12	29	29	0
Joint venture........................	—	3	0	16	8	0	41
Franchise............................	—	—	—	22	22	18	8
Total for year...................	17	11	22	50	59	47	49
Cumulative total................	17	28	50	100	159	206	255
(Carrefour/industry) cumulative.........	.87	.46	.37	.25	.24	.24	.24

Note: Data in Exhibit 6 differ somewhat from data in Exhibit 4 because (1) not all stores operating under the Carrefour name were located in France, and (2) Carrefour constructed three stores prior to 1966 which were not large enough to be classified as hypermarkets.

Source: *Enterprise*, March 6, 1971, p. 10; September 15, 1972; p. 75; and *Carrefour Annual Report*, 1971, p. 21.

Exhibit 7

CARREFOUR, S.A.

FINANCIAL DATA FOR LARGE RETAIL FIRMS IN EUROPE, 1967–1971

Sales (millions of French francs)

Country	Firm	1967–68	1968–69	1969–70	1970–71
France	Au Printemps	5,151*	5,480*	6,120*	6,719*
	Carrefour	524	1,025	1,445	2,234
	Casino	1,245	1,380	1,589	1,868
	Docks Remois	586	627	683	732
	Galeries Lafayette	556	484	545	582
Belgium	G. B. Enterprises	664	812	1,343	1,719
	S. A. Innovation	419	381	853	971
Germany	Karstadt	4,888	5,281	5,745	6,644
	Kaufhof	4,459	4,929	5,218	5,928
	Nechermann	2,048	2,190	2,348	2,697
U.K.	Great Universal	4,084	4,370	4,856	5,079
	Marks and Spencer	3,226	3,626	4,129	4,766
Italy	La Rinascente	1,366	1,426	1,564	1,744

Net Worth (millions of French francs)

Country	Firm	1967–68	1968–69	1969–70	1970–71
France	Au Printemps	372	373	378	372
	Carrefour	39	89	98	112
	Casino	79	110	118	141
	Docks Remois	85	89	92	95
	Galeries Lafayette	275	267	243	160
Belgium	G. B. Enterprises	138	145	225	247
	S. A. Innovation	145	152	262	260
Germany	Karstadt	1,029	1,102	1,190	1,272
	Kaufhof	759	816	858	931
	Nechermann	210	216	209	222
U.K.	Great Universal	1,971	2,002	2,154	2,364
	Marks and Spencer	1,328	1,371	1,424	1,858
Italy	La Rinascente	298	306	324	314

Net Profit/Net Worth (percent)

Country	Firm	1967–68	1968–69	1969–70	1970–71
France	Au Printemps	4.7	4.9	1.9	0.5
	Carrefour	26	18	23	39
	Casino	21	14	14	16
	Docks Remois	5.3	5.3	5.9	6.9
	Galeries Lafayette	(1.9)	(1.5)	(9.9)	(52)
Belgium	G. B. Enterprises	9.9	11	11	15
	S. A. Innovation	6.8	4.5	6.0	4.8
Germany	Karstadt	13	13	13	13
	Kaufhof	13	14	15	14
	Nechermann	10	11	5	7
U.K.	Great Universal	15	15	15	15
	Marks and Spencer	18	18	20	24
Italy	La Rinascente	8.2	8.1	7.8	8.3

Current Ratio

Country	Firm	1967–68	1968–69	1969–70	1970–71
France	Au Printemps	1.0	1.0	1.2	0.9
	Carrefour	0.9	0.9	0.9	0.9
	Casino	1.1	1.1	1.2	1.0
	Docks Remois	1.2	1.3	1.2	1.4
	Galeries Lafayette	1.2	1.0	1.1	1.0
Belgium	G. B. Enterprises	1.7	1.6	1.6	1.4
	S. A. Innovation	2.6	3.1	1.5	1.1
Germany	Karstadt	4.1	3.4	2.6	2.0
	Kaufhof	1.7	1.9	2.7	2.1
	Nechermann	1.6	2.0	2.0	1.6
U.K.	Great Universal	2.8	2.6	2.6	2.8
	Marks and Spencer	1.1	1.1	1.0	1.1
Italy	La Rinascente	0.9	0.8	0.8	0.7

Total Debt/Shareholders' Equity

Country	Firm	1967–68	1968–69	1969–70	1970–71
France	Au Printemps	0.9	1.1	1.2	1.4
	Carrefour	3.8	2.4	3.7	4.6
	Casino	3.5	2.8	3.6	4.0
	Docks Remois	1.3	1.7	2.0	2.1
	Galeries Lafayette	0.8	1.0	1.2	1.6
Belgium	G. B. Enterprises	1.0	1.3	1.1	1.9
	S. A. Innovation	0.8	0.8	1.3	1.4
Germany	Karstadt	0.8	0.8	0.9	0.9
	Kaufhof	1.5	1.4	1.5	1.6
	Nechermann	2.2	2.6	2.8	3.3
U.K.	Great Universal	0.5	0.7	0.7	0.7
	Marks and Spencer	0.6	0.7	0.8	0.8
Italy	La Rinascente	1.5	1.6	1.8	2.0

* Includes sales of affiliated stores.

Part II
long-term financing

NOTE ON THE THEORY OF OPTIMAL
CAPITAL STRUCTURE

This note examines the interrelationships between the objective of maximizing shareholder value and the objective of achieving an optimal capital structure. The problem of meeting these objectives will be approached from the standpoint of theory since a basic understanding of the theory is important in dealing with the practical problems encountered in attempting to achieve an optimal capital structure for a specific firm.

In raising funds to finance operations, firms can utilize a number of alternatives including issuing debt or equity. Exhibit 1 illustrates the capital structure choice in a highly simplified context. A firm has invested $500,000 in plant, equipment, and working capital. The investment generates earnings before interest and taxes (EBIT) of $120,000 in perpetuity. Annual depreciation charges exactly equal capital expenditures, and the firm pays out all of its earnings as dividends. The firm's sales do not grow, but remain stable over time. The firm has the opportunity to select its capital structure from among the debt/total capital ratios presented in line 1 of Exhibit 1.

Locating the optimum capital structure for our hypothetical firm, given the data in Exhibit 1, is a trivial problem. Simply locating this optimum point is not our objective. The educational usefulness of Exhibit 1 comes from achieving an understanding of the logic behind the assumptions utilized in the exhibit and the interrelationships among the variables presented in the exhibit. These assumptions and interrelationships need to be explored in some detail.

Impact of leverage on total payments to security holders

Lines 1–8 of Exhibit 1 show the impact of leverage on the firm's income statement. The firm's earnings stream, EBIT, is unaffected by leverage. As debt is added to the capital structure, interest charges increase and profit after taxes falls. Total payments to security holders (i.e., interest plus profit after taxes) increase with leverage. This increase can be attributed entirely to tax savings resulting from the tax deductibility of interest payments. The increase in total

103

payments to security holders is a key advantage flowing from the use of debt capital.

The cost of funds

Lines 9 and 10 of Exhibit 1 show the rates of return required to induce investors to acquire the debt and equity securities of our hypothetical firm. As leverage increases, both bondholders and shareholders are subjected to increased risk. This risk includes both the risk of bankruptcy and the risk of increased variability in annual returns. As the level of debt increases, investors require higher returns to compensate them for accepting increased risk. The required (expected) returns (lines 9 and 10) represent the critical assumptions in the optimal capital structure analysis which follows. These assumptions reflect a fundamental trade-off between risk and return. Since the returns must be paid to investors in order to allow the firm to raise funds, these returns represent capital costs. The required return on the firm's debt is the cost of debt capital, k_D (line 9), and the required return on the firm's equity is the cost of equity capital, k_E (line 10).

Market value of securities

In theory, the market value of any security can be determined by calculating the present value of its expected cash flows. The discount rate employed in the present value calculation must be the investors' required return on a security of comparable risk (i.e., the rates in lines 9 and 10). The resulting present value is an estimate of the aggregate market value and price of the security. If investors purchase the security at this price, they expect to earn the required return on their investment. If the price was higher, investors would not purchase the security since their expected return would be less than the return on other securities with comparable risk. If the price was less, investors would promptly purchase the security since it would offer a higher return than other securities of comparable risk. The actions of investors would bid up the price of the security until its value equaled the present value calculated as described above.

The example in Exhibit 1 employs cash flows which are expected to continue in perpetuity. The present value (V) of a stream of cash payments (CF) which is expected to continue in perpetuity is calculated in the following way. $V = CF/r$ where r is the appropriate discount rate. The market value of the firm's equity can be estimated as the present value of the future cash flows expected by shareholders (i.e., dividends) discounted at the cost of equity capital or $V_E = DIV/k_E$ (line 12). Similarly, the market value of the firm's debt is $V_D = $ interest$/k_D$ (line 11). The market value of the firm as a whole is simply the sum of the market value of its debt and equity or $V_F = V_D + V_E$ (line 13). Note that as debt is added to the capital structure, the market value of the firm, V_F (line 13) first rises and later falls. The reasons for this phenomenon will be explored below. The maximum value of the firm, $540,274, occurs with $150,000 of debt in the capital structure.

Profitability and "business" versus "investor" returns

Lines 14–18 of Exhibit 1 present book value and profitability data for the firm. The *market* values of both the firm's equity (line 12) and its total capital (line 13) are greater than the *book* values (lines 15 and 16) of the firm's equity and total capital. The use of leverage has created this incremental value. The entire value increase accrues to the shareholders, since they are the residual owners of the firm. This value increase is a one-time windfall gain to the shareholders. Thereafter the shareholders can expect to receive only their required rate of return (i.e., the firm's cost of equity capital).

The return on total capital (ROTC) is simply EBIT after tax divided by total invested capital. Total capital is measured at book values. Return on total capital is unaffected by leverage. Return on equity (ROE) is profit after taxes divided by the book value of equity: $ROE = PAT/BV_E$. With no debt, $ROTC = ROE$. However, the addition of debt "leverages" the return on equity and ROE rises above ROTC. While ROE represents the return on the book value of equity, investors do not necessarily receive this same return. Investors instead receive the *market* return which reflects dividends received plus any changes in the price of their shares. ROE is thus a measure of *business* return not *investor* return. This is a critical distinction.

Earnings per share and price-earnings ratios

Lines 19–22 of Exhibit 1 demonstrate the effects of changes in a firm's capital structure on its earnings per share (EPS) and on its price-earnings ratio. The calculations assume the firm has no debt initially. In adding a given amount of debt to the capital structure, it is assumed that the firm issues debt and repurchases shares of stock with the proceeds of the debt issue. Specifically, the following sequence of events is assumed: (1) the firm announces its intention to carry out an alteration in its long-run capital structure, (2) the price of its stock changes to reflect the new anticipated value of the firm (thereby producing a one-time windfall gain for shareholders), and then, (3) the firm markets a debt issue and repurchases stock at the new price. Note that EPS increases with additional debt. However, this does not *necessarily* imply that shareholders are always better off with higher levels of debt. The price-earnings ratio of the stock falls with increased leverage since EPS is riskier.[1] As debt increases, investors pay a smaller price per dollar of expected earnings per share in order to reflect the increased risk (or lower "quality") of earnings. By definition $P = (P/EPS) \times (EPS)$. As leverage increases, EPS rises, and the stock's price-earnings ratio falls. The impact on stock price of leverage is determined by the trade-off of these two effects. Note that for low levels of leverage, the increase in EPS dominates the reduction in the price-earnings ratio, and the stock price rises with leverage. For high levels of debt, the opposite occurs; thus, the price of the stock first rises and then falls with leverage.

---

[1] In this simple perpetuity example, the cost of equity capital is equal to the inverse of the price-earnings ratio (i.e., $k_E = EPS/P$). This is *not* true in general.

The weighted average cost of capital

The weighted average cost of capital is the percentage of debt in the capital structure multiplied by the aftertax cost of debt plus the percentage of equity in the capital structure multiplied by the aftertax cost of equity. Because of the tax deductibility of interest payments, the aftertax cost of debt to the firm, k_D^t, is less than the return paid to bondholders, k_D. With $t = .50$, the aftertax cost of debt is only one half its pretax cost. The cost of equity is already in aftertax terms. Thus, using market value weights, the weighted average cost of the firm's capital is

$$ k = \left(\frac{V_D}{V_E + V_D} \right) k_D (1 - t) + \left(\frac{V_E}{V_E + V_D} \right) k_E = \left(\frac{V_D}{V_F} \right) k_D^t + \left(\frac{V_E}{V_F} \right) k_E $$

Most financial theorists recommend calculating a firm's cost of capital using *market* value weights rather than *book* value weights for debt and equity in the firm's capital structure. Although market values are used in the calculation of k in line 25, the use of book values would have very little impact on the results. This is a particularly happy outcome since financial managers, lenders, and rating agencies characterize a firm's capital structure, almost without exception, in terms of *book value* weights. It is important to note also that when a firm sells a new issue of common stock, the issue is sold at market prices. For this incremental equity addition the book value and the market value of the capital raised are equal. This equality removes the potential for any conflict in the use of market versus book value weights in setting hurdle rates for capital investments financed in part via new equity additions.

In lines 11–13, the value of the firm was calculated by adding the value of the firm's debt and equity securities. In a capital budgeting analysis, a comparable valuation is reached in a more direct manner. The technique involves calculating the firm's (or investment project's) free cash flow (FCF). Free cash flow is the aftertax cash flow generated by the firm's investments ignoring all payments to providers of capital (i.e., ignoring all financing charges such as interest and dividends and ignoring the tax savings attributable to the use of debt). In the example outlined in Exhibit 1, free cash flow is simply EBIT after tax. The value of the firm is the present value of FCF discounted at the weighted average cost of the capital invested in the firm. In our perpetuity example, $V_F = FCF/k$. The costs of financing are not deducted in the calculation of FCF. They are incorporated by discounting FCF at the weighted average cost of capital which includes these capital costs. Thus, using free cash flow and the weighted average cost of capital, the value of the firm (or the investment project) can be calculated directly. Note that the resulting values of V_F in line 27 are the same as those in line 13 which are derived by valuing debt and equity separately.

Implications

The most important results of the Exhibit 1 example are contained in lines 13, 20, and 25. In the simple world outlined in Exhibit 1, the firm's optimal capital structure *simultaneously* (a) maximizes the value of the firm and (b) its share price, and (c) minimizes the firm's weighted average cost of capital. Given the assumptions concerning the cost of debt and equity (lines 9 and 10), as debt is added to the capital structure, the weighted average cost of capital falls. This increases the value of the firm. Since this increase in the firm's value accrues to the owners of the firm, the price of the firm's stock rises. In this example, the firm's optimal (or target) book value debt ratio is in the range of 30%–40%. The determination of the firm's optimal (or target) capital structure is also displayed in the graphs in Exhibit 2.

Exhibits 1 and 2 are based on very simple assumptions. They are designed to delineate the mechanics of the capital structure decision. The exhibits do not provide a detailed explanation of the economic rationale for the behavior portrayed. One common rationale is that as debt is added, V_F rises (P rises, k falls) due to the tax savings provided by debt. Recall that these tax savings increase the total cash payments to security holders (line 8). The value of the firm is therefore increased by the present value of these tax savings. This is a major benefit of leverage. As leverage is increased, however, so is the probability of financial distress. Firms with very high debt ratios (and low bond ratings) may have difficulty raising funds in periods of tight money. This affects the firm's ability to make investments and remain competitive. Higher debt ratios also increase the chances that in periods of difficulty, management decisions will be constrained by creditors. Violation of debt covenants could restrict the freedom of managers to make decisions which are in the best interest of shareholders. The firm might be unable to undertake attractive investment opportunities or might be forced by creditors to sell assets or issue equity at extremely unattractive times. At worst, the firm could face bankruptcy or liquidation. Such decisions would probably not be in the long-term interests of shareholders.

The other side of the argument has also been advanced as an explanation of the limits to leverage, however. During a period of extreme financial distress, a management group might feel that it has little to lose by making operating or investment decisions with a very high potential payoff (i.e., high enough to save the firm from bankruptcy if the projects were successful) but with a very low probability that the projects would actually be successful. Such decisions could serve the interests of managers and equity shareholders, but work to the detriment of creditors. To insure against this risk, the return required by bondholders, k_D (the cost of debt), rises precipitously at high levels of debt.

There are many potential costs associated with financial distress. These costs are embedded implicitly in the costs of capital assumed in this example (lines 9 and 10). As a firm's debt ratio rises, the probability of financial distress increases, and the value of the firm is reduced by the present value of these expected costs. At low levels of debt, the disadvantages of leverage are outweighed by the advantages of leverage, and the value of the firm rises. At high debt ratios, the present value of the expected costs of financial distress is larger than the present value of the tax savings, and increased leverage reduces the value of the firm. An intermediate level of debt which represents the optimal trade-off between these two factors maximizes the value of the firm (and the price of the stock) and minimizes the cost of capital.

Conclusions

The example outlined in this note is based on many simplifications; that is, perpetuity cash flows, 100% dividend payout, capital expenditures equal to depreciation, no sales growth, and so forth. However, the analysis in Exhibits 1 and 2 does provide a conceptual framework for the determination of optimal capital structure. Unfortunately, in practice it is not easy to apply these concepts in a straightforward manner. It is quite difficult to accurately estimate the cost of capital for a firm given its existing capital structure. It is no simpler to estimate the firm's capital cost given some proposed *new* capital structure. To further complicate the problem, in contrast to the Exhibit 1 example, firms' capital structures can include not only straight debt and common equity but also preferred stock and convertible securities.

While there are significant practical problems associated with determining a firm's optimum capital structure, some statistical tools and benchmarks are available to aid financial decision makers in their search for the best capital structure.[2] These tools provide substantial insight concerning the levels of debt which are clearly too high or too low. In the last analysis, the capital structure decision rests heavily upon the financial manager's business judgment. The conceptual framework for dealing with the capital structure decision can be combined with available benchmarks and the financial manager's business judgment to facilitate the setting of a reasonable target debt policy for the firm.

---

[2] For example, bond ratings and their determinants, interest rates by bond rating, statistics on the availability of debt in credit crunches by bond rating, interest coverage and cash flow coverage ratios as measures of leverage, statistical studies of similar firms with different debt ratios, statistical estimates of the cost of equity capital, and so forth. A statistical method for estimating the cost of equity capital for a firm can be found in "Diversification, the Capital Asset Pricing Model, and the Cost of Equity Capital," pp. 140–57, and "Financial Leverage, the Capital Asset Pricing Model, and the Cost of Equity Capital," pp. 163–72.

Exhibit 1

NOTE ON THE THEORY OF OPTIMAL CAPITAL STRUCTURE

HYPOTHETICAL CALCULATION OF THE IMPACT OF CAPITAL STRUCTURE ON SECURITIES VALUATION

		0%	10%	20%	30%	40%	50%
1	Debt in the capital structure*						
2	Earnings before interest and taxes, EBIT	$120,000	$120,000	$120,000	$120,000	$120,000	$120,000
3	Interest	0	4,125	8,750	14,625	22,000	31,250
4	Profit before taxes, PBT	$120,000	$115,875	$111,250	$105,375	$98,000	$88,750
5	Taxes	60,000	57,938	55,625	52,688	49,000	44,375
6	Profit after taxes, PAT	$60,000	$57,937	$55,625	$52,687	$49,000	$44,375
7	Dividends, DIV	60,000	57,937	55,625	52,687	49,000	44,375
8	Total payments to security holders (line 3 + line 7)	$60,000	$62,062	$64,375	$67,312	$71,000	$75,625
9	Required return on debt capital, k_D (cost of debt capital)	8.00%	8.25%	8.75%	9.75%	11.00%	12.50%
10	Required return on equity capital, k_E (cost of equity capital)	12.00%	12.50%	13.00%	13.50%	14.50%	16.00%
11	Market value of debt, V_D (line 3 ÷ line 9)	$ 0	$ 50,000	$100,000	$150,000	$200,000	$250,000
12	Market value of equity, V_E (line 7 ÷ line 10)	500,000	463,496	427,885	390,274	337,931	277,344
13	Market value of the firm, V_F (line 11 + line 12)	$500,000	$513,496	$527,885	$540,274	$537,931	$527,344
14	Book value of debt, BV_D	$ 0	$ 50,000	$100,000	$150,000	$200,000	$250,000
15	Book value of equity, BV_E	500,000	450,000	400,000	350,000	300,000	250,000
16	Book value of the firm, BV_F (total capital)	$500,000	$500,000	$500,000	$500,000	$500,000	$500,000
17	Return on total capital, ROTC (EBIT(1-t) ÷ line 16)	12.0%	12.0%	12.0%	12.0%	12.0%	12.0%
18	Return on equity, ROE (line 6 ÷ line 15)	12.0%	12.9%	13.9%	15.1%	16.3%	17.8%
19	Number of shares outstanding, N	5,000	4,513	4,053	3,612	3,141	2,630
20	Price per share of common stock, P($) (line 12 ÷ line 19)	$ 100.0	$ 102.7	$ 105.6	$ 108.1	$ 107.6	$ 105.5
21	Earnings per share of common stock, EPS ($) (line 6 ÷ line 19)	$ 12.00	$ 12.84	$ 13.72	$ 14.59	$ 15.60	$ 16.87
22	Price-earnings ratio, P/EPS (line 20 ÷ line 21 = line 12 ÷ line 6)	8.3	8.0	7.7	7.4	6.9	6.3
23	Book value debt ratio (line 14 ÷ line 16)	0%	10%	20%	30%	40%	50%
24	Market value debt ratio, V_D/V_F (line 11 ÷ line 13)	0%	9.7%	18.9%	27.8%	37.2%	47.7%
25	Weighted average cost of capital, k (using market values; see text)	12.0%	11.7%	11.4%	11.1%	11.2%	11.4%
26	Free cash flow, FCF (EBIT (1-t) = line 2 x .50)	$ 60,000	$ 60,000	$ 60,000	$ 60,000	$ 60,000	$ 60,000
27	Market value of the firm, V_F (line 26 ÷ line 25)	$500,000	$513,496	$527,885	$540,274	$537,931	$527,344

*Calculated using book value weights for debt and equity.

Exhibit 2

NOTE ON THE THEORY OF OPTIMAL CAPITAL STRUCTURE

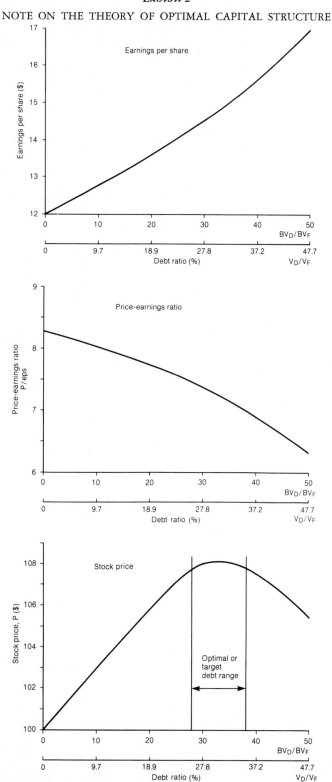

Exhibit 2—Continued

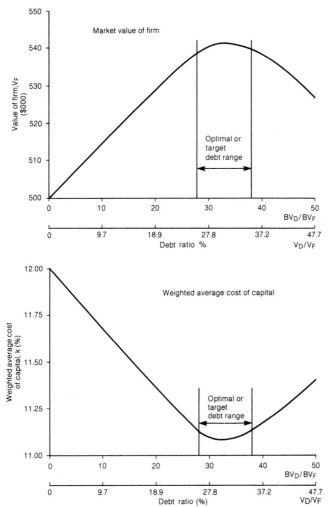

CHEM-CAL CORPORATION*

^^

For several months, Mr. Jay Cochran, vice-president for finance of Chem-Cal Corporation, had been considering two methods for measuring proposed capital expenditures: the net present value (NPV) method and the internal rate of return (IRR) method. Mr. Cochran had become convinced that, once he had obtained reliable estimates of project cash flows, his biggest problem would lie in choosing the appropriate discount rate to use with the NPV method or in selecting the proper cutoff rate to use with the IRR method of evaluating projects. According to Mr. Cochran, it would be unwise to consider a discount rate or cutoff rate for Chem-Cal without first discussing the company's cost of capital. As chairman of the finance committee, he had planned to present an estimate of the company's cost of capital at the next meeting of the committee on January 24, 1979. This estimate would serve as a discount rate or cutoff rate by which the acceptability of proposed investments could be determined.

At Chem-Cal's headquarters in Los Angeles, company officials directed the operations of three large manufacturing facilities, two in Southern California and one in Akron, Ohio. During World War II, Chem-Cal had pioneered in the development and production of organic polymers. In 1965, Mr. James Semester, corporation president, had remarked in a speech before the New York Security Analysts that Chem-Cal was "first in fibers, films, and foams"— a phrase later used in Chem-Cal advertising. In addition, the company manufactured a large number of chemical products for industrial, agricultural, and consumer use. Chem-Cal had concentrated its research efforts on the development of new products with widespread commercial use. The company's sales and after-tax earnings had grown steadily since World War II, reflecting both Chem-Cal's success and the overall expansion of the chemical industry in the postwar period. However, in Mr. Cochran's opinion, the company's sales growth since 1974 had been largely the result of price increases.

While they had been sympathetic with Mr. Cochran's interest in the theory of capital budgeting, several Chem-Cal officials had some reservations about

* Reprinted from *Stanford Business Cases 1980* with permission of the publishers, Stanford University Graduate School of Business, © 1980 by the Board of Trustees of the Leland Stanford Junior University.

the value of quantitative analysis in evaluating proposed projects. Mr. Semester had made the following comments in December 1978:

Capital budgeting and the evaluation of capital projects in a large company are not, and cannot be, the precise jobs that textbooks seem to imply that they are. There are literally hundreds of projects considered every year, and responsibility for approval is delegated downward depending upon the size of the expenditure. Our overall policy is to maintain or improve the rate of return on investment for the company. Most projects can only be appraised as a matter of judgment under this policy and precise numerical evaluation is relatively seldom possible.

I don't want to give you the impression that we don't make detailed economic analyses of specific projects—we do and will probably do more in the future. But the use of quantitative techniques for analyzing many of our investments would not only waste time and money on a fruitless search but would tend to give a spurious impression of accuracy. The problem seems, to me, to be the same as that faced in introducing other quantitative techniques into business use; you want to retain the overriding protection of experience and judgment.

Chem-Cal's executive vice president and member of the finance committee, Mr. Richard Bergeron, had this to say about the company's existing policy regarding capital investment decisions:

The company does not set a firm cutoff rate which is applied automatically to all investment proposals. However, required minimum rates of return are set as a guide in considering proposed investments for which a rate of return analysis is applicable. These cutoff rates differ among proposals for (1) construction of new facilities and (2) improvement of existing facilities. However, a particular project that does not meet the required minimum rates of return will be considered if there are sufficient collateral considerations. Also, there are certain types of projects which are not susceptible to rate-of-return analysis, such as those involving power, service and office facilities, air and water pollution abatement, and employee safety and welfare.

When individual projects are submitted for final approval, we use the discounted-cash-flow rate of return technique when this technique is applicable. In a large company such as ours, however, I feel this technique is applicable for relatively few projects—probably fewer than 40%. The cash flow technique is most useful down at the research-engineering level, where there are always many alternatives to consider. These are sifted out in the planning stage, however, and seldom become an issue when a decision is made as to whether or not to undertake the project.

On January 19, 1979, Mr. Cochran and Mr. Bergeron joined Mr. Semester in his office for a preliminary discussion of the topics on the agenda for the finance committee meeting scheduled for January 24.

Cochran: As I mentioned before, we've been doing some work with our staff people on improving our capital budgeting procedures. Next Wednesday I'd like to present to the committee my estimates of our costs of debt and equity capital, so that we can get an idea what our cutoff rate or discount rate should really be.

Semester: Those academic guys really got through to you last summer, didn't they, Jay?

Cochran: Well, frankly, I think that's the big value in a management program like that. You get back to the campus for a few weeks and get some new ideas on the old problems.

Semester: O.K., shoot, Jay.

Cochran: First of all, we have come up with estimates of initial investment and future cash flows for *all* the projects proposed by the divisions in November. It was a little painful on some of the R&D and safety projects, but at least we have some numbers to look at and compare. Here are the ten major projects in our new budget.

Project	Initial Investment	Project Life	Net Present Value (at 10%)	Internal Rate of Return
A...........	$ 800,000	8	$ 920,000	37%
B...........	3,000,000	20	4,200,000	28%
C...........	3,600,000	10	1,680,000	20%
D...........	600,000	2	66,000	18%
E...........	4,800,000	15	1,140,000	14%
F...........	1,800,000	6	108,000	12%
G...........	300,000	5	(Negative)	9%
H...........	1,200,000	20	(Negative)	4%
I...........	2,400,000	4	(Negative)	3%
J...........	150,000	(?)	(Negative)	(—)
	$18,650,000			

Bergeron: How do you come up with the internal rate of return again?

Cochran: Actually, we find it by trial and error, Dick. For example, with Project D we estimated that an investment of $600,000 will give us a net cash inflow after taxes of $384,000 a year for two years. We found that 18% is the discount rate at which the present value of the two $384,000 inflows is equal to the initial investment of $600,000.

Bergeron: And all your figures are net of taxes?

Cochran: Right.

Semester: What's the rate of return on Project J?

Cochran: That's the safety program I mentioned before. It's almost impossible to estimate the cash flows, but when we did, the rate of return was less than zero. It's just one of those projects that we have to take even though the numbers alone don't justify it. The projects are ranked by rate of return, but obviously, other factors affect their acceptability.

This year we will have internally generated funds of about $8.2 million available for capital investments as you can see in my table. [See following page.]

So the cost of funds is particularly important, I feel, since we'll either have to obtain outside capital or limit our capital spending to the amount available internally.

Semester: If we were to limit our capital budget to $8.2 million, we wouldn't need a cutoff rate.

MR. COCHRAN'S TABLE

	Millions
Profit before taxes	$17.0
Taxes (overall tax rate of 50%)	8.5
Profit after taxes	$ 8.5
Depreciation	2.5
Cash flow	$11.0
Dividends*	2.8
Internally generated funds available	$ 8.2

*Dividends include $300,000 on preferred stock and $2.5 million on common stock.

Cochran: Right, if we were using the IRR method. But we'd still have to choose an appropriate discount rate if we were evaluating new projects by the NPV method.

Bergeron: We could sell debentures at 6½–7% ten years ago, but those days are gone forever.

Cochran: There's no doubt about that. New issues with an "A" rating are going at about 10 right now. I have talked with David Towers and a few other underwriters, and the consensus seems to be that we could add about $5 million in debt at a little over 10½. That would raise our debt ratio to 30%, pretty close to the industry average. The next $5 million issue would probably cost closer to 11%.

Semester: We'll be working toward that industry average as a long-run goal, but I'd hate to have Moody's revise our rating.

Cochran: Well, if we went to $40–45 million in debt with our present equity position, we might slip to a "Baa."

Semester: It seems to me that there is a hidden cost in new long-term debt. The increase in financial risk may have an effect on the market price of our stock.

Bergeron: With these bonds, are you talking about coupon rate or effective yield, Jay?

Cochran: Either one. The difference is small.

Semester: Are you sure about that? I heard last week ConRad received only 98 on their issue of 9⅛s, so their cost must have been something over 9½%.

Cochran: O.K., O.K., right. But the difference is still small.

Semester: How about a sinking fund?

Cochran: I think we can bank on it. It'll probably be the standard trustee arrangement. With a 20-year maturity, the first payment to the trustee could probably be deferred for five years. This would mean retiring the full amount of the issue over 15 equal annual payments.

Semester: Doesn't the sinking fund provision increase our net cost?

Cochran: Well, I don't know, Jim. There are obviously some trustee's fees to pay, but beyond that, I can't think of any other costs involved.

Semester: There must be some opportunity costs involved in these sinking fund payments.

Cochran: I don't think so. As the trustee retires the bonds, it opens up the top for new debt.

Bergeron: What about a preferred issue?

Semester: We've been over that a dozen times, Dick. Preferred issues are a thing of the past. They've got all the disadvantages of debt and common.

Bergeron: I don't want to beat a dead horse, but it still seems to me that with preferred we can avoid the risk of debt without diluting our common equity.

Semester: Yes, I know, Dick, we've been through all that before. The big thing is that bond interest is deductible[1] and preferred dividends aren't. As long as we can sell bonds at any reasonable price, we're better off than with preferred. Our existing preferred cost us only 6%, but I'll bet that new preferred would cost at least 9%.

Cochran: Well, I guess maybe the cost of preferred isn't too relevant to our present budget. How about the cost of the new common?

Bergeron: We'd have to maintain our dividend on the new shares. So our annual cost would be at least $1.25 a share.[2]

Semester: What could we realize from a new issue, Jay?

Cochran: Well, the market price has been running around $23 to $25. I think we could net at least $21 a share after issue costs on a new offering.

Bergeron: Then that's cheaper than debt. We get $21 a share and pay out only $1.25 a share each year. That's 6% money. You can't beat that.

Cochran: This is one thing I wanted to discuss. Last summer at the management program, the consensus seemed to be that the cost of common equity was equal to the earnings-price ratio.

Bergeron: Do you mean the price-earnings ratio?

Cochran: No. The reciprocal of the price-earnings ratio.

Bergeron: I don't follow you.

Cochran: Well, it has to do with diluting present earnings per share. If you don't earn a return on the new funds of at least the earnings-price ratio, then you dilute the earnings of the old stockholders. In our case, this works out to a 20% return.

Semester: I wonder if we should look at present earnings or future earnings.

Cochran: Well, that gets into the fine points of the calculations. As a rough cut, I think we can use present earnings. It looks like competition will be tougher and our product prices will be weaker in the foreseeable future, so our earnings will probably level off for a few years.

Semester: At any rate, this would be a good point to bring up at the meeting. Is there anything else we should talk about now?

Cochran: I'd like to hit one more point, briefly. How should we figure our overall cost of capital? The big trend seems to be toward using a weighted average cost of capital as a cutoff rate or discount rate.

Semester: I've read about that, Jay, and I've wondered about this weighting business.

---

[1] The company's tax rate was approximately 50%. A recent survey of Chem-Cal stockholders revealed that the "average stockholder," taking into account number of shares owned, had a marginal tax rate of 36%.

[2] Chem-Cal had paid a cash dividend of $1.25 per share each year for the past six years.

Cochran: Well, the cost of each type of capital is weighted by its proportion of the total capital structure.

Semester: Using book values, right?

Cochran: Right.

Semester: That's one point I've wondered about. Our common stock is selling for less than book value, so why not use the market value of the securities instead of the book values in weighting the cost?

Bergeron: I can't see why you go through this weighting business at all. It's a simple matter of economics. You just match the cheapest source of capital with the best available return on investment. For example, start with retained earnings: since they are already available for investment, the cost is effectively nil. Then debt might be the next cheapest source, and so on.

MR. BERGERON'S SKETCH

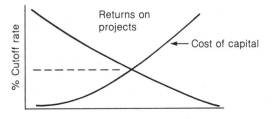

When you get to the point where your cost of capital is greater than your expected return, you stop investing. It's as simple as that.

Semester: I think we'd better get our ideas firmed up before the full committee meets next week.

CAPITAL STRUCTURE*

Millions

Long-term debt	
7% debentures due 1985	$ 30.0
Preferred stock	
Cumulative, non-callable, $100 par value,	
6% Series, 100,000 shares authorized,	
50,000 shares outstanding	5.0
Common stock	
No par, 3,000,000 shares authorized,	
2,000,000 shares outstanding	12.1
Retained earnings	67.9
	$115.0

*Source: Chem-Cal Corporation balance sheet of December 31, 1978.

COMMUNICATIONS SATELLITE CORPORATION

^^

In January 1975, the Federal Communications Commission (FCC) concluded an 11-year investigation of the appropriate economic regulation of the Communications Satellite Corporation (Comsat). In the coming months, the Commissioners would deliver a decision which would address the full range of regulatory issues. One of the most important of these was the determination of a fair rate of return on Comsat's capital. The company had requested a 12% rate of return for the period 1964 to 1974 and 15% thereafter. However, the FCC's trial staff[1] had recommended setting Comsat's allowable return at 7% for the years between 1964 and 1971 and at 8.33% for 1972 with annual increases to 9.42% by 1975 (Exhibit 1). If the FCC rejected Comsat's request for 1975 in favor of the staff's recommendation, the company's revenues in that year might be reduced by as much as 30%, its net operating income could decline by 45%, and earnings per share could drop by 35%.

History and role of Comsat

The Communications Satellite Act of 1962 (the Satellite Act) set forth a national policy mandating the establishment of a worldwide communications satellite system in cooperation with other nations. This act authorized the formation of a new private company to represent the United States in the proposed satellite system. Comsat was incorporated on February 1, 1963 to fulfill this role. Under the Satellite Act it was charged with establishing "as expeditiously as practicable" a commercial communications satellite system as part of an improved global communications network. The act specifically required the inclusion of economically less-developed countries in the development of this system. Although Comsat was incorporated as a private company, it was obliged under the Satellite Act to offer its customers the benefits of the new communications technology in terms both of improved quality and of reduced charges.

Comsat, under the provisions of the Satellite Act and as a U.S. communications carrier, was subject to regulation by the FCC. Other elements of the government were also involved in Comsat's operations. The National Aero-

---

[1] In the FCC proceeding, representatives of the Common Carrier Bureau's trial staff took the role of public advocate. To fulfill this role, they were segregated from the Commission's decision-making personnel.

nautics and Space Administration (NASA) was authorized to assist Comsat with satellite launchings and other such technical activities. The assistance of the State Department was authorized to facilitate in the negotiation and maintenance of international agreements necessary to implement a global system. The President of the United States was also given certain supervisory powers over Comsat.

In August 1964, the International Telecommunications Satellite Corporation (INTELSAT) was created as an international partnership for the purposes of owning and developing the global satellite system. Comsat was designated the manager of INTELSAT and was accordingly responsible for the research, design, development, construction, establishment, and operation of the space segment of the system. By 1972, INTELSAT's initial 18-nation membership had increased to more than 84. These nations owned both the satellites and their related ground-control facilities. Voting rights and ownership interests in the partnership were based on the proportion a nation's usage of the system bore to total usage. Although Comsat still held the largest ownership interest in INTELSAT, its share had declined from about 52% in 1972 to 40% in 1973 and was expected to drop even lower as other nations increased their use of the system.

Establishment and growth of the worldwide communications system

Comsat's founders had a number of important technological and business decisions to make. One of the most important was choosing a satellite technology from among several alternatives, each of which had different technological and economic characteristics. Comsat's selection of a geostationary (or synchronous orbit) satellite system was, to a large extent, responsible for its rapid and successful development. A synchronous satellite is placed in circular orbit in the plane of the earth's equator and revolves about the polar axis in the same direction and with the same period as the earth's rotation. Such a geostationary-orbit satellite system requires fewer satellites than alternative lower-altitude, nongeostationary orbit systems.

In April 1965, Early Bird, the world's first commercial communications satellite, was launched from Cape Kennedy by a Comsat-NASA team. Commercial service was established in June 1965, two years ahead of schedule. Although Early Bird's capacity was limited by comparison with later-generation satellites, it increased trans-Atlantic telephone capacity by nearly two thirds, and it was the only transmitter of live transoceanic television.

Early Bird (later designated INTELSAT I) was the first of four generations of Comsat communications satellites. In 1966, the INTELSAT II series was designed by Hughes Aircraft in order to provide the expanded communication services required by early Apollo missions and by commercial users. Three of the four INTELSAT II satellites launched achieved synchronous orbit—one over the Atlantic and two over the Pacific.

In 1966, TRW, Inc. began work for Comsat on the INTELSAT III series. These satellites, the first designed expressly for global service, provided five times the power of the previous generation. Although the program was delayed by TRW's inability to meet delivery dates, it was eventually successful in placing five of eight satellites launched (between September 1968 and February 1969) in regular commercial service.

In late 1968, Comsat contracted with Hughes to develop the INTELSAT IV series. These satellites were designed to provide five times the capacity of the third generation, hopefully sufficient to meet global requirements through 1975. INTELSAT IV provided great flexibility in permitting simultaneous use for different types of services. The reliability of the system was enhanced by increased on-board redundancy (reserve capacity to be used when problems developed in the system). Five INTELSAT IVs were successfully placed in orbit by August 1973, providing complete global coverage.

In September 1975, the first INTELSAT IV-A, a modified version of the fourth generation series, was placed into orbit. These satellites had twice the capacity of the INTELSAT IV and were developed to meet traffic demands in the latter half of the 1970s.

Comsat's early operations were very successful. It had experienced fewer launched failures in its start-up years than anticipated, and most satellites had achieved their design lives. The company's ability to maintain service was excellent, with only a single instance of a satellite outage causing a revenue loss (for one month in 1969). Beginning in 1972, Comsat had at least one spare satellite over each ocean basin for the purpose of restoring traffic during an outage. In addition to its redundancy in space, Comsat always maintained spares on the ground.

The earth stations which were part of the communications satellite system had also been technologically improved. Seven of the 68 earth stations existing in 1974 were located in the United States. Over a span of less than a decade, these stations had evolved through four distinct generations. Each successive generation was characterized by lower unit costs, greater and more diverse capabilities, increased reliability, and simpler operation and maintenance. By 1975, Comsat was approaching full earth station redundancy.

By 1975, Comsat had established a reliable global satellite system which exceeded all expectations. Its network, accessible to even the most remote areas of the earth, provided much of the world's transoceanic telephone, facsimile, teletype, telex, and television communications.

Commercial and financial performance

In 1964, Comsat's managers estimated the development costs for its satellite system to be between $190 and $230 million. They considered it impractical and undesirable to issue debt to meet these needs in view of the company's lack of mortgageable property, the absence of established earning power, and the unforeseeable risks of the satellite project. Therefore, they decided to fund the entire capital requirement with an equity offering. In June 1964, Comsat sold half of its $200 million initial stock offering to 163 U.S. communication carriers and the other half to the public through a syndicate of 385 underwriting firms. Priced at $20 per share, the issue was oversubscribed with over 130,000 individuals and institutions eventually acquiring shares. The price quickly rose to $27 in hectic over-the-counter trading. Three months later, the stock was listed on the New York, Midwest, and Pacific Coast Stock Exchanges.[2] The net proceeds of the issue were invested in a portfolio of marketable securities which was drawn down as needed over the following ten years to finance the communications satellite program.

Comsat's operating revenue was generated by the leasing of satellite half-circuits, transmitting channels between U.S. earth stations and INTELSAT satellites. Comsat leased half the channel; the other half-circuit was the responsibility of a foreign entity. Although half-circuit leases accounted for only 20% of 1965 revenues, they had increased to over 90% of 1971 revenues. Income from investment in marketable securities provided the balance of Comsat's revenues.

Comsat's customers were U.S. communications carriers which provided international interconnecting facilities and leased service directly to their customers. Comsat provided these carriers with television, telephone, data, and message services. Although telephone service accounted for the greatest volume by far of traffic in Comsat's first decade, data transmission and television revenues were small but growing. The advantages of Comsat's mature global system included its low cost (due to economies of scale), flexibility, reliability, and high-quality transmission.

Although Comsat's network represented the only technology capable of transmitting color television signals, most of the other services it provided were also offered by other carriers. Comsat's system received a large portion of its business from these carriers during cable outages and periods of excessive demand. Thus, Comsat's customers were also its chief competitors. Such competition among international carriers was regulated by the FCC.

Comsat's managers believed that the high start-up costs and the low operating revenues which characterized the company's development period justified its charging higher rates than its competition.[3] Thus, it adopted a "market-oriented" (versus a cost-plus-profit) approach to pricing. Ignoring the fact that the costs of providing satellite transmission were not sensitive to transmitting distance, they added a premium to the rates charged for competing undersea cable services. In certain instances, the market bore this premium based on Comsat's superior service; in others (such as television), it was borne only as the result

---

[2] Reflecting investor interest, the NYSE waived its stringent listing requirements concerning the duration of a firm's earnings history.

[3] Rates had been reduced substantially for some services (e.g., television) which were thought to be demand elastic. Rates had also been reduced somewhat to reflect lower costs due to technological advances and greater system use (i.e., economies of scale). For instance, a voice grade half-circuit for service from the United States to Europe cost $2,850 per month in 1972, down from $4,200 per month in 1965.

of Comsat's monopolistic position. In the FCC hearings, Comsat's witnesses admitted that they had set "the highest possible rate we felt our customers would accept."[4]

Comsat's financial growth during its formative years was dramatic (Exhibits 2, 3, and 4). From 1965 to 1974, its revenues had grown at a 40% annual rate. In its early years, earnings consisted primarily of interest earned on marketable securities. However, in the fourth quarter of 1967, Comsat realized its first net operating profit on satellite operations. Net income had increased almost tenfold from $4.6 million in 1967 to $44.9 million in 1974. In October 1970, Comsat had declared its first quarterly dividend (12½ cents per share), and by 1973, dividends had been increased to $1 per share. However, Comsat's stock, which had traded as high as $84 in 1971 (Exhibit 5), was trading in the mid-30s early in 1975, reflecting investors' uncertainty about the outcome of the FCC investigation.

Comsat's pioneering efforts in communications technology represented the major commercial benefit of the U.S. space program. The company's financial performance had been as dramatic as the operating performance of the satellite system it managed. However, the pending FCC proceeding could have a far-reaching impact on its future.

The FCC proceeding

The FCC proceeding was initiated in 1965 when the Commission tentatively approved Comsat's first rate request. In approving the request, the Commission authorized an investigation to consider the economic regulation of Comsat. However, the Commission did not initiate a full investigation immediately due to the national policy, outlined in the Satellite Act, of "expeditiously" establishing the satellite system and because of Comsat's lack of operating history. After several years of proposals and rulings, formal hearings commenced in March 1972 and continued intermittently through the summer of 1974. A major issue to be settled in the hearings was the determination of Comsat's fair rate of return. The rate case proceeding concerned the regulation of Comsat since its formation. Although Comsat argued that retroactive reductions of rates were unwarranted, the Commission claimed the general authority to order refunds. Even if refunds were not ordered, the determination of Comsat's cost of capital and its rate base for past years was considered important as precedent for future regulatory decisions. The FCC delineated its guiding principles in a decision concerning American Telephone and Telegraph Company (AT&T):

Generally, the rate of return to be set should be sufficient to enable a utility to maintain its credit and cover the cost of capital already committed to the enterprise as well as to attract additional capital, as needed, in competitive money markets at reasonable costs. . . . *In its simplest terms, rate of return is a percentage expression of the cost of capital.* It is just as real a cost as that paid for

---

[4] FCC Docket 16070, FCC 75–1304, 38249 at 331. The trial staff argued that Comsat's rates were excessive. It took the position that the rates should be based on Comsat's costs.

labor, material, supplies, or any other item necessary for the conduct of business. A return which is too low could impair the ability of a utility to raise additional needed capital, thus imperiling the integrity of existing investment, with adverse effects on the quality of service. A return which is set too high results in charges to the ratepayer above the just and reasonable level. [Emphasis supplied.][5]

The legal standards for determining the fair rate of return were articulated in several landmark cases, among them the *Federal Power Commission* v. *Hope Natural Gas Company*, 320 U.S., 591 (1944). The court opined (at 603) :

. . . The fixing of "just and reasonable" rates, involves a balancing of the investor and the consumer interests. Thus we stated in the *Natural Pipeline Co.* case that "regulation does not insure that the business shall produce net revenues" . . . the investor interest has a legitimate concern with the financial integrity of the company whose rates are being regulated. From the investor or company point of view it is important that there be enough revenue not only for operating expenses but also for capital costs of the business. These include service on debt and dividends on stock. *By that standard the return to the equity owner should be commensurate with returns on investments in other enterprises having corresponding risks.* That return, moreover, should be sufficient to assure confidence in the financial integrity of the enterprise, so as to maintain its credit and to attract capital. [Emphasis supplied.]

Evaluation of Comsat's operating risk

The *Hope* case emphasized the need to consider the returns of "enterprises having corresponding risks" in setting a company's fair rate of return. Consistent with this standard, several parties to the proceeding attempted to compare Comsat's risk with that of other regulated carriers. AT&T was chosen as a benchmark because of its prominent position in the telecommunications industry and its long regulatory history. The trial staff took the position that Comsat was no more risky (and probably somewhat less risky) than AT&T in 1964, and that by 1974, Comsat was certainly less risky. The staff asserted that in Comsat's earlier days, its operating risks had been minimized owing to its government mandate and assistance. Furthermore, the nature of its risks had been fully disclosed to investors in Comsat's prospectus. The staff claimed that by 1974, the company (which still enjoyed government support) was a mature enterprise facing technical and business risks similar to those confronting AT&T. It argued further than Comsat's shareholders bore less risk than did AT&T shareholders as a result of Comsat's much more conservative financial policies. Comsat argued that it was subject to unique risks, substantially greater than those of a large established firm providing a proven technology. It contended that the international telecommunications market which it served was fundamentally riskier than the domestic telecommunications market, AT&T's primary revenue base. It believed that this higher level of risk justified a higher return to its shareholders. Lengthy debates ensued over the evaluation

---

[5] American Telephone and Telegraph Company, 9 FCC 2d at 51–52.

of Comsat's specific operating and financial risks. The company presented evidence concerning significant technological, business, demand, competitive, regulatory, and political risks.

Comsat's witnesses asserted that the company's *technological risk* was substantial, utilizing as it did a new and relatively untried technology. Among the early uncertainties were the risk of launch failures and the risk that satellites' operating lives might be significantly shorter than anticipated. The trial staff took the position that Comsat exaggerated these risks. It argued that in hindsight, Comsat's overstatement of risk was obvious: the satellite network's orderly technological evolution and relatively trouble-free operation demonstrated that Comsat's fears were unfounded. It was further argued that "only risks which can be foreseen are entitled to consideration in the formulation of an appropriate risk premium."[6]

In examining the company's *business risk*, Comsat's witnesses noted that in 1964 the company had had no demonstrated earnings capability and no historical record of earnings. They stated that investors' consequent uncertainty as to the level and timing of future earnings and dividends had exerted upward pressure on Comsat's cost of capital. Trial staff witnesses rebutted this argument, claiming that Comsat's prospectus, the Satellite Act of 1962, and various investment analysts' reports had preempted significant investor uncertainty: these documents had made it clear that although there was no government guarantee, there was a very strong mandate to provide Comsat the opportunity to earn a fair return.

Although Comsat's witnesses conceded that *demand risk* had abated somewhat by 1972, they testified that "in 1964 Comsat [had] faced substantial risks related to the demand for international telecommunications services."[7] Dr. Eugene F. Brigham asserted that the company still encountered "a great deal of difficulty in forecasting demand because its customers are a few large public utilities and because there have been only a relatively few years of dynamic growth."[8] The company characterized the international telecommunications market as highly variable. Trial staff witnesses countered that the demand risk was negligible based on a high average historic rate of growth and the forecast for continued rapid growth: they presented evidence demonstrating that the annual rate of growth for overseas telephone message services (expected to be Comsat's major source of revenues in its early years) between 1964 and 1972 varied between 19% and 35%.[9] They believed that this record and the expected continuing rapid growth in demand nearly eliminated the demand risk of operating in the international telecommunications market. They believed that Comsat's demand risk was no greater than that faced by AT&T and other international carriers.

---

[6] FCC Docket 16070, FCC 75–1304, 38249, at 217.

[7] Ibid., at 226.

[8] Ibid., at 227.

[9] FCC Docket 16070, Trial Staff Exhibit No. 170.

Comsat asserted that it had also faced significant *competitive risks* in 1964 in the form of planned and existing cable system, high-frequency radio facilities, and the possible emergence of regional or domestic satellite systems. Moreover, company witnesses noted that an unusual competitive threat existed in the fact that Comsat's principal customers were also its principal competitors (as owners of alternative communication facilities such as cables). The trial staff argued that Comsat had faced only nominal risks regarding market share in 1964 and that by 1972, it faced no appreciable risk. They contended that Comsat would clearly benefit from the strong national policy recommendation that the satellite system should share in the growing international telecommunications traffic. They cited many FCC rulings which manifested the Commission's desire to maintain a reasonable balance between cable and satellite circuits on international routes. In their opinion these decisions constituted strong assurance to Comsat of a reasonable market share.

Comsat's witnesses testified that the company faced substantial *regulatory uncertainty* because of the undefined nature of Comsat's prospective regulation. They felt this uncertainty was greater than that facing well-established regulated enterprises, and that this should be reflected by an upward adjustment in its authorized rate of return. Comsat supported this claim by introducing as evidence investment brokers' reports. The trial staff rebutted Comsat's claims by again falling back on the significance of the national policy mandate for a global satellite system: presumably such policy support precluded unfair regulation. The staff argued that allowing Comsat "an additional risk premium based on the speculation that the Commission might not grant all the regulatory benefits a utility desires, constitutes a grant of those benefits in another form."[10] Furthermore, it was noted that the brokers' reports introduced suggested that the investment community believed that the regulatory agencies would not allow large, speculative rewards. Rather, they expected the FCC to regulate Comsat on a common carrier basis with a rate of return in the range of 8% to 10%.[11]

Comsat's witnesses also claimed that the company faced substantial *political or international risk* in that its commercial success depended heavily on the cooperation and the participation of foreign entities. The trial staff responded that such operating uncertainties were minimized by the assistance received from the State Department and by the ratification of various relevant international agreements.

Evaluation of Comsat's financial risk

The trial staff took the offensive in the discussion of Comsat's financial risk. Throughout its history, Comsat, a public utility, had maintained a 100% equity capital structure. The staff claimed that this policy reflected a degree of financial security unparalleled in the field of telecommunications common carriage: AT&T's 1973 debt-to-capitalization ratio was about 50%; the average debt ra-

[10] FCC Docket 16070, FCC 75–1304, 38249, at 238.
[11] FCC Docket 16070, Comsat's Exhibit 47B and 48.

tios of 87 telephone and 7 telegraph carriers were 49% and 40%, respectively;[12] and the average debt ratio for all utilities was 61%.[13] The staff asserted that since debt is less costly than equity, Comsat's capital structure was unreasonably conservative and as such, it adversely affected both ratepayers and stockholders. The staff cited precedents demonstrating that ratepayers should not be penalized by managerial conservatism and that debt may be imputed in the determination of fair rates. Thus, it recommended that the Commission impute debt at 45% of total capital in the determination of Comsat's rate of return from 1972 to the present.[14] The staff contended that such a level of imputed debt would not create appreciable financial risk and therefore would not warrant an increase in Comsat's allowable cost of equity. In determining Comsat's cost of debt, the staff reasoned that the company's all-equity capital structure and its recent operating performance would allow it to sell debt at AA or AAA utility rates. Thus, the trial staff recommended imputing a 45% debt level at the AA rate in computing Comsat's cost of capital.

Comsat's witnesses maintained that the firm could not have raised debt before 1972. It supported this by recalling its operating risks and by noting that in 1964 Comsat had had no security to offer creditors and no demonstrated earnings power. (The staff pointed out that Western Union International, operating without monopoly power or government backing, had raised large amounts of debt in its first few years of operation while competing with other international carriers.) After the 1964 equity issue, the firm's capital requirements had not been sufficiently large to require another issue of either debt or equity. However, Comsat's managers did agree that "in the long run it would be desirable . . . to include some debt in its capital structure. . . ."[15]

Another subject under discussion was the appropriate rate base to be used in determining a fair pricing structure for Comsat. Briefly, the FCC determines a firm's allowable revenues by multiplying its rate base (or revenue-producing plant) by the authorized rate of return and adding operating expenses to that product.[16] In 1964, Comsat had decided to raise at the outset all

---

[12] From the FCC's 1974 compilation of *Statistics of Communications Common Carriers*.

[13] FCC Docket 16070, testimony of E. F. Brigham.

[14] The year 1972 was recognized as the date Comsat was considered a "mature" enterprise (i.e., had demonstrated operational success). Witnesses for the trial staff did not recommend imputing debt during Comsat's developmental stages (i.e., before 1972). They characterized not doing so as "generous."

[15] FCC Docket 16070, Comsat's Summary of Reply and Brief.

[16] Regulatory decisions interact to determine a firm's prices through the revenue requirements formula:

$$R = (RB)r + E$$

where:

R = total revenue (i.e., revenue requirement)
RB = the firm's rate base; its capital employed in rendering service
r = the authorized or fair rate of return (i.e., cost of capital)
E = operating expenses (including taxes)

By setting RB and r, the regulators determine the firm's maximum allowable revenue (i.e., the revenue requirement). The firm must then set its prices accordingly.

capital necessary to establish the satellite system. This decision reflected the favorable stock market conditions at the time, the desire to minimize the substantial fixed transaction costs typical of equity issues, and the high degree of uncertainty associated with Comsat's early years. However, several fortuitous technical, political, and financial developments combined to reduce the capital investment required to establish the system.[17] Thus, Comsat had held a large portfolio of liquid assets for a longer period of time than anticipated. This portfolio had amounted to $193 million in 1964 (96% of total assets) but had been reduced to $35 million by 1974 (8.9% of total assets). Comsat argued that a portion of its portfolio of liquid assets should be included in the rate base. Comsat maintained that the rate base for 1964 and subsequent years should include (1) all funds which were ultimately used in establishing the satellite system and (2) all additional funds used as a contingency reserve against adversities. The company claimed that investors who had supplied these funds in 1964 were entitled to earn a full and fair return.

The trial staff's response cited the FCC's established practice of allowing a return on investors' capital only to the extent it was actually employed in rendering consumer service. The staff argued further that business interruption insurance and such alternative sources of capital as bank credit lines were available at reasonable costs to cover contingencies, making Comsat's large liquid holdings unnecessary. The trial staff believed that Comsat's sizable portfolio of cash and marketable securities was yet another example of its extreme fiscal conservatism. As a consumer advocate, it felt strongly that allowing liquid holdings as part of the rate base would unduly penalize ratepayers. The staff also noted that Comsat's large liquid portfolio reduced its financial risks. It believed that this fact should be reflected in a lower authorized rate of return. The Department of Defense, another party to the proceedings, suggested that if the FCC were to allow a return on Comsat's cash and marketable securities, it should be no more than that actually earned in the competitive investment marketplace.

Evaluation of Comsat's cost of capital

The *Hope* standard for determining a fair rate of return implied that the appropriate return is actually that required (or expected) by a firm's investors. Thus, Comsat's cost of capital would be equivalent to its fair rate of return. Several expert witnesses applied various methodologies designed to determine the market's expected return.

Dr. Eugene F. Brigham, a Comsat witness, suggested a discounted cash flow (DCF) approach, a dividend growth model. However, due to Comsat's short

---

[17] For instance, when Comsat issued equity in 1964, it planned to initiate parallel development of both nongeostationary and synchronous satellites. This was not necessary due to the advances in synchronous technology made by Hughes Aircraft and NASA in the successful SYNCOM program in the mid-1960s. Comsat's ability to exploit this technology reduced substantially both the cost and the time required to establish the global system.

operating history, the difficulty in forecasting its cash flows and the fact that Comsat had only recently begun paying dividends (1970), Dr. Brigham was convinced that a direct application of the DCF method was not feasible. Therefore, he calculated the rates of return on common stock for a sample consisting of 602 industrial firms and 56 utilities listed on Standard and Poor's Compustat computer files. He found that the average return on his sample between 1946 and 1964 was 12.4%. He felt that "one could argue that investors might assume similar returns would be earned in the future on equity investments."[18] Dr. Brigham also cited a study (by Arthur Andersen and Company) of the equity returns authorized in four utility cases in 1964. The four cases had allowed equity returns of 9.26% to 11.7%. Because they were utilities, Dr. Brigham considered these firms as belonging to a "low-risk class." He relied on this "indirect" approach of using returns on other firm's equity as a "benchmark" for determining Comsat's cost of equity in 1964. Since he considered Comsat's risk as roughly equivalent to that of the Compustat sample and as higher than the utilities, his estimate of Comsat's cost of equity for 1964 was 12%–14%.

Dr. Brigham estimated that Comsat's cost of equity in 1971 was between 11% and 13% with a midpoint of 12%. He felt that Comsat was less risky in 1971 than in 1964 but that this had been partially offset by the general increase in interest rates over this period. His estimate was based on another Arthur Andersen survey of rate cases in 1970 which showed that the authorized rate of return in 26 utility decisions was between 9.3% and 13.7% with an average of 11.1%.

Consistent with the testimony of Dr. Brigham and its other witnesses, Comsat asked for a 12% rate of return for the period 1964 to September 30, 1974 and 15% since October 1, 1974.

The trial staff agreed that there was insufficient company history to allow a direct DCF calculation. However, they criticized Dr. Brigham's results as not comparable with Comsat. They noted that his Compustat study included mostly industrial firms rather than utilities such as Comsat. Furthermore, Dr. Brigham's study did not reveal whether any of the sample firms were capitalized on a 100% equity basis as Comsat was. Since most firms have debt in their capital structures, the returns in the sample might contain premiums for risk attributable to leveraged capital structure. Thus, the staff argued that the sample firms were not "other enterprises having corresponding risks" as required by the *Hope* standard.

Furthermore, the staff felt that the holding period of 1946 to 1964 was too short, resulting in a long-term average equity return which was unjustifiably high. A witness testified that the average return on common equity from 1926 to 1970 was 9.3%.

Concerning Dr. Brigham's use of the four rate-case decisions in 1964, the staff argued that these firms were not relevant to Comsat's case because these firms were all highly leveraged. The staff questioned Dr. Brigham's belief that

---

[18] FCC Docket 16070, testimony of E. F. Brigham.

these utilities were "low risk" while Comsat, a public utility, was not. Furthermore, no evidence was presented to demonstrate that these results were representative of rate cases in 1964. Indeed, a fifth case was omitted from the study under the assumption that the authorized return, 4.6%, was a typographical error.

The same points were raised in objection to Dr. Brigham's study of authorized returns in 1970. Furthermore, his study did not state whether these authorized returns were the cost of equity or the overall cost of capital. In general, the staff's chief criticism of Dr. Brigham's studies was his assumption that Comsat was riskier than other utilities and should be compared with riskier industrial firms.

The trial staff's recommendation was based on the testimony of Dr. Willard T. Carleton. Dr. Carleton agreed with Dr. Brigham that Comsat's short operating history and the difficulty in projecting future earnings and dividends precluded the use of DCF formulas to determine investors' required return. His alternative methodology could be expressed by the relation:

$$k_E = R_F + \text{risk premium}$$

where:

k_E = the cost of equity

R_F = the return on the least-risk (or risk-free) security

risk premium = the additional return investors require as compensation for bearing the business and financial risks of the firm's equity.

Dr. Carleton used long-term U.S. government bond yields as the relevant least-risk rate. For example, to determine Comsat's cost of equity for 1964, Dr. Carlton added a risk premium of 2% to 4% to the U.S. Treasury bond interest rate in 1964 of 4%. Thus, his estimate for 1964 was 6% to 8% with a midpoint of 7%. The relatively small risk premium is consistent with the staff's position that Comsat's investors faced relatively little risk.

Based on Dr. Carleton's analysis, the trial staff computed Comsat's cost of capital, imputing a 45% debt ratio for the period 1972 through 1975. The resulting weighted average costs of capital, also Comsat's recommended fair return, were 7% for the period 1964–1971 and 8.33% for 1972 with increases to 9.42% for 1975. These recommendations were consistent with the trial staff's position that AT&T's cost of capital represented an appropriate benchmark for estimating Comsat's allowable return: using a dividend growth model Dr. Carleton estimated AT&T's 1964 cost of equity to be 8.1%. The staff's recommendations for other years were also consistent with its interpretation of Comsat's risk relative to that of AT&T.[19]

Following the presentation of the direct cases, Dr. Stewart C. Myers, a re-

---

[19] For instance, the staff's recommended 1972 cost of capital for Comsat was 8.33%. In a widely publicized rate-case decision announced in 1971, the FCC ruled that AT&T's authorized rate of return (i.e., its cost of capital) was 9.75%. In the same case, AT&T's cost of equity was set at 10.5%.

buttal witness for Comsat, testified in support of Comsat's request. He asserted that applying the methodology of modern portfolio theory would reveal the only direct evidence of the risk of Comsat's equity as perceived by investors in the market. Thus, Dr. Myers relied on the capital asset pricing model (CAPM) to make his estimates of investors' required returns. This methodology involves the statistical estimation of a security's systematic, nondiversifiable (or market-related) risk as measured by its beta. The following formulation was used:

$$k_E = R_F + \beta(k_M - R_F)$$

where:

k_E = The cost of equity capital
R_F = The return on the least-risk (or risk-free) security
k_M = The cost of equity (or the expected return) for the market as a whole
β = The beta of the firm's stock.

Dr. Myers' study, conducted with Dr. Gerald A. Pogue, was not designed to yield a specific estimate of Comsat's cost of equity: it was intended both to determine whether Dr. Brigham's estimate of Comsat's cost of capital at 12% was too high and to determine whether Comsat's equity was riskier than that of AT&T. Dr. Myers also hoped that his work would shed some light on whether Comsat had become riskier over the period 1964 to 1972.

Dr. Myers estimated Comsat's beta at approximately 1.7 over the period 1964 to 1972, with only a 16% probability that the "true" beta was less than 1.4 (the standard error of the beta was .3). Drs. Myers and Pogue assumed an expected return on the market of 11.5% with a range of 10% to 13%. They arrived at several estimates of Comsat's cost of equity by varying their assumptions about market return and the risk-free (or least-risk) rate. Additional estimates were made to account for discrepancies which have been found in empirical tests of the model. All of Dr. Myers' estimates of Comsat's cost of equity ranged between 11.2% and 17.2% with a midpoint of 14%. (Exhibits 8 and 9 present the methodology for estimating the cost of equity using CAPM.)

Although Dr. Myers found Comsat's beta to be relatively stable over time, his evidence did reveal a gradual increase in this measure of risk between 1964 and 1973. Therefore, he argued that Comsat's risk as perceived by investors had been increasing rather than decreasing as the trial staff suggested. Dr. Myers suggested that this effect may have been caused by the decrease over time in Comsat's liquid holdings relative to plant investment.

In the 1971 AT&T rate case, Drs. Myers and Pogue (testifying for the trial staff) had prepared a study which estimated AT&T's beta at approximately .7 and its cost of equity at 10.5%. Based on his analyses, Dr. Myers stated that the odds that Comsat's risk as measured by beta was less than that of AT&T's were "miniscule." This was also true of Comsat's total risk (or total variability in return as measured by the standard deviation of return). Dr. Myers also compared Comsat's systematic and total risk to major firms in other industries (Exhibits 6 and 7). He found that Comsat's risk was more than twice that of electric utilities and natural gas pipelines and roughly the same as a typical major airline. Furthermore, of the 921 stocks in his sample of data, only 145 had estimated betas higher than Comsat's; only 184 had higher estimates of total risk (standard deviations).[20]

Dr. Myers concluded that "Comsat's cost of equity capital is at least as large as a typical industrial firm's and well in excess of AT&T's. Twelve percent (Dr. Brigham's estimate and Comsat's request) is a reasonable estimate of Comsat's cost of capital—if anything, it is conservative." He considered CAPM sufficiently valid to "warrant according independent significance to beta evidence. . . . If there were no other evidence . . . in this proceeding, I would not hesitate in recommending that the Commission rely on beta in determining relative risk."[21]

Dr. Myers acknowledged that CAPM ignores "unsystematic" reasons (those unrelated to the market) for observed stock price movement. However, if stock prices are determined by investors holding large portfolios, only systematic, market-related risk is relevant in determining a stock's risk premium. Dr. Carleton argued that the issue at hand was to determine a rate of return such that Comsat would be enabled to attract capital and maintain its financial integrity. He stated that the issue was not—as Dr. Myers contended it was—to determine the "extent to which Comsat's stock contributes to the risk of a diversified portfolio."[22]

The decision

In the spring of 1975, the FCC held the complete, 20,000-page record of the Comsat proceedings for evaluation. Its task was to act as a surrogate for market competition in prescribing Comsat's economic regulation under the Satellite Act of 1962. At issue were Comsat's appropriate rate base, its fair rate of return, and its price structure.

Perhaps the most important of these issues was that of determining Comsat's fair rate of return—its cost of capital. The decision reached would have a major impact on the thousands of shareholders who had invested in Comsat securities. It would also directly affect Comsat's customers because the allowed return was an important variable in the company's pricing formula. Furthermore, the Commissioners' ruling would inevitably influence Comsat's internal capital budgeting process: the cost of capital they set would represent the relevant hurdle rate to be applied to proposed new investments.

---

[20] Dr. Myers used the file of security returns compiled by the Center for the Research in Security Prices at the University of Chicago. His version contained almost all stocks listed on the New York Stock Exchange.

[21] FCC Docket 16070, testimony of S. C. Myers.

[22] FCC Docket 16070, testimony of S. C. Myers. In the 1971 AT&T rate case, Dr. Myers' estimate of the cost of capital using CAPM was accepted, while other estimates were rejected. This was also true of beta estimates (by Dr. Robert Haugen and Dr. Howard Thompson) of the costs of capital of Armco Steel and Republic Steel in a landmark civil case, the Reserve Mining Case, involving Reserve Mining's dumping of wastes into Lake Superior.

The Commissioners' task was complicated by the need to consider Comsat's unique government mandate to supply a new and complex technology for commercial use. Moreover, the tools ordinarily employed to measure empirically investors' required rate of return were of questionable value given Comsat's brief operating history. The role of the FCC, as stated in the *Hope* standard, was to consider all such factors in balancing investor and consumer interests, consistent with generally accepted judicial guidelines.

Exhibit 1

COMMUNICATIONS SATELLITE CORPORATION
PROPOSED FAIR RATES OF RETURN, 1964–1975

	Comsat Proposal	FCC Proposal
1964–1971	12%	7.00%
1972	12%	8.33%
1973	12%	8.70%
1974	12%	9.15%
1975	15%	9.42%

Exhibit 2

COMMUNICATIONS SATELLITE CORPORATION
BALANCE SHEETS, 1968 AND 1972–1974
(Dollar figures in millions)

ASSETS	1968	1972	1973	1974
Cash	$ .8	$ .7	$ 1.2	$ .4
Marketable securities	133.3	94.3	129.9	49.7
Accounts receivable	11.5	14.4	14.9	30.6
Accrued interest receivable	1.9	1.1	3.0	.6
Other current assets	.8	1.8	1.0	3.4
Current Assets	$148.3	$112.3	$150.0	$ 84.7
Property, plant, and equipment:				
Satellites	21.7	137.9	121.4	129.8
Earth stations	24.6	47.5	41.8	41.9
Headquarters and laboratory	5.5	27.5	29.3	30.2
Total	$ 51.8	$212.9	$192.5	$201.9
Less: accumulated depreciation	20.3	71.7	83.6	100.9
Construction in progress	47.1	35.7	99.5	206.5
Satellite system development costs	20.9	12.9	9.5	6.8
Research and development costs	3.6	20.6	21.7	21.0
Net property, plant, and equipment	$103.1	$210.4	$239.6	$335.3
Investments, deferred charges, and other assets	1.8	6.5	6.0	10.2
Total assets	$253.2	$329.2	$395.6	$430.2
LIABILITIES AND NET WORTH				
Accounts payable and accrued liabilities	$ 17.1	$ 14.0	$ 36.0	$ 36.5
Income taxes payable	...	2.0	14.8	9.1
Current liabilities	$ 17.1	$ 16.0	$ 50.8	$ 45.6
Deferred taxes and investment credit	18.1	34.8	36.3	40.2
Stockholders' equity				
Common stock	195.2	195.2	195.2	195.2
Retained earnings	22.8	83.2	113.3	149.2
Net worth	$218.0	$278.4	$308.5	$344.4
Total liabilities and net worth	$253.2	$329.2	$395.6	$430.2

Exhibit 3

COMMUNICATIONS SATELLITE CORPORATION
INCOME STATEMENTS, 1968 AND 1972–1974
(Dollar figures in millions)

	1968	1972	1973	1974
Operating revenues..............................	$ 30.5	$105.9	$119.3	$133.
Operating expenses:				
Operations and maintenance......................	18.8	30.5	28.5	29.
Depreciation.................................	7.2	24.7	22.8	20.
Amortization.................................	2.3	7.3	8.5	9.
Operating income..............................	$ 2.2	$ 43.4	$ 59.5	$ 73.
Interest income................................	8.6	4.5	8.8	7.
Other income (expense)........................	1.7	(.3)	2.1	5.
Income before taxes...........................	$ 12.5	$ 47.6	$ 70.4	$ 86.
Income taxes				
On operating income.........................	1.2	22.0	30.1	37.
On net other income.........................	4.5	.6	4.0	3.
Total taxes............................	$ 5.7	$ 22.6	$ 34.1	$ 41.
Net income...................................	$ 6.8	$ 25.0	$ 36.3	$ 44.
Dividends.....................................	$ —	$ 5.5	$ 6.2	$ 9.
Retained earnings..............................	6.8	19.5	30.1	35.

Exhibit 4

COMMUNICATIONS SATELLITE CORPORATION
Operating and Financial Performance, 1967–1974
(Dollar figures in millions except per share data)

	1967	1968	1969	1970	1971	1972	1973	1974
Operating revenues............	$ 18.5	$ 30.5	$ 47.0	$ 69.6	$ 88.4	$105.9	$119.3	$133.5
Net operating income (after tax).....	(.6)	1.0	1.8	10.5	16.4	21.4	29.4	36.3
Interest income..............	7.9	8.6	7.5	7.9	6.1	4.5	8.8	7.4
Net income................	4.6	6.8	7.1	17.5	22.5	25.0	36.3	44.9
Net operating income/average equity.....	—	.5%	.8%	4.5%	6.6%	8.0%	10.0%	11.1%
Net income/average equity........	2.2%	3.2%	3.2%	7.5%	9.0%	9.3%	12.4%	13.8%
Net property, plant, and equipment.....	$ 70.6	$103.1	$138.5	$182.5	$208.6	$210.3	$239.5	$335.3
Cash and marketable securities.......	155.6	134.1	102.1	100.6	104.7	95.0	131.2	50.1
Earnings per share.............	$ .46	$ .68	$ .71	$ 1.75	$ 2.25	$ 2.50	$ 3.63	$ 4.49
Dividends per share............	—	—	—	.125	.50	.545	.62	.90
Book value per share...........	21.11	21.80	22.51	24.14	25.89	27.84	30.85	34.44
Full-time leased half circuits—Comsat....	717	951	1,433	2,139	2,537	2,971	3,583	3,942
Full-time leased half circuits—global....	1,050	1,525	2,984	4,388	5,834	7,527	9,837	10,969

Exhibit 5

COMMUNICATIONS SATELLITE CORPORATION
COMPARATIVE STOCK MARKET DATA FOR COMSAT AND AT&T, 1967–1974

	Comsat*			AT&T†		
	Price per Share		Price-Earnings	Price per Share		Price-Earnings
	High	Low	Ratio	High	Low	Ratio
1967	$77⅞	$41⅛	129.3	$62	$49	15
1968	64¾	41½	78.1	58	48	14
1969	60⅞	41¾	72.3	58	48	13
1970	57¾	25	23.6	54	40	12
1971	84½	49⅛	29.7	54	41	12
1972	75⅜	52	25.5	54	41	11
1973	64½	37⅛	14.0	55	45	10
1974	40⅜	22¾	7.0	53	40	9

*Comsat's Annual Reports and The Wall Street Journal.
†The Wall Street Journal (rounded figures).

Exhibit 6

COMMUNICATIONS SATELLITE CORPORATION
ANNUAL MARKET RETURNS ON SELECTED SECURITIES, 1967–1974

	Comsat* Common Stock	AT&T† Common Stock	Moody's Industrials‡ Common Stock Index	Baa Industrial Bonds§	Aa Utility Bonds‖
1967	17.51%	−.92%	29.2%	6.21%	5.66%
1968	9.60	8.28	8.7	6.90	6.35
1969	5.07	−3.13	−5.4	7.76	7.34
1970	−12.06	4.00	3.0	9.00	8.52
1971	29.25	−2.87	14.8	8.37	8.00
1972	.65	25.03	19.7	7.99	7.60
1973	−37.51	−.71	−14.3	8.07	7.72
1974	−22.16	−1.52	−27.5	9.48	9.04
Average	−1.21	3.52	3.52	7.97	7.53

*Comsat's Annual Reports and The Wall Street Journal.
†AT&T's Annual Reports and The Wall Street Journal.
‡Moody's Industrial Manual.
§Moody's Industrial Manual.
‖Moody's Public Utility Manual.

Exhibit 7

COMMUNICATIONS SATELLITE CORPORATION
RISK MEASURES FOR THE COMMON STOCK OF SELECTED FIRMS AND INDUSTRY GROUPS,
October 1964 to June 1970*

| Company | Time Period | *Systematic Risk* | | *Total Risk* |
		Estimated Beta	Standard Error of Estimated Beta	Estimated Standard Deviation of Returns
Comsat.............	Oct. 1964–June 1970	1.69	.30	11.2
Comsat.............	Oct. 1964–July 1967	1.39	.55	11.1
Comsat.............	Aug. 1967–June 1970	1.79	.34	10.9
AT&T.............	Oct. 1964–June 1970	.62	.11	4.0
AT&T.............	Oct. 1964–July 1967	.54	.18	3.7
AT&T.............	Aug. 1967–June 1970	.70	.14	4.3
Average of Moody's 24 utilities...........	Oct. 1964–June 1970	.74		5.3
Average of 7 gas pipeline companies...........	Oct. 1964–June 1970	.79		6.4
Average of 14 major grocery chains.............	Oct. 1964–June 1970	.83		6.8
Average of 33 major chemical companies...........	Oct. 1964–June 1970	1.19		7.8
Average of 20 major department stores.............	Oct. 1964–June 1970	1.36		9.1
Average of 21 office machine manufacturers.........	Oct. 1964–June 1970	1.58		11.5
Average of 11 major airlines...........	Oct. 1964–June 1970	1.69		11.7

*FCC Docket 16070, Testimony of S. C. Meyers.

Exhibit 8

COMMUNICATIONS SATELLITE CORPORATION
EXAMPLES OF ESTIMATING COMSAT'S COST OF EQUITY CAPITAL
USING CAPM WITH DIFFERENT EXPECTED MARKET RETURNS

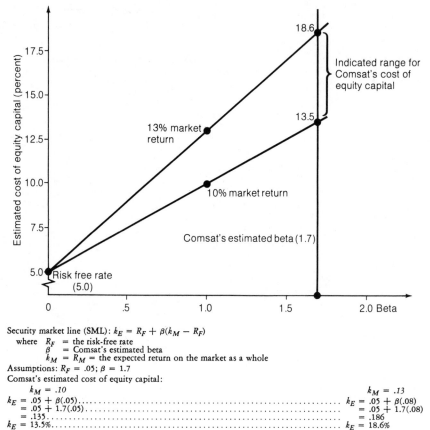

Security market line (SML): $k_E = R_F + \beta(k_M - R_F)$

where R_F = the risk-free rate
β = Comsat's estimated beta
$k_M = R_M$ = the expected return on the market as a whole

Assumptions: $R_F = .05; \beta = 1.7$

Comsat's estimated cost of equity capital:

$k_M = .10$

$k_E = .05 + \beta(.05)$ ....
$\quad = .05 + 1.7(.05)$ ....
$\quad = .135$ ....
$k_E = 13.5\%$ ....

$k_M = .13$

$k_E = .05 + \beta(.08)$
$\quad = .05 + 1.7(.08)$
$\quad = .186$
$k_E = 18.6\%$

Exhibit 9

COMMUNICATIONS SATELLITE CORPORATION
Lower Bound Estimates of Comsat's Cost of Equity Capital Using CAPM

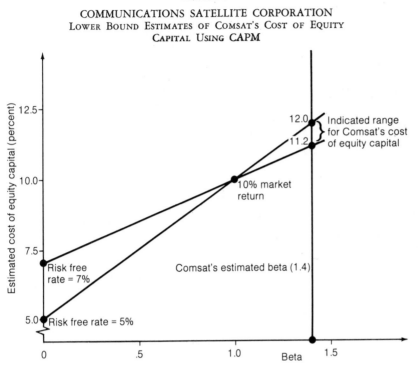

Security market line (SML): $k_E = R_F + \beta(k_M - R_F)$

Assumptions:

$k_M = .10$ = low estimate of the return on the market
$\beta = 1.4$ = low estimate of Comsat's beta

Comsat's estimated cost of equity capital:

$R_F = .05$

$k_E = .05 + \beta(.05)$
$= .05 + 1.4(.05)$
$= .12$
$k_E = 12\%$

$R_F = .07$

$k_E = .07 + \beta(.03)$
$= .07 + 1.4(.03)$
$= .112$
$k_E = 11.2\%$

DIVERSIFICATION, THE CAPITAL
ASSET PRICING MODEL, AND
THE COST OF EQUITY CAPITAL

∧∧∧

Risk as variability in return

The rate of return an investor receives from holding a stock for a given period of time is equal to the dividends received plus the capital gains in the period divided by the initial market value of the security.

$$R = \frac{\text{dividends} + (\text{ending price} - \text{beginning price})}{\text{beginning price}}$$

Alternatively, return can be viewed as the dividend yield plus the percentage capital appreciation.

$$R = \text{dividend yield} + \text{percentage capital appreciation}$$

Suppose an investor buys one common share of Du Pont for \$100 on January 1. Over the year the investor receives \$4 in dividends and sells the share for \$108 on December 31. The return is 12%.

$$R_{\text{Du Pont}} = \frac{\$4 + (\$108 - \$100)}{\$100} = \frac{12}{100} = .12$$

or

$$R_{\text{Du Pont}} = 4\% \text{ dividend yield} + 8\% \text{ appreciation} = 12\%$$

If the ending price is \$85, the return is −11%.

In general, the return on any security can be viewed as the cash the security holder receives (including liquidation at the end of the period) divided by the initial investment. Investing in a savings account which offers a 5% interest rate results in an annual return of 5%.

$$R_{\text{savings account}} = \frac{\$5 + (\$100 - \$100)}{\$100} = .05$$

There is an important difference, however, between investing in a savings account and investing in common stocks. An investor knows before committing funds that the savings account will earn a return of 5%. The return on the savings account is certain since the investor knows that the actual return will not be different from the expected return of 5%. Thus, savings accounts are considered a safe or riskless security.

Although an investor may expect a return of 12% on Du Pont's common shares, the investor may be disappointed or pleasantly surprised. The actual return on Du Pont may be less than or greater than 12% since (1) Du Pont may change its dividend and, more important, (2) the market price at the end of the period might be different than the investor anticipated. Actual returns on common stock vary widely from year to year. An investor committing funds at the beginning of any period cannot be confident of receiving the average or expected return.

In general, an investment whose actual returns are not likely to depart from the expected or average return is considered a low risk investment. One whose returns from year to year are quite volatile is said to be risky. Thus, risk can be viewed as variability in return (see Exhibit 1).

Risk reduction through diversification

Risky stocks can be combined in such a way that the combination of securities, called a portfolio of securities, is less risky than any one of the component individual stocks. Consider the example outlined in Exhibit 2. Suppose we have two firms located on an isolated Caribbean island. The chief industry on the island is tourism. Firm A manufactures and sells suntan lotion. Its sales, earnings, and cash flows are highest during sunny years. Thus, its stock does well in sunny years and poorly in rainy years. Firm B manufactures and sells disposable umbrellas. Returns on its stock reflect its higher earnings in rainy years. In purchasing either stock A or B, an investor is subject to considerable risk or variability in return. For instance, the return on an investment in the stock of Firm B will vary from −9% to 33% depending on weather conditions.

Suppose, however, instead of buying only one security, an investor puts half of the funds in stock A and half in stock B. The possible returns on this portfolio of securities are calculated in Exhibit 2. For example, in a sunny year, a $50 investment in stock A returns $16.50, while $50 invested in stock B loses $4.50. The total return on $100 invested in the portfolio is 12% ([16.50 − 4.50]/ 100). Note that the return on this portfolio is 12% *regardless* of which weather condition prevails.

Combining these two risky securities yields a portfolio with a certain return. Since we are sure of earning 12% on the portfolio, it is a very low-risk investment comparable to a riskless security such as a savings account. This example demonstrates risk reduction through diversification. By diversifying the investment over both firms, the investor creates a portfolio which is less risky than its two component stocks.

Total risk elimination is possible in this example because there is a perfect negative relationship between the returns on stocks A and B. In practice, such a perfect relationship is very rare. Most firms' securities tend to move together

Exhibit 1

RISK AS VARIABILITY IN RETURN

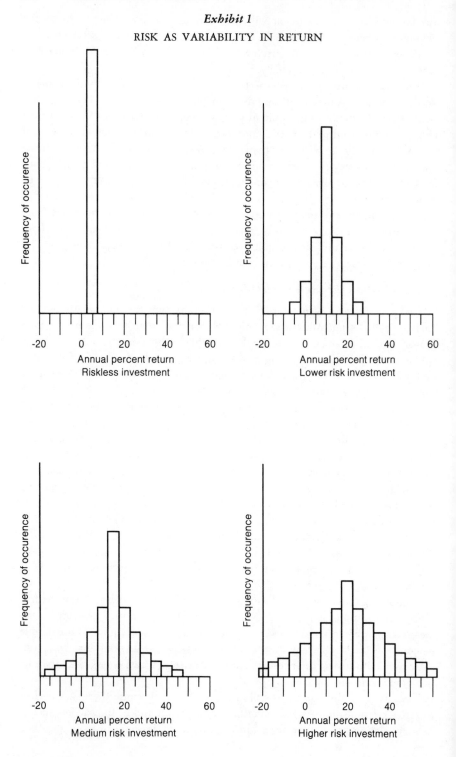

Exhibit 2

AN EXAMPLE OF RISK REDUCTION THROUGH DIVERSIFICATION

Source of Risk: Weather Conditions	Return on Stock of Firm A, Suntan Lotion Manufacturer	Return on Stock of Firm B, Disposable Umbrella Manufacturer	Return on a Portfolio Consisting of 50% Invested in Stock A and 50% Invested in Stock B
Sunny year..............	33%	−9%	.50(33%) + .50(−9%) = 12%
Normal year............	12	12	.50(12%) + .50(12%) = 12%
Rainy year..............	−9	33	.50(−9%) + .50(33%) = 12%
Average return*........	12%	12%	12%

*Assumes sunny and rainy years are equally likely to occur.

and, therefore, complete elimination of risk is not possible. However, as long as there is some lack of parallelism in the returns of securities, diversification will always reduce risk. Since companies' fortunes and therefore their stocks' returns do not move completely in parallel, investment in a diversified portfolio composed of many securities is less risky than investing in a few individual stocks.

Systematic and unsystematic risk

Combining securities into portfolios reduces risk. When combined with other securities, a portion of a stock's variability in return is canceled by complementary variations in the returns of other securities. Some firms represented in the portfolio may experience unanticipated adverse conditions (e.g., a wildcat strike). However, this may well be offset by the unexpected good fortune of other firms in the portfolio. Nevertheless, since to some extent stock prices (and returns) tend to move in tandem, not all variability can be eliminated through diversification. Even investors holding diversified portfolios are exposed to the risk inherent in the overall performance of the stock market (e.g., the Bear Market of 1974). Thus, it is convenient to divide a security's total risk into that portion which is peculiar to a specific firm and can be diversified away (called unsystematic risk) and that portion which is market related and nondiversifiable (called systematic risk). Thus,

total risk	=	unsystematic risk (diversifiable risk, firm specific)	+	systematic risk (nondiversifiable risk, market related)

Exhibit 3 illustrates the reduction of total risk as securities are added to a portfolio. Unsystematic risk is virtually eliminated in portfolios of 30 or 40 securities drawn from industries which are not closely related. Since the remaining (systematic) risk is market related, diversified portfolios tend to move in tandem with the market. The popular market indices (e.g., Dow Jones Average of 30 Industrials, Standard & Poor's Index of 500 Stocks, New York Stock Exchange Index) are themselves diversified portfolios, and they tend to move in parallel. Thus, there is a close correspondence between swings in the

Exhibit 3

ELIMINATION OF UNSYSTEMATIC RISK THROUGH DIVERSIFICATION

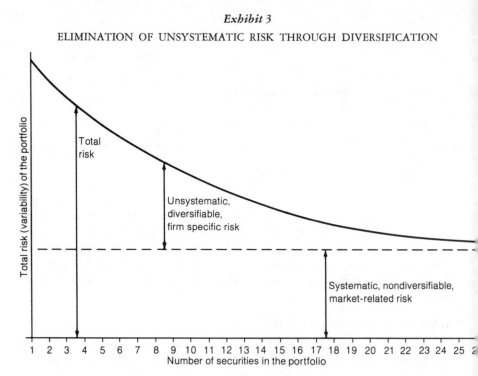

returns of any diversified portfolio and in the returns on market indices such as the Dow. Examples of systematic and unsystematic risk factors are listed in Exhibit 4.

Exhibit 4

SYSTEMATIC AND UNSYSTEMATIC RISK FACTORS

Examples of unsystematic risk factors:

A firm's technical wizard is killed in an auto accident.
A wildcat strike is declared.
A lower-cost, foreign competitor unexpectedly enters a firm's product market.
Oil is discovered on a firm's property.

Examples of systematic risk factors:

Oil-producing countries institute a boycott.
Congress votes a massive tax cut.
The Federal Reserve follows a restrictive monetary policy.
There is a precipitous rise in long-term interest rates.

Risk, return, and market equilibrium

If investors are risk averse, they must be compensated for taking on risk. Thus, risky securities are priced by the market to yield a higher expected return than riskless securities. The extra reward or risk premium is necessary to induce risk-averse investors to hold risky securities. Thus, in a market dominated by risk-averse investors, there must be a positive relationship between risk and expected return to achieve equilibrium. The expected return on a riskless security (e.g., Treasury bill) is the risk-free rate. The expected return on risky securities can be thought of as this risk-free rate plus a premium for risk.

$$R_S = R_F + \text{risk premium}$$

The market's risk/return trade-off is illustrated in Exhibit 5.

Exhibit 5

THE MARKET'S RISK/EXPECTED RETURN TRADE-OFF IN EQUILIBRIUM

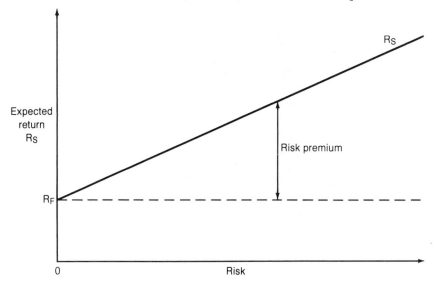

Capital asset pricing model (CAPM)

CAPM represents an idealized view of how the market prices securities and determines expected returns. It provides a measure of the risk premium and a method of estimating the market's risk/expected return curve.

The model's assumptions result in a world in which, to minimize risk, investors hold diversified portfolios. Therefore, the only risk investors are sensitive to is systematic or market related risk. Since they hold portfolios consisting of many securities, events peculiar to specific firms (i.e., unsystematic risk) have a negligible impact on their overall return. Only a small fraction of an investor's funds are invested in each security. Furthermore, variations in returns from one security will, as likely as not, be canceled by complementary variations in the returns of other securities.

Since such unsystematic risk can be eliminated simply by holding large portfolios, investors are not compensated for bearing unsystematic risk. Investors holding diversified portfolios are exposed only to systematic (nondiversifiable), market related risk. Therefore, the relevant risk in the markets' risk/expected return trade-off is systematic risk not total risk. The investor is rewarded with a higher expected return for bearing systematic or market related risks. Only systematic risk is relevant in determining the premiums for bearing risk. Thus, the result of CAPM is that a security's return is related to that portion of risk which cannot be eliminated by portfolio combination.

An individual investor who invests in only one stock is still exposed to both systematic and unsystematic risk. However, the investor is rewarded in terms of a higher expected return only for the systematic risk borne. There is no reward for bearing unsystematic risk since it can be eliminated by adequate diversification.

The CAPM provides a convenient measure of systematic risk. This measure, called beta (β), gages the tendency of a security's return to move in parallel with the overall market's return (e.g., the return on the S&P 500). One way to think of beta is as a measure of a security's volatility relative to the market's volatility. A stock with a beta of 1.0 tends to rise and fall the same percentage as the market (i.e., S&P 500 index). Thus, $\beta = 1.0$ indicates an average level of systematic risk. Stocks with a beta greater than 1 tend to rise and fall by a greater percentage than the market. They have a high level of systematic risk and are very sensitive to market changes. Similarly, a stock with a beta less than one has a low level of systematic risk and is less sensitive to market swings.

These results determine the risk/expected return trade-off under CAPM.

In general,

$$R_S = R_F + \text{risk premium}$$

If CAPM correctly describes market behavior,

$$R_S = R_F + \beta_S(R_M - R_F)$$

The expected return on a security (R_S) is equal to the risk-free rate plus a risk premium. With CAPM the risk premium is beta times the return on the market (R_M) minus the risk-free rate. Alternatively, the relationship can be expressed in terms of the risk premium (i.e., the return over and above the risk-free rate).

$$R_S - R_F = \beta_S(R_M - R_F) = \text{risk premium for security (S)}$$

Thus, the risk premium on a stock (or portfolio or any security) varies directly with the level of systematic risk, β_S. This risk/expected return trade-off with CAPM is called the security market line (SML) and is illustrated graphically in Exhibit 6.[1]

One perhaps counter-intuitive aspect of the determination of expected re-

---

[1] It should be noted that the SML is more general than CAPM. It is also the risk/expected return trade-off in other models of market behavior.

Exhibit 6

THE SECURITY MARKET LINE: THE RISK/EXPECTED RETURN
TRADE-OFF WITH CAPM

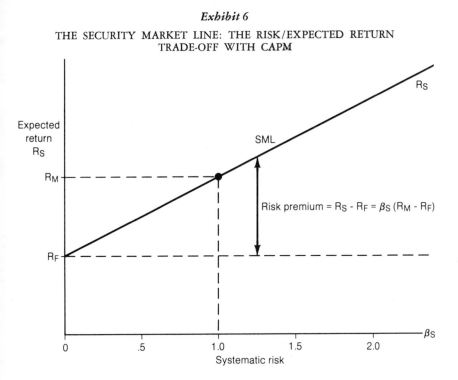

turns with CAPM can be illustrated with a simple example. Consider a firm engaged in oil exploration. The return (denoted R_A) to the shareholders in such a firm is very variable. If oil is found, the return is very high. If no oil is discovered, shareholders lose all their investment, and the return is negative. The stock's total risk is very high. However, much of the variability in return is generated by factors independent of the returns on other stocks (i.e., the return on the market). This risk is unique to the firm and is, therefore, unsystematic risk. Since the stock's return is not closely related to the return on the market as a whole, it contributes little to the variability of a diversified portfolio. Its unsystematic risk can be diversified away by holding large portfolios. Nevertheless, the costs of exploration and the price of oil are related to the general level of economic activity. Therefore, the stock does contain some systematic or market related risk. However, most of its total risk is unsystematic risk associated with the chances of finding oil. Thus, in spite of the fact the firm's stock looks very risky (i.e., in terms of total risk), it has a low level of systematic risk. Its beta might be .8. The market will therefore price this stock to yield a relatively low expected return. From the viewpoint of investors holding large portfolios, it is a low-risk security. Its expected return is denoted R_A in Exhibit 7. Note that the return on this stock (R_A) is less than the return on the average stock in the market (R_M).

Exhibit 7

AN EXAMPLE OF THE DETERMINATION OF EXPECTED
RETURNS WITH CAPM

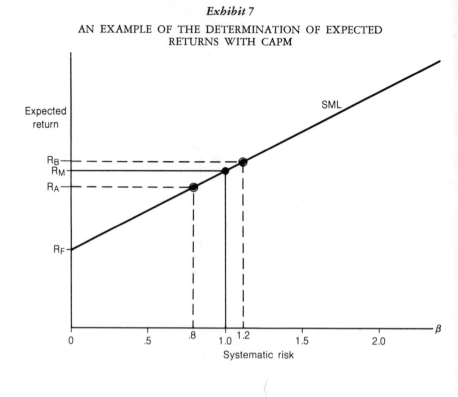

In contrast, consider a firm which manufactures computers. As a large, stable firm, its total variability in return might be less than that of the oil exploration firm. However, its sales, earnings, and, therefore, stock returns are closely related to changes in overall economic activity. The return on its stock is very sensitive to changes in the return on the market as a whole. Therefore, its risk cannot be eliminated by diversification. When combined with other securities in a diversified portfolio, changes in its return tend to reinforce swings in the returns of the other securities. It has a relatively high level of systematic risk and a beta of perhaps 1.2. Viewed as an individual security, it appears less risky (total risk) than the oil exploitation firm. Nevertheless, because of its high level of nondiversifiable risk, the market considers it the riskier security. Therefore, it is priced to yield a high expected return. Its return is labeled R_B in Exhibit 7. Such counter intuitive examples are rare, however. Most firms with high total risk also have high betas (and vice versa).

In summary, if CAPM correctly describes market behavior, the relevant measure of a security's risk is its market related or systematic risk (measured by beta). If a security's return bears a strong positive relationship with the return on the market (i.e., has a high beta), it will be priced to yield a high expected return (and vice versa). Since unsystematic risk can be easily eliminated through diversification, it does not increase a security's expected return.

The market cares only about systematic risk. These results are summarized in Exhibit 8.

Exhibit 8
SUMMARY OF THE DETERMINATION OF EXPECTED RETURNS WITH CAPM

1. Risk is defined as variability in return.
2. The investor can reduce risk by holding a diversified portfolio.
3. The total risk of a security can be divided into unsystematic and systematic risk.
   a. Risk which can be eliminated through diversification is called unsystematic risk. It is associated with events unique to the firm and independent of other firms.
   b. The risk remaining in a diversified portfolio is called systematic risk. It is associated with the movement of other securities and the market as a whole.
4. If CAPM correctly describes market behavior, investors hold diversified portfolios in order to minimize risk.
5. Since investors hold diversified portfolios with CAPM, they are exposed only to systematic risk. In such a market, investors are rewarded in terms of a higher expected return only for bearing systematic, market related risk. There is no reward associated with unsystematic risk, for it can be eliminated through diversification. Thus, relevant risk is systematic or market related risk, and it is measured by beta.
6. The risk/expected return trade-off with CAPM is called the security market line (SML).

Securities are priced such that

$$R_S = R_F + \text{risk premium}$$
or
$$R_S = R_F + \beta_S (R_M - R_F)$$

Thus, the SML gives us an estimate of the expected return on any security (R_S).

Application of CAPM to corporate finance: Estimating the cost of equity capital

CAPM provides insight into the market's pricing of securities and the determination of expected returns. Thus, it has clear applications in investment management. CAPM has an important application to corporate finance as well. A firm's cost of equity capital, k_E, is the expected (or required) return on the firm's common stock. The firm must be expected to earn k_E on the equity financed portion of investments in order to keep the price of its stock from falling. If the firm cannot expect to earn at least k_E, funds should be returned to the shareholders who can earn k_E on marketable securities of the same risk level. Since k_E involves the market's expectations, it is difficult to measure. The CAPM can be used by financial managers to obtain an estimate of k_E.

Since CAPM provides a conceptual framework for the determination of the expected return on common stocks, it can be used to estimate a firm's cost of equity capital.

If CAPM correctly describes market behavior, the market's expected return on a common stock is given by the security market line (SML).

$$R_S = R_F + \beta_S(R_M - R_F)$$

However, the expected return on a firm's stock is by definition its cost of equity capital. Therefore, in terms of costs of capital, the SML is

$$k_E = R_F + \beta_S(k_M - R_F)$$

where k_E ($=R_S$) is the firm's cost of equity capital, k_M ($=R_M$), the cost of equity for the market as a whole (or for an average firm in the market), and β_S is the beta of the firm's stock.

Thus, to estimate k_E we need estimates of:

1. R_F, the risk-free rate
2. $k_M = R_M$, the expected return on the market as a whole
3. $\beta_S =$ the level of systematic risk associated with the firm's stock.

The R_F can be estimated as the average or expected rate of return on Treasury bills in the future. In recent years, this rate has averaged about 5% to 8%. A reasonable estimate might be 6% per year.[2]

The expected return on the market in the future (k_M) is more difficult to estimate. A common approach is to assume investors expect returns in the future to be about the same as returns in the past. The average annual return on the market as a whole (or an index such as the S&P 500) over the past 25 to 35 years has been in the range of 10% to 12%. Some would argue that this return needs to be increased to adjust for an expected inflation rate in the future which is higher than that experienced in the past. Adjusting for higher long-term inflation might yield an estimate of k_M in the range of 14% to 16% with a midpoint of 15%.[3]

The stock's beta (β_S) can be estimated by linear regression.[4] Betas are also available from many brokerage firms and investment advisory services. Furthermore, one can get an intuitive estimate simply by observing the stock's reaction to swings in the market as a whole. Finally, a rough guess at beta can be made by noting the tendency of the firm's earnings and cash flows to move in parallel with the earnings and cash flows of other firms in the economy.

Betas for selected firms in three industries are presented in Exhibit 9. Despite relatively high degrees of operating and financial leverage, electric utilities have very stable earnings streams. Swings in the earnings and stock returns of utilities are modest relative to swings in the earnings and returns of most firms in the economy. Therefore, electric utilities have a low level of systematic risk and low betas.

At the other extreme, airline revenues are closely tied to passenger miles, which in turn is very sensitive to changes in economic activity. This basic variability in revenues is amplified by high operating and financial leverage. The

---

[2] A methodology for estimating the Treasury bill rate expected in the future is presented in the Appendix.

[3] A methodology for estimating R_M is presented in the Appendix.

[4] The regression equation estimated is $(R_S - R_F) = a + \beta_S (R_M - R_F) + e$. Given past values of R_F, R_S, and R_M, the regression yields estimates of a (which should be zero) and the stock's beta, β_S.

Exhibit 9

BETAS FOR SELECTED FIRMS IN THREE INDUSTRIES

Electric Utilities		Tire Manufacturers		Airlines	
Company	β	Company	β	Company	β
Commonwealth Edison	.84	Firestone	.96	American Airlines	1.41
Idaho Power	.68	B. F. Goodrich	1.10	Braniff Airways	1.95
Illinois Power	.81	Goodyear	1.06	Eastern Airlines	1.44
Kansas Power & Light	.63	Uniroyal	1.11	National Airlines	1.78
Pacific Power & Light	.81			Northwest Airlines	1.46
Philadelphia Electric	.82			Pan Am World	
Southern California				Airways	1.78
Edison	.83			TWA	1.87
Utah Power & Light	.81			UAL	1.26

result is earnings and returns which show wide variations relative to swings in the earnings and returns of most firms. Thus, airlines have high betas.

Estimates of three firms' cost of equity capital are presented in Exhibit 10.

Exhibit 10

EXAMPLES OF ESTIMATING THE COST OF EQUITY CAPITAL USING CAPM

Assumptions:

$R_F = .06 =$ the risk-free rate
$k_M = R_M = .15 =$ the expected return on the market as a whole

SML:

$$k_E = R_F + \beta(k_M - R_F)$$
$$= .06 + \beta(.15 - .06)$$
$$= .06 + \beta(.09)$$

Kansas Power and Light	*B. F. Goodrich*	*American Airlines*
$\beta_{KPL} = .63$	$\beta_{BFG} = 1.10$	$\beta_{AA} = 1.41$
$k_E = .06 + \beta_{KPL} (.09)$	$k_E = .06 + \beta_{BFG} (.09)$	$k_E = .06 + \beta_{AA} (.09)$
$= .06 + .63(.09)$	$= .06 + 1.10(.09)$	$= .06 + 1.41 (.09)$
$= .1167$	$= .159$	$= .1869$
$k_E = 12\%$	$k_E = 16\%$	$k_E = 19\%$

Plugging the assumed values of R_F, k_M, and β into the SML generates estimates of k_E. As expected, the low-risk utility has an estimated cost of equity below that of the other two firms.

The assumed value of k_M represents a major potential source of error in these estimates. A high and low estimate of k_M can be used to generate a reasonable range of estimates of k_E. The estimation of β also introduces error into the estimate of k_E.

CAPM and risk-adjusted discount rates

Consider the holding company structure outlined in Exhibit 11. The parent company owns all the equity in its subsidiaries, and the holding company's stock is publicly traded. Such a firm can be viewed as a portfolio of assets. Its stock's beta will be a weighted average of the betas associated with the riskiness of

Exhibit 11

CORPORATE STRUCTURE OF A HOLDING COMPANY
WITH THREE SUBSIDIARIES

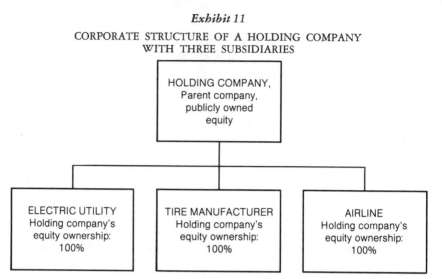

each industry. For example, the parent company's beta might be 1.0. However, the appropriate cost of equity capital for capital budgeting purposes is not the k_E derived from the beta of the holding company's stock. The cost of equity capital used in evaluating investment proposals for any subsidiary should reflect the risk associated with the industry in which that subsidiary operates. Thus, in spite of the fact the holding company's beta of 1.0 yields a k_E of 15%, investments in the utility subsidiary should be evaluated using a lower k_E. The utility industry is less risky than the other subsidiaries. Therefore, the market's expected (or required) return is lower for investments in the utility subsidiary. Since the airline industry is risky, a higher k_E should be used in capital budgeting. Application of the firm's overall k_E in all subsidiaries will result in poor decisions. Good projects in the utility subsidiary will be rejected and poor projects in the airline subsidiary will be accepted. Thus, the cost of equity capital used in a subsidiary's capital budgeting decisions should reflect the risk associated with that subsidiary's line of business. This insures that projects' returns are measured against those returns shareholders would expect to receive on alternative investments of corresponding risk.

How can we estimate the beta appropriate for a subsidiary? An obvious approach is to use the beta on similar, independent firms operating in the same industry. These firms' betas and the resulting estimates of k_E reflect the risk level of the industry and are therefore appropriate for investment decisions concerning a subsidiary operating in the same industry. If there are no independent firms in the industry, an intuitive estimate of beta can be made. This estimate would reflect the degree to which the subsidiary's earnings and cash flows tend to move in tandem with other firms' earnings and cash flows.

Thus, CAPM provides a conceptual framework for determining the k_E appropriate for a subsidiary's capital budgeting decisions.

Conclusion and caveats

Although it has been applied widely in investment management, CAPM's extension to corporate financial management is a relatively recent development. Therefore, its use is not widespread in industry today. Although some of the model's assumptions are clearly unrealistic, empirical tests demonstrate that there is a strong relationship between returns and risk as measured by beta. However, the nature and stability of the relationship predicted by the SML is not fully supported by these tests. Furthermore, application of CAPM requires ad hoc estimates of R_M, the expected return on the market, and R_F, the risk-free rate. The estimates of beta are also subject to error. Thus, it is clear that CAPM should not be relied upon as the complete answer to cost of capital determination.

Nevertheless, tests of the model confirm that it has much to say about the way returns are determined in the securities market. The shortcomings of CAPM appear no more severe than those of alternative methods of estimating the cost of equity capital (e.g., the dividend growth model). The cost of equity capital is inherently difficult to measure. Though imperfect, CAPM represents a new and different approach to this difficult task. Thus, corporate financial managers can use CAPM in conjunction with traditional approaches to develop a realistic, useful estimate of k_E.

READINGS ON CAPM
(in increasing order of difficulty)

Malkiel, Burton G., 1975. *A Random Walk Down Wall Street*, College ed. rev. New York: W. W. Norton.

Lorie, James H., and Hamilton, Mary T., 1973. *The Stock Market: Theories and Evidence*. Homewood, Ill.: Richard D. Irwin, Inc.

Modigliani, Franco, and Pogue, Gerald A., 1974. "An Introduction to Risk and Return I." *Financial Analysts Journal*. March–April.

Modigliani, Franco, and Pogue, Gerald A., 1974. "An Introduction to Risk and Return II," *Financial Analysts Journal*, May–June.

Sharpe, William F., 1970. *Portfolio Theory and Capital Markets*. New York: McGraw-Hill.

Fama, Eugene F., 1976. *Foundations of Finance*. New York: Basic Books.

Mossin, Jan, 1973. *Theory of Financial Markets*. New York: Prentice-Hall.

APPENDIX

THE ESTIMATION OF INPUTS FOR THE SECURITY MARKET LINE

The expected return on the market

One input required in the security market line is the expected return on the stock market as a whole, R_M. Although past realized returns on the Standard and Poor's Index of 500 Stocks (S&P 500) can be observed, the return expected in the future cannot be observed. However, the expected returns on some fixed income securities can be observed. For Treasury bills, long-term government bonds, and high-grade corporate bonds, the expected return is equal to the security's yield to maturity.[1] These observed expected returns can be used to estimate the expected return on the stock market, R_M.

One approach to estimating R_M is based upon the assumption that the nominal return on the market is equal to the real return on the market (exclusive of inflation) plus a premium for inflation necessary to maintain the investor's purchasing power. The R_M could be estimated by adding an estimate of future inflation to the historic average real return on the stock market. There are both theoretical and empirical difficulties with this approach. First, there is some disagreement among economists concerning the underlying relationship between inflation and nominal returns. Secondly, the approach requires a forecast of future inflation, and this forecast should be the market's inflation forecast. The alternative approach described below is more easily applied and is consistent with the inflation premium approach.

The alternative methodology involves two steps. First, the average difference between the actual returns realized in the past on the stock market (i.e., the S&P 500) and the actual past returns on the fixed income security is calculated. Secondly, this historical spread is added to the currently prevailing expected return (i.e., yield to maturity) on the fixed-income security. The second step automatically adjusts for inflation because the prevailing rate on the fixed-income security includes a premium reflecting the market's forecast of future inflation. The approach yields an estimate of the expected return on the market, R_M. The rationale is that stocks are expected to yield a return greater than that on lower risk, fixed-income securities and the additional return on stocks, the spread, is expected to be the same as in the past.

Presented in Exhibit A1 are average historical, realized rates of return for Treasury bills, long-term government bonds, high-grade corporate bonds, and stocks (the S&P 500) calculated by Ibbotson and Sinquefield in a recent study.[2] Historical spreads between the returns on the market and fixed income securities are also listed in Exhibit A1.

The appropriate fixed-income security to be used in estimating R_M depends upon the length of time to maturity. In estimating R_M we are normally focusing

---

[1] This is not strictly true for corporate bonds which include some risk of default. The yield to maturity implicitly assumes all the bond's obligations are met (i.e., no default). With some risk of default (or delay in meeting obligations), the expected return on a bond is less than its yield to maturity. The expected return with default risk incorporates the expectation that there is some chance that the bond's obligations will not be paid on time. For high-grade corporate bonds, this difference might be expected to be sufficiently small to be safely ignored.

[2] See Ibbotson and Sinquefield, "Stocks, Bonds, Bills, and Inflation: Year-by-Year Historical Returns (1926–1974)," *Journal of Business*, January 1976; and Ibbotson and Sinquefield, "Stocks, Bonds, Bills and Inflation: Simulations of the Future (1976–2000)," *Journal of Business*, July 1976.

on a long time horizon. The inflation premium incorporated in a security's nominal return is the rate of inflation expected by the market over the life of the security. Therefore, to estimate the nominal return on stocks which the market expects over the long haul, we need to employ a long-term bond rate which reflects the market's long-term inflation forecast. Hence, Treasury bills are not a good security to use as a benchmark in estimating R_M. The nominal rate of return on a new, one-year Treasury bill includes the market's forecast of inflation for the next year. This short-term inflation forecast may be much higher or lower than the long-term inflation forecast, and it is the long-term inflation forecast that needs to be incorporated in our estimate of R_M. Thus, the use of Treasury bills in this methodology for estimating R_M will not always yield good results. Use of long-term bond rates yields better results.

The methodology employing long-term government bond rates is illustrated in Exhibit A2. To estimate the expected return on the market in late 1976, the average historical spread between the return on stocks and long-term government bonds, 7.5%, is added to the currently prevailing government bond rate of 7.3%. The resulting estimate of R_M is 14.8%, and the analogous estimate using corporate bonds is 15%. The estimated R_M is then used as an input in the security market line in estimating costs of equity capital. These estimates incorporate the market's long-term inflation forecast which is reflected in the currently prevailing bond rate.[3]

It is important to recognize that due to the extreme variability in the return on the market in the past, the return expected in the future is very difficult to measure accurately. Furthermore, a number of simplifying assumptions are implicit in the methodology described above. Nonetheless, the approach is a standard methodology employed in attempting to estimate R_M.

The risk-free rate

In estimating a stock's expected return, we are typically seeking a cost of equity to be applied to cash flows projected for many years in the future. If this is the case, use of the currently prevailing Treasury bill rate in the security market line may not yield good results. The reason is the same as described above. The currently prevailing Treasury bill rate reflects the market's short-term inflation forecast while we seek a cost of equity incorporating a long-term inflation forecast. One approach to correcting for short-term fluctuations in the Treasury bill rate (and in the inflation rate) is to estimate the Treasury bill rate expected to prevail on average in the future. This estimated future Treasury bill rate is then used as the risk-free rate in the security market line in estimating costs of equity capital.

The future expected Treasury bill rate can be estimated by a methodology

---

[3] The market's long-term inflation forecast can be estimated as the currently prevailing bond rate minus the historical real return on the bond. Thus, for long-term government bonds, the inflation forecast is 7.5% − 1.3% = 6.2%. An equivalent way of estimating R_M is to add this inflation forecast to the historic real return on stocks. This approach also results in an estimated R_M of about 15%.

similar to that employed above. The approach involves subtracting the average historical spread between the long-term government bond return and the Treasury bill return from the currently prevailing long-term government bond rate. The resulting estimated risk-free rate incorporates the long-term inflation forecast inherent in the long-term government bond rate rather than the short-term inflation forecast reflected in the currently prevailing Treasury bill rate.[4] This methodology is illustrated in Exhibit A3. In the example, the currently prevailing Treasury bill rate may be temporarily very high or low reflecting short-term inflation forecasts. The currently prevailing long-term government bond rate reflects the long-term inflation forecast. Subtracting the historic government bond Treasury bill spread from the prevailing long-term government bond rate yields an estimate of the Treasury bill rate which reflects the market's long-term inflation forecast. Using this estimated risk-free rate in the security market line yields a cost of equity capital applicable to cash flows projected over a long time horizon.

---

[4] It should be noted that there is an alternative methodology which may yield more precise estimates of future Treasury bill rates. This alternative approach consists of estimating the future Treasury bill rates implicit in the government securities yield curve. Use of these future estimated risk-free rates in the security market line yields different estimates for the cost of equity for different future years.

Exhibit A1

HISTORICAL RETURNS AND SPREADS, 1926–1974
(Ibbotson and Sinquefield)

	Average* Real Return	Average* Nominal Return	Average Historical Spread†
Treasury bills..........	.2%	2.3%	8.6%
Long-term government bonds........	1.3%	3.4%	7.5%
Long-term high-grade corporate bonds..........	1.7%	3.7%	7.2%
Common stocks, the S&P 500............	8.6%	10.9%	—

Note: In estimating $R_F = k_E$ = cost of equity capital, the estimates of R_M and R_F are used as inputs in the security market line equation.

* Arithmetic averages.

† The historical spread is defined as the average return on stocks minus the average return on the fixed-income security. For example, the historical spread between stocks and corporate bonds is the average return on corporate bonds, 3.7%, resulting in a spread of 7.2%.

Exhibit A2

EXAMPLE OF ESTIMATING R_M, LATE 1976

	Long-Term Government Bonds	Long-Term High-Grade Corporate Bonds
Historical spread†......	7.5%	7.2%
Currently prevailing rate..............	7.3%	7.8%
Estimated R_M.........	14.8%	15.0%

Exhibit A3

EXAMPLE OF ESTIMATING FUTURE R_F, LATE 1976

Currently prevailing long-term government bond rate...... 7.5%

Less:

Historic spread between the long-term government bond rate and the Treasury bill rate 1.1%

Estimated future R_F............ 6.4%

Currently prevailing Treasury bill rate............ 4.6%

ENZONE PETROLEUM CORPORATION

One of the critical problems confronting management and the board of Enzone Petroleum Corporation in July 1975 was the determination of a minimum acceptable rate of return on new capital investments. While this question had been under discussion within the company for several years, so far the people involved had been unable to agree even on what general concept of a minimum acceptable rate they should adopt. They were about evenly divided between using a single cutoff rate based on the company's overall weighted average cost of capital and a system of multiple cutoff rates said to reflect the risk-profit characteristics of the several businesses or economic sectors in which the company's subsidiaries operated. In early 1975, management was asked by the board to restudy the issue of single versus multiple cutoff rates and to recommend which approach the company should follow in the future. The issue had assumed increased importance as the result of management's decision to extend the use of the cutoff rate to the evaluation of existing operations and investments. It was planned to evaluate divisional managers on the basis of their net profits after the deduction of a charge for capital employed by the division.

Enzone Petroleum was formed in 1924 with the merger of several formerly independent firms operating in the oil refining, pipeline transportation, and industrial chemical fields. Over the following 50 years, the company integrated vertically into exploration and production of crude oil and marketing refined petroleum products and horizontally into plastics, agricultural chemicals, and real-estate development. The company was organized as a holding company with semiautonomous operating subsidiaries working in each of the above areas of activity. However, the need to balance upstream crude production capacity with the requirements of downstream refining and marketing necessitated collaboration and coordination among divisions to ensure optimization of overall systems performance and to dampen overall risk.

Total operating revenues exceeded $6 billion in 1974, and its capital expenditures averaged about $450 million a year in recent years. (See Exhibit 1 for a financial summary of recent operations.) Profitability had lagged that of other companies in the industry—a situation that management hoped to correct by a major expansion of its petrochemical operations. "You're driven in the direction of the most profits, so you go to petrochemicals. Everybody sees that, so the job is to get there first with the most." Management also placed heavy emphasis on reversing the decline in Enzone's domestic crude oil and natural gas reserves and production and on the development of such alternative energy sources as coal, nuclear power, and synthetic fuels.

Although management was unable to decide whether the company should use single or multiple cutoff rates, they had worked tentatively with a single corporate-wide rate for about ten years. The company's basic capital budgeting approach during this period had been to accept all proposed investments with a positive net present value when discounted at the company's estimated weighted average cost of capital.

The cost of capital discount rate used in the above net present value discounting procedure had been fixed at 10% in 1966 as follows: first, an estimate had been made of the expected proportions of future funds sources. Second, costs had been assigned to each of these sources. Third, a weighted average cost of capital had been calculated on the basis of these proportions and costs. Finally, this weighted average had been adjusted upward to reflect the fact that no return at all was earned on a substantial proportion of the company's investments.

1966 COST OF CAPITAL CALCULATION

Source	Estimated Proportions of Future Funds Sources	Estimated Future Aftertax Cost	Weighted Cost
Debt	.25	3%	.0075
Retained earnings	.65	10%	.0650
New equity	.10	10%	.0100
	1.00		8.25%

There was a general consensus in management on the mix of future funds sources. A firm policy had been adopted that funded debt should represent approximately 25% of total capital (defined as funded debt plus book equity) in the belief that an Aa bond rating would assure access to the bond markets. This policy had been reaffirmed in recent years as management contemplated the enormous financing requirements to develop its North Slope Alaskan properties and alternative energy sources such as coal, shale oil deposits, and solar.

Some argument had developed on the cost of retained earnings and new equity. It had been very straightforward to assign an aftertax cost to debt. Stevens, Mitchell, O'Hara—Enzone's investment bankers—had forecast early in 1966 that the company's future debt issues would require a coupon of 6%, assuming continuation of its debt policy and Aa rating. This represented a 3% aftertax cost. The cost of equity had been more difficult to understand conceptually or to estimate. After prolonged debate, it was decided to use the current earnings yield on the stock as the cost of both new equity and retained earnings. Advocates pointed out that no dilution of earnings per share would occur if the company earned at least this return on new equity. With earnings per share estimated at $2.52 in 1966 and a market price of $26, cost of equity had been set at 10%.

Some members of top management had expressed dissatisfaction with Enzone's cutoff rate in recent years for two reasons. First, they questioned the appropriateness in 1975 of the costs assigned in 1966 to each of the sources of finance. Bond issues rated Aa were priced to yield 9% in 1975 and most economists and business leaders spoke alarmingly of a long-term capital shortage. Second, several of Enzone's operating subsidiaries had strongly opposed the use of a single discount rate from the beginning; and the recent proposal to charge profit center managers for the capital employed in their operations had heightened their opposition. These subsidiaries argued that the internal allocation of funds by the parent company among its principal operating subsidiaries should be based upon a system of multiple-target rates of return reflecting the unique risk-profit characteristics of the industry, or economic sector, or country in which each subsidiary operated.

The specific alternative proposed by the supporters of multiple cutoff rates in lieu of a single company-wide rate involved determining several rates, based on the estimated cost of capital inherent in each of the economic sectors or industries in which the company's principal operating subsidiaries worked. Weighted average cost of capital cutoff rates reflecting their specific risk-profit environments would be determined for the company's production-exploration, pipeline transportation, refining, and marketing affiliates in the oil industry, as well as for its plastics, industrial chemicals, agricultural chemicals, and real-estate subsidiaries operating outside the oil industry. For example, cutoff rates of 18%, 13%, 10% and 8%, respectively, were proposed for the production-exploration, chemicals, real-estate, and transportation parts of the business. All the other rates proposed fell within this range. The suggestion was that these multiple cutoff rates determine the minimum acceptable rate of return on proposed capital investments in each of the main operating areas of the company, as well as represent the rate charged to each of the various profit centers for capital employed.

It was proposed that the weighted average cost of capital in each operating sector be developed as follows: first, an estimate would be made of the usual debt and equity proportions of independently financed firms operating in each sector. Several such independents competed against each of the company's affiliates. Second, the costs of debt and equity given these proportions and sectors would be estimated in accordance with the concepts followed by the company in estimating its own costs of capital in the past. Third, these costs and proportions would be combined to determine the weighted average cost of capital, or minimum acceptable rate of return, for net present value discounting purposes in each sector.

These multiple hurdle or discount rates had been calculated for several periods in the past, and it invariably turned out that their weighted average, when weighted according to the company's relative investment in each sector, exceeded the company's actual overall average cost of capital. This differential was attributed to the fact that the sector hurdle rates calculated as described above tended to overlook the risk diversification benefits of many investments undertaken by Enzone Petroleum. As compared to nonintegrated enterprise operating in any given branch, a vertically and horizontally integrated firm such as Enzone Petroleum enjoyed some built-in asset diversification as well as important captive markets between certain of its vertically integrated parts. For example, the risks associated with a refinery investment by an integrated company like Enzone Petroleum were said to be much less than for an identical investment made by an independent. It was proposed that this diversification premium be allocated back and deducted from the multiple subsidiary discount rates as calculated above in proportion to the relationship between the investment in each subsidiary to the company's total assets.

While it had been impossible to appraise accurately the overall impact of changing from single- to multiple-target rates, it could be foreseen that both the company's asset structure and the probable size of its future capital expenditures would be affected. It was anticipated, for example, that up to one third of future capital expenditures might be shifted from one to another operating sector or affiliate with the adoption of multiple hurdle rates. In addition, the company's expected average annual capital budget could easily increase from $600 million to $700 million or more. An annual budget of this magnitude might force reconsideration of the company's traditional debt, common stock, and dividend policies.

As management and the board of Enzone Petroleum began their latest review of the controversy between using single or multiple minimum acceptable cutoff rates, the officers of the operating subsidiaries were asked to restate their positions. Those behind the present single-target rate contended that the stockholders of Enzone Petroleum would expect the company to invest their funds in the highest return projects available. They suggested that without exception, the affiliates backing multiple rates were those that were unable to compete effectively for new funds when measured against the corporate group's actual cost of capital. Furthermore, it was not obvious that the categories suggested by the advocates of multiple rates were very helpful in grouping projects according to their riskiness. For example, recent experience in tankers had been disastrous for many companies, and yet tanker investments would be initiated by the transportation division and would therefore be subjected to an unrealistically low hurdle rate. Against this, the multiple-hurdle rate proponents pointed out again that if the parent company was serious about competing over the long run in industries with such disparate risk-profit characteristics as they faced, it was absolutely essential to relate internal target rates of return to these circumstances. It was against this background that the final choice between single- versus multiple-cutoff rates had to be decided.

Exhibit 1

ENZONE PETROLEUM CORPORATION
FINANCIAL SUMMARY

	1969	1970	1971	1972	1973	1974	Est. 1975
Sales (in millions)	$2,260	$2,473	$2,633	$2,790	$3,346	$6,020	$6,100
Net income (in millions)	193	176	177	162	227	399	292
Earnings per share	3.49	3.11	3.13	2.86	4.00	7.02	5.12
Dividends per share	1.60	1.68	1.68	1.68	1.68	2.12	2.30
Mean market price	60	56	57	53	76	70	36*
Return on book equity	10%	9%	8%	7%	10%	15%	10%
Beta (β)	—	—	—	—	—	—	.90

*Closing price on July 13, 1975

Exhibit 2

ENZONE PETROLEUM CORPORATION
INFORMATION ON U.S. CAPITAL MARKETS

	1966	1967	1968	1969	1970	1971	1972	1973	1974	197!
Yields on newly issued:										
Aa industrials	5.2%	5.6%	6.2%	7.1%	7.9%	7.2%	7.1%	7.4%	8.6%	8.9%
91-day Treasury bills	4.7	5.0	6.2	8.1	4.8	3.7	5.1	7.4	7.1	5.2
Estimate of the total return that investors expect to earn on a broadly diversified portfolio of common stocks	~10%									~13%

FINANCIAL LEVERAGE, THE CAPITAL ASSET PRICING MODEL, AND THE COST OF EQUITY CAPITAL

A stock's expected return, its dividend yield plus expected price appreciation, is related to risk. Risk-averse investors must be compensated with higher expected returns for bearing risk. One source of risk is the financial risk incurred by shareholders in a firm which has debt in its capital structure. The objective of this note is to delineate a methodology for measuring the risk associated with financial leverage and estimating its impact on the cost of equity capital.

Financial leverage and risk

The presence of debt in a firm's capital structure has an impact on the risk borne by its shareholders. In the absence of debt, shareholders are subjected only to basic business or operating risk. This business risk is determined by factors such as the volatility of a firm's sales and its level of operating leverage. As compensation for incurring business risk, investors require a premium in excess of the return they could earn on a riskless security such as a Treasury bill. Thus, in the absence of financial leverage, a stock's expected return can be thought of as the risk-free rate plus a premium for business risk.

The addition of debt to a firm's capital structure increases the risk borne by its shareholders. One source of additional risk is the increased risk of financial distress (e.g., bankruptcy). A second source is the effect of financial leverage on the volatility of shareholders' returns. The fixed obligations associated with debt amplify the variations in a firm's operating cash flows. The result is a more volatile stream of shareholders' returns. For investors to hold the shares of firms with debt in their capital structures, they must be compensated for the additional risk generated by financial leverage. The additional risk premium associated with the presence of debt in a firm's capital structure is the financial risk premium.

Therefore, the expected return on a firm's stock can be thought of as the risk-free rate plus a premium for risk.

$$\text{expected return} = \text{risk-free rate} + \text{risk premium}$$

The risk premium consists of a premium for business risk and a premium for financial risk.

$$\begin{matrix} \text{expected} \\ \text{return} \end{matrix} = \begin{matrix} \text{risk-} \\ \text{free} \\ \text{rate} \end{matrix} + \begin{matrix} \text{business} \\ \text{risk} \\ \text{premium} \end{matrix} + \begin{matrix} \text{financial} \\ \text{risk} \\ \text{premium} \end{matrix}$$

This relation can be expressed in symbols.

$$R_S = R_F + BRP + FRP$$

Thus, the expected return on a firm's stock can be decomposed into three components. These components are (1) the return on a riskless security, R_F, (2) a premium reflecting the firm's basic business (or operating) risk in the absence of financial leverage, BRP, and (3) a premium for the additional risk created by the existence of debt in a firm's capital structure, FRP. This relationship is illustrated graphically in Exhibit 1. The capital asset pricing model

Exhibit 1

THE RELATIONSHIP BETWEEN A FIRM'S FINANCIAL LEVERAGE
AND THE EXPECTED RETURN ON ITS STOCK

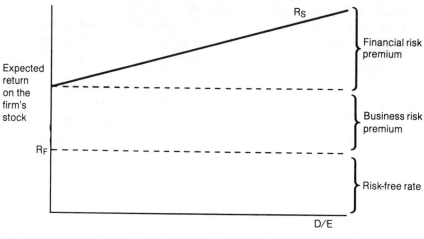

The firm's ratio of debt to equity

(CAPM) provides a methodology for measuring these risk premiums and estimating the impact of financial leverage on expected returns.

The effect of financial leverage on beta

The CAPM is an idealized representation of the manner in which capital markets price securities and thereby determine expected returns.[1] Since CAPM

---

[1] For a more complete description of CAPM see "Diversification, the Capital Asset Pricing Model, and the Cost of Equity Capital," pp. 140–57.

models the risk/expected return trade-off in the capital markets, it can be used to examine the impact of financial leverage on expected returns.

In CAPM, systematic (or market related) risk is the only risk relevant in the pricing of securities and the determination of expected returns. Systematic risk is measured by beta (β). The CAPM provides a measure of a stock's risk premium employing beta which facilitates the estimation of the stock's expected return.

In general,

$$R_S = R_F + \text{risk premium}$$

If CAPM correctly describes market behavior,

$$R_S = R_F + \beta(R_M - R_F)$$

A stock's expected return is equal to the risk-free rate, R_F, plus a premium for risk. With CAPM the risk premium is beta times the return on the market, R_M, minus the risk-free rate. This basic CAPM expression is known as the security market line, the SML.

If a firm has no debt in its capital structure, the stock's risk premium consists solely of a business risk premium. The stock's beta therefore reflects the systematic risk inherent in its basic business operations. With no financial leverage, this beta is its unlevered beta, β^U. This unlevered beta is the beta the stock would have if the firm had no debt in its capital structure.

The presence of debt in a firm's capital structure results in additional risk. The systematic risk inherent in the firm's basic business operations is amplified by financial leverage. With financial leverage, the beta on a firm's stock reflects both business and financial risk. This beta is called a levered beta, β^L. Employing a levered beta in the CAPM expression, the SML measures both the business risk premium and the financial risk premium. The beta published by various investment advisory services reflects *both* the business and the financial risk experienced during the time period over which the beta was determined.

Under the assumptions of CAPM there is a simple relationship between levered and unlevered betas.

$$\beta^L = \beta^U[1 + (1 - t)D/E]$$

Alternatively,

$$\beta^U = \frac{\beta^L}{[1 + (1 - t)D/E]}$$

A stock's levered beta is equal to its unlevered beta multiplied by a factor which includes the firm's ratio of debt to equity, D/E, and its tax rate, t. The tax rate appears in the equations because of the tax deductibility of interest payments. Therefore, a stock's beta (and its expected return) increases as its debt ratio increases. The increase in beta reflects the additional systematic risk generated by financial leverage. The resulting increase in expected return reflects the increase in the financial risk premium required by investors as compensation for additional risk.

These results can be employed to estimate the impact on expected return of a change in a firm's capital structure. The approach is illustrated in Exhibit 2.

Exhibit 2

THE RELATIONSHIP OF EXPECTED RETURN AND FINANCIAL LEVERAGE WITH CAPM

Definitions:

R_S = the stock's expected return.

R_M = the expected return on the market.

t = the firm's tax rate.

D/E = the firm's ratio of debt to equity.

β^L = the (levered) beta on the stock of a firm with $D/E > 0$.

β^U = the (unlevered) beta on the stock of the same firm if $D/E = 0$.

CAPM equations:

Security market line (SML): $R_S = R_F + \beta (R_M - R_F)$

Levering beta: $\beta^L = \beta^U [1 + (1 - t) D/E]$

Unlevering beta: $\beta^U = \dfrac{\beta^L}{[1 + (1 - t) D/E]}$

To estimate the impact of a change in capital structure:

Step 1: Estimate the unlevered beta.
Given: current D/E, current estimated β^L, and t.
Unlever the beta by solving: $\beta^U = \dfrac{\beta^L}{[1 + (1 - t) D/E]}$

Step 2: Estimate the levered beta associated with the new D/E.
Given: β^U from Step 1, the new D/E, and t.
Lever the beta by solving: $\beta^L = \beta^U [1 + (1 - t) D/E]$

The estimated beta for the new debt ratio is then used in the SML equation to estimate the expected return associated with the new D/E.

Assuming the firm currently employs debt in its capital structure, its observed beta will be the levered beta associated with its current ratio of debt to equity. The beta which the stock would have if it changed its debt ratio can be estimated by a two-step procedure. The first step involves unlevering the stock's beta. Given its current debt ratio, D/E, its tax rate, t, and its current beta, β^L, its unlevered beta, β^U, can be calculated from the equation presented above. The second step consists of relevering the stock's beta to reflect a change in capital structure. Given β^U, the tax rate, t, and the new, hypothetical debt ratio, D/E, the other equation presented above can be used to calculate the stock's new leveraged beta, β^L. This levered beta is an estimate of the beta the stock would have if it changed its debt ratio to that employed in the second stage of the procedure. The resulting estimate of beta can then be plugged into the familiar CAPM expression presented earlier, the security market line, to estimate the stock's expected return associated with the proposed debt ratio.

An example of levering and unlevering, General Electric's beta and expected return, is presented in Exhibit 3. A reduction in GE's ratio of debt to equity from approximately .33 to .11 would result in a decrease in its beta from 1.24 to 1.12.

Exhibit 3

SAMPLE ANALYSIS OF THE IMPACT ON EXPECTED RETURN OF FINANCIAL LEVERAGE WITH CAPM, GENERAL ELECTRIC COMPANY

Assumptions:

$R_M = 15\%$; $R_F = 7\%$; $t = .50$

GE's current $D/E = .33$

Current $\beta^L_{GE} = 1.24$

Unlevering GE's beta:

$$\beta^U_{GE} = \frac{\beta^L_{GE}}{[1 + (1 - t)\, D/E]} = \frac{1.24}{[1 + (.50)\,(.33)]} = 1.06$$

CAPM:

Equations:

Levering Beta

$$\beta^L_{GE} = \beta^U_{GE}\,[1 + (1 - t)\, D/E]$$

The Security Market Line (SML)

$$R_S = R_F + \beta_{GE}\,(R_M - R_F)$$

Example:

Proposed $D/E = 1.00$

$$\beta^L_{GE} = 1.06\,[1 + (.50)\,(1.0)] = 1.59$$

$$R_S = 7\% + 1.59\,(15\% - 7\%) = 19.72\%$$

Summary results:

Debt Ratio		GE's Beta	GE's Expected Return, R_S
Currently, D/E =	.33	1.24	16.92%
Unlevered, D/E =	0	1.06	15.48%
Proposed, D/E =	.11	1.12	15.96%
Proposed, D/E =	1.00	1.59	19.72%

The reduction in financial risk would result in a reduction in the financial risk premium required by investors. Therefore the estimated expected return on GE's stock falls from about 17% to roughly 16%. Similarly, an increase in GE's debt ratio would increase its beta and expected return.

The decomposition of expected return into the risk-free rate, business risk premium, and financial risk premium

CAPM can be employed to decompose a stock's expected return into its basic components. This can be accomplished by combining the equation relating levered and unlevered beta and the basic CAPM expression, the SML. The general and CAPM versions of this decomposition are:

$$\begin{matrix} \text{expected} \\ \text{return} \end{matrix} = \begin{matrix} \text{risk-} \\ \text{free} \\ \text{rate} \end{matrix} + \begin{matrix} \text{business} \\ \text{risk} \\ \text{premium} \end{matrix} + \begin{matrix} \text{financial} \\ \text{risk} \\ \text{premium} \end{matrix}$$

$$R_S = R_F + \beta^U \left[R_M - R_F \right] + \beta^U \left(1 - t \right) D/E \left[R_M - R_F \right]$$

Alternatively,

$$R_S = R_F + \beta^U \left[R_M - R_F \right] + \left(\beta^L - \beta^U \right) \left[R_M - R_F \right]$$

Thus, the expected return on a stock can be decomposed into (1) the risk-free rate, (2) a business risk premium present with no debt in the firm's capital structure (i.e., $D/E = 0$), and (3) the additional risk premium created by the existence of debt in the capital structure. With no debt in a firm's capital structure, the expected return on its stock consists only of the first two components. The effects of financial leverage are captured entirely in the third component. With CAPM this third component, the financial risk premium, is simply the increase in its beta, $\beta^L - \beta^U$, caused by financial leverage, multiplied by the risk premium on the market as a whole, $R_M - R_F$. Additional debt amplifies the systematic risk inherent in a firm's basic business operations and drives up the beta and expected return on its stock.

The example presented in Exhibit 4 demonstrates the use of these concepts to decompose the expected returns on two stocks, Procter & Gamble (P&G) and Colgate-Palmolive. As one might suspect, Colgate's business (or operating) risk is substantially greater than Procter & Gamble's. Colgate's unlevered beta is 1.01 versus .8 for P&G, leading to a business risk premium of 8.08% for Colgate compared with 6.4% for P&G. Colgate's basic business risk is amplified by the higher level of debt in its capital structure resulting in a financial risk premium which is roughly 0.5% more than P&G's. Thus, Colgate's overall risk premium, business risk premium plus financial risk premium, is substantially larger than P&G's. Consequently, Colgate's levered beta and the expected return on its stock reflect its higher level of business and financial risk relative to P&G.

An example of the decomposition of the expected return on GE's stock at different debt ratios is presented in Exhibit 5. Note that changing the firm's debt ratio effects only its financial risk premium. As expected, the financial risk pre-

Exhibit 4

SAMPLE DECOMPOSITION OF EXPECTED RETURN, PROCTER & GAMBLE COMPANY AND COLGATE-PALMOLIVE COMPANY

Unlevering betas:

	Procter & Gamble	Colgate-Palmolive
Debt ratio..........	$D/E = .25$	$D/E = .34$
Levered beta........	$\beta^L_{PG} = .90$	$\beta^L_{CP} = 1.18$

To unlever beta..........

$$\beta^U = \frac{\beta^L}{[1 + (1 - t)\, D/E]}$$

Unlevered beta.......... $\beta^U_{PG} = .80$ $\beta^U_{CP} = 1.01$

Expected return calculation and decomposition:

Assumptions: $R_M = 15\%$, $R_F = 7\%$, $t = .50$

Definitions: BRP = business risk premium, FRP = financial risk premium

Procter & Gamble

Expected return decomposition: $R_{PG} = R_F + \beta^U_{PG}\,[R_M - R_F] + (\beta^L_{PG} - \beta^U_{PG})\,[R_M - R_F]$

Substituting assumed values: $R_{PG} = 7\% + .80\,[15\% - 7\%] + (.90 - .80)\,[15\% - 7\%]$

Results.:: $14.20\% = 7\% + \quad 6.40\% + \quad\quad .80\%$

$R_{PG} = R_F + \quad BRP_{PG} + \quad\quad FRP_{PG}$

Colgate-Palmolive

Expected return decomposition: $R_{CP} = R_F + \beta^U_{CP}\,[R_M - R_F] + (\beta^L_{CP} - \beta^U_{CP})\,[R_M - R_F]$

Substituting assumed values: $R_{CP} = 7\% + 1.01\,[15\% - 7\%] + (1.18 - 1.01)\,[15\% - 7\%]$

Results.:: $16.44\% = 7\% + \quad 8.08\% + \quad\quad 1.36\%$

$R_{CP} = R_F + \quad BRP_{CP} + \quad\quad FRP_{CP}$

Exhibit 5

SAMPLE DECOMPOSITION OF EXPECTED RETURN AT
VARIOUS DEBT RATIOS, GENERAL ELECTRIC COMPANY

From Exhibit 3:

Assumptions:			*Debt Ratio*			*GE's Beta*	
R_M	=	15%	Currently, D/E =	.33	β^L_{GE}	=	1.24
R_F	=	7%	Unlevered, D/E =	0	β^U_{GE}	=	1.06
t	=	.50	Proposed, D/E =	.11	β^L_{GE}	=	1.12
			Proposed, D/E =	1.00	β^L_{GE}	=	1.59

Expected return decomposition:

$$R_{GE} = R_F + BRP_{GE} + FRP_{GE}$$
$$R_{GE} = R_F + \beta^U_{GE}[R_M - R_F] + (\beta^L_{GE} - \beta^U_{GE})[R_M - R_F]$$

Example:
Proposed

$$D/E = 1.00 \quad R_{GE} = 7\% + 1.06[15\% - 7\%] + (1.59 - 1.06)[15\% - 7\%]$$
$$19.72\% = 7\% + 8.48\% + 4.24\%$$

Summary results:

Debt Ratio			R_{GE}	=	R_F	+	BRP_{GE}	+	FRP_{GE}
Currently, D/E	=	.33	16.92%	=	7%	+	8.48%	+	1.44%
Unlevered, D/E	=	0	15.48%	=	7%	+	8.48%	+	0%
Proposed, D/E	=	.11	15.96%	=	7%	+	8.48%	+	.48%
Proposed, D/E	=	1.00	19.72%	=	7%	+	8.48%	+	4.24%

mium, the levered beta, and the expected return on GE's stock all increase with additional financial leverage.

Application to corporate finance

The CAPM facilitates the examination of the impact of financial leverage on expected returns. It therefore has an important application to corporate finance. A firm's cost of equity capital, k_E, is the expected (or required) return on the firm's stock. If the firm cannot expect to earn at least k_E on the equity-financed portion of its investments, funds should be returned to its shareholders who can earn k_E on other securities of the same risk level in the financial marketplace. The CAPM can be used by financial managers to obtain an estimate of k_E and to examine the impact on k_E of financial leverage.

A firm's cost of equity capital is by definition the expected return on its stock. Since the basic CAPM expression, the security market line, yields estimates of expected returns, it can also be used to estimate costs of equity capital. Similarly, the CAPM concepts and techniques relating expected returns and financial leverage can be applied in examining the impact of financial leverage on the cost of equity capital. *The results presented earlier can be applied directly simply by recognizing that R_S, a stock's expected return, is equal to k_E, its cost of equity capital.*

To apply these concepts requires as inputs the risk-free rate, R_F, the expected return on the market as a whole, R_M, the stock's beta, its tax rate, t, and its ratio of debt to equity, D/E. As with any CAPM application, R_F can be estimated as the return on Treasury bills and R_M as the expected return on the

Standard and Poor's Index of 500 Stocks. Betas can be estimated by linear regression and are also published by various investment advisory services. The firm's tax rate, t, can be estimated easily from its financial statements. In estimating the debt ratio, the CAPM approach assumes that market values of debt and equity are employed. By definition, market values reflect the current values of debt and equity. In contrast, book values represent values prevailing in the past when the securities were issued. In addition, betas are themselves market-determined variables. Nevertheless, for convenience, book value debt ratios are often used in practice.

To examine the relationship between the cost of equity capital and financial leverage, the estimated inputs are simply plugged into the equations presented earlier. The resulting expected returns are by definition costs of equity capital. The approach demonstrates that a firm's cost of equity is positively related to the level of debt in its capital structure, and the increment to the cost of equity generated by financial leverage can be estimated in the manner described earlier.

Conclusion

The capital asset pricing model is based upon extremely simple and clearly unrealistic assumptions. Empirical studies demonstrate that, consistent with CAPM, there is a strong relationship between stock returns and risk as measured by beta. Studies also generally support the relationship between returns and financial leverage posited by CAPM. However, these studies are by no means conclusive in establishing the validity of CAPM. The application of CAPM is also limited by problems associated with the model's inputs. Use of the model requires ad hoc estimates of several inputs and the betas employed are subject to substantial estimation errors.

Thus, CAPM should not be viewed as a wholly reliable method of estimating the cost of equity and examining the impact of financial leverage. However, in view of the deficiencies in alternative approaches, CAPM represents a useful tool which managers may apply to an inherently difficult area of corporate finance. Finally, an alternative approach relating expected returns and financial leverage is outlined briefly in the Appendix.

APPENDIX

The CAPM methodology described in the text of this note incorporates the implicit assumption that the firm's cost of debt is equal to the risk-free rate. An alternative approach which relaxes this restrictive assumption is presented in this appendix. This more general approach examines the relationship between the cost of equity capital and financial leverage. This relationship expressed in cost of equity terms is:

$$k_E^L = k_E^U + [k_E^U - k_D] (1 - t) D/E$$

where k_E^L is the levered cost of equity capital, k_E^U is the unlevered cost of equity, k_D is the cost of debt, t is the firm's tax rate, and D/E its ratio of debt to equity. In this equation k_E^U is the cost of equity if the firm had no debt in its capital structure. Therefore, k_E^U reflects the risk-free rate and a premium for business risk. The second term on the right-hand side of the equation captures the impact of financial leverage—the financial risk premium. With additional debt, the increase in the levered cost of equity is related to the difference between the unlevered cost of equity and the cost of debt. Solving for k_E^U, the equation becomes:

$$k_E^U = \frac{k_E^L + k_D\,(1-t)\,D/E}{[1 + (1-t)\,D/E]}$$

Thus, given estimates of k_E^L, k_D, t, and D/E, the firm's unlevered cost of equity, k_E^U, can be calculated. The value of k_D will change with the degree of leverage in the firm's capital structure. Thus, the schedule of debt cost versus leverage must be known in order to estimate a new equity capital cost at a new debt ratio. To estimate the levered cost of equity associated with some new debt ratio, k_E^U, t, the new k_D, and the proposed D/E can be used as inputs in the previous equation.

Therefore, this alternative approach can be employed in a manner analogous to that described in the text of this note. The equations can be manipulated to yield estimates of the cost of equity associated with various debt ratios and to decompose the cost of equity into its components. The advantage of this approach is that it is not tied exclusively to the assumptions of CAPM. Specifically, it avoids the assumption that the firm's cost of debt is the risk-free rate. The advantage of the CAPM approach is the simple methodology it provides for levering and unlevering betas.

CENTRAL EXPRESS CORPORATION

^^^

In May, 1973, Mr. Thorp, treasurer of Central Express Corporation, was considering the relative advantages and disadvantages of several alternative methods of financing Central's acquisition of Midland Freight, Incorporated. At a recent meeting of the board of directors, there had been substantial disagreement as to the best method of financing the acquisition. After the meeting Mr. Thorp had been asked by Mr. Evans, president of Central, to assess the arguments presented by the various directors, and to outline a position to be taken by the management at the June directors meeting.

Central Express was a regulated general commodities motor carrier whose routes ran the length of the Pacific Coast, from Oregon and California to the industrial Midwest, and from Chicago to several Texas points. Founded in 1932 by three brothers, the firm had experienced little growth until the early 1960's. At that point Mr. Evans had joined the firm as president after many years as an executive of a major eastern carrier. Mr. Evans had first concentrated his efforts on expanding Central's revenues on existing routes through an intensive marketing effort and a renewed emphasis on improving service. In 1967, utilizing the proceeds of Central's initial public offering of common stock, Mr. Evans had begun a program designed to reduce operating costs through a combination of extensive computerization of operations and improvement in terminal facilities. As a result of these changes, Central had become a large and profitable concern, widely respected in the industry for its aggressive management.

In 1973, Mr. Evans and the directors of the firm had come to the conclusion that the key to continued expansion in revenues and income was a policy of selected acquisitions. After a study of potential candidates for acquisition, negotiations had begun with Midland Freight, Inc., a common carrier serving Michigan and Indiana from Chicago. The owners of Midland had agreed to sell the firm to Central for $10,000,000 in cash. Mr. Evans felt that Midland was an outstanding acquisition in that it would expand Central's route system and seemed well suited for the type of marketing and cost reduction programs that had fostered Central's growth. The board had unanimously approved the merger.

Central's lawyers felt that no difficulty would be encountered in gaining the approval of the Interstate Commerce Commission for the merger, and the closing date for the acquisition was set for October 1, 1973. Mr. Evans realized that the funds for the Midland acquisition would have to be raised from outside sources. Given that Midland would add $1,680,000 in earnings before interest and taxes (EBIT) to Central on an annual basis, he felt that such external financing would not be difficult to obtain.

The management had followed a consistent policy of avoiding long-term debt. The company had met its needs through use of retained earnings supplemented with the proceeds of the 1967 stock offering and infrequent short-term bank loans. As of 1973, Central's capitalization consisted of common stock and surplus with no fixed debt of any kind. The common stock was held in large amounts by the management. While the stock was widely distributed, there was no real dominant interest other than management. The shares were transferred infrequently and were traded over the counter. Discussions with an investment banker led Mr. Thorp to believe that, barring a major market decline, common stock could be sold to the public at $26.50 a share. After underwriting fees and expenses, the net proceeds to the company would be $25.00 a share. Thus, if common stock was used, the acquisition would require issuance of 400,000 shares.

For the past few years, Mr. Thorp and Mr. Evans had been disappointed in the market performance of Central common stock (Exhibit 1). Thus, they had decided to reconsider the firm's policy of avoiding long-term debt. It was felt that such a change might be justified by the anticipated stability of Central's future earnings. Mr. Thorp had determined that the firm could sell $10,000,000 in bonds to a California insurance company. The interest rate on these bonds would be 8% and they would mature in 15 years. An annual sinking fund of $500,000 would be required, leaving $2,500,000 outstanding at maturity. Although the bond terms would create a sizable need for cash, Mr. Thorp felt that they were the best that could be obtained.

In addition, Mr. Thorp had calculated that, given the tax deductibility of bond interest and Central's current effective tax rate of 50%, the 8% rate was the equivalent of 4% on an after-tax basis. In contrast, he felt that the stock at $25 a share and a dividend of $2.00 a share would cost Central 8%. This cost comparison made the debt alternative seem desirable to Mr. Thorp.

At the May directors meeting, the Midland acquisition received enthusiastic approval. Mr. Thorp then decided to sound out the board as to their sentiments regarding the possibility of financing the acquisition with long-term debt, rather than with common stock. He presented the cost calculations given above. To Mr. Thorp's concern, an acrimonious debate broke out among all the directors concerning financing policy.

Mr. Thorp was immediately questioned as to the cost of the debt issue since his figures did not include the annual payment to the sinking fund. One director argued that this represented 8% of the average size of the bond issue over its 15-year life, and he felt that the stock issue had a smaller cost than the bonds. In addition, he emphasized the cash outlay called for in the bond alternative and the $2,500,000 maturity, especially in view of Central's already existing lease commitments. He felt that the use of debt thus added risks to the company, making the common stock more speculative and causing greater variation in market price.

Another director argued for the issuance of common stock because "simple arithmetic" showed that Central would net 8.4% or $840,000 a year after taxes from the acquisition. Yet, if an additional 400,000 shares of common stock were sold, the dividend requirements, at the current rate of $2.00 a share, would be only $800,000 a year. Since management was not considering raising the dividend rate, he could not see how the sale of the common stock would hurt the interests of present stockholders. Further, if there were any immediate sacrifice by existing shareholders, he argued that it would be overcome as expansion of the firm continued. Under these circumstances, he argued that the bond issue should be rejected, given the cash demands it would place on the firm.

On the other hand, one director became very agitated in arguing that the stock was a "steal" at $26.50 a share. He pointed out that Central's policy of retaining earnings had built the book value of the firm to $45.00 a share as of December, 1972. In addition, he felt that the true value of the company was understated since book value of Central's assets was considerably below current replacement cost. This director was also worried by the substantial dilution of management's voting control of Central that was implicit in the 400,000 share offering. Thus, he concluded that the sale of common stock at this time would be a "gift" to new shareholders of the substantial value held by current stockholders.

Two directors agreed that sale of stock would dilute the stock's value, but they measured this dilution in terms of earnings per share instead of book or replacement value. These directors anticipated that postacquisition earnings would equal $6,800,000 before interest and taxes. If common stock was sold, earnings per share would be diluted to $2.62. In contrast, the directors argued that the sole use of debt would increase earnings per share to $3.33. The two directors felt that it was not important that the sinking fund equaled $0.56 a share each year.

Finally, a director spoke about some personal observations he had made about financing in the trucking industry. First, he noted that Central was one of the few major common carriers that had no long-term debt in their capital structures, while Central's price-earnings ratio was among the lowest in the industry. Second, he wondered whether Mr. Thorp had given consideration to the possibility of issuing preferred stock. This director had determined that Central could sell 100,000 shares of preferred stock bearing a dividend rate of $8.25 and a par value of $100. The director criticized Mr. Thorp for failing to deal with the issues he had raised.

This debate had caused the directors meeting to run over its scheduled conclusion and no signs of agreement had developed. Mr. Thorp asked that the discussion of financing alternatives be held over until the June meeting to allow him time to prepare additional material. Now, as the date for the meeting approached, Mr. Thorp once again turned his attention to the issues raised at the board meeting. He realized that a considerable number of issues raised by the directors needed to be considered, and he had designed a chart to aid in the comparison of the debt and stock alternatives (shown as Exhibit 3).

Exhibit 1

CENTRAL EXPRESS CORPORATION

SELECTED INCOME AND DIVIDEND DATA, 1967–73

(In thousands except per share data)

	Operating Revenue	Income before Taxes	Income after Taxes	Income per Share	Dividends per Share	Market Prices per Share of Common Stock	
						High	Low
1967	$126,000	$2,898	$1,449	$1.61	$1.00	19¼	11¼
1968	138,750	3,330	1,665	1.85	1.20	24	14¾
1969	147,461	3,834	1,917	2.13	1.20	25½	15
1970	171,692	4,464	2,232	2.48	1.20	27¼	17⅜
1971	185,333	5,004	2,502	2.78	2.00	38¾	22¼
1972	205,714	5,760	2,880	3.20	2.00	34	25½
1973 Est.*	216,000	5,120	2,560	2.85	2.00†	28¾‡	23½‡

* Excluding the proposed acquisition and its financing.
† Annual rate.
‡ To May 1 (May 1 prices were 28⅜-28⅛).

Exhibit 2

CENTRAL EXPRESS CORPORATION

SUMMARY BALANCE SHEET AS OF DECEMBER 31, 1972

(In thousands)

ASSETS

Cash	$ 3,800	
Accounts receivable	7,690	
Inventory	1,620	
Prepaid expenses	1,820	
Current assets		$14,930
Carrier operating property (cost)	47,330	
Less: Accumulated depreciation	17,820	
Net carrier operating property		29,510
Other assets		6,180
Total assets		$50,620

LIABILITIES AND STOCKHOLDERS' EQUITY

Accounts payable	$ 5,060	
Miscellaneous payables and accruals	4,050	
Taxes payable	1,010	
Current liabilities		$10,120
Common stock ($1 par)	900	
Paid-in surplus	8,000	
Retained earnings	31,600	
Stockholders' equity		40,500
Total liabilities and stockholders' equity		$50,620

Exhibit 3

CENTRAL EXPRESS CORPORATION

ANALYSIS OF FINANCIAL ALTERNATIVES

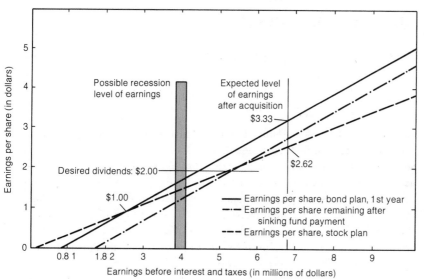

CALCULATION OF POINTS TO DETERMINE LINES

(In thousands except per share data)

	Bonds	Stock	Bonds	Stock
EBIT	$2,600	$2,600	$6,800	$6,800
Interest, 1st year	800	...	800	...
Taxable earnings	1,800	2,600	6,000	6,800
Tax at 50%	900	1,300	3,000	3,400
After-tax earnings	900	1,300	3,000	3,400
Earnings per share				
÷ 900,000	$ 1.00		$ 3.33	
÷ 1,300,000		$ 1.00		$ 2.62
Annual sinking fund	500	...	500	...

Note: The effects of leverage and dilution are indicated by the differing slopes of the lines, and can be expressed:

"For each million change of EBIT, the bond plan brings a change in earnings per share which is $0.17 greater than the stock plan. Leverage is favorable from EBIT of $2.6 million upward."

CROWN CORPORATION

^^

In February, 1969, Mr. Walter Bennett, treasurer of Crown Corporation, was considering several financing alternatives. Crown's decision to integrate backwards into the production of primary aluminum ingot had resulted in very heavy capital expenditures. Its need for funds for working capital and for completion of a large aluminum plant now outstripped the company's internal cash generation and it would be necessary to raise $30 million within the next six months to cover capital needs for 1969. Mr. Bennett hoped to develop a financing program that would meet the immediate and the longer-term needs without jeopardizing Crown's seventy-cent dividend rate.

Company description

A series of acquisitions and divestitures during the 1960's had totally transformed Crown Corporation from a mining company into a manufacturer of superalloy castings for aircraft and industrial uses and aluminum products for the building, packaging, and aircraft industries. Sales were evenly divided between castings and aluminum products.

Crown's castings were for the most part designed for operation in the "hot part" of the gas turbine engine. The company worked from designs prepared chiefly by aircraft engine manufacturers. These manufacturers, in their endeavor to obtain greater thrust, designed parts that would function at engine operating temperatures ranging to 2,150 degrees Fahrenheit. The high temperatures required the use of precision castings for blades and vanes. The techniques and know-how involved in casting operations were important and the commercial success of such an operation was in large measure dependent upon achieving a low ratio of rejects. Crown's constant emphasis on quality and technical excellence had established a high level of confidence among its customers. For adherence to a rigid standard of performance and quality, it had been selected to participate in the majority of United States jet engine programs in the past ten years. (Exhibit 1 provides information on jet engine production in the United States.)

The other half of Crown's sales comprised aluminum products, including a broad product line for the building and construction industry. Major efforts had been made to increase the company's captive source of primary aluminum ingot for consumption by its fabricating operations. To assure a steady and

178

economical source, Crown had become a producer of primary aluminum in 1966 through participation with American Metal Climax, Inc. in a project known as Intalco. Crown's share of Intalco's output was 130 million pounds, roughly 81% of its total need.

In 1967 the decision was made to build a second aluminum ingot plant, named Eastalco, at a cost of $50 million. Eastalco was expected to start operations in mid-1970, providing Crown with additional primary aluminum capacity of 85 million pounds a year and increased net income of $3–4 million. A planned addition of 85 million pounds in 1972 would raise Eastalco's capacity to 170 million pounds and would meet the company's objective to be a fully-integrated producer.

	Actual (Millions of Pounds)				Estimates (Millions of Pounds)		
	1965	1966	1967	1968	1969	1970	1973
Consumption of primary aluminum by Crown's fabricating divisions	94	107	116	135	160	185	290
Production of primary aluminum:							
at Intalco	0	16	69	88	130	130	130
at Eastalco	0	0	0	0	0	85	170
Purchases (sales) of primary aluminum by Crown	94	91	47	47	30	(30)	(10)

Company performance[1]

Crown's sales had risen sharply from $60 million in 1958 to $230 million in 1968 on the strength of 23 acquisitions, strong internal growth, and a firming of aluminum prices. The company's earnings had been considerably more erratic, however, with the volatility the result largely of instability in its aluminum business. After reaching a peak of $1.13 in 1959, earnings per share fell to $0.34 in 1963 as overcapacity developed in the aluminum business and prices of fabricated products were eroded. (Crown's operating results are shown in Exhibit 2.) The "great growth potential" of aluminum had encouraged major capacity additions by established producers and entry by new producers during the 1950's. Domestic industry capacity rose by 79% between 1954 and 1960. American producers were also faced with a tremendous buildup in capacity elsewhere in the world. After a decade of generally rising prices, excess capacity began to take its toll in 1958. In April of that year, the producer price for American ingot was lowered from 26 to 24 cents a pound to match a similar reduction initiated by Canadian firms in the world market. By December, 1962, the quotation had dropped to 22.5 cents a pound.

In the fabricated products market, where the relative ease of entry had

---

[1] The history of the aluminum industry is drawn in large part from *Aluminum: Past and Future*, by Yvonne Levy (San Francisco: Federal Reserve Bank of San Francisco, 1971).

brought in many small and medium-sized independent concerns, competition for the available business was even keener and price erosion more severe. List prices of fabricated products dropped on the average about 20% between late 1961 and late 1963. (Exhibit 3 provides data on aluminum shipments and prices.) The decline in actual market prices undoubtedly was even sharper because of a method of discounting—called "commodity pricing"—that was undertaken in order to penetrate new markets. This method, most prevalent in sheet, strip, coil, and plate products, involved selling a product for a specific application at a price lower than the published price. The seller then attempted to confine the lower price to specific product areas so as not to reduce revenues. However, in the late 1950's, the whole price structure came tumbling down and profits came tumbling after. Profits of the three major aluminum companies collapsed from $175 million in 1956 to a low of $88 million in 1960.

Demand–supply conditions in the industry finally improved in the early 1960's and with the improvement came sharply higher earnings for Crown and other aluminum producers. Over the 1961–66 period, industry shipments of aluminum increased by 14% annually. Despite increases in supply, the price of ingot went up four times between October, 1963 and November, 1964, from a low of 22.5 cents a pound to 24.5 cents a pound. But price weakness continued at the fabricating level during this period. The hundreds of small fabricators lowered prices to obtain business for their idle machinery, while consumers increasingly came to disregard published mill prices.

Prices of fabricated products remained weak until 1965, when strike-anticipation hedge buying bolstered demand and pushed up operating rates. Producers raised prices several times early in the year, and then again after a new three-year labor contract was signed in June. For the next three years shipments of aluminum products continued to rise 8–10% annually and prices firmed further. Shortly after a new three-year labor contract was signed in 1968, producers raised the price of ingot by 4%, to 26 cents a pound, and the price of fabricated products by a comparable amount. After a brief period of discounting in the wake of the labor settlement, the new list prices apparently took hold. In January, 1969, producers raised the price of ingot from 26 to 27 cents a pound and prices on a wide range of mill products by an average of 5%, and further price increases were anticipated.

The strong price situation improved industry profitability dramatically. Profits of the three major aluminum firms rebounded from the 1960 low of $88 million to $230 million in 1966. (See Exhibit 4.) Crown's record was no less dramatic. Rising from a low of $0.34 a share in 1963, Crown's earnings reached $2.03 a share in 1967. Its stock, which had sold at less than $5 a share in 1963, reached a high of $51 in mid 1968 on the strength of record earnings and an increased dividend rate.

Surpluses of the seventies?

The improved industry price structure in the late 1960's encouraged aluminum producers to move forward to meet the demands and the opportunities of the 1970's. Throughout the world, producers began to build new smelters and enlarge older ones. In the United States the expansion in capacity contemplated over the next three years seemed moderate in terms of past trends in demand. American producers were scheduled to boost their primary production potential from almost 4.2 million tons in 1970 to 5 million tons by 1973, or at a 6.4% annual rate. This rate of expansion, although substantial, was below the 10% rate of growth of domestic aluminum consumption during the 1960's.

In reducing their rate of expansion, U.S. producers recognized that they were facing the strongest counterattack from other materials in their history. Aluminum's success in penetrating the territory staked out by other metals had been phenomenal. Shipments of aluminum ingot and mill products grew at more than twice the rate of durable goods output and construction activity over the 1960's. The industry was successful, through research and development and aggressive marketing techniques, in creating new uses for the metal and in displacing traditional materials in older applications.

The steel industry, the giant of the metal field with 1968 ingot production of 130 million tons as against aluminum's 3 million tons, had initiated a strong fight to ward off the lightweight metal's further advances. In particular, steel was fighting hard to protect its position in the $3.5 billion can market and in the rapid transit market, which could evolve into a $10 billion outlet over the 1970's. The copper industry was also fighting to protect its markets and the plastics industry was challenging aluminum in each of aluminum's principal markets—construction, transportation, and packaging.

However, the most effective dampening influence on the domestic industry was the huge increase in aluminum capacity abroad. Plans in 1969 called for capacity elsewhere in the non-Communist world to rise at well over double the U.S. rate between 1970 and 1973, as major European and Asian nations built up their own production in an effort to reduce their dependence on imports. With almost 4.4 million tons of new capacity—3.5 million tons overseas plus 0.9 million tons in the United States—scheduled to come on stream in the 1970–73 period, world capacity could rise from about 9.4 million to 13.7 million tons, or at a 14% annual rate.

This expansion in capacity would exceed the anticipated growth in demand, since most industry analysts expected that world aluminum consumption would not exceed the 9% rate of growth registered during the 1960–68 period. If all the capacity programmed was brought in on schedule, growth in consumption at the 9% level over the next several years could result in as much as 2 million tons of excess capacity by 1973, representing about 15% of the industry's total production capability.

Before jumping to the conclusion that the industry's price structure was in danger of weakening, however, Mr. Bennett realized that the major aluminum producers might stretch out their expansion projects over a longer period, especially where expansion was scheduled through incremental additions to existing plants. Projects not yet started might be postponed or canceled.

Furthermore, he did not underestimate the ability of the industry to boost consumption above anticipated levels by imaginative research and development and marketing programs.

Crown's expected growth

Mr. Bennett expected that Crown's sales would increase at 6–8% annually, exclusive of acquisitions, over the foreseeable future. No growth was forecast through 1974 in the precision castings business as sharp reductions in defense procurement needs would offset the 15% per year increase in commercial sales. However, sales of aluminum products were expected to rise by 15–20% annually as the company broadened its penetration of major aluminum consuming markets. This sales growth would necessitate heavy spending on aluminum reduction facilities and fabricating capacity. Total capital expenditures, including the Eastalco project, were forecast at $39 million in 1969, $32 million in 1970, $7 million in 1971, and $50 million in 1972. The heavy capital spending would require that Crown raise $30 million in 1969, $22 million in 1970, and $30 million in 1972.

Financing alternatives

Several alternatives were open to Crown to meet its financing needs in 1969. (See the balance sheets for 1965–68 shown in Exhibit 5.) The company's investment bankers believed that a $30 million common stock issue was possible and pointed to the future financing flexibility afforded by the use of equity financing. On the other hand, the dilution of earnings per share that would result from sale of additional stock was a matter of concern to Mr. Bennett. Crown stock had fallen from $51 a share in May, 1968 to a level of $30 a share as investors reacted to disappointing earnings in 1968. (Comparative industry stock price data are provided in Exhibit 6.) Further near-term price weakness seemed likely as earnings per share remained depressed as Crown absorbed heavy start-up costs for the production of the main landing gear for the McDonnell Douglas DC–10 in 1969. Under these conditions, announcement of a large equity issue would drive the stock price down to the low twenties, at which price it would be necessary to sell 1.4 million shares to raise the $30 million net to the company. Mr. Bennett wondered whether equity financing should be deferred until the company resumed its pattern of earnings gains.

As an alternative to equity financing, a consortium of commercial banks had agreed to lend the company up to $30 million at $7\frac{1}{4}$% interest. The term loan would be repayable at an annual rate of $5 million beginning in 1970 and ending in 1975. Under the provisions of the loan agreement, net working capital must exceed $55 million, dividend payments were restricted to earnings accumulated after the date of the loan agreement, and additional funded debt was limited to $20 million.

It would also be possible to place a $30 million subordinated convertible debenture issue privately with the Northern Life Insurance Company. The debentures would carry a coupon of 6% with annual debt retirement of $2 million in years six through twenty. The issue would not be callable for ten years, except at par for mandatory debt retirement, and would be convertible into common stock at $31.50.

Mr. Bennett was interested in the debt alternatives. Although the company's use of debt had increased sharply and coverage ratios had narrowed, its coverage of interest costs was still considered adequate. On the other hand, the flexibility afforded by use of equity financing could be valuable in future years.

Exhibit 1

CROWN CORPORATION

AIRCRAFT ENGINE PRODUCTION

(Number of engines)

		Military			Civil		
Year	*Total*	*Total Military*	*Recip-rocal*	*Jet*	*Total Civil*	*Recip-rocal*	*Jet*
1946..............	43,407	2,585	1,680	905	40,822	40,822	...
1947..............	20,912	4,561	2,683	1,878	16,351	16,351	...
1948..............	14,027	4,988	2,495	2,493	9,039	9,039	...
1949..............	11,972	7,990	2,981	5,009	3,982	3,982	...
1950..............	13,675	9,361	3,122	6,239	4,314	4,314	...
1951..............	20,867	16,287	6,471	9,816	4,580	4,580	...
1952..............	31,041	25,659	8,731	16,928	5,382	5,382	...
1953..............	40,263	33,616	13,365	20,251	6,647	6,647	...
1954..............	26,959	21,440	7,868	13,572	5,519	5,519	...
1955..............	21,108	13,469	3,875	9,594	7,639	7,639	...
1956..............	21,348	9,849	2,663	7,186	11,499	11,499	...
1957..............	21,984	11,087	2,429	8,658	10,897	10,859	38
1958..............	18,869	8,121	1,452	6,669	10,748	10,233	515
1959..............	17,162	4,626	661	3,965	12,536	11,152	1,384
1960..............	16,189	3,673	756	2,917	12,516	10,891	1,625
1961..............	15,832	5,172	417	4,755	10,660	9,669	991
1962..............	15,919	5,441	241	5,200	10,478	9,921	557
1963..............	17,185	5,390	155	5,235	11,795	11,322	473
1964..............	19,585	5,380	175	5,205	14,205	13,346	859
1965..............	23,378	5,191	92	5,099	18,187	17,018	1,169
1966..............	30,810	7,548	45	7,503	23,262	21,324	1,938
1967..............	28,858	8,046	...	8,046	20,812	18,324	2,488
1968..............	29,761	8,542	...	8,542	21,219	17,806	3,413

Source: *Aerospace Facts and Figures 1973/1974* (New York: Aerospace Industries Association of America, Inc., 1973), p. 48.

*

Exhibit 2

CROWN CORPORATION

SELECTED OPERATING DATA, 1963–68

(In millions except per share data)

	1962	1963	1964	1965	1966	1967	1968
Net sales	$ 110	$ 122	$ 122	$ 141	$ 176	$ 213	$ 230
Operating profit*	8.3	4.6	5.5	9.1	18.5	27.8	28.5
Other income (expense)†	(0.4)	(0.6)	(0.3)	(0.8)	(0.1)	(0.7)	(1.0)
Income before taxes	$ 7.9	$ 4.0	$ 5.2	$ 8.3	$18.4	$27.1	$27.5
Federal income taxes	3.7	1.5	2.3	3.6	7.6	12.3	13.8
Net income	$ 4.2	$ 2.5	$ 2.9	$ 4.7	$10.8	$14.8	$13.6

Per Share Data

Earnings	$0.57	$0.34	$0.42	$0.66	$1.50	$2.03	$1.87
Dividends	0	0.20	0.20	0.23	0.40	0.60	0.70
Market price:							
High	9	7	7	11	27	51	51
Low	5	5	5	6	10	22	32
Price-earnings ratio:							
High	16	21	17	17	18	25	27
Low	9	15	12	9	7	11	17

* After deduction of depreciation expense ($5 million in 1968).
† Other income and other expenses including interest expense are offset against each other.

Exhibit 3

CROWN CORPORATION

STATISTICS ON INDUSTRY SHIPMENTS AND PRICES:
TOTAL ALUMINUM INDUSTRY SHIPMENTS, 1942–69
(Millions of pounds, net shipments)

Year	Total	Ingot	Domestic Mill Products	Imported Mill Products
1942	1,452.7	507.4	933.6	11.7
1943	2,217.2	724.6	1,492.4	0.2
1944	2,566.4	952.0	1,613.0	1.4
1945	1,886.4	549.2	1,329.8	7.4
1946	1,672.4	529.2	1,140.8	2.4
1947	2,040.1	631.8	1,408.2	0.1
1948	2,282.0	629.8	1,640.2	12.0
1949	1,654.1	479.9	1,158.1	16.1
1950	2,460.6	724.6	1,713.4	22.6
1951	2,506.6	709.8	1,756.2	40.6
1952	2,694.5	811.2	1,850.4	32.9
1953	3,276.8	982.9	2,228.2	65.7
1954	3,036.0	920.2	2,086.6	29.2
1955	4,035.1	1,205.4	2,791.8	37.9
1956	4,154.6	1,223.5	2,885.8	45.3
1957	3,880.1	1,161.6	2,677.6	40.9
1958	3,631.2	974.0	2,597.1	60.1
1959	5,061.0	1,575.0	3,386.1	100.1
1960	4,732.5	1,608.6	3,049.1	74.8
1961	4,970.1	1,536.6	3,345.1	88.4
1962	5,772.5	1,858.6	3,811.3	102.7
1963	6,377.0	2,032.6	4,257.2	87.2
1964	7,171.3	2,228.6	4,834.9	107.8
1965	8,150.2	2,337.3	5,679.4	133.5
1966	9,031.6	2,340.1	6,457.5	234.1
1967	8,946.4	2,486.4	6,350.6	109.5
1968	9,977.4	2,694.8	7,167.0	115.6
1969f	10,825.0	3,050.0	7,660.0	115.0

Notes: f = forecast.
Detail may not add to totals due to rounding.
Sources: Ingot and mill products, domestic: 1942–45—Aluminum and Magnesium Division, War Production Board; 1946 to date—U.S. Department of Commerce, Bureau of the Census, Industry Division, and Bureau of Domestic Commerce, Aluminum and Magnesium Industries Operations, Facts for Industry 1946–1959, and Current Industrial Report Series M33–2, 1960 to date.
Mill products, imported: U.S. Department of Commerce, Bureau of the Census, Foreign Trade Division, and CIR Series M33–2.

Exhibit 3—Continued

PRICE CHRONOLOGY

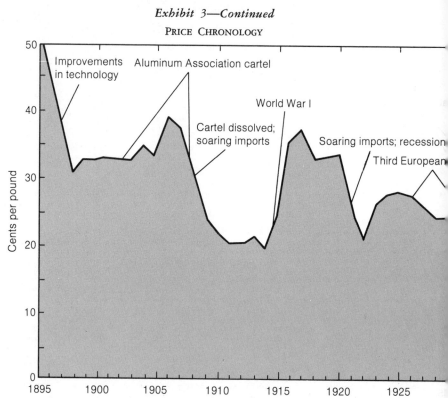

Little over a century ago, aluminum was still a rare metal, costing $545 a pound in 1852. Yet after several decades of technological advance, the price dropped to $8 a pound in 1885. Then, with the development of the electrolytic process for producing aluminum, the metal began to come within the reach of the average consumer . . . On the eve of World War I, aluminum was selling for 19½ cents a pound, thanks to the growth of a technologically advanced industry in Europe and North America—and despite the efforts of producers' cartels to maintain a high price structure for the metal. As a consequence of this price decline, aluminum markets were no longer confined to specialty items in the cooking, military, and surgical fields, but had spread also to tonnage items in the fast-growing electrical and automotive industries . . . During World War I, prices practically doubled despite the rapid expansion of production facilities. But by the end of 1921, prices were back to prewar levels as producers here and abroad fought to find peacetime markets for wartime-swollen supplies . . . During the next several decades, aluminum prices trended down-

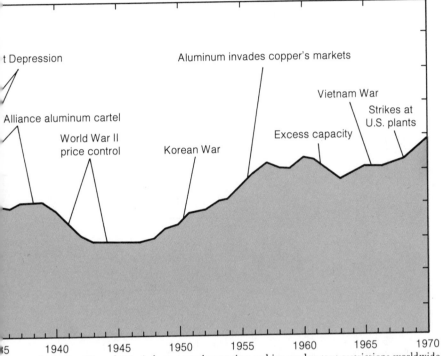

t Depression

Aluminum invades copper's markets

Vietnam War

Strikes at
U.S. plants

Alliance aluminum cartel

World War II
price control

Korean War

Excess capacity

5   1940   1945   1950   1955   1960   1965   1970

wards. In the 20's and 30's, industry cartels set prices and imposed output restrictions worldwide in an attempt to manage markets that had been unsettled by lagging demand and increasing capacity. In the 40's, as the domestic industry expanded rapidly to meet insatiable wartime demands, the government held the price line by setting the ingot price at 14 cents a pound . . . Prices have generally moved upward since World War II. The surprisingly high level of civilian reconversion demand, plus the heavy Korean-war and strategic-stock-pile demand, helped push prices from 14 to 25½ cents a pound between 1947 and 1957. But then prices slumped, reaching 22½ cents a pound in 1963, as military and civilian demand turned sluggish in the face of a tremendous buildup in capacity throughout the world. Finally, with the industrial expansion and the war boom of the late 60's, prices increased again.

Source: *Aluminum: Past and Future*, by Yvonne Levy (San Francisco: Federal Reserve Bank of San Francisco, 1971).

Exhibit 4

CROWN CORPORATION

CHARTS SHOWING IMPROVEMENT IN PROFITS OF THE THREE MAJOR
ALUMINUM FIRMS IN THE LATE 1960's
ALONG WITH RISING PRICES

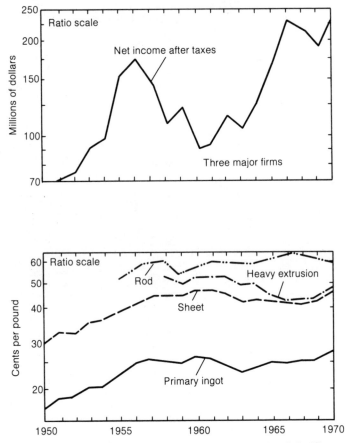

Source: *Aluminum: Past and Future*, by Yvonne Levy (San Francisco: Federal Reserve
Bank of San Francisco, 1971).

Exhibit 5

CROWN CORPORATION

BALANCE SHEETS AS OF DECEMBER 31, 1965–68

(In millions)

	1965	1966	1967	1968
ASSETS				
Cash	$ 3	$ 3	$ 5	$ 4
Marketable securities	7	10	23	6
Accounts receivable	20	23	35	42
Inventories	28	38	45	50
Other	0	0	1	1
Total current assets	$ 58	$ 74	$109	$103
Investments in aluminum plants				
Intalco	32	29	34	36
Eastalco	0	0	0	4
Other net property, plant and equipment	28	31	34	42
Other	3	4	4	4
Total assets	$121	$138	$181	$189
LIABILITIES				
Accounts payable	$ 8	$ 10	$ 13	$ 14
Accrued liabilities	6	7	7	10
Accrued taxes	4	8	8	6
Dividends payable	1	1	1	1
Current maturities—long-term debt	2	2	2	4
Total current liabilities	$ 21	$ 28	$ 31	$ 35
Long-term debt*	30	28	56	52
Deferred federal taxes	1	2	3	3
Stockholders' equity (7,273,000 shares outstanding at year-end 1968)	69	80	91	99
Total liabilities and net worth	$121	$138	$181	$189

* Crown Corporation placed a $56 million debt issue directly with several life insurance companies in 1967. Of the proceeds, $26 million represented a refinancing of existing debt and the balance of $30 million represented new money to the company. The debentures have a coupon of 6% with debt retirement of $4 million annually beginning in 1968 and ending in 1981.

Exhibit 6

CROWN CORPORATION

COMPARATIVE DATA ON ALUMINUM COMPANIES

	Alcan	Alcoa	Harvey	Crown	Braun*	Standard & Poor's 425 Industrials
Earnings per share:						
1962..............	$1.14	$2.52	$1.19	$ .57	$1.74	$3.87
1963..............	1.01	2.27	.90	.34	1.23	4.24
1964..............	1.57	2.72	.77	.42	1.55	4.83
1965..............	1.93	3.41	.53	.66	2.14	5.51
1966..............	2.41	4.83	2.24	1.50	3.30	5.89
1967..............	1.94	4.93	2.36	2.03	3.00	5.66
1968..............	2.14	4.75	2.16	1.87	2.81	6.15
1969 est...........	2.30	5.40	1.75	1.85†	3.00	6.25
Price-earnings ratio:						
1962..............	15–25	18–27	13–25	9–16	14–21	17
1963..............	20–28	23–31	20–27	15–21	25–34	18
1964..............	17–21	22–30	22–29	12–19	18–27	18
1965..............	13–17	18–23	34–44	9–17	13–19	17
1966..............	10–18	14–20	9–13	7–18	9–16	15
1967..............	12–17	14–19	11–25	11–25	13–20	18
1968..............	10–13	13–17	15–25	17–27	15–17	18
Feb. 1969..........	13	14	20	16	13	18
1968 sales (in millions)..........	$1,081	$1,353	$177	$230	$850	
Book value per share (1968)............	$23	$49	$20	$13	$25	
Current dividend rate..............	$1.10	$1.80	$1.20	$0.70	$1.00	$3.21
Long-term debt as % of total capital.....	46%	39%	41%	34%	55%	
Times interest earned..	5.2	6.6	6.7	9.1	4.8	
Debt rating:						
Senior debt.........	A	A	...	not rated	not rated	
Convertible sub-ordinated debt...	...	BBB	BBB	...	...	

* Affiliated with Braun Industries.
† Before any new financing.

SYNERDYNE, INC.

∧∧

Henry Middleton, president of Synerdyne, was both surprised and a bit upset. A month earlier, on October 16, 1972, the company had made a tender offer for one million shares of its own stock. Synerdyne was loaded with cash and its stock seemed to be dragging bottom. Repurchase of one million shares at $20 a share seemed certain to benefit stockholders who retained their shares, especially in view of the expected upswing in earnings.

To Middleton's surprise the company was flooded with stock from disenchanted stockholders eager to unload their shares. Eight million shares—over 28% of the total outstanding—were tendered during the 30-day offer period. Although Synerdyne was under no obligation to purchase more than the one million shares tendered for, Middleton's strong inclination was to accept all eight million and be rid of those who did not share his enthusiasm about the company. However, he first wanted to consider carefully all the implications of such a major stock repurchase.

Synerdyne's history[1]

Henry Middleton started Synerdyne in 1960 from scratch. Leaving Litton Industries, Inc., where he had been in charge of the electronic equipment division, Middleton and another Litton alumnus each put up $225,000 to form the company. It was from this humble start—and with the help of a few technical wizards—that Middleton made Synerdyne one of the most impressive conglomerates in the 1960's through one acquisition after another. Touted all over the Street, no conglomerate rode higher. Its sales soared from $4 million in 1961 to $969 million in 1970, and earnings went from an almost invisible 3¢ a share to $1.86—a spectacular average annual compound growth rate of over 70%. Happy investors pinned on it a sizzling price-earnings ratio of 60 at its peak.

The conglomerate movement, of which Synerdyne was a part, originally sprang from several considerations. One was that it allowed businessmen to put together huge corporate entities quickly, through merger. Another element was the possibility of dampening earnings volatility by combining companies

---

[1] The discussion of Synerdyne's history is based, in part, on "The Trouble at Synerdyne," *Dun's Review*, April, 1972, pp. 66 ff. The discussion of the conglomerate movement is based, in part, on John Brooks, *The Go-Go Years* (New York: Weybright & Talley, 1973), pp. 180–81.

with offsetting cyclical swings. Finally, there was the theory of synergism—a way to make two plus two equal five. By wise mergers companies could be made to yield a better return on a combined basis than they would separately. For one thing, managerial talent and capital expenditures could be channeled into growth areas.

Fortuitously, the stock market boom of the mid and late 1960's provided a means of putting together huge conglomerates almost instantly. Avid investors were bidding up the stocks of "growth" companies—those with rapidly rising earnings per share—regardless of the quality of earnings. Acquisition-minded companies were able to buy up solid, old-line firms with stock and convertible securities. And the simple mathematical fact was that any time a company with a high multiple bought one with a lower multiple a kind of magic came into play. Earnings per share of the new, merged company in the first year of its life came out higher than those of the acquiring company in the previous year even though neither company did any more business than before. (See Exhibit 1.)

Synerdyne was no exception to this pattern. After a slow start, acquisition activity rose from three companies in 1962 to sixteen companies in 1966 and to thirty-eight in 1968. The resultant tenfold increase in earnings per share

NUMBER OF ACQUISITIONS BY SYNERDYNE

1961	1962	1963	1964	1965	1966	1967	1968	1969	1970	1971
1	3	9	6	6	16	18	38	10	0	0

pushed the stock price from $4 in 1963 to a high of $60 in 1968. The high price-earnings multiple relative to the prices paid for acquired companies provided built-in earnings per share which in turn helped to sustain the high stock price. (See Exhibit 2.)

In less than four years, however, all that changed. The start of the decline can be dated. By 1967, Litton Industries had become the pacesetter among conglomerates—its reputation impeccable, its stock soaring, its earnings rising steadily as they had been doing for a decade. But that January, when Litton's top officers met at the company's Beverly Hills headquarters, a totally unanticipated state of affairs was revealed. Several of the divisions were discovered, apparently for the first time, to be in serious trouble; and as a result profits for the quarter ending January 31, 1968 would fail to rise at all and in fact were headed substantially down.

When the public earnings announcement was made—21¢ profit a share against 63¢ for the same quarter of the previous year—it was, as a Wall Street pundit put it, the day the cake of Ivory soap sank. Litton stock dropped 18 points in a week and within a month or so it had lost almost half of its 1967 value. Gulf & Western Industries, Inc. and Ling-Temco-Vought, Inc. slumped in apparent sympathy and the first tremors of panic shook the whole conglomerate world.

Plagued by flat sales and earnings, Synerdyne also lost its glamour. In early 1970 Middleton announced the end of the acquisition era at Synerdyne. Investors, to be sure, had given him good reason to do so. Mirroring the general disenchantment with conglomerates, they had swiftly downgraded Synerdyne's multiple to a low of ten—hardly an attractive grist for the acquisition trading mill. So henceforth, Middleton said, the company would grow from within.

The result was that in fiscal 1970 Synerdyne's sales slipped for the first time in its history. Then in fiscal 1971 the company's earnings—Middleton's own primary measure of success—also fell for the first time, declining 14% to $44 million, or $1.58 a share. Sales fell another 9% to $880 million. The acquisition spree was over and now that all the Synerdyne companies were on the line to produce, the caliber of some of them seemed questionable.

To begin with, a number of Synerdyne's major commercial markets were particularly hard hit during the business slowdown in 1971. Added to that, Synerdyne's government business—one third of total sales—was hard hit by cutbacks in government spending. The company took its biggest lumps in two of its most technically advanced and supposedly fastest growing areas: aviation and electronics, and specialty metals. Net income in aviation and electronics fell 61%; in specialty metals, 42%. Of the other three major groups, industrial products fell 13%; consumer products, 30%. Only insurance and finance showed an increase. (See Exhibit 3.)

The 15 Synerdyne companies encompassed tool steels, refractory metals, super-alloys, and exotic metals. Many of the markets for these metals simply shriveled up during 1970–71. Especially hard hit were sales of dies and tool steels for the machine-tool market.

A far greater impact, however, was felt in the company's aviation- and industrial-engine business, which depended on a strong economy. Synerdyne's Waukegan Motors supplied about half of all private aircraft piston engines in the United States and a major segment of the liquid- and air-cooled engines used in industrial plants and various off-the-road vehicles. Both markets slipped sharply during the 1970–71 mini-recession.

At the same time the United States was upsetting Synerdyne's electronic-systems business. First Synerdyne lost a major contract to provide guidance systems for the U.S. Navy's Cheyenne helicopters in 1970. The company was stunned again in early 1972 when a military avionics contract it was expecting went instead to Lear Siegler, Inc. Fortunately, these disappointments were offset by a strong performance by Synerdyne's biggest company, Phillips Aeronautical Company. Contributing well over $80 million a year in revenues, Phillips monopolized the military market for pilotless jet target aircraft. Military men, pleased with the results of unmanned surveillance aircraft in Vietnam, envisioned a variety of new uses. Phillips, with the technological edge developed in recent years, was in a good position to gain a healthy share of the market when it developed.

Finally, the limping consumer economy had restrained the growth of Synerdyne's line of television sets and high-fidelity speakers.

Slumping sales and earnings, coupled with investor wariness of con- glomerates, triggered a sharp sell-off of the stock from its 1968 high of $62 to only $16 in October, 1972. For Henry Middleton, with personal holdings of over 500,000 shares, the decline represented a paper loss of $23 million. It also represented an opportunity for the company to repurchase shares at the lowest price-earnings multiple since the founding of Synerdyne and at a time when a cyclical rebound of earnings seemed imminent. (See Exhibit 2.)

On October 16, Synerdyne advertised its tender for one million shares of its stock at $20—a $3½ premium over the closing price on the previous day. Management planned to use funds raised by the sale of its holdings of marketable securities to finance the stock repurchase.[2] (Synerdyne's financial condition is shown in Exhibit 4.)

To Middleton's surprise, stockholders tendered eight million shares during the 30-day period of the tender offer. Acceptance of all shares tendered would increase the company's earnings per share by 21–27%, depending upon its future level of profitability. (See Exhibit 5.) It would also cost $160 million and would necessitate new debt financing. Several banks and insurance com- panies had already agreed to loan Synerdyne $140 million on terms outlined in Exhibit 6. While troubled by the tight loan restrictions, Middleton be- lieved that the company could service the additional debt, especially if the sinking fund payments were spaced appropriately, and could meet the loan restrictions. (See Exhibit 7.) However, it was feared that a recapitalization of the magnitude under consideration might damage investor confidence in Synerdyne's securities. The riskiness of the stock was already in line with that of the overall market, as reflected in a beta of 1.0. A large share repurchase program funded by debt would increase the volatility substantially. (Exhibit 8 provides financial information on other conglomerates.) Clearly, a final decision could be reached only after a thorough review of these factors.

---

[2] The market return and the risk-free rate of interest were estimated at 13% and 5%, respectively, in November 1972.

Exhibit 1

SYNERDYNE, INC.

IMPACT OF ACQUISITIONS ON EARNINGS PER SHARE

I. Example where company with a high multiple stock acquires a company for a low price.

	Acquired Company	Acquiring Company	Combined Companies
Net income	$ 80	$200	$280
Number of shares		100 ——→	110
Earnings per share		$2.00	$2.55 +28%
Price-earnings ratio		40	
Market price		$ 80	
Acquisition price (10X)	$800		
Number of shares issued for the acquired company		10	

II. Example where company with a low multiple stock acquires a company for a low price.

	Acquired Company	Acquiring Company	Combined Companies
Net income	$ 80	$200	$280
Number of shares		100 ——→	140
Earnings per share		$2.00	$2.00 +0%
Price-earnings ratio		10	
Market price		$ 20	
Acquisition price (10X)	$800		
Number of shares issued for the acquired company		40	

Exhibit 2

SYNERDYNE, INC.

SUMMARY OF OPERATIONS AND FINANCIAL CONDITION FOR FISCAL YEARS ENDING SEPTEMBER 30, 1963–72

	1963	1964	1965	1966	1967	1968	1969	1970	1971	1972
Operations (In millions):										
Sales	$ 26	$ 30	$ 70	$ 206	$361	$643	$1,032	$969	$880	$969
Income before interest and taxes	$1.66	$2.97	$6.01	$19.6	$ 36	$ 74	$ 109	$106	$ 80	$ 87
Interest expense	0.45	0.59	0.81	1.9	4	11	18	18	15	16
Income before taxes	$1.21	$2.38	$5.20	$17.7	$ 32	$ 63	$ 91	$ 88	$ 65	$ 71
Taxes	0.62	1.23	2.47	8.2	15	30	43	37	21	26
Net income*	$0.59	$1.15	$2.73	$ 9.5	$ 17	$ 33	$ 48	$ 51	$ 44	$ 45
Per Share:										
Market price	4–7	4–10	5–15	10–27	16–60	39–62	26–49	12–36	14–32	15–28
Earnings per share	0.16	0.27	0.41	0.75	1.02	1.47	1.84	1.86	1.58	1.60
Dividends per share	0	0	0	0	0	0	0	0	0	0
Price-earnings ratio (PER)†	34	26	24	25	37	34	20	13	15	13
PER as % of Dow Jones Industrial PER	189%	137%	134%	167%	217%	212%	143%	90%	91%	84%
PER as % of conglomerate index PER	170%	162%	141%	167%	205%	162%	118%	72%	100%	118%
Financial Condition:										
Long-term debt as % of total capital	53%	53%	36%	33%	43%	50%	47%	36%	31%	30%
Times interest earned	3.6	5.0	7.4	10.2	9.1	6.5	6.1	6.0	5.4	5.4

* Of the $45 million of net income in 1972, $18 million represented Synerdyne's equity in the net income of unconsolidated subsidiaries. The low average tax rate in 1972, as well as in 1969–71, reflected the inclusion of the equity in the net income of unconsolidated subsidiaries, which is included in Synerdyne's income statement on an after-tax basis. Thus, Synerdyne's income before taxes from *consolidated* subsidiaries was $53 million in 1972 ($71 million minus $18 million). After provision for taxes of $26 million, income after taxes from *consolidated* subsidiaries was $27 million. The reported net income of $45 million was the total of the $27 million from *consolidated* subsidiaries plus the $18 million equity in the net income of unconsolidated subsidiaries. (The unconsolidated subsidiaries were active in the finance and insurance businesses and could not be consolidated under existing generally accepted accounting principles.)

† Based on average of the high and the low market price.

Exhibit 3

SYNERDYNE, INC.

CONTRIBUTION TO AFTER-TAX PROFITS OF VARIOUS
SYNERDYNE OPERATIONS, 1968–72

(In millions)

	1968	1969	1970	1971	1972 % of Total
Industrial products and services.........	$ 9.5	$13.9	$14.3	$12.4	$13.6 — 26%
Aviation and electronics...............	8.5	14.7	14.4	5.6	7.2 — 14%
Specialty metals......................	9.1	11.7	10.8	6.3	7.0 — 13%
Consumer products...................	6.0	6.2	5.4	3.8	1.0 — 2%
Total of consolidated subsidiaries.	$33.1	$46.5	$44.9	$28.1	$28.8 — 55%
Unicoa (insurance)...................	N.A.	N.A.	6.9	8.0	9.6 — 18%
Argonaut (insurance).................	N.A.	N.A.	6.9	14.5	13.2 — 25%
Other...............................	N.A.	N.A.	1.3	1.4	1.4 — 2%
Total of unconsolidated subsidiaries.....................	$ 4.9	$10.5	$15.1	$23.9	$24.2 — 45%
Total net income*..............	$38	$57	$60	$52	$53 — 100%

* Total net income *before* interest expense.

Exhibit 4

SYNERDYNE, INC.

CONSOLIDATED BALANCE SHEETS AS OF SEPTEMBER 30, 1971–72

(In millions)

	1971	1972
ASSETS		
Cash...	$ 43	$ 39
Marketable securities....................................	6	30
Accounts receivable.....................................	126	131
Inventories..	148	149
Prepaid expenses..	10	9
Total current assets.............................	$333	$358
Investments in unconsolidated subsidiaries..................	265	304
Net property and equipment..............................	220	229
Other...	42	39
Total assets.....................................	$860	$930
LIABILITIES AND NET WORTH		
Accounts payable..	$ 39	$ 42
Accrued liabilities.......................................	59	69
Accrued income taxes....................................	6	2
Current portion of long-term debt........................	4	18
Total current liabilities............................	$108	$131
Other long-term liabilities...............................	35	34
Long-term debt*..	122	121
Subordinated debentures†...............................	100	100
Common stock‡...	495	544
Total liabilities and net worth.....................	$860	$930

* Sinking fund payments are scheduled as follows for the years 1973 through 1977, respectively (in millions of dollars): $18; $14; $14; $7; $5. Fifty million dollars of the subordinated debentures are convertible into common stock at $52.40 per share.
† Sinking fund payments are scheduled to start in 1977 at a rate of $8 million per year.
‡ Outstanding shares of common stock were 27,782,409 and 28,037,125 at year-end 1971 and 1972, respectively.

Exhibit 5

SYNERDYNE, INC.

IMPACT OF REPURCHASE OF EIGHT MILLION SHARES OF STOCK
ON EARNINGS PER SHARE

(Dollar figures in millions except per share data)

	EBIT = $87 Million		EBIT = $120 Million	
	Without Repurchase	*With Repurchase*	*Without Repurchase*	*With Repurchase*
Earnings before interest and taxes.....	$87	$ 87	$120	$120
Interest on existing debt.............	16	16	16	16
Interest on new debt (first year)......	—	11	—	11
Profit before taxes..................	$ 71	$ 60	$104	$ 93
Taxes*............................	26	21	42	37
Profit after taxes...................	$ 45	$ 39	$ 62	$ 56
Millions of shares outstanding.......	28	20	28	20
Earnings per share.................	$1.61	$1.95	$2.21	$2.80
		+21%		+27%

* The relationship of taxes to profit before taxes is explained in the footnote to Exhibit 2.

Exhibit 6

SYNERDYNE, INC.

TERMS OF THE PROPOSED $140 MILLION FINANCING

Amount: $140 million promissory notes

Date: November 18, 1972

Purpose: Repurchase of Synerdyne common stock

Maturities: (*a*) $50 million loan from commercial banks due on 8/15/76. Loan may be prepaid in part or in whole without penalty.

(*b*) $90 million loan from life insurance companies due in ten equal annual payments commencing in 1977.

Interest Rate: (*a*) On $50 million bank loan: 7% interest and compensating balances equal to 15% of the bank loan outstanding.

(*b*) On $90 million life insurance loan: 8%.

Restrictions: (*a*) Dividends on Synerdyne common stock are limited to 30% of the cumulative consolidated net income subsequent to the date of this agreement.

(*b*) Consolidated net worth must be maintained at not less than $340 million through September 30, 1973, $375 million thereafter through September 30, 1974, and $400 million thereafter.

(*c*) The ratio of consolidated current assets to consolidated current liabilities must be maintained at not less than 1.75 to 1.

(*d*) The ratio of (i) all consolidated liabilities (exclusive of subordinated debentures) to (ii) the sum of consolidated net worth plus subordinated debentures, may not exceed 1.2 to 1. The $140 million promissory notes would be included in consolidated liabilities.

(*e*) Unconsolidated subsidiaries may not increase the ratio of (i) all liabilities (exclusive of subordinated debentures) to (ii) the sum of their net worth plus their subordinated debentures, from the level that existed on September 31, 1972.

(*f*) Subsidiaries may not be sold for other than cash.

(*g*) Cash acquisitions are prohibited.

(*h*) Unconsolidated subsidiaries may not be sold and are prohibited from repurchasing shares of their own stock.

(*i*) Total cumulative dividends to Synerdyne from unconsolidated subsidiaries subsequent to September 30, 1972 may not exceed 50% of Synerdyne's cumulative equity in the net income of its unconsolidated subsidiaries subsequent to September 30, 1972.

Exhibit 6—Continued

SYNERDYNE, INC.

PRO FORMA BALANCE SHEETS AS OF SEPTEMBER 30, 1972–77

(Dollar figures in millions)

	Actual 1972	Pro Forma 1972	1973	1974	1975	1976	1977
ASSETS							
Cash and equivalent	$ 69	$ 49	$ 45	$ 45	$ 45	$ 45	$ 45
Accounts receivable	131	131	139	152	165	177	191
Inventories	149	149	161	174	188	203	219
Prepaid expenses	9	9	9	9	9	9	9
Total current assets	$358	$338	$354	$380	$ 407	$ 434	$ 464
Investment in subsidiaries	304	304	320	336	352	368	384
Net property and equipment	229	229	228	229	232	237	246
Other	39	39	39	39	39	39	39
Total assets	$930	$910	$941	$984	$1,030	$1,078	$1,133
LIABILITIES AND NET WORTH							
Accounts payable	$ 42	$ 42	$ 45	$ 49	$ 53	$ 57	$ 62
Accrued liabilities	69	69	75	81	87	94	102
Accrued taxes	2	2	2	2	3	3	4
Bank loan	0	0	0	0	0	6	0
Current portion of long-term debt	18	18	14	14	32	22	22
Total current liabilities	$131	$131	$136	$146	$ 175	$ 182	$ 190
Other long-term liabilities	34	34	34	34	34	34	34
Long-term debt	121	261	240	218	176	162	148
Subordinated debentures	100	100	100	100	100	92	84
Common stock	544	384	431	486	545	608	677
Total liabilities and net worth	$930	$910	$941	$984	$1,030	$1,078	$1,133
COMPLIANCE WITH LOAN RESTRICTIONS							
a. Consolidated net worth		$384	$431	$486	$ 545	$ 608	$ 677
b. Ratio of consolidated current assets to consolidated current liabilities		2.6	2.6	2.6	2.3	2.4	2.4
c. Ratio of consolidated liabilities (exclusive of subordinated debentures) to the sum of consolidated net worth plus subordinated debentures		.9	.8	.7	.6	.5	.5

Exhibit 7

SYNERDYNE, INC.

Forecast of Sales, Earnings, and Financing Needs Including Impact of the Proposed Stock Repurchase

(In millions)

	Actual 1972	1973	1974	1975	1976	1977
Income Statement						
Net sales	$969	$1,080	$1,160	$1,240	$1,320	$1,410
Profit after taxes from consolidated subsidiaries	27	32	38	40	42	44
Equity in net income of unconsolidated subsidiaries	18	20	22	24	26	28
Net income before interest on new debt	$ 45	$ 52	$ 60	$ 64	$ 68	$ 72
After tax interest expense on $140 million new debt		5	5	5	5	3
Net income (including impact of stock repurchase)		$ 47	$ 55	$ 59	$ 63	$ 69
Financing Need						
Profit after taxes from consolidated subsidiaries		$ 32	$ 38	$ 40	$ 42	$ 44
Non-cash charges		30	32	34	35	37
Cash potential from consolidated operations		$ 62	$ 70	$ 74	$ 77	$ 81
Dividend from unconsolidated operations*		4	6	8	10	12
Total sources		$ 66	$ 76	$ 82	$ 87	$ 93
Less:						
Cash dividends on common stock		0	0	0	0	0
Additions to working capital		7	16	16	16	16
Investment in plant and equipment		29	33	37	40	46
Sinking fund payments on existing debt		18	14	14	7	13
Total		$ 54	$ 63	$ 67	$ 63	$ 75
Available to service $140 million new debt		$ 12	$ 13	$ 15	$ 24	$ 18
Less:						
After-tax interest expense on $140 million new debt		5	5	5	5	3
Sinking fund payments on $140 million new debt		7	8	10	25†	9
Total		$ 12	$ 13	$ 15	$ 30	$ 12
Financing (shortfall) excess		$ 0	$ 0	$ 0	$ (6)	$ 6

* Only the dividend from the unconsolidated subsidiaries would be available to Synerdyne for debt service. The remainder of the net income of the unconsolidated subsidiaries would be reinvested in the subsidiaries.

† The last $25 million of the bank loan must be paid off in 1976 according to the terms of the loan.

Exhibit 8

SYNERDYNE, INC.

FINANCIAL SUMMARY ON EIGHT CONGLOMERATES

	Avco	Colt	Gulf & Western	Kidde	Litton	Signal	Textron	Synerdyne
1971 Operations:								
Net sales (in millions)	$1,117	$637	$1,566	$703	$2,342	$1,315	$1,604	$880
Net income (in millions)	$28	$13	$55	$27	$50	$27	$72	$44
% sales	2.5%	2.0%	3.5%	3.8%	2.1%	2.1%	4.5%	5.0%
Return on equity	8%	5%	9%	10%	6%	5%	14%	9%
Return on capital	5%	4%	5%	8%	5%	4%	11%	7%
Per Share:								
1972 estimated earnings	$2.00	$1.60	$3.31	$2.90	$(2.29)	$1.80	$2.25	$1.60
1971 earnings	.97	1.27	2.61	2.44	1.21	1.19	2.06	1.58
1966 earnings	2.88	2.15	1.68	2.20	1.87	3.08	1.94	.75
% increase: 1966–72	(31%)	(26%)	97%	32%	—	(42%)	16%	113%
1971 cash dividends	$0	$0.80	$0.50	$0	$0	$0.58	$0.90	$0
Market price on 11–16–72	$15	$17	$33	$27	$13	$19	$32	$16
Price-earnings ratio on 11–16–72*	8	11	10	9	—	11	14	10
1971 Financial Condition:								
Long-term debt as % of total capital	56%	38%	63%	35%	41%	39%	22%	31%
Times interest earned	1.23	3.4	2.1	8.0	2.8	2.4	13.2	5.4
Bond rating								
Senior debt	—	BBB	BBB	NR	BBB	BBB	A	BBB
Subordinated debt	B	—	B	NR	BB	BB	BBB	BB

* Based on 1972 estimated earnings.

AMERICAN TELEPHONE AND TELEGRAPH COMPANY—1974

^^

Early in 1974, the treasurer of the American Telephone and Telegraph Company[1] was reviewing the company's major financial policies. One major concern was the company's debt position, which had risen in recent years to a level that put the company's triple-A bond rating in jeopardy. For years, AT&T had carefully maintained the highest credit rating and the treasurer was hesitant to adopt a financing plan that might lead to its loss. However, a depressed stock price made common equity financing undesirable.

The company

The American Telephone and Telegraph Company and its 21 principal operating telephone subsidiaries furnished local and toll telephone service to over 80% of the telephones in the United States. Other communication services included data transmission, private line teletypewriter service, and the transmission of radio and television programs. A subsidiary, the Western Electric Company, manufactured telephone equipment and apparatus for the company and its telephone subsidiaries. Another affiliate, the Bell Telephone Laboratories, conducted scientific research and development work for AT&T and Western Electric.

Characteristics

Several characteristics distinguished AT&T from most other private enterprise in the United States. The company was the world's largest utility and the nation's largest private employer, with over one million employees. Its assets at the end of 1973 exceeded $67 billion and were greater than the combined assets of General Motors Corporation, Exxon Corporation, International Business Machines Corporation, and General Electric Company. In 1973, it spent $9.3 billion on construction, which exceeded the total assets of General Electric and approached those of IBM. Western Electric by itself was the nation's tenth largest manufacturing company and Bell Telephone Laboratories was the largest corporate research organization in the world.

As a regulated public utility, the size and profitability of its investments

---

[1] Although AT&T is the parent company, AT&T, as used herein, refers to the consolidated operation of AT&T and its subsidiaries.

were determined in large measure by forces not fully under the control of management. The company and its telephone affiliates were typically required to provide whatever level of service the public demanded at prices set by the regulatory bodies.

The communications business, moreover, was capital-intensive, i.e., large quantities of capital were required to meet service demands. For AT&T, over $2.60 of capital was required to produce $1.00 of annual revenue (sales); by contrast, the average manufacturing company needed $0.60 to produce a dollar of annual revenues.

In addition, the communications business was becoming more competitive. The Federal Communications Commission had adopted the policy of fostering competition. Customer owned devices were permitted to be connected to the telephone network through protective interconnecting devices. In addition, some firms had been authorized to provide specialized intercity services, and open competition appeared to be the policy with respect to domestic satellite communications.

Recent operating results

Demand for communication services had grown throughout the period following World War II at a rate almost twice that of the economy overall. The number of AT&T telephones quintupled from 22 million in 1945 to 110 million in 1973 and the total number of conversations (toll and local) rose in each consecutive year from 30 billion to an estimated 143 billion. Total revenues increased steadily from $1.9 billion in 1945 to $23.5 billion in 1973.

Beginning in 1969, the company experienced some service problems. Demand for telephone service had temporarily outpaced the company's capacity in a few large metropolitan areas and service quality had suffered. In these areas, public criticism had quickly mounted and the issue of quality of telephone service had become a political football for some regulators, politicians, and consumer groups. As a result of these service problems, the company spent large sums of construction dollars to expand its plant capacity. By the end of 1973, most of the service problems had been corrected.

The second half of the 1960's also saw the company's earning rate begin to fall. Inflation had caused a sharp rise in operating and capital costs, which could not be fully offset by productivity gains. For the first time in years, AT&T needed numerous rate increases to maintain its profitability and to insure access to the capital markets. For the remainder of the decade, appreciation of the need for rate relief in an inflationary environment by the various regulatory bodies was essential if the company was to achieve the earnings level necessary to finance its construction program on reasonable terms.

Construction and financing needs

As a result of the growth in the demand for service, AT&T's capital expenditures had been large. In 1973, the company spent $9.3 billion on new construction: $6.0 billion was spent to expand service; another $2.1 billion resulted from customer movement and plant relocations; and $1.2 billion was needed to modernize the system. For the rest of the 1970's, assuming inflation would not be greater than 3–5%, the construction program was expected to grow somewhat below the 1960–73 average of 9.3%.

On average, only 50% of the construction program had been financed internally. In recent years the deferred taxes from the normalization of the investment tax credit and accelerated depreciation had become an important source of internal funds, and by 1973, along with higher reinvested earnings, the internally-generated funds were 61% of the construction program. For the remainder of the decade, the percentage of internal sources was expected to increase further. However, the external financing requirement was expected to remain in the $3.5–4.0 billion range annually.

Financial policy

The company had always recognized the importance of the dividend to its shareowners. Since 1885, AT&T had never passed a dividend payment or lowered its dividend rate, even during the depression. In recent years, the dividend policy had been to increase the dividend when warranted by increased reinvested earnings and when the increase could be maintained at that level. This resulted in a payout rate in the range of 60–65%. The management felt that this policy maximized the attractiveness of the stock by achieving a reasonable mix between dividend income and capital gain.

The company's debt policy was designed to maintain a strong financial structure. The strong financial structure entitled AT&T's debt to the highest credit rating and maximized the access to all major sources of new capital. Public statements by the company continually stressed the intention of maintaining an appropriate capital structure to assure an ongoing top-quality rating for its bonds and to maintain a relatively low level of volatility for the share price. (In 1974, the beta of AT&T's stock was estimated at .75.)

Until the late 1950's, the company's debt ratio objective had been between 30–40%. In the late 1950's, it became generally accepted that depression-boom swings in the economy could be prevented or at least mitigated and that a higher debt level could be safely carried by the company. At the same time, however, the company's stock price was very favorable. Accordingly, the company issued common stock in 1961 and 1964. Beginning in 1965, the company's debt ratio moved steadily upward from 32% in 1965 to 47.6% in 1973, the latter being somewhat above its long-term objective. During this time, debt was used almost exclusively to raise outside money except for the issuance of $3 billion of preferred stock. The rapid increase in the debt ratio beyond 40% since 1970 also reflected the substantial decline in the company's stock price. The sale of common stock between 1970–73 would have been below book value, which was undesirable because it would inhibit the growth rate in earnings per share.

Even though interest coverage stabilized in 1971–73, the precipitous decline from 1966 to 1971 had not gone unnoticed. Standard & Poor's had recently downgraded the bonds of three companies to a double-A rating—The Southern New England Telephone Company, New England Telephone and Telegraph Company, and The Pacific Telephone and Telegraph Company. The reduction had been attributed to a steady downward trend in interest coverage and the continuing need for considerable external financing. Additional downgradings of other subsidiaries seemed probable unless the unsatisfactory trends were reversed.

At the end of 1973, the company was somewhat below the borderline for a triple-A rating and the treasurer believed that it was essential to maintain the triple-A rating. He said:

It is most important that any company determine its capital structure on the relevant business and financial characteristics of the business. A company's capital requirement is one important characteristic. The frequency and volume of our debt issues to be marketed in the years ahead require that we maintain a top-flight credit standing. This is *not* simply a provincial wish on the part of the financial officers to have things comfortably in hand, but rather, it is a very practical need. Both debt ratio and interest coverage impinge on the credit rating. The credit rating of a bond is a major determinant in both the cost and availability of long-term debt. Lower-rated bonds pay more in interest charges because the risk is judged greater, and these cost differentials can be substantial, particularly in difficult markets.[2] Perhaps more importantly, lower-rated firms can find money difficult and perhaps impossible to obtain in periods of financial trauma such as we experienced in 1970.[3]

The treasurer also recognized that the company's heavy external financing needs during the rest of the 1970's would necessitate the sale of common stock and an improved stock price would reduce the number of shares that would have to be sold. It was within this context that he embarked upon a review of AT&T's financial policies. Exhibits 1–9 provide information on AT&T's operating results, financial needs, and policies. Exhibits 10–13 provide background information on bond ratings and on the capital markets. As of early 1974, the market return and the risk-free rate of interest were estimated at 14% and 6%, respectively.

---

[2] In 1973 yields on seasoned Public Utility bonds averaged 7.60%, 7.71%, 7.84%, and 8.17% for bonds rated AAA, AA, A, and BBB respectively. For AT&T, an increase of 10 basis points (one-tenth of one percent) in its average borrowing cost would mean increased interest expense of $28 million per year. [Footnote added.]

[3] Interview with casewriter.

Exhibit 1

AMERICAN TELEPHONE AND TELEGRAPH COMPANY—1974
GROWTH IN TELEPHONES IN THE UNITED STATES*

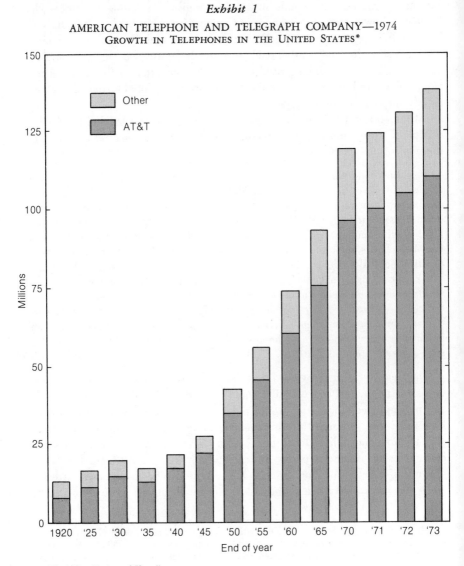

* Excluding Alaska and Hawaii.

Exhibit 2

AMERICAN TELEPHONE AND TELEGRAPH COMPANY—1974

RECENT OPERATING HISTORY

(Dollar figures in billions except per share data)

	1960	1965	1966	1967	1968	1969	1970	1971	1972	1973
Operating revenues—total	$ 7.9	$11.1	$12.1	$13.0	$14.1	$15.7	$17.0	$18.5	$20.9	$23.5
Local	4.5	6.0	6.4	6.7	7.2	7.8	8.5	9.2	10.4	11.4
Toll	3.0	4.6	5.3	5.7	6.3	7.3	7.9	8.7	9.8	11.3
Other	0.4	0.5	0.4	0.6	0.6	0.6	0.6	0.6	0.7	0.8
Net income	1.20	1.80	1.98	2.05	2.05	2.20	2.19	2.20	2.53	2.99
Return on average equity	10.0%	9.5%	9.9%	9.7%	9.3%	9.5%	9.2%	8.7%	9.4%	10.47%
Return on average total capital	7.7%	7.7%	7.9%	7.8%	7.5%	7.7%	7.6%	7.4%	7.7%	8.3%
Earnings per share	$ 2.77	$ 3.41	$ 3.69	$ 3.79	$ 3.75	$ 4.00	$ 3.99	$ 3.92	$ 4.34	$ 5.06
Dividends per share	1.65	2.05	2.20	2.25	2.40	2.45	2.60	2.60	2.70	2.87
Stock price range	39–54	60–70	49–63	49–62	48–58	48–58	40–54	41–54	41–54	46–55
Median price-earnings ratio	17	19	15	15	14	13	12	12	11	10
Telephones in service (millions)	61	76	80	84	88	93	97	100	105	110
Average conversations per day (millions)	219	280	295	307	323	350	368	388	410	N.A.
Toll messages (millions)	2,844	4,278	4,798	5,206	5,794	6,522	7,154	7,734	8,554	9,461
Revenues per message	$ 1.05	$ 1.08	$ 1.10	$ 1.10	$ 1.09	$ 1.13	$ 1.10	$ 1.12	$ 1.14	$ 1.19

Note: N.A. = not available.

Exhibit 3

AMERICAN TELEPHONE AND TELEGRAPH COMPANY—1974

COST AND RATE INFORMATION

	1960	1961	1962	1963	1964	1965	1966	1967	1968	1969	1970	1971	1972	1973
Applications for rate increases..	2	0	1	1	2	1	1	3	10	11	13	33	19	15
Amount requested (in millions).								$ 191	$ 257	$ 500	$ 898	$1,594	$1,315*	$357*
Amount granted (in millions)..								...	$ 56	$ 83	$ 396	$ 788	$ 792	$854
Telephone rates index (1960 = 100)														
Local.	100	100	100	100	100	100	99	99	100	101	106	111	117	N.A.
Long distance.	100	100	99	98	98	95	94	92	93	93	92	95	98	N.A.
Wage and other employee benefits per telephone.	$48.07	$47.69	$47.48	$47.13	$48.96	$49.99	$51.74	$52.99	$53.86	$59.26	$64.73	$69.99	$76.75	N.A.

* Some applications still pending.
Note: N.A. = not available.

Exhibit 4

AMERICAN TELEPHONE AND TELEGRAPH COMPANY—1974

INSTABILITY OF RATE EARNED ON TOTAL CAPITAL

(Measured by change from year to year)

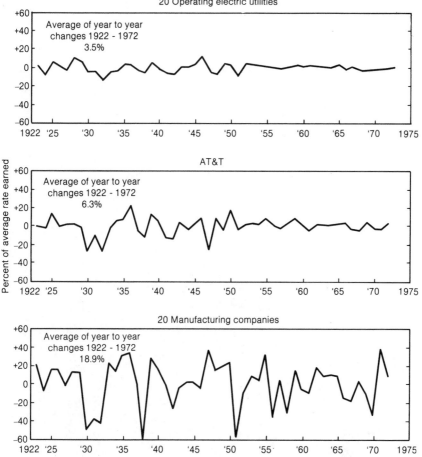

Exhibit 5

AMERICAN TELEPHONE AND TELEGRAPH COMPANY—1974

CONSTRUCTION EXPENDITURES AND NEW MONEY REQUIREMENTS

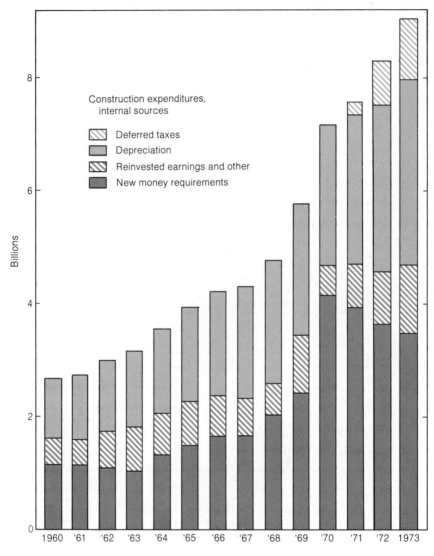

Exhibit 6

AMERICAN TELEPHONE AND TELEGRAPH COMPANY—1974

DEBT RATIO

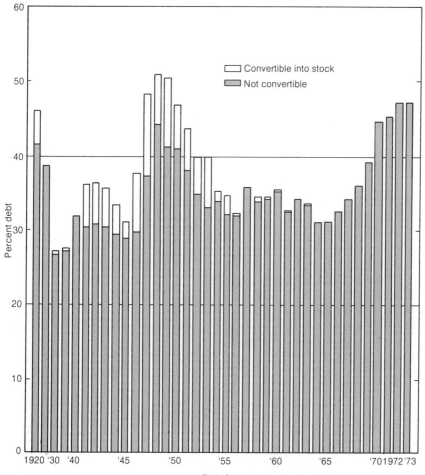

Exhibit 7

AMERICAN TELEPHONE AND TELEGRAPH COMPANY—1974

INTEREST COVERAGE

(Pre-tax)

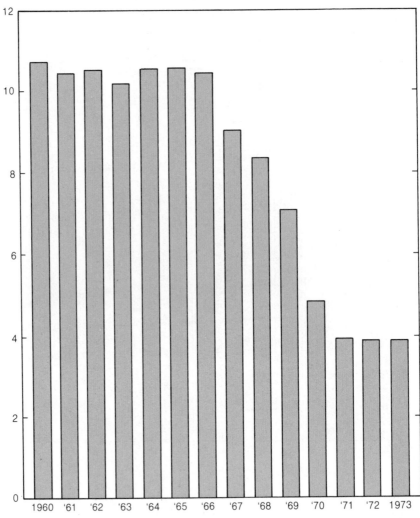

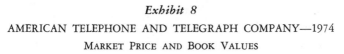

Exhibit 8

AMERICAN TELEPHONE AND TELEGRAPH COMPANY—1974

MARKET PRICE AND BOOK VALUES

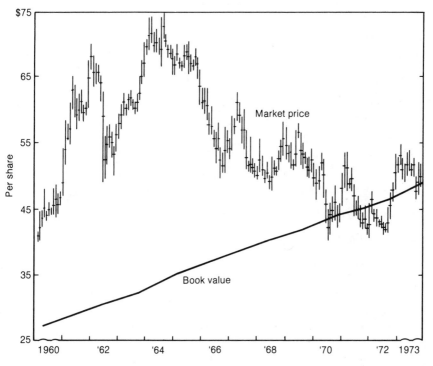

Exhibit 9

AMERICAN TELEPHONE AND TELEGRAPH COMPANY—1974

IMPACT OF VARIOUS DEBT POLICIES ON INTEREST COVERAGE, EARNINGS PER SHARE,
AND DIVIDENDS

	1973	1974	1975	1976	1977
Debt = 48% Capital by 1977					
Debt ratio..........................	48%	48%	48%	48%	48%
Interest coverage (pre-tax)............	3.90	3.84	3.83	3.82	3.81
Earnings per share..................	$ 5.06	$ 5.36	$ 5.69	$ 6.03	$ 6.39
Dividends per share.................	$ 2.87	$ 3.08	$ 3.40	$ 3.60	$ 3.80
Payout ratio........................	57%	58%	60%	60%	60%
Return on equity...................	10.47%	10.59%	10.77%	10.93%	11.06%
Debt = 40% Capital by 1977					
Debt ratio..........................	48%	45%	43%	42%	40%
Interest coverage (pre-tax)............	3.90	4.07	4.25	4.43	4.60
Earnings per share..................	$ 5.06	$ 5.28	$ 5.46	$ 5.65	$ 5.89
Dividends per share.................	$ 2.87	$ 3.08	$ 3.25	$ 3.35	$ 3.50
Payout ratio........................	57%	58%	60%	60%	60%
Return on equity...................	10.47%	10.44%	10.35%	10.28%	10.26%
Debt = 55% Capital by 1977					
Debt ratio..........................	48%	50%	52%	54%	55%
Interest coverage (pre-tax)............	3.90	3.72	3.52	3.35	3.21
Earnings per share..................	$ 5.06	$ 5.43	$ 5.92	$ 6.44	$ 6.99
Dividends per share.................	$ 2.87	$ 3.08	$ 3.55	$ 3.85	$ 4.15
Payout ratio........................	57%	57%	60%	60%	60%
Return on equity...................	10.47%	10.73%	11.18%	11.61%	12.02%

Note: These forecasts are based on estimates and assumptions by the casewriter about future capital expenditures, interest rate levels, and the allowed return on capital. Assumed cost of debt for 48% capital = 8% for 1974–77.

Exhibit 10

AMERICAN TELEPHONE AND TELEGRAPH COMPANY—1974

BOND RATING GUIDELINES FOR INDUSTRY GROUPS

	AAA	AA	A	Baa	Ba
Telephone (Senior)					
Debt ratio..............................	43%	48%	53%	60%	70%
Pre-tax interest coverage.................	4.50X	4.00X	3.50X	3.00X	2.00X
Electric (Senior)					
Debt ratio..............................	49%	52%	55%	58%	60%
Pre-tax interest coverage.................	4.50X	3.50X	3.00X	2.50X	2.0X
Industrial—Manufacturing (Sinking Fund Debentures)					
Debt ratio..............................	15%	20%	30%	40%	50%
Pre-tax interest coverage.................	11.0X	9.0X	7.0X	4.0X	2.5X
Industrial—Retail (Sinking Fund Debentures)					
Debt ratio..............................	40%	50%	60%	68%	75%
Pre-tax fixed payment coverage............	5.00X	3.50X	2.50X	2.00X	1.75X
Finance Companies (Sinking Fund Debentures)					
Debt ratio..............................	...	75%	77%	82%	85%
Pre-tax interest coverage.................	...	2.25X	1.80X	1.60X	1.30X

Source: Internal memorandum of the Pacific Mutual Life Insurance Company, May, 1972.

Exhibit 11

AMERICAN TELEPHONE AND TELEGRAPH COMPANY—1974

TOTAL CASH OFFERINGS OF NEW CORPORATE SECURITIES

(Dollar figures in billions)

	1967	1968	1969	1970	1971	1972	1973e	1974e
Corporate stock issues (Common and preferred)	$ 2.6	$ 4.1	$ 7.2	$ 7.6	$12.0	$11.9	$ 8.3	$ 9.0
Corporate bonds								
Public straight debt	10.8	8.1	9.5	23.1	21.3	15.7	12.6	23.0
Privately placed straight debt	5.9	5.6	4.0	3.5	6.9	9.0	9.0	10.0
Convertible debt	4.4	3.3	4.0	2.7	3.6	2.3	0.4	1.0
Total corporate bonds	$21.1	$17.0	$17.5	$29.3	$31.8	$27.0	$22.0	$34.0
Total gross new cash offerings*	$23.7	$21.1	$24.7	$36.9	$43.8	$38.9	$30.3	$43.0
AT&T external financing needs	$ 1.6	$ 2.0	$ 2.4	$ 4.2	$ 3.9	$ 3.7	$ 3.5	$ 3.7
AT&T as percent of total gross new cash offerings	7%	9%	10%	11%	9%	10%	12%	9%

Note: e = estimate.
* Gross offerings including refinancing of maturing debt.
Source: Salomon Brothers, *Supply and Demand for Credit in 1974* (New York: Salomon Brothers, 1974).

1. Evaluation of opportunity cost to keeping AAA ratings 2.

Exhibit 12

AMERICAN TELEPHONE AND TELEGRAPH COMPANY—1974

PORTFOLIO INVESTMENTS OF SELECTED FINANCIAL INSTITUTIONS AND INDIVIDUALS IN THE UNITED STATES

AMOUNTS HELD AS OF DECEMBER 31, 1972

(In billions)

	U.S. Government Securities	Federal Agency Securities	Commercial Paper	State and Local Bonds	Corporate and Foreign Bonds	Corporate Stocks*	Mortgages	Loans	Total Credit†	Annual Net Increases in Amounts of Total Credit 1967-72		
										High	Low	Average
Mutual savings banks	$ 3.5	$ 4.2	$ 0	$ 0.9	$ 14.2	$ 4.1	$ 67.6	$ 1.8	$ 96.3	$10.6	$ 2.8	$ 6.1
Savings and loan associations	13.8	10.5	0.2	0	0	0	206.4	1.8	232.7	35.8	9.1	17.9
Life insurance companies	3.7	0.6	3.2	3.3	86.8	27.3	77.3	…	202.2	12.5	6.1	6.3
Fire and casualty companies	5.0	0.6	…	23.9	9.1	20.4	0	…	59.0	6.2	2.0	4.2
Private noninsured pension funds	3.1	0.6	0.5	…	27.4	107.1	3.0	…	141.7	7.2	5.8	6.4
State and local retirement funds	2.6	1.1	0.5	1.7	42.2	15.4	7.2	…	70.7	7.2	3.7	5.7
Open-end mutual funds	0.6	…	1.5	…	5.2	52.9	…	…	60.2	3.4	(1.4)	1.2
Commercial banks	67.0	21.8	10.1	89.8	5.5	…	99.3	280.5	574.0	70.0	15.6	41.1
Finance companies	…	…	…	…	…	…	11.1	59.8	70.9	7.9	0.6	4.5
Credit unions	3.0	…	…	…	…	…	1.0	16.7	20.7	3.4	0.8	2.0
Business corporations	6.2	3.1	19.6	5.4	…	…	…	34.5	68.8	7.6	(1.8)	3.8
State and local governments	19.1	3.5	0.6	…	…	…	…	…	23.2	4.1	(1.5)	1.6
Foreigners	55.5	3.8	3.7	…	2.9	26.8	…	…	92.7	27.7	.9	9.3
Individuals and miscellaneous	77.6	10.5	1.7	53.3	59.6	966.0	46.3	…	1,214.4	18.1	(9.8)	1.8
Total privately held	$260.7	$60.3	$41.6	$178.3	$252.9	$1,220.0	$519.2	$395.1	$2,927.5			
Federal agencies‡	189.1	3.2					45.3		237.6			
Total outstanding	$449.8	$63.5	$41.6	$178.3	$252.9	$1,220.0	$564.5	$395.1	$3,165.1			

* At market.
† Including holdings of corporate stock at market.
‡ U.S. trust funds, federal agencies, Federal Reserve banks.
Source: Salomon Brothers, op. cit.

Exhibit 13

AMERICAN TELEPHONE AND TELEGRAPH COMPANY—1974

TOTAL CORPORATE EXTERNAL FINANCING REQUIREMENTS* (1971–85)

(In billions)

Electric power industry.................	$ 175
Fossil fuel industry....................	200
Communications......................	100
Metal industries......................	75
All other............................	550
Total........................	$1,100†
Average annual 1967–71.................	28
Average annual 1971–85................	73

* Net new issuance excludes refinancing of maturing debt.
† In constant 1971 dollars.
Source: Economic Report, "Financial Implications of Material Shortages," Manufacturers Hanover Trust Company, November, 1973.

GEORGIA POWER COMPANY

∧∧

Late in 1974, the management of Georgia Power Company (a subsidiary of The Southern Company) was reviewing the firm's alternatives for dealing with a financial crisis of major proportions. Georgia Power was spending close to $2 million per day in its construction program, and the company was rapidly running out of cash. The markets for first mortgage debt and preferred stock were closed to Georgia Power because of a combination of the company's deteriorating earnings coverage and a recent aversion demonstrated by investors toward the purchase of electric-utility securities rated Baa or lower. Given Georgia Power's limited access to the long-term capital markets, the company's bank lenders were showing considerable nervousness about granting additional short-term advances.

Finally, Georgia Power's parent, The Southern Company, was having such severe financial problems of its own that it was unclear how much help the subsidiary could expect from its parent.

Background data

Georgia Power was the largest subsidiary of The Southern Company which was, in turn, the largest electric utility holding company in the United States. Southern owned all of the common stock of Georgia Power Company, Alabama Power Company, and two smaller electric utilities in Florida and Mississippi.

While Southern owned 100% of the stock of its subsidiaries and periodically contributed additional common equity capital to finance the growth of these firms, the debt and preferred stock financing of these subsidiaries was all accomplished externally. Georgia Power, for example, had 31 separate issues of first mortgage bonds and 16 separate issues of preferred stock trading in the public markets as of September 30, 1974. Key financial data for Georgia Power are presented in Exhibit 1.

Selected *consolidated* financial data for Southern are presented in Exhibit 2. Comparable data for Southern on an *unconsolidated* basis are presented in Exhibit 3. The unconsolidated data of Exhibit 3 indicate the degree to which Southern acted as a financial conduit between its subsidiaries and the equity capital markets. The Southern Company collected dividends from its subsidiaries (lines 11–13, Exhibit 3) and raised capital via the sale of common stock (line 14, Exhibit 3). Short-term borrowings were occasionally used as a financial source (line 15, Exhibit 3) on a temporary basis[1] when Southern believed that temporarily delaying an equity offering might result in a more favorable offering price at a later date.

Southern utilized its funds sources primarily to pay dividends to its common shareholders (line 17, Exhibit 3) and to fund the common equity capital needs of its subsidiaries (lines 18–20, Exhibit 3). These infusions of new equity capital were needed by Southern's subsidiaries to help finance the construction of new facilities for the generation, transmission, and distribution of electric power.

For many years, Southern and its affiliated companies had, in relation to the investor-owned electric utility industry overall, experienced:

1. Rapid growth (columns 1 and 2, Exhibit 4).

2. Somewhat lower profitability (columns 3 and 4, Exhibit 4).

3. Noticeably higher levels of market value for the firm's common stock measured in relation to either book value (columns 5 and 6, Exhibit 4) or price-earnings ratios.

Southern's affiliates enjoyed adequate coverage of their interest charges (columns 7 and 8, Exhibit 4), and, until 1974, high credit ratings for their first mortgage debt securities (columns 9 and 10, Exhibit 4). All of the above facts combined to give Southern and its affiliates, prior to 1973–74, full access to the debt and equity capital markets on attractive terms. In 1973–74, however, this situation changed dramatically.

Downgrading Georgia Power's bond rating

In December 1972, the first mortgage debt securities of Georgia Power, Southern's largest affiliate, were downgraded in rating from Aa to A. As was the case for both industrial and utility borrowers generally, Georgia Power's earnings coverage ratios had been declining since the mid-1960s (column 7, Exhibit 4), in part due to a rise in average interest rates on embedded debt. Georgia Power's coverage problems went deeper, however, than the rise in average interest cost. An erosion in the company's return on assets in the early 1970s (line 9 versus line 19, Exhibit 1) contributed to the pressure on coverage ratios.

In early January 1973, Georgia Power announced that its capital spending for 1973 and 1974 would amount to $1.056 billion. Later that month, after regulatory authorities granted only $17.8 million of a requested $47.9 million rate

---

[1] The U.S. Securities and Exchange Commission (SEC), through the Public Utility Holding Company Act of 1935, regulated the use of debt by utility holding companies. In part, this regulation was designed to preclude the pyramiding of debt by utilities through the use of the parent-subsidiary ownership structure. The SEC, as a matter of policy, limited the permanent financing of holding companies (with subsidiaries having publicly held senior securities) to common stock. In a few isolated instances, the SEC has permitted holding companies to issue long-term debt. In addition, holding companies were permitted to incur short-term debt aggregating up to 5% of total capital without receiving specific approval from the SEC.

increase, the company announced that "after a careful review of our present financial situation, we have no choice but to suspend or delay construction of some of our planned projects."[2,3] The capital spending forecast for 1973–74 was pared back to $973 million, a reduction of about 8%.

Financing Georgia Power's capital expenditures

Georgia Power announced its intention to finance the externally funded portion of its 1973 capital expenditure program in the following way.[4]

Date of Planned Issue	First Mortgage Bond Issue ($ millions)	Preferred Stock Issue ($ millions)
June 6................	$ 150	$ —
Nov. 7................	150	25

By March 1973, however, the utility announced that its pretax profits might not be adequate to permit the sale of the planned securities in the desired amounts on the proposed dates. Indentures relating to Georgia Power's previous first mortgage bond issues prohibited the firm from selling additional first mortgage bonds if pretax profits (during 12 consecutive calendar months out of the last 15 months) would not cover pro forma interest charges at least twice. Similar covenants prevented the sale of preferred stock if the firm's aftertax earnings would not cover pro forma interest and preferred dividends at least 1.5 times.

True to the firm's prior disclosure, in June 1973, Georgia Power was able to sell only $115 million of 30-year first mortgage bonds at an interest rate of 7⅞% due to the indenture limitation.

Improving coverage ratios via rate increases

Just prior to the $115 million bond financing, Georgia Power filed with its state regulatory agency (the Georgia Public Service Commission [PSC]) for an emergency interim rate increase of $86 million. This was equivalent to a 7.5% price and revenue increase. If granted, this increase would have positioned Georgia Power to have the earnings coverage needed to successfully complete its proposed November $175 million financing program. The Georgia Public Service Commission responded to this request in August with an $11.1 million *interim* increase, which would remain in effect until such time as the appropriate level for a *permanent* increase could be determined. The amount of the per-

---

[2] *The Wall Street Journal*, January 18, 1973.

[3] The suspension included work on two hydroelectric projects (Wallace Dam and Rocky Mountain) in which Georgia Power had already invested $9.5 million. If later events were to force the cancellation and abandonment of these projects, the aftertax loss (net of salvage, contract cancellation costs, and so forth) was estimated at about $6.5 million. The Wallace Dam project (in which Georgia Power had invested $8.7 million) was reinstated one year later in early 1974.

[4] *The Wall Street Journal*, January 24, 1973.

manent increase was expected to be decided by year-end. In September 1973, Georgia Power had to cancel its plans for the November financing. The announcement of the cancellation of the proposed offering was punctuated with the following comments from the president of Georgia Power:

We have been warning people for the past several years that the future power supply of this state and its economic growth are in jeopardy. If we don't get additional relief on customer rates, we are going to be facing power shortages in the very near future that we are powerless to correct under present circumstances.[5]

The energy crisis—a changed economic environment

Within a month after Georgia Power canceled its proposed $175 million financing, (1) the Arab-Israeli War, (2) a Middle-East oil embargo, and (3) the fourfold increase in OPEC prices for crude oil combined to begin a transformation in the economics of electric-power production. While Georgia Power utilized fuel oil for less than 10% of its total electrical power generation, the increase in oil prices after October 1973 prompted a sharp rise in coal prices. Georgia Power was heavily dependent upon coal as its principal fuel source. Following the oil embargo, Georgia Power's average cost of fuel per kilowatt-hour of power generated increased as indicated below:

GEORGIA POWER COMPANY AVERAGE COST
OF FUEL PER KILOWATT-HOUR
GENERATED* (MILLS)

	1973	1974
January	5.34	6.12
February	4.45	7.34
March	4.39	7.26
April	3.99	7.23
May	5.01	7.57
June	4.91	7.29
July	5.99	8.51
August	5.46	9.38
September	6.12	11.09
October	5.32	11.33
November	6.28	12.80
December	6.88	

* Excludes hydroelectric power.

Rate actions bordering on confiscation

In November 1973, the Supreme Court of Georgia issued its opinion on an appeal by Georgia Power which alleged that in a previous rate hearing, the Georgia PSC's rate actions had been confiscatory. The court held that while the PSC's rate order had not "been confiscatory in the constitutional sense . . . [it was] within that 'area of unreasonableness' which is barely above the point of confiscation." Perhaps with an eye to the court's November finding, in De-

---

[5] *The Wall Street Journal,* September 19, 1973.

cember 1973, the PSC authorized a permanent annual rate increase of about $68 million, some $57 more than it had granted as interim relief back in August.[6]

Armed with its improved profit prospects, Georgia Power offered $150 million of 30-year debt at 8⅝% on January 21, 1974. The issue was only 25% sold by the underwriters on the day of the offering. Four business days later, the offering was still only 60% sold. This was an extremely slow sale. Fortunately, a brief rally in bond prices during the last few days of January allowed Georgia Power's underwriters to fully distribute the issue at no loss to themselves.

While Georgia Power faced considerable financing difficulties, other public utilities throughout the country were facing problems of equal severity. In April 1974, Consolidated Edison failed to declare its usual quarterly cash dividend. Consolidated Edison's stock price promptly fell more than 50%, and the market for all public utility financing was depressed even further than it had been previously (column 7, Exhibit 5).

The financing window begins to close

In June 1974, Georgia Power announced its intention to sell $130 million of 30-year first mortgage bonds and $60 million of preferred stock in July. Earnings coverage ratios were barely sufficient to permit financing at the announced levels (columns 4 and 5, Exhibit 6). On July 17, bids from competing groups of underwriters were scheduled to be received by Georgia Power. The company had indicated that its interest coverage limitation would allow it to receive bids at rates of up to 11⅝% for the $130 million of bonds. At interest rates above 11⅝%, the firm would have to scale back the amount of bonds offered in order to remain within its coverage ratio limits. The 11⅝% rate was ⅝% above the yield accepted on a comparably rated bond sold by Virginia Electric & Power Company in the prior week (line 1, Exhibit 7). No bids were submitted for either Georgia Power's bonds or its preferred stock, thereby underscoring the depth of the financing crisis facing public utilities in general, and Georgia Power in particular. Immediately following the failure of Georgia Power's proposed offering, the U.S. Securities and Exchange Commission suspended for nine months its requirement that public utilities sell their securities via competitive bid.[7] Georgia Power then turned to Blyth, Eastman, Dillon &

---

[6] In December 1973, the PSC also appproved shortening the time lag from *twelve* to *three* months between the incurrence of increased fuel cost and its full recovery under fuel-adjustment clauses in Georgia Power's rate schedules. In spite of shortening the lags during periods of rising costs, substantial portions of increased fuel costs were not fully recovered for *five months* due to the fact that the fuel-adjustment rate formula was based on a three-month moving average fuel cost applied to sales in the second succeeding month thereafter.

[7] The SEC, as empowered by the Public Utility Holding Company Act of 1935, requires all registered public utility holding companies and their subsidiaries to sell their securities through competitive bidding as opposed to negotiating a price with underwriters. The intent of this regulation is to encourage competition among investment bankers to quote the highest possible price (net of underwriting commissions) to the seller. Some reasoning why competitive bidding might not be as successful a marketing approach as negotiated offerings in an unstable capital market environment are offered in D. E. Logue and Robert A. Jarrow,

Company, Inc., and on a noncompetitive bid basis, negotiated $130 million of first mortgage debt with a *five-year maturity* (the shortest ever)[8] at an 11% interest rate. The issue was successfully concluded on August 1, 1974 (line 7, Exhibit 7).

The innumerable postponements, reductions, and cancellations of Georgia Power's financings caused the utility to borrow extraordinary sums on a short-term basis from both commercial banks and the commercial paper markets. The firm also had to rely more heavily on its parent company to meet its immediate financing needs. This put considerable stress on Southern Company, the parent firm. At June 30, 1974, for example, Georgia Power had accumulated $221 million of short-term debt (column 1, Exhibit 6). Southern had $133 million in short-term debt outstanding at the parent-company level (column 1, Exhibit 6). All of the proceeds from these borrowings had been transferred as paid-in capital to various Southern Company affiliates. Such heavy reliance on short-term debt required special approval from both the SEC and Georgia Power's preferred shareholders.

A forced sale of equity under disastrous circumstances

In spite of a terribly poor equity market environment (columns 7 and 8, Exhibit 5; and column 7, Exhibit 6), in August 1974, Southern's management felt that the firm could delay no longer in reducing its short-term debt position. The company filed a 17.5 million share offering which was scheduled for sale on September 18. The offering was to be the largest ever (in terms of the number of shares sold) for an electric-utility holding company. On this basis, it was 65% larger than any previous Southern offering, although the total amount of capital raised was smaller than the offering completed in 1972 as noted below.

Date of Southern Company Offering	Number of Shares Sold (millions)	Price per Share	Amount of Capital Raised ($ millions)	Underwriting Discount and Commission
Nov. 12, 1970	3.8	$22	$ 83.6	2.0%
Dec. 14, 1971	7.0	19¼	134.8	2.4
Nov. 14, 1972	8.3	21¼	176.4	2.3
Nov. 28, 1973	10.5	14⅞	156.2	4.9
Sept. 18, 1974	17.5	9½	166.3	8.0

It took (1) the combined efforts of Morgan Stanley, Salomon Brothers, and Merrill Lynch; (2) the highest underwriting commission on a large electric-

---

"Negotiation vs. Competitive Bidding in the Sale of Securities by Public Utilities," *Financial Management*, Fall 1978; and J. F. Curley, "Comment," *Financial Management*, Winter 1978.

[8] All previous issues of Georgia Power first mortgage debt had 30-year maturities, as was the norm for the electric-utility industry, in general, prior to the 1974 financing crisis.

utility offering in history; and (3) a 15% dividend yield[9] to successfully market the issue. The offering was sold at a price equal to only 52% of book value of Southern's common stock.[10] The issue produced a decline in the book value of Southern's common stock from $18.21 to $16.53 per share. The intensity of the selling effort and the significant dilution suffered by Southern's shareholders combined to make this issue extremely painful. One syndicate manager described the transaction as being comparable to "passing a kidney stone."

The Southern stock offering in September 1974 temporarily removed the pressure of excessive levels of short-term debt from the *parent* company. The offering did little to help Georgia Power's financial plight, however.

The financing window closes for Georgia Power

As 1974 drew to a close, financial deterioration at Georgia Power began to approach crisis proportions. The firm's first mortgage debt was unmarketable due to the lack of adequate earnings coverage, and rating agencies were on the verge of reducing the rating on the firm's first mortgage debt and preferred stock to Baa (column 9, Exhibit 4). The Duke Power Company note offering of September 11 (line 19, Exhibit 7) had demonstrated the implications of such a downgrading. The rating on Duke Power's first mortgage bonds was A at the time of its note issue, but the firm, like Georgia Power, had insufficient earnings coverage to permit the issuance of first mortgage debt. Instead, the firm chose to sell *unsecured* debt in the form of a five-year note.[11] This debt was rated Baa. Duke Power paid 13% for the five-year debt. If Georgia Power tried to sell unsecured debt when its *first mortgage* debt was rated Baa, the rating on its unsecured debt might fall to Ba. Since the Duke Power offering, each passing day made it look less likely that an electric utility with a Baa rating on its *first mortgage* debt could sell *unsecured* debt at any price.

The cash drain on Georgia Power for construction outlays was running at the rate of about $2.0 million per day, capital sources (including short-term debt) were drying up, and the company was rapidly approaching the point of insolvency. The firm was aggressively pursuing all alternatives on a broad front in an attempt to rebalance its precarious position.

---

[9] The company had indicated (according to Merrill Lynch's syndicate manager for the offering) "that the dividend would not be cut." *Institutional Investor*, November 1974, p. 129.

[10] At the Southern Company annual shareholder meeting of May 22, 1974, a shareholder resolution proposed that: "future public offerings of the common stock of the company . . . shall not be accepted at prices less than book value per share." Southern's management and directors advised shareholders that the proposed limitation "as to the sale price of the Corporation's future issues of stock would be most decidedly contrary to the best interests of the Corporation and each and all of its stockholders." The resolution received the affirmative vote of only about 4% of the votes cast at the meeting.

[11] Interest on unsecured debt was not included in the calculation of the earnings tests contained in the first mortgage debt indentures for electric utilities.

Some action alternatives for alleviating the crisis

The most obvious alternative for assuring Georgia Power's viability over the longer term included rate relief. On this front, the company was preparing an application to the Georgia PSC for an emergency rate increase of 28%. If a substantial rate increase was granted, the capital markets might permit the firm to market its securities shortly after the boost went into effect.

On another front, Georgia Power could halt construction on various portions (or indeed, even all) of its facilities expansion program. As indicated below, many electric utilities had cut back their projected future capital expenditure programs during 1974.

1974 ELECTRIC UTILITY CONSTRUCTION CUTS

	Planning Horizon Covered (years)	Old Construction Program ($ millions)	Revised Construction Program ($ millions)	Amount Cut ($ millions)	Percent Cut
Commonwealth Edison	6	$ 4,900	$ 4,300	$ 600	12.2%
Duke Power	6	4,700	3,200	1,500	31.9
Middle South Utilities	5	3,700	3,200	500	13.5
Detroit Edison	5	3,600	2,700	900	25.0
Philadelphia Electric	5	3,300	2,700	600	18.2
So. California Edison	6	3,000	2,500	500	16.7
Public Service Electric & Gas	5	2,800	1,900	900	32.1
American Electric Power	3	2,300	1,350	950	41.3
Pennsylvania Power & Light	5	2,100	1,800	300	14.3
General Public Utilities	3	1,790	1,000	790	44.1
Total for 10 Firms		$32,190	$24,650	$7,540	23.4%

Source: *Electrical World*, December 1, 1974.

As shown in Exhibit 8, the suspension or cancellation of some new generating units could have a significant impact on capital spending for 1975 and beyond. Suspensions or cancellations would, however, have an impact on Georgia Power's earnings.

Suspensions tended to be less costly than outright contract cancellations. The costs of suspensions could be capitalized as a cost of the projects and, for rate purposes, would be allowable as a base for depreciation charges and rate-of-return computations. Georgia Power could not, however, capitalize[12] the cost of

[12] An income item entitled "allowance for funds used during construction" (line 7, Exhibit 1) represented an important component of reported income for Georgia Power. It represented the estimated composite interest and equity costs of capital funds used in financing construction in progress. The portion of the allowance for funds used during construction that could be allocated to common equity, as a percentage of net income available for common stock, was 3% in 1969, 6% in 1970, 13% in 1971, 16% in 1972, 19% in 1973, and 16% for the nine months ended 9/30/74. As is evident from a comparison of lines 7 and 15 of Exhibit 1, the absence of some method for offsetting the cost of financing non-earning assets (that is, construction in progress) would have a disastrous impact on reported earnings.

funds used to finance construction of partially completed facilities during the suspension period. Since the rate used to capitalize funds used in construction was about 7.5% per year after taxes, this could amount to a substantial earnings penalty, particularly on suspended projects that were well along toward completion.

Contract cancellations, on the other hand, would subject Georgia Power to (1) write-offs relating to contract termination costs; (2) the risk of loss on the resale of equipment contracted for but no longer needed; and (3) write-offs relating to much of the construction work already completed. For projects still in the preconstruction stages, however, the costs of cancellation were manageable. The cost of canceling Vogtle units 3 and 4 in late 1974, for example, were estimated at less than $10 million pretax. To cancel Vogtle units 1 and 2, however, might involve the write-off of all the cumulative work in progress plus as much as $30 million in additional costs.

In addition to rate increases and reductions in its construction program, Georgia Power had another possible method for dealing with its financial crisis —that was to sell[13] some of its existing plants or plants under construction (or some percentage of the ownership in selected plants) to its competitors in the retail distribution of electric power, many of whom were also wholesale customers of Georgia Power. These competitors-customers consisted of 39 rural electrical cooperatives (which purchased about 4.8 billion kilowatt-hours per year, or 12% of Georgia Power's total sales of electrical energy), and 50 municipally owned electric distribution systems (which purchased about 3.5 billion kilowatt-hours per year, or 9% of Georgia Power's total sales of electrical energy).

The sale of interests in generating capacity to Georgia Power's competitors-customers offered some disadvantages as well as some advantages. The firm's management and employees would have to overcome the difficult psychological hurdle of being in business with the principal advocates of public power. The conflict between public and private power throughout the United States had deep historical roots. Some might view this form of financing as a sellout to the enemy. In addition, Georgia Power's management and employees might view the sale of generating capacity as compromising both the firm's growth potential and their own individual opportunities for career advancement. At a minimum, Georgia Power would lose the opportunity to earn a return on the facilities sold to its competitors-customers.

On the plus side of the ledger, the sale of generating capacity to Georgia Power's competitors-customers did have considerable appeal from the standpoint of helping to resolve Georgia Power's immediate financial crisis. It was also true that Georgia Power's earnings on existing bulk sales of power to these same customers were not particularly attractive. Rates charged for this power

---

[13] Because substantially all of Georgia Power's properties were mortgaged, the proceeds from any property sale would have to be utilized solely to finance new property additions. In effect, new property would have to be substituted as collateral for old property released from a mortgage so that the old property could be sold.

were determined by the U.S. Federal Power Commission and were usually less remunerative than sales to other customers.

The two other opportunities which Georgia Power had for alleviating its financial crisis included the possible sale of unsecured notes, as Duke Power had done in September 1974 as noted on page 224. However, it was not entirely clear that this was a real option.

Finally, Georgia Power could have sold and then leased back some of its plant. Any leased plant could not be included in the asset base on which Georgia Power was permitted to earn an investment return, however. Rates would be set so as to simply cover the lease cost on a dollar-for-dollar basis.

Exhibit 1

GEORGIA POWER COMPANY
OPERATING AND FINANCIAL DATA, 1969–1974
(Dollar figures in millions except kilowatt-hour data)

	1969	1970	1971	1972	1973	12 Mos. 9/30/74
Operating items:						
1 Kilowatt-hours sold (billions)	26.8	30.1	31.8	34.7	38.4	38.5
Revenue items:						
2 Revenues	$ 334.2	$ 379.5	$ 429.4	$ 511.4	$ 603.1	$ 736.9
3 Fuel	63.6	82.9	111.0	132.9	157.8	239.3
4 Depreciation and amortization	39.0	42.5	49.4	57.0	68.6	75.9
5 Other expenses	123.7	144.2	162.2	181.8	212.0	237.0
6 Operating income	$ 107.9	$ 109.9	$ 106.8	$ 139.7	$ 164.7	$ 184.7
7 Allowance for funds used during construction	7.1	13.9	19.5	31.1	45.9	60.8
8 Other income	2.2	2.8	2.6	1.9	2.1	2.0
9 Earnings before interest and taxes	$ 117.2	$ 126.6	$ 128.9	$ 172.7	$ 212.7	$ 247.5
10 Interest expense	28.9	38.9	52.1	67.9	91.5	116.0
11 Profit before taxes	$ 88.3	$ 87.7	$ 76.8	$ 104.8	$ 121.2	$ 131.5
12 Taxes	38.6	31.1	20.9	29.4	33.1	30.4
13 Profit after taxes	$ 49.7	$ 56.6	$ 55.9	$ 75.4	$ 88.1	$ 101.1
14 Preferred dividends	6.4	8.1	11.0	12.3	17.2	17.2
15 Net income available for common stock	$ 43.3	$ 48.5	$ 44.9	$ 63.1	$ 70.9	$ 83.9
Balance sheet items:						
16 Net plant in service	$1,069.4	$1,224.0	$1,420.5	$1,657.8	$1,790.4	$1,974.6
17 Construction work in progress	149.7	198.5	337.8	515.8	840.5	1,067.1
18 Other assets	76.6	80.6	111.1	131.0	155.6	185.7
19 Total assets	$1,295.7	$1,503.1	$1,869.4	$2,304.6	$2,786.5	$3,227.4
20 Common equity	$ 370.6	$ 438.3	$ 540.0	$ 652.1	$ 785.4	$ 872.1
21 Preferred stock	133.2	153.3	183.3	257.8	257.8	257.8
22 Borrowed money	635.8	742.4	940.1	1,150.4	1,449.5	1,720.3
23 Other liabilities	156.1	169.1	206.0	244.3	293.8	377.2
24 Total liabilities	$1,295.7	$1,503.1	$1,869.4	$2,304.6	$2,786.5	$3,227.4

					9 Mos. 9/30/74
Sources and uses of funds:					
25 Reinvested earnings*	$ 10.8	$ 8.4	$ 12.1	$ 8.8	$ 6.7
26 Depreciation and amortization	39.0	49.5	57.1	68.8	59.4
27 Deferred taxes and ITC's	11.0	22.0	26.4	36.0	28.1
28 Allowance for funds used during construction	(7.1)	(19.5)	(31.1)	(45.9)	(47.0)
29 Borrowed money (net additions)†	84.7	197.7	210.3	299.1	270.8
30 Preferred stock sales	15.0	30.0	74.5	—	—
31 Equity contribution from Southern Co.	30.5	93.3	100.0	124.0	80.0
32 Other (net)	12.2	(14.4)	(6.1)	(12.3)	31.5
33 Total sources for gross property additions	$ 196.1	$ 367.0	$ 443.2	$ 478.5	$ 429.5
34 Gross property additions‡	196.1	367.0	443.2	478.5	429.5
* After dividends on common stock to Southern Co. of:	$32.5	$36.5	$51.0	$62.1	$56.8
† Includes short-term debt additions of:	19.8	41.6	(13.1)	147.7	(11.1)
‡ Does not include allowance for funds used during construction of:	7.1	19.5	31.1	45.9	47.0

Exhibit 2

GEORGIA POWER COMPANY

The Southern Company and Consolidated Subsidiaries Operating and Financial Data, 1969–1974

(Dollar figures in millions except kilowatt-hour data)

	1969	1970	1971	1972	1973	12 Mos. 9/30/74
Operating items:						
1 Kilowatt-hours sold (billions)	53.0	58.5	61.6	66.7	73.1	n.a.
Revenue items:						
2 Revenues	$ 666.3	$ 738.1	$ 828.7	$ 983.2	$1,165.8	$1,388.1
3 Fuel	141.7	174.5	222.6	270.5	339.2	512.8
4 Depreciation and amortization	83.3	91.3	101.7	114.9	132.8	145.7
5 Other expenses	195.5	224.4	256.7	306.9	330.1	372.3
6 Operating income	$ 245.8	$ 247.9	$ 247.7	$ 290.9	$ 363.7	$ 357.3
7 Allowance for funds used during construction	12.7	19.9	32.3	52.0	83.3	101.0
8 Other income	1.1	2.5	1.7	0.8	2.4	13.3
9 Earnings before interest and taxes	$ 259.6	$ 270.3	$ 281.7	$ 343.7	$ 449.4	$ 471.6
10 Interest expense	63.5	79.4	102.9	132.3	176.2	218.0
11 Profit before taxes	$ 196.1	$ 190.9	$ 178.8	$ 211.4	$ 273.2	$ 253.6
12 Taxes	89.0	76.1	61.4	66.2	94.5	75.0
13 Profit after taxes	$ 107.1	$ 114.8	$ 117.4	$ 145.2	$ 178.7	$ 178.6
14 Preferred dividends of subsidiaries	12.2	14.1	18.1	24.7	30.5	35.7
15 Net income available for common stock	$ 94.9	$ 100.7	$ 99.3	$ 120.5	$ 148.2	$ 142.9
Balance sheet items:						
16 Net plant in service	$2,372.4	$2,591.8	$2,928.5	$3,323.0	$3,677.8	$4,047.8
17 Construction work in progress	223.1	335.5	566.5	902.9	1,406.1	1,762.1
18 Other assets	143.3	172.1	213.9	271.8	289.9	377.5
19 Total assets	$2,738.8	$3,099.4	$3,708.9	$4,497.7	$5,373.8	$6,187.4
20 Common equity	$ 785.1	$ 905.6	$1,066.6	$1,278.4	$1,480.3	$1,654.2
21 Preferred stock	252.0	281.4	324.8	462.8	512.8	562.8
22 Borrowed money	1,372.0	1,549.3	1,885.2	2,239.6	2,767.3	3,207.7
23 Other liabilities	329.7	363.1	432.3	516.9	613.4	762.7
24 Total liabilities	$2,738.8	$3,099.4	$3,708.9	$4,497.7	$5,373.8	$6,187.4

Sources and uses of funds:

						9 Mos. 9/30/74
25 Reinvested earnings*	$ 36.0	$ 37.9	$ 29.4	$ 39.3	$ 53.4	$ 20.8
26 Depreciation and amortization	87.3	95.3	106.1	120.7	139.5	116.6
27 Deferred taxes and ITC's	20.5	17.9	38.5	51.6	71.5	52.4
28 Allowance for funds used during construction	(12.7)	(19.9)	(32.3)	(52.0)	(83.3)	(78.6)
29 Borrowed money (net additions)†	93.2	177.3	335.9	354.4	527.7	440.4
30 Preferred stock sales	20.0	29.4	43.4	138.0	50.0	50.0
31 Common stock sales	64.3	81.9	131.5	172.3	148.5	153.0
32 Other (net)	16.4	(9.2)	(4.0)	(16.9)	11.7	23.4
33 Total sources for gross property additions	$ 325.0	$ 410.6	$ 648.5	$ 807.4	$ 919.0	$ 778.0
34 Gross property additions‡	325.0	410.6	648.5	807.4	919.0	778.0
* After dividends on common stock of:	$58.9	$62.8	$69.9	$81.2	$ 94.8	$84.9
† Includes short-term debt additions of:	(18.3)	(45.1)	74.5	(36.2)	165.8	24.0
‡ Does not include allowance for funds used during construction of:	12.7	19.9	32.3	52.0	83.3	78.6

Exhibit 3

GEORGIA POWER COMPANY

The Southern Company—Parent Company Financial Data (Unconsolidated), 1969–1974

(Dollar figures in millions)

	1969	1970	1971	1972	1973	12 Mos. 9/30/74
Income items:						
1 Net income*	$ 94.9	$ 100.7	$ 99.3	$ 120.5	$ 148.2	$ 142.8
Balance sheet items:						
Investments in subsidiaries†						
2 Georgia Power	$ 277.1	$ 334.6	$ 427.9	$ 527.9	$ 651.9	$ 731.9
3 Alabama Power	195.3	219.3	261.3	305.8	370.8	428.3
4 Other subsidiaries	72.6	80.1	98.2	126.3	139.6	144.1
5 Other assets	7.2	15.0	4.1	16.0	4.8	9.1
6 Total assets	$ 552.2	$ 649.0	$ 791.5	$ 976.0	$1,167.1	$1,313.4
7 Short-term debt	$ 0.0	$ 0.0	$ 3.7	$ 0.0	$ 19.2	$ 2.6
8 Other liabilities	0.3	0.3	0.3	0.3	0.5	0.8
9 Common equity	551.9	648.7	787.5	975.7	1,147.4	1,310.0
10 Total liabilities	$ 552.2	$ 649.0	$ 791.5	$ 976.0	$1,167.1	$1,313.4
						9 Mos. 9/30/74
Sources and uses of funds:						
Dividends from subsidiaries						
11 Georgia Power	$ 32.5	$ 38.3	$ 36.5	$ 51.0	$ 62.1	$ 56.8
12 Alabama Power	25.0	29.6	31.3	35.5	45.8	35.1
13 Other subsidiaries	10.7	11.7	12.3	14.0	17.2	11.3
14 Sale of Southern Co. common stock	64.3	81.9	131.5	172.3	148.5	153.0
15 Increase in short-term debt	(30.0)	0.0	3.7	(3.7)	19.2	(16.6)
16 Total sources	$ 102.5	$ 161.5	$ 215.3	$ 269.1	$ 292.8	$ 239.6
17 Dividends to Southern Co. shareholders	$ 58.9	$ 62.8	$ 69.9	$ 81.2	$ 94.8	$ 84.9
Investments in common equity of:						
18 Georgia Power	30.5	57.5	93.3	100.0	124.0	80.0
19 Alabama Power	6.0	24.0	42.0	44.5	65.0	57.5
20 Other subsidiaries	2.5	6.5	15.0	26.0	10.5	2.5
21 Other uses (net)	4.6	10.7	(4.9)	17.4	(1.5)	14.7
22 Total uses	$ 102.5	$ 161.5	$ 215.3	$ 269.1	$ 292.8	$ 239.6

* Includes equity in earnings of subsidiaries.
† Does not include earnings retained by subsidiaries. Data in line 2 do not, therefore, reconcile with line 20 of Exhibit 1.

Exhibit 4

GEORGIA POWER COMPANY

GROWTH, PROFITABILITY, AND CAPITAL MARKETS DATA FOR ELECTRIC UTILITIES AND THE SOUTHERN COMPANY AND SUBSIDIARIES, 1960–1974

	(1) Growth in Production of Electric Energy	(2)	(3) Profit to Common Equity/Common Equity	(4)	(5) Market Value/Book Value of Common Stock	(6)	(7) Interest Coverage before Taxes†	(8)	(9) Credit Rating on Bonded Indebtedness	(10)
	Electric Utility Industry (Percent)	Southern Co. (Percent)	Electric Utility Industry	Southern Co.	Electric Utility Industry	Southern Co.	Georgia Power Co.	Alabama Power Co.	Georgia Power Co.	Alabama Power Co.
1960	5.9	6.5	.113	.114	1.9	2.7	5.11	4.73	A	A
1961	5.2	4.9	.112	.101	2.3	2.8	4.64	4.44	A	A
1962	7.6	10.2	.117	.111	2.2	2.5	5.11	4.65	A	A
1963	7.6	8.1	.118	.112	2.1	2.6	5.05	4.76	A	A
1964	7.3	7.9	.123	.116	2.3	2.9	5.21	4.87	A	A
1965	7.2	14.2	.126	.117	2.2	2.8	4.77	4.64	Aa	A
1966	8.4	9.9	.128	.118	1.9	2.3	4.74	4.22	Aa	A
1967	6.1	6.6	.128	.116	1.7	2.1	4.37	4.26	Aa	A
1968	9.5	15.5	.123	.117	1.7	2.0	4.12	4.32	Aa	A
1969	8.5	8.9	.122	.120	1.3	1.7	4.06	4.50	Aa	A
1970	6.2	7.3	.118	.111	1.3	1.6	3.25	3.67	Aa	A
1971	5.4	5.1	.117	.093	1.2	1.3	2.47	3.02	Aa	A
1972	8.2	8.4	.118	.094	1.1	1.1	2.55	2.64	A	A
1973	6.2	13.7	.115	.100	0.8	0.9	2.32	3.14	A	A
1974 (12 mos. to 9/30)	0.6	1.6	.107	.086	0.5	0.6	2.13	2.47	Baa‡	A
Average 1960–74	7.1*	8.7*								
Average 1969–74	5.3*	7.2*								

* Compound growth rate over period.
† Calculated as (earnings before interest and taxes) ÷ (interest) per Standard & Poor's.
‡ While Georgia Power's debt was still rated A at 9/30/74, this rating was being reviewed for probable downgrading to Baa at 9/30/74.

Exhibit 5

GEORGIA POWER COMPANY

	(1)	(2)	(3)	(4)	(5)	(6)	Electric Utility Industry	
			Yields and Yield Spreads for Long-Term New Utility Debt, By Rating					
	Bank Prime Rate (Percent)	90-Day Commercial Paper (Percent)	A (Percent)	Baa (Percent)	Aaa-A (Percent)	Baa-Aaa (Percent)	Market Value/Book Value of Common Stock	Dividend Yield on Common Stock (Percent)
January, 1973	6.25	5.50	7.50	7.75	0.20	0.45	1.06	6.23
February	6.25	6.13	7.60	7.77	0.20	0.37	1.03	6.42
March	6.50	6.25	7.60	7.85	0.20	0.45	1.00	6.64
April	6.75	7.13	7.75	8.00	0.20	0.45	0.99	6.68
May	7.25	7.25	7.65	7.90	0.15	0.40	0.99	6.68
June	7.75	7.75	7.80	8.05	0.18	0.43	0.96	6.86
July	8.75	8.63	8.00	8.25	0.23	0.48	0.92	7.19
August	9.75	10.13	8.85	9.10	0.45	0.70	0.89	7.40
September	10.00	10.63	8.40	8.75	0.45	0.80	0.95	6.95
October	9.75	9.75	7.85	8.35	0.30	0.80	0.89	7.37
November	9.75	8.88	8.15	8.60	0.30	0.75	0.79	8.25
December	9.75	9.25	8.00	8.45	0.30	0.75	0.79	8.28
January, 1974	9.50	9.25	8.30	8.75	0.35	0.80	0.82	8.03
February	8.75	8.25	8.35	8.75	0.35	0.75	0.82	7.99
March	9.25	8.25	8.55	8.75	0.45	0.65	0.79	8.35
April	10.50	9.25	8.95	9.40	0.35	0.80	0.65	9.06
May	11.50	11.00	9.40	9.75	0.40	0.75	0.61	9.62
June	11.75	10.25	9.75	10.25	0.85	1.35	0.55	10.52
July	12.00	12.00	10.75	11.75	1.25	2.25	0.57	10.74
August	12.00	11.50	11.00	12.00	1.25	2.25	0.51	12.07
September	12.00	11.88	10.75	12.00	0.75	2.00	0.49	12.36

Exhibit 6

GEORGIA POWER COMPANY

SHORT-TERM DEBT POSITION, PROFITS, COVERAGE RATIOS, AND DIVIDEND YIELDS FOR THE SOUTHERN COMPANY AND GEORGIA POWER
(by quarters, December 1972 to September 1974)

	(1) Short-Term Debt Outstanding* ($ millions)	(2) Net Income Available for Common Stock, 3 Months ($ millions)	(3) 12 Months ($ millions)	(4) Coverage Ratios† Debt	(5) Preferred Stock	(6) Dividend Yields, Preferred Stock (Percent)	(7) Common Stock (Percent)
Southern Co.							
Dec. 31, 1972	$ 0.0	$29.5	$120.5	n.a.	n.a.	n.a.	6.46%
March 31, 1973	39.1	34.2	127.9	n.a.	n.a.	n.a.	6.85
June 30, 1973	73.3	29.7	133.9	n.a.	n.a.	n.a.	7.13
Sept. 30, 1973	116.9	47.1	140.5	n.a.	n.a.	n.a.	7.29
Dec. 31, 1973	19.2	37.2	148.2	n.a.	n.a.	n.a.	8.38
March 31, 1974	75.0	42.0	156.0	n.a.	n.a.	n.a.	8.24
June 30, 1974	132.7	26.7	153.0	n.a.	n.a.	n.a.	10.40
Sept. 30, 1974	2.6	37.1	142.9	n.a.	n.a.	n.a.	13.80
Georgia Power Co.							
Dec. 31, 1972	$ 37.0	$14.7	$63.1	2.18	1.53	7.35%	n.a.
March 31, 1973	105.7	13.6	63.2	2.22	1.53	7.56	n.a.
June 30, 1973	118.1	13.4	62.3	2.02	1.44	7.64	n.a.
Sept. 30, 1973	131.2	23.5	65.2	2.15	1.46	7.80	n.a.
Dec. 31, 1973	166.9	20.4	70.9	2.27	1.50	8.30	n.a.
March 31, 1974	121.4	24.3	81.5	2.19	1.58	8.48	n.a.
June 30, 1974	221.1	18.1	86.2	2.26	1.56	9.53	n.a.
Sept. 31, 1974	187.1	21.1	83.9	1.96	1.48	12.21	n.a.

n.a. = not applicable.
* Parent company debt only for Southern Co.
† These coverage ratios are calculated according to the definitions in Georgia Power's indentures and charter.
They are not comparable to the coverage data presented in column 7 of Exhibit 4. Also, these data exclude any revenue subject to customer refund.

Exhibit 7

GEORGIA POWER COMPANY

JULY–SEPT. 1974 ELECTRIC UTILITY DEBT OFFERINGS

		(1) Date of Offering	(2) Size of Offering ($ millions)	(3) Type of Debt*	(4) Debt Maturity (Years)	(5) Interest Coupon (Percent)	(6) Interest Yield† (Percent)	(7) Gross Underwriting Spread (Percent)	(8) Bond Rating Moody's/S&P
1	Virginia Electric & Power Co.	July 10	$100	M	20	11 %	—%	1.00 %	A/A
2	South Carolina Electric & Gas	16	35	M	5	10½	—	.95	A/A
3	Consumers Power Co.	17	60	M	20	11⅜	—	1.50	A/A
4	Toledo Edison	23	40	M	8	10	—	.85	Aa/A
5	Narragansett Electric Co.	24	25	M	6	10½	10.36	1.06	A/A
6	Iowa Power & Light	Aug. 1	20	M	30	10¾	—	.875	Aa/A
7	Georgia Power Co.	1	130	M	5	11	—	.925	A/A
8	Rochester Gas & Electric	7	30	M	9	10¾	—	.875	A/A
9	Indianapolis Power & Light	8	60	M	7	9⅜	—	.850	Aa/AA
10	Public Service Co. of Indiana	13	75	M	7	9⅝	9.65	.825	Aa/AA
11	Boston Edison	15	60	M	5	12½	12.33	1.35	/BBB
12	Potomac Electric Power Co.	20	50	M	30	10¾	—	.95	A/A
13	Potomac Electric Power Co.	20	50	M	7	10¼	10.30	.85	A/A
14	Ohio Edison Co.	20	150	M	7	10	—	.889	Aa/AA
15	Consumers Power Co.	21	50	M	8	11¼	11.19	1.15	A/A
16	Houston Lighting and Power Co.	28	100	M	30	10⅛	10.18	.875	Aaa/AAA
17	Illinois Power Co.	Sept. 5	50	M	30	10½	—	.875	Aa/AA
18	Northern Indiana Public Service Co.	10	50	M	30	10.40	—	.875	Aa/AA
19	Duke Power Co.	11	100	Notes	5	13	—	1.35	Baa/BBB‡
20	Baltimore Gas & Electric	12	50	M	9	10⅛	10.16	.85	Aa/AA
21	Hawaiian Electric Co.	19	35	M	30	11¼	—	.875	A/A
22	Utah Power & Light	30	40	M	9	10¼	10.19	1.022	A/A

* M equals first mortgage for all issues except Duke Power.

† Utility issues were occasionally offered at a slight premium or discount from face value. This produced a yield somewhat different from the interest coupon shown on the face of the debt security. Data are shown only when the yield differs from the coupon.

‡ Duke Power's first mortgage bonds were rated A by Moody's, whereas the unsecured notes issued in September 1974 were rated Baa.

Source: Investment Dealers' Digest, Corporate Financing Directory, March 11, 1975.

Exhibit 8

GEORGIA POWER COMPANY

GEORGIA POWER COMPANY PLANT CONSTRUCTION IN PROGRESS AT 8/31/74

	Planned Commercial Operation Date	Fuel Type	Cumulative Expenditures Estimated Through 1974 ($ millions)	1974 Estimated Expenditures ($ millions)	1975 Estimated Expenditures ($ millions)	1976 Estimated Expenditures ($ millions)	Total Estimated Cost at Completion ($ millions)	Kilowatt Capacity (thousands)
Bowen unit no. 3	1974	Coal	$123	$ 21	$ 1	$ —	$126	880
no. 4	1975	Coal	107	66	18	—	126	880
Hatch unit no. 1	1974	Nuclear	363	63	2	—	365	810
no. 2	1978	Nuclear	96	44	89	95	410	820
Yates unit nos. 6 and 7	1974	Coal	170	25	—	—	170	700
Wansley unit no. 1	1976	Coal	104	45	73	9	187	880
no. 2	1977	Coal	24	35	44	73	162	880
Vogtle unit no. 1	1980	Nuclear	52	29	109	148	638	1,160
no. 2	1981	Nuclear	8	7	47	97	549	1,160
no. 3	1982	Nuclear	4	4	5	18	634	1,160
no. 4	1983	Nuclear	2	2	2	6	596	1,160
Scherer unit no. 1	1979	Coal	4	4	20	56	260	880
no. 2	1980	Coal	—	—	—	4	260	880
Wallace Dam	1978	Hydro	20	8	32	37	110	325
Rocky Mountain	1979	Hydro	3	3	4	10	103	675
Others	—	—		35	37	88		
Total generating plant				$391	$483	$641		
Transmission plant				81	127	142		
Distribution plant				83	101	114		
General plant				19	17	17		
Nuclear fuel				11	7	32		
Total plant				$585	$735	$946		

SYSTEMS ENGINEERING LABORATORIES, INC.

^^

In early 1978, Systems Engineering Laboratories, Inc. was considering how to raise $10 to $15 million of new capital to finance its rapid growth. Systems was incorporated in 1961. At first, the firm produced components for data acquisition systems. Later, the firm began to produce digital computers for the high-speed acquisition and control of real-time data. The company's sales grew rapidly from $1.0 million in 1962 to $6.2 million by 1966.

In March 1966, Systems first sold stock publicly through an offering of 240,000 shares at $4.50 per share. In a second public offering in November 1967, the firm sold 100,000 shares at $22.00 per share. Two years later, the firm sold stock in a third public offering. The sale of 250,000 shares at a price of $40.25 per share raised approximately $10 million in this public offering.

In the decade following its initial public offering, Systems' financial record was somewhat erratic. The firm's progress was interrupted twice (Exhibit 1). Sales declines and major losses were sustained in 1971 and again in 1974. In 1971, a soft economy, several disastrous acquisitions, and a significant write-down of obsolete inventory resulted in a sales decline from $21 to $13 million and a loss exceeding $10 million. This loss eliminated almost one half of the firm's net worth.

In 1972, Systems introduced three new major products which helped to re-build the company's sales. Progress continued until 1974 when sales declined from $17 million to $15 million, and a net loss of $3.8 million was incurred (Exhibit 1). The loss in 1974 consisted of $2.6 million from operations, $1.2 million from the write-off of obsolete inventory, and $1.3 million from the discontinuation of an obsolete product line. This $5.1 million loss was reduced by a $1.3 million gain on the sale of land.

In 1974, Systems commenced a major new product development effort. This effort was quite successful, and the first models of a newly developed computer series were shipped in October 1975. Shipments of this equipment had a major impact on Systems' sales, profits, and financing requirements (Exhibit 2).

Systems felt that its new products represented a significant improvement in machine performance/price ratios. An improvement of substantial magnitude was usually necessary to prompt users to consider changing their computer vendor, since "computer users characteristically become attached to computer

238

suppliers because of their extensive investments in applications software operable only on the machines for which it is written."[1] In Systems' view, opportunities of the type presented by its new products "do not occur often in the computer industry, and we intend to focus resources to benefit from this situation."[2] In this effort, Systems would be facing some competitors with substantially greater financial resources. Indeed, all of Systems' principal competitors were larger firms. These competitors included Digital Equipment Corporation, Data General Corporation, Prime Computer, Inc., and Perkin-Elmer Corporation (Exhibit 4).

The bulk of Systems' computer sales were to manufacturers whose products served three markets. These markets were (1) energy monitoring and control systems (primarily for electric utilities); (2) flight-training simulators; and (3) laboratory and computation uses. Systems' 1977 share of market and the growth in the computer segment of these markets between 1977 and 1981 was estimated as shown below.

	Systems' 1977 Share of Market (Percent)	Size of Market in 1977 ($ millions)	Estimated Size of Market in 1981 ($ millions)	Estimated Annual Market Growth 1977–1981 (Percent)
Energy monitoring and control	35%	$ 25	$ 65	27%
Flight-training simulators	25	30	60	19
Laboratory and computation	5	195	300	16

Revolving credit financing arrangement

Through June of 1977, Systems had been able to finance its operations through the use of a revolving credit agreement which the firm had established with two banks in 1972. This agreement allowed Systems to borrow (on a fully secured basis) amounts which had, in the past, adequately met the firm's operating needs. Southeast First National Bank of Miami was the lead bank in the credit, and the Chemical Bank joined in the credit with a 50% participation. The revolving credit agreement had been modified many times in the past in order to meet the needs of both Systems and its lenders (Exhibit 3). By year-end 1977, however, it was clear that Systems would very soon encounter a level of funds needs that would exhaust the desires of the firm's lenders for granting additional credit. The various markets served by Systems had been growing at annual rates of 18% to 40% in fiscal 1978, a rate somewhat higher than the longer-run average forecasted above. These growth rates were not expected to diminish in the immediate future. Systems would thus easily require $10 million to $15 million of new externally supplied capital over the next two years to simply keep pace with the growth in its markets, even ignoring the financing

---

[1] Systems Engineering Laboratories, Inc., Annual Report-1977, p. 2.

[2] Ibid., p. 2.

requirements associated with Systems' *increased* market share objective. As the need for additional funds grew, Systems began encountering difficulty meeting the restrictive covenants on its existing debt.

Indeed, Systems had been unable to fulfill the loan restriction relating to the ratio of total liabilities to tangible net worth as of September 23, 1977, and had to obtain a waiver of this restriction from its bankers. At December 23, 1977, Systems was in default of *two* covenants (i.e., those relating to debt to worth and inventory turnover) and had received waivers. During December 1977, the Chemical Bank dropped out of the credit agreement after declining to increase Systems' line of credit, and the First National Bank of Boston became the lead bank in the loan. The maximum loan limit was raised from $6.5 million to $8.5 million. On March 3, 1978, this loan limit was raised to $10.0 million. By March 24, 1978, Systems was in default of *three* covenants (i.e., those relating to debt to worth, inventory turnover, and current ratio) and had again received waivers. On May 8, 1978, the Continental Illinois National Bank joined in the credit agreement, raising Systems' maximum credit limit to $12.0 million.

A need for new financing

Systems' lenders were endeavoring to assist the firm in achieving its full growth potential. Nonetheless, by 1978, Systems' lenders were insistent that the firm either had to seek new long-term financing or find a way to live within its existing credit limits. The latter choice would require Systems to forgo highly profitable sales, an outcome that the firm was unwilling to accept. Systems simply had to find one or more new sources of financing, and the firm was exploring all available options. By the end of March 1978, it was clear that the sale of two quite different financing instruments was feasible, as were a number of intermediate choices utilizing some variation on the two polar choices.

A possible sale of common equity

At one extreme, Systems might sell common equity. As shown in Exhibit 5, Systems' stock price had risen sharply in the prior four months as the firm's improved prospects began to be reflected in reported earnings per share (lines 12, 13 of Exhibit 2). This increase in stock price for Systems came at a time, however, when the prices of equity securities were declining overall. The weak tone of the broader market for equities added significant risk to a Systems' equity offering that would have to be completed under considerable time pressure. In addition, the market for newly issued securities of small firms was not terribly robust in early 1978. For example, initial public offerings for firms with net worth only slightly below that of Systems had not been well received by the market in recent years (Exhibit 6). While an equity offering by Systems in early 1978 would have been its fourth registered public offering, the relative receptivity of the equity markets to offerings by small firms over the last decade, as shown by Exhibit 6, was revealing.

A $10 million equity offering could put considerable pressure on Systems' stock price. Indeed, the mere announcement of an offering of such significant size in a declining general market environment might easily wipe away the share-price progress which Systems had achieved over the past several months. It was entirely conceivable that a $10 million transaction might require an offering price of only $8 per share which, after underwriting discounts and expenses, might produce as little as $7.25 per share for Systems. While net proceeds of $7.25 per share might look quite reasonable in relation to Systems' book value of $4.55 per share, this price looked less attractive in terms of Systems' potential earnings per share in the near future. It also looked less attractive in terms of the price/earnings ratios and market value/book value ratios achieved by Systems' principal competitors.

	Price/Earnings* Ratio of Common Stock at 3/31/78	Market Value/Book Value Ratio of Common Stock at 3/31/78
Digital Equipment Corp.	11.8	1.9
Data General Corp.	13.4	2.6
Prime Computer, Inc.	17.9	5.0
Perkin-Elmer Corp.	12.5	1.6
Systems Engineering Labs @ $12⅜ per share	16.4	2.8
Systems Engineering Labs @ $7¼ per share	9.4	1.6

*Calculation based on earnings per share for the 12 months ended 3/31/78.

Systems did have at least one other, quite different financing alternative, however. That alternative was to issue a high-coupon subordinated debenture.

A possible sale of subordinated debentures

Systems' size and profit history were such that a large, subordinated debt issue would probably receive an extremely low rating (such as CCC[3]) from bond-rating agencies such as Moody's or Standard & Poor's. Historically, a nonconvertible debt security carrying such a low rating could not be sold for cash. In fact, the volume of publicly traded debt in this rating category was quite small.[4] Most of the debt found in similar rating categories was either convertible debt, had been downgraded from earlier, higher ratings, or was originally issued in exchange for other securities. Starting in late 1976, however, significant quantities of high-coupon, low-rated, nonconvertible debt began to be sold publicly in fairly significant volume. Whereas not a single issue of public debt rated below A was sold by an industrial firm in 1975, debt offerings aggregating several hundred million dollars rated BB or lower (two full rating categories below A) were sold in 1977 (Exhibit 7).

---

[3] According to Standard & Poor's: "Bonds rated BB, B, CCC, and CC are regarded, on balance, as predominantly speculative with respect to capacity to pay interest and repay principal in accordance with the terms of the obligation. BB indicates the lowest degree of speculation and CC the highest degree of speculation. While such bonds will likely have some quality and protective characteristics, these are outweighed by large uncertainties or major risk exposures to adverse conditions."

[4] Salomon Brothers estimated that 2.6% of all publicly traded debt of industrial firms was rated CCC or lower. Indeed, only 7.2% of all publicly traded debt of industrial firms was rated below BBB.

A few investment bankers had begun to specialize in underwriting such debt, and a market for this type of security had developed to the point where at least five mutual funds were specializing in low-rated, high-coupon debt (Exhibit 8). Some measure of the degree to which investors were beginning to find lower-rated debt attractive can be seen in Exhibit 9. Between January 1977 and March 1978, the yields on Aaa rated industrials rose 59 basis points from 7.77% to 8.36%. Over this same time period, the yields on Baa industrials rose by only eight basis points. The yield spreads separating bond rating categories narrowed sharply in 1977 and early 1978. Investors were willing to reach into lower rating categories in order to achieve high yields.

Systems' investment bankers felt that the climate for low-rated debt was sufficiently attractive in early 1978 that Systems might be able to raise $10 million to $15 million of subordinated debt with an interest coupon of 12.5%.[5] This would represent the highest coupon rate for an industrial borrower in the history of the long-term, public-debt markets. It was thought that such debt could be sold with a 15-year maturity and would require mandatory sinking fund payments equal to 10% of the amount of debt issued. Sinking fund payments would not be required during the first seven years that the debt was outstanding.[6]

If Systems' sales volume were to expand by 30% per year from the sales rate anticipated for the last fiscal quarter of 1978, Systems' sales, debt ratios, and earnings per share over the period 1978–81 would be as indicated in Exhibit 10. This exhibit assumes that Systems' capital intensity and operating profit margins would remain at the levels experienced in the most recent fiscal quarters.

In the light of the above facts, Systems had to determine promptly the size and form of its next financing. As Systems considered its alternatives, rumors indicated that Prime Computer, Inc., one of Systems' competitors, was preparing to file a registration statement with the SEC indicating its intention to offer $15 million of 15-year, nonconvertible subordinated debentures.

---

[5] One other option that Systems could consider was the issuance of a 15-year convertible debenture. Systems' investment bankers felt that if the debenture was made convertible at a 20% premium over the market price on the day of issuance, it might be sold at an 8.5% interest rate. If the debenture was made convertible at a 50% premium over the market on the day of issuance, it might be sold at an 11% interest rate.

[6] The issue would be callable at any time at an initial redemption price of 106.75% of the price paid by the public. For a period of eight years, no redemption would be allowed from money borrowed at an interest cost of less than 12.5%. The debt would be subordinated to all other current and future borrowings, and Systems would be unable to pay a dividend until its net worth reached $18 million.

Exhibit 1

SYSTEMS ENGINEERING LABORATORIES, INC.
FINANCIAL HISTORY, 1968–1978
($ thousands except per share data)

		Fiscal Years Ended June 30										9 Months Ended	
		1968	1969	1970	1971	1972	1973	1974	1975	1976	1977	3/31/77	3/31/78
1	Revenues	$12,032	$17,298	$21,153	$12,773	$15,719	$17,082	$14,951	$17,457	$20,003	$30,774	$21,762	$35,368
2	Cost of sales	6,980	9,766	11,592	17,179	9,350	11,404	12,941	11,034	11,832	17,029	12,049	18,750
3	Gross profit	$ 5,052	$ 7,532	$ 9,561	$ (4,406)	$ 6,369	$ 5,678	$ 2,010	$ 6,423	$ 8,171	$13,745	$ 9,713	$16,618
4	Selling, general, and administrative	2,202	3,267	4,639	4,393	3,304	3,699	3,857	4,063	5,186	7,651	5,522	8,672
5	Research and development	969	1,269	1,580	3,523	1,253	1,168	1,894	2,218	2,279	3,737	2,792	3,446
6	Interest	62	173	194	456	631	687	902	513	510	655	512	696
7	Other income (expenses)	—	—	—	—	21	210	(816)	123	(203)	(72)	—	—
8	Income before taxes and extraordinary items	$ 1,819	$ 2,823	$ 3,148	$(12,778)	$ 1,202	$ 334	$(5,459)	$ (248)	$ (7)	$ 1,630	$ 887	$ 3,804
9	Provision for taxes	830	1,374	1,316	(3,799)	398	39	(270)	199	197	951	479	1,864
10	Income after taxes	$ 989	$ 1,449	$ 1,832	$ (8,979)	$ 804	$ 295	$(5,189)	$ (447)	$ (204)	$ 679	$ 408	$ 1,940
11	Extraordinary items	—	—	—	(3,464)	308	343	1,336	136	197	870	479	1,551
12	Profit after taxes	$ 989	$ 1,449	$ 1,832	$(12,443)	$ 1,112	$ 638	$(3,853)	$ (311)	$ (7)	$ 1,549	$ 887	$ 3,491
13	EPS (excluding extraordinary items) ($'s)	$ .50	$ .69	$ .77	$ (3.50)	$ .31	$ .11	$ (2.01)	$ (.17)	$ (.07)	$ .24	$ .15	$ .68
14	Share price range in period—high	42⅞	53⅞	49⅛	18¼	16⅜	8⅜	2⅞	6¾	10⅜	12	9⅞	13¾
15	—low	23¾	26⅛	10⅛	6¾	6⅞	1⅛	¾	⅞	4⅞	5	5¼	6¼
16	Trading volume in period† (000's)	1,096	3,646	6,325	3,124	2,713	1,160	566	1,236	1,815	1,817	754	2,035
17	β of common stock												1.72
18	Book value per share	$ 2.47	$ 3.23	$ 7.85*	$ 3.78	$ 4.07	$ 4.28	$ 2.90	$ 2.76	$ 2.63	$ 3.19	$ 3.05	$ 4.55
19	Shares outstanding (000's)	2,049	2,091	2,374	2,565	2,620	2,602	2,582	2,582	2,778	2,799	2,727	2,774
20	Total assets	$ 8,760	$15,555	$30,616	$21,797	$21,366	$24,232	$15,430	$13,662	$17,642	$23,565	$21,144	$35,604
21	Net worth	5,059	6,764	18,684*	9,691	10,665	11,146	7,500	7,115	7,294	8,940	8,321	12,623
22	Income after taxes/net worth	.195	.214	.098	(1.28)	.075	.026	(.692)	(.063)	(.027)	.079		

* In October 1969, Systems raised $9.4 million via the sale of 250,000 shares of common stock.

† Calendar year volume data are shown for the fiscal years. Data for nine months cover the periods as indicated.

Exhibit 2

SYSTEMS ENGINEERING LABORATORIES, INC.
QUARTERLY FINANCIAL DATA, JUNE 1976–JUNE 1978

	6/25/76	9/24/76	12/24/76	3/25/77	6/24/77	9/23/77	12/23/77	3/24/78	6/30/78e
1 Orders ($ millions)	11.5	8.2	9.8	7.9	14.7	14.3	14.1	14.3	15.3
2 Backlog ($ millions)	20.2	22.4	24.3	24.3	30.0	34.6	37.1	37.5	35.2
3 New computer series shipments (units)	n.a.	20	24	31	37	50	59	72	72
					—($ million)—				
4 Revenues	6.3	6.0	7.9	7.8	9.0	9.8	11.6	13.9	17.6
5 Earnings before interest and taxes	.5	.3	.5	.6	.9	1.1	1.6	1.8	2.1
6 Interest	.2	.1	.2	.2	.2	.2	.2	.3	.6
7 Profit before taxes	.3	.2	.3	.4	.7	.9	1.4	1.5	1.5
8 Taxes	.1	.2	.1	.2	.4	.4	.7	.7	.6
9 Profit after taxes (before extraordinary items)	.2	.0	.2	.2	.3	.5	.7	.8	.9
10 Extraordinary items	.1	.1	.1	.2	.4	.4	.5	.6	.6
11 Profit after taxes	.3	.1	.3	.4	.7	.9	1.2	1.4	1.5
					$ per share				
12 EPS (before extraordinary items)	.02	.01	.06	.07	.09	.16	.25	.27	.32
13 EPS (after extraordinary items)	.03	.06	.11	.15	.23	.31	.44	.48	.54

	6/25/76	9/24/76	12/24/76	3/25/77	6/24/77	9/23/77	12/23/77	3/24/78	6/30/78e
					($ million)				
14 Cash	.7	—	.7	.5	.5	.2	—	1.2	
15 Accounts receivable	7.0	8.3	7.8	9.1	9.7	11.7	13.3	16.2	
16 Inventories	5.8	6.1	6.2	6.3	7.0	7.6	9.5	11.3	
17 Other current assets	.3	.4	.5	.5	.8	1.1	1.1	1.0	
18 Total current assets	13.8	14.8	15.2	16.4	18.0	20.6	23.9	29.7	
19 Net equipment leased to others	1.3	1.2	1.0	1.0	1.5	.9	.5	.5	
20 Net property, plant, and equipment	2.2	2.1	2.1	3.5	3.8	3.9	4.3	5.2	
21 Other assets	.4	.4	.4	.3	.2	.2	.3	.2	
22 Total assets	17.7	18.5	18.7	21.2	23.5	25.6	29.0	35.6	44.0
23 Short-term debt—revolving credit*	5.8	6.5	6.8	6.5	6.5	6.5	8.5	10.0	
24 other	.4	.1	—	.4	.7	.4	—	—	
25 Accounts payable and accruals	3.2	3.2	3.1	4.4	5.6	6.7	6.9	9.9	
26 Other current liabilities	.4	.7	.6	.5	.8	1.0	1.0	1.2	
27 Total current liabilities	9.8	10.5	10.5	11.8	13.6	14.6	16.4	21.1	
28 Long term debt and other liabilities	.6	.6	.4	1.1	1.0	1.2	1.5	1.9	
29 Total liabilities	10.4	11.1	10.9	12.9	14.6	15.8	17.9	23.0	30.0
30 Net worth	7.3	7.4	7.8	8.3	8.9	9.8	11.1	12.6	14.0§
31 Total liabilities and net worth	17.7	18.5	18.7	21.2	23.5	25.6	29.0	35.6	44.0
					Ratio Data				
32 Revenues†/assets	1.95	1.30	1.69	1.47	1.53	1.53	1.60	1.56	1.60
33 Profit after taxes†/revenues	.045	.004	.023	.024	.030	.046	.060	.057	.053
34 Assets/net worth	2.42	2.50	2.40	2.55	2.64	2.61	2.61	2.83	3.14§
35 Profit after taxes‡/net worth	.212	.013	.093	.090	.121	.184	.251	.252	.266
36 Earnings before interest and taxes/revenues	.087	.050	.065	.074	.098	.113	.137	.129	.120

n.a. = not available.
* Assumes that all debt under the revolving credit agreement is short term, even though for some quarters the maturity date was more than 12 months away.
† Equal to the annualized rate; that is 400% of the results for the quarter.
‡ Not including extraordinary credits resulting from the utilization of tax-loss carryforwards.
§ Assuming no new equity raised via sale of stock prior to 6/30/78.

Exhibit 3

SYSTEMS ENGINEERING LABORATORIES, INC.

KEY TERMS AND CONDITIONS OF SYSTEMS' REVOLVING CREDIT AGREEMENT, 1972–1978

Date of Agreement	Expiration Date	Maximum Credit ($ millions)	Interest Rate*	Loan Participants	Loan Covenants†
8/24/72	1/31/75	8.0	1.17 (prime + ½%)	Southeast @ $4.0 Chemical @ $4.0	(1) Tangible net worth $\geq$ $8.5 million until 6/30/73 after which $9.5 million. (2) Liabilities/net worth $\leq$ 1.4 times tangible net worth until 6/30/70 after which 1.1 times. (3) Minimum net working capital of at least $3.0 million plus amount of borrowing hereunder. (4) Capital expenditures less than $.8 million per year.
8/27/74	9/30/75	6.0	Same as above	Southeast @ $3.0 Chemical @ $3.0	(1) Tangible net worth $\geq$ $6.65 million + any profits or equity sales. (2) Liabilities/net worth $\leq$ 1.3 times. (3) Minimum net working capital of at least $3.0 million. (4) Capital expenditures limited to greater of $250,000 per year or 50% of cumulative profits after tax from date of agreement.
9/9/76	9/30/77	6.5	1.20 (prime + 1%)	Southeast @ $3.25 Chemical @ $3.25	(1) Tangible net worth $\geq$ $6.5 million to 9/23/76; rising to $8.6 million at 9/30/77. (2) Liabilities/net worth $\leq$1.6 until 12/29/76, and $\leq$1.5 thereafter. (3) Minimum net working capital of at least $3.8 million plus borrowings hereunder until 12/24/76, and at least $4.0 million thereafter. (4) No capital expenditures in excess of $400,000 per year. (5) Equity sales reduce commitment by 100% of the amount issued up to $2.0 million, plus 50% of the amount issued in excess of $2.0 million.

Date of Agreement	Expiration Date	Maximum Credit ($ millions)	Interest Rate*	Loan Participants	Loan Covenants†
12/20/77	12/20/78	8.5	Prime + 1% + compensating balance‡ of 10% of loan + 10% of total commitment	FNB-Boston @ $4.5 Southeast @ $4.0	(1) Tangible net worth ≥ $9.45 million until 12/22/77, after which amounts rising to $13.5 million at 9/29/78. (2) Liabilities/net worth ≤ 1.72 until 12/22/77, after which ratio must decline to 1.20 by 9/29/78. (3) Minimum net working capital ≥ $5.0 million until 12/22/77, after which amount rises to $9.25 million at 6/30/78. (4) Capital expenditures limited to $1.5 million per year. (5) Annualized inventory turnover rate will exceed 2.25x during each quarter. (6) No distributions while tangible net worth less than $20 million. (7) R&D expenditures not to exceed 10% of sales.
3/3/78		10.0	Prime + 1% for $8.5 million; prime + 1½% for balance; + compensating balance‡ of 10% of loan + 10% of commitment	FNB-Boston @ $6.0 Southeast @ $4.0	Same as above except: (a) The ratio of liabilities/net worth could decline more slowly in the early period to 1.20 by 9/29/78. (b) Inventory turnover requirement dropped to 2.0 for the quarter ending 3/23/78.
5/8/78		12.0	Same as above‡	FNB-Boston @ $6.0 Southeast @ $4.0 Continental Ill. @ $2.0	Same as above.

*The loan terms also included a commitment fee equal to ½% of any unused portion of the maximum credit available.
†The loan covenants included the condition that essentially all of Systems' assets would be pledged to secure the bank loans, and that the total loan outstanding would not exceed 90% of qualified accounts receivable.
‡Interest equivalent to the lenders' earnings on the compensating balances could be paid in lieu of maintaining these balances.

Exhibit 4

SYSTEMS ENGINEERING LABORATORIES, INC.

KEY FINANCIAL DATA FOR SYSTEMS' PRINCIPAL COMPETITORS

	1974	1975	1976	1977
Sales (millions):				
Digital Equipment............	$ 421.9	$ 533.8	$ 736.3	$1,058.6
Data General................	93.0	119.6	178.7	254.7
Prime Computer..............	6.5	11.4	22.8	50.0
Perkin-Elmer Corp............	293.6	323.0	354.7	432.4
Systems Engineering Labs......	15.0	17.5	20.0	30.8
Profit after taxes (millions):				
Digital Equipment............	$ 44.0	$ 46.0	$ 73.4	$ 108.5
Data General................	10.1	13.5	20.8	28.6
Prime Computer..............	(.5)	.7	2.4	3.9
Perkin-Elmer Corp............	19.2	20.5	21.0	26.6
Systems Engineering Labs......	(3.9)	(.3)	0.0	1.5
Borrowing ratio:*				
Digital Equipment...........	(.12)	(.02)	(.35)	.04
Data General................	(.02)	(.79)	(.37)	(.25)
Prime Computer..............	.59	.53	.59	.39
Perkin-Elmer Corp............	(.09)	(.08)	(.09)	.02
Systems Engineering Labs......	.40	.31	.46	.46
(Profit after taxes)/net worth:				
Digital Equipment...........	.131	.117	.121	.148
Data General................	.216	.151	.181	.196
Prime Computer..............	(.250)	.250	.453	.255
Perkin-Elmer Corp............	.133	.123	.113	.127
Systems Engineering Labs......	(.520)	(.042)	000	.169
Common stock β:				
Digital Equipment...........				1.21
Data General................				1.46
Prime Computer..............				2.18
Perkin-Elmer Corp............				1.48
Systems Engineering Labs......				1.72

* The borrowing ratio is defined as debt versus total capitalization where cash and marketable securities have been removed from both the numerator and the denominator of the ratio. That is (borrowed money − cash − marketable securities)/(net worth + borrowed money − cash − marketable securities). This ratio will be negative in those situations where the firm has more cash and marketable securities than it has borrowed money. Under such circumstances the firm has negative leverage.

Source: *Moody's Industrial Manual.*

Exhibit 5

SYSTEMS ENGINEERING LABORATORIES, INC.
STOCK PRICE VERSUS THE S&P 500, 1974–1978

Exhibit 6

SYSTEMS ENGINEERING LABORATORIES, INC.

UNDERWRITTEN INITIAL PUBLIC EQUITY OFFERINGS OF SMALL* FIRMS VERSUS
THE OVERALL LEVEL OF STOCK MARKET PRICES, 1968–1977

Year	Number of Issues Underwritten	Total Size of Offerings ($ millions)	S&P 500 Average
1968	358	$ 745	106.5
1969	698	1,367	91.1
1970	198	375	90.1
1971	248	551	99.2
1972	409	896	117.5
1973	101	205	94.8
1974	9	16	67.1
1975	4	16	88.7
1976	38	168	104.7
1977	29	110	93.8
1978 3 mos.	2	12	89.2

*Small firms are defined as those with less than $5 million of net worth prior to their initial public offering through 1975. In 1976, the cutoff point was raised to include all firms with less than $10 million of net worth prior to their initial public offering.

Sources: (1) *Venture Capital*, March 1976, p. 8; January 1977, p. 12; January 1978, p. 7; and (2) "Security Price Index Record," *Standard & Poor's Statistical Service*, 1978.

Exhibit 7

SYSTEMS ENGINEERING LABORATORIES, INC.
Public Offerings of Low-Rated, Nonconvertible Debentures

Issuer	*Date*	*Amount ($ millions)*	*Security*	*Rating Moody's/ S & P*	*Pro Forma Debt Percent Total Capital*	*Yield to Maturity at Issue Date*	*Lead Manager*	*Underwriting Cost (Percent of Total Issue)*
Western Air Lines	4/76	$ 23.0	10% Sub. S.F. notes 1984	Ba/B	57%	10.19%	E. F. Hutton	2.50%
Hospital Affiliates	10/76	12.0	10% Sr. debs. 1991	NR/BB+	65	10.00	Goldman Sachs	4.00
City Investing	12/76	125.0	9% S.F. debs. 1996	NR/BB	54	11.02	Blyth Eastman Dillon	2.80
LTV Corp.	2/77	75.0	9¼% S.F. debs. 1997	B/B	75	11.40	Lehman Brothers	3.30
Zapata Corp.	3/77	75.0	10¼% Sub. debs. 1997	B/B	68	11.44	Lehman Brothers	3.30
Fuqua Inds.	3/77	60.0	9⅞% Sr. Sub. debs. 1997	B/B	50	11.27	Lehman Brothers	3.30
Texas International Co.	4/77	30.0	11½% Sub. debs. 1997	B/B	52	11.50	Drexel Burnham Lambert	3.00
UV Inds.	4/77	25.0	9¼% Sr. Sub. notes 1987	Ba/BB−	53	9.25	E. F. Hutton	1.70
APL Corp.	7/77	35.0	10¾% Sub. debs. 1997	B/BB	44	10.75	Bear Stearns	2.75
Michigan Gen'l. Corp.	8/77	27.5	10⅞% Sr. S.F. debs. 1992	B/BB	66	10.875	Drexel Burnham Lambert	3.50
Buttes Gas & Oil Co.	8/77	70.0	10¼% Sub. debs. 1997	B/B	67	11.10	E. F. Hutton	3.30
U.S. Home Corp.	8/77	50.0	10% Notes 1987	NR/BB	52	10.00	White Weld	1.75
City Investing Co.	8/77	100.0	9⅛% S.F. debs. 1997	NR/BB	50	10.43	Blyth Eastman Dillon	2.80
Western Co. of N. Amer.	9/77	32.5	10⅞% Sub. debs. 1997	B/B	55	11.29	Smith Barney, Harris Upham	6.40
Loral Corp.	9/77	20.0	10¾% Sub. S.F. debs. 1997	B/BB−	48	10.75	Paine Webber	2.50
Action Inds.	9/77	12.0	11% Sr. S.F. debs. 1992	B/BB−	55	11.00	Drexel Burnham Lambert	2.50
Gulf Resources & Chem.	10/77	50.0	10⅞% Sub. S.F. debs. 1997	B/B	50	10.875	Bear Stearns	2.25
Emerson Radio Corp.	10/77	7.5	11% Sr. S.F. debs. 1992	B/B	53	11.49	Drexel Burnham Lambert	4.00
Polychrome Corp.	10/77	20.0	10½% Sr. S.F. debs. 1997	Ba/BB	39	10.50	Drexel Burnham Lambert	2.00
Tannetics	12/77	12.5	10½% Sr. S.F. debs. 1992	NR/B	46	11.31	Drexel Burnham Lambert	3.75
Cascade Natural Gas	12/77	10.0	10½% Sr. Sub. debs. 1992	Ba/BB	61	10.50	Hornblower Weeks, Noyes & Trask	3.00
Comdisco	12/77	15.0	11½% Sub. debs. 1992	B/B	91	11.50	Drexel Burnham Lambert	3.40
Caesars World	12/77	25.0	11¼% Sr. S.F. debs. 1997	NR/B	75	12.29	E. F. Hutton	3.75
Lear Petroleum Corp.	12/77	13.0	11½% Sub. debs. 1992	NR/CCC	75	11.50	Bateman Eichler, Hill Richards	4.00
Petro-Lewis Corp.	1/78	25.0	11% Sub. debs. 1997	NR/B	70	11.79	Oppenheimer	3.60
Midland Glass Co.	2/78	25.0	10¾% Sub. S.F. debs. 1998	B/B	43	10.75	Bear Stearns	2.50
Charter Medical Corp.	2/78	12.0	11% S.F. debs. 1993	NR/B	70	11.00	Drexel Burnham Lambert	3.30
California Life Corp.	3/78	20.0	11% S.F. debs. 1998	NR/BB	48	11.00	First Boston	2.50
A-T-O	3/78	20.0	10⅜% Sub. debs. 1998	Ba/B	52	10.375	E.F. Hutton	2.20
Western Co. of N. Amer.	3/78	30.0	10.70% Sub. debs. 1998	B/B	58	10.70	Smith Barney, Harris Upham	2.75

Source: *Institutional Investor*, August 1978, pp. 36–37.

Exhibit 8

SYSTEMS ENGINEERING LABORATORIES, INC.

NET ASSETS OF MUTUAL FUNDS SPECIALIZING
IN LOW-RATED, HIGH-YIELD DEBT SECURITIES

| Fund | Net Assets ($ millions) | | | | |
	1973	1974	1975	1976	1977
Keystone Custodian Fund, series B-4....	$243	$236	$324	$449	$477
First Investors Fund for Income, Inc......	18	43	105	223	363
Lord Abbett Bond-Debenture Fund.....	99	102	137	175	182
National Bond Fund..................	40	55	86	120	140
Fidelity Aggressive Income Fund.......	—	—	—	—	5

Source: *Investment Companies 1978*, Wiesenberger Investment Company Service.

Exhibit 9

SYSTEMS ENGINEERING LABORATORIES, INC.

YIELDS ON LONG-TERM AAA AND BAA INDUSTRIAL BONDS, 90-DAY TREASURY BILLS,
AND THE COMMERCIAL BANK PRIME RATE,
FIRST QUARTER 1974–FOURTH QUARTER 1976
AND JANUARY 1977–MARCH 1978
(Percent)

| | Industrial Bond Yields | | | 90-Day Treasury Bill Rate | Commercial Bank Prime Rate |
	Aaa	Baa	Difference		
March 1974...........	7.87	8.42	.55	7.99	9.25
June.................	8.34	9.03	.69	8.15	11.75
Sept.................	9.12	9.78	.66	8.36	12.00
Dec.................	8.74	9.85	1.11	7.18	10.50
March 1975...........	8.52	10.01	1.49	5.54	7.75
June.................	8.61	10.39	1.78	5.19	7.00
Sept.................	8.68	10.35	1.67	6.38	8.00
Dec.................	8.51	10.33	1.82	5.50	7.25
March 1976...........	8.30	10.07	1.77	5.05	6.75
June.................	8.40	9.76	1.36	5.44	7.25
Sept.................	8.18	9.33	1.15	5.08	7.00
Dec.................	7.81	9.03	1.22	4.35	6.25
Jan. 1977............	7.77	8.99	1.22	4.60	6.25
Feb.................	7.86	9.04	1.18	4.66	6.25
March...............	7.92	9.04	1.12	4.61	6.25
April................	7.86	8.97	1.11	4.54	6.25
May.................	7.87	8.88	1.01	4.94	6.75
June.....:..........	7.77	8.80	1.03	5.00	6.75
July.................	7.78	8.75	.97	5.14	6.75
Aug.................	7.82	8.72	.90	5.50	7.00
Sept.................	7.76	8.74	.98	5.77	7.25
Oct.................	7.88	8.77	.89	6.19	7.75
Nov.................	7.93	8.84	.91	6.16	7.75
Dec.................	8.04	8.90	.86	6.06	7.75
Jan. 1978............	8.31	9.07	.76	6.44	8.00
Feb.................	8.37	9.11	.74	6.45	8.00
March...............	8.36	9.07	.71	6.29	8.00

Exhibit 10

SYSTEMS ENGINEERING LABORATORIES, INC.

PRO FORMA REVENUES, PROFITS, EPS, AND DEBT/TOTAL CAPITAL RATIOS FOR SYSTEMS ENGINEERING LABORATORIES OVER THE PERIOD 1978–1981 UNDER VARIOUS FINANCING ASSUMPTIONS

($ millions except per share data)

	6/30/78	Raise $10 Million Equity in 1978			Raise $10 Million Debt in 1978		
		6/30/79	6/30/80	6/30/81	6/30/79	6/30/80	6/30/81
1 Revenues (quarterly data for fiscal 4th quarter)	$ 17.6	$ 22.9	$ 29.7	$ 38.7	$ 22.9	$ 29.7	$ 38.7
2 Revenues*	52.9	81.0	105.2	136.8	81.0	105.2	136.8
3 Earnings before interest and taxes†	$ 6.6	$ 10.5	$ 13.7	$ 17.8	$ 10.5	$ 13.7	$ 17.8
4 Interest‡	1.3	1.3	2.1	3.1	2.7	3.5	4.6
5 Profit before taxes	$ 5.3	$ 9.2	$ 11.6	$ 14.7	$ 7.8	$ 10.2	$ 13.2
6 Taxes	2.4	4.4	5.6	7.1	3.7	4.9	6.3
7 Profit after taxes (before extraordinary items)	$ 2.9	$ 4.8	$ 6.0	$ 7.6	$ 4.1	$ 5.3	$ 6.9
8 Extraordinary items§	2.2	.6	—	—	.6	—	—
9 Profit after taxes	$ 5.1	$ 5.4	$ 6.0	$ 7.6	$ 4.7	$ 5.3	$ 6.9
10 Total assets‖	$ 44.0	$ 57.3	$ 74.3	$ 96.8	$ 57.3	$ 74.3	$ 96.8
11 Liabilities other than borrowed money#	$ 13.2	$ 17.2	$ 22.3	$ 29.0	$ 17.2	$ 22.3	$ 29.0
12 Borrowed money	16.8	10.7	16.6	24.8	21.4	28.0	36.9
13 Net worth	14.0‡‡	29.4	35.4	43.0	18.7	24.0	30.9
14 Total liabilities and net worth	$ 44.0	$ 57.3	$ 74.3	$ 96.8	$ 57.3	$ 74.3	$ 96.8
15 Shares outstanding** (in thousands)	2,800	4,180	4,180	4,180	2,800	2,800	2,800
16 EPS (before extraordinary items) ($'s)	$ 1.04	$ 1.15	$ 1.44	$ 1.82	$ 1.46	$ 1.89	$ 2.46
17 Debt/total capital††	.55	.27	.32	.37	.53	.54	.54
18 Senior borrowings/(net worth and subordinated debt)	1.20	.36	.47	.58	.40	.53	.66

* Assumes revenues in the 4th quarter of each year are 30% higher than the level achieved in the 4th quarter of the prior year, and that sales for the year equal four times the average of the [4th quarter rate of the year in question plus the 4th quarter rate of the prior year].

† Assumes earnings before interest and taxes equal 13% of revenues per line 36, Exhibit 2.

‡ Interest is calculated as 12.5% of year-end borrowed money.

§ Extraordinary item equal to .6 in 1979 represents the utilization of Systems' remaining tax loss carryforward.

‖ Assumes that the assets required to support sales at the 4th quarter rate each year would equal (4th quarter revenues) × (4) ÷ 1.6 per line 32, Exhibit 2.

Assumes that liabilities other than borrowed money remain at 30% of total assets.

** Assumes that in order to net $10 million at a share price of $7.25 net to Systems, 1.38 million Systems shares would be sold in an equity offering.

†† Borrowed money/(borrowed money plus net worth).

‡‡ Assumes no new equity raised via sale of stock prior to 6/30/78.

Source: Casewriter estimates.

LING-TEMCO-VOUGHT, INC.

In early, 1971, Ling-Temco-Vought, Inc. (LTV) faced a serious financial crisis. The company had just completed calendar year 1970 with a loss of about $70 million (line 24, Exhibit 1). This amount, combined with the loss of $38 million reported for 1969, more than wiped out the entire profit earned by the firm from its inception in 1953. By year-end 1970, LTV had a debt/equity ratio of 4.48 (line 26, Exhibit 2), a cash deficit from operations for the year exceeding $15 million (line 11, Exhibit 3) and debt maturities within one year equal to $77 million (line 18, Exhibit 2). While it appeared that this debt could be retired as it matured with cash raised from the sale of assets, it was equally clear that such a move would represent only a holding action at best. To many creditors and investors, LTV's capital structure at the end of 1970 appeared dangerously unbalanced, and they looked to the company for some significant corrective action in the not too distant future.

Corporate structure and business strategy

LTV's corporate structure had always been very complex. In many ways the firm resembled a holding company. As of December 31, 1970, for example, it owned a control position in seven other large and well-known corporations (Exhibit 4). On the other hand, LTV was so active in acquiring and disposing of securities, whole companies, or portions of companies (Exhibit 5) that in some ways it bore a closer resemblance to a mutual fund than to a holding company.

While LTV's corporate structure was complex, its operating strategy as a business enterprise was simple. LTV's business consisted of buying the common stock of large publicly held companies and then "redeploying"[1] the assets of these companies. LTV borrowed very aggressively, and often used this source of cash to finance tender offers made directly to the shareholders of companies it wished to acquire. The companies selected by LTV as acquisition targets generally had (a) low price-to-earnings ratios, (b) substantial unused borrowing capacity; and (c) one or more easily separable operating divisions which competed in industries characterized by relatively higher price-to-earnings ratios.

---

[1] LTV's concept of "redeployment" is explained in the text that immediately follows.

254

Once a company had been successfully acquired and was wholly owned, LTV would (1) break it up into several different independent firms, usually along the lines of previously separate divisions, (2) have each of these new firms assume a portion of the debt LTV initially used to acquire them (thus reducing LTV's investment), and finally (3) sell a portion (usually about 25%) of the equity in each newly constituted firm to the public in order to return to LTV another large fraction of its investment in the acquisition. The goal of a complete transaction cycle was to leave LTV with a large ownership fraction of some highly leveraged subsidiary companies at no (or very little) cost to LTV. At the conclusion of each transaction, LTV would have the use of an increased reserve of borrowing power generated by its growing portfolio of marketable securities of subsidiary companies. LTV's increased borrowing power could then be used to finance the acquisition of additional and generally larger companies.

This approach to the management of corporate assets was a unique and integral part of the business strategy of LTV and its founder, Mr. James J. Ling. In 1969, Mr. Ling elaborated on his strategy (which he dubbed "Redeployment") and philosophized about the future of LTV as follows:

> Thus you see, from my point of view, redeploying assets in this way is building values [in terms of the securities of acquired subsidiaries which LTV retained] and these values are measured on the stock market. And in turn they [the retained securities] are useful financially as the means of building new values.
>
> . . . . .
>
> I personally believe that the best background for corporate life in a company such as LTV is that of a financial analyst working in the Wall Street arena— someone who . . . knows the basic ways of getting good information in and out about companies.
>
> . . . . .
>
> The principles on which we operate—essentially the redeployment concept of managing corporate assets—have general validity for business and are consistent with the general rules of a competitive economy. . . . [But] suppose that for some reason or other [such as Justice Department intervention] the growth of LTV [were] impeded; it might [then] very well benefit all of the underlying LTV companies if LTV disposed of its shares in those companies, and suppose that came to pass. LTV now has no operating connection with any other company. Suppose as a result of our dispositions of our interests in all the underlying companies, we have developed $1.5 billion in assets, and, to simplify the model, let's say that they are in the form of cash in the bank. Now we want to redeploy those assets; at this stage we have the responsibility of building earnings per share—more than we would get from C/D's[2] and the like. And so, hopefully, we purchase control of one of the top twenty corporations on FORTUNE's list of the 500 largest industrials, say a company having a number of major subsidiaries and divisions—one that is suitable for redeployment under our concept of building assets, managing assets (to the best advantage of the shareholders). Having over a period of time ac-

---

[2] C/D's (certificates of deposit) are interest bearing time deposits in banks. [Footnote added.]

complished that, our assets become worth, say $2.5 billion, and we are fenced in again as regards growth. Then, speaking abstractly in terms of the model, we might very well sell out again and buy a bigger company, one, say, in the top ten. Remember, this is all iffy. I believe that we can very well go forward by maintaining the investments that we have in the underlying subsidiary companies. Fenced in or not, we are still in the business of managing assets. That's what, in the multi-industry companies, is really the name of the game.[3]

Creative management of capital structure

While LTV was extremely innovative in the asset management area, the firm was equally creative in its approach to liabilities management. Some of Mr. Ling's views on capital structure follow:

. . . get all the money you can without using equity, or use equity as infrequently as possible. I backed up this thought with a study of the Dow-Jones averages, a personal study. I went back to the last day of December, 1922, the day I was born—I usually think that's far back enough for me to go. I checked the Dow-Jones averages and found that there have been only a few times that the annual averages have been lower than a P/E ratio of 10, and the historical averages have usually been somewhat above that. Money rates, on the other hand, have increasingly risen from 1½ to 2 percent to 3, 4, 5, 6, 7, 8, 9, 10 percent, with intermediate ups and downs. The result is that debentures and bonds that were sold at 2½ percent and 3 percent, and which a lot of banks had and still have in their portfolios, turned out to be the worst investment in the world. Hence the most desirable thing to issue when you buy a company, if you can buy good, solid operating assets and recurring earnings, is debt.

. . . . .

The economic environment we live in demands that we alter capital structure every chance that we get when it's constructive to do so.

. . . . .

As for those [investors] who can't keep up with our changing financial structure . . . we'll use that to our advantage, perhaps by buying in our stock if the P/E remains low enough long enough. Certainly that's an option that we've executed in times past in similar conditions. If the market puts us too high we'll take advantage by selling LTV stock, and if it puts us too low, we take advantage by buying.[4]

Between 1964 and 1968, LTV's operating strategy was extremely successful in terms of the traditional financial measures reported to shareholders. With the aid of several large acquisitions at the parent company level (Exhibit 5), sales grew from $300 million to $2.8 billion;[5] earnings per share rose from $0.91 to $5.01; and the price of LTV common stock moved from $6 to over $100 a share. During this period LTV made three acquisitions of firms in

---

[3] John McDonald, "Some Candid Answers from James J. Ling," *Fortune*, Part I, August 1, 1969, pp. 163–64; Part II, September 1969, p. 185.

[4] John McDonald, *op. cit.*, Part II, pp. 137–38 and 178.

[5] This figure represents consolidated sales. It is derived by adding the sales of all LTV subsidiary companies together and then deducting any sales between subsidiaries.

the $1 billion class.[6] These acquisitions included Wilson & Co. in 1967, Greatamerica Corporation in 1968, and Jones & Laughlin Steel Corporation in 1968. It was this last acquisition and the method used to finance it that ultimately led to LTV's difficulties.

The move into steel

Early in 1968, LTV moved to acquire the Jones & Laughlin Steel Corporation (J&L), a firm larger in terms of earnings than LTV itself. Mr. Ling cited several reasons for his decision to make a major acquisition in the steel industry at that time. His reasons related mostly to the economic and political environment existing in 1968.

Now here we were, early 1968. . . . More and more tenders are being made, and a hostile climate is slowly developing against making them. You are looking at the possibility that there will be clampdowns on acquisitions. This has been coming for a long, long period of time. Thus, we thought, if you want to make not a big terminal acquisition but at least a big one for the time being, this was the time.

. . . . .

At the same time I felt the money market getting tighter and tighter [Exhibit 6] and recognized that we might not be able to borrow 225, 230, 240 million dollars [needed for a tender offer] in three months or six months or nine months. [Any acquisition] had to be a big one. . . . We came down to a choice of going into steel or into capital goods. . . . You look at your ability, hopefully, to recapture part of the cost of buying a company, so that you wind up . . . with a big percentage interest in the company but with no real cost in it. We concluded that we couldn't really do that in some of the capital-goods businesses, but I had an idea of how to do it in the steel industry.[7]

Having made this decision, in May, 1968, LTV tendered for and ultimately received 5 million shares of J&L common stock. For its equity position, which represented 63% ownership, LTV paid $85 a share in cash, a total of $425 million. This was the largest cash tender offer in history, and it was made at a premium of 75% above J&L's pre-tender offer market price of $48.50. LTV financed the tender offer by:

(a) Raising $75 million in cash through the sale of two subsidiary companies acquired in the Greatamerica acquisition,[8] (Exhibit 5),
(b) Selling 5-year notes for $130 million, and
(c) Borrowing $220 million through one-year loans from a group of 25 banks.

---

[6] Measured in terms of sales for Wilson & Co. and Jones & Laughlin Steel Corporation and in terms of assets for Greatamerica Corporation.

[7] John McDonald, op. cit., Part I, pp. 93–94.

[8] The Greatamerica acquisition was financed with $490 million of LTV subordinated long-term debt (Exhibit 5) which did not mature until 1988. The proceeds from this sale of subsidiary companies were not immediately needed for debt retirement, as the related maturities were far in the future.

In the nine months following the successful tender offer for 63% of J&L common stock, LTV made plans for acquiring the rest of the J&L stock in anticipation of a recapitalization that would relieve LTV of its potentially hazardous $200 million short-term debt position (line 16, Exhibit 2). Standing on the LTV parent company balance sheet, the $200 million short-term debt obligation was rather threatening. A "redeployed" J&L, however, could easily have absorbed this amount of additional debt from its LTV parent since at the end of 1968 J&L's debt position was only $230 million versus an equity base exceeding $700 million.

Unfortunately for LTV, in early 1969, the U.S. Department of Justice, after announcing an antitrust suit aimed at requiring complete divestiture of LTV's ownership interest in J&L, forced LTV to agree that:

Pending the final adjudication of this litigation, the business and financial operations of Jones & Laughlin Steel Corporation shall be maintained completely separate and independent from those of Ling-Temco-Vought, Inc.[9]

This action foreclosed any alternative LTV may have had to transfer some of its debt directly into J&L, and left LTV dangerously overextended. The company could not reverse its acquisition of J&L stock (by selling it in the open market, for example) without losing the premium it had paid in the tender offer. This premium represented $182.5 million or 63% of LTV's net worth at the end of 1968; so LTV was not anxious to exploit this alternative. Unfortunately, even though the company could not afford to divest J&L, neither could it afford to continue holding J&L as an essentially dormant asset. As a holding company, LTV had a tiny revenue base, which in the company's recent history had never come close to covering its expenses (lines 4 and 7, Exhibit 3). By 1968, for example, interest requirements of $46.5 million (line 5, Exhibit 3) on LTV's outstanding debt of $950.0 million (line 24, Exhibit 2) had caused the company to incur a $21.8 million negative cash flow from operations (line 11, Exhibit 3). Since LTV was clearly unable to service its interest costs and debt repayments from internally generated cash flow, the firm could look only to the sale of assets or new financings to satisfy its cash needs.

Again unfortunately for LTV, its legal and financial problems emerged just as the economic climate in the United States began showing signs of weakness. Corporate profits began sliding in the fourth quarter of 1968, as did stock market prices (lines 2–3, Exhibit 6). In addition, interest rates began rising precipitously (lines 4–5, Exhibit 6) just as Mr. Ling had predicted. Perhaps worst of all, the profits of LTV's subsidiary companies fell sharply from $81.4 million to $58.5 million between 1968 and 1969 (lines 1–9, Exhibit 1).

The decline in profitability of LTV's subsidiary companies was accompanied by an even faster decline in the market value of their common stocks.

---

[9] U.S. Department of Justice, Memorandum of Agreement with Ling-Temco-Vought, Inc., March 26, 1969.

This erosion in market values was naturally reflected in LTV's principal asset (its ownership of subsidiary company common stocks) and in LTV's borrowing power against these assets. So sharp was the decline in the stock price of LTV subsidiary companies (Exhibit 6) that between 12/31/68 and 12/31/69 LTV saw the spread between the market value and the cost of its security portfolio move from a positive $300 million to a negative $440 million (Exhibit 7).

The loss of flexibility, then control

The deterioration in LTV's position made it essentially impossible for the company to raise additional capital.[10] This fact coupled with LTV's negative operating cash flow meant that the only way LTV could satisfy its creditors was through the sale of assets or the refinancing of existing debt as it matured. LTV's bank loans were originally scheduled to be completely retired in 1969, but the firm was unable to accomplish this objective. LTV did, however, reduce its bank debt from $201 million to $111 million during 1969. The $90 million reduction was accomplished through the sale of LTV's entire interest in two subsidiary companies and the sale of a large block of Braniff Airways stock (Exhibit 5). By the end of 1969, LTV had managed to extend the maturity on its remaining $111 million in bank loans to January, 1971.

If 1969 could be described as a difficult year for LTV, 1970 could only be called a disaster. There were two major factors contributing to this condition. First, the earnings of J&L, LTV's most important subsidiary, fell from $22.1 million to a deficit of $15.4 million. This profit reversal of $37.5 million dropped LTV's equity in the earnings of all subsidiaries to below $10 million (line 20, Exhibit 1). Second, the market prices of LTV subsidiary company common stocks were hit very hard in the general market decline of 1970 (Exhibit 6). Indeed, if LTV's entire portfolio of securities in these companies had been liquidated at December 31, 1970 prices and LTV's other assets liquidated at book value, the company would have been unable to pay off its subordinated debt at even close to face value (Exhibit 8).

In an effort to further reduce its bank debt and stave off a possible bankruptcy, LTV sold off all its stock holdings in two subsidiaries during the first quarter of 1970, prompting *Forbes* magazine to write:

Want to buy a glamour company at bargain prices? You should have been in Dallas last month. James J. Ling . . . was selling them off at a pace that would make a used car salesman proud.[11]

In May, 1970, Robert H. Stewart, III, chairman of the First National Bank in Dallas, was elected chairman of LTV replacing Mr. Ling, who became

---

[10] The indenture agreement relating to the 5% subordinated debentures used to acquire the Greatamerica Corporation prohibited additional borrowings when LTV's long-term debt exceeded 150% of the sum of book net worth plus the spread between the market value and the cost of its security holdings in subsidiary companies (line 3, Exhibit 7).

[11] *Forbes*, March 15, 1970.

president. LTV's banks were evidently anxious to salvage what they could on their loans, as might be inferred from Mr. Stewart's comment that:

My responsibility to the First National Bank in Dallas will continue foremost in my mind, but I have confidence in the future of LTV and will be pleased to work with its officers and directors.[12]

Fears that LTV's banks might move precipitously in converting the firm's assets into cash (so as to pay off bank loans) led some analysts to question whether LTV's other creditor and investor groups might not fare better if LTV were forced to file a bankruptcy petition.

. . . Bankruptcy . . . does have certain advantages: By keeping the creditors at arm's length, it gives the troubled company time to get its house in order.

What's happening at LTV, by contrast, is that the creditors, mainly the bankers, hold the reins. Whether that's in the best interests of everyone else with an interest in LTV and its subsidiaries remains to be seen.[13]

So serious was LTV's situation in May, 1970, that at one point the market price of the company's 5% subordinated debentures (which had been issued in the Greatamerica acquisition) fell to 15% of their face value (Exhibit 9). At this price, their yield to maturity in 1988 reached 34%.

YIELD TO MATURITY AS A FUNCTION OF PURCHASE PRICE IN 1971 FOR
LTV 5% SUBORDINATED DEBENTURES, DUE 1988

Market Price*	Yield to Maturity
$60	9.5%
50	11.5
40	14.2
30	18.4
20	26.2
15	34.0

* Bond prices are quoted in terms of dollars per $100 of face amount, in spite of the fact that most bonds are traded in minimum multiples of $1,000 face amount.

The financial picture at LTV improves

LTV management was able to stave off bankruptcy in 1970, and by year-end had reduced the company's bank indebtedness from $111 million to $75 million. The maturity of this $75 million had been extended in the early weeks of 1971 from January 31, 1971 to July 31, 1971. This loan was secured by essentially all the assets of the company.

Perhaps the most significant event of 1970 occurred when LTV negotiated an agreement with the Department of Justice relating to its ownership interest in J&L. That agreement permitted LTV to gain operating control of J&L as soon as LTV divested all its holdings in both Braniff Airways and Okonite (Exhibit 4).

---

[12] *The Wall Street Journal*, May 18, 1970.
[13] *Forbes*, "A Fate Worse Than Bankruptcy," August 15, 1970, p. 18.

In order both to comply with the Justice Department agreement and also to reduce its short-term debt, in early 1971, LTV sold off (1) 4.5 million of its 10.5 million Braniff shares for $44 million cash; (2) 1.15 million of its 4.5 million Wilson & Co. shares for $15 million cash,[14] and (3) all of its stock in Okonite for $40.5 million (roughly half of which was paid in cash—Exhibit 5). The cumulative impact of these transactions, had they been completed by December 31, 1970, would have placed LTV in the year-end position shown (on a retroactive basis) in column 5 of Exhibit 2. Following these three transactions, under the Justice Department agreement, LTV had only to dispose of its remaining 6 million shares of Braniff before it could take control of J&L.

The receipts from the three transactions just described provided almost enough cash to get LTV out from under its bank debt in the spring of 1971. In addition LTV was strengthened by an apparent upturn in the economy during the first quarter of 1971 (Exhibit 6). Estimates of LTV subsidiary company earnings for the first quarter were up sharply (Exhibit 1). By the spring of 1971, it appeared that LTV had solved its immediate problem in that bankruptcy had at least been temporarily averted, but the firm now faced the perhaps more difficult problem of assuring its long-run survival and good health. With a debt/equity ratio of 4.2 (column 5, Exhibit 2), its long-term debentures selling in the $30 range, and its common stock collapsed to the $10 area (Exhibit 9), investors had hardly pronounced the LTV crisis at an end.

Some alternatives for strengthening LTV's capital structure

The management of LTV had numerous options for dealing with the company's financial problems as of the spring of 1971. Of the myriad courses of action open, two (representing more or less opposite ends of the spectrum of alternatives) are sketched in the text which follows and in Exhibit 2.

First, the company might have sold its remaining interest in Braniff for cash, and used the proceeds from this transaction to retire debt. If debt with the nearest term maturities were paid down, LTV would have eliminated its problem with debt repayments until mid-1973 (line 20, column 6, Exhibit 2). Under this alternative the company would continue to suffer under a tremendous debt load in relation to its equity base,[15] (line 26, column 6, Exhibit 2) but it would have purchased two years of "breathing room" in which cash pressures would be absent for the first time in many years. A booming economy and substantial improvement in both the earnings record and stock prices of its remaining subsidiaries (should such events have transpired between 1971 and mid-1973) might then have permitted LTV to (1) meet its

---

[14] These shares were purchased by Wilson & Co. at $13 a share. In the two weeks prior to the announcement of the purchase, Wilson & Co. common stock sold in the $23 range. The sale was thus made at a 43% discount from the market.

[15] LTV's equity base would actually be reduced by the Braniff stock sale (line 13, column 6, Exhibit 2) since the market value of Braniff stock was significantly below the price LTV had originally paid to acquire it.

next debt maturity problem in mid-1973 without difficulty, and (2) make whatever long-term alterations in capital structure it deemed necessary away from the crisis atmosphere and low security valuations characterizing LTV's environment in the spring of 1971. Had this approach been chosen, LTV's position on a pro forma basis retroactive to 12/31/70 would have appeared as shown in column 6 of Exhibit 2.

A second alternative, which LTV could have considered in dealing with its financing and capital structure problems in the spring of 1971, consisted of swapping a package of LTV's stock in Braniff plus LTV's own common stock in exchange for a large fraction of the $475 million face value of 5% subordinated LTV debentures which were then outstanding and selling in the public market at a very large discount from face value. A package consisting of 20 shares of Braniff stock and 20 shares of LTV stock had a market value of about $500 as of 3/10/71. If such a package were offered in exchange for each $1000 face value debenture (with a market value of $310 on 3/10/71), a large number of debenture holders might accept the swap.

If LTV were able to attract enough exchanges so as to exhaust its remaining supply of 6 million Braniff shares, the result of the transaction (restated retroactive to 12/31/70) would have left LTV in the pro forma financial position shown in column 7 of Exhibit 2. This alternative, while increasing the number of outstanding LTV shares from 4.3 to 10.3 million, would have immediately moved the company a long way in the direction of strengthening its capital structure.

Exhibit 1

LING-TEMCO-VOUGHT, INC.

INCOME STATEMENTS FOR LTV, INC., PARENT AND SUBSIDIARY
COMPANIES, 1967–71

(In millions of dollars except per share data)

		1967	1968	1969	1970	3 Months 3/31/70	3 Months 3/31/71
	Total Earnings of LTV Subsidiary Companies						
1	Braniff Airlines....................	4.7	10.4	6.2	(2.6)	(.8)	(1.1)
2	Jones & Laughlin Steel..............	35.8	27.6	22.1	(15.4)	(1.0)	10.7
3	LTV Aerospace....................	9.6	15.0	17.0	11.1	3.0	1.1
4	LTV Electrosystems................	5.4	3.3	(3.4)	2.9	0.5	0.5
5	LTV Ling Altec...........:.......	2.9	2.0	(0.3)	—	0.2	0.1
6	Okonite.........................	9.0	6.5	(0.8)	2.0	§	§
7	Wilson & Co......................	11.0	10.1	8.3	12.7	1.6	4.0
8	Wilson Pharmaceutical..............	1.7	1.5	1.8	1.2	§	§
9	Wilson Sporting Goods..............	4.0	4.4	3.0	3.3	§	§
10	Combined extraordinary items of all... subsidiaries.....................	—	0.6	4.6	(24.5)		
		84.1	81.4	58.5	(9.3)		
	LTV "Equity in Earnings"# of Subsidiary Companies						
1	Braniff Airlines...................	§	7.7†	3.5	(1.5)		
2	Jones & Laughlin Steel.............	§	2.6†	15.7	(13.1)		8.6
3	LTV Aerospace....................	7.9	10.6	18.3*	7.7		0.7
4	LTV Electrosystems................	4.0	2.6	(2.8)	2.0		0.4
5	LTV Ling Altec...................	1.0	1.1	(2.8)	(0.7)		—
6	Okonite.........................	7.9	5.5‡	(0.9)‡	1.9	§	§
7	Wilson & Co......................	9.0	8.2	3.8	11.3		3.5
8	Wilson Pharmaceutical..............	1.3	1.2	1.4	§	§	§
9	Wilson Sporting Goods.............	3.0	3.3	2.3	§	§	§
10	LTV share of earnings from continuing operations of subsidiaries.......	34.1	42.8	38.5	7.6		13.2
	LTV parent company operations:						
11	Interest expense + debt discount..	(6.7)	(46.5)	(63.6)	(66.1)		(15.9)
12	Other non-extraordinary items‖....	5.9	30.3	29.4	7.4		4.6
13	Extraordinary items.................	—	2.8	(42.6)	(18.5)		0.8
14	Net income (loss) of LTV and subsidiaries on consolidated basis........	33.2	29.4	(38.3)	(69.6)	(15.3)	2.7
15	Earnings/share per LTV shareholder reports...........................	$ 6.85	$ 5.01	$(10.15)	$(17.09)	$ (3.95)	$0.32

* Includes extraordinary profit equal to 40% of this figure.
† Included for only a portion of year.
‡ After preferred dividends.
§ Not yet acquired by LTV on this date, or sold by LTV prior to this date.
‖ Includes the tax benefits resulting from consolidation (for tax purposes) of 80% or more owned subsidiaries with the LTV parent, and other miscellaneous income statement items which for the sake of convenience have been added together by the case-writer.
LTV's equity in the earnings of each subsidiary was simply equal to its percentage ownership of that subsidiary's common stock multiplied by the subsidiary's profit after taxes.
Sources: (1) LTV annual reports, 1967–70.
　　　　　 (2) Ling-Temco-Vought, Inc., Prospectus, May 21, 1971.
　　　　　 (3) LTV and subsidiary company quarterly reports.

Exhibit 2

LING-TEMCO-VOUGHT, INC.

BALANCE SHEETS FOR LTV, INC. (PARENT COMPANY) FOR 1967–70 PLUS PRO FORMA
BALANCE SHEETS AS OF 12/31/70 FOR SEVERAL RECAPITALIZATION ALTERNATIVES
(In millions of dollars)

		1 1967	2 1968	3 1969	4 1970	5 12/31/70 With Adjust- ment[1]	6 12/31/70 Pro Forma Recapital- ization[1,2]	7 12/31/70 Pro Forma Recapital- ization[1]
1	Current assets..............	84.7	107.6	82.1	31.8	31.8	31.8	31.8
2	Investments in subsidiaries...	181.5	987.8	1,020.3	953.8	788.7	656.4	656.4
3	Unamortized debt discount...	0.5	113.2	103.8	93.5	93.6	93.6	41.6
4	Other assets................	45.7	79.6	23.7	13.9	19.6	19.6	19.6
5	Total.................	312.4	1,288.2	1,229.9	1,093.0	933.7	801.4	749.4
	Current liabilities							
6	Current portion of long- term debt..............	1.5	0.4	22.7	77.3	28.6	—	28.6
7	Notes payable to banks....	—	201.4	0.1	0.1	0.1	—	0.1
8	Other...................	9.6	36.9	40.0	23.4	23.4	23.4	27.4
	Long-term debt							
9	Due subsidiaries..........	—	76.1	113.0	108.4	94.0	94.0	94.0
10	Due others..............	51.5	672.1	752.6	627.0	599.2	547.8	296.0
11	Reserve for investment losses.	—	—	30.0	65.3	7.5	—	—
12	Other deferrals.............	4.7	12.7	10.9	10.0	10.0	10.0	10.0
13	Net worth................	245.1	288.6	260.6	181.5	170.9	126.2	293.3
14	Total.................	312.4	1,288.2	1,229.9	1,093.0	933.7	801.4	749.4
	Maturity schedule of debt*							
15	due in 1968...........	1.5						
16	1969...........	2.5	201.8					
17	1970...........	32.5	27.8	22.9				
18	1971...........	2.5	2.9	127.9	77.5	28.8	—	28.7
19	1972...........	2.5	2.8	2.4	2.4	2.4	—	2.4
20	1973..........	⎫	116.1	115.7	115.7	115.7	66.7	115.7
21	1974..........	⎬ 11.5	⎫	2.4	2.4	2.4	2.4	2.4
22	1975..........		⎬ 598.6	24.4	24.4	24.4	24.4	24.4
23	1976 and beyond	⎭	⎭	⎬ 504.2	482.1	454.3	454.3	151.1
24	Total..................	53.0	950.0	775.5	704.5	628.0	547.8	324.7
25	Ratio of earnings to fixed charges..................	.38	.08	.24	.32	.39	—	1.29
26	Total debt†/equity.........	.22	3.29	3.41	4.48	4.22	5.09	1.43

* Includes all amounts shown in lines 6, 7, and 10. Does not include long-term debt due subsidiaries.
† Includes all amounts shown in lines 6, 7, 9, and 10.
Note: (1) Includes the effects of the early 1971 sale of assets (mentioned on page 465) restated as though the sale had been made prior to 12/31/70.
(2) Includes the effects of Alternative 1 (mentioned on pages 465–66)—an early 1971 sale of LTV's remaining shares in Braniff and the use of the proceeds of this sale to retire all debt maturing prior to mid-1973—all restated as though the transaction had occurred prior to 12/31/70.
(3) Includes the effects of Alternative 2 (mentioned on page 466)—an early 1971 swap of LTV's remaining shares in Braniff plus LTV's common stock in exchange for $300 million in LTV debt due in 1988—all restated as though the transaction had occurred prior to 12/31/70.
Sources: (1) LTV annual reports, 1966–70.
(2) Ling-Temco-Vought, Inc., Prospectus, May 21, 1971.
(3) The data in column 6 include some estimates made by the casewriter.

Exhibit 3

LING-TEMCO-VOUGHT, INC.

STATEMENT OF CASH FLOW FOR LTV, INC. (PARENT COMPANY) FOR 1967–70
(Dollar figures in millions)

		1967	1968	1969	1970
	Income:				
1	Dividends from subsidiaries	$ 1.9	$ 2.9	$ 8.5	$ 8.8
2	Interest earned	1.5	2.0	9.8	14.4
3	Other	3.8	3.3	3.6	3.1
4	Total	$ 7.2	$ 8.2	$21.9	$26.3
	Costs and expenses:				
5	Interest and debt discount	6.7	46.5	63.6	59.3
6	Other expenses	5.3	5.7	6.8	7.5
7	Total	$12.0	$52.2	$70.4	$66.8
8	Loss before income tax and extraordinary items	(4.8)	(44.0)	(48.5)	(40.5)
	Elimination of noncash charges:				
9	Amortization of debt discount plus depreciation	2.7	10.0	13.1	11.1
10	Tax payments received*	6.7	12.2	27.1	14.1
11	Cash flow from operations	4.6	(21.8)	(8.3)	(15.3)
	Liabilities management decisions:				
12	Repayment of debts	(2.1)	(2.2)	(90.7)	(84.9)
13	New debt and equity financings	66.1	428.5	22.0	—
	Asset management decisions:				
14	Investments in and advances to subsidiaries	—	(428.5)	(7.7)	(18.8)
15	Proceeds from sale of assets	—	18.0	97.0	79.0
16	Dividends	(7.8)	(9.3)	(5.5)	(2.8)
17	Other items	1.0	(3.7)	5.7	(8.7)
18	Net increase (decrease) in cash	61.8	(19.0)	12.5	(51.5)
19	Ratio of earnings to fixed charges	.38	.08	.24	.32

* From carryback of operating losses, and from subsidiaries under tax agreements.
Source: (1) Ling-Temco-Vought, Inc., Prospectus, May 21, 1971.

Exhibit 4

LING-TEMCO-VOUGHT, INC.

LTV PARENT AND SUBSIDIARY COMPANIES AS OF 12/31/70

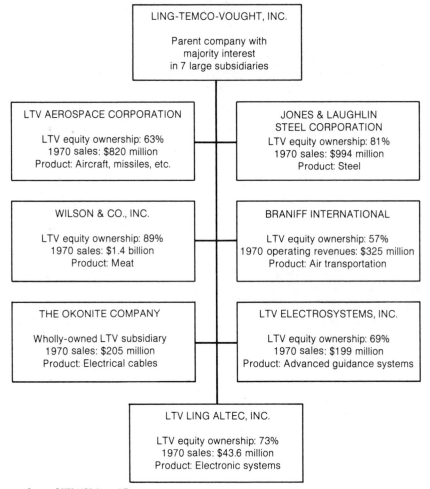

Source: LTV 1970 Annual Report.

Exhibit 5

LING-TEMCO-VOUGHT, INC.

SUMMARY OF LTV, INC. ACQUISITION AND DIVESTITURE ACTIVITY
FROM JANUARY 1, 1964 TO MID-1971

Acquisitions
(*Companies having assets in excess of $2,000,000*)

Name of the Acquired Company	Date of Acquisition	Total Consideration
e Okonite Co.	January 10, 1966	$31,697,127 cash.
	May, 1970	261,976 shares LTV common stock + 224,999 shares of preferred stock issued to eliminate minority interest.
Ilson & Co., Inc.	December, 1966	$81,505,000 cash.
(Later split into Wilson & Co., Wilson Sporting Goods Co., and Wilson Pharmaceutical Co.).	April 27, 1967	1,153,206 shares of $5 series A preferred stock (redemption value $100 per share).
eatamerica Corp. (Later split into Braniff Airways, Inc.; National Car Rental Systems, Inc.; Stonewall Insurance Co.; First Western Bank & Trust Co., Inc.; American Amicable Life Insurance Co., Inc.).	February–April, 1968	$489,761,000, 5 percent subordinated debentures due January 15, 1988; 1,632,539 warrants expiring January 15, 1978.
es & Laughlin Steel Corp.	May, 1968	$428,500,000 cash for 63 percent of stock.
	March, 1969	Jones & Laughlin Industries, Inc., issued the following for 18 percent of the stock; $124,040,600, 6¾ percent subordinated debentures, 1,459,301 warrants, 291,862 common shares.

Divestitures
(*Over $1,000,000 in stock or assets*)

Company	Date Sold	Net Proceeds
Friedrich & Friedrich Refrigerators, Inc. (100 percent).	May 23, 1964	$6,064,000.
TV Aerospace Corp. (122,570 common shares); LTV Electrosystems, Inc. (122,570 common shares); LTV Ling-Altec, Inc. (122,570 common shares).	May 27, 1965	$3,145,000 (245,140 shares of LTV common at 22⅝ less $9 cash per share).
TV Aerospace Corp. (500,000 common shares).	March 1, 1966	$11,175,000 (cash-public offering).
turn Industries, Inc.	March 30, 1966	None (distributable as dividend to shareholders of LTV; net worth as of date sold: $1,245,000).
TV Electrosystems, Inc. (400,000 common shares).	April 27, 1966	$5,500,000 (cash—public offering).
conite Co. (500,000 common shares).	June 22, 1966	$7,900,000 (cash—public offering).
ilson & Co., Inc. (1,000,000 common shares).	July 27, 1967	$21,750,000 (cash—public offering).
ilson Sporting Goods Co. (600,000 common shares).	August 2, 1967	$17,000,000 (cash—public offering).
ilson Pharmaceutical & Chemical Corp. (350,000 common shares).	August 15, 1967	$5,635,000 (cash—public offering).
onewall Insurance Co. (entire LTV interest).	May 9, 1968	$15,000,000 (cash).
rst Western Bank & Trust Co. (entire LTV interest).	June 7, 1968	$62,500,000 (cash).
merican Amicable Life Insurance Co. (entire LTV interest).	October 25, 1968	$18,000,000 cash and $26,000 face value of notes and warrants.
raniff Airways (2,456,227 class A special shares); National Car Rental Systems, Inc. (2,456,227 class A special shares); Computer Technology (810,430 common shares). (In addition to the securities of the above companies, 2,701,567 LTV $115 warrants were issued in the exchange offer.)	December 16, 1968	1,947,001 shares LTV common; $14,822,000 principal amount of LTV 6½ percent notes; $5,000,000 principal amount of 6¾ debentures; $15,306,000 principal amount of LTV 5 percent debentures and $1,811,000 principal amount LTV 5¾ percent debentures.
raniff Airways, Inc. (2,000,000 class A special shares).	February 24, 1969	$33,900,000 (cash—secondary offering to public).
omputer Technology, Inc. (entire LTV interest).	March 28, 1969	$18,169,000 (cash—secondary offering to public).
ational Car Rental Systems, Inc. (entire LTV interest).	May 2, 1969	$31,610,000 (cash).
nes & Laughlin Industries, Inc. (291,862 common shares—issued pursuant to exchange offer).	May 15, 1969	$7,588,400 (based on an assigned value of $26 per share, its estimated value at the time the exchange offer was made).
hitehall Electronics Corp. (1,800,000 shares).	July 25, 1969 September 23, 1969	$7,500,000 ($6,140,000 cash and $1,359,500 note receivable).
ilson Sporting Goods (entire LTV interest).	February 22, 1970	$63,000,000 (cash).
ilson Pharmaceutical (entire LTV interest).	July 10, 1970	$16,000,000 (cash).
konite (entire LTV interest).	Spring, 1971	$40,500,000 ($22 million cash and notes).
raniff Airways (4,500,000 class A shares).	Spring, 1971	$43,856,000 (cash—secondary offering to public).
ilson & Co. (1,150,000 common shares).	Spring, 1971	$15,000,000 (cash—repurchased by Wilson).

Exhibit 5 is not included for the purpose of generating insight into individual transactions. It is presented instead to show the xtent and variety of LTV's acquisition and divestiture activity.

Sources: (1) U.S. House of Representatives, Antitrust Subcommittee of the Committee on the Judiciary, "Investigation of Conglomerate Corporations," June 1, 1971, pp. 335, 337.
(2) Ling-Temco-Vought, Inc., Prospectus, May 21, 1971.

Exhibit 6

LING-TEMCO-VOUGHT, INC.

Selected Macro Economic Data and LTV Subsidiary Security Prices from 12/31/67 to 3/31/71

	12/31/67	12/31/68	3/31/69	6/30/69	9/30/69	12/31/69	3/31/70	6/30/70	9/30/70	12/31/70	3/31/71
1. GNP seasonally adjusted (billions of 1958 dollars)	683.6	716.5	721.4	724.2	727.8	725.2	719.8	721.1	723.3	715.9	729.7
2. Corporate profits (billions of dollars)	80.0	84.7	82.7	80.7	78.0	73.3	69.8	71.5	73.0	69.0	75.5
3. Dow Jones industrial average	905	944	935	873	813	800	786	683	760	839	904
4. Average yield on medium-grade industrial bonds (%)	6.53	6.82	7.44	7.65	8.02	8.58	8.57	9.05	9.29	8.92	8.18
5. Bank prime rate of interest (%)	6	6¾	7½	8½	8½	8½	8	8	7½	6¾	5¼
Price/Share of LTV Subsidiary Company Common Stocks											
6. Braniff Airlines	15½*	21⅛	17⅞	14½	13⅝	10⅛	9¼	8¼	7½	8¼	9½
7. Jones & Laughlin Steel	27⅞*	38¼	29⅝	27¼	31½	17⅝	17⅝	11½	11½	9⅝	12
8. LTV Aerospace	44⅞	41¾	36	24	22½	15⅜	12⅝	7¾	10⅜	7⅜	10
9. LTV Electrosystems	35½	19½	13⅜	10	8⅝	5⅛	5¼	5⅜	5⅜	3⅞	6⅝
10. LTV Ling Altec	22	13½	10¾	7¼	5⅝	2⅜	3⅞	2½	2⅝	1¾	2¾
11. Okonite	30⅛	27⅜	21½	15⅛	10⅝	8	8¾	†	†	†	†
12. Wilson & Co.	28	37⅛	29½	24¼	20	19¼	16	9½	14	16¾	26⅛
13. Wilson Pharmaceutical	18⅝	19⅛	13⅛	11½	9	8⅝	8⅞	6⅛	6¼*	6¾*	9½*
14. Wilson Sporting Goods	26⅛	20	18	14¼	9⅞	10⅝	16¼*	13⅞*	13¾*	14½*	14⅝*

* Not yet acquired by LTV on this date, or sold by LTV prior to this date.
† Security not publicly traded.
Sources: (1) U.S. Department of Commerce, *Survey of Current Business.*
(2) *Bank and Quotation Record*, William B. Dana Co.
(3) U.S. Board of Governors of the Federal Reserve System, *The Federal Reserve Bulletin.*

Exhibit 7

LING-TEMCO-VOUGHT, INC.

MARKET VALUE VERSUS BOOK VALUE FOR LTV'S
PORTFOLIO OF SUBSIDIARY COMPANY SECURITIES

(In millions)

	12/31/67	12/31/68	12/31/69	12/31/70	3/31/71
LTV Investment Portfolio					
1. Market value..........................	$620	$1,320	$ 600	$ 380	$ 480
2. Book* value..........................	170	1,020	1,040	940	940
3. Market-book spread..................	$450	$ 300	$ (440)	$(560)	$(460)

* Differs from line 2, Exhibit 2 because of miscellaneous items.
Sources: (1) LTV Annual Report—1967.
          (2) LTV Annual Report—1968.
          (3) U.S. House of Representatives, Antitrust Subcommittee of the Committee on the Judiciary "Investigation of Conglomerate Corporations," Part 6, April, 1970, p. 79.
          (4) Line 1 data for 12/31/70 and 3/31/71 were calculated by the casewriter.

Exhibit 8

LING-TEMCO-VOUGHT, INC.

ESTIMATED PAYMENTS TO VARIOUS CREDITOR CLASSES IF LTV'S SECURITY
PORTFOLIO HAD BEEN LIQUIDATED AT 12/31/70 PRICES AND THE
COMPANY'S OTHER ASSETS SOLD AT BOOK VALUE

(Dollar figures in millions)

Creditors (In order of priority)	Book Value	Payment in Liquidation	% of Claim Satisfied
Accrued compensation, taxes, etc..................	$ 15.4	$ 15.4	100%
Secured debt			
banks.....................................	75.0	75.0	100
9¼% notes...............................	27.8	27.8	100
Unsubordinated claims			
borrowed money............................	227.8	227.8	100
other.....................................	4.8	2.7	56‡
Subordinated claims............................	485.5	184.3	38‡
Preferred stock (liquidation claim)................	60.2	—	0
Residual*...................................	196.5	—	0
Total..................................	$1,093.0	$533.0†	

* Includes shareholders' equity and reserves and deferrals less liquidating value of preferred stock.
† Equals the book value of LTV's total assets plus the spread between the market value and the cost of its security holdings in subsidiary companies (line 3, Exhibit 7).
‡ This calculation might significantly overstate the potential realizations on the lowest level claims, since LTV had guaranteed (and in one case collateralized) loans of over $100 million to subsidiary companies.
Source: Casewriter's estimates.

Exhibit 9

LING-TEMCO-VOUGHT, INC.

PRICE PERFORMANCE OF SELECTED LTV, INC. SECURITIES
APRIL, 1969–FEBRUARY, 1971

(Month end prices except for May, 1970 data)

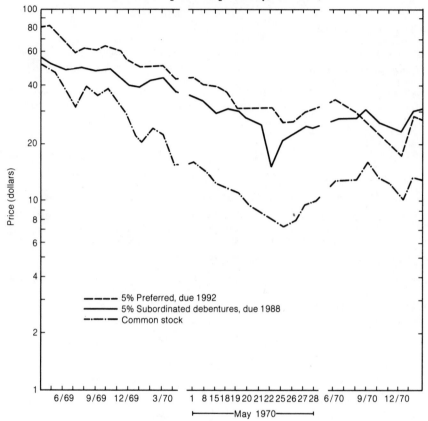

Note: Since these prices are plotted on a semi-log scale, equal percentage price changes are represented by equal vertical distance.
Data for May, 1970 are presented first weekly, then daily.

CYCLOPS CEMENT COMPANY (Abridged)

On May 27, 1965, Mr. Clinton Howe, a director of the Cyclops Cement Company, received from the president of the company a copy of the consultant's report on cash flows in recession conditions, a summary of which is reproduced as an Appendix to this case. Mr. Howe had been present at the directors meeting on March 15, when the scope and methodology to be used in the study had been discussed. Therefore he knew that the consultant planned to use his analysis of recession cash flows as a basis for recommendations on the company's future debt policy. Mr. Howe also knew that the president, Mr. Patrick Dean, had a number of proposals for expansion (by acquisition as well as internally) under study, and that he was prepared to consider an increase in Cyclops' borrowing ratio rather than issue stock at its currently depressed level. Mr. Dean had assured the directors, however, that he would not consider a debt/capitalization ratio of over 50%.

The report was likely to be discussed at the next meeting of the board of directors on June 5, and Mr. Howe undertook a study of the consultant's recommendations.

The Cyclops Cement Company had been established in the upper Mississippi Valley area in the late 19th century, and approximately 50% of company sales still came from this area. The remaining sales were evenly distributed among three widely separated areas: the Southwest, the Southeast, and New England, which Cyclops had entered through mergers with three smaller companies. In terms of production volume, Cyclops ranked among the top 15 companies in the industry in 1965, with six plants and a total productive capacity of 18,200,000 barrels a year.

The cement industry

The broadly based use of cement and concrete products in most types of construction provides the industry with considerable stability. The historical record has demonstrated this. The only exceptions have been the major depression of the 1930's and World War II (see Chart I in the Appendix).

The production of cement is very capital intensive, utilizing a highly mechanized process involving very old, well-established, and well-known technology. Significant reductions in unit production costs are possible from the operation of large plants, since coordination requires no more effort for large- than for small-scale operations. The cost of a barrel of production capacity also declines with increased plant size.

Plant size is limited, however, by the high cost of transport of cement—a bulky, low-value product. Since the raw materials used in cement production are readily available in most regions of the country, it is generally less expensive to operate a number of regional plants close to cement users than to incur high transport costs by shipping cement long distances from a few very large plants. Ninety percent of total U.S. cement production is shipped less than 160 miles, with the primary exceptions being the output of some new and very large plants where ready access to low-cost water transportation permits competitive pricing in markets up to 1,300 miles away. Competition, therefore, is generally on a regional basis, with three or four producers operating plants in the region and accounting for the great majority of total cement sales. The plants are small, but the relatively high production costs are offset by low distribution expense.

The ruinous trade conditions of the 1930's produced chronic overcapacity in the cement industry and made most companies reluctant to expand their facilities.[1] The 10-year period ending in 1955 saw very little increase in productive capacity despite strong gains in construction activity and use of cement. The resulting rise in operating rates combined with firm product prices to yield profit rates considerably above the average for manufacturing as a whole. By 1955 the industry was operating at 94% of capacity and was earning almost 19% on net worth. This high return resulted in part from the use of fully depreciated plant. Exhibit 1 provides data on this period.

Exhibit 1

CYCLOPS CEMENT COMPANY

OPERATING RATES, PRICES, AND PROFITS IN THE CEMENT INDUSTRY, 1950–55

	1950	1951	1952	1953	1954	1955
Industry capacity (mil. bbls.)	268	282	284	292	298	315
Cement production (mil. bbls.)	226	246	249	264	272	297
Percent capacity utilization	84	87	88	90	91	94
Annual increase in capacity (mil. bbls.)		14	2	8	6	17
Annual increase in production (mil. bbls.)		20	3	15	8	25
Bureau of Mines cement price index (1950 = 100)	100	108	108	114	117	122
Profit after tax as % of net worth:						
All manufacturing companies	17.1	14.4	12.3	12.7	12.3	14.9
Cement industry	17.8	14.5	14.3	15.0	17.6	18.6

Source: Standard & Poor's *Trade and Securities Statistics.*

The prosperity was short-lived, however. A number of factors spurred companies to invest heavily in new capacity in the years 1955–62, most important of which were (a) the high operating rates and profits of the industry,

---

[1] Shipments of Portland cement fell from 170 million barrels in 1929 to 81 million barrels in 1932, while the average realized price of cement at the mills fell from $1.48 per barrel in 1929 to $1.01 in 1932.

(*b*) inauguration of the federal highway program, and (*c*) a favorable ruling on depletion allowance (reversed by legislation in 1960). Existing cement producers expanded their facilities and entered new regional markets both by acquisition and by construction of new plants. In addition, a number of new companies entered the cement business during this period. By 1962 the industry's operating rate had declined to 72% under the pressure of substantial additions to capacity and a slowdown in cement consumption (see Exhibit 2).

Exhibit 2

CYCLOPS CEMENT COMPANY

OPERATING RATES, PRICES, AND PROFITS IN THE CEMENT INDUSTRY, 1956–62

	1956	1957	1958	1959	1960	1961	1962
Industry capacity (mil. bbls.)	349	380	403	420	433	443	469
Cement production (mil. bbls.)	316	298	312	339	319	324	337
Percent capacity utilization	91	78	77	81	74	73	72
Annual increase in capacity (mil. bbls.)	34	31	23	17	13	10	26
Annual increase in production (mil. bbls.)	19	−18	14	27	−20	5	13
Bureau of Mines cement price index (1950 = 100)	130	135	138	140	143	141	140
Profit after tax as % of net worth:							
All manufacturing companies	13.8	12.9	9.8	11.7	10.6	9.9	10.9
Cement industry	18.5	14.2	14.7	14.3	11.2	10.2	9.8

Source: Standard & Poor's *Trade and Securities Statistics.*

Despite the decline in operating rates, product prices were reasonably well maintained until 1960. Typically, the largest producer in each regional market set the base price, subject to the right to meet any lower price quoted by a competitor. The base prices were announced quarterly and were generally followed by the other competitors.

The combination of excess capacity, high fixed costs, and new entrants eager to secure a share of the market eroded the oligopolistic competitive structure in the early 1960's and producers adopted several strategies to offset the heightened competition. Financial support was provided by some cement producers to ready-mixed concrete companies in the form of lengthened payment periods and guarantees of bank loans. Typically short on capital, the ready-mix companies accounted for 60% of the cement industry's sales, and their business was essential to the profitable operation of a cement plant.

"Off-list" price reductions in the form of larger discounts for prompt payment, special "competitive" discounts, and "phantom delivery point" billing increased sharply. The average realized mill price of cement, which had risen in each year since 1940, fell in each year from 1961 through 1964.

AVERAGE REALIZED MILL PRICE PER BARREL

1955	1956	1957	1958	1959	1960	1961	1962	1963	1964
$2.86	$3.05	$3.18	$3.25	$3.28	$3.35	$3.32	$3.29	$3.20	$3.19

Customer service was improved by the establishment of distribution terminals that could insure prompt delivery of cement to users, thereby reducing the importance *to the user* of buffer inventories. The terminals also permitted the adoption of separate pricing policies for each terminal, in place of the historical reliance on a single policy for an entire region.

NUMBER OF NEW DISTRIBUTION TERMINALS

1950-59	1960-61	1962	1963	1964
69	32	42	44	43

By 1964 profitability of the cement industry had fallen to a 15-year low as product prices continued to erode (see Exhibit 3). Heavy investments in

Exhibit 3

CYCLOPS CEMENT COMPANY
OPERATING RATES, PRICES, AND PROFITS IN THE CEMENT INDUSTRY, 1963-64

	1963	1964
Industry capacity (mil. bbls.)......................	478	479
Cement production (mil. bbls.).....................	353	369
Percent capacity utilization........................	74	77
Annual increase in capacity (mil. bbls.).............	9	1
Annual increase in production (mil. bbls.)...........	16	16
Bureau of Mines cement price index (1950 = 100)......	136	136
Profit after tax as % of net worth:		
All manufacturing companies.....................	11.6	12.7
Cement industry................................	8.9	8.8

Source: Standard & Poor's *Trade and Securities Statistics.*

plant modernization and automation and in distribution terminals were widespread in the industry and resulted in little competitive advantage for any one company. Rather than being a source of higher reported earnings, the savings merely offset (and possibly contributed to) price cuts. There was, however, one encouraging sign; namely, industry investment in capacity additions was low in 1963 and 1964 and, on the basis of announced investment plans, it seemed likely that the low level of capacity additions would continue into 1966. Some industry observers hoped that rising operating rates might permit a firming of product prices and a recovery in profits.

Financial history of Cyclops Cement Company

Cyclops did not escape the industrywide competitive pressures. Earnings plummeted by 35% in the two-year period 1959-60 and then rebounded in 1962-64 (see Exhibit 4 for a summary of operations). Capital expenditures were very heavy, and the company sold an issue of $15 million 5% debentures in 1958. The restriction in this issue that funded debt was not to exceed 33⅓% of net tangible assets was suggested by the company's investment bankers, who stated that this was in line with recent issues by other firms in a variety of industries. At the time, the provision seemed to allow for a

Exhibit 4

CYCLOPS CEMENT COMPANY
SEVEN-YEAR STATISTICAL AND FINANCIAL SUMMARY
(Dollar figures in millions except per share data)

	1958	1959	1960	1961	1962	1963	1964
Sales	$44.2	$49.4	$45.3	$48.9	$55.5	$54.3	$53.1
Net earnings after tax	4.7	4.4	3.1	3.3	4.35	3.8	4.75
Capital expenditures	12.0	13.3	7.1	5.5	5.7	9.7	11.8
Net working capital	11.0	2.0	8.0	9.1	12.2	9.2	5.8
Total assets	70.5	74.5	85.2	79.6	83.4	88.9	88.0
Long-term debt	15.0	15.0	19.75	19.75	19.75	19.75	19.3
Preferred stock	4.5	4.5	9.2	9.2	9.2	9.2	9.0
Common stockholders' equity	38.6	39.7	39.8	41.0	43.4	44.9	47.3
Cement capacity (mil. bbls.)	13.9	15.9	15.9	16.8	16.8	16.8	18.1
Employees	1,457	1,503	1,491	1,470	1,498	1,489	1,421
Common shareholders	5,600	6,300	6,700	7,200	7,300	7,300	7,400
Earned per share	$2.75	$2.57	$1.81	$1.93	$2.54	$2.22	$2.77
Dividends per share	2.00	2.00	1.60	0.90	0.80	0.95	1.00

considerable increase in the company's funded debt and had been accepted without comment by the officers and directors of Cyclops.

In 1960, however, the company's large plant-rebuilding programs and an adverse tax ruling forced Cyclops to go to the market for additional long-term funds. The $33\frac{1}{3}\%$ restriction limited borrowing to an issue of $4.75 million of 5% debentures, and it was necessary to raise an additional $4.7 million by means of 6% cumulative preferred stock. Both issues were placed privately with groups of insurance companies.

Exhibit 5 presents the capitalization ratios of several cement companies. Except for Cyclops the list is in the order of debt ratio, with the highest ratio at the top. Companies A, B, and C are "captives" of larger companies whose financial strength in a sense guarantees their solvency. Consequently, their very high debt ratios cannot be considered as typical of the industry. With the exception of these three companies Cyclops is near the median position in this listing.

Future financing needs

Cyclops had a number of proposals for expansion under study. Capital expenditures were expected to average $7–$7.5 million over the next few years, although technological changes in the industry might make major investments necessary at some stage if Cyclops was to remain cost competitive. The directors were also interested in further mergers and acquisitions including the possibility of diversifying outside the cement industry. They wished to develop financial policies that would give the company sufficient flexibility to take advantage of any opportunities that might arise.

However, it was clear that there would be considerable resistance from the board of directors to any reduction in the current dividend rate to finance

Exhibit 5

CYCLOPS CEMENT COMPANY

TYPICAL CAPITALIZATION RATIOS IN THE CEMENT INDUSTRY

	⌐Total Capitalization 100%⌐		
	Debt	Preferred	Common
Cyclops Cement Company...............	25%	13%	62%
A†....................................	78	11*	11
B†....................................	82	—	18
C†....................................	79	—	21
D.....................................	33	18	49
E.....................................	33	30	37
F.....................................	31	—	69
G.....................................	30	—	70
H.....................................	27	12	61
I.....................................	24	—	76
J.....................................	24	—	76
K.....................................	22	3	75
L.....................................	20	—	80
M.....................................	11	—	89
N.....................................	11	20	69
O.....................................	—	—	100
P.....................................	—	—	100
Q.....................................	—	—	100

* Subordinated notes.
† These companies were captives of larger corporations so that their financial structures cannot be taken to be representative of independently owned companies in the cement industry.

the planned expansion. In Mr. Dean's words, "The board would take a hard and long look before cutting or omitting a dividend." Dividends had nevertheless been cut substantially in recent years from $2.00 a share in 1958 to $0.80 in 1962. The rate had been increased slightly to $1.00 in 1964. A recent study by the company had indicated that the stock prices of publicly owned cement companies were very closely correlated with dividend yields, and Mr. Dean had decided that the cash dividend should be increasd to $1.20 a share and had instructed the consultant to use this figure in his projections of future cash flows. It was hoped that the increased dividend rate would raise the stock price from its recent range of $25–$28.

APPENDIX

CYCLOPS CEMENT COMPANY
SUMMARY OF CONSULTANT'S REPORT

Introduction

In this section we shall explain briefly the importance of cash flows in any appraisal of the risk of default in a recession period. We shall make use of the recent history of Cyclops to indicate the advantages of cash flow analysis over income statements and balance sheets in an analysis of this kind.

The ability of a firm to meet its financial obligations in any given period or set of circumstances can only be determined after a study of each and every one of the sources and uses of funds expected to arise during that period. Attention to income and expense is not enough. Many profitable firms suffer temporary shortages of funds. For example, in the year 1964 Cyclops reported a net profit of $4.750 million; yet the net cash gain available for common and preferred dividends was a *negative* figure of $3.604 million. The disparity between these figures alone is sufficient evidence that profitability by itself is no guarantee of solvency. Other firms remain safely solvent during periods in which losses are being experienced. Some firms have enjoyed an adequate cash flow to keep them solvent through long periods of unprofitability.

Financial obligations are undertaken in order to obtain funds to be used to create income (and therefore value) in the firm. Properly used, low-cost senior securities add to the value of the common stock equity position by increasing the earnings available per common share. But the degree to which the fixed-charge burden associated with these senior securities may be accepted depends not on income but on cash flows. If the sources of cash provide a flow sufficient to meet all uses, *including the demands of the financial obligations*, without exhausting the organization's cash balances, then solvency is assured. If not, even if profits are earned, then there will be default unless either new sources of cash are found or uses are reduced.

To determine what financial burden is acceptable, it is necessary to examine the flows likely to arise during a recession period, making a realistic assessment of these flows on the basis of the organization's past experience in recession conditions. Only then can a debt-financing policy safely be made part of the company's long-range plans. In this study, therefore, the sources and uses of funds in Cyclops Cement Company will be forecast under various sets of assumptions about business recession, and under each set of assumed conditions the total burden of proposed financial obligations will be compared with net funds changes arising from other activities. Where the difference is positive—that is, the net positive cash flow from all other sources exceeds the financial burden—then that burden will be safely covered, whatever the reported earnings may be.

This method may be illustrated by examining the experience of Cyclops during the period 1961–64 in terms of funds movements. These data are presented in Table 1. In terms of the method of analysis we are here introducing, solvency was in fact threatened in 1964, but the reserves available in the form of cash balances were more than adequate to overcome the threat.

It should be noted that the financial burden sections of the "uses" columns are further subdivided between "contractual" and "policy" burden. Contractual burden includes those financial obligations, like bond interest and sinking fund payments, that are matters of contract and so must not be defaulted. Policy burden is made up of those obligations, such as dividends, that are at the discretion of the board of directors. The annual retirement of $225,000 of the 6% cumulative preferred issue is considered discretionary in view of the mild penalties for failure to do so.

Table 1

CASH FLOWS, 1961–64
(Dollar figures in millions)

	1961	1962	1963	1964
Reported earnings after taxes	$ 3.3	$ 4.4	$ 3.8	$ 4.8
Sources of funds:				
Operations before lease payments, interest, noncash charges, and taxes	$ 12.1	$ 13.2	$ 12.8	$ 12.8
Working capital excluding cash	8.3*	—	3.6	—
Total sources	$ 20.4	$ 13.2	$ 16.4	$ 12.8
Uses of funds—operating:				
Working capital excluding cash and accrued taxes	—	$ (0.6)	—	$ (0.8)
Plant and equipment	$ (5.0)	(4.7)	$ (8.4)	(11.7)
Other needs	(1.2)	—	(0.7)	(0.4)
Total operating uses	$ (6.2)	$ (5.3)	$ (9.1)	$(12.9)
Available for financial uses	$ 14.2	$ 7.9	$ 7.3	$ (0.1)
Uses of funds—financial:				
Income tax payments	$ (5.0)	$ (2.1)	$ (0.8)	$ (0.5)
Contractual burden:				
Lease payments	$ (0.5)	$ (0.6)	$ (0.7)	$ (0.7)
Interest	(1.2)	(0.9)	(1.0)	(1.0)
Debt reduction	(3.8)	—	(0.8)	(0.8)
Total contractual burden	$ (5.5)	$ (1.5)	$ (2.5)	$ (2.5)
Policy burden:				
Preferred dividends	$ (0.6)	$ (0.6)	$ (0.5)	$ (0.5)
Preferred redemption	—	—	(0.2)	(0.4)
Common dividends	(1.6)	(1.4)	(1.6)	(1.7)
Total policy burden	$ (2.2)	$ (2.0)	$ (2.3)	$ (2.6)
Total financial uses	$(12.7)	$ (5.6)	$ (5.6)	$ (5.6)
Balance—change in cash	$ 1.5	$ 2.3	$ 1.7	$ (5.7)

* Primarily reduction of receivables by use of new financing.

The choice of a recession to be studied

The risks arising from debt-servicing burden are often too vaguely presented. Any debt increases the risk of default by some degree, however small. The question should be not whether there is or is not some abstract risk but whether or not there is a real risk of cash inadequacy in any foreseeable depression. To answer this question it is necessary to specify, after study of the economic conditions of the industry, the dimensions that a depression might assume.

Volume. The cement industry trends shown in Chart 1 (which is drawn on a semilogarithmic scale to emphasize relative changes) demonstrate a generally stable upwards tendency in both consumption and cement prices. The only major interruptions in this trend occurred during the depression of the 1930's and in World War II. Only two declines in volume have been experienced since World War II, neither of them involving a drop of more than 7% from the previous peak or lasting more than three years. The recession of 1936–38 was of similar magnitude.

Cyclops Cement Company has experienced a greater fluctuation in post-war volume than that shown in the industry trends. No decrease experienced by the company has involved a decline of more than 17% from the previous peak, however, and no division has experienced a volume decline greater than 18%. It did take Cyclops five years to return to 1956 volumes after the 1957 decline. The author has concluded, therefore, that a recession of four years' duration with a return to previous volumes in the fifth year is for this company a conservative but not unrealistic basis for this study of recession cash flows. Volume levels during the five-year period are assumed to be:

Year preceding............... 100%
Year 1...................... 90
Year 2...................... 85
Year 3...................... 80
Year 4...................... 80
Year 5...................... 100

Chart 1

CEMENT INDUSTRY TRENDS

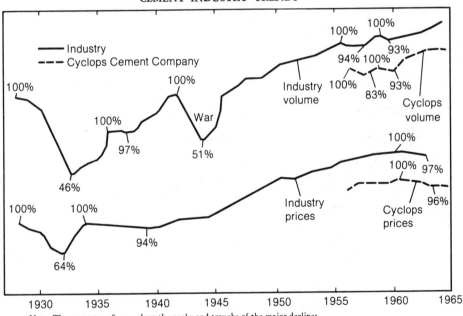

Note: The percentage figures show the peaks and troughs of the major declines.

In Chart 1 the upper long, unbroken line represents total industry volume plotted on a semilogarithmic scale and the lower unbroken line represents industry prices similarly plotted. The shorter dashed lines to the right of the chart represent Cyclops' actual volume and price performance for the years 1956–65. It is clear from these data that the author's assumptions concerning possible recession conditions and Cyclops' response to these conditions reflect more severe fluctuations than have actually been experienced since World War II.

Price. Cement prices have fallen surprisingly little in view of the severe competition in the industry in recent years. Certain areas have experienced marked fluctuations in prices, but the general pattern is one of considerable stability. The average industry price has fallen only twice since the 1930's: by 6% after 1934 and by 5% in the early 1960's. For the purposes of this study, however, since we are studying a particular company, a price decline of up to 10% of the prerecession price is assumed to be possible, distributed over the recession period as follows:

Year preceding	100%
Year 1	100
Year 2	95
Year 3	90
Year 4	90
Year 5	95

These assumptions as to the volume and price declines likely to be experienced in the recession period have been used as the basis for the analysis that follows. Although prices of delivered products were assumed to fall, there has been no adjustment for the reduction of prices of the elements of cost.

The recommendations concerning financial policy, which will be made in the final section of this study, will be designed to insure that the company is able to survive a recession of the dimensions specified above without appreciable danger of being unable to meet its contractual financial burdens and without contraction of the common stock dividends.

Forecast of cash movements related to operations

The information presented in Table 2 was obtained from detailed studies made by the divisions of Cyclops and coordinated by the headquarters staff. This table shows the cash receipts and expenditures arising from operations for each year of the recession as deliveries fall below 1965 levels. In each year except recession year 4 the assumption is made that this year is the first at that particular volume: the fourth-year column demonstrates the results of stabilizing volume for a second year at 80% of the 1965 level. Deliveries are assumed to return to their prerecession level in year 5.

Table 2 seeks to show the cash flow effects of changes in volume separately from those of changes in price. Thus, in the upper part of the table, cement prices are assumed to remain constant at their 1965 levels ($3.76 per barrel, delivered) so that the effect of volume changes may be seen in isolation. The slow decline in net operating inflow as a percentage of receipts is strikingly portrayed and demonstrates that the cash elements in the cost of production are dominated by variable costs. This fact is overlooked when one thinks of cost as including the heavy depreciation charges of a capital-intensive company such as Cyclops.

In the lower part of Table 2 the results of price declines of various

Table 2

FORECAST OF CASH FLOWS FROM OPERATIONS AT VARIOUS PRICE LEVELS
(Dollar figures in millions)

	Year Preceding Recession	Recession Year				
		1	2	3	4	5
Shipments (mil. bbls.).........	13.7	12.3	11.6	11.0	11.0	13.7
As % of 1965 levels..........	100	90	85	80	80	100
As % of capacity.............	77	69	65	62	62	77
Receipts at 1965 prices..........	$ 51.43	$ 46.29	$ 43.22	$ 41.15	$ 41.15	$ 51.43
Other income.................	0.58	0.52	0.49	0.46	0.46	0.58
	$ 52.01	$ 46.81	$ 43.71	$ 41.61	$ 41.61	$ 52.01
Cash operating expenditures*....	(35.17)	(33.60)	(31.37)	(30.27)	(28.51)	(35.17)
Net operating inflow:						
At 1965 prices...............	$ 16.84	$ 13.21	$ 12.34	$ 11.34	$ 13.10	$ 16.84
As % of receipts.............	32%	28%	28%	27%	31%	32%
Net operating inflow:						
Assuming 5% price decline....	$ 14.24	$ 10.87	$ 10.18	$ 9.28	$ 11.04	$ 14.24
Assuming 10% price decline...	11.64	8.53	8.02	7.22	8.98	11.64
Assuming 15% price decline...	9.04	6.19	5.86	5.16	6.92	9.04
Net operating inflow under assumed recession volumes and price levels...............	$ 16.84	$ 13.21	$ 10.18	$ 7.22	$ 8.98	$ 14.24

* Does not include headquarters expenditures, pension fund contributions, interest and lease payments, and taxes.

magnitudes are superimposed on the volume changes and the effects on net operating inflows are shown. Whenever the consequences of a price change are being considered, it is necessary to take into account the change in income tax liability consequent on this reduction in revenues. Finally, the table shows the net operating inflows likely to be experienced under the combination of volume and price changes selected by this report as the dimensions of the recession to be studied. These inflow figures will be used in Table 5 below.

Forecast of other cash flows (excluding taxes on income and financial burden)

All nonoperating cash flows that may be expected under recession conditions, with the exception of changes in the company's cash balances, income taxes, and financial obligations, are set out in Table 3.

After discussion with company officers it was decided that it would be reasonable to assume that the onset of a recession would not bring about immediate adjustments in any items other than those directly related to volume. There are two reasons for this. First, it is unlikely that the recession will be recognized as such immediately, especially as short-term fluctuations of as much as 10% may be encountered in a normal year. Second, there will be considerable pressure to continue normal investment expenditures. The column representing the first year of the recession in Table 3 therefore uses "normal" levels of expenditure. Further columns depict the flows in years 2 and 3 and thereafter as investments are reduced in response to the continuing recession.

Table 3

FORECAST OF NONOPERATING FLOWS

(Dollar figures in millions)

	Year Preceding Recession	Recession Year			Subsequent Severe Years	Recovery to Prerecession Volumes
		1	*2*	*3*		
Headquarters expenditures*...	$(1.97)	$(1.95)	$(1.83)	$(1.79)	$(1.33)	$(1.87)
Plant and equipment..........	(7.50)	(7.50)	(2.50)	(1.00)	(1.00)	(5.00)
Subtotal..............	$(9.47)	$(9.45)	$(4.33)	$(2.79)	$(2.33)	$(6.87)
In-house resources:						
Reduction in pension fund contributions...........	0	0	0.20	0.20	0.20	0
Reduction of cash balances..	0	0.87	0	0	0	0
Special market expenditures.	0	0	(0.43)	0	0	0
Reduction (increase) in non-cash working capital (below)................	0	(1.00)	0.18	0.21	0	(0.80)
Total................	$(9.47)	$(9.58)	$(4.38)	$(2.38)	$(2.13)	$(7.67)

DETAILS OF CHANGES IN NONCASH WORKING CAPITAL ACCOUNTS

Volume as percentage of base (prerecession) year.......	100	90	85	80	80	100
Accounts receivable..........	$ 5.36	$ 6.04	$ 5.70	$ 5.36	$ 5.36	$ 6.77
Inventories (direct cost portion)................	1.43	1.28	1.21	1.13	1.13	1.44
	$ 6.79	$ 7.32	$ 6.91	$ 6.49	$ 6.49	$ 8.21
Accounts payable............	4.68	4.21	3.98	3.77	3.77	4.69
	$ 2.11	$ 3.11	$ 2.93	$ 2.72	$ 2.72	$ 3.52
Change in working capital account from previous year.		(1.00)	0.18	0.21	0	(0.80)

* Nonfinancial cash expenditures excluding leases.

It is clear that the dominant factors affecting these flows are, on the outflow side, the plant and capital equipment budget, and on the other side, the amount of liquid reserves that are quickly available. The December 31, 1964, cash level of $3.12 million is probably a minimum for the next several years, and even this figure is well in excess of management's comfortable assessment of minimum operating cash requirement of $2.25 million. It is assumed, therefore, that excess cash of $0.87 million is available and is used in year 1 of the recession.

The lower portion of Table 3 shows the amounts forecast for those working capital items that fluctuate with volume. An explanation of the amounts chosen and of other items in Table 3 follows.

Detailed discussion of Table 3

Headquarters expenses. An estimate was made by company officers of the needs to support the central office. They were made at four possible recession levels, keyed to earnings rather than to cash flow. Therefore, with a one-year lag, from the onset of the recession, the level of headquarters expense has been reduced according to plan.

Plant and equipment. At the beginning of 1965 the company projected $7.5 million for capital expenditures during the year. Although $11.7 million (net funds) was spent in 1964 and $8.5 million in 1963, management believes that no further major modernization expenditures will be required for several years and that an average of $7.5 million would be a generous allowance for normal years in the next decade. The five-year plan, already adopted, shows lower levels of expenditure than those in the last two years.

In recession, a much less ample program can be anticipated, but there will always be an important time lag before cutbacks can become a reality. Many projects require one to two years for construction, and it seems unlikely that they would be halted prior to completion in response to a recession. The author has been assured that the lower figures used in recession years are feasible, without any damage to the company's need to return to high levels of production in the recovery period. The figure of $5.0 million is used in the year of recovery, because it is believed that this is all that could be spent effectively in the first year following a period of retrenchment.

In-house resources. Most companies possess considerably more capacity to produce funds under the pressure of need than is apparent at first glance. The following in-house resources have been considered in picturing the funds flow of Cyclops Cement Company in a recession period.

Use of accumulated contributions to pension reserve: Since the company has built up $0.6 million above the legally required minimum, it is estimated by company officers that the present outflow of about $0.3 million annually could be reduced to $0.1 million for three years, without creating any need for higher levels of payment than previous levels when prosperity is restored. This estimate has been used with a one-year time lag. The saving appears in each of three years because the full pension charge was taken as an operating expense.

Liquidation of outside investments: Although there is a considerable investment in real estate that could be liquidated, the policy given to us by management is not to rely on this source of funds.

Use of cash reserves: The $3.12 million of cash funds shown at December 31, 1964, is well in excess of operating needs, which have been estimated at $1.3 million by a careful study recently made. A larger figure, $2.25 million, has been chosen on the authority of management, which feels that it is desirable to maintain liberal balances in the company's banks. So a reduction of only $0.87 million is taken.

Drawing down the liquid position as indicated would require the increased use of short-term credit to meet seasonal requirements. This credit is certainly available under present conditions, but the author's forecast that it would also be available under recession conditions should be checked.

Since the company manifests a large cash-generating capacity in normal years, the idea of recession use of the present cash reserves does not present the risk of permanent reduction of the firm's strength.

Special promotion fund: At the request of management, a special fund of

$0.43 million is appropriated in the second recession year, to permit special sales efforts and the absorption of bad debts beyond normal figures.

Working capital items related to sales volume. Significant changes would also occur in certain working capital items.

Accounts receivable: These are currently 10.3% of 1965 estimated sales volume. Since it is known that the granting of liberal credit terms is an important source of sales in a buyer's market, an increase of the collection period by 25% (about $1.5 million at current volume) is assumed.

Accounts payable: Since the maintenance of a strong credit position requires prompt payment, the "last ditch" resort to slowness on the part of Cyclops is rejected, and payables are maintained at 9% of sales, the recent average level.

Inventories: The nature of the production process and the present inventory control systems should permit the maintenance of inventories at approximately a constant relationship to shipments. This relationship is assumed here. Consistent with the objective of this analysis only the cash costs of production are reflected in Table 3.

Financial burdens

The year 1967 was chosen as the source of the figures for financing burden in the year preceding the recession, because in that year all the sinking fund requirements rise to their fullest amounts. They are presented in Table 4. The amounts are shown on a pretax basis. The tax deductibility of interest and lease payments is included in calculating the estimated tax payments shown in Table 5.

The "Contractual Burden," strictly defined, is the sum of interest and lease

Table 4

FINANCIAL BURDENS
(Dollar figures in millions)

	As in 1967	Recession Year				
		1	2	3	4	5
Contractual:						
Interest, debentures (5%).......	$0.82	$0.76	$0.71	$0.67	$0.60	$0.54
Lease payments...............	0.56	0.56	0.56	0.56	0.56	0.56
	$1.38	$1.32	$1.27	$1.23	$1.16	$1.10
Debenture sinking funds........	1.07	1.07	1.07	1.07	1.07	1.07
Total contractual.........	$2.45	$2.39	$2.34	$2.30	$2.23	$2.17
Policy:						
Preferred sinking fund*........	$0.45	$0.23	$0.23	$0.23	$0.23	$0.23
Preferred dividend (6%)........	0.49	0.47	0.46	0.44	0.43	0.42
	$0.94	$0.70	$0.69	$0.67	$0.66	$0.65
Total contractual and preferred burdens....................	$3.39	$3.09	$3.03	$2.97	$2.89	$2.82
Common dividend ($1.20).......	2.07	2.07	2.07	2.07	2.07	2.07
Total burden.............	$5.46	$5.16	$5.10	$5.04	$4.96	$4.89

* It is assumed that Cyclops will exercise its option to retire an additional $225,000 of preferred stock in the year prior to the downturn.

payments and debenture sinking funds, but the author feels that Cyclops will always plan to meet the dividend and sinking fund requirements on the preferred stock. Not only is it in the spirit of a preferred stock agreement to pay dividends as long as possible, but also an accumulation of preferred dividends has disastrous effects on the value of the common stock. Therefore, the author proposes that the figures in Table 4 be interpreted to show a continuing burden of approximately $3.1 million, of which $1.3 million represents deductions due to sinking fund operations.

By making sinking fund payments, Cyclops is regularly restoring its borrowing power. Perhaps in recession this fact is not important, but it is a matter of long-run importance which will enter the final recommendations of this report. Debt of $5.36 million is scheduled for retirement in the five years shown.

A forecast of recession cash flows

Table 5 combines the cash flow patterns developed in Tables 2–4 and indicates the impact of the selected recession on the borrowing needs of Cyclops. The financial burdens are based on the present capital structure and on an increase to $1.20 in the dividend rate on the common stock.

The following conclusions seem important.

1. The pattern of changes in cash is very different from the pattern of reported earnings.[2] In contrast to net earnings, which decline through year 3, peak borrowing needs are reached in the first year of the recession.

2. Sharp curtailment in investment in plant and equipment by the second year of the recession is a key influence on the company's low borrowing needs during the recession. In view of the long construction period for many of Cyclops' projects, this assumes quick perception of, and response to, the onslaught of a recession.

3. Even at low levels of volume and price, and after maintaining the $1.20 annual dividend on the common stock, there is not a cash deficit after the volume of investment in new assets is reduced. Income tax carry-backs are important contributors to this result. [The tax calculations are not included in the report but are available from the vice president–finance.]

4. In interpreting Table 5 the reader should keep in mind that several additional elements of conservatism are built into the calculations. The cash balance is set at a level $1.0 million above operating needs. A four-year recession with declines in volume and in price below the experience of any recession since the 1930's has been assumed. While prices of delivered goods have been assumed to decline, no decline has been assumed in the prices of the elements of cost. Finally, Cyclops has an excellent credit standing. The

---

[2] The consultant and the Cyclops management elected to omit the earnings figures from the report to ensure that the board of directors would focus on the critical numbers —namely, the cash flow figures. The tax payment figures provide some insight, however, into the pattern of earnings. The differences between earnings and cash flow patterns are also shown in Table 1, which provides historical data for the 1961–64 period.

Table 5

A FORECAST OF RECESSION CASH FLOWS

(Dollar figures in millions)

	Year Preceding Recession	Recession Year 1	Recession Year 2	Recession Year 3	Recession Year 4	Recession Year 5
SUMMARY OF OPERATIONS						
Shipments (mil. bbls.)...........	13.7	12.3	11.6	11.0	11.0	13.7
Percent of base year..............	100	90	85	80	80	100
Percent of capacity...............	77	69	65	62	62	77
Price per barrel..................	$ 3.76	$ 3.76	$ 3.57	$ 3.38	$ 3.38	$ 3.57
Percent of base year.............	100	100	95	90	90	95
SUMMARY OF CASH FLOWS*						
Operating inflows (from Table 2)	$ 16.84	$ 13.21	$10.18	$ 7.22	$ 8.98	$ 14.24
Headquarters expenditures (from Table 3)..............	(1.97)	(1.95)	(1.83)	(1.79)	(1.33)	(1.87)
Investment in plant and equipment (from Table 3).........	(7.50)	(7.50)	(2.50)	(1.00)	(1.00)	(5.00)
Reduction (increase) in working capital (from Table 3).......	0	(0.13)	0.18	0.21	0	(0.80)
Reduction in pension fund contributions (from Table 3)	0	0	0.20	0.20	0.20	0
Special marketing expenditures (from Table 3)..............	0	0	(0.43)	0	0	0
Contractual financial burden (from Table 4)..............	(2.45)	(2.39)	(2.34)	(2.30)	(2.23)	(2.17)
Tax (payments) or refunds........	(2.25)	(1.03)	(0.29)	1.02	0.46	(1.91)
Subtotal..................	$ 2.67	$ 0.21	$ 3.17	$ 3.56	$ 5.08	$ 2.49
Preferred burden (from Table 4)...	(0.94)	(0.70)	(0.69)	(0.67)	(0.66)	(0.65)
Common dividend at $1.20.......	(2.07)	(2.07)	(2.07)	(2.07)	(2.07)	(2.07)
Total cash flow............	$ (0.34)	$ (2.56)	$ 0.41	$ 0.82	$ 2.35	$ (0.23)
Effect on cash, excluding preferred burden and common dividend...................	2.67	0.21	3.17	3.56	5.08	2.49
Cumulative effect, excluding preferred burden and common dividend...................	2.67	2.88	6.05	9.61	14.69	17.18
Effect on cash, including preferred burden and common dividend	(0.34)	(2.56)	0.41	0.82	2.35	(0.23)
Cumulative effect, including preferred burden and common dividend†...................	(0.34)	(2.92)	(2.66)	(1.97)	0.28	0.05

* Figures in ( ) are cash outflows.
† The cumulative effect includes interest on the prior-year cash deficit.

company obviously has an untapped source of short-term funds not shown in Table 5.

Recession cash flows and various debt policies

It seems desirable to expand the recession cash flow analysis to include a range of possible capital structures. Three specific capital structures are considered:

1. The present capital structure, which includes debt, 25%; preferred stock, 12%; common stock, 63% (based on book values).

2. The capital structure that would result from refinancing the two preferred issues with a new debt issue and would include debt, 37%; common stock, 63%.

3. An increase in debt to 50% of total capitalization, with the balance as common stock.

The implications of each of the three capital structures for Cyclops' cash flows and cyclical borrowing needs are shown in Table 6 and are discussed in the recommendations that follow.

Table 6

CASH FLOWS UNDER VARIOUS CAPITAL STRUCTURES
(Dollar figures in millions)

	Year Preceding Decline	Recession Year 1	2	3	4	5
Current Policy: debt, 25%; preferred, 12%; common, 63%:						
Eflect on cash, excluding preferred burdens and common dividend	$ 2.67	$ 0.21	$ 3.17	$ 3.56	$ 5.08	$ 2.49
Cumulative effect, excluding preferred burdens and common dividend	2.67	2.88	6.05	9.61	14.69	17.18
Effect on cash, including preferred burdens and common dividend	(0.34)	(2.56)	0.41	0.82	2.35	(0.23)
Cumulative effect, including preferred burdens and common dividend*	(0.34)	(2.92)	(2.66)	(1.97)	0.28	0.05
Capital Structure: debt, 37%; common, 63%:†						
Eflect on cash, excluding common dividend	1.94	(0.51)	2.47	2.86	4.40	1.82
Cumulative effect, excluding common dividend	1.94	1.43	3.90	6.76	11.16	12.98
Effect on cash, including common dividend ($2.07 million)	(0.13)	(2.58)	0.40	0.79	2.33	(0.25)
Cumulative effect, including common dividend*	(0.13)	(2.72)	(2.46)	(1.79)	0.45	0.20
Capital Structure: debt, 50%; common, 50%‡ (and repurchase of common):						
Eflect on cash, excluding common dividend	1.18	(1.24)	1.74	2.16	3.69	1.14
Cumulative effect, excluding common dividend	1.18	(0.06)	1.68	3.84	7.53	8.67
Effect on cash, including common dividend ($1.72 million)	(0.54)	(2.96)	0.02	0.44	1.97	(0.58)
Cumulative effect, including common dividend*	(0.54)	(3.53)	(3.64)	(3.38)	(1.58)	(2.24)

* The cumulative figures include interest on the prior year's deficit cash position. The preferred burden and common dividend in the year preceding the decline are $0.94 million and $2.07 million respectively.

† Assumes funding the retirement of the preferred issues with 20-year debt issue at 5½% on which sinking fund payments start immediately.

‡ Assumes a negotiated increase of ¼% in the rate on the existing debt in exchange for relaxation of the restriction on debt and issuance of an additional $18.6 million of 20-year debt at 5¾% (sinking fund payments start immediately). The proceeds from the $18.6 million debt issue are used to retire the preferred stock and to repurchase 300,000 shares of common stock at $30 per share. The common stock dividend in each year is $1.72 million. The reduction reflects the smaller number of shares outstanding as a result of recapitalizing the company. It is recognized that the company would probably not repurchase its stock but would use its newly discovered borrowing power in a series of steps through acquisitions to reach the desired goal over a period of years.

Recommendations

1. Since the first recession year shows large drains because of the continuation of expenditures for plant and equipment, it is recommended that the company maintain reserves in liquid funds or assured credit in amounts roughly equivalent to the capital commitments that are considered irreversible. Such an arrangement as a banker's commitment for a term loan might be considered and would bolster the certainty of the common dividend rate.

2. Since there appears to be no reason to pay the high cost of preferred stock, because the reduction of preferred dividends is not required to preserve solvency, it is recommended that this type of security be eliminated from the capital structure by the use of (*a*) funds generated in prosperous years and (*b*) increased long-term indebtedness.

On December 31, 1964, total long-term debt amounted to $19 million, or 25% of net tangible assets ($76 million). The ratio of 33⅓% imposed under the terms of the 5% debentures of 1958 permitted long-term debt of $25 million with net tangible assets at this level. Unused debt capacity of $6 million was therefore available without offending existing contracts. The extent of the funds available from operations for the retirement of the preferred stock was dependent upon the size of new capital investment projects being undertaken. In a year of normal sales volume in which investment in new plant and equipment did not exceed $5 million (e.g., 1961–62) approximately $2 million might be expected to be available for preferred retirement. The total sum required to accomplish the retirement of both preferred issues as of June 30, 1965, is $9 million.

3. Since dividend payments are an important key to value of the common stock of cement companies, it is recommended that the net savings of retiring preferred stock be passed on in the form of increased dividends on the common stock.

4. At present Cyclops Cement Company's flexibility in financial policy is greatly constrained by the existing indentures and preferred stock agreements. Thus, at the moment the only major available reductions in expenditures to meet recessions (other than in the control of operations) are in the budget for plant and equipment or the common dividend.

It is recommended that the company study its present indentures and consider how they might be changed to introduce needed flexibility. Raising the debt limit to make unnecessary the use of preferred stock is one goal. Another is to arrange an alternative to the sinking fund in the form of investment in approved types of assets. A third is the introduction of flexibility by specifically authorizing that advance payments could be made on sinking fund payments with the provision that an equal amount of later payments could be skipped over in times of stress if necessary. All these changes might be arranged by amendment of the existing indentures, and this step should be attempted first. But in the long run, if calling the present issues is necessary, it is a step worth taking.

CHINON, S.A.

∧∧

In July 1974, Henri Perrier, vice president of Banque de Paris, was reviewing a request by the treasurer of Chinon, S.A. for an increase in its lending facility from FF 30 million to FF 40 million. The request came at a difficult time for the bank. Severe credit restrictions had been imposed by the Conseil National du Crédit, resulting in a jump in short-term interest rates from a low of 7¾% to a level of 10% to 11%. The banking community was also wary of the possible consequences on the French economy of the recent, sharp increase in world oil prices. However, Perrier and other bankers felt a responsibility to help firms such as Chinon that were major contributors to the nation's balance of payments. Furthermore, the bank's relationship with Chinon had been excellent since the late 1950s in terms of both profitability and growth. Perrier was reluctant to do anything that would jeopardize this relationship.

HISTORY OF CHINON, S.A.

Louis Jacquard, a corn and beet farmer in the rich agricultural region of La Touraine, southwest of Paris, had always liked tinkering with machinery. In 1928, he set up a workshop to repair agricultural equipment and to manufacture his own creations. He gave it the name of the place where he lived—Chinon.

The hydraulic excavator was invented by Mr. Jacquard in 1951 and gave the company a technological lead that it would carry into the early 1970s. Under his guidance, the company channeled all of its resources into the one product line, sold principally to the building and public works market, and became the world's largest producer of hydraulic excavators. Four factories were built and 14 models of hydraulic excavators were launched and distributed through a network of 11 commercial subsidiaries and 87 independent agents. When Mr. Jacquard retired in 1967 to return to pottering, he handed over to his four sons a concern generating revenues of FF 262 million per year, 45% of which were export, and net profits of FF 9 million.

Under the management of the four Jacquard sons, Chinon embarked on a fast sprint for world status. Sales of the parent company rose from FF 262 million in 1967 to FF 1,021 million in 1973, a compound growth rate of 23% per year. (See Exhibit 1.) Consolidated sales, which included the results of foreign subsidiaries, were FF 1,402 million in 1973. In part, the rapid sales growth resulted from diversification into hydraulic mobile cranes in 1969 and hydraulic loaders in 1972. Chinon also established a hydraulics division in 1969 to market its hydraulic components outside of the firm. However, the bulk of the sales growth stemmed from intensified marketing of the hydraulic excavator line on a worldwide basis. In 1973, 90% of the company's sales were still from excavators.

In 1974, Chinon was at an all-time high. Annual revenues were forecast at FF 1.8 billion. The firm had 60,000 excavator units in service, a 60% share of the French market, and an 18% share of the world market for hydraulic excavators. It had 14 manufacturing facilities, 11 commercial subsidiaries, and sales represenatives in over 100 countries. Roughly two thirds of its sales were made outside France. For its success, Chinon was lauded in France for its high level of exports, excellent product and service, and strong technological base.

THE HYDRAULIC EXCAVATOR BUSINESS

Product

A hydraulic excavator was essentially a tractor with a shovel attachment propelled by a hydraulic transmission system. (See Exhibit 2.) It performed three basic functions: digging, lifting, and laying. It was useful, for example, in digging holes for building foundations, in pulling out breakwater blocks on a beach, in laying water pipes, or in loading scrap metal onto a cargo ship.

There were two types of hydraulic excavators: tracked and wheeled. Tracked models represented about two thirds of all hydraulic excavators sold. To these basic models could be added a comprehensive range of over 200 attachments, from the basic backhoe bucket to the hydraulic auger, and including scrap grapples, deep digging clamshells, and specialized rehandling attachments, to provide a contractor with a machine tailor-made for any application.

Market

The hydraulic excavator market was estimated in 1973 to be FF 4.4 billion in sales worldwide, excluding the East Bloc countries, and growing at 10% per year. Seventy percent of all sales, or FF 3.1 billion, were made to the building and public works sector. This market had flourished during the 1960s when many countries initiated mammoth highway construction projects requiring large, heavy-duty machines. In the early 1970s, however, highway construction activity began to decline, and the emphasis shifted to urban demolition and reconstruction projects requiring smaller, less costly excavating machines. The remaining 30%, or FF 1.3 billion, of hydraulic excavator sales were made to the agriculture, extraction, stockpiling, and forestry sectors.

Although the worldwide unit volume had increased at an average rate of 6% per year, certain geographic markets had grown more rapidly in importance than others, namely the American and German markets. (See Exhibit 3.) The buoyant economic climate of these nations made them large producers as well as consumers of construction equipment during the 1960s and early 1970s. In fact in 1973, 50% of all construction equipment sold worldwide was manufactured in the United States and 15% in Germany.

The machine life of hydraulic excavators played an important role in determining unit sales in a given year. Manufacturers claimed that a well-maintained machine could last as long as eight years, considering five years of active use and three less so, or 10,000 to 15,000 total hours of work. In general, the smaller hydraulic excavators lasted 5 to 6 years, while the larger machines lasted only 2 to 3 years, due to their tougher jobs and more constant use.

Sales of hydraulic excavators also varied by season. In Europe, for example, 50% of a year's sales took place from April through June in anticipation of the summer's construction activity. Firms with a worldwide distribution were less affected by the seasonality and cyclicality of sales than those concentrating on a single geographic region.

Changing competitive environment

Until 1974, there were three major world competitors in hydraulic excavators: Chinon and two German firms, Liebherr and O. & K. Chinon was the clear market leader, with an estimated 18% of worldwide sales in 1973, versus 14% for Liebherr and 13% for O. & K. However, Liebherr and O. & K. had intensified their competitive challenges recently with bold price-cutting measures, broadened product lines, and more liberal credit and trade-in policies. They had also caught up with Chinon on hydraulics technology and had strengthened their dealership networks in Europe.

Aside from these firms, there were many national producers of hydraulic excavators such as Hymac and Priestman in the United Kingdom and Ackerman in Scandinavia. These small firms lacked the financial resources and dealership networks to expand abroad, yet they operated profitably in their own countries due to the preference of many national governments to steer public works and military orders to local equipment and manufacturers.

However, the most serious longer-term challenge seemed likely to come from several North American latecomers to the hydraulic excavator market. Massey-Ferguson had purchased Hanomag in 1974; J. I. Case was aggressively entering the European backhoe-loader market, which it dominated in the United States. Allis-Chalmers and Fiat had combined their construction-equipment operations. And Ford and International Harvester had acquired the French construction equipment manufacturers, Richier and Yumbo, respectively, in the early 1970s, each of which had hydraulic excavators in its product lines.

Basis for competition

By 1974, hydraulic technology and product quality were no longer a successful basis on which to compete. Success under the new market conditions was a question of "market penetration and cash." A strong presence in a geographic market, in terms of machines in use and loyal, effective dealers offering a full range of services, was paramount. Additionally, manufacturers needed the sales volume to price aggressively and the resources to finance dealers and customers.

In the changing competitive environment, smaller firms were left with four options:

They could steer clear of direct confrontation with the giants and stick to specialized items.

They could attack on a broad front, such as J. C. Bamford of the United Kingdom had done with its presence in all of the high-volume segments of the construction-equipment field, thus offering its dealers a full line of products.

They could fight on a narrower front, aiming at excellence in one or two selected products, such as Chinon had done as the world leader in hydraulic excavators.

They could choose to compete on a regional basis only, particularly if they lacked financial resources, as Ackerman had done with its hydraulic excavators in Scandinavia and as Weatherill had done with its loading shovels in the United Kingdom.

CHINON'S OPERATIONS IN 1974

Product line and development

In 1974, Chinon offered a construction equipment product line consisting of 31 excavators, 10 mobile cranes, and 4 loaders. Of the hydraulic excavators, 16 were on tracks and 10 on wheels, ranging from 8 to 137 tons and from 33 to 850 c.v. motor power. The TY45 wheeled model at nine tons has been the firm's best seller, accounting for 80% of excavator sales in 1962, but by 1974, unit sales were dispersed evenly among the light, medium, and heavyweight models. In describing the Chinon excavators, Marcel Jacquard had once said:

Versatility is the most useful quality of all Chinon machines. Whether it is a problem of digging, lifting, or laying, there's always a Chinon with the right attachment available to do the job with maximum speed and efficiency. . . . Versatility is a great source of profit for an excavator owner. Profit not only comes from efficiency but also from full machine utilization. The TY45, designed to utilize over 100 attachments, is the best example of Chinon versatility.

Indeed, Chinon had by far the broadest line of excavators of any manufacturer.

It had been the Chinon policy to introduce new or updated models of its products on a periodic basis. For example, in 1972, three new hydraulic excavator models were introduced; in 1974, four new excavator models and three new crane models were scheduled; and in 1975, plans included the replacement of 14 existing models with 19 new ones. Also in 1974, the firm was preparing for the introduction of a completely new generation of hydraulic excavators, equipped with a new motor system called "varidyn," scheduled to be introduced in 1976. Ten percent of the Chinon employees were engaged in research and development (R&D) at an annual expense to the company of FF 50 million by 1974, or about 4% of revenues.

Markets

In 1974, on a consolidated sales basis, Chinon served the following customer markets: building and public works (67%), extraction (7%), agriculture (6%), and diverse applications (20%). In the building and public works sector, Chinon's principal customers were small contractors whose purchase decisions depended heavily on levels of public spending and interest rates.

On a geographic basis, Chinon's market penetration had expanded from France to Europe to the entire world, except for the East Bloc countries, following the introduction of the hydraulic excavator in 1951. By 1974, sales outside France represented roughly two thirds of Chinon's estimated consolidated sales, up from 24% ten years earlier.

The geographic diversification was considered by management to provide substantial strength by dampening the business cycles in specific countries. (See Exhibit 4 for information on specific markets.) In a speech made before a group of international investors in 1974, Marcel Jacquard related Chinon's market positions to the firm's continued and rapid growth by saying:

The activity of public works is cyclical, but because of our product range and updating of materials, Chinon is not a cyclical business, but a growth business. In a period of inflation, the private customer dominates; and in a period of recession, it's the public powers. . . .

In conclusion, it is the variety of our customers and our deep penetration in expanding markets which are the best guarantees of our development.

Despite its worldwide market penetration, Chinon still considered its major market to be Europe, particularly France, Germany, Spain, and Italy. In 1974, 66% of the firm's consolidated sales were attributed to Europe. France alone accounted for 32%, and Germany 10%. Chinon held a 60% market share in France, a 25% share in the other Common Market countries, and an 18% share worldwide. By country, Chinon's market shares varied widely depending upon the strength of local competitors and whether the Chinon product line fit the country's market needs. For example, Chinon was first in hydraulic excavators in France, Belgium, and Spain but always third, or even fourth, in Germany behind Liebherr and O. & K. In the United States, Chinon's penetration was a mere 4%.

Manufacturing

Marcel Jacquard once defined the Chinon production strategy as two-fold: cost reduction and quality control. To obtain a level production volume, Chinon produced its hydraulic excavators for inventory, except for the very large models which were produced to order. On average, the production time was 4 to 5 months. Cost reductions came from lengthening the production runs of particular series and by standardizing models, although some adaptations had to be made to accommodate the market needs of each country. Product quality had always been a Chinon trademark, and rigorous control standards were applied along the production lines, and demanding technical standards were applied in R&D.

Chinon concentrated its machine production in the region of La Touraine, southwest of Paris, where it was the major employer with almost 5,000 workers. In 1974, there were four ultramodern factories: La Hayes-Descartes, Loches, Amboise, and Vouvray, all within a 40 kilometer radius of one another. Together the first three had a production capacity of 3,000 hydraulic excavator units; the Vouvray plant housed the hydraulics division.

The concentration of production within a small area minimized the cost of transporting parts from the various plants to the final assembly area. However, it did add some risk to Chinon's operations. French law had traditionally favored workers' rights, and it seemed unlikely that the work force could be reduced quickly. Any fall in orders would be met by a combination of no new hiring, early retirements, and a reduction in hours worked per week.

There were four subsidiary plants in France and six plants abroad. Mobile cranes were manufactured in Villeurbanne near Lyons. Loaders were produced in Caudry near the Belgium border. Hydraulic equipment and machine parts were produced in Mantes (Seine Valley) and Saumur (La Touraine). Its production subsidiaries abroad were in Spain, Belgium, Mexico, Brazil, the United States, and Ireland and had an annual capacity of 1,500 units.

A fairly elaborate system of reports had been devised to link the three-year marketing plans of each of the 13 sales subsidiaries and the manufacturing divisions. However, one industry official close to the firm implied that the system, while well-intentioned, was not vigorously enforced and the flow of information was accordingly sporadic.

Finance

The Jacquard family felt strongly that Chinon should be controlled and managed by the family responsible for its development and success. The company did go public in August of 1969 with the issuance of 196,000 shares of common stock of FF 90 per share. An additional 157,000 shares were sold in 1970 at a price of FF 300. However, very few new shares were issued after 1970. In 1974, the family held 37.6% of the common stock and 50.7% of the shareholders' voting rights. At the recent price of FF 525 per share, the Jacquards held shares worth approximately FF 186 million.

The reluctance to sell additional equity necessitated substantial borrowing by Chinon to finance its rapid sales growth and its seasonal sales pattern. (See Exhibit 5.) The construction-equipment business was fairly capital intensive, with considerable sums tied up in accounts receivables and inventories. The expansion had also required major investments in plant and equipment. Capital expenditures were expected to exceed FF 125 million in 1974 alone and to continue at that rate in 1975 and 1976.

Commenting on the firm's high debt to total capital ratio in an interview in the *Journal des Finances* in June 1972, Marcel Jacquard had said:

It is not excessive; it's sound and normal. It's even a little deficient. The net worth is in the order of FF 170 million (1971) for FF 83 million of total medium- and long-term debt. That makes a ratio indicating that we can support more debt.

Future prospects

Marcel Jacquard's comments in the *Journal des Finances* interview summarized his objectives for the future of the firm:

I don't think much about it (the fact that other French firms were merging with foreign companies) except that the foreigners and especially the Americans are powerful people and the Europeans, one after the other, have had their problems. Chinon has gone it alone for 20 years and has benefited from no one else. When you look at the situation of our principal international competitors, you see that they are generally profiting from very big public markets, such as Caterpilla· in the United States and Fiat in Italy. We have had at a time the weakness of being alone, but always the strength to have overcome . . . I believe that we can continue this way in the future and achieve a minimum of 10% growth per year (in unit volume) on a consolidated basis.

Exhibit 1

CHINON, S.A.

COMPARATIVE INCOME STATEMENTS, YEARS ENDING DECEMBER 31

(FF in millions except per share data)

	Parent Company				Consolidated	
	1970	1971	1972	1973	1972	1973
Sales...................	FF 566	FF 610	FF 761	FF 1,021	FF 1,109	FF 1,402
Cost of sales............	306	333	416	588		644
Depreciation............	15	13	16	18		38
Gross profit............	FF 245	FF 264	FF 329	FF 415		FF 720
Selling expense.........	176	190	237	295		493
General and administrative expenses.............	19	22	25	29		89
Interest expense........	25	27	24	37		60
Other expense (income)..	(6)	(8)	(1)	6		9
Income before tax.......	FF 31	FF 33	FF 44	FF 48		FF 69
Income taxes...........	13	15	22	23		37
Net income.............	FF 18	FF 18	FF 22	FF 25	FF 28	FF 32
Per share of common stock						
Earnings per share.....	FF 19	FF 19	FF 23	FF 26	FF 30	FF 34
Dividends per share....	7.5	7.5	9.0	12	9	12
Dividend payout......	40%	39%	39%	46%	33%	35%
Share price range......	360–490	230–400	285–500	400–810	285–500	400–810
Price-earnings range...	19–26	12–21	12–22	15–31	10–17	12–24
Shares outstanding....	940,800	940,800	941,040	944,367	941,040	944,367

Exhibit 2

CHINON, S.A.

Exhibit 3

CHINON, S.A.

INDUSTRY SALES OF HYDRAULIC EXCAVATORS, SELECTED COUNTRIES, 1973

France	2,700 units	Spain	600 units
West Germany	4,200 units	Austria	440 units
Great Britain	1,700 units	Europe—other	1,460 units
Italy	1,300 units	Africa	450 units
Sweden	700 units	Middle-East	170 units
Holland	500 units	Far-East	560 units
Switzerland	600 units	North America	4,700 units

Exhibit 4

CHINON, S.A.
SELECTED NATIONAL STATISTICS

	Period Averages					Second Quarter	
	1969	*1970*	*1971*	*1972*	*1973*	*1973*	*1974*
France							
Industrial production.....	94	100	106	114	120	120	125
Industrial prices..........	93	100	192	107	123	119	163
Short-term interest rates...	7.6%	8.1%	7.7%	7.4%	8.3%	8.0%	10.4%
West Germany							
Industrial production.....	94	100	102	106	113	112	112
Industrial prices..........	95	100	104	107	114	113	129
Short-term interest rates...	6.8%	8.3%	8.0%	7.9%	9.3%	9.3%	10.6%
Italy							
Industrial production.....	94	100	100	104	114	114	124
Industrial prices..........	93	100	103	108	126	122	175
Government bond yields..	6.9%	9.0%	8.3%	7.5%	7.4%	7.4%	9.2%
Spain							
Industrial production.....	91	100	103	119	138	134	153
Industrial prices..........	98	100	106	113	125	125	148
United Kingdom							
Industrial production.....	100	100	101	103	110	110	108
Industrial prices..........	93	100	109	115	123	120	149
Government bond yields..	9.0%	9.2%	8.9%	8.9%	10.7%	10.0%	14.1%
United States							
Industrial production.....	103	100	102	111	120	120	121
Industrial prices..........	96	100	104	107	115	114	137
Government bond yields..	6.1%	6.6%	5.7%	5.6%	6.3%	6.2%	7.1%

Exhibit 5

CHINON, S.A.

CONSOLIDATED BALANCE SHEETS, AT DECEMBER 31

(FF millions)

ASSETS	1972	1973
Cash...........................	FF 61	FF 44
Accounts receivable...............	305	399
Inventories......................	456	682
Other..........................	52	80
Total current assets............	FF 874	FF 1,205
Long-term accounts receivable.......	31	45
Net plant and equipment...........	187	239
Other..........................	7	10
Total assets.................	FF 1,099	FF 1,499
LIABILITIES AND NET WORTH		
Bank loans......................	FF 86	FF 181
Trade notes payable...............	240	322
Accounts payable.................	53	86
Short-term export loans*...........	136	153
Other loans.....................	91	162
Accruals........................	35	49
Other..........................	78	93
Total current liabilities.........	FF 719	FF 1,406
Long-term debt..................	136	180
Minority interest.................	21	21
Net worth......................	223	252
Total liabilities and net worth....	FF 1,099	FF 1,499

* The export financing program was established by the French Government to enhance export development. Participating banks were insured against credit risk by the French government and were able to refinance a substantial portion of the loans with the Banque Française de Commerce Exterieur.

MIDWEST COMMUNICATIONS, INC.*

In June, 1974, the management of Midwest Communications, Inc. decided to acquire $1 million in new broadcasting equipment for one of its television stations. Various means of financing this acquisition had been considered during the past several months. Mr. Jonathan Stone, vice president of finance of Midwest Communications, Inc., had narrowed the financing decision to two alternatives: (1) a seven-year lease proposed by the manufacturer of the equipment to be acquired, Audionics Corporation, or (2) a seven-year term loan for $1 million from a major insurance company. Mr. Stone knew that a final choice between these two alternatives would have to be made within a matter of days.

Midwest Communications and the broadcasting industry

Prior to 1960, Midwest Communications was a privately-held business engaged in magazine publishing and distribution. The corporation raised external equity capital in 1960 with an initial public issue of common stock. In 1961, Midwest purchased its first radio station and embarked on a program of investment in the broadcasting industry. A second radio station was acquired in 1963, and in the period 1963–66 both stations produced operating losses.

As a result of management changes and significant promotional work, the two radio stations were profitable in every year of the period 1967–73. Several additional radio and television stations were purchased in the late 1960's and early 1970's, and by 1973 operating revenues from broadcasting had grown to $9.7 million, representing 28% of Midwest's total operating revenues of $34.6 million. A five-year summary of income statements is shown in Exhibit 1, and balance sheets for 1971–73 are summarized in Exhibit 2.

Midwest ranked in the "second tier" of the broadcasting industry in terms of total broadcasting revenues, as the company was significantly smaller than the ten major broadcasters in the United States. The largest independent companies in the radio and television broadcasting industry were Columbia Broadcasting Systems, Inc. (sales revenues of $1.5 billion) and American Broadcasting Companies, Inc. ($880 million).

* Reprinted from *Stanford Business Cases 1974* with the permission of the publishers, Stanford University Graduate School of Business, © 1974 by the Board of Trustees of the Leland Stanford Junior University.

Early in 1974, observers of the broadcasting industry noted widespread Wall Street pessimism about rising operating costs (reflecting an 8% increase in costs reported for 1973) with only modest increases in total advertising revenues. One prominent New York Stock Exchange member firm anticipated that advertising revenues to broadcasters would grow at only 3% to 5% in 1974, down from a 9% increase in 1973. Under these industry conditions the price of the common stock of most major broadcasters had dropped 50% from the market highs of 1973, and Midwest's stock price had declined from its 1973 peak of $31 a share to around $10 by mid-1974. In the light of this development the management of Midwest had ruled out a new issue of common stock as a source of financing capital expenditures so long as the price of the company's common stock remained depressed.

The lease proposal

The seven-year lease under consideration had been proposed by the manufacturer of the new equipment to be acquired, Audionics Corporation. Audionics Corporation was a leading manufacturer of audio and video broadcasting equipment with total sales of several hundred million dollars. Audionics had recently organized a new financial subsidiary, Audionics Finance Corporation (AFC), whose purpose was to extend lease financing to customers interested in acquiring Audionics equipment. AFC customarily retained new leases in its portfolio, but it reserved the right to place some of its leases with third-party institutions.

The principal terms of the seven-year lease proposed to Midwest by Audionics to cover the acquisition of the $1 million of Audionics equipment were as follows:

1. *Annual lease payment for duration of lease.* Midwest would be obligated to pay AFC seven equal annual lease payments of $166,611 a year, payments to be made at the end of each year.[1]
2. *Maintenance, taxes, and insurance.* All payments for maintenance of the equipment and any taxes and assessments thereon would be the responsibility of Midwest. Midwest would also be obligated to carry a specified level of insurance on the equipment. (Mr. Stone estimated that Midwest's outlays for these purposes would be the same whether the equipment was leased or purchased.)

The annual lease payments quoted by AFC were computed so as to amortize the full $1 million sales price of the equipment over the seven-year period at an implicit interest rate of 4%. At the end of the seven-year period ownership of the equipment would, of course, reside in the hands of AFC. If Midwest desired to continue to use the equipment beyond the expiration of the lease, it would have to negotiate a renewal of the lease or a purchase of the equipment from AFC as of the expiration of the lease in 1981.

---

[1] Actually, most leases provide for monthly or quarterly rental payments, with payments due at the beginning of the period. The terms as here stated have been modified to simplify the analysis of the case.

In the course of his investigations of possible financing arrangements for the new equipment Mr. Stone had read an article in *Fortune* magazine on "Leveraged Leasing." This article, a portion of which is reproduced in Exhibit 3, described a leveraged lease of Anaconda Company on the plant and equipment of a new aluminum reduction mill. Mr. Stone had inquired of AFC whether a leveraged lease might be an attractive means of financing the equipment that Midwest was acquiring. The representative of AFC had responded that leveraged leases were seldom used in transactions of less than $5 million because of sizable legal and administrative costs involved. He advised Mr. Stone that a leveraged lease would not be appropriate in a $1 million transaction. He recommended instead a standard lease such as that described above.

The loan proposal

The only practical alternative to the lease proposal was for Midwest to buy the new equipment outright from Audionics and to finance it from available funds or by new borrowing. Since all of Midwest's internal funds were fully committed to projects previously undertaken, a decision to purchase the $1 million of equipment from Audionics would necessitate a new loan of $1 million. After investigating a number of loan possibilities Mr. Stone had decided that a seven-year term loan from a major insurance company was the most attractive source of additional debt available to Midwest.

The provisions of this loan were straightforward. Interest on the loan would be set at a rate of 12% on the outstanding balance of the loan for the duration of the loan. Repayments of principal would be made in equal annual installments at the rate of $142,857 a year, the payments to be made on each anniversary date of the loan. The loan proposal contained standard covenants on the usual subjects such as the maintenance of a required minimum level of working capital, incurrence of additional indebtedness, and repurchases of stock. All such provisions were regarded as reasonable by Mr. Stone.

Additional considerations relevant to lease versus buy-borrow decision

One of the considerations important in the decision as to whether to lease or buy the Audionic equipment was the tax consequences of the two transactions. Mr. Stone had been advised by his tax counsel that under the lease proposal the full amount of the annual lease payments would be deductible for income tax purposes as rental payments. In the event the property was purchased the tax consequences would be as follows: (1) Midwest would be entitled to an investment tax credit in the year of purchase equal to 7% of the purchase price, or $70,000; (2) the full $1 million purchase price could be depreciated on an accelerated basis over an eight-year life. Under the sum-of-the-years-digits method the depreciation allowances to which Midwest would be entitled would be:

Year	Allowable Depreciation
1	$222,222
2	194,444
3	166,667
4	138,889
5	111,111
6	83,333
7	55,556
8	27,778

In addition, under the purchase alternative the interest payments on the term loan obtained to finance the purchase would be deductible.

A second consideration involved in the decision was whether the equipment would have continued usefulness to Midwest at the end of the seven-year lease period, either for use within the company or for resale purposes. Mr. Stone estimated that under normal conditions the Audionics equipment package would be worth $200,000, or 20% of its initial value, at the end of seven years, even though the equipment would be fully depreciated by the end of the eighth year. Mr. Stone recognized, however, that technological developments might render the equipment obsolete sooner than he anticipated. On the other hand, a sustained rapid rate of inflation over the next seven years might mean that the dollar value of the equipment at the end of seven years would substantially exceed Mr. Stone's estimate of $200,000.

A third consideration that troubled Mr. Stone was the appropriate discount rate or discount rates to use in comparing the cash flows involved in the lease versus the buy-borrow alternatives. Mr. Stone had asked his assistant, Mr. Young, a recent MBA graduate, to prepare a memorandum for him discussing this issue. Mr. Young's memorandum, which is reproduced as Exhibit 4, did not fully resolve Mr. Stone's uncertainty on this point.

The decision

In order to obtain a better feel for the merits of the two alternatives Mr. Stone gave Mr. Young another assignment. First, he requested Mr. Young to lay out precisely the cash flows involved under the two alternatives. Where uncertainties were involved, such as the residual value of the equipment at the end of the seven years, Mr. Stone asked Mr. Young to prepare multiple estimates that would bracket the reasonable range of probable outcomes. Finally, Mr. Stone asked Mr. Young to compute the present value of the lease versus the buy-borrow alternative over the range of discount rates that might conceivably be justified on the basis of his earlier memorandum (Exhibit 4). Mr. Stone hoped that this additional information would resolve the uncertainty regarding the relative attractiveness of the two alternatives. In any event, he knew that he had to make a firm decision on the appropriate method of financing within the next two or three days.

Exhibit 1

MIDWEST COMMUNICATIONS, INC.

INCOME STATEMENTS FOR YEARS ENDING DECEMBER 31, 1969–73

(In millions except for per share data)

	1969	1970	1971	1972	1973
Newspaper operating revenues	$10.6	$17.1	$18.2	$19.7	$22.1
Broadcasting operating revenues	6.8	7.1	7.4	7.8	9.7
Other operating revenues	0.2	1.5	2.3	2.6	2.8
Total operating revenues	$17.6	$25.7	$27.9	$30.1	$34.6
Operating expenses	12.3	17.8	19.5	20.9	23.9
Depreciation	0.7	1.1	1.1	1.2	1.4
Interest expense	···	1.3	1.2	0.5	0.3
Other income	0.1	0.3	0.1	0.1	···
Net income before taxes	$ 4.7	$ 5.9	$ 6.2	$ 7.6	$ 9.0
Provision for income taxes	2.6	3.2	3.2	3.7	4.3
Net income after taxes	$ 2.1	$ 2.7	$ 3.0	$ 3.9	$ 4.7
Earnings per share (in dollars)	$ 0.57	$ 0.67	$ 0.73	$ 0.89	$ 1.06

Note: Figures may not add because of rounding.

Exhibit 2

MIDWEST COMMUNICATIONS, INC.

BALANCE SHEETS AS OF DECEMBER 31, 1971–73

(In millions)

	1971	1972	1973
ASSETS			
Cash and marketable securities	$ 2.7	$ 2.1	$ 2.0
Accounts receivable	2.7	2.8	3.6
Inventories	0.5	0.5	0.4
Other current assets	0.5	0.4	0.6
Total current assets	$ 6.3	$ 5.8	$ 6.7
Land and land improvements	1.1	1.1	1.8
Buildings	6.7	7.0	8.9
Equipment and fixtures	12.9	13.7	17.5
	$20.7	$21.8	$28.2
Less: Accumulated depreciation	9.4	10.1	11.1
Net fixed assets	$11.3	$11.7	$17.1
Intangible assets	16.6	16.6	18.7
Other assets	1.0	1.0	1.3
Total assets	$35.3	$35.0	$43.8
LIABILITIES			
Long-term debt due within one year	$ 1.2	$ 1.2	$ 1.3
Accounts payable	0.7	0.9	0.8
Dividends payable on common stock	. . .	. . .	0.3
Accrued income taxes	0.9	1.0	0.5
Film contracts, payments due in one year	0.1	0.2	0.4
Accrued expenses and other current liabilities	0.9	1.0	1.1
Total current liabilities	$ 3.9	$ 4.3	$ 4.4
Long-term debt	11.0	3.5	7.8
Film contracts, payments due after one year	0.1	0.1	0.6
Deferred income taxes	0.5	0.5	0.8
Total liabilities	$15.4	$ 8.4	$13.5
Convertible cumulative preferred stock	9.1	8.5	. . .
Net common equity	10.8	18.1	30.2
Total liabilities and net worth	$35.3	$35.0	$43.8

Note: Figures may not add because of rounding.

Exhibit 3

MIDWEST COMMUNICATIONS, INC.

LEVERAGED LEASING: HOW TO SAVE $74 MILLION, MAYBE

Leasing deals tend to be complicated, and Anaconda Company's new Sebree plant—an aluminum reduction mill—is an interesting example. Fourteen other companies were involved in the deal that raised $110.7 million and brought the plant into being. (Anaconda itself financed another $28 million not involved in the lease.)

Two of the companies did a lot of consulting and arranging for Anaconda. U.S. Leasing (upper left of the diagram), a company that specializes in "packaging" leasing deals, helped to design this one after it outbid another packager and several banks.

First Boston (upper right in the diagram), which has served for many years as Anaconda's investment banker, arranged for 65 percent of the financing by lining up three insurance companies, Prudential, Metropolitan, and Aetna Life (lower right), which together agreed to lend $72 million. The insurance companies will earn 9⅛ percent on this investment, with interest and principal coming out of Anaconda's annual lease payments.

The other 35 percent is "equity capital," put up by those six banks and Chrysler (lower left). In return for putting up $38.7 million, the seven get the rest of the lease payments. They also get to own the plant itself, which means that they receive the tax benefits from depreciation and the federal investment tax credit on the plant.

The property is held in the banks' name by First Kentucky Trust Company (center of the diagram), which took in both the debt and equity capital needed for construction and paid it out to the builder-contractor, the Aluminum Company of America. In addition, First Kentucky will funnel the lease payments from Anaconda to the insurance companies and banks. (The banks, as owners of the property, pay the trustee's expenses, which will be deducted from those lease payments.)

The point of this involved exercise, from Anaconda's point of view, is to reduce the cost of financing the plant. The company has calculated that over the twenty-year term of the lease, its lease payments will total some $74 million less than would the cost of interest payments on bonded debt. This calculation assumes, however, that Anaconda's effective tax rate, which has been extremely low recently (because of heavy losses in 1971), will stay low. If the company's tax rate should rise sharply, then it will miss the tax shelter it has given up by forgoing ownership of the plant.

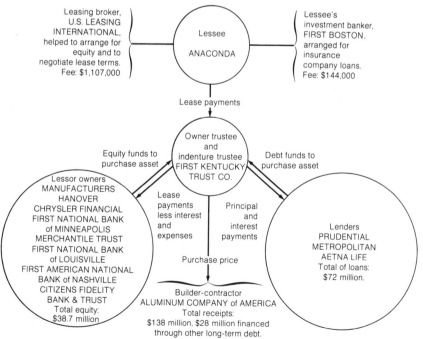

Source: *Fortune* (November 1973), p. 133.

Exhibit 4
MIDWEST COMMUNICATIONS, INC.
MEMORANDUM

June 15, 1974

TO: Mr. Stone

FROM: Mr. Young

SUBJECT: *Discount Rate to Use in Computing Present Values in Lease versus Buy-Borrow Decisions*

There seems to be a big difference of opinion these days about the right discount rate to use in computing present values in lease versus buy-borrow decisions. As you know, we have always used Midwest's (weighted average) cost of capital in *all* discounted cash flow calculations, in the interests of consistency. Our target debt ratio is 0.30 (long-term debt to total long-term capital), and in 1973 we were comfortably below that figure (0.23).

Under the term-loan alternative, with a 12% interest rate, the cost of debt to us currently would be about 6% on an after-tax basis. The cost of equity capital represents one number on which we have never had total agreement. The fundamental point is that this figure should reflect the basic business and financial risk of the company. Nearly everyone would agree that the broadcasting industry is subject to above-average risk—a look at our current stock price versus the high of last year will confirm that assessment. We assume the average public corporation in this country has a cost of equity of about 12%. Adding a 3% margin for additional risk would place our cost of equity in the area of 15%. Under current conditions in the capital markets even these figures may be too low.

At a level of abstraction commonly found in academic finance journals, it seems to make sense to discount each item of cash flow in a project at a rate commensurate with its risk. The problem is that any one project has many individual components of cash flow, all more or less risky, so that some degree of aggregation must be used in practice. The traditional approach has been to apply a single rate to the whole company as a "risk class" as well. At a practical level, we have to decide whether to apply one rate, our (weighted average) cost of capital, in all discounted cash flow calculations, or to use a higher or lower rate depending on some judgment of the risk of future cash flows in each specific instance in Midwest.

A case can be made for discounting lease payments at a rate lower than our cost of capital, on grounds that the payments are legal commitments that we certainly intend to honor. In this sense a lease payment is very similar to a loan payment. Both are legal obligations which can be treated as virtually certain over the term of the lease or loan. On the other hand, our estimates of residual equipment values are subject to all the obvious uncertainties concerning the state of new technology, new competing products, and demand for used audio/video broadcasting equipment. The argument for discounting everything at our cost of capital is based on simplicity. It has the great virtue of being workable and understandable, although it seems to be less elegant from a conceptual standpoint than applying different rates to different cash flows of different risk.

DIGI TERMINAL, INC.

∧∧

Howard Moore, president of Digi Terminal, Inc. (DTI), sat in his office wishing he knew the refinements of bankruptcy proceedings. Six days earlier on November 6, 1974, he had filed a petition under Chapter XI. Since then, the remaining 65 employees had been laid off and the phones had been disconnected. Moore wondered when the electricity would be cut.

While DTI was officially seeking an arrangement under Chapter XI of the Bankruptcy Act, many employees remained on the premises preparing resumes and intermittently walking into the president's office to offer ideas and ask Moore whether there was any possibility that the company could survive. A few minutes earlier, two co-founders, Elliott Wilson, the executive vice president, and Stan Jones, vice president-operations, had said they were giving up. Moore feared that they may have made the right decision, but he doggedly declared, "I'm going to work two more weeks—24 hours a day if I have to—to save DTI."

Formation of DTI

Like many of the enterprises which had sprung up around Philadelphia in the late 1960s, Digi Terminal was an offshoot of a large electronics manufacturing firm. Howard Moore, 32, had been a sales training manager at Maxwell, a major producer of minicomputers. He and Elliott Wilson, 33, a district sales manager, left that company in early 1969 to found a business of their own. Although they had not crystallized their plans at that time, Moore and Wilson ultimately determined to focus on the production and marketing of three computer interface devices designed to expand the telecommunication capabilities of various well-known systems. At Purdue University where Moore had earned his master's degree in industrial administration, models for these three products had been constructed and tested. On the basis of these tests, it appeared that production would require only a few commonplace manufacturing processes and would be mainly a simple assembly operation. Although market studies for the three products had not been undertaken, Moore and Wilson felt confident that sales would reach $1 million in the first year of operations, $2 million in the second year, and $4 million in the third year.

Believing that they had adequately dealt with the product issue, Moore and Wilson turned to the preparation of a business plan. This task consumed all of their waking hours for the next three weeks, but the final draft was complete in every detail. It contained layouts of production, warehouse, and office space, estimates of equipment and inventory requirements, projections of personnel needs, and pro forma financial statements setting forth expected income and cash financing requirements for the first three years of operations. This plan called for Moore to assume the position of president and chief financial officer and for Wilson to become vice president of sales. The vice presidents of production and engineering were to be, respectively, Stan Jones and Sid Herman, Maxwell employees who had agreed to join DTI when it commenced operations.

The final step was to arrange financing for the fledgling company. In the spring of 1969, Moore and Wilson approached Brown and Novax, a Philadelphia investment banking firm, with the hope of raising $275,000. Armed with their business plan they arrived for a half-hour appointment with the underwriters. Four hours later, they left with a tentative offer to raise $400,000 through the private sale of preferred stock. In April 1969, $435,000 of 6¼% convertible cumulative preferred shares were placed with a small group of investors, netting $391,500 for DTI after expenses. The stock was priced at $100 per share and was convertible at $4 per share.

DTI also issued 325,000 shares of common stock at $.04 per share to help defray the costs of organization and initial operations. Additionally, $12,500 was raised by selling 25,000 shares, or 8% of the total, to friends at $.50 per share. The remaining 300,000 shares were retained by the founders, giving them a 92% interest in the common stock. These men considered the terms of the preferred issue very attractive because they provided for a 70% controlling interest even if all of the preferred shares were eventually converted.

Operations commenced in May 1969, shortly after the financing. Moore leased a 7,000-square-foot building in an industrial park in Swarthmore, Pennsylvania, but decided not to hire the production staff until the first orders were received. On the marketing side, Elliott Wilson began to build a direct sales force for the company.

Credit authorization system

The strategy of delaying production proved to be fortuitous: once the selling effort began, it became clear that the market for the three interface devices was quite limited. With that unsettling discovery, Moore and his partners recognized the need to re-evaluate their product and market strategy. Subsequently, they decided to emphasize in their marketing effort not only the equipment but also possible service applications.

At roughly the same time that DTI made the decision to concentrate on product end uses, a potential customer in the retail trade expressed considerable interest in a systems application of one of DTI's telecommunication interfaces —a point-of-sale credit authorization system. This application was subsequently developed and sold to the customer, the first systems sale DTI had made.

Although DTI continued work on each of its initial three products, Moore and Wilson recognized the potential of their credit authorization system and began to market it for use in both the retail and the banking industries.

The retail market included dozens of department, discount, and specialty stores that required reliable, high-speed systems to control the large volume of credit purchases at the point of sale. All such stores with annual sales of more than $20 million were part of the target market. The second market, banks having assets greater than $100 million, included over 400 commercial institutions. The system would allow tellers at these banks to access daily trial balances and other account information as they handled such routine customer transactions as check cashing.

DTI designed a single system for use in both markets. It included a small general-purpose computer for central control, one or more disc units for storing information, a magnetic tape unit for accumulating and updating data, and a communications unit for accessing other data banks. High volume systems would be outfitted with terminals at the point of transaction and would cost between $200,000 and $600,000. Low volume systems were designed to use telephones and would be priced between $50,000 and $200,000.

Each system would be offered as a "turnkey" operation, engineered for the individual customer and covered by a long-term service contract. Because much of the optional equipment (additional processors, disc storage units, display terminals, and printers) was standardized and could be combined in numerous ways, it would be relatively easy to customize hardware. However, designing unique software was likely to be expensive, because programs would have to be written and debugged entirely by DTI, a time-consuming undertaking.

In early 1971, when DTI completed its first prototype system, there were only a few competitors in the credit authorization market, and no one company dominated the industry. The largest producer was TRW, a diversified manufacturer of electronics equipment. Other companies which had gained some acceptance in the field, such as Credit Systems, Inc. in Pennsylvania and Digital Data Systems in New Jersey, were quite small. Moore believed that DTI's systems were superior in quality and marketable at equal or slightly higher prices than any of its competitors' products.

In contrast to its computer interface products, DTI's credit authorization systems met with immediate market success. Companies in both target markets placed orders, and by the end of 1971, DTI had completed installations of retail credit authorization systems for its first three customers, the Thomas Jenks Company in San Francisco, Boltman's in New York City, and Markham Stores in Cleveland. By year-end it became clear that DTI was seriously undercapitalized for the volume of business that appeared to lie within its grasp.

1971 and 1972 financings

Upon receipt of DTI's first firm orders, Moore had been able to establish a $200,000 line of credit for the company with the Bank of Pennsylvania in Philadelphia. He had drawn on this line in early 1971 and again in early 1972 to finance capital needs which had developed between private offerings placed by Brown and Novax in April 1971 and March 1972. In the first issue, they raised $126,000 through the sale of 90,000 shares of common stock. The second offering grossed $780,000 through the sale of 260 "investment units."[1] Each unit consisted of common stock, warrants, and a subordinated five-year note. The cumulative effect of the offerings was to reduce the founders' ownership of the company to 46% initially and to 40% if and when all outstanding warrants were exercised.

As operations gained momentum, DTI would have required even more external financing were it not for its billing policy which provided for a regular inflow of production-progress payments. Because six to eight months were required to produce a finished credit authorization system from the signing of a contract to final installation, DTI had insisted from the start on contracts calling for progress payments: 10% of the purchase price was required on signing of a contract, 30% on completion of specifications, 50% on delivery of equipment, and the final 10% on completion of contract. Because manufacturing costs were less than 40% of sales, this plan not only financed production but also provided funds for software development and for general corporate purposes.

Expansion

Every three or four months, Howard Moore revised his detailed business plan for the coming year. In mid-1972, he became increasingly concerned with the strains of rapid growth on DTI. Production could not keep pace with sales, and improvisation became necessary, particularly for warehousing space. Loft footage was rented in an adjacent building, component parts were moved from the main plant to the nearest available warehouse (10 miles away) for storage, and nine 45-foot trailers were leased and parked next to the main plant to relieve congestion therein. Sales for the fiscal year ending April 30, 1972 jumped to $862,000 from $331,000 in fiscal 1971. However, Moore expected and planned for an even larger increase for fiscal 1973, to at least $2.5 million in sales. (Yearly income statements and balance sheets are presented in Exhibits 1 and 2, and quarterly sales and income results are shown in Exhibit 3. Exhibit 4 gives the distribution of sales by product line.)

In early 1973, DTI moved into a new 24,000-square-foot building located in the same industrial park, leaving only its field service operations in the old building. New workers were hired to begin production of many subassembly parts which had previously been brought in. By July, when operations had been settled into the new plant, DTI was equipped, staffed, and financed for the increased sales levels which Moore had projected.

During the early months of 1973, four large orders for credit authorization

---

[1] The common offered in 1971 was priced at $1.60 per share to net DTI $1.40 per share after issue costs. The 260 "investment units" sold in 1972 were priced at $3,000 per unit. Each unit included 500 shares of common stock valued at $3.27 per share, warrants to purchase 417 shares of common at $2.40 per share prior to mid-1977, and an 8%, $1,000 subordinated five-year note to be surrendered as payment for the warrants upon exercise.

systems materialized, making Moore's expansion plans seem overly conservative. Bonham and North of Chicago and Broadmore Stores of Los Angeles came in for systems of 300 terminals each, and Jayson Moss of Kansas City and Barings of New Orleans each ordered systems of 1,000 terminals each.

Another large order, in the amount of $1.2 million, was received at this time from National Retail Stores, a holding company for several regional department-store chains. However, this order was for a totally new product, a full point-of-sale (POS) system. The retailer wanted DTI to add a cash drawer and some data keys to its credit authorization terminals to produce a more versatile system. National reasoned that because the terminals were already connected to a computer, it would be easy to design software to incorporate into the existing system such functions as sales recording, inventory updating, and customer billing. Because all these operations could be performed simultaneously, such a system would produce considerable savings in hourly wages and would additionally reduce errors. This order clearly offered DTI the prospect of much larger follow-on sales to National, but more important, it paved the way for entry to a multibillion dollar industry.

National calculated that such a system should cost between $500 and $1,500 per terminal, as opposed to the $3,000 to $4,500 price then being charged for similar units by such market leaders as NCR. At the lower price, it would be economical to replace existing mechanical registers with the DTI system, whereas the higher-priced units were only cost-justified for new stores. Therefore, Moore was persuaded that the replacement market offered a much higher sales potential for DTI than did the new-store market served by its competitors.

More financing, March 1973

Observing the surge in new orders, DTI's salesmen revised their short-term sales forecast to an optimistic $18 to $20 million. Moore, however, remembered how badly he and Wilson had erred in their initial sales forecasts and was much more conservative in his estimate, although even he increased his 18-month sales projection to within a range of $4.4 to $5.5 million.

Faced with the demands of financing such growth and the costs of developing the POS system, Moore turned to Brown and Novax for the fourth time in four years. Together they calculated that DTI would require $1.7 million of new capital, $1.2 million to support higher sales, and $500,000 to develop the POS system. The large amount to be raised and the likelihood of future calls on the market convinced everyone that the time had come "to take DTI public." That was accomplished with a March 1973 offering of 220,000 shares of common at $8 per share. The issue netted $1.5 million for the company after $250,000 of expenses and was very well timed. Shortly thereafter, the new-issues market for companies such as DTI completely disappeared.

Soon after going public, with the stock price still near $8 (see Exhibit 5 for 1974 and 1975 high-low bids), Moore took the opportunity to force conversion of the outstanding preferred stock. In this way, he eliminated DTI's only dividend requirement, effected a wider distribution of the common stock, and paved the way for a repeat offering of preferred should that be needed.

With the proceeds of the issue, Moore paid off all overdue payables and $450,000 of short-term loans from the Bank of Pennsylvania. Then he rapidly took on more production personnel, hiring 50 new workers over a two-month period. This raised total employment to 169 (see Exhibit 3) and increased break-even volume to about $4 million.

Problems—mid-1973

Although retail sales surged in early 1973, by midyear they had leveled off. Consequently, retailers became hesitant to make any postponable investments. In this climate, Pitney Bowes, one of the largest forces in the point-of-sale cash register field, decided to discontinue that business and wrote off $40 million in the process.

DTI had not escaped the effects of retailers' uncertainties; although there was active interest in DTI's systems and small orders continued strong, no large orders were booked in 1973 other than those made early in the year. By late summer, Moore began to worry. Adding to his concern, Credit Systems and Digital Data, both manufacturers of point-of-sale credit authorization systems, announced that they were bankrupt and were leaving the field. Moore wondered whether the failures were good or bad news for DTI; although they reduced competition, they might also make potential customers skeptical about other small companies such as DTI.

In fact, such concern was justified, because DTI was beginning to lose money. Its very high break-even sales volume would not be reached unless it could make some of the elusive "big-ticket" sales. Furthermore, production of the last four credit authorization systems was nearly finished, and the inflow of cash production payments was dwindling. The unexpectedly costly and slow development of the software further aggravated the cash-flow problem. After assessing the situation in September, Moore reported to his board that massive layoffs would be required if business did not pick up soon.

As a result of these developments, Moore was forced to begin drawing again on DTI's line of credit with the Bank of Pennsylvania, which had been increased in early 1973. Borrowings rose to $600,000 in July 1973 and to $1.1 million in October (see Exhibit 3).

Part-time employees were laid off in October, and when new large orders failed to materialize by December, another 30 people, or roughly 20% of the work force, were cut. The remaining employees worked with added determination to keep the company afloat. Field service moved out of the old building and into the main building to reduce overhead; leased warehouse space was reduced by moving inventory into the central building; more subassembly operations were performed in-house to cut production costs as operations declined.

The situation continued to deteriorate into 1974, and DTI drew more heavily on the Bank of Pennsylvania until fiscal 1974 results were released in May, revealing a $2 million loss.[2] At that point, William Stephens from the loan collection department visited DTI. "I'm here to deloan this place, not loan it up," he told Moore. No more money was to be advanced until George Hannekin, a consultant hired by the company at urging of the bank, could complete a thorough examination of the company. In the meantime, Stephens required DTI to pledge all of its assets as security against the $1.7 million loan outstanding.

During the next two weeks, the consultant virtually lived at DTI, studying every aspect of the company's operations. After Hannekin submitted his report, Stephens revised the bank's position: DTI could borrow up to $200,000 more, but that would be the absolute limit of its credit. The further advances would be extended only to keep DTI alive while Moore arranged for a merger or secured some other source of financing.

Both Moore and Stephens believed that DTI was an attractive acquisition candidate. It had: 1) a base of blue-chip customers using 8,000 of the company's terminals and 200 processors; 2) a reputation for excellent product reliability; 3) excellent, up-to-date technology; and 4) an intact marketing organization and experienced management team. Thus, DTI offered an inexpensive but strong foothold in the POS and the credit authorization system markets.

Merger search—1974

Moore began immediately to look for a suitable merger partner. He met with some 35 companies, three of them major customers, trying to arouse some interest in DTI. Despite his determination, he was unsuccessful in this effort. He met with similar failure at this time in his attempt to help DTI close two critical $750,000 orders. It seemed that neither potential buyers nor potential customers were interested in a company teetering on bankruptcy, regardless of the acknowledged superiority of its product: availability of critical maintenance and long-term service were too uncertain.

In late August, Moore contacted Computer General, the fourth largest minicomputer company in the country. After several meetings, the president, John Wyler, made an oral offer for $1.1 million. Recognizing that this price would not allow both the bank and the shareholders to fully recover their investment, Moore asked Stephens for how much the bank would settle. When Stephens responded that he required full repayment, Moore declared, "Unless our shareholders get a fair share of the deal, management will walk away from DTI." He reasoned that Stephens would be willing to bargain for less than 100% repayment if he were faced with the alternative of a quick liquidation; he estimated that the "fire-sale" value to the bank of DTI's inventory was only about

---

[2] A large part of the loss was caused by an accounting change. In earlier years, it had been the company's policy to defer major software costs, anticipating they would be fully recovered in future sales over a three-year period. With sales falling below projected levels, the company decided to take a conservative approach and amortize $1.3 million of capitalized software costs. The write-off left only about $250,000 of software charges outstanding, the amount considered applicable to business which was expected under present market conditions (Exhibit 2).

$300,000,[3] significantly less than Stephens could expect in a merger agreement. With this in mind, Moore proposed a $1.2 million deal to Computer General: $950,000 for the bank and $250,000 for DTI's shareholders. Wyler accepted the offer orally and even the bank's consultant, George Hannekin, agreed that it was a favorable arrangement for all concerned. Nevertheless, Stephens was intractable. "Fifty cents on the dollar isn't good enough for me or for the bank."

Stephens believed that DTI was worth more than $1.2 million to the right corporate partner and consequently recommended a second consultant, Robert Stein, a specialist in the merger and acquisition field. After a two-week study of DTI, Stein began to prospect among his own contacts.

In early October, Wyler tried to force Moore's hand. He indicated that Computer General's offer was still good but that the price would drop $100,000 per week from that time forward. Stephens was still not willing to approve the deal.

Stein contacted Delaware Electronics Corporation later that month. Although its management expressed some interest in acquiring DTI, it was unwilling to match Computer General's $1.2 million offer on short notice. Stein's other prospects showed no interest at all after examining DTI's most recent financial statements (Exhibits 1, 2, and 3). This fact, coupled with DTI's continuing losses, convinced Stephens that Computer General's offer was probably the best that could be obtained. In early November, he authorized Moore and Stein to proceed with that deal.

The following Tuesday, Moore and Stein visited Wyler and were shocked to hear his new offer: $300,000 for the bank and $200,000 for the shareholders. Even after accounting for the $100,000-per-week reduction, $500,000 seemed to them an absurdly low price. Hours of haggling only increased the offer to $700,000.

Later, in the hotel, Moore told Stein that he was very disappointed with the price but that he felt forced to accept Wyler's offer. When they called Stephens, he surprisingly agreed to the deal. Moore than contacted Computer General and accepted the offer. After confirming the deal with his chairman, Wyler reported that the proposed acquisition would be presented to the board of directors the following day.

Moore waited all day Wednesday in his hotel room for word of the board's confirmation. The call never came. Before leaving for the airport, he called Computer General, but the only person he could reach was the treasurer. He told Moore that the company had just reported its first losing quarter in 2½ years and that, consequently, the board had vetoed the deal at any price.

Bankruptcy

Computer General's withdrawal left DTI with no merger prospects other

---

[3] The October 31, 1974 balance sheet in Exhibit 2 notes $1,305,000 of inventory. Moore guessed that a third of the physical volume of this inventory was work-in-process, that another third was saleable components, and that the final third was made up of material that would be considered worthless in a liquidation sale.

than Delaware Electronics. Stein urged Moore to reopen discussion with that company now that the formerly prohibitive $1.2 million price was substantially reduced. Delaware Electronics manufactured aerospace equipment for Defense Department prime contractors and was interested in acquiring DTI as a means of diversifying its operations into nongovernment fields. (Exhibit 6 presents Delaware Electronics' financial statements.)

At this point the Bank of Pennsylvania was no longer advancing additional funds to DTI, but it was releasing cash to the company's deposit account as collections were received on outstanding receivables. When Moore and Stein met with Stephens and explained the Computer General fiasco and the plan to approach Delaware Electronics, Stephens expressed considerable pessimism and said that he wanted to discuss the situation with other bank officials. Moore interpreted this as an indication that Stephens was seriously considering foreclosing on DTI. For his part, Stephens interpreted a portion of their discussion relating to the management of DTI's deposit account as an indication that Moore was considering filing for bankruptcy. This exchange of veiled meanings took place on Friday afternoon.

The following Tuesday both men acted. Stephens dispatched an official of the bank to DTI's head office to "take open, peaceful, and unopposed possession" of the debtor's assets. Two hours later, Moore filed a petition for bankruptcy under Chapter XI in the U.S. District Court of Pennsylvania. (Exhibit 7 presents a copy of this petition).

In the hearing which followed, the court did not appoint a receiver but instead left DTI's management and directors in charge of operations pending their submission of a plan of arrangement. In assenting to the bank's seizure prior to the filing, DTI had—upon advice of its counsel—given the bank the position it desired as a secured creditor in possession.[4] However, all creditors were prevented under Chapter XI from taking legal action against DTI to satisfy their claims. Thus, Moore was given a brief lease on life to devise a survival plan for his company.

Moore's negotiations with creditors

The six days following the bankruptcy filing were a blur of activity. Endless trips to the courthouse and numerous discussions with DTI's officers, directors, employees, and lawyers consumed much of Moore's time. However, the three most important meetings he scheduled were with Stephens and other interested bank officers, with John Symmington, the president of Delaware Electronics, and with the financial vice president of National Retail Stores. Their cooperation, individually and collectively, would be required to revitalize DTI.

In his meeting with Stephens, Moore requested that the prebankruptcy management of the deposit account be continued for as long as was required to make a deal with Delaware Electronics. Receivables of DTI were small, but

---

[4] Taking legal possession of pledged assets prior to the filing of a Chapter XI petition eliminates the uncertainty involved in petitioning the court to recognize the lender's security and to award possession to the lender.

collections which might come in were desperately needed to meet daily expenses. Stephens could have refused and prevailed upon the court for release of such funds to the bank, but he agreed. The long-shot possibility of a merger offered better financial prospects for the bank than did the liquidation of all DTI's assets and receivables. Stephens' paramount concern was negotiating a favorable disposition of the bank's $1.9 million claim in the plan of arrangement which Moore was obliged to submit to the court.

Having dealt with the bank, Moore flew to Wilmington to talk to John Symmington of Delaware Electronics. He was relieved to discover that Symmington also had a strong entrepreneurial spirit and had himself gone through voluntary arrangement proceedings. Thus, his interest in DTI was not dampened by its Chapter XI status. He was well acquainted with DTI's products and its market position, and furthermore, he believed that the future of the company rested largely on the success of the POS system. The discussion therefore moved quickly to the financing required to keep DTI alive. Moore's estimates showed that the company could operate on a gross cash inflow of about $100,000 per month: payroll and overhead expenses for field maintenance would approximate $45,000; manufacturing, marketing, and general corporate administration costs would be about $55,000. These expenses would be applied to income from field maintenance of about $55,000 per month and from manufacturing of about $35,000 (provided customers made progress payments on existing orders). Thus, the monthly *net* cash requirement would be about $10,000, and any new orders received would further reduce that amount.

Because the continued flow of manufacturing progress payments on existing orders was critical in minimizing the amount of funds required monthly, Symmington had considerable interest in Moore's upcoming meeting with DTI's largest customer, National Retail Stores. Both he and Moore recognized the likelihood that customers would not make payments before delivery or place new orders with a company in Chapter XI without a performance guarantee from a responsible third party such as Delaware Electronics.

Symmington was also concerned about the quid pro quo for Delaware Electronics if it were to advance DTI cash and to quarantee its production. He indicated that further discussion was pointless unless Delaware Electronics was given majority control of DTI on confirmation of an arrangement and an assured means of increasing that interest above 80% when desired (to permit consolidation of financial statements). Symmington said that he was not authorized to make a specific proposal at this time; however, he promised to do so after a week's detailed financial and marketing investigation.

Moore was understandably apprehensive about National Retail Stores' attitude toward the Chapter XI petition. Fifty of the 550 POS units ordered had been installed in a Rochester, New York division the week before Moore had filed the bankruptcy petition. These units were 95% debugged, and National was pleased with the system but was concerned about advancing further funds. The retailer had already paid two thirds of the $1.2 million contract price but had received only 9% of its order. National would obviously not want to see that investment go down the drain, but neither would it knowingly throw good money after bad.

National's financial vice president repeatedly focused on this dilemma in his meeting with Moore. He wanted some form of assurance that DTI would complete the existing contract and, if not, that National would not lose its investment in the work it had already financed. He indicated that National would consider its investment protected if DTI would place the POS drawings, computer programs, patent applications, and related materials in trust with the understanding that they were to be transferred to National if DTI failed. Moore knew that it was very important to accommodate National's wishes in return for its continued payment on the POS order. While DTI faced the prospect of doing little better than breaking even on the remaining 500 units after accounting for cost overruns, the company would need every bit of cash it could obtain to sustain operations.

The final group of interested parties consisted of some 450 general creditors, primarily suppliers, to whom DTI owed $860,000. Some concession would have to be made to their position because the law required that a proposed arrangement must be accepted by a majority, both in number and in amount of claims, of all unsecured creditors. However, because there was no single claimant who required immediate attention, Moore felt that he was at last free to take the time he needed to assess the current situation and to consider the plan of arrangement he must prepare.

*   *   *   *   *

Moore was determined to persist in his efforts to save his company. He reflected that he felt a deep personal commitment to the people of DTI. They were responsible for the company's rapid growth, and their loyalty and extra effort had fended off bankruptcy for as long as they had. He was also keenly aware of the trust that the shareholders had placed in his leadership.

DTI had made great progress, and Moore believed in what it was doing. Its credit authorization systems were marketable, reliable, and economical. The POS system, now fully developed, offered particularly useful capabilities to retailers. As he had told Symmington, he firmly believed that with adequate financial support DTI could reach $4.0 to $4.5 million in sales in the coming year, earning 12% pretax on sales after taking all write-offs. Much larger sales volumes were likely in future years.

Turning then to the pressing problem of formulating a plan of arrangement for the court, Moore jotted down a preliminary proposal.

1. Offer both the general creditors and the holders of the 8% debentures five cents on the dollar.

2. Offer the Bank of Pennsylvania $950,000, representing 50% settlement in the form of (a) cash (from Delaware Electronics) and/or notes; and (b) preferred stock redeemable on or before December 31, 1984.

3. Offer Delaware Electronics (a) 1,600,000 newly issued shares, cal-

culated to equal 61% of the total outstanding; (b) warrants to purchase an additional 3,000,000 shares at $.10 per share; (c) a contract
with National Retail Stores to complete the 500-unit POS order, thus
giving assurance of a continuing cash flow from progress payments.

4. Offer National Retail Stores (a) a performance guarantee by Delaware
Electronics assuring delivery, as contracted, of the remaining 500 POS
units, and (b) the deposit with a bank trustee for ten years of POS
drawings, patent applications, and related documents.

Moore knew that time was becoming critically short and that the court would
not wait more than a few more days for him to submit a reasonable plan. He
poured himself a cup of coffee and mulled over the question of whether such
proposals were likely to be accepted.

Exhibit 1

DIGI TERMINAL, INC.

INCOME STATEMENTS, 1970–1974

(Dollar figures in thousands)

	Fiscal Years Ending April 30					Six Month to Oct. 31,
	1970	1971	1972	1973	1974	1974
Sales*............................	$ 15	$ 331	$ 862	$2,840	$ 2,666	$ 750
Less:						
Software costs			52	273	1,756	488
Manufacturing and field service...	8	196	421	1,263	1,233	650
Selling and administrative						
expenses....................	236	253	251	549	1,047	486
Research and development........	97	103	118	311	474	299
Operating income (loss)...............	$(326)	$(221)	$ 20	$444	$(1,844)	$(1,173)
Interest expense....................		4	16	12	126	109
Other income......................	13			5	4	
Income before taxes (loss)...........	$(313)	$(225)	$ 4	$437	$(1,966)	$(1,282)
Federal and state income taxes.......				6		
Net income (loss)..................	$(313)	$(225)	$ 4	$431	$(1,966)	$(1,282)

*The company records sales and cost of sales on its contracts by the percentage-of-completion method. Under this method, income is based on that percentage of the contract price that costs incurred to date bear to total estimated costs except that 5% of the income so calculated is deferred until final customer acceptance.

Exhibit 2

DIGI TERMINAL, INC.
BALANCE SHEETS, 1970–1974
(Dollar figures in thousands)

	Year Ending April 30					Oct. 31
	1970	1971	1972	1973	1974	1974
ASSETS						
‹sh............................	$ 26	$ 17	$ 334	$ 213	$ 25	$ 16
›counts receivable.................	12	10	50	19	51	47
‹billed receivables*..............			282	1,803	979	325
‹entories.......................	94	208	172	911	1,156	1,305
‹her...........................	3	3	3	8	12	9
Current assets.................	$ 135	$ 238	$ 841	$2,954	$2,223	$1,702
‹nt and equipment...............	32	34	46	303	658	609
‹ferred charges†..................			104	365	257	78
Total assets..................	$ 167	$ 272	$ 991	$3,622	$3,138	$2,389
LIABILITIES AND CAPITAL						
‹counts payable...................	$ 43	$ 87	$ 207	$ 766	$ 586	$ 865
›tes payable—bank...............		131			1,675	1,900
›gress billings...................		37				
‹vidends payable.................				26		
‹her...........................	8	12	43	157	158	187
Current liabilities..............	$ 51	$ 267	$ 250	$ 949	$2,419	$2,952
‹bordinated long-term debt........			260	260	253	253
Total liabilities...............	$ 51	$ 267	$ 510	$1,209	$2,672	$3,205
‹eferred stock....................	435	435	435			
‹mmon stock (par value, $.04).....	13	16	22	36	36	36
‹pital surplus...................	12	123	589	2,537	2,556	2,556
‹tained earnings.................	(344)	(569)	(565)	(160)	(2,126)	(3,408)
‹t worth.......................	$ 116	$ 5	$ 481	$2,413	$ 466	$ (816)
Total liabilities and capital......	$ 167	$ 272	$ 991	$3,622	$3,138	$2,389

*The company records sales and cost of sales on its contracts by the percentage-of-completion method. Under this ‹thod, income is based on that percentage of the contract price that costs incurred to date bear to total estimated costs, ‹ept that 5% of the income so calculated is deferred until final customer acceptance.

†Deferred charges consist of unamortized software costs and unamortized debt-issue expense.

Exhibit 3

DIGI TERMINAL, INC.
SELECTED QUARTERLY DATA
(Dollar figures in thousands)

	Fiscal 1972		Fiscal 1973				Fiscal 1974				Fiscal 1975	
	Jan. 31, 1972	Apr. 30, 1972	July 31, 1972	Oct. 31, 1972	Jan. 31, 1973	Apr. 30, 1973	July 31, 1973	Oct. 31, 1973	Jan. 31, 1974	Apr. 30, 1974	July 31, 1974	Oct. 31, 1974
						Operating Data						
Sales	$ 167	$ 247	$ 485	612	$ 733	$1,010	$1,163	$ 774	$ 482	$ 247	$ 444	$ 305
Cost of sales	77	124	281	328	375	552	697	376	379	1,537	505	632
Selling and administrative	64	65	101	121	163	164	244	271	260	272	235	251
Research and development	16	56	57	72	62	120	117	90	107	160	168	131
Operating income (loss)	$ 10	$ 2	$ 46	$ 91	$ 133	$ 174	$ 105	$ 37	$ (264)	$(1,722)	$ (464)	$ (710)
Net interest expense	4	5	(1)	4	7	(3)	10	26	41	45	64	44
Income before tax	$ 6	$ (3)	$ 47	$ 87	$ 126	$ 177	$ 95	$ 11	$ (305)	$(1,767)	$ (528)	$ (754)
New orders	n.a.	n.a.	180	250	1,100	700	550	500	700	850	475	380
Number of employees	19	23	38	50	79	119	169	158	128	117	109	68
						Balance Sheet Items						
Cash	$ 2	$ 266	$ 9	$ 175	$ 44	$ 213	$ 35	$ 23	$ 84	$ 25	$ 27	$ 16
Accounts receivable	5	50	4	341	173	19	184	175	114	51	53	47
Unbilled receivables	109	282	754	612	1,104	1,803	2,129	2,025	1,302	979	528	325
Unamortized software	32	92	82	130	252	353	454	838	1,142	247	98	69
Bank loans	210	—	—	350	440	—	600	1,100	1,300	1,675	1,965	1,900

n.a. = not available.

Exhibit 4

DIGI TERMINAL, INC.
SALES BY PRODUCT LINE
(Dollar figures in thousands)

Year Ending April 30	Credit Authorization Systems	Bank Teller Information Systems	Other	Total
1970	$ —	$ —	$15	$ 15
1971	286	—	45	331
1972	571	201	90	862
1973	2,295	495	50	2,840
1974	2,164	462	40	2,666

Exhibit 5

DIGI TERMINAL, INC.
MARKET PRICE OF COMMON STOCK

	High Bid	Low Bid
Fiscal year 1974, quarters		
First quarter	8	4½
Second	6½	4¼
Third	6¼	3¼
Fourth	4	1½
Fiscal year 1975, quarters		
First	2¾	½
Second	1	⅛
Third (to Nov. 10)	⅜	.01

Source: National Daily Quotation Service.

Exhibit 6

DIGI TERMINAL, INC.
DELAWARE ELECTRONICS CORPORATION

GENERAL INFORMATION

Delaware Electronics, with headquarters in Wilmington, Delaware, was primarily a Defense Department contractor. In fiscal 1974, military sales accounted for more than 85% of total company sales. Military products included gyromagnetic compasses for use in airplanes, radar sets for the Navy, gunnery trainers for artillery and tank crews, and missile simulators. Sales increased rapidly in 1973 and 1974, and with an order backlog of $20 million, further gains appeared certain. Profits of the military division equaled 110% of the company's net income.

The company's civilian branch provided computer programming and computer based information systems to the transportation industry.

Exhibit 6—Continued

INCOME STATEMENTS

(Dollar figures in thousands)

	1973	1974
Sales.................................	$8,760	$12,573
Less:		
Cost of sales........................	6,652	9,710
Selling and administrative expenses......	1,320	1,724
Operating income........................	$ 788	$ 1,139
Interest expense........................	173	145
Income before tax.......................	$ 615	$ 964
Income after tax........................	$ 615	$ 964

BALANCE SHEETS

(Dollar figures in thousands)

ASSETS	1973	1974
Cash.................................	$ 311	$ 954
Accounts receivable....................	1,225	1,350
Unbilled receivables (net of progress billings and advances)...............	910	1,132
Recoverable federal income taxes.........	131	131
Other................................	1,043	444
Current assets.....................	$ 3,620	$ 4,011
Plant and equipment (net)..............	656	715
Other assets..........................	60	37
Total assets.....................	$ 4,336	$ 4,763

LIABILITIES AND CAPITAL		
Accounts payable......................	$ 1,537	$ 1,470
Notes payable.........................	1,087	
Accrued expenses......................	454	854
Advances from customers on contract.....	144	309
Current portion of long-term debt........	258	460
Current liabilities.................	$ 3,480	$ 3,093
Long-term debt........................	559	412
Total liabilities...................	$ 4,039	$ 3,505
Preferred stock.......................	200	65
Common stock ($.01 par)..............	1,250	1,386
Paid-in surplus.......................	12,178	12,144
Retained earnings (deficit).............	(13,331)	(12,337)
Net worth.............................	$ 297	$ 1,258
Total liabilities and capital..........	$ 4,336	$ 4,763

Exhibit 7

DIGI TERMINAL INC.

CHAPTER XI PETITION

UNITED STATES DISTRICT COURT
DISTRICT OF PENNSYLVANIA

In re:

DIGI TERMINAL, INC.   Bankruptcy No. 74 1965

Debtor

ORIGINAL PETITION UNDER
CHAPTER XI

1. Petitioner's post office address is: Menlo Industrial Park, Swarthmore, Delaware County, Pennsylvania.

2. Petitioner has had its principal place of business within this district for the preceding six months.

3. No other case under the Bankruptcy Act initiated on a petition by or against petitioner is now pending.

4. Petitioner is qualified to file this petition and is entitled to the benefits of Chapter XI of the Act.

5. Petitioner is insolvent.

6. Petitioner intends to file a plan pursuant to Chapter XI of the Act.

7. Exhibit "A" is attached to and made part of this petition. [Officers' certificate attesting board of directors' vote to authorize Moore to prepare and file a Petition for an Arrangement under Chapter XI of the Bankruptcy Act—omitted here].

WHEREFORE petitioner prays for relief in accordance with Chapter XI of the Act.

_____

Attorneys for Petitioner

Commonwealth of Pennsylvania
County of Philadelphia

I, Howard P. Moore, president of the petitioner named in the foregoing petition, do hereby swear that the statements contained therein are true according to the best of my knowledge, information, and belief.

_____

Howard P. Moore
President

Subscribed and sworn to before me on November 6, 1974.

_____

Notary Public

SCM CORPORATION (A)

^^^

In October, 1965, Mr. Paul Elicker, vice president and treasurer of SCM Corporation, was considering possible changes in SCM's dividend policy. He knew that this topic would be discussed at the December meeting of the board of directors, and he wanted to be adequately prepared to make a sound recommendation on this matter to Mr. Mead, president of SCM, and to the board of directors.

Earlier in October, Mr. Elicker had received a comprehensive report on dividend policy for SCM from the Corporate Services Division of Irving Trust Company (see Appendix). This report recommended that SCM resume paying cash dividends in December and eliminate its stock dividend at the same time. After reviewing this recommendation, Mr. Elicker had asked Mr. Anthony H. Meyer of Irving Trust Company for his opinion about the implications of deferring the resumption of cash dividend payments until a later time. Mr. Meyer's reply is contained in Exhibit 5.

SCM's business had been founded in 1903 to manufacture and sell typewriters. In the early 1950's the company, then known as the Smith-Corona Typewriter Company, had two main product lines. Office typewriters were expected to provide a fairly stable earnings base regardless of swings in the business cycle. Portable typewriters were thought to be more subject to consumer whims and economic conditions, and thus were expected to contribute to the company's profits primarily during periods of prosperity. On a cash basis, sales of office typewriters (with relatively short collection periods) were expected to provide a steady net inflow of cash throughout the year. Portables, on the other hand, were subject to a pronounced seasonal sales pattern, which required a seasonal buildup of inventories, and were sold through dealers who were often slow in paying SCM for the typewriters, necessitating a seasonal swing in receivables.

Because of the stability of the office typewriter line, and because many of the 300,000 shares of common stock then outstanding were held by a family group who had special dividend interests, the company had adopted what it considered to be a fairly liberal cash dividend policy in the early 1950's. For example, the dividend payout ratio ranged from 36% to 64% in the 1951–53 period.

During the 1950's, however, sales of manual office typewriters proved to be unstable for SCM, and as IBM electric typewriters began to command an increasing share of the office typewriter market, SCM's manual typewriter line began to generate large losses. Portable typewriter sales grew rapidly during this period and proved to be relatively insensitive to general business conditions. While SCM's share of the market for portables increased from 30% in 1953 to 35% in 1960, this growth of sales plus the seasonal pattern of inventories and receivables for this line created a growing need for funds at a time when losses on office typewriters were also consuming funds. By the late 1950's, these developments had created a severe cash shortage.

Despite the cash squeeze and the necessity for additional debt financing in the late 1950's, cash dividends were continued. Earnings declined to $0.30 per share in fiscal 1959, but SCM maintained its dividend payment of $0.85 per share in the hope that earnings would improve in the following year. In addition, the company planned to force conversion of its outstanding convertible debentures in fiscal 1959 to strengthen its equity base in anticipation of future debt financing, and an adverse market price reaction to a dividend cut could have made it impossible to force conversion of the debentures. In fiscal 1960, however, when SCM reported a loss of $0.24 per share, the directors voted—in a close vote—to eliminate the cash dividend payment entirely. Modest earnings of $301,747 (or $0.16 per share) were reported in fiscal 1961, but special charges and write-offs of $2,398,000 were made directly to Earned Surplus.

SCM's management had begun taking steps in the late 1950's to improve the company's long-range prospects. The acquisition of Kleinschmidt Laboratories (1956) and Marchant Company (1958) added teletype equipment and calculators to the product line; and by 1965 other product lines, such as office supplies, photocopy machines, peripheral data processing equipment, electronic calculators, adding machines, and accounting machines, had been developed or acquired.

This restructuring of SCM's business began to show results in fiscal 1962 as earnings improved to $2,592,000 ($1.35 per share), and a 2% stock dividend was paid. Management's rationale for the 2% stock dividend was that it should enable stockholders to benefit from the improving earnings outlook. Cash dividends were not considered appropriate at that time because of the company's continuing cash squeeze.

Earnings in 1963 and 1964 were somewhat below the 1962 level, but stock dividends of 3% were paid in each of these years. In fiscal 1965 earnings had increased to $3,815,477 ($1.47 per share) and management was very optimistic about the outlook for SCM's photocopy equipment, particularly a new model of the Coronastat electrostatic office copier scheduled for introduction in fiscal 1968. The directors had discussed resuming cash dividend payments during fiscal 1965; but the company's cash needs were still considerable, and additional external financing was planned to raise additional cash. As a result of the optimistic earnings outlook during a period of continuing cash stringency, the directors declared a 5% stock dividend during fiscal 1965.

As Mr. Elicker approached the study of the Irving Trust Company material in October, he had certain additional data available for consideration. SCM's annual report for fiscal 1965 had recently been sent to stockholders; so Mr. Elicker knew that investors were aware of the company's improved situation. (Exhibits 1 and 2 contain financial data about the company.) The cash situation was still tight in view of SCM's projected need for funds, but he felt that the worst part of the cash squeeze was past. (Exhibit 3 shows an historical record of sources and uses of funds; Exhibit 4 is the company's forecast of sources and uses of funds for a four-year period, based upon the assumption that SCM adopts Irving Trust Company's recommendation of a $0.10 cash dividend per quarter.)

Mr. Elicker's own research had suggested that "glamour companies" which paid modest cash dividends might have higher price-earnings ratios than those in the nondividend-paying group, but he was not sure whether the apparent difference in price-earnings ratios was due to dividend policy differences or to other factors. It was possible, but not certain, that a cash dividend might help maintain the current high market price of SCM's stock or push it up even further.

Since external financing was contemplated in the future, Mr. Elicker desired to take legitimate steps to create a better and more solid market value for the common stock. On the other hand, SCM had not paid a cash dividend for five years, the image of the company had changed significantly during that time, and SCM's stock was actively traded. The market price had risen from $25¾ to $51⅝ during September, and the shares had been trading in late October between $44 and $52 per share. Consequently, Mr. Elicker doubted whether SCM's present shareholders really cared very much about cash dividends.

Since Mr. Elicker expected dividend policy to be a main topic for discussion at the December meeting of directors, he planned to review the Irving Trust Company report again and then decide what type of dividend action he would recommend. If he decided that resumption of cash dividends was desirable, he would have to decide on a recommendation about the amount of the cash dividend as well as whether a stock dividend should also be declared.

Exhibit 1

SCM CORPORATION (A)
CONSOLIDATED BALANCE SHEETS AS OF JUNE 30, 1964–65
(In millions)

ASSETS	1964	1965
Current assets:		
Cash	$ 1.2	$ 2.1
Accounts receivable	25.0	28.0
Inventories	41.2	41.5
Total current assets	$67.4	$71.6
Fixed assets, net	22.5	23.9
Other assets	1.8	1.4
Total	$91.7	$96.9

LIABILITIES		
Current liabilities	$18.0	$20.7
Long-term debt	23.3	21.9
Deferred income taxes	0.5	1.4
Stockholders' equity	49.9	52.9
Total	$91.7	$96.9

Notes:

1. Under the provisions of the long-term debt, approximately $2.5 million of retained earnings was available for cash dividends at June 30, 1965.

2. In June, 1965, the company announced that it would redeem for cash any shares of its convertible preferred stock still outstanding on July 8, 1965. As a result of this announcement, over 99% of the outstanding preferred stock was converted into common stock in June and early July.

3. At June 30, 1965, 2,694,178 shares of common stock were issued and outstanding, and an additional 235,445 shares were reserved (and subsequently issued) for conversion of the preferred stock.

Exhibit 2

SCM CORPORATION (A)
EIGHT-YEAR STATISTICAL SUMMARY
FISCAL YEARS ENDED JUNE 30, 1958–65

	1958	*1959*	*1960*	*1961*	*1962*	*1963*	*1964*	*1965*
Net sales (in thousands)	$ 87,146	$ 90,411	$ 93,359	$ 96,476	$103,165	$117,343	$ 124,704	$ 149,657
Net income (loss) (in thousands)	2,244	482	(455)	302	2,592	1,656	2,437	3,815
Earnings per common share*	$ 1.22	$ 0.23	$ (0.21)	$ 0.14	$ 1.21	$ 0.57	$ 0.83	$ 1.47
Dividends paid on common stock:								
Cash dividends per share	$ 0.77	$ 0.75	—	—	—	—	—	—
Stock dividends	—	—	—	—	2%	3%	3%	5%
Market price of common stock (calendar years)	$13¼–20¼	$11–19½	$9⅞–16¼	$10¾–26⅞	$8⅞–24⅞	$9⅛–15	$12½–19⅛	$15⅞–52½†
Price-earnings ratio‡								
SCM Corporation	14.5	66.3	—	134.4	13.9	21.2	19.0	23.3
Dow-Jones Industrials	18.2	18.3	19.4	21.5	17.3	17.2	17.8	16.8

* 1965 on average shares outstanding after stock dividend; prior years adjusted for subsequent stock dividends.
† Range for year to October 25, 1965.
‡ Based on midpoint of price range.

Exhibit 3

SCM CORPORATION (A)
SOURCE AND USE OF FUNDS
FISCAL YEARS ENDED JUNE 30, 1958–65
(In millions)

	1958	1959	1960	1961	1962	1963	1964	1965
Beginning cash balance	$ 2.4	$ 4.2	$ 4.0	$ 3.2	$ 3.2	$ 2.3	$ 3.9	$ 1.0
Add:								
Income after taxes	2.2	0.5	(0.5)	0.3	2.6	1.7	2.4	3.8
Depreciation	1.2	1.6	2.0	2.0	2.3	2.7	2.4	2.5
Other increases (decreases) in current liabilities	1.0	(2.0)	(0.5)	1.5	1.7	(0.1)	1.9	1.9
Borrowings from (repayments to) banks	(3.1)	(6.7)	7.4	2.4	0.9	(10.7)	0.5	1.6
Debentures	4.2	7.4						
Other long-term debt	9.7	6.0						
Increases (decreases) in stockholders' equity	0.2	4.9†	(1.7)‡	(2.0)§	(0.6)¶	11.4**	0.1	0.1
Total available	$17.8	$15.9	$10.7	$ 7.4	$10.1	$ 7.3	$11.2	$10.9
Less:								
Increase (decrease) in accounts receivable	$ 5.0	$(4.0)	$ 3.0	$ 0.6	$ 1.1	$ 1.0	$ 1.1	$ 3.0
Increase (decrease) in inventories	1.0	4.8	(0.2)	2.8	2.2	(0.9)	4.8	0.3
Capital expenditures*	6.2	3.7	3.0	2.5	2.2	1.4	2.8	3.8
Long-term debt repayments		4.9†	1.5	1.1	2.6	1.4	1.5	1.4
Other increases (decreases) in assets		1.0	0.2	(2.8)‖	(0.3)	0.1	(0.7)	(0.4)
Cash dividends paid	1.4	1.5				0.4††	0.7††	0.7††
Total cash employed	$13.6	$11.9	$ 7.5	$ 4.2	$ 7.8	$ 3.4	$10.2	$ 8.8
Ending cash balance	$ 4.2	$ 4.0	$ 3.2	$ 3.2	$ 2.3	$ 3.9	$ 1.0	$ 2.1
Interest expense—long-term debt*	$ 1.2	$ 1.5	$ 2.0	$ 2.2	$ 2.0	$ 1.7	$ 1.4	$ 1.6

* Casewriter's estimate, based upon analysis of published financial statements.
† Increase in equity in 1959 represents conversion of outstanding 6% convertible subordinated debentures into 229,128 shares of common stock. An equivalent reduction in long-term debt is included in "debt repayments" for 1959.
‡ Net special charges to retained earnings amounted to $1,737,349 in 1960, and represented provision for nonrecurring costs and write-downs of assets (less estimated reduction in U.S. income taxes).
§ Reduction in equity in 1961 was due to special charges to retained earnings ($2,144,850), less proceeds from issuance of common stock for acquisitions and stock options.
‖ Includes write-offs and sales of assets.
¶ Due primarily to change in accounting method in one corporate division.
** Represents net proceeds from sale of $12,002,200 (par value) 5½% convertible preferred stock, after issuance and distribution expenses of $561,050.
†† Dividends paid on 5½% convertible preferred stock.

Exhibit 4

SCM CORPORATION (A)

SOURCE AND USE OF FUNDS FORECAST

FISCAL YEARS ENDED JUNE 30, 1966–69

(In millions)

	1966	*1967*	*1968*	*1969*	*Total*
Beginning cash balance..............	$ 2.1	$ 4.8	$ 4.7	$ 5.0	$ 2.1
Add:					
Income after taxes *..............	8.6	10.9	11.9	18.7	50.1
Depreciation....................	2.1	5.6	8.1	10.4	26.2
Borrowings—banks and payables...	15.5	4.3	(20.5)	5.5	4.8
Debentures.....................	—	—	33.0	—	33.0
Other long-term debt.............	—	10.0	—	—	10.0
Increase in equity†...............	1.9	5.5	—	—	7.4
Total available..............	$30.2	$41.1	$ 37.2	$39.6	$133.6
Less:					
Increase in accounts receivable......	$ 6.0	$ 5.3	$ 5.7	$ 7.5	$ 24.5
Increase in inventories.............	6.1	7.5	8.0	10.5	32.1
Increase in lease inventories........	1.3	6.7	7.0	9.2	24.9
Capital expenditures..............	5.0	8.5	6.7	3.9	24.1
Debt repayments†................	3.0	6.9	1.9	1.9	13.7
Other increases in assets...........	3.4	0.2	0.8	0.2	4.6
Cash dividend‡..................	0.6	1.3	1.4	1.4	4.7
Total cash employed..........	$25.4	$36.4	$ 32.2	$34.6	$128.6
Ending cash balance................	$ 4.8	$ 4.7	$ 5.0	$ 5.0	$ 5.0
Interest on long-term debt at 7%§.....	$ 1.4	$ 1.6	$ 3.1	$ 4.2	$ 10.3

* The reader may assume an income tax rate of 50% in his study of this exhibit.
† Increases in equity in 1966 and 1967 represent anticipated conversion of $7,441,900 of outstanding 5¼% convertible subordinated debentures for 377,378 shares of common stock. An equivalent reduction in long-term debt is included in "debt repayments" for 1966 and 1967.
‡ Assuming dividends of $0.10 per quarter (two quarters in fiscal 1966) on outstanding shares (including shares issued for conversion of convertible preferred stock in fiscal 1966 and shares expected to be issued for conversion of the 5¼% convertible subordinated debentures in fiscal 1966 and 1967).
§ Casewriter's estimate.

Exhibit 5

SCM CORPORATION (A)

IRVING TRUST COMPANY

ONE WALL STREET

NEW YORK, N.Y.   10015

Anthony H. Meyer   Telephone: LL3–3283
    Assistant Vice President

October 20, 1965

Mr. Paul Elicker
Vice President and Treasurer
SCM Corporation
410 Park Avenue
New York, New York

Dear Paul:

You asked me to comment on our dividend policy recommendations for SCM with re-spect to what the results might be if you decide to defer the resumption of cash dividends for the time being.

Short range, we would not expect any very significant reaction. As we stated in our report, SCM's shareholders at this point are not likely to be dividend oriented. Even if they were, no reasonable dividend would provide a yield of any consequence.

However, you'll recall that Mr. Mead's remarks at the New York Society of Security Analysts last summer implied that the time to resume dividends was not too far distant. The market may be looking for a dividend declaration, not for yield but as an ex-pression of management's confidence in the future, and may expect it to come when the

Exhibit 5—Continued

stock dividend is usually declared. To avoid any possible adverse reaction, SCM should make it clear if dividends are deferred that this decision is in no way a reflection of management's thinking about earnings prospects.

We would also have to recommend that you pay a stock dividend again this year if you don't reinstitute a cash payout. Again we are considering short-range market effect. As you know we don't believe there are any permanent market effects from stock dividends, but you could get an unfavorable temporary reaction by taking no dividend action whatever in December.

Long range, we are back in never-never land because of the difficulty of relating payout policy to price-earnings ratio. We do believe that the ultimate effect of a regular cash dividend policy is to enhance a stock's investment quality, thereby broadening its owner-ship base and improving both its price-earnings ratio and its price stability. If SCM defers the resumption of cash dividends, it is doing no more than deferring the time when it begins to acquire the improved investment quality a regular dividend record would give it.

If current cash needs merit a higher priority than enhancing your image a bit sooner, we would see no serious objection to delaying the dividend. At the same time, we would hate to see a "cash needs" argument marshaled against dividends year after year. There is a positive value to a cash dividend record, even if the dividend is modest. On the other side of the coin, the difference between retaining 75% of earnings and retaining them all is relatively minor in terms of helping to meet SCM's capital needs.

You sometimes hear people say that dividends can't matter for growth companies because there are nondividend-paying growth companies whose stocks sell at very fancy earnings multiples. What this argument overlooks is that there is no way of knowing where these stocks would sell if they did pay a dividend. Statistics can't tell us much, but just to take a couple of examples:

	Year	% Increase in Earnings per Share over Prior Year	Average Price-Earnings Ratio	Payout Ratio
Litton Industries	1962	56	34X	0
	1963	40	31X	0
	1964	25	25X	0
IBM	1962	19	40X	27%
	1963	19	34X	31
	1964	18	36X	39

There are a great many differences between Litton and IBM, and dividends aren't likely to be the most important one—but the devil can quote scripture to his purposes, and some-one could argue from these figures that Litton should adopt a dividend policy like IBM's.

I hope some of these thoughts will be useful to you. Let me know if we can do anything more.

With best regards,

Sincerely,

(*Signed*) Tony

APPENDIX

SCM CORPORATION (A)
DIVIDEND POLICY FOR SCM CORPORATION [1]

I. Summary

In this report we set forth what we consider the underlying principles on which to base an effective dividend policy and then apply these criteria to

---

[1] A report prepared by Corporate Services Division, Irving Trust Co., Oct., 1965.

SCM. Briefly stated, we believe an effective dividend policy involves:

1. The establishment of a consistent dividend record on which investors can reasonably base their future dividend expectations; and
2. The selection of an appropriate dividend payout ratio based on earnings expectations, earnings volatility, the nature of investment interest in the company's stock, and in some cases credit considerations.

Applied to SCM, all criteria point to the resumption of cash dividends with a low payout target. Our recommendation is that the company resume cash dividends at an initial $0.40 annual rate and eliminate its stock dividend at the same time.

II. INTRODUCTORY COMMENTS

The ultimate goal of corporate financial policy is to maximize the stockholder's return on investment in the long run. Return on investment usually takes only two forms—dividends and capital appreciation. Dividend policy is an important aspect of overall financial policy because it influences, directly and significantly, both forms of return.

A simple example can be used to highlight the main elements in the dividend policy problem. Assume that two companies, A and B, both earn a steady 12% on equity. Equity in each case consists of one share of stock with a book value of $100. Company A elects to pay out 25% of its earnings in dividends, and Company B pays 75%. The results would be as follows:

Company A

Year	Equity	Earnings at 12%	Dividends Paid (25%)	Earnings Retained (75%)
1	$100.00	$12.00	$3.00	$ 9.00
2	109.00	13.08	3.27	9.81
3	118.81	14.26	3.56	10.70
4	129.51	15.54	3.89	11.65
5	141.16	16.94	4.24	12.70

Company B

Year	Equity	Earnings at 12%	Dividends Paid (75%)	Earnings Retained (25%)
1	$100.00	$12.00	$ 9.00	$3.00
2	103.00	12.36	9.27	3.09
3	106.09	12.73	9.55	3.18
4	109.27	13.11	9.83	3.28
5	112.55	13.51	10.13	3.38

Effect on dividend return

The differing dividend payout policies of A and B clearly result in radically differing dividend returns to their owners. B's dividend is initially three times as great as A's. As time goes on, however, A's dividend will overtake and pass B's, since A's dividend, in keeping with its earnings, is growing at 9% annually, whereas B's is growing at only 3%. The effect of any payout policy on future dividend returns is easily measurable to the extent that future earnings can be predicted.

Effect on appreciation return

The impact of dividend policy on future capital gains is more nebulous and more complex. On the one hand a cash dividend is a certain, current return compared with the uncertain, future return offered by potential capital gains. Therefore, investors like cash dividends, and a stock which pays a higher dividend, all other things being equal, will command a higher price.

However, all other things are not equal. The effect of dividend payout policy on earnings growth shows up very clearly in the Company A–Company B illustration. Simply stated, the higher the payout the slower the growth. More precisely, the rate of internal growth in earnings per share can be expressed as the percentage return on equity times the percentage of earnings retained. 12% return × 25% retained = 3% growth. 12% return × 75% retained = 9% growth. Since investors like earnings growth, they will pay a higher price for a stock if its earnings are growing more rapidly.

Moreover, a fast earnings growth obviously implies higher earnings per share in the future than slow earnings growth, starting from the same earnings base. Companies A and B each earned the same amount in the first year. In the fifth year A's earnings were 25% greater than B's. And earnings are a major determinant in stock market prices.

To summarize, payout policy affects appreciation return in three ways. Payout exerts pressure on the price-earnings ratio (the rate at which earnings are capitalized) in one direction because of investor interest in dividends. It exerts pressure in an opposite direction because of investor interest in earnings growth. Finally, it affects the future earnings to which the capitalization rate will be applied.

Combined effect on overall return

Clearly a low payout policy, because it accelerates earnings growth, will produce a higher stock price eventually. However, this does not necessarily argue for a low payout in all cases. A higher eventual capital gain return resulting from a low payout may be more than offset by a lower dividend return in the meanwhile.

Even if management can make a reasonably close estimate of future earning power, it is left with the problem of what capital gain returns would result from various payout policies. If a correlation between price-earnings ratio and payout ratio could be found, the capital gain question could be answered and the effect of dividend policy on overall return to investors could be determined with some fairly simple mathematics.

However, the market prices of industrial common stocks are a reflection of so many factors that the long-range effect of payout on price-earnings ratio is usually impossible to isolate. It is equally difficult to find the precise payout ratio which is sure to produce the highest overall return to investors. Nevertheless, careful evaluation of a number of relevant factors can direct a company toward a payout range appropriate to its particular circumstances.

III.   DIVIDEND PATTERN

Before selecting a target payout ratio it is necessary to consider what constitutes an effective dividend pattern, since the company's goal with respect to pattern will influence its decision on payout.

The importance of dividend pattern cannot be overstressed. The company's dividend record influences the future dividend expectations of investors, and these expectations in turn affect the market price of the company's stock. Investors learn about a company's dividend policy primarily by looking at its dividend history. A regular pattern in the past implies a regular pattern in the future. A dividend cut in the past makes future payments less certain. And the more certain investors feel about future dividends, the more they will pay for them.

With this in mind, what is the most effective dividend pattern a company can hope to achieve?

A regular dividend increasing regularly would be highly effective, but a record like this can be established only by companies which enjoy extremely stable and predictable earnings growth. Many public utilities are in this category, but most industrial companies are not.

A regular dividend increasing irregularly as earnings permit is probably the best pattern which can be accomplished by typical industrial companies, subject as they are to fairly wide earnings fluctuations.

A regular dividend is somewhat less desirable, since it implies flat earnings. Unless a company suffers from a steadily declining return on equity, earnings retention should result in earnings and dividend growth.

Variable dividends offer an investor little on which to base his future dividend expectations, so they are unlikely to exert much influence on the market price of the stock.

The same is true of *irregular extra dividends.* As for *regular extras,* most analysts feel that companies which can pay them would do more for their stock by incorporating the extra amount into the regular dividend rate. Extra dividends may in some cases be a perfectly sound way of disposing of excess cash, but they probably have no appreciable effect on stock prices.

Stock dividends were the subject of an exhaustive and rigorous statistical analysis by C. Austin Barker, a partner at Hornblower & Weeks, Hemphill Noyes & Co. He reported on his work in a *Harvard Business Review* article, "Evaluation of Stock Dividends," which appeared in the July–August, 1958, issue. Barker's principal finding was that stock dividends have no lasting effect on stock prices. This being the case, and bearing in mind that stock dividends are costly[2] and tend to confuse a company's record, it is hard to

---

[2] Note also that stock dividend issuing costs are not deductible for tax purposes.

see much merit in a policy of paying stock dividends either to supplement or to replace cash dividends.

Credibility of pattern

No dividend record, however regular, will have a favorable long-run market effect if the dividend pattern is clearly unsustainable. To illustrate:

Year	Company A Earnings per Share	Dividend	Payout Ratio	Company B Earnings per Share	Dividend	Payout Ratio
1	$1.15	$0.60	52%	$1.05	$0.60	57%
2	1.35	0.60	44	0.92	0.60	65
3	1.60	0.80	50	1.10	0.80	73
4	1.73	0.80	46	0.93	0.80	86
5	2.05	1.00	49	1.00	1.00	100

Company A's dividend policy is right in line with its earnings growth. Investors will feel fairly certain about a continuation of orderly dividend increases if they believe the company has good prospects for continued earnings growth. For Company B, the same dividend record makes no sense in terms of its earnings record. If no earnings improvement is in sight, investors will expect no dividend increases in spite of the past pattern—in fact they will recognize that the future of the $1.00 dividend is in jeopardy. The future of A's dividend is therefore very much more valuable than the future of B's, even though the patterns are identical.

Payout ratio and pattern

Since corporate earnings tend to fluctuate from year to year around the line of their long-term trend, the maintenance of a precise payout ratio every year would result in a variable cash dividend. It is usually necessary, and entirely in order, to take liberties with the payout target in any given year in order to maintain an effective dividend pattern.

IV. PAYOUT RATIO

The question of payout for most industrial companies can be approached by thinking in terms of three broad payout categories:

	Payout Percentage
Small payout	25
Average payout	50
Full payout	75

The factors which would govern the choice of one of these payout areas are discussed below.

Payout and return on equity

The rate of return a company earns on its equity investment is an extremely important element in the payout decision. A few mathematical relationships are worth reviewing to bring out the points involved:

1. *Return to investors through yield and growth.* If a stock is bought and later sold at the same price-earnings ratio and the dividend payout ratio remains constant, the total return to investors is the sum of the dividend yield when the stock is bought and the annual rate of growth in earnings per share. For example, suppose a stock's cash dividend yield on its market price is 3%, and earnings per share are growing at 7% annually. With a constant price-earnings ratio, the price of the stock will appreciate at 7% per year in keeping with earnings, thereby giving the investor a 7% appreciation return when he sells it. Meanwhile he will have been receiving another 3% return from dividends, or a total of 10%.

2. *Price-earnings ratio, payout, and yield on market value.* Dividend yield on market value is entirely unaffected by return on equity. It is a function of only two things—price-earnings ratio and payout ratio.

3. *Earnings retention, rate of return, and rate of growth.* Earnings growth is directly affected by return on equity. As we noted in the Introductory Comments, the rate of growth in earnings per share is the percentage return on equity times the percentage of earnings retained.

With these relationships in mind we can examine how varying rates of return on equity and varying payout ratios will tend to affect overall return to stockholders.

Table 1 illustrates the returns to investors which would result from various payout ratios at various rates of return on equity, assuming the investor buys and sells at the same price-earnings ratio. Appreciation return on this basis is always percentage earned on equity times percentage of earnings retained. Since yield return is affected by price-earnings ratio, we show a range of possible price-earnings ratios in the table, and the range of yields and overall returns these price-earnings ratios would produce.

Although it isn't possible to pinpoint price-earnings ratios, it is likely that Company A, whose earning power is low, would tend to sell at closer to 10 times earnings than 25. Company C, with its substantially greater earnings potential, would tend to sell at closer to 25 times earnings than 10. This being

Table 1

PAYOUT AND RETURNS TO INVESTORS

				Range of Percentage Returns to Investors				
				From Yield, Assuming Price-Earnings			Overall	
	% Return	Payout	From	Ratios of			At 10×	At 25×
Company	on Equity	%	Appreciation	10×	and	25×	Earnings	Earnings
A	5	25	3.75	2.50		1.00	6.25	4.75
		50	2.50	5.00		2.00	7.50	4.50
		75	1.25	7.50		3.00	8.75	4.25
B	10	25	7.50	2.50		1.00	10.00	8.50
		50	5.00	5.00		2.00	10.00	7.00
		75	2.50	7.50		3.00	10.00	5.50
C	15	25	11.25	2.50		1.00	13.75	12.25
		50	7.50	5.00		2.00	12.50	9.50
		75	3.75	7.50		3.00	11.25	6.75

the case, high payout adds up to higher overall return for Company A, while low payout produces higher overall return for Company C. At 10 times earnings, A gains 5% in yield and loses only 2½% in appreciation if its payout is 75% rather than 25%.[3] At 25 times earnings, C gains 7½% in appreciation and loses only 2% in yield if its payout is 25% rather than 75%.

This seems to suggest that companies like A should pay out all their earnings in dividends, and companies like C should pay none. However, several factors are present which would make this unwise.

For low-earning, low price-earnings ratio companies like A, the higher the payout, the better, *provided* an effective pattern of well-protected dividends can be maintained. A payout of 75% pushes very hard at the upper limit of what would be considered well protected. Investors would have serious doubts about the company's ability to maintain a dividend rate which represented a higher payout. Moreover, investors might well be proved right. Several years of poorer earnings might force the company to cut its dividend, which would hurt its dividend record and the price of its stock.

For high-earning, high price-earnings ratio companies like C, the question of why pay dividends at all is a hard one to answer, but the major factor is the degree of uncertainty investors feel about appreciation return. Our illustrations have assumed steady earnings growth and a constant price-earnings ratio. However, investors are properly uncertain about both these assumptions. Earnings growth, particularly when it reflects a high return which will tend to attract competition, may decelerate. The future price-earnings ratio may decline, either because earnings fall short of expectations or because of a generally poorer stock market period. Moreover, investors recognize that stocks which sell at a high multiple of earnings are particularly vulnerable to market fluctuation. Cash dividends, on the other hand, are a more certain return to investors. Even a small one is to some extent an anchor to windward.

A final consideration is that some investors, particularly institutions and fiduciaries, restrict their common stock investments to dividend-paying securities.[4] Omitting cash dividends would deprive a company of this pool of potential investment interest in its stock.

Payout and stability of earnings

Because of the importance of dividend pattern, a company must choose a dividend rate which it can sustain. If earnings are volatile, a low target pay-

---

[3] Actually, A would be unlikely to sell as low as 10 times earnings with a 75% payout, since the resulting 7½% yield is extremely high. Analysts tend to think of a well-protected dividend yield of 4½ to 5% as quite attractive, and the market price of a stock with a higher yield would tend to rise until the yield declined to this level. With a 75% payout A's stock would probably sell at 15 times earnings so as to yield 5%. This tendency of dividends to put a floor on a stock's market price is a very significant consideration for companies which earn a low return on equity.

[4] For example, a stock which does not have a 10-year uninterrupted cash dividend record does not qualify as a legal investment for insurance companies under New York State insurance law.

out ratio is indicated, since this would produce a dividend rate which could be sustained even during a period of sharply reduced earnings. If earnings are stable, on the other hand, a high target payout ratio can be set if other factors make high payout desirable. Several factors influence earnings stability. The major ones are these:

Level of earnings. In our economy, a company which earns an abnormally high return tends to attract competition which will force earnings down to an average level sometime in the future. Conversely, when a company is earning a low return, chances are good that this condition will remain stable or improve as time goes on. New competition is unlikely to rush into an essentially unpromising area, and companies with poor earnings are likely to be very active in seeking ways to improve profits.

Nature of the business. By their nature some companies are far more stable than others. A company supplying parts to one auto manufacturer runs a higher risk of earnings fluctuation than a chain of department stores. Electronics companies are less predictable than electric utilities.

Debt leverage. The stability of a company's earnings is also affected by the percentage of debt in its capital structure. Debt leverage magnifies fluctuations in operating earnings into larger fluctuations in common stock earnings. For this reason, a decision on capital structure should normally be made before a decision is reached on dividend policy.

Payout and the nature of investment interest

Stockholders differ on the returns they seek on their investments. They may be seeking cash dividends, or growth in market price, or both. Each company must decide, in the light of the nature of its business, what sort of investment interest it is likely to attract. At one end of the spectrum is the investor in a new and speculative venture, hoping for market gain. He is not particularly interested in receiving dividends. He wants earnings to be plowed back into the business and feels that a large dividend would limit the company's internal growth rate. At the other end of the spectrum is the investor in a stable, low-growth company who plans on income from cash dividends.

The speculative investor is unlikely to pay a premium price for stock in consideration of its dividend, but the income-seeking investor probably will.

Summary—selection of a payout ratio

In selecting a payout ratio, we would suggest that potential return on retained earnings be used as a starting point. On this basis, a 25% payout would constitute a sound preliminary target for companies which visualize a future return of 15% or better on new investment. The payout target should move up toward the 50% area if future return expectations range down toward 10%. A payout of up to 75% would produce the best overall results if future earnings expectations are substantially lower than 10%.

The target area selected on the basis of potential earnings on equity should then be reviewed and perhaps modified in the light of (1) the earnings stability factor and (2) the probable nature of investment interest in the company's stock.

As a matter of interest, the average payout ratio of Moody's 125 Industrials during the 1960–64 period declined from 63% to 53%, averaging 59%. Return on equity during this period climbed from 11% to 14% and averaged 12%.

Special situations—nominal payout or none

Companies which are financially strong can consider their capital needs aside from their dividend policy, since strong companies can raise capital externally on a reasonable basis. Weaker companies are forced to subordinate dividend policy to their capital needs to the extent that avenues for raising capital externally on a satisfactory basis are closed to them.

Typically, new companies have a very thin equity base; their growth potential is high; and raising capital externally is a considerable problem for them. The success of these companies may well depend on the reinvestment of every dollar of earnings they can generate, and their stockholders are almost certain to have no interest whatever in dividends. Cash dividends would make no sense for these companies.

A policy of paying nominal cash dividends is one into which a young company might evolve temporarily. The company would presumably still need virtually all of its earnings for reinvestment in the business. However, a nominal dividend payout would establish a basis for eventual purchases of the company's stock by institutional investors who prefer or require a dividend record. Nominal payout would also accord recognition to the belief of many investors that a cash dividend is an indication of some measure of investment quality.

Payout and changing the dividend

Since investors know that most seasoned companies do in fact have a target payout ratio, a change in the dividend rate carries with it strong implications about management's future earnings expectations. In raising the rate, for example, management is saying that earnings will rise, or have risen already to a sustainable new plateau high enough to justify the increase. Holding the rate if earnings go off implies management's faith that previous earnings levels will be restored. Cutting the dividend implies a permanent downtrend. The market for the company's stock will react accordingly. Since one of the objectives of financial management is to minimize fluctuations in the price of a stock, it is important to change the dividend rate only when future expectations warrant such a change. Increasing the dividend capriciously can give the stock a short-term lift, but in the long run will tend to undermine investor confidence.

Payout and tax considerations

The personal income tax treatment of dividend income as distinguished from capital gains is well known to us all. Stated briefly, dividend income is taxed at full income tax rates, which range up to a current maximum of 70%, while capital gains are taxed at either half the income tax rate or 25%, whichever is less. Consequently, the argument is sometimes advanced that dividend payout should be minimized so as to permit investors to receive most of their return on a capital gains basis.

For companies with great earning capacity, selling at high price-earnings ratios, the personal income tax aspect reinforces other powerful arguments for a low payout. However, for companies with poor earnings the tax factor does not, on careful examination, justify disregarding other arguments for high payout. Consider what might happen to investors in Company A in Table 1 if it changed its payout from 75% to 25%. It will be recalled that Company A earned 5% on equity, and we suggested that a 75% payout might cause it to sell at 15 times earnings so as to yield 5%. Assume a personal income tax rate of 40%, which would mean a captial gains rate of 20%.

		Percentage Gross Return			Percentage Return to Investors after Payment of Personal Income Taxes		
Payout %	Price-Earnings Ratio	Yield	Appreciation	Total	Yield	Appreciation	Total
75	15✕	5.0	1.25	6.25	3.0	1.0	4.0
25	15✕	1.67	3.75	5.42	1.0	3.0	4.0

In spite of tax savings, net return has not improved in amount. Moreover, it has declined in quality, since the return now has a larger component of appreciation, which is relatively uncertain, and a smaller component of dividends, which are relatively certain. Finally, a stock yielding 1⅔% and expected to grow in earnings at 3¾% is unlikely to sell at 15 times earnings. It might well drop to 10 times or below. At that level yield will be somewhat improved, but the stockholder will have sustained a capital loss of a third or more of his investment.

A final aspect of the personal income tax question is the fact that not all investors are taxed at the same rate. Speculative investors are likely to be in a higher bracket than income-seeking investors, and some income-seeking investors—charitable trusts, pension funds, etc.—are entirely tax-free. Differences in the extent to which investors are taxed will thus tend to coincide with other factors favoring high payout with low earnings and low payout with high earnings.

V. DIVIDEND POLICY FOR SCM

A review of SCM's present situation convinces us that a low payout target is the company's best dividend policy for the time being. Each factor in this decision is discussed below.

Return on common equity

SCM's historical return on common equity has been subnormal in recent years, but has shown marked improvement which the company expects to continue. The following returns for 1963–65 and an estimated return for 1966 are based on the company's equity at the beginning of each year and its net income for that year. Equity includes preferred equity in each year and net income has not been reduced by the preferred dividend. This gives us a good comparative performance measure.

Fiscal Year	Return on Equity
1963	4.6%
1964	5.1%
1965	7.6%
1966	9.0%–10.0% (est.)

Since these are overall returns which are partially a reflection of losses in the Data Processing Systems Division and unsatisfactory results in some other areas, opportunities clearly exist in the more profitable sectors of SCM's business to invest retained earnings at potential returns substantially greater than the 10% which is average for American industry. Moreover, SCM is currently selling at a high price-earnings ratio. Earnings retained might add considerably to future appreciation return; earnings paid out wouldn't constitute a very significant yield return. It is difficult to pin down SCM's price-earnings ratio because of the stock's recent market behavior; but our analysis suggests that a 20× price-earnings ratio is, on the average, a reasonable expectation for SCM. A price-earnings ratio of 20× would result in the following yields:[5]

Payout Ratio	Yield
25%	1.25%
50	2.50
75	3.75

On the basis of our return-on-equity criterion, a low payout appears to be indicated.

Earnings stability

SCM's management is in a better position than we are to judge how stable its business is, but we would be inclined to classify it as relatively unstable. Factors we would cite are strong competition in those sectors of its business which are actually or potentially highly profitable, a market demand subject to cyclical fluctuations, heavy dependence on continuously productive R & D, and the risks associated with capital commitments abroad and reliance on foreign sales.

---

[5] Yield on current market of about $44⅛ (October 5, 1965, closing price) would of course be somewhat lower.

Debt leverage is also present to a significant extent, and increases the potential for variance in earnings available for common. SCM's 1966 budgeted figures indicate interest coverages will be just under seven times pretax and just under four times after-tax—rather low, although they represent a substantial improvement over recent years' results.

All told, the stability factor also suggests a low payout policy.

Nature of investment interest in SCM

SCM's stock has been extremely volatile this year, ranging from $16¼ to $51⅝ so far. Most of the move occurred during the month of September, when the stock rose from $25¾ to $51⅝ and then backed off to $42. There is little doubt that recent interest in SCM is concentrated on the company's Coronastat line, principally the Model 55, and the potential for future earnings growth arising from this source. Under the circumstances, we believe SCM investors are almost entirely seekers of capital gains, and we would not anticipate that any cash dividend the company could reasonably pay would have an appreciable effect on the price of SCM stock. Consequently, we don't think the company should penalize its rate of internal earnings growth at this point by paying out a substantial part of its earnings in dividends.

Financial strength

We suggested above that financially strong companies can consider dividend policy apart from capital needs because they are able to raise capital externally on a reasonable basis. However, SCM's budgeted capital requirements, at least for the coming year, are very substantial indeed. Its 1966 budget indicates capitalization will be as follows:

	Millions of Dollars	Percent
Current bank loans*	14	15
Senior long-term debt	14	15
Conv. subordinated debt	7	8
Common equity	58	62
Total	93	100

* Included because they appear to represent permanently needed capital.

This compares with debt of about 20% of total capital for typical major industrial companies, whose earnings records are generally better than SCM's. We note also that the company's convertible debentures are rated double B by two rating agencies, and single B by the third, indicating that there is not a great deal of extra long-term borrowing capacity. We do not know if management is considering an equity financing. However, an offering of normal proportions would still leave SCM somewhat short on equity in terms of its growth expectations. Consequently, we believe that credit considerations suggest the minimization of cash dividends.

Statistical correlations

As we stated earlier, there are so many elements present in the market's appraisal of an industrial common stock that the effects of dividend policy are usually impossible to isolate. However, we did examine the office equipment industry, as well as a group of other companies which have some of the characteristics of SCM, to see if any significant correlations could be found between price-earnings and payout ratios. As we anticipated, the results did not show any clear relationship. Consequently, we are basing our dividend policy recommendations for SCM strictly on the general principles reviewed in this report.[6]

Recommendations

1. We believe that the establishment of a regular cash dividend would add to SCM's investment quality and would begin to lay the groundwork for eventual ownership of SCM stock by institutional investors with a dividend requirement or a dividend preference. We recommend that cash dividends be instituted in December coinciding with the time when the stock dividend is usually declared.
2. We recommend a $0.10 dividend—a $0.40 annual rate—as a starter. Our reasons for suggesting this low payout are: (1) our assumption that reinvestment of retained earnings offers a high potential return; (2) the fact that current interest in the stock is not dividend-oriented; and (3) SCM's need for capital.
3. We do not believe that stock dividends result in any real benefits to stockholders and recommend that SCM's stock dividend policy be dropped.

Comparable situations

[This section of the Report states that the record of listed stocks was studied to try to find situations comparable to SCM. Three companies were located that had eliminated cash dividends, switched to stock, and then switched back. A study of the data for these companies, the Irving Trust Report states, fails to show any significant change in market price as an immediate result of replacing stock dividends with cash. The Irving Trust Report states, however, that the experience of these companies "says nothing about the possible long-range benefits of such a transition."]

Dividend policy—long range

We believe that a long-range dividend policy for SCM can be designed on the basis of the principles reviewed in this report. There are several important factors we are not able to evaluate at the present time—the company's potential earning power and its capital structure goal—and we would be glad to review these points with SCM's management if this would be of interest. At the same time, we are satisfied that a low payout target is in order for the time being.

---

[6] Note: The full Irving Trust Report contained about 10 pages of supporting data and charts. This portion of the report is omitted from the case since the results, as anticipated, were inconclusive.

CONSOLIDATED EDISON COMPANY (Abridged)

Charles F. Luce, chairman of the board of Consolidated Edison Company (Con Ed), faced a difficult decision on April 22, 1974. The board of trustees was scheduled to meet on the next day to decide whether Con Ed should pay a cash dividend in the second quarter and if so, how much the dividend should be. The company had paid a dividend every year since 1885, and many of its stockholders counted on this regular source of income. However, Con Ed desperately needed to conserve funds as sale of equity at the currently depressed stock price was painful.

Background

When Charles F. Luce became chief executive of Con Ed in 1967, the giant utility was already a favorite target for criticism from customers, public officials, the press, and even some business consultants. After citing the company's difficulties with customers, *Fortune* magazine labeled it "the company you love to hate." *The Wall Street Journal* noted that Con Ed "seems to have a unique capacity for alienating its 4.2 million customers, including the biggest customer of all, the city."

The article in *The Wall Street Journal* presented a list of complaints that had become standard for Con Ed critics: "Con Ed charges the highest electric rates of any big-city utility, contributes a major share of New York's air pollution, noisily chops 40,000 holes in the streets each year, inefficiently operates an aging system that produces nearly 1,900 neighborhood power failures annually —and is rude in the bargain."

Management conceded that its rates were high and that service needed improvement but pointed out in defense that the problems of doing business in New York City were without parallel. Con Ed's bill of $193 million for state and local taxes in 1967 was several times that of other large utilities, and the city requirement that much of its transmission lines be placed underground added considerably to the costs of construction and maintenance.

Continuing difficulties

Mr. Luce attempted a variety of reforms to rejuvenate Con Ed. He began a huge construction program to replace more than 2 million kilowatts of obsolete

344

capacity and to add 2.8 million kilowatts of new generating capacity by 1972. (Total system generating capacity was 7.5 million kilowatts in 1967.) He tried diligently to introduce modern business techniques throughout an organization deemed "hidebound" by *Fortune* in 1966. He instituted a formal budgeting system, put procurement on a competitive basis, and dismissed personnel who had received favors from contractors doing business with Con Ed. He was instrumental in the installation of a modern computer-based billing and customer service system to expedite the handling of customer complaints.

Progress was slow and results were not always apparent. Between 1968 and 1973, many of the problems which Mr. Luce had first encountered seemed to worsen. Brownouts increased during the summer months through 1970, and there were three network failures—two in 1972 and one in 1973. Breakdowns of equipment already on line were the direct cause of these difficulties, but the more basic cause was the inability of Con Ed to meet power-plant construction deadlines.

However, by September 1973, Con Ed appeared to be coming out of its difficulties: the generating and transmission systems had performed well during the hottest summer in 15 years; 3 million kilowatts of new generating capacity was near completion; the Public Service Commission[1] had recently granted a 13.8% permanent rate increase; earnings were on the rise; and the new customer service system was showing impressive results. Then, without warning, the energy crisis struck.

The energy crisis

The Arab oil embargo and energy crisis placed Con Ed in an extremely tight, almost helpless situation. The company had been forced by the city council in 1971 to burn only low-sulphur oil—oil that was available principally from OPEC-member countries. At best, Con Ed seemed to be confronted with sharply higher fuel prices; oil priced at $172 million in 1972 was $293 million in 1973, and on the basis of prices quoted in early 1974, Con Ed's bill for that year was estimated at $800 million. At worst, the company ran the risk of absolute shortages of fuel.

Con Ed responded to the crisis by appealing for *reduced* energy consumption. Total electric send-out was reduced in the first quarter of 1974 by 10%—this in spite of a "normal" growth of from 3½% to 4%. As fuel was conserved, however, finances deteriorated. Many of the utility's costs—taxes, maintenance, labor, interest charges—were high, and increasing, and largely unrelated to send-out. Lower revenues and higher costs meant drastically lower earnings. Had it not been for an accounting change (approved by the Public Service Commission), Con Ed would have reported a loss in both November and December of 1973. (See Exhibit 1 for a financial summary.)

---

[1] Public Service Commission is the New York State agency authorized to regulate public utilities. Its powers include approving rate schedules for gas, steam, and electricity, and approving utility stock and bond offerings.

Need for rate relief

Con Ed needed a massive rate increase to cover sharply higher fuel and interest costs, as well as the adverse impact of lower volume. The full amount of the increase in fuel costs was automatically passed through to the consumers under a fuel-adjustment clause. In addition, a $315 million electric rate-increase request was submitted to the Public Service Commission. The company also requested a $108 million "conservation adjustment" rate increase, arguing that, since decreased energy send-out could not be matched by decreased costs, a higher rate per unit of energy sold was necessary to maintain the same corporate rate of return. The total rate request of $423 million represented a 30% increase over a two-year period (1974–75). Approval of the entire increase, coupled with the automatic fuel adjustment pass-throughs, would increase the typical customer's monthly bill from $15.59 to $26.

The Public Service Commission was not wholly sympathetic. There had been a series of rate hikes since 1958, and the City of New York had grown increasingly vehement in its opposition to them. The city itself was a huge consumer of power; it felt an obligation to represent the interests of millions of its residents, many of them poor; and it claimed that high electricity costs were to the detriment "not only of the ordinary user of electric current but also of commerce and industry and the general economy of the city." If the rate increase were approved, the utility's residential customers would pay the highest electric rates in the United States—8¢ a kilowatt-hour for the average residential customers, nearly double the rate in other major cities. High rates for satisfactory service were bad enough, critics charged, but high rates from a utility as negligent as Con Ed were intolerable. (Some observers added that it was good politics for elected officials to take a stand against Con Ed and in "the public interest.")

The Public Service Commission granted a temporary increase of $175 million in February 1974—substantially less than the minimum felt necessary by Con Ed. It was announced concurrently that a final decision on a permanent rate increase would not be rendered for months.

Financial needs and plans

The Commission's decision introduced substantial uncertainty to the company's financing plans. A planned January offering of $50 million of preferred stock and $50 million of bonds was postponed. In March, $150 million of 9⅛% bonds were finally issued. Almost immediately, they were bid down to a market yield of 10.45%, the highest in the utility industry. Investor confidence in the company was obviously quite low.

The situation was extremely serious. Con Ed's construction program was enormous, swollen in recent years by inflation. Management planned to spend $3.5 billion on new plant and equipment during 1974 to 1978, and any major delays would increase the likelihood of brownouts and system breakdowns.

An additional $1.5 billion would be needed for repayment of existing debt and for cash dividends on the preferred and common stock. (See Exhibit 2.)

Of the $5.0 billion funds needs, $2.2 billion would be generated by operations. It was planned to raise the remaining $2.8 billion in a mix consistent with management's policy that debt, preferred stock, and common stock represent 51%, 13%, and 35% of total capital, respectively. Con Ed's senior debt had been downgraded recently to a BBB by Standard & Poor, reflecting a substantial deterioration in interest coverage. (See Exhibit 1.) Furthermore, the $150 million bond issue in March 1974 had dropped the company's interest coverage to a level only slightly above the minimum set in its existing bond indentures. Management felt that it was essential that debt be limited to no more than 51% of total capital.

Financing alternatives

Con Ed's "cash crisis" demanded total external financing of $610 million in 1974. (See Exhibit 2.) An alternative to issuing additional equity, long-term debt, and preferred stock in the proportions set by management debt-structure policy was to use short-term bank loans. Con Ed had total bank lines of $300 million, of which only $64 million was in use at year-end 1973. An increase of $236 million in the company's bank loans, combined with the $150 million debt issue in March, represented a large percentage of Con Ed's total external financing need in 1974. (See Exhibit 2.) It would still be necessary, however, to raise an additional $224 million somehow during 1974.

Management was hesitant to sell large amounts of new equity. The company's stock had suffered along with those of most electric utilities and was selling at $18—a ten-year low and substantially below book value. Investors were increasingly attracted to historically high bond yields and the prices of utility stocks had found little support in recent months. (See Exhibit 3.) Large new issues of common stock seemed likely to dilute per-share results excessively.

As an alternative, Mr. Luce was considering the sale of two of its power plants to the State of New York. It was proposed that the New York State Power Authority pay Con Ed $500 million for two partially completed generating plants. The State would need to spend an additional $300 million to complete the two plants and might then lease the plants back to Con Ed.

A bill had been submitted to the state legislature in early April. The outcome of the legislative debate was uncertain, however, at the time of the board meeting. Constituents of many New York City and Westchester County Democrats and Republicans had complained bitterly about Con Ed's higher rates. These legislators were also concerned that city and county tax revenues would be lost if the tax-exempt New York State Power Authority took over the plants as proposed in the legislation. Furthermore, they were reluctant to believe that Con Ed was really in as bad shape as it claimed. The problem was complicated by the apparent disinterest of some upstate Republican legislators in the difficulties of Democratically controlled New York City.

Mr. Luce was thus faced with the dividend question. On the one hand, the cash shortage was quite critical and would deteriorate further in the months ahead. Customer complaints about rate increases had risen sharply. There was reason to suppose that some legislators would vote against the plant purchase if any money were to be used for dividend payments.

On the other hand, a regular quarterly or semiannual dividend had been paid faithfully by Con Ed and its predecessors since 1885. Although the dividend had not been increased in seven years, Con Ed stock was still acquired for income purposes. For many stockholders—especially older ones on social security—the average $360 of annual dividends was extremely important. Any cut in the dividend would inflict widespread personal hardship and possibly damage Con Ed's reputation in the capital markets.

Exhibit 1

CONSOLIDATED EDISON COMPANY (Abridged)
SUMMARY OF FINANCIAL RESULTS
($ in millions except per share data)

	1969	1970	1971	1972	1973	First Quarter 1973	1974
Operating revenues.............	$1,027	$1,128	$1,314	$1,480	$1,736	$ 425	$ 553
Net income....................	135	128	145	148	182	55	41
Preferred stock dividends.......	34	34	38	40	44	11	11
Net income for common stock...	$ 101	$ 94	$ 107	$ 108	$ 138	$ 44	$ 30
Per share of common							
Earnings per share.............	$ 2.68	$ 2.30	$ 2.35	$2.06	$ 2.32	$ .80	$ .49
Dividends per share...........	$ 1.80	$ 1.80	$ 1.80	$ 1.80	$ 1.80	$ .45	$ .45
Market price.................	$ 30	$ 25	$ 27	$ 26	$ 22	$ 25	$ 20
Price-earnings ratio...........	11	11	11	13	9	—	—
Dividend yield...............	6.0%	7.2%	6.7%	6.9%	8.2%	—	—
Debt position							
Interest coverage..............	2.6	2.2	2.2	2.1	2.2	2.2	1.8
Debt, percent of total capital....	52%	53%	52%	51%	52%	—	—
Bond rating..................	A	A	A	A	BBB	—	—
Operating statistics							
Capital expenditures...........	$ 305	$ 401	$ 430	$ 519	$ 686		
Percent earned on capital........	5.4%	5.5%	5.6%	5.6%	6.1%		
Percent earned on book equity...	8.6%	7.5%	7.5%	6.7%	7.6%		
Percent earned on market equity..	8.9%	9.1%	8.9%	8.0%	10.7%		
Number of customers (thousands)	2,903	2,895	2,866	2,842	2,847		
Sales, kilowatt-hours (millions)...	30,296	32,399	32,997	33,144	34,733		

Exhibit 2

CONSOLIDATED EDISON COMPANY (Abridged)
FUTURE SOURCES AND USES OF FUNDS
($ in millions except per share data)

	1974	1975	1976	1977	1978	Total
Sources						
Cash flow from operations						
Net income...................	$ 210	$ 250	$ 280	$ 310	$ 340	$1,390
Noncash charges..............	140	155	170	190	205	860
External sources*						
Bond issues..................	330	338	280	410	374	1,732
Preferred stock issues...........	100	67	72	88	72	399
Common stock issues..........	180	123	127	145	113	688
Total sources...............	$ 960	$ 933	$ 929	$1,143	$1,104	$5,069
Uses						
Construction expenditures.........	$ 625	$ 650	$ 700	$ 800	$ 725	$3,500
Preferred dividends..............	55	58	65	73	82	333
Common dividends.............	122	139	155	170	188	774
Repayment of debt..............	80	86	9	100	109	384
Repayment of current liability.....	78	—	—	—	—	78
Total uses..................	$ 960	$ 933	$ 929	$1,143	$1,104	$5,069
Memoranda:						
Common dividend..............	$ 1.80	$ 1.80	$ 1.80	$ 1.80	$ 1.80	
Common shares outstanding.......	73M	81M	88M	98M	105M	
Assumed net issue price...........	$ 16	$ 16	$ 17	$ 16	$ 16	
Long term debt, percent of capital..	51%	51%	51%	51%	51%	
Times interest earned.............	2.22	2.20	2.17	2.12	2.08	
Rate increases (excluding						
fuel adjustment increases).......	15%	15%	10%	10%	10%	
Earnings per share (average						
shares outstanding).............	$ 2.33	$ 2.49	$ 2.54	$ 2.55	$ 2.54	

* External financing raised in proportions demanded by management policy.
Source: Casewriter estimates.

Exhibit 3

CONSOLIDATED EDISON COMPANY (Abridged)

HISTORICAL COMPARISON OF STOCK PRICES AND INTEREST RATES

	1965	1966	1967	1968	1969	1970	1971	1972	1973
Moody's Utilities Index									
Market price...........	$ 117	$ 103	$ 102	$ 98	$ 95	$ 79	$ 84	$ 80	$ 71
Earnings per share.......	$5.92	$6.30	$6.67	$6.67	$6.92	$6.89	$7.14	$7.73	$7.55
Dividends per share.....	$3.86	$4.11	$4.34	$4.50	$4.61	$4.70	$4.77	$4.87	$5.01
Price-earnings ratio......	20	16	15	15	14	11	12	10	9
Dividend yield..........	3.3%	4.0%	4.3%	4.6%	4.9%	5.9%	5.7%	6.1%	7.0%
Consolidated Edison									
Market price...........	$ 45	$ 37	$ 33	$ 33	$ 30	$25	$ 26	$ 26	$ 22
Earnings per share.......	$2.42	$2.31	$2.58	$2.57	$2.68	$2.30	$2.35	$2.07	$2.34
Dividends per share.....	$1.80	$1.80	$1.80	$1.80	$1.80	$1.80	$1.80	$1.80	$1.80
Price-earnings ratio......	19	17	13	13	12	11	11	12	9
Dividend yield..........	4.0%	4.9%	5.5%	5.5%	6.0%	7.2%	6.9%	6.9%	8.2%
Book value............	$ 28	$ 29	$ 30	$ 30	$ 31	$ 31	$ 31	$ 31	$ 31
Cost of money									
BBB Utility bonds......	5.0%	6.1%	6.9%	7.2%	8.9%	9.0%	8.4%	7.8%	8.5%
Medium-grade utility									
preferred stocks.......	4.9%	5.7%	6.5%	6.5%	7.8%	7.6%	7.4%	7.6%	8.4%

* * * * *

RISING YIELDS ENHANCE BONDS' APPEAL*

This is an unusually good time for investors who need income—as well as for those who are apprehensive about the stock market—to look into what the bond market has to offer. The basic attractions of bonds now are largely self-evident: yields are exceptionally high—in most areas close to the record levels of 1970.

Buying bonds now with a view to long-term holding can lock in the high returns currently available. When yields peak out, a process that may not be too far off, prices of most bonds, which move inversely to yields, should begin to rise. Finally, the bond market normally offers in some degree a refuge against the generally volatile price action of stocks.

It must be recognized, however, that the bond market, except for convertible issues, does not provide protection against the long-term erosion of buying power that continued inflation—even at a pace slower than in recent months—will exact on the dollars invested.

The immensity of the credit markets and the diversity of choices they offer may be somewhat surprising even to experienced investors accustomed to dealing mainly in stocks. One recent study placed the total amount of credit outstanding in the U.S. at the end of 1973 at almost $1.9 trillion, or more than 2½ times the market value of all New York Stock Exchange issues.

Including private placements, corporate financing in 1973 totaled $33.4 billion, of which two-thirds ($22.3 billion) consisted of bonds and notes, with preferred ($3.4 billion) and common stock ($7.7 billion) accounting for the remainder. In addition, the U.S. Government offered ove $19 billion and state and local governments sol over $22 billion in various debt issues.

Three major bond areas

There are three major areas of bond investmen for the individual: corporate, U.S. Governmen and tax-exempt. Bonds range in maturity from few months (for some Governments and munici pals) to over 30 years.

Yields, currently at or near all-time peaks, ar close to 9% for new AA-rated corporates, 8.5% fo 90-day Treasury bills and 5.60% for recent Ne York State (AA) bonds.

Most brokers dealing in stocks also trade i bonds. In general, bonds are bought and sold i units of $1,000, with a minimum commission o $2.50 per bond by New York Stock Exchang firms; on small orders, the charge is frequentl higher.

Many factors play a part in determining th amounts of debt financing and the yield at whic new offerings can be brought to market, but th key determinants are the demand for and suppl of funds. In general, when economic factors ar favorable, the need to borrow tends to rise, an lenders get a better price.

* Reprinted from *The Outlook*, vol. 46, no. 15, April 15, 1974, with permission of the publishe Standard & Poor's Corporation.

Exhibit 3—Continued

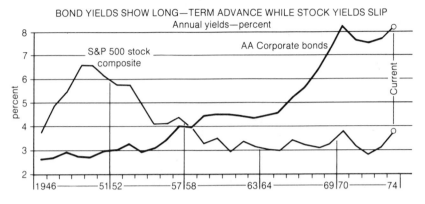

BOND YIELDS SHOW LONG—TERM ADVANCE WHILE STOCK YIELDS SLIP
Annual yields—percent

Inflation and inflationary expectations, par-cularly in recent years, have also had a profound ffect on yields. This is so because lenders tend to emand compensation, in the form of higher ields, for the reduced value of the dollars in hich the bonds will eventually be paid off. The hart showing "real" yields illustrates this—the al rate of return on AA-rated corporate bonds, djusted for inflation, has traditionally tended to an at 2% to 4%. The difference between this and ае yields shown by the upper line represents al->wance for the effects of inflation.

Short-term rates are also basically determined y supply-demand factors, and these in turn can e strongly influenced by Federal Reserve policy. he Fed has these main tools: (1) It can buy or ll Government securities in the open market, ising or lowering the amount of lendable funds the banking system. (2) It can alter reserve re-uirements for member banks, tighten them when considers credit to be too freely available, and ce versa. (3) It can raise or lower the discount te to help accomplish similar objectives. Finally -as it has done frequently in recent years—it can sort to moral suasion, or jawboning, to affect anks' lending policies.

hort-term yields rise

Traditionally, short-term yields have been lower an those available from long-term obligations. ut in recent years heavy demand for short-term nds and the assumption that present rates of flation will moderate have reversed the pattern. s charted, interest rates for short-term credit now enerally equal or exceed those for long-term edit. For example, three-month negotiable cer-ficates of deposit are now at about 10%, while w issues of 20-year high-grade utilities are lling to yield just under 9%.

There has also been a marked shift in the rela-tion of bond to stock yields. Typical yields on high-quality bonds are now well over twice that of the S&P 500-stock price index, whereas prior to the mid-1950s stock yields consistently ex-ceeded bond yields (see chart).

Two considerations help to explain the shift. First, a rather steady rise in price-earnings mul-tiples of stocks in the years following World War II had the effect of bringing stock yields down. Second, surging inflation has augmented the yield compensation demanded by bond investors.

Where matters stand

In the past two months, with demand for funds still exceedingly heavy, short-term rates have swung dramatically upward and bond prices have deteriorated. But special factors have entered into this bulge in rates, and it may even now be not too far from cresting, including the bank prime lending rate, which has now returned to its 10% record.

As for inflationary pressures, the worst may be behind us for at least the time being. If, as we fore-see, there is some easing in inflation over the next several months, existing yield levels would look attractive in retrospect.

Attractive areas of the bond market

Representative top-quality seasoned corporate bonds now yield over 8%, and still higher returns are available from new issues, which tend to re-flect current money-market trends. Top-grade utilities, for example, are now being offered on close to a 9% basis with five-year call protection.

The relative safety of individual issues of bonds is identifiable by the quality ratings assigned by S&P. Issues rated AAA are of highest grade, but

Exhibit 3—Continued

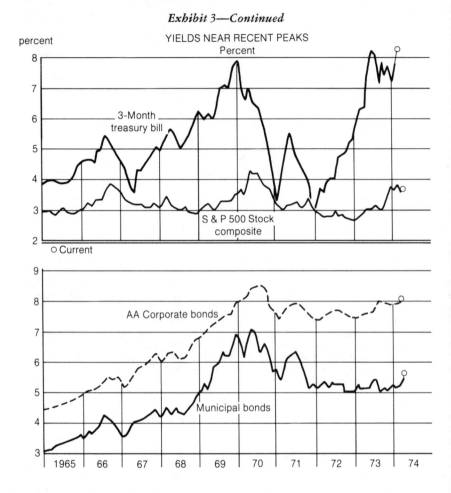

percent   YIELDS NEAR RECENT PEAKS
Percent

○ Current

1965 | 66 | 67 | 68 | 69 | 70 | 71 | 72 | 73 | 74

AA bonds differ from them in only a small degree. A-rated issues are regarded as upper-medium grade. The BBB rating is borderline between definitely sound obligations and those in which the speculative element begins to predominate. The BBB group is the lowest qualifying for commercial bank investment; most individual investors probably will not want to buy bonds that ᴀre more speculative than this.

Discount bonds

While the bond market should not be regarded as a trading area except for professional investors, there is much to be said for the capital-gain potentials of discount bonds, particularly for high-bracket taxpayers. Consider for example the AT&T 2¾s, maturing in October, 1975, and now selling around 94. When they are paid off at par,

the holder will have realized $60 per $1,000 bon as a long-term capital gain, in addition to th annual interest of $27.50. The yield to maturit works out at about 5.35%, with well over half th total in the form of capital gain taxable at lower rate.

Municipals afford tax exemption

Investors requiring a degree of tax protectio should not overlook municipal bonds, the intere on which is free from federal income taxes an sometimes also from state and city income taxe They are payable from taxes imposed by the i suer, or in the case of revenue bonds, from re enues received from the users of the faciliti financed thereby.

Municipal bond yields, rising steeply recentl are still somewhat below record highs. For eː

Exhibit 3—Continued

A SHOPPING LIST OF YIELDS
Percent

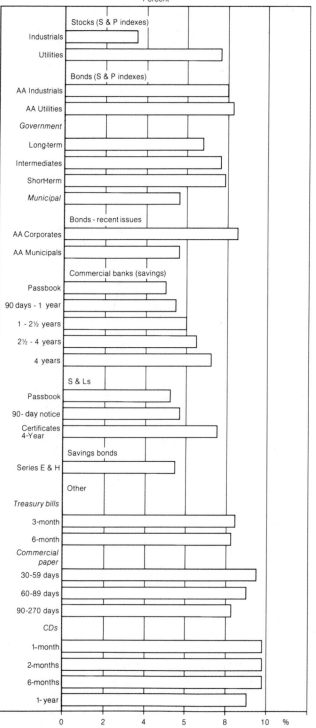

Exhibit 3—Continued

ample, an A-rated 20-year bond yielding 6.00% to maturity can be purchased in today's market. An investor in the 36% tax bracket (taxable income of $24,000 to $28,000) filing a joint return would have to purchase a taxable bond with an equivalent 9.3% yield to match this return. Profits from the sale of municipal bonds are not exempt from capital gains taxes.

Shorter governments preferable

In the Government sector, long-term Treasury bonds, typically yielding about 7.8%, fully taxable, appear comparatively unattractive relative to shorter maturities—three-month bills, for example, which are currently around an 8.5% basis. So-called "flower bonds" fit a special need.

These are U.S. Treasury bonds that can be bought at discounts but applied at par value against estate taxes. Issuance of this type of obligation was halted by law a few years ago, so the list is shrinking. However, a number of bonds are still available at prices in the 70s and 80s, bearing current returns of between 4% and close to 6%.

Convertibles as a middle ground

Convertible bonds, most of which may be converted into a stated number of shares of common stock, offer an interesting middle ground for investing in fixed-income securities that may also in strong stock markets, show rewarding appreciation.

The basic features of attraction of convertible

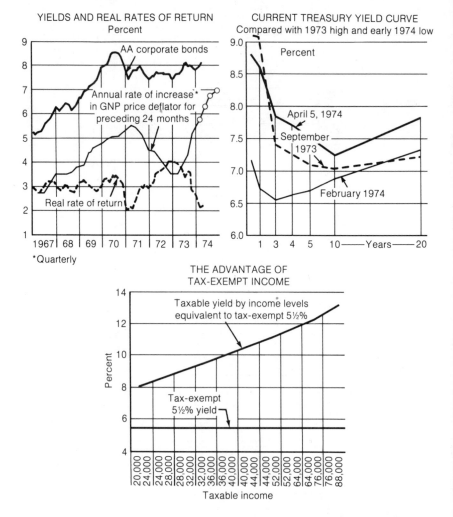

YIELDS AND REAL RATES OF RETURN
Percent

AA corporate bonds

Annual rate of increase* in GNP price deflator for preceding 24 months

Real rate of return

1967 68 69 70 71 72 73 74

*Quarterly

CURRENT TREASURY YIELD CURVE
Compared with 1973 high and early 1974 low

Percent

April 5, 1974

September 1973

February 1974

1 3 4 5 10———Years———20

THE ADVANTAGE OF
TAX-EXEMPT INCOME

Taxable yield by income levels equivalent to tax-exempt 5½%

Tax-exempt 5½% yield

Percent

Taxable income

ecurities are that (1) those selling at no more than moderate premiums over their values in common stock tend to participate in any sizable price appreciation in the stock, (2) their yields as bonds are almost always higher than the returns on the commons, and (3) they are in some degree protected by their interest-rate "floors."

In the tables below we list a number of bonds in each of five categories, to fit various needs.

Who should buy bonds

Are bonds suitable for you? A categorical yes or no answer would be hard to defend, for requirements differ widely. Those whose primary concerns are income and safety of principal would in almost all cases be well advised to have adequate bond representation. Even young married people, for whom estate building may be vital, should not overlook convertibles. Others whose current income suffices for their needs and who may have considerable capital committed in other ways—such as bank deposits, stocks, or real estate—may wish to sweeten over-all yields by buying some bonds.

In general, bonds are not an appropriate vehicle for those willing to accept stock market risks in order to obtain long-run growth of capital. In today's circumstances, however, it is possible to nail down yields that are not too far from average total-return performance of stocks historically. Thus the average investor may find some participation in bonds worthwhile, with a view to maintaining reasonable portfolio balance.

Part III

investment decisions, mergers,
and acquisitions

EVALUATION OF INVESTMENT ALTERNATIVES

∧∧

1. In September 1974, American Brands, Inc. issued $150 million of five-year notes that were scheduled to mature September 1, 1979. The annual interest rate was $9\frac{5}{8}\%$ with interest to be paid semiannually on March 1 and September 1. Assume that on September 2, 1975, new four-year notes of equivalent risk could be purchased at face value with an interest rate of 8% and that you had purchased a $1,000 American Brands note when the notes were originally issued. What would be its market value on September 2, 1975? (Note: As an approximation, assume that the appropriate discount rate for semiannual periods is $8\%/2$, or 4%.)

2. Most home mortgages require monthly payments and have long maturities of 20 to 30 years, but assume you have applied for a $10,000 four-year mortgage with payments to be made to the bank at the end of each year. The mortgage-loan officer at the Gordon Road Savings Bank says that their current interest rate on such mortgages is 5% and, after a quick reference to a nearby copy of the mortgage-tables book, further states that the annual payment would be $2,820. Show that this annual cash flow provides a rate of return of 5% on the bank's investment of $10,000. Is 5% the true interest rate to you? In other words, if you pay interest of 5% on your outstanding balance each year, will the remainder of the $2,820 payments be sufficient to just repay the loan?

3. If you went to the consumer installment-loan department of the same savings bank and applied for a $10,000 four-year loan to finance your new car, the loan officer might also quote a 5% rate, but the annual payments might be computed in a different manner.

Principal..........................	$10,000
Four years of interest	
at 5% (.05 × 4 × $10,000).........	2,000
Total due bank....................	$12,000
Annual payments ($12,000 ÷ 4).......	$ 3,000

    What is the rate of return to the bank, that is, the internal rate of return the banks will earn on your loan?

4.   A company has an opportunity to invest funds in the following series of projects:

Project	Required Investment (Beginning of Year 1)	Net Cash Proceeds after Taxes at End of Each Year		
		Year 1	Year 2	Year 3
A..........	$10,000	$10,000	—	—
B..........	$10,000	$ 7,500	$ 7,500	—
C..........	$10,000	$ 2,000	$ 4,000	$12,000
D.........	$10,000	$10,000	$ 3,000	$ 3,000

Each of these projects has an equal element of risk. Investment outlays are made at the beginning of the first year, while cash inflows after taxes are received in a lump sum at the end of each year. There is assumed to be no salvage value with any of the projects.

QUESTIONS

In answering the following questions, ignore any effects that arise from tax considerations.

1.   Rank the four projects according to each of the following commonly used methods (see definitions below):
  a.   Payback period.
  b.   Unadjusted or accounting rate of return.
  c.   Rate of return on investment—that is, internal rate of return.
  d.   Net present value—assuming a discount rate of 6% and 30%.
2.   Why do the rankings differ?
3.   What does each rule measure, and what does it assume?
4.   Assuming the projects are independent, which should be accepted? Assuming the projects are mutually exclusive, which is best?

DEFINITIONS

Payback period: the payback period is defined as the length of time required for the stream of cash proceeds produced by an investment to equal the original cash outlay required by the investment.

Unadjusted or accounting rate of return (this is only one of many possible versions of unadjusted [i.e., undiscounted] computations of rates of return):

$$\frac{\text{average annual cash inflow} - \dfrac{\text{required investment}}{n}}{\dfrac{\text{required investment}}{2}}$$

where n is the number of years of anticipated cash inflow. In this case, n equals one for Project A, two for B, and three for C and D.

Rate of return on investment (i.e., internal rate of return): the internal rate of return is the discount rate which will make the present value of the cash proceeds expected from an investment equal to the present value of the cash outlays required by the investment.

Net present value: the discounted value of the cash flows, using the indicated discount rate.

PRESSCO, INC. (Abridged)

^^^

In June 1979, Mr. John Smythe, a marketing representative for Pressco, Inc., was attempting to put together a financial presentation designed to help close the sale of mechanical drying equipment to Paperco, Inc. The equipment which Mr. Smythe hoped to sell to Paperco would replace less efficient facilities which had been placed in service only 2½ years previously by Paperco. The cost savings (exclusive of depreciation charges) which Mr. Smythe felt certain Paperco would realize from the proposed new-equipment installation amounted to $700,000 per year. Of this amount, $450,000 in savings was expected to come from more efficient fuel utilization, a factor which Mr. Smythe believed would qualify the full $2.9 million investment for a tax credit of 20%.[1] Capital expenditures without such energy saving features normally qualified for only a 10% investment tax credit. (See Exhibit 1 for a discussion of the investment tax credit.)

In its internal management reports and in its reports to shareholders, Paperco utilized straight-line depreciation. However, in its tax reports (and thus in calculating relevant cash flows on investment), Paperco utilized double-

---

[1] The actual amount of the tax credit was subject to some uncertainty. As noted in *The New York Times* financial pages:

At this point, the business energy tax credit, too, lacks quality and performance standards.

. . . The I.R.S. has not yet drawn up any regulations implementing the act [Energy Tax Act of 1978], and none are expected before year-end.

. . . the revenue service's slow pace has drawn criticism from many quarters. Senator John H. Chafee, Republican of Rhode Island, has said that because many energy-saving projects take years to engineer and construct, they may be abandoned unless regulations are proposed and issued promptly. On a similar note, the Business Roundtable has sent a memorandum to the Treasury Department complaining that the absence of I.R.S. regulations may defeat the objectives of the act. Many energy-saving projects have lead times of five years or more, the memorandum says, and a termination date for the credit is less than three and a half years away.

The I.R.S. has said that business need not wait until it issues standards before investing in energy property, but many businesses remain skittish about making such commitments.

"It's a Catch-22 situation," says Steven F. Meyer of the Washington office of Peat, Marwick, Mitchell & Co. "In the absence of regulations, the only thing you can do is look for the intent of Congress as evidenced in the House, Senate and Committee reports," he notes.

declining-balance depreciation.[2] (See Exhibits 2 and 3 for a breakdown of the relevant depreciation projections.)

The assumptions which Mr. Smythe planned to utilize in his presentation of the investment opportunity to Paperco's management are outlined below:

1. Equipment cost, $2,100,000.
   Shipment—12 months following receipt of order.
   Start-up of facility—18 months following receipt of order.

2. Equipment payment terms.
   20% ($420,000) with order.
   20% ($420,000) 120 days after order.
   60% ($1,260,000) 30 days after equipment delivery.

3. Installation cost, $800,000.
   $80,000 per month for the last 10 of the 18 months from receipt of order to start-up.

4. Paperco cost of capital.
   12%

5. Depreciable life and estimated salvage value.

	Proposed New Facility	Facility to Be Replaced
Equipment depreciation period.......	10 years	10 years
Installation depreciation period......	8 years	8 years
Estimated salvage value at end of life....................	$250,000	$ 60,000

6. Facility to be replaced

Original equipment cost.........................	$500,000
Original installation cost.........................	$500,000
Estimated market value of equipment if sold in 18 months (when displaced)...........	$150,000
Estimated remaining physical life as of June 1979 was...........................	11½ years

7. Paperco paid federal income taxes at the rate of 48%.

---

[2] The IRS permitted taxpayers to switch from the double-declining-balance method of depreciation to the straight-line method of depreciation whenever the switch became advantageous. A switch to straight-line depreciation at the most advantageous time is incorporated in the data presented in Exhibits 2 and 3.

Exhibit 1

PRESSCO, INC.
INVESTMENT TAX CREDIT

The IRS regulations allow a credit against tax for investment in certain depreciable property. To get the full investment credit available, the investment must have a useful life of seven years or more when acquired. If useful life is five or six years, the full credit is allowed on two thirds (66⅔%) of the investment. If life is three or four years, only one third (33⅓%) of the investment qualifies. But if useful life is less than three years, there is no credit.

If equipment is retired before seven years, investment credits relating to that equipment are recaptured in accordance with the amount of time the equipment was actually in service.

The current investment credit rate is 10%. An additional 10% investment credit for the period beginning October 1, 1978 and ending December 31, 1982 is added to the credit noted above for investment in property that qualifies as energy property under the rules outlined below. The additional 10% investment tax credit was part of the Energy Tax Act of 1978.

a. *Alternative energy property* includes certain equipment that uses an alternate substance, a substance other than oil, gas, or oil and gas products, as a fuel or that aids in the use of such a substance. Specifically it includes: (1) a boiler, or a burner for a combuster other than a boiler, if its primary fuel is an alternate substance; (2) equipment for converting an alternate substance into a synthetic fuel (other than coke or coke gas); (3) equipment for modifying oil- and gas-using equipment to use another fuel or an oil mixture that is 25% made up of another substance; (4) equipment using coal as a feedstock for manufacturing products other than coke or coke gas; (5) pollution-control equipment required by government regulations to be installed in connection with equipment in categories (1) through (4), except equipment required to be installed by regulations in effect on October 1, 1978, which is installed in connection with property using coal or lignite as of that date; (6) equipment used to handle, store, or prepare an alternate substance at the point of use for use in equipment described in categories (1) through (5); and (7) equipment to produce, distribute, or use geothermal energy, but only, in the case of electrical generation, equipment up to the electrical transmission state. Sec. 48(1)(3).

b. *Solar or wind energy property* includes equipment that uses solar or wind energy to generate electricity or to heat or cool (or provide hot water for use in) a structure. Sec. 48(1)(4).

c. *Specifically defined energy property* includes certain listed equipment installed in connection with an existing industrial or commercial facility to reduce the amount of energy consumed in an existing industrial or commercial process. The IRS may specify other similar items of energy conservation equipment eligible for the credit. The listed items are: recuperators, heat wheels, regenerators, heat exchangers, waste-heat boilers, heat pipes, automatic energy control systems, turbulators, preheaters, combustible gas recovery systems, and economizers. Sec. 48(1)(5).

d. *Recycling equipment* means equipment used exclusively to recycle solid waste or to sort and prepare it for recycling. It does not include equipment used after the point where a marketable product, such as newsprint, paperboard, metal ingots, or textile fibers, has been produced. In the iron and steel industry the credit is limited to equipment used before the reduction of solid waste to a molten state. No more than 10% use of virgin materials is permissible. Equipment used to convert solid waste into fuel or useful energy is recycling equipment. Sec. 48(1)(6).

e. *Shale oil equipment* is equipment for producing oil from shale. Equipment for hydrogenation, refining, or other processes subsequent to retorting is not included. Sec. 48(1)(7).

f. *Equipment for producing natural gas from geopressured brine* is energy property. Whether a well qualifies as producing natural gas from geopressured brine will be determined by the Federal Energy Regulatory Commission under the definition in the Natural Gas Pricing Act, but the Secretary of the Treasury will determine if equipment used in connection with a well qualifies for the credit. Sec. 48(1)(8).

Exhibit 2

PRESSCO, INC.
DEPRECIATION EXPENSE—NEW EQUIPMENT AND INSTALLATION
(In thousands of dollars)

Year	Double-Declining-Balance Method*			Straight-Line Method		
	Equipment	Installation	Total	Equipment	Installation	Total
1	$ 370	$ 160	$ 530	$ 185	$ 100	$ 285
2	296	128	424			
3	237	102	339			
4	189	82	271			
5	152	82	234			
6	122	82	204			
7	121	82	203			
8	121	82	203			
9	121		121			185
10	121		121			
	$1,850	$ 800	$2,650	$1,850	$ 800	$2,650

* See footnote 2 regarding the switch to straight-line depreciation in the first year that this switch becomes advantageous.

Exhibit 3

PRESSCO, INC.
DEPRECIATION EXPENSE—REPLACED EQUIPMENT AND INSTALLATION
(In thousands of dollars)

Year	Double-Declining-Balance Method*			Straight-Line Method		
	Equipment	Installation	Total	Equipment	Installation	Total
1	$ 88	$125	$213	$ 44	$ 63	$107
2	70	75	145		62	106
3	56	60	116		63	107
4	45	48	93		62	106
5	36	48	84		63	107
6	29	48	77		62	106
7	29	48	77		63	107
8	29	48	77		62	106
9	29		29			44
10	29		29			44
	$440	$500	$940	$440	$500	$940

* See footnote 2 regarding the switch to straight-line depreciation in the first year that this switch becomes advantageous.

THE SUPER PROJECT

^^

In March, 1967, Mr. Crosby Sanberg, manager, financial analysis at General Foods Corporation, told a casewriter, "What I learned about incremental analysis at the Business School doesn't always work." He was convinced that under some circumstances "sunk costs" were relevant to capital project evaluations. He was also concerned that financial and accounting systems did not provide an accurate estimate of "incremental costs and revenues" and that this was one of the most difficult problems in measuring the value of capital investment proposals. Mr. Sanberg used the Super project[1] as an example.

Super was a new instant dessert, based on a flavored, water soluble, agglomerated powder. Although a four-flavor line would be introduced, it was estimated that chocolate would account for 80% of total sales.

General Foods was organized along product lines in the United States. Foreign operations were under a separate division. Major U.S. product divisions included Post, Kool-Aid, Maxwell House, Jell-O, and Birds Eye. Financial data for General Foods are given in Exhibits 1, 2, and 3.

The capital investment project request for Super involved $200,000 as follows:

Building modifications	$ 80,000
Machinery and equipment	120,000
	$200,000

Part of the expenditure was required for modifying an existing building, where Jell-O was manufactured. Available capacity of a Jell-O agglomerator[2] would be used in the manufacture of Super, so that no cost for the key machine was included in the project. The $120,000 machinery and equipment item represented packaging machinery.

The market

The total dessert market was defined as including powdered desserts, ice creams, pie fillings, and cake mixes. According to a Nielsen survey, powdered

---

[1] The name and nature of this new product have been disguised to avoid the disclosure of confidential information.

[2] Agglomeration is a process by which the processed powder is passed through a steam bath and then dried. This "fluffs up" the powder particles and increases solubility.

desserts constituted a significant and growing segment of the market; their 1966 market share had increased over the preceding year. Results of the Nielsen survey follow:

DESSERT MARKET
AUGUST–SEPTEMBER, 1966, COMPARED WITH AUGUST–SEPTEMBER, 1965

	Market Share August–September, 1966	% Change from ⌐August–September, 1965⌐ Share	Volume
Jell-O...........................	19.0%	+3.6	+40.0
Tasty...........................	4.0	+4.0	(New)
Total powders..................	25.3	+7.6	+62.0
Pie fillings and cake mixes.........	32.0	−3.9	(No change)
Ice cream.......................	42.7	−3.4	+ 5.0
Total market...................	100.0%		+13.0

On the basis of test market experience, General Foods expected Super to capture a 10% share of the total dessert market. Eighty percent of the expected volume of Super would come from a growth in total market share or growth in the total powdered segment, and 20% would come from erosion of Jell-O sales.

Production facilities

Test market volume was packaged on an existing line, inadequate to handle long-run requirements. Filling and packaging equipment to be purchased had a capacity of 1.9 million units on a two-shift, five-day workweek basis. This represented considerable excess capacity, since 1968 requirements were expected to reach 1.1 million units and the national potential was regarded as 1.6 million units. However, the extra capacity resulted from purchasing standard equipment, and a more economical alternative did not exist.

Capital budgeting procedure

Capital investment project proposals submitted under procedures covered in the General Foods Accounting and Financial Manual were identified as falling into one of the following classifications:

1. Safety and Convenience
2. Quality
3. Increase Profit
4. Other

These classifications served as a basis for establishing different procedures and criteria for accepting projects. For example, the Super project fell in the third classification, "increase profit." Criteria for evaluating projects are given in Exhibit 4. In discussing these criteria, Mr. Sanberg noted that the payback and return guidelines were not used as "cutoff" measures. Mr. Sanberg added: "Payback and return on investment are rarely the only measure of acceptability. Criteria vary significantly by type of project. A relatively high return might be required for a new product in a new business category. On the other hand, a much lower return might be acceptable for a new product entry which represented a continuing effort to maintain leadership in an existing business by, for example, filling out the product line."

Estimates of payback and return on funds employed were required for each profit-increasing project requiring a total of $50,000 or more of new capital funds and expense before taxes. The payback period was the length of time required for the project to repay the investment from the date the project became operational. In calculating the repayment period, only incremental income and expenses related to the project were used.

Return on funds employed (ROFE) was calculated by dividing 10-year average profit before taxes by the 10-year average funds employed. Funds employed included incremental net fixed assets plus or minus related working capital. Start-up costs and any profits or losses incurred prior to the time when the project became operational were included in the first profit and loss period in the financial evaluation calculation.

Capital budgeting atmosphere

A General Foods accounting executive commented on the atmosphere within which capital projects were reviewed, as follows: "Our problem is not one of capital rationing. Our problem is to find enough good solid projects to employ capital at an attractive return on investment. Of course, the rate of capital inputs must be balanced against a steady growth in earnings per share. The short-term impact of capital investments is usually an increase in the capital base without an immediate realization of profit potential. This is particularly true in the case of new products.

"The food industry should show a continuous growth. A cyclical industry can afford to let its profits vary. We want to expand faster than the gross national product. The key to our capital budgeting is to integrate the plans of our eight divisions into a balanced company plan which meets our overall growth objectives. Most new products show a loss in the first two or three years, but our divisions are big enough to introduce new products without showing a loss."

Documentation for the Super project

Exhibits 5 and 6 document the financial evaluation of the Super project. Exhibit 5 is the summary appropriation request prepared to justify the project to management and to secure management's authorization to expend funds on a capital project. Exhibit 6 presents the backup detail. Cost of the market test was included as "Other" expense in the first period because a new product had to pay for its test market expense, even though this might be a sunk cost at the time capital funds were requested. The "Adjustments" item represented erosion of the Jell-O market and was calculated by multiplying the volume of erosion times a variable profit contribution. In the preparation of Exhibit 6 costs of acquiring packaging machinery were included, but no cost was attributed to the 50% of the capacity of a Jell-O agglomerator to be used for the Super project because the General Foods Accounting and Financial Manual requested that capital projects be prepared on an incremental basis as follows:

"The incremental concept requires that project requests, profit projections, and funds-employed statements include only items of income and expense and investment in assets which will be realized, incurred, or made directly as a result of, or are attributed to, the new project."

Exchange of memos on the Super project

After receiving the paper work on the Super project, Mr. Sanberg studied the situation and wrote a memorandum arguing that the principle of the preceding quotation should not be applied to the Super project. His superior agreed with the memorandum and forwarded it to the corporate controller with the covering note contained in Appendix I. The controller's reply is given in Appendix II.

APPENDIX I

March 2, 1967

TO: J. C. Kresslin, Corporate Controller
FROM: J. E. Hooting, Director, Corporate Budgets and Analysis

Super Project

At the time we reviewed the Super project, I indicated to you that the return on investment looked significantly different if an allocation of the agglomerator and building, originally justified as a Jell-O project, were included in the Super investment. The pro rata allocation of these facilities, based on the share of capacity used, triples the initial gross investment in Super facilities from $200,000 to about $672,000.

I am forwarding a memorandum from Crosby Sanberg summarizing the results of three analyses evaluating the project on an:
   I.   Incremental basis
   II. Facilities-used basis
   III. Fully allocated facilities and costs basis
Crosby has calculated a 10-year average ROFE using these techniques.

Please read Crosby's memo before continuing with my note.
                    *   *   *   *   *

Crosby concludes that the fully allocated basis, or some variation of it, is necessary to understand the long-range potential of the project.

I agree. We launch a new project because of its potential to increase our sales and earning power for many years into the future. We must be mindful of short-term consequences, as indicated by an incremental analysis, but we must also have a long-range frame of reference if we are to really understand what we are committing ourselves to. This long-range frame of reference is best approximated by looking at fully allocated investment and "accounted" profits, which recognize fully allocated costs because, in fact, over the long run all costs are variable unless some major change occurs in the structure of the business.

Our current GF preoccupation with only the incremental costs and investment causes some real anomalies that confuse our decision making. Super is a good example. On an incremental basis the project looks particularly attractive because by using a share of the excess capacity built on the coattails of the lucrative Jell-O project, the incremental investment in Super is low. If the excess Jell-O capacity did not exist, would the project be any less attractive? In the short term, perhaps yes because it would entail higher initial risk, but in the long term it is not a better project just because it fits a facility that is temporarily unused.

Looking at this point from a different angle, if the project exceeded our investment hurdle rate on a short-term basis but fell below it on a long-term basis (and Super comes close to doing this), should we reject the project? I say yes because over the long run as "fixed" costs become variable and as we have to commit new capital to support the business, the continuing ROFE will go under water.

In sum, we have to look at new project proposals from both the long-range and the short-term point of view. We plan to refine our techniques of using a fully allocated basis as a long-term point of reference and will hammer out a policy recommendation for your consideration. We would appreciate your comments.

February 17, 1967

TO: J. E. Hooting, Director, Corporate Budgets and Analysis
FROM: C. Sanberg, Manager, Financial Analysis

**Super Project: A Case Example of
Investment Evaluation Techniques**

This will review the merits of alternative techniques of evaluating capital investment decisions using the Super project as an example. The purpose of the review is to provide an illustration of the problems and limitations inherent in using incremental ROFE and payback and thereby provide a rationale for adopting new techniques.

ALTERNATIVE TECHNIQUES

The alternative techniques to be reviewed are differentiated by the level of revenue and investment charged to the Super project in figuring a payback and ROFE, starting with incremental revenues and investment. Data related to the alternative techniques outlined below are summarized [at the end of this appendix].

Alternative I Incremental Basis

Method.   The Super project as originally evaluated considered only incremental revenue and investment, which could be directly identified with the decision to produce Super. Incremental fixed capital ($200M) basically included packaging equipment.

Result.   On this basis the project paid back in seven years with a ROFE of 63%.

Discussion.   Although it is General Foods' current policy to evaluate capital projects on an incremental basis, this technique does not apply to the Super project. The reason is that Super extensively utilizes existing facilities, which are readily adaptable to known future alternative uses.

Super should be charged with the "opportunity loss" of agglomerating capacity and building space. Because of Super the opportunity is lost to use a portion of agglomerating capacity for Jell-O and other products that could potentially be agglomerated. In addition, the opportunity is lost to use the building space for existing or new product volume expansion. To the extent there is an opportunity loss of existing facilities, new facilities must be built to accommodate future expansion. In other words, because the business is expanding Super utilizes facilities that are adaptable to predictable alternative uses.

Alternative II Facilities-Used Basis

Method. Recognizing that Super will use half of an existing agglomerator and two thirds of an existing building, which were justified earlier in the Jell-O project, we added Super's pro rata share of these facilities ($453M) to the incremental capital. Overhead costs directly related to these existing facilities were also subtracted from incremental revenue on a shared basis.

Result. ROFE, 34%.

Discussion. Although the existing facilities utilized by Super are not incremental to this project, they are relevant to the evaluation of the project because potentially they can be put to alternative uses. Despite a high return on an incremental basis, if the ROFE on a project was unattractive after consideration of the shared use of existing facilities, the project would be questionable. Under these circumstances, we might look for a more profitable product for the facilities.

In summary, the facilities-used basis is a useful way of putting various projects on a common ground for purposes of *relative* evaluation. One product using existing capacity should not necessarily be judged to be more attractive than another practically identical product which necessitates an investment in additional facilities.

Alternative III Fully Allocated Basis

Method. Further recognizing that individual decisions to expand inevitably add to a higher overhead base, we increased the costs and investment base developed in Alternative II by a provision for overhead expenses and overhead capital. These increases were made in year 5 of the 10-year evaluation period, on the theory that at this point a number of decisions would result in more fixed costs and facilities. Overhead expenses included manufacturing costs, plus selling and general and administrative costs on a per unit basis equivalent to Jell-O. Overhead capital included a share of the distribution system assets ($40M).

Result. ROFE, 25%.

Discussion. Charging Super with an overhead burden recognizes that overhead costs in the long-run increase in proportion to the level of business activity, even though decisions to spend more overhead dollars are made separately from decisions to increase volume and provide the incremental facilities to support the higher volume level. To illustrate, the Division-F1968 Financial Plan budgets about a 75% increase in headquarters' overhead spending in F1968 over F1964. A contributing factor was the decision to increase the sales force by 50% to meet the demands of a growing and increasingly complex business. To further illustrate, about half the capital projects in the F1968 three-year Financial Plan are in the "nonpayback" category. This group of projects comprises largely "overhead facilities" (warehouses, utilities, etc.), which are not directly related to the manufacture of products but are necessary components of the total business. These facilities are made necessary by an increase in total business activity as a result of the cumulative effect of many decisions taken in the past.

The Super project is a significant decision which will most likely add to more overhead dollars as illustrated above. Super volume doubles the powdered dessert business category; it increases the Division businesses by 10%. Furthermore, Super requires a new production technology: agglomeration and packaging on a high-speed line.

CONCLUSIONS

1. The incremental basis for evaluating a project is an inadequate measure of a project's worth when existing facilities with a known future use will be utilized extensively.

2. A fully allocated basis of reviewing major new product proposals recognizes that overheads increase in proportion to the size and complexity of the business, and provides the best long-range projection of the financial consequences.

ALTERNATIVE EVALUATIONS OF SUPER PROJECT
(FIGURES BASED ON 10-YEAR AVERAGES; IN THOUSANDS OF DOLLARS)

	I *Incremental* *Basis*	II *Facilities-* *Used Basis*	III *Fully Allocated* *Basis*
Investment:			
Working capital	267	267	267
Fixed capital:			
Gross	200	653	672
Net	113	358	367
Total net investment	380	625	634
*Profit before taxes**	239	211	157
ROFE	63%	34%	25%
Jell-O Project:			
Building	$200 × ⅔ = $133		
Agglomerator	640 × ½ = 320		
	$453		

* Note: Assumes 20% of Super volume will replace existing Jell-O business.

APPENDIX II

TO: Mr. J. E. Hooting, Director, Corporate Budgets and Analysis
FROM: Mr. J. C. Kresslin, Corporate Controller
SUBJECT: SUPER PROJECT

March 7, 1967

On March 2 you sent me a note describing Crosby Sanberg's and your thoughts about evaluating the Super project. In this memo you suggest that the project should be appraised on the basis of fully allocated facilities and production costs.

In order to continue the dialogue, I am raising a couple of questions below.

It seems to me that in a situation such as you describe for Super, the real question is a *management decision* as to whether to go ahead with the Super project or not go ahead. Or to put it another way, are we better off in the aggregate if we use half the agglomerator and two thirds of an existing building for Super, or are we not, on the basis of our current knowledge?

It might be assumed that, for example, half of the agglomerator is being used and half is not and that a minimum economical size agglomerator was necessary for Jell-O and, consequently, should be justified by the Jell-O project itself. If we find a way to utilize it sooner by producing Super on it, aren't we better off in the aggregate, and the different ROFE figure for the Super project by itself becomes somewhat irrelevant? A similar point of view might be applied to the portion of the building. Or if we charge the Super project with half an agglomerator and two thirds of an existing building, should we then go back and relieve the Jell-O projects of these costs in evaluating the management's original proposal?

To put it another way, since we are faced with making decisions at a certain time on the basis of what we then know, I see very little value in looking at the Super project all by itself. Better we should look at the total situation before and after to see how we fare.

As to allocated production costs, the point is not so clear. Undoubtedly, over the long haul, the selling prices will need to be determined on the basis of a satisfactory margin over fully allocated costs. Perhaps this should be an additional requirement in the course of evaluating capital projects, since we seem to have been surprised at the low margins for "Tasty" after allocating all costs to the product.

I look forward to discussing this subject with you and with Crosby at some length.

Exhibit 1

THE SUPER PROJECT

CONSOLIDATED BALANCE SHEET OF GENERAL FOODS CORPORATION
FISCAL YEAR ENDED APRIL 1, 1967
(Dollar figures in millions)

ASSETS

Cash..	$ 20
Marketable securities..	89
Receivables...	180
Inventories...	261
Prepaid expenses...	14
Total current assets..	$564
Land, buildings, equipment (at cost, less depreciation)..........	332
Long-term receivables and sundry assets......................	7
Goodwill..	26
Total assets...	$929

LIABILITIES AND STOCKHOLDERS' EQUITY

Notes payable..	$ 22
Accounts payable...	86
Accrued liabilities...	73
Accrued income taxes..	57
Total current liabilities....................................	$238
Long-term notes...	39
3⅜% debentures...	22
Other noncurrent liabilities..................................	10
Deferred investment tax credit...............................	9
Stockholders' equity:	
Common stock issued......................................	164
Retained earnings...	449
Common stock held in treasury, at cost......................	(2)
Total stockholders' equity.................................	$611
Total liabilities and stockholders' equity...................	$929
Common stock—shares outstanding at year-end.................	25,127,007

Exhibit 2

THE SUPER PROJECT

COMMON STOCK PRICES OF GENERAL
FOODS CORPORATION
1958–67

Year	Price Range
1958	$24 –$ 39¾
1959	37⅛– 53⅞
1960	49⅛– 75½
1961	68⅝– 107¾
1962	57¾– 96
1963	77⅝– 90½
1964	78¼– 93¼
1965	77½– 89⅞
1966	62¾– 83
1967	65¼– 81¾

Exhibit 3

THE SUPER PROJECT

TEN-YEAR SUMMARY OF STATISTICAL DATA OF GENERAL FOODS CORPORATION, 1958–67

(All dollar amounts in millions, except assets per employee and figures on a share basis)

Fiscal years	1958	1959	1960	1961	1962	1963	1964	1965	1966	1967
EARNINGS										
Sales to customers (net)	$1,009	$1,053	$1,087	$1,160	$1,189	$1,216	$1,338	$1,478	$1,555	$1,652
Cost of sales	724	734	725	764	769	769	838	937	965	1,012
Marketing, administrative, and general expenses	181	205	236	261	267	274	322	362	406	449
Earnings before income taxes	$ 105	$ 115	$ 130	$ 138	$ 156	$ 170	$ 179	$ 177	$ 185	$ 193
Taxes on income	57	61	69	71	84	91	95	91	91	94
Net earnings	$ 48	$ 54	$ 61	$ 67	$ 72	$ 79	$ 84	$ 86	$ 94	$ 99
Dividends on common shares	24	28	32	35	40	45	50	50	53	55
Retained earnings—current year	24	26	29	32	32	34	34	36	41	44
Net earnings per common share	$ 1.99	$ 2.21	$ 2.48	$ 2.69	$ 2.90	$ 3.14	$ 3.33	$ 3.44	$ 3.73	$ 3.93
Dividends per common share	$ 1.00	$ 1.15	$ 1.30	$ 1.40	$ 1.60	$ 1.80	$ 2.00	$ 2.00	$ 2.10	$ 2.20
ASSETS, LIABILITIES, AND STOCKHOLDERS' EQUITY										
Inventories	$ 169	$ 149	$ 157	$ 189	$ 183	$ 205	$ 256	$ 214	$ 261	$ 261
Other current assets	144	180	200	171	204	206	180	230	266	303
Current liabilities	107	107	126	123	142	162	202	173	219	238
Working capital	$ 206	$ 222	$ 230	$ 237	$ 245	$ 249	$ 234	$ 271	$ 308	$ 326
Land, buildings, equipment, gross	$ 203	$ 221	$ 247	$ 289	$ 328	$ 375	$ 436	$ 477	$ 517	$ 569
Land, buildings, equipment, net	125	132	148	173	193	233	264	283	308	332
Long-term debt	49	44	40	37	35	34	23	37	54	61
Stockholders' equity	$ 287	$ 315	$ 347	$ 384	$ 419	$ 454	$ 490	$ 527	$ 569	$ 611
Stockholders' equity per common share	$11.78	$12.87	$14.07	$15.46	$16.80	$18.17	$19.53	$20.99	$22.64	$24.32
CAPITAL PROGRAM										
Capital additions	$ 28	$ 24	$ 35	$ 40	$ 42	$ 57	$ 70	$ 54	$ 65	$ 59
Depreciation	11	14	15	18	21	24	26	29	32	34
EMPLOYMENT DATA										
Wages, salaries, and benefits	$ 128	$ 138	$ 147	$ 162	$ 171	$ 180	$ 195	$ 204	$ 218	$ 237
Number of employees (in thousands)	21	22	22	25	28	28	30	30	30	32
Assets per employee (in thousands)	$ 21	$ 22	$ 23	$ 22	$ 22	$ 23	$ 24	$ 25	$ 29	$ 29

Per share figures calculated on shares outstanding at year-end and adjusted for 2 for 1 stock split in August, 1960.

Exhibit 4

THE SUPER PROJECT

CRITERIA FOR EVALUATING PROJECTS BY GENERAL FOODS CORPORATION

The basic criteria to be applied in evaluating projects within each of the classifications are set forth in the following schedule:

Purpose of Project

a) SAFETY AND CONVENIENCE:

1. Projects required for reasons of safety, sanitation, health, public convenience, or other overriding reason with no reasonable alternatives. Examples: sprinkler systems, elevators, fire escapes, smoke control, waste disposal, treatment of water pollution, etc.

2. Additional nonproductive space requirements for which there are no financial criteria. Examples: office space, laboratories, service areas (kitchens, restrooms, etc.).

b) QUALITY:

Projects designed primarily to improve quality.

c) INCREASE PROFIT:

1. Projects that are justified primarily by reduced costs.

2. Projects that are designed primarily to increase production capacity for an existing product.

3. Projects designed to provide facilities to manufacture and distribute a new product or product line.

d) OTHER:

This category includes projects which by definition are excluded from the three preceding categories. Examples: standby facilities intended to insure uninterrupted production, additional equipment not expected to improve profits or product quality and not required for reasons of safety and convenience, equipment to satisfy marketing requirements, etc.

Payback and ROFE Criteria

Payback—return on funds projections not required but the request must clearly demonstrate the *immediate* need for the project and the lack or inadequacy of alternative solutions.

Requests for nonproductive facilities, such as warehouses, laboratories, and offices should indicate the advantages of owning rather than leasing, unless no possibility to lease exists. In those cases where the company owns a group of integrated facilities and wherein the introduction of rented or leased properties might complicate the long-range planning or development of the area, owning rather than leasing is recommended. If the project is designed to improve customer service (such as market centered warehouses) this factor is to be noted on the project request.

If payback and ROFE cannot be computed, it must be clearly demonstrated that the improvement is identifiable and desirable.

Projects with a payback period *up to 10 years* and a 10-year return *on* funds *as low as* 20% PBT are considered worthy of consideration, provided (1) the end product involved is believed to be a reasonably permanent part of our line or (2) the facilities involved are so flexible that they may be usable for successor products.

Projects for a proven product where the risk of mortality is small, such as coffee, Jell-O Gelatin, and cereals, should assure a payback in *no more than 10 years* and a 10-year PBT return on funds of *no less* than 20%.

Because of the greater risk involved such projects should show a high potential return *on* funds (not less than a 10-year PBT return of 40%). Payback period, however, might be as much as *10 years* because of losses incurred during the market development period.*

While standards of return may be difficult to set, some calculation of financial benefits should be made where possible.

* These criteria apply to the United States and Canada only. Profit-increasing capital projects in other areas in categories c1 and c2 should offer at least a 10-year PBT return of 24% to compensate for the greater risk involved. Likewise, foreign operation projects in the c3 category should offer a 10-year PBT return of at least 48%.

Exhibit 5

THE SUPER PROJECT
CAPITAL PROJECT REQUEST FORM OF GENERAL FOODS CORPORATION

NY 1292-A 12-63
PTD. IN U.S.A.

December 23, 1966
Date

"Super" Facilities   66-42
Project Title & Number

Jell-O Division - St. Louis
Division & Location

New Request [X]   Supplement [ ]

Expansion-New Product   [X] A
Purpose   [ ] R

PROJECT DESCRIPTION

To provide facilities for production of Super, chocolate dessert. This project included finishing a packing room in addition to filling and packaging equipment.

· SUMMARY OF INVESTMENT	
NEW CAPITAL FUNDS REQUIRED	$ 200M
EXPENSE BEFORE TAXES	--
LESS: TRADE-IN OR SALVAGE, IF ANY	--
Total This Request	$ 200M
PREVIOUSLY APPROPRIATED	--
Total Project Cost	$ 200M

FINANCIAL JUSTIFICATION*		
ROFE (PBT BASIS) - 10 YR. AVERAGE	62.9	%
PAYBACK PERIOD April, F'68 Feb. F'75	6.83	YRS.
FROM TO		
NOT REQUIRED ·	[ ]	
* BASED ON TOTAL PROJECT COST AND WORKING FUNDS OF	$ 510M	

ESTIMATED EXPENDITURE RATE		
QUARTER ENDING Mar. F19 67	$	160M
QUARTER ENDING June F19 68		40M
QUARTER ENDING F19		
QUARTER ENDING F19		
REMAINDER		

OTHER INFORMATION		
MAJOR [ ] SPECIFIC ORDINARY [ ]	BLANKET [ ]	
INCLUDED IN ANNUAL PROGRAM YES [ ] NO [ ]		
PER CENT OF ENGINEERING COMPLETED	80	%
ESTIMATED START-UP COSTS	$	1M
ESTIMATED START-UP DATE	April	

LEVEL OF APPROVAL REQUIRED
[ ] BOARD [ ] CHAIRMAN [ ] EXEC. V.P. [ ] GEN. MGR.

SIGNATURES		DATE
DIRECTOR CORP. ENG.		
DIRECTOR B & A		
GENERAL MANAGER		
VICE PRESIDENT		
EXEC. VICE PRESIDENT		
PRESIDENT		
CHAIRMAN		

For Division Use - Signatures	
NAME AND TITLE	DATE

Exhibit 5—Continued

INSTRUCTIONS FOR CAPITAL PROJECT REQUEST FORM NY 1292-A

The purpose of this form is to secure management's authorization to commit or expend funds on a capital project. Refer to Accounting and Financial Manual Statement No. 19 for information regarding projects to which this form applies.

NEW REQUEST—SUPPLEMENT: Check the appropriate box.

PURPOSE: Identify the primary purpose of the project in accordance with the classifications established in Accounting and Financial Statement No. 19, i.e., Sanitation, Health and Public Convenience, Non-Productive Space, Safety, Quality, Reduce Cost, Expansion— Existing Products, Expansion—New Products, Other (specify). Also indicate in the appropriate box whether the equipment represents an addition or a replacement.

PROJECT DESCRIPTION: Comments should be in sufficient detail to enable Corporate Management to appraise the benefits of the project. Where necessary, supplemental data should be attached to provide complete background for project evaluation.

SUMMARY OF INVESTMENT:

New Capital Funds Required: Show gross cost of assets to be acquired.
Expense before Taxes: Show incremental expense resulting from project.
Trade-in or Salvage: Show the amount expected to be realized on trade-in or sale of a replaced asset.
Previously Appropriated: When requesting a supplement to an approved project, show the amount previously appropriated even though authorization was given in a prior year.

FINANCIAL JUSTIFICATION:

ROFE: Show the return on funds employed (PBT basis) as calculated on Financial Evaluation Form NY 1292-C or 1292-F. The appropriate Financial Evaluation Form is to be attached to this form.
Not Required: Where financial benefits are not applicable or required or are not expected, check the box provided. The non-financial benefits should be explained in the comments.
In the space provided, show the sum of The Total Project Cost plus Total Working Funds (line 20, Form NY 1292-C or line 5, Form NY 1292-F) in either of the first three periods, whichever is higher.

ESTIMATED EXPENDITURE RATE: Expenditures are to be reported in accordance with accounting treatment of the asset and related expense portion of the project. Insert estimated quarterly expenditures beginning with the quarter in which the first expenditure will be made. The balance of authorized funds unspent after the fourth quarter should be reported in total.

OTHER INFORMATION: Check whether the project is a major, specific ordinary, or blanket, and whether or not the project was included in the Annual Program. Show estimated percentage of engineering completed; this is intended to give management an indication of the degree of reliability of the funds requested. Indicate the estimated start-up costs as shown on line 32 of Financial Evaluation Form NY 1292-C. Insert anticipated start-up date for the project; if start-up is to be staggered, explain in comments.

LEVEL OF APPROVAL REQUIRED: Check the appropriate box.

Exhibit 6

THE SUPER PROJECT
FINANCIAL EVALUATION FORM OF GENERAL FOODS CORPORATION
(Dollar figures in thousands)

MY 1292-C   10-64
PTD. IN U.S.A.

Jell-O / Division   St. Louis / Location   The Super Project / Project Title   67-89 / Project No.   Date   Supplement Sc.

PROJECT REQUEST DETAIL	1ST PER.	2ND PER.	___PER.	___PER.	___PER.
1. LAND	$				
2. BUILDINGS	80				
3. MACHINERY & EQUIPMENT	120				
4. ENGINEERING					
5. OTHER (EXPLAIN)					
6. EXPENSE PORTION (BEFORE TAX)					
7. SUB-TOTAL	$ 200				
8. LESS: SALVAGE VALUE (OLD ASSET)	200				
9. TOTAL PROJECT COST*					
10. LESS: TAXES ON EXP. PORTION					
11. NET PROJECT COST	$ 200				

RETURN ON NEW FUNDS EMPLOYED – 10-YR. AVG.

		PAT (C ÷ A)	PBT (B ÷ A)
A - NEW FUNDS EMPLOYED (LINE 21)		$ 380	$ 380
B - PROFIT BEFORE TAXES (LINE 35)		///////	239
C - NET PROFIT (LINE 37)		$ 115	///////
D - CALCULATED RETURN		30.2 %	62.9 %

PAYBACK YEARS FROM OPERATIONAL DATE

PART YEAR CALCULATION FOR FIRST PERIOD	–	YRS.
NUMBER OF FULL YEARS TO PAY BACK	6.00	YRS.
PART YEAR CALCULATION FOR LAST PERIOD	0.83	YRS.
TOTAL YEARS TO PAY BACK	6.83	Yrs.

*Same as Project Request

FUNDS EMPLOYED

	1ST PER. E.68	2ND PER. F 69	3RD PER. F 70	4TH PER. F 71	5TH PER. F 72	6TH PER. F 73	7TH PER. F 74	8TH PER. F 75	9TH PER. F 76	10TH PER. F 77	11TH PER.	10-YR. AVG.
12. NET PROJECT COST (LINE 11)	$ 200	200	200	200	200	200	200	200	200	200		
13. DEDUCT DEPRECIATION (CUM.)	19	37	54	70	85	98	110	121	131	140		
14. CAPITAL FUNDS EMPLOYED	$ 181	163	146	130	115	102	90	79	69	60		113
15. CASH	124	134	142	151	160	160	169	169	178	173		157
16. RECEIVABLES												
17. INVENTORIES	207	222	237	251	266	266	281	281	296	296		260
18. PREPAID & DEFERRED EXP.												
19. LESS CURRENT LIABILITIES	(2)	(82)	(108)	(138)	(185)	(184)	(195)	(195)	(207)	(207)		(150)
20. TOTAL WORKING FUNDS (15 THRU 19)	329	274	271	264	241	242	255	255	267	267		267
21. TOTAL NEW FUNDS EMPLOYED (14 + 20)	$ 510	437	417	394	356	344	345	334	336	327		380

PROFIT AND LOSS

	1ST	2ND	3RD	4TH	5TH	6TH	7TH	8TH	9TH	10TH	11TH	10-YR. AVG.
22. UNIT VOLUME (in thousands)	1100	1200	1300	1400	1500	1500	1600	1600	1700	1700		1460
23. GROSS SALES	2200	2400	2600	2800	3000	3000	3200	3200	3400	3400		2920
24. DEDUCTIONS	88	96	104	112	120	120	128	128	136	136		117
25. NET SALES	2112	2304	2496	2688	2880	2880	3072	3072	3264	3264		2803
26. COST OF GOODS SOLD	1100	1200	1300	1400	1500	1500	1600	1600	1700	1700		1460
27. GROSS PROFIT	1012	1104	1196	1288	1380	1380	1472	1472	1564	1564		1343
GROSS PROFIT % NET SALES	%											
28. ADVERTISING EXPENSE												
29. SELLING EXPENSE	1100	1050	1000	900	700	700	730	730	750	750		841
30. GEN. AND ADMIN. COSTS												
31. RESEARCH EXPENSE												
32. START-UP COSTS	15											2
33. OTHER (EXPLAIN) Test Mkt.	360											36
34. ADJUSTMENTS (EXPLAIN) Erosion	180	200	210	220	230	230	240	240	250	250		225
35. PROFIT BEFORE TAXES	(643)	(146)	(14)	168	450	450	502	502	564	564		239
36. TAXES	(334)	(76)	(7)	87	234	234	261	261	293	293		125
36A. ADD: INVESTMENT CREDIT	(1)	(1)	(1)	(1)	(1)	(1)	(1)	(1)	-	-		(1)
37. NET PROFIT	(308)	(69)	(6)	82	217	217	242	242	271	271		115
38. CUMULATIVE NET PROFIT	(308)	(377)	(383)	(301)	(84)	133	375	617	888	1159		
39. NEW FUNDS TO REPAY (21 LESS 38)	$ 818	814	800	695	440	211	(30)	(283)	(552)	(832)		

Exhibit 6—Continued

INSTRUCTIONS FOR PREPARATION OF FORM NY 1292-C
FINANCIAL EVALUATION

This form is to be submitted to Corporate Budget and Analysis with each profit-increasing capital project request requiring $50,000 or more of capital funds and expense before taxes.

Note that the ten-year term has been divided into eleven periods. The first period is to end on the March 31st following the operational date of the project, and the P & L projection may thereby encompass any number of months from one to twelve, e.g., if the project becomes operational on November 1, 1964, the first period for P & L purposes would be 5 months (November 1, 1964 through March 31, 1965). The next nine periods would be fiscal years (F'66, F'67, etc.) and the eleventh period would be 7 months (April 1, 1974 through October 30, 1974). This has been done primarily to facilitate reporting of projected and actual P & L data by providing for fiscal years. See categorized instructions below for more specific details.

Project Request Detail: Lines 1 through 11 show the breakdown of the Net Project Cost to be used in the financial evaluation. *Line 8* is to show the amount expected to be realized on trade-in or sale of a replaced asset. *Line 9* should be the same as the "Total Project Cost" shown on Form NY 1292-A, Capital Project Request. Space has been provided for capital expenditures related to this project which are projected to take place subsequent to the first period. Indicate in such space the additional costs only; do not accumulate them.

Funds Employed:

Capital Funds Employed: *Line 12* will show the net project cost appearing on line 11 as a constant for the first ten periods except in any period in which additional expenditures are incurred; in that event show the accumulated amounts of line 11 in such period and in all future periods.

Deduct cumulative depreciation on *line 13*. Depreciation is to be computed on an incremental basis i.e., the net increase in depreciation over present depreciation will be computed at one half of the first year's annual rate; no depreciation is to be taken in the eleventh period. Depreciation rates are to be the same as those used for accounting purposes. *Exception:* When the depreciation rate used for accounting purposes differs materially from the rate for tax purposes, the higher rate should be used. A variation will be considered material when the first full year's depreciation on a book basis varies 20% or more from the first full year's depreciation on a tax basis.

The ten-year average of Capital Funds Employed shall be computed by adding line 14 in each of the first ten periods and dividing the total by ten.

Total Working Funds: Refer to Financial Policy No. 21 as a guide in computing new working fund requirements. Items which are not on a formula basis and which are normally computed on a five-quarter average shall be handled proportionately in the first period. For example, since the period involved may be less than 12 months, the average would be computed on the number of quarters involved. Generally, the balances should be approximately the same as they would be if the first period were a full year.

Cash, based on a formula which theorizes a two weeks' supply $(2/52$nds), should follow the same theory. If the first period is for three months, two-thirteenths $(2/13$ths) should be used; if it is for 5 months, two-twenty-firsts $(2/21$sts) should be used, and so forth. Current liabilities are to include one half of the tax expense as the tax liability. The ten-year averages of Working Funds shall be computed by adding each line across for the first ten periods and dividing each total by ten.

Profit and Loss Projection

P & L Categories (Lines 22 through 37): Reflect only the incremental amounts which will result from the proposed project; exclude all allocated charges. Include the P & L results expected in the individual periods comprising the first ten years of the project. Refer to the second paragraph of these instructions regarding the fractional years' calculations during the first and eleventh periods.

Any loss or gain on the sale of a replaced asset (see line 8) shall be included in line 33.

As indicated in the caption Capital Funds Employed, no depreciation is to be taken in the eleventh period.

The ten-year averages of the P & L items shall be computed by adding each line across for the eleven periods (10 full years from the operational date) and dividing the total by ten.

Adjustments (Line 34): Show the adjustment necessary, on a before-tax basis, to indicate any adverse or favorable incremental effect the proposed project will have on any other products currently being produced by the corporation.

Investment Credit is to be included on Line 36-A. The Investment Credit will be spread over 8 years, or fractions thereof, as an addition to PAT.

Return on New Funds Employed: Ten-year average returns are to be calculated for PAT (projects requiring Board approval only) and PBT. The PAT return is calculated by dividing average PAT (line 37) by average new funds employed (line 21); the PBT return is derived by dividing average PBT (line 35) by average new funds employed (line 21).

Payback Years from Operational Date:

Part Year Calculation for First Period: Divide number of months in the first period by twelve. If five months are involved, the calculation is $5/12 = .4$ years.

Number of Full Years to Pay Back: Determined by the last period, excluding the first period, in which an amount is shown on line 39.

Part Year Calculation for Last Period: Divide amount still to be repaid at the end of the last full period (line 39) by net profit plus the *annual* depreciation in the following year when payback is completed.

Total Years to Pay Back: Sum of full and part years.

MRC, INC. (A)

∧∧

In late March, 1961, Archibald Brinton, president of MRC, Inc., was grappling with the question of whether to acquire American Rayon, Inc. (ARI). Mr. Brinton was troubled by ARI's erratic earnings record and mediocre long-run outlook. However, he recognized that MRC could benefit greatly from ARI's liquidity and borrowing capacity. He was therefore inclined to go through with the acquisition, provided ARI could be purchased at a price that promised to yield MRC an adequate return on its money.

BACKGROUND INFORMATION ON MRC

MRC was a Cleveland based manufacturing concern with 1960 earnings of $3.9 million on sales of over $118 million. The most important product lines were power brake systems for trucks, buses, and automobiles; industrial furnaces and heat treating equipment; and automobile, truck, and bus frames. Exhibit 1 presents data on the operating results and financial position of MRC.

Diversification program

Upon becoming chief executive officer in 1957, Mr. Brinton had initiated an active program of diversification by acquisition. The need for rapid diversification seemed compelling. Until 1957, virtually all sales were made to less than a dozen large companies in the automotive industry, with car and truck frames accounting for 85% of the $70 million sales total. As a result, earnings, cash flow, and growth were constantly exposed to the risks inherent in selling to a few customers, all of which operated in a highly cyclical and competitive market. Previous attempts at internal diversification had floundered on management's lack of expertise in markets and technologies outside the automotive area. Mr. Brinton had therefore turned to acquisitions as a means of buying up established sales and earnings as well as managerial and technical knowhow. In Mr. Brinton's words, the acquisition strategy was "intended (1) to achieve related diversification and thus lessen vulnerability to technological change in a single industry; (2) to stabilize earnings and cash flow; (3) to uncouple growth prospects from the cyclical and unexciting automotive industry; and (4) to escape the constant threat of backward integration by one or more major customers." The drive for diversification had been intensified in 1959 when Chrysler announced a move toward unitized, i.e., "frameless" body construction.

By the end of 1960, the diversification campaign had resulted in the completion of five acquisitions, two of which were major transactions. Acquisition of Ross Engineering Corporation increased MRC sales by $27 million in 1957, and the purchase of Surface Combustion Corporation in 1959 added about $38 million to annual sales. The acquisition history of MRC is shown in Exhibit 2. Significantly, total sales increased almost $50 million between 1956 and 1960, despite a $30 million decline in automotive sales over that period.

Management structure

While the diversification program had reduced MRC's dependence on any one industry, it had also created significant strains on the company's organization structure and financial position.

As the acquisition program carried MRC into a widening variety of markets and technologies, it had become increasingly apparent that the company's highly centralized decision making processes were ill suited to the needs of a diversified corporation. By the end of 1959, it was clear the headquarters management group could not acquire or maintain detailed knowledge of all the products, markets and technologies embraced by MRC. Since continued rapid diversification was considered imperative, the company had shifted to a highly decentralized management structure, which transferred substantial decision making power to division managers.

In 1961, there were seven divisions. All marketing, purchasing, manufacturing, research and development, personnel matters, and accounting were handled at the division level. Each division had its own general manager (usually a vice president), who reported directly to Mr. Brinton and had the primary responsibility for the growth and profitability of his division. A division manager could get stock options and earn an annual bonus of up to 60% of his base salary, depending on the earnings and growth of his division. Divisional sales and earnings goals were formalized in an annual budget and in a rolling five-year plan, which were formulated by each general manager and submitted each November to the head office for review by Mr. Brinton and the corporate staff.

The corporate staff provided legal, administrative, and financial support to the divisions and handled external affairs, financing, and acquisitions as well. The staff, including corporate officers, numbered less than 60 people about half of whom would be classified as secretarial and clerical.

Mr. Brinton felt that he could exercise adequate control over the decentralized organization through his power to hire and fire at the division manager level and, more importantly, through control of the elaborate capital budgeting system. Appendix A discusses MRC's capital budgeting procedures.

No acquisitions were made in 1960. But by 1961, Mr. Brinton was confident that the organization was capable of smoothly assimilating new operations, and his staff had identified and opened preliminary discussions with a number of attractive acquisition prospects. However, the financial problems brought on by the strain of financing past acquisitions had become pressing.

Finances

The acquisition campaign had been hampered from the outset by MRC's low price-earnings (P/E) multiple. Although growth was an explicit objective of the acquisition program, MRC could not exchange its shares for those of high P/E, growth companies without absorbing a stiff dilution in per share earnings. It was feared that such dilution of earnings per share would further depress the P/E ratio and thus make it still more difficult to swap stock with growth companies. Consequently, MRC had been forced to rely heavily on debt financing for most of its acquisitions.

By early 1961, MRC had largely exhausted its borrowing capacity. Between 1956 and 1960, long-term debt had risen from less than $4 million to more than $22 million. Although it appeared that capital expenditures planned for 1961 could be funded with internally generated funds, the near exhaustion of debt capacity posed a serious threat to the acquisition strategy. Discussions with commercial banks, life insurance companies, and investment bankers had made it clear that any further increases in long-term debt, without a substantial infusion of new equity, would be extremely difficult, and probably impossible. Investment bankers had further pointed out that long-term lenders would probably insist on severely restricting the company's flexibility to make cash acquisitions, even if it should prove feasible to raise new debt. With MRC near its debt limit and the P/E ratio around 10 times, the entire diversification campaign was in danger of collapsing.

ARI, with its $20 million of marketable securities, appeared to provide a convenient new source of funds with which to fuel the acquisition program.

BACKGROUND INFORMATION ON ARI

American Rayon, Inc., a Philadelphia based corporation, was the third largest producer of rayon in the United States.[1] In 1960, ARI had recorded sales of $55 million and a pretax profit of $5 million, after three years of severe profit problems (see Exhibits 3 and 4). By early 1961 the company's stock was trading at less than half of book value on the New York Stock Exchange and top management feared that the company's new-found profitability, along with its great liquidity and a disenchanted shareholder group, would make ARI attractive to raiders. Consequently, management was seeking to arrange a marriage with a congenial partner. ARI's investment banker had brought the company to the attention of Mr. Brinton, who had expressed tentative interest in a deal.

---
[1] Rayon is a glossy fiber made by forcing a viscous solution of modified cellulose (wood pulp) through minute holes and drying the resulting filaments.

Acquisition investigation

The results of MRC's investigation were mixed. On the plus side, ARI had over $20 million in liquid assets that were not needed for operations, no short or long-term debt, and a modern central manufacturing facility. It appeared that the company could be purchased for about $40 million worth of MRC common stock. Moreover, although ARI top management was elderly, James Clinton, the 64-year-old president, was willing to stay on for two years after the acquisition to give MRC personnel a chance to learn the business before his retirement.

On the other hand, the longer-term outlook for the rayon industry was grim. The rayon industry had enjoyed one of the most spectacular successes in the history of American enterprise. For example, the American Viscose Corporation, which founded the industry in 1910, achieved in its first 24 years aggregate net earnings of $354,000,000 or 38,000% of original investment, while financing rapid expansion entirely out of earnings.[2] But rayon began to falter in the early 1950's as competing synthetics such as nylon and acrylic became popular. Style and fashion shifts also made cotton more attractive. The net effect was to force production cutbacks in rayon, and by the end of the 1950's many companies, including Du Pont, had withdrawn from the rayon industry altogether.

With shrinking industry volume, ARI had experienced increasing earnings difficulties. These difficulties could be traced directly to the declining use of rayon in automobile tire cord, the market accounting for upwards of 60% of ARI's output. First tried in tire construction in 1940, the use of rayon in tire manufacture reached an annual peak around 1955.[3] With the advent of nylon cord, however, rayon's market share in tire cord began to decline. Between 1955 and 1960, rayon's share of the total tire cord market dropped from 86% to 64%, and the total poundage of rayon so used dropped 38% (see Exhibit 5).

Prospects for ARI

It was clear to MRC management that the medium to long-run future must hold continuing decline and eventual liquidation for ARI. If purchased, ARI could not be expected to contribute to the MRC growth objectives, and in time it might well become a serious drag on earnings. Consequently, Mr. Brinton was somewhat leery of pushing through to an acquisition. He was not at all sure that ARI, trapped in a decaying industry, would contribute to the strategic objectives of the diversification program. He was afraid that MRC would get entangled in a dying business, and he knew that MRC management lacked the technical know-how to contribute to the profitability of ARI, should the

---

[2] Jesse W. Markham, *Competition in the Rayon Industry* (Cambridge, Mass.: Harvard University Press, 1952), p. 16.

[3] C. A. Litzler, "The Fluid Tire Cord Situation," *Modern Textiles Magazine*, September 1966, p. 20.

forecasts for this business prove optimistic. Moreover, he was not at all sure that the recently overhauled organization structure could easily assimilate a company as large as ARI. In the face of these concerns, he was reluctant to move quickly, whatever the DCF-ROI (discounted cash flow-return on investment) numbers might show.

However, the near-term picture, as presented by Richard Victor, vice president for mergers and acquisitions, was not entirely unappealing. Although losses were sustained in 1957 and 1958 the company had subsequently returned to profitability as a result of substantial reductions in overhead, sale or liquidation of marginal and unprofitable operations, streamlining the marketing and R&D organizations, and consolidating production in a new manufacturing facility. Based on the investigation and analysis of his staff, he estimated that ARI would be able to maintain current volume, prices and margins through 1964, followed thereafter by annual sales declines of 10% to 15%. He also estimated that assumption of numerous staff responsibilities by the MRC corporate staff would add about one percentage point to ARI's before tax profit margin. Exhibit 6 shows pro forma income statements for ARI prepared by the MRC acquisition team.

From a financing point of view, it was thought that capital spending needs over the next six to eight years would average no more than $300,000 annually. Mr. Victor felt that, if anything, his estimates understated future profits, since he expected ARI to pick up market share as smaller companies continued to withdraw from the rayon industry.

VALUATION

At a price of $40 million, ARI looked cheap. But Mr. Brinton insisted that any acquisition undertaken by MRC must promise to yield an adequate return, as measured by its discounted cash flow rate of return (DCF-ROI).[4] Mr. Brinton regarded an acquisition decision as a special case of the capital budgeting decision. Like a capital budgeting project, an acquisition required the commitment of economic resources, cash or common stock or debt capacity, in the expectation of realizing a future income stream. Consequently, the primary valuation procedure used in acquisitions was conceptually identical to the capital budgeting procedure (see Appendix A). All outlays and all cash inflows that were expected to result from undertaking a particular transaction were projected, and the DCF-ROI was found. In terms of required rates of return, acquisitions were considered to be very similar to new product introductions.

Exhibit 7 shows management's forecast of MRC's per share income for the next three years.

MRC's common stock had closed the day before at 14½. ARI had closed at 15.

---

[4] This measure of effectiveness is also commonly known as the internal rate of return, the time adjusted rate of return, and the yield.

Exhibit 1

MRC, INC. (A)

FOUR-YEAR SUMMARY OF FINANCIAL DATA

(Dollar figures in millions except per share data)

	1957	1958	1959	1960
Results of Operations				
Sales:				
Automotive and transportation................	$ 76.4	$49.7	$56.8	$ 41.3
Capital goods.............................	30.0	26.0	27.5	54.3
Building and construction....................	—	—	2.7	14.2
Aerospace and defense.......................	0.9	0.7	1.8	8.3
Total...............................	$107.3	$76.4	$88.8	$118.1
Net earnings..................................	5.5	3.0	4.0	3.9
Depreciation and amortization..................	1.4	1.5	1.7	2.3
Cash funds from operations*...................	6.2	3.8	4.9	5.5
Return on total capital.......................	12.6%	8.1%	7.8%	9.3%
Return on common equity......................	18.4%	8.9%	14.3%	13.2%
Common Stock				
Net earnings per share[†]........................	$ 1.73	$ 0.82	$ 1.18	$ 1.16
Common dividends per share...................	0.94	0.79	0.75	0.75
Market price................................	13–8	10–8	15–9	13–9
Average price-earnings ratio....................	6.5	12.1	10.3	9.5
Average dividend yield........................	8.4%	7.9%	6.2%	6.8%
Financial Position				
Working capital.............................	$ 26.9	$22.5	$28.7	$ 31.3
Net property, plant, and equipment.............	15.6	16.0	23.1	28.4
Long-term debt..............................	4.3	9.6	16.5	22.7
Preferred and common shareholders' equity.......	39.6	39.5	40.5	41.6

* Net earnings plus depreciation, amortization, and deferred taxes, less preferred dividends.
† Calculated on average number of shares outstanding during the year.

Exhibit 2

MRC, INC. (A)

ACQUISITION HISTORY OF MRC, INC.

December, 1957........ Acquired J. O. Ross Engineering Corporation in exchange for 281,000 shares.

March, 1958.......... Acquired Hartig Engine and Machine Company, Mountainside, New Jersey, for cash and notes.

October, 1958........ Acquired Transportation Division of Consolidated Metal Products Corporation, Albany, New York, and moved operations to Owosso, Michigan, Division.

April, 1959........... Acquired Nelson Metal Products Company, Grand Rapids, Michigan, for cash.

November, 1959....... Acquired Surface Combustion Corporation, Toledo, Ohio, for $23 million cash.

Exhibit 3

MRC, INC. (A)

FIVE-YEAR SUMMARY OF FINANCIAL DATA ON AMERICAN RAYON, INC.

(Dollar figures in millions except per share data)

	1956	1957	1958	1959	1960
Results of Operations					
Net sales.............................	$59.3	$58.1	$47.9	$62.1	$54.5
Earnings before taxes.................	9.4	(2.3)	(6.2)	1.7	4.8
Pretax profit margin..................	15.9%	—	—	2.7%	8.8%
Net earnings.........................	$ 4.5	$(1.2)	$(3.2)	$ 0.8	$ 2.5
Depreciation and amortization.........	3.9	4.0	4.1	4.3	3.3
Cash funds from operations............	8.4	2.8	0.9	5.1	5.8
Return on total capital...............	5.3%	—	—	1.0%	3.4%
Return on common equity.............	5.9%	—	—	1.1%	3.8%
Common Stock					
Net earnings per share*...............	$ 2.45	$(0.65)	$(1.69)	$ 0.44	$ 1.34
Common dividend per share*..........	3.00	1.75	—	—	—
Book value per share*................	39.68	39.05	37.37	37.79	36.42
Market price.........................	48–37	24–11	14–6	13–8	19–9
Average price-earnings ratio...........	17	—	—	23.9	10.4
Financial Position					
Working capital......................	$39.1	$38.8	$36.6	$37.9	$41.2
Net property, plant, and equipment. ..	36.6	34.1	34.2	33.8	23.9
Long-term debt.......................	—	—	—	—	—
Common shareholders' equity.........	75.4	74.2	71.0	71.8	65.2

* Based on 1,851,255 common shares outstanding.

Exhibit 4

MRC, INC. (A)

BALANCE SHEET OF AMERICAN RAYON, INC.
AS OF DECEMBER 31, 1960

(In thousands)

ASSETS

Cash	$ 2,564
U.S. Government securities*	20,024
Accounts receivable, net	11,863
Inventories:	
Finished goods	4,376
In process	2,161
Raw materials and supplies	3,919
	$10,456
Prepaid expenses	283
Current assets	$45,190
Property, plant, and equipment, net	23,912
Other	125
Total assets	$69,227

LIABILITIES AND SHAREHOLDERS' EQUITY

Accounts payable	$ 2,863
Accrued items	1,145
Current liabilities	$ 4,008
Common stock	26,959
Retained earnings	38,260
Shareholders' equity	$65,219
Total liabilities and shareholders' equity	$69,227

* Carried at cost plus accrued interest which approximates market.

Exhibit 5

MRC, INC. (A)

CONSUMPTION OF TIRE CORD

(In millions)

	Rayon		Nylon		Cotton		Total
Year	Pounds	Market Share	Pounds	Market Share	Pounds	Market Share	Pounds
1947	214.6	43%	n.a.	—	285.1	57%	499.7
1950	297.0	64	n.a.	—	165.4	36	462.4
1955	406.9	86	49.2	10%	16.7	4	472.8
1956	343.0	83	58.6	14	10.6	3	412.2
1957	318.5	77	83.2	20	10.3	3	412.0
1958	253.0	71	97.9	27	7.1	2	358.0
1959	287.1	70	120.3	29	3.9	1	411.2
1960	251.3	64	138.1	35	3.1	1	392.5

Sources: 1947–55: U.S. Bureau of the Census, *Statistical Abstract of the United States–1967* (Washington, D.C.: U.S. Government Printing Office), p. 761; 1956–60: American Rayon, Inc., Proxy Statement, March 28, 1961, p. 6.

Exhibit 6

MRC, INC. (A)

PRO FORMA INCOME STATEMENTS OF AMERICAN RAYON, INC.

(In thousands)

Year Ended	1961	1962	1963	1964	1965	1966	1967
Net sales..................	$55,000	$55,000	$55,000	$52,000	$48,000	$42,600	$40,070
Earnings before taxes........	4,840	5,390	5,390	3,640	2,724	1,917	841
Federal income taxes........	2,323	2,587	2,587	1,747	1,308	920	404
Net earnings..............	2,517	2,803	2,803	1,893	1,416	997	437
Depreciation..............	3,000	3,000	3,000	3,000	3,000	3,000	3,000
Cash funds from operations...	5,517	5,803	5,803	4,893	4,416	3,997	3,437

Exhibit 7

MRC, INC. (A)

THREE-YEAR FORECAST OF MRC EARNINGS

Year Ended	1961	1962	1963
Net earnings*..............	$4,723,000	$5,054,000	$5,458,000
Earnings per share†.........	$ 1.46	$ 1.59	$ 1.74

* Assumes funding for all projects tentatively approved in 1961 capital budget, but no new acquisitions.

† Based on 2,706,896 common shares outstanding and preferred dividends of $760,000.

APPENDIX A

MRC, INC. (A)

CAPITAL BUDGETING PROCEDURES OF MRC, INC.

The formal capital budgeting procedures of MRC were outlined in a 49-page manual written for use at the divisional level and entitled "Expenditure Control Procedures." This document outlined (1) the classification scheme for types of funds requests, (2) the minimum levels of expenditure for which formal requests were required, (3) the maximum expenditure which could be authorized on the signature of corporate officers at various levels, (4) the format of the financial analysis required in a request for funds to carry out a project, and finally (5) the format of the report which followed the completion of the project and evaluated its success in terms of the original financial analysis outlined in (4).

Classification scheme for funds requests

The manual defined two basic classes of projects: profit improvement and necessity. Profit improvement projects included:

a) Cost reduction projects.
b) Capacity expansion projects in existing product lines.
c) New product line introductions.

Necessity projects included:

All projects where profit improvement was not the basic purpose of the project, such as those for service facilities, plant security, improved working conditions, employee relations and welfare, pollution and contamination prevention, extensive repairs and replacements, profit maintenance, and services of outside research and consultant agencies. Expense projects of an unusual or extraordinary character included in this class were those expenses which did not lend themselves to inclusion in the operating budget and could normally be expected to occur less than once per year.

Minimum amounts subject to formal request

Not all divisional requests for funds required formal and specific economic justification. Obviously, normal operating expenditures for items such as raw materials and wages were managed completely at the level of the divisions. Capital expenditures and certain nonrecurring operating expenditures were subject to formal requests and specific economic justification if they exceeded certain minimum amount levels specified below.

Project Appropriation Requests were to be issued as follows:

1. Capital:

Projects with a unit cost equal to or more than the unit cost in the following schedule shall be covered by a Project Appropriation Request: items with lesser unit costs shall be expensed.

Land improvements and buildings	$1,000
Machinery and equipment	500
Tools, patterns, dies, and jigs	250
Office furniture and office machines	100

2. Expense:

Expenses of an unusual or extraordinary character which do not lend themselves to inclusion in the operating budget and could normally be expected to occur less than once per year shall be covered by a Project Appropriation Request.

The minimum amount at which a Project Appropriation Request for expense is required is $10,000.

Approval limits of corporate officers

Officers at various management levels within MRC had the authority to approve a division's formal request for funds to carry out a project subject to the maximum limitations shown below.

Approvals. Requests shall be processed from a lower approval level to a higher approval level in accordance with the chart below to secure the approving authorities' initials (and date approved) signifying approval. Lower approvals shall be completed in advance of submission to a higher level.

Highest Approval
Level Required

Expense projects:
Minimum up to $10,000................... Division manager
$10,000 up to $50,000...................... Corporate president
$50,000 and over......................... Board of directors

Capital projects:
Minimum up to $5,000.................... Division manager
$5,000 up to $50,000...................... Corporate president
$50,000 and over......................... Board of directors

Expense and capital combinations:
Required approvals shall be the higher approval level required for either the capital or expense section in accordance with the above limits.

Project Appropriation Request

The formal financial analysis required in a request for funds was called a Project Appropriation Request (PAR). The format of a PAR is shown in Exhibit A–1. The key output factors in the analysis (which included the amount of the total appropriation, the discounted cash flow rate of return on the investment, and the payback period) were summarized on the opening page under "Financial Summary" for easy reference.

The PAR originated at the divisional level and circulated to the officers whose signatures were necessary to authorize the expenditure. If the project was large enough to require the approval of an officer higher than the division manager, then five other members of the corporate financial group also reviewed the proposal. This group included the controller, the tax manager, the director of financial planning, the treasurer, and the vice president of finance. These managers did not review very small projects, however, since capital items under $5000 never reached the corporate office. Division managers could authorize these small projects on their own signature.

Project Evaluation Report

On each PAR, the corporate controller had the option of indicating whether or not he desired a Project Evaluation Report (PER). When requested, the division manager submitted this report one year after the approved project was completed. The report indicated how well the project was performing in relation to its original cost, return on investment (ROI), and payback estimates.

The stream of PARs reaching the corporate office

During 1960, MRC approved 70 PARs calling for the expenditure of more than $17 million.

A sample evaluation made in 1961 of some of the projects which the board of directors had approved in earlier years is reproduced as Exhibit A–2.

Scrutinizing a PAR at the presidential level

In discussing capital budgeting at MRC, Mr. Brinton stated that the largest projects, involving more than a million dollars, were almost always discussed informally between the president and the division manager at least a year before a formal PAR was submitted. He said:

Let's look at a project involving a facilities expansion. The need for a new plant addition in most of our business areas doesn't sneak up on you. It can be foreseen at least a couple of years in advance. An enormous amount of work is involved in submitting a detailed economic proposal for something like a new plant. Architects have to draft plans, proposed sites have to be outlined, and construction lead times need to be established. No division manager would submit a complete request for a new facilities addition without first getting an informal green light that such a proposal could receive favorable attention. By the time a formal PAR is completed on a large plant addition, most of us are pretty well sold on the project.

In response to the question, "What are the most significant items that you look at when a new PAR lands on your desk?" Mr. Brinton responded as follows:

The size of the project is probably the first thing that I look at. Obviously, I won't spend much time on a $15,000 request for a new fork-lift truck from a division manager with an annual sales volume of $50 million.

I'd next look at the type of project we're dealing with to get a feel for the degree of certainty in the rate of return calculation. I feel a whole lot more comfortable with a cost reduction project promising a 20% return than I would with a volume expansion project which promises the same rate of return. Cost reduction is usually an engineering problem. You know exactly how much a new machine will cost and you can be fairly certain about how many man-hours will be saved. On a volume expansion you're betting on a marketing estimate and maybe the date for getting a plant on stream. These are fairly uncertain variables.

On a new product appropriation, things get even worse. Here you're betting on both price and volume estimates, and supporting data can get awfully thin. Over all, I think our cost reduction projects have probably yielded higher returns and have been less risky than either plant expansion or new product proposals. They don't, of course, eat up anything like the amount of capital that the other two types of projects can require.

The third and perhaps most important item that I look for is the name of the division manager who sent the project up. We've got managers at the top and at the bottom of the class just like any organization. If I get a project from an individual who has been with the company for a few years, who has turned a division around, or shown that he has a better command of his business than anyone else in his industry, then I'll usually go with his judgment. If his business is going to pot, however, I may take a long hard look, challenge a lot of the assumptions, and ask for more justification.

Fourth, I look at the ROI figure. If the project is a large one, I have the finance people massage the numbers to see what happens to the ROI if some of the critical variables like volume, prices, and costs are varied. This is an area where knowing your division manager is enormously important. Some managers, particularly those with a sales background, may be very optimistic on volume projections. In this kind of situation you feel more comfortable if you can knock the volume down 25% and still see a reasonable return.

I haven't established formal and inviolable hurdle rates which each and every project must clear. I want to avoid giving the division people an incentive to stretch their estimates on marginal projects or, alternatively, to build in fat cushions—insurance policies—on great projects. Still, I generally look for a minimum DCF-ROI of about 12% on cost reduction proposals, 15% to 16% on large volume expansion projects and 18% to 20% or even more on new product introductions. But these aren't magic numbers. Projects showing lower yields are sometimes accepted.

Strategic capital investments

Mr. Brinton later commented on a question regarding the role of capital budgeting in overall corporate strategy.

In general we'll invest our capital in those business areas that promise the highest return. Usually you can't afford to establish a position in a market on just the hope that a return will materialize in the future. Du Pont can afford to invest $75 million in a new fiber, but MRC can't. We can afford to invest a few million dollars in projects of this nature—and we have in areas like continuous casting and iron ore pelletizing—but most of our projects have to promise a prompt return.

Exhibit A–1

MRC, INC. (A)

PROJECT APPROPRIATION REQUEST

Division		Department	Location	
Power Controls				

Title

Disc Brake Manufacturing Facility

Profit Improvement	Necessity	Predicted Life	Underrun	Overrun	Starting Date	Completion Date
X		15 Years			July 1961	April 1963

1. DESCRIPTION AND JUSTIFICATION

The U.S. automotive industry is experiencing a trend to the use of disc braking systems for passenger cars and light trucks. Our market research indicates this type of braking system will be widespread within 5 years and the Power Controls Division can be a major supplier of these systems if we act now to provide the required manufacturing facilities.

2. FINANCIAL SUMMARY

	This Request	Previous Approved Requests	Total Project	Approval and Distribution of Copies					
				Division	Date	No.	Corporate	Date	No.
Capital	4,875,000	———	4,875,000	Issued By			Group V.P.		
Working Capital	1,950,000		1,950,000				Group V.P.		
Expense	975,000		975,000						
Total	7,800,000		7,800,000				Controller		
Less Salvage Value of Disposals							Tax Manager		
Net							Mgr. Fin. Planning		
Book Value of Disposals							Treasurer		
Project Budgeted Amount			7,800,000				Financial V.P.		
Return on Investment (after Tax)			16%	Division Controller			President		
Period to Amortize (after Tax)			3.6 Years	Division Manager			For the Board		
Accounting Distribution				Project Evaluation Report Required	Yes	No			

Estimated Timing of Expenditures – By Quarter and Year							
3/61	4/61	1/62	2/62	3/62	4/62	1/63	2/63
$ 75,000	$125,000	$1,125,000	$1,500,000	$1,500,000	$1,875,000	$ 900,000	$ 700,000

Exhibit A-1—Continued

PRESENT VALUE OF CASH FLOWS

YEAR	YEAR OF OPER- ATION	DISBURSEMENTS	CASH RETURNS	15% TRIAL INTEREST RATE Factor	15% PRESENT WORTH Disbursements	15% PRESENT WORTH Cash Returns	16% TRIAL INTEREST RATE Factor	16% PRESENT WORTH Disbursements	16% PRESENT WORTH Cash Returns	% TRIAL INTEREST RATE Factor	% PRESENT WORTH Disbursements	% PRESENT WORTH Cash Returns
1961	2 Prior	200					1.346	269				
1962	1 Prior	6,000	218				1.160	6,960	253			↑
			Beginning of Operations									
1963	At 1	'1,600	468	1.000	xxxxxxxxxxxx	xxxxxxxxxxx	1.000	1,132	xxxxxxxxxx	1.000		xxxxxxxxxxx
1963	1		641		xxxxxxxxxxxx		.862	xxxxxxxxxxxx	553		xxxxxxxxxxx	
	2		1,792				.743		1,331			
	3		1,686				.641		1,081			
	4		1,601				.552		884			
	5		1,523				.476		725			
	6		1,473				.410		604			
	7		1,443				.354		511			
	8		1,439				.305		439			
	9		1,434				.263		377			
	10		1,432				.227		325			
	11		1,337				.195		261			
	12		1,241				.168		208			
	13		1,241				.145		180			
	14		1,241				.125		155			
	15		1,400				.108		151			
	15 Return Work Cap.		1,950				.108		210			
	15 Residual Plant		885				.108		96			
	18											
	19											
	20											
	21											
	22											
	23											
	24											
	25											
	26											
	27											
	28											
	29											
	30											
	TOTALS	7,800	24,445					8,361	8,344			
	CASH RETURNS LESS DISBURSEMENTS	xxxxxxxxxxx			xxxxxxxxxxx			xxxxxxxxxxx	(17)		xxxxxxxxxxx	
	DISBURSEMENTS CASH RETURNS	xxxxxxxxxxx			xxxxxxxxxxx			xxxxxxxxxxx	1.0		xxxxxxxxxxx	

Exhibit A–2

MRC, INC. (A)

SUMMARY OF SELECTED PROJECT EVALUATION REPORTS, AUGUST, 1960

(Dollar figures in thousands)

Project Number	Description	Date Approved	Project Amount		Rate of Return		Payback Period (Years)	
			Forecast	Actual	Forecast	Actual	Forecast	Actual
FA-157............	Roll Forming Mill	1/58	$193	$193	37%	42%	2.5	2.3
FA-151............	Univ. Paint Mach. Unloader	7/59	98	43	>30	>30	2.6	1.6
FA-147............	Loading Equip. '65 Buick	7/57	80	79	29	29	3.1	3.3
P 352–51.........	"V" Band Couplings Program	8/59	58	90	>30	Loss	0.7	Loss
P 328–29.........	New Gas Furnace Line	6/56	495	491	>50	43 est.	1.0	1.7 est.
P-532............	Aluminum Die Cast Equipment	5/59	86	86	>30	>30	2.2	2.0
P-547............	(2) W-S #1 AC Chuckers	7/59	66	66	>30	>30	2.0	1.4
64-129C..........	(2) W-S Chuckers	12/58	116	114	12	Loss	5.5	Loss

MRC, INC. (B)

^^^

In mid-1966, top management of MRC, Inc. was considering a $30,500,000 capital budget proposal which would carry one of the company's divisions into the production of polyester fiber. Through its ARI division, the company was already heavily involved in the production of rayon fiber for tire cord, but this market was rapidly shrinking because of competitive inroads made by both nylon and polyester. An entry into polyester fiber, then, might allow MRC to preserve its market position in tire cord, and also move the company into the production of polyester fiber for other end uses.

BACKGROUND INFORMATION ON MRC, INC.

In 1966, sales of the 13 divisions of MRC were running at an annual rate of $340 million. No single division accounted for as much as 20% of total sales, but the largest five divisions contributed 70% of the total. The product lines of the various MRC divisions are shown in Exhibit 1.

The most important product lines in terms of sales were: (1) industrial furnaces and heat treating equipment; (2) parts used in the manufacture of railroad rolling stock and other foundry products; (3) rayon fiber for automobile tire cord and apparel fabrics; (4) auto, truck, and bus frames; and (5) power brake systems for autos, trucks, and buses.

Diversification through acquisition

Between 1961 and 1965, MRC had nearly tripled sales and earnings. (See Exhibit 2 for financial data for 1961–66.) During this period the company had an active program of diversification by acquisition and concluded acquisitions at an average rate of one new company per year. Exhibit 3 shows the acquisition history of MRC. Five of these transactions were major. Ross Engineering increased MRC sales in 1957 by $27 million. The purchase of Surface Combustion in 1959 added about $38 million to annual sales. In 1961, American Rayon boosted the company's growing sales volume by about $55 million. And the acquisition of Steel City Electric and National Castings in 1963 and 1965 added about $16 million and $73 million, respectively, to annual sales.

For background information on the diversification program and the resultant decentralization of the management structure see MRC, Inc. (A).

BACKGROUND INFORMATION ON AMERICAN RAYON, INC.

In the spring of 1961, MRC had merged with American Rayon, Inc. (ARI) by an exchange of common stock. Almost all of ARI's sales consisted of rayon fiber, and more than 60% of these sales consisted of rayon tire cord for use in the production of automobile tires. At the time of the merger, ARI was the third largest U.S. producer of rayon and the future of this fiber was extremely uncertain. See the (A) case for background on this transaction and on the outlook for the rayon industry.

Efforts to diversify ARI

Over the period 1961–66, ARI performed profitably, although not satisfactorily in the later years, as shown below:

Year	Sales Index of ARI Fibers Division	Pretax Profit as a % of Sales
1961	100	6%
1962	100	8
1963	112	10
1964	115	9
1965	118	7
1966	124	4

The aggregate use of rayon in tire cord continued to decline during this period, and efforts were undertaken to reduce the division's dependence on the tire cord market. In 1964, after retirement of the original division manager, MRC invested $8 million in a facility to produce high-wet modulus rayon staple fiber, which was used principally in wearing apparel.[1] At the time this project was proposed by the new division manager, the selling price of the fiber was between 44 and 45 cents a pound. ARI management had felt that the price would decline to about 36 cents a pound within five years and stabilize there. At this reduced price level, the plant addition promised a five-year payback and a healthy DCF–ROI.

According to Archibald Brinton, president of MRC:

ARI had process problems during the first year after the facility opened. These problems cut heavily into the division's profits. We also had some problem in getting the textile manufacturers to switch to our fiber. The textile people won't switch to the fiber of a new manufacturer until it's been thoroughly tested and evaluated. This testing is a costly and time-consuming process.

By the beginning of the second year after the plant was completed, the selling price of high-wet modulus rayon was down to 26 cents a pound.

---

[1] Staple fiber is "short length" fiber (approximately 1 to 1½ inches) such as is found in cotton bolls.

Man-made fiber manufacture is a continuous process production operation. You run the plants 24 hours a day, 7 days a week. The production costs are such that you have to run at close to capacity to make any profit. If you cut back production very far, you might as well shut down entirely. We had a choice. If you cut production, your unit costs skyrocket; if you keep producing, your inventories skyrocket. With us it was a question of whether we might be better off shutting the plant down completely until prices firmed. We finally decided to keep it running, and made staple fiber until it was coming out of our ears. Prices are firming now, but although we've had three price rises in the last nine months, they are still not up to 36 cents a pound.

In 1966, ARI was still heavily dependent on rayon tire cord as the principal source of its business. During 1965, total industry production of rayon tire cord amounted to 210 million pounds. This production was split about equally by ARI—25%; American Viscose Corporation Division of FMC—30%; Beaunit Corporation—23%; and American Enka Corporation—23%.

Threats to the tire cord market

By 1966, the only real market remaining for rayon tire cord was the original equipment tire market.[2] Of the 210 million pounds of rayon tire cord used for all classes of tires in 1965, about 150 million pounds went into the 50 million passenger car tires required by the original equipment manufacturers (OEMs). The OEMs had purchased rayon cord tires almost exclusively through 1965, but nylon started to break into this market when Chevrolet Division of General Motors Corporation indicated in 1966 that it would provide tires with nylon cord on the 1968 models. "The use of . . . nylon for Chevrolet production for this first year could mean a market of approximately 10,000,000 tires. . . ."[3]

If rayon cord were ultimately displaced from OEM passenger car tires, the rayon industry stood to lose approximately 150 million pounds of its market. As this last market started to switch, rayon producers would find it increasingly difficult to remain price competitive with nylon.

The nylon producers may be in a position . . . to further reduce the price of their material. However, the rayon producers most probably will not be in a position to do the same because of the decrease . . . in usage of their materials.[4]

Du Pont recently pointed to acetate yarn as an example of a fiber having passed the low point in raw material price and already having capitalized fully on the lower cost attainable through very large scale of production. . . . This may also be the case for rayon staple fiber.[5]

---

[2] Original equipment tires are purchased from tire manufacturers and placed on new cars by auto manufacturers.

[3] C. A. Litzler, "The Fluid Tire Cord Situation," *Modern Textiles Magazine*, September, 1966, p. 22.

[4] Ibid.

[5] National Advisory Commission on Food and Fiber, *Cotton and Other Fiber Problems and Policies in the United States*, Technical Papers, Vol. 2 (Washington, D.C., 1967), p. 43.

The rise of polyester

While nylon was rapidly replacing rayon as the principal fiber in tire cord, a new fiber, polyester, was becoming important.[6] Five million pounds of this fiber were used in 1963 by tire manufacturers, 19 million pounds was the estimated use in 1966, and a Goodyear spokesman predicted that over 100 million pounds would be used in tire cord by 1970.[7]

Polyester was considered by some to be the "third generation" man-made fiber after rayon and nylon. The fiber had shown very rapid growth in recent years (Exhibit 4). After Du Pont's polyester patent expired in July, 1961, competition rapidly appeared, prices declined, and new markets opened up to the fiber. Much of polyester's success up to 1966 was due to the enthusiasm that greeted the introduction of stay-press fabric in wearing apparel. In 1956, the total production of polyester fiber for all uses was about 20 million pounds. By 1965, polyester output reached over 400 million pounds. Du Pont was the major producer of polyester fiber, accounting for well over one half of total U.S. production.

ALTERNATIVE COURSES OF ACTION IN THE FACE OF CHANGE

In mid-1966, the management of MRC was considering alternative courses of action with regard to the ARI division. The profits of this division were unsatisfactory when viewed in relation to the amount of capital required to support its operations. With the market for ARI's major product line facing even greater near-term difficulty than in the past (owing to the Chevrolet decision), the company had to (1) continue realizing progressively less satisfactory returns on the assets employed by ARI, or (2) commit a substantial amount of new capital to production facilities for new fibers, or (3) get out of certain areas of the rayon business.

Leaving the market

The alternative of getting out of the rayon business entirely or in part presented a problem since the physical plant of ARI was on the books of the company at a net book value of about $20 million. If this was sold substantially below book value, MRC would have to absorb a substantial nonrecurring loss on the sale, which would probably reduce the company's 1966 earnings per share below the level achieved in 1965. Although this loss would be nonrecurring, MRC management felt that investors might confuse it with a downturn in earnings from normal operations. The company was in the middle of its fifth consecutive year of earnings progress in 1966. Its stock prices had

---

[6] Polyester (polyethylene terephthalate) is a long chain polymer formed in the condensation reaction between ethylene glycol (permanent antifreeze) and dimethyl terephthalate. Du Pont's dacron is the best-known brand of polyester fiber.

[7] *Oil, Paint and Drug Reporter*, November 21, 1966, pp. 4 and 52.

been moving up steadily since 1961 in response to these earnings gains, and management was reluctant to risk this share-price progress to investor misunderstanding.

Investing in new fibers

While selling the ARI division was not a particularly attractive alternative, investing in facilities for producing newer fibers also raised some difficult problems. First, since nylon seemed to have already neared a peak in tire cord use, an investment in a facility to produce this fiber would be practically obsolete by the time it was completed. On the other hand, polyester had not reached the point of acceptance in tire production to justify the construction of a large new plant just to serve this segment of the polyester market. New fiber plants had to be large to be economically competitive. As a representative example, Exhibit 5 shows the variation in production costs of rayon fiber as the size of the producing plant increases. Economies of scale are clearly evident here, as they are in most chemical production processes.[8] Similar production economies could be expected in polyester fiber production. For this reason, if MRC went into the production of polyester tire cord, it would be necessary to produce polyester fiber for other uses as well. This would put the company into the textile fiber business against firms such as Du Pont. Except for the venture into high-wet modulus rayon staple fiber in 1964, the company had had little contact with textile mills, and had competed directly with large apparel fiber manufacturers such as Du Pont only to a limited extent.

THE POLYESTER PROPOSAL

In mid-1966, top management of MRC was considering a specific proposal that would carry the corporation heavily into the production of polyester fiber for tire cord and apparel fabrics. This proposal had been initiated by the ARI division general manager, John Wentworth, an experienced and extremely well-regarded young executive who had been lured away from Monsanto Company after MRC's experience with high-wet modulus rayon staple fiber.

During the period 1966–71, the project would call for an investment of $30.5 million (Exhibit 6). About $20.2 million of this amount would be used to construct a new plant for the production of polyester fiber, $5.3 million would be used for plant additions to reduce the production costs of high-wet modulus rayon fiber and expand production capacity, and $5.0 million would be added to working capital in support of the increased level of sales.

Over a period of three years, the new facility would give ARI the capacity to produce up to 50 million pounds a year of polyester fiber and resin. Ten million pounds would go into tire cord, 30 million pounds would be marketed as staple fiber in competition with firms such as Du Pont, and 10 million pounds of resin chips would be sold to other polyester fabricators.

---

[8] S. C. Schuman, "How Plant Size Affects Unit Costs," *Chemical Engineering*, May, 1965, pp. 173–76.

Economics of the polyester venture

Exhibit 7 shows the profit, cash flow, and DCF-ROI projections over the 15-year life of the facility assuming that the volume and price projections of 1971 continue through 1981. The second ROI calculation assumes that all polyester selling prices decline 10% in 1972 and remain at those levels for the final 10 years of the project's life. Exhibit 8 shows the profit and cash flow projections for the first five years of the project's life. The volume and price assumptions underlying these calculations are shown at the bottom of the exhibit. Although polyester staple fiber was selling for 84 cents a pound in mid-1966, the analysis assumes that this price will have declined to 70.5 cents a pound by 1969.

The competitive environment

During the months that the MRC management was mulling over the new fiber project, the competitive situation in polyester was in considerable turmoil. In late March, 1966, Du Pont announced that it would build a new polyester facility capable of producing 200 million pounds a year by the end of 1968. The plant was to be twice the size of Du Pont's two other polyester plants and was to be called the Cape Fear plant. This facility, plus other announced additions at Du Pont's other polyester plants, would raise the company's capacity in polyester fiber from 240 million pounds a year in February, 1966 (versus 456 million pounds for the industry at that date), to over 600 million pounds a year by the end of 1968. Exhibit 9 shows the production capacity of the U.S. companies producing polyester resins at February, 1966, plus the announced capacity additions due to come on-stream at least by the end of 1968. The exhibit also shows the 1965 total sales volume of these companies, the other fibers they manufactured, and their average return on total capital during the period 1961–65.

In April, 1966, an article in *Chemical Week* mentioned a number of other important competitive factors in the polyester situation:[9]

Polyester sales in '65 increased 50% over '64 and '66 growth is projected for at least 35% to 500 million lbs. Demand got out of hand last year because a 14¢/lb. price decrease was coupled with an unexpectedly enthusiastic acceptance of polyester blends in durable-press apparel. . . .

If all announced new capacity is built as scheduled, by the end of '68 U.S. production capability would be nearly 1.25 billion lbs./year. . . .

With the Du Pont capacity disclosure, other polyester fiber producers theorize that marginal producers may scale down expansion plans and potential producers may think twice before entering the market. Intense competition in other fibers is in store as well.

THE POINT OF DECISION

It was in this environment that the management of MRC had to make its decision on the polyester fiber proposal.

---

[9] *Chemical Week*, April 2, 1966, p. 21.

Exhibit 1
MRC, INC. (B)
DIVISIONS OF MRC

Capitol Foundry
Cast alloy steel grinding balls; volume or job-lot production of gray, white, and nickel-chrome iron; chrome-molybdenum and austenitic-manganese steel castings.

ARI Fibers
Tyrex rayon tire yarns, cords, and fabrics; high tenacity rayon yarns, plied yarns, cords (adhesive-treated and untreated) for mechanical rubber goods; rayon textile yarns; rayon staple fiber; polyester tire yarn, cord, and fabric.

Janitrol Aero
Heat transfer equipment for aircraft and missiles; electronic cooling equipment; pneumatic, hydraulic, and cryogenic controls; high pressure couplings and duct supports; liquid heaters for ground support; aircraft and portable heaters; gas turbine combustion systems; gas turbine accessories; hot fuel priming units.

Janitrol
Heating and air conditioning equipment for residential, commercial, and industrial applications, including gas and oil-fired furnaces, unit heaters, gas conversion burners, gas and oil-fired boilers, central air conditioning systems, electric/gas year-round heat/cool packages, rooftop heating and cooling units, electric heat pumps, makeup air heaters.

Midland Frame
Passenger car, truck, and bus chassis frames; miscellaneous stampings and weldments.

National Castings
Couplers, draft gears, car trucks, cushioned underframes for railroad, mine, and industrial haulage systems; malleable, pearlitic malleable steel castings for metalworking industries.

Power Controls
Air-brake systems; vacuum power brake systems; power controls; electro-pneumatic door controls; air compressors; air actuating cylinders; emergency relay valves; zinc and aluminum die castings.

Ross Engineering
"Engineered Atmospheres" for processing, drying or curing pulp, paper, rubber, chemicals, food, textiles, wood and wood products, et al.; coil processing and metal decorating lines; textile dryers and curing machinery; air heaters; fume incinerators; web conditioners; dryer drainage systems; SUPERTHERM high temperature hot fluid heating systems.

Steel City
Switch, outlet, and floor boxes; conduit and cable fittings; hangers and supports; metal framing systems for conduit lighting and electrical equipment; slotted angle.

Surface Combustion
Industrial burners; heat-treat furnaces; heat-processing equipment for glass and ceramics; steel mill equipment; process and comfort air dehumidification and bacterial removal systems; continuous dryers; iron pelletizing and reducing equipment and plants; gas generators for metallurgical, food, and chemical applications.

Waldron-Hartig
Machinery for paper, film, foil, and textile coating, converting, laminating, embossing, and treating; metal coil coating and processing lines; plastics extruders, blow molding machinery, and film and sheeting lines; power transmission couplings.

Webster Engineering
Gas and oil burners for boilers in large buildings and industry; FANDAIRE air-cooled condensers, condensing units, and chillers.

MRC of Canada, Ltd.
Power Controls
Surface Combustion
Products similar to those of the Power Controls, Ross Engineering, and Surface Combustion Divisions in the United States.

Exhibit 2

MRC, INC. (B)

SIX-YEAR SUMMARY OF FINANCIAL DATA

(Dollar figures in millions except for per share data)

	1961	1962	1963	1964	1965	1966
OPERATIONS						
?es:						
.utomotive and transportation.........	$ 57.8	$ 73.2	$ 80.9	$ 82.5	$ 94.2	$102.6
.apital goods.........................	42.7	48.2	47.3	65.1	94.8	125.7
.uilding and construction..............	12.4	18.3	31.2	33.4	34.5	33.5
.ailroad..............................	—	—	—	—	39.6	42.7
.onsumer goods.......................	16.5	15.0	14.9	16.2	18.7	18.0
.erospace and defense.................	8.3	11.6	15.7	13.9	14.3	21.6
Total..........................	$137.6	$166.3	$190.1	$211.1	$296.1	$344.1
? income...........................	5.5	5.9	7.6	8.7	14.1	17.6
?reciation and amortization of						
intangibles......................	4.3	4.6	5.2	5.1	6.9	7.4
.h funds generated*..................	9.0	9.8	12.0	14.0	19.8	24.1
.eral income taxes....................	3.2	6.1	8.2	8.5	12.5	16.6
.fit margin...........................	7.4%	9.1%	10.5%	9.8%	10.7%	11.4%
.reciation rate.......................	4.5	4.7	4.8	4.5	4.7	4.7
.ned on total capital.................	5.3	6.3	7.8	9.1	10.4	12.1
.ned on common equity...............	5.3	6.5	8.2	9.7	12.6	13.7
COMMON STOCK						
? income per share††.................	$ 0.84	$ 0.97	$ 1.47	$ 1.82	$ 2.66	$ 3.33
.idends per share†....................	0.75	0.75	0.75	0.85	0.95	1.22
.h funds generated per share*†‡.........	1.60	1.85	2.57	2.96	4.15	4.90
.: tangible book value—per share†.......	15.86	17.00	17.64	18.63	20.70	22.52
.rket price†...........................	13–11	14–10	16–12	19–15	26–18	30–22
.idend payout ratio...................	49%	45%	33%	31%	28%	31%
.erage annual price-earnings ratio........	15.1	11.3	10.5	10.3	8.2	7.9
.erage annual dividend yield...........	5.8%	6.0%	4.9%	4.6%	4.4%	4.7%
.mber of shareholders.................	13,125	12,165	11,750	12,725	12,750	15,150
FINANCIAL POSITION						
.rking capital.........................	$ 58.6	$ 47.4	$ 50.1	$ 49.3	$ 69.4	$ 70.2
.t property, plant, and equipment........	42.4	43.8	44.6	49.3	66.6	72.4
.ng-term debt........................	—	—	—	13.5	9.0	7.9
.ferred and common shareholders' equity.	105.6	96.5	100.6	91.9	134.2	142.3
.ditions to property, plant, and						
equipment......................	1.4	2.5	3.2	9.9	9.1	14.4
.mber of employees...................	8,000	8,500	9,000	9,300	14,000	14,600

* Net income and provisions for depreciation, amortization of intangibles, and deferred income taxes, less preferred dividends.
† Adjusted for 2 for 1 splits in 1964 and 1966.
‡ Calculated on average number of shares outstanding during the year.

Exhibit 3

MRC, INC. (B)

ACQUISITION HISTORY OF MRC

December, 1957:	Acquired J. O. Ross Engineering Corporation in exchange for 281,000 shares.
March, 1958:	Acquired Hartig Engine and Machine Company, Mountainside, New Jersey, for cash and notes.
October, 1958:	Acquired Transportation Division of Consolidated Metal Products Corporation, Albany, New York, and moved operations to Owosso, Michigan Division.
April, 1959:	Acquired Nelson Metal Products Company, Grand Rapids, Michigan, for cash.
November, 1959:	Acquired Surface Combustion Corporation, Toledo, Ohio, for $23 million cash.
May, 1961:	Merged American Rayon, Inc. by exchange of common stock.
January, 1962:	Acquired Wright Manufacturing Company, Phoenix, producer of air conditioning equipment.
March, 1962:	Acquired Fandaire Division, a producer of commercial air conditioning systems, from Yuba Consolidated Industries, Inc.
December 31, 1962:	Acquired the precision machine business of J. Leukart Machine Company, Columbus, Ohio.
April 1, 1963:	Purchased Steel City Electric Company from Martin Marietta Corporation.
April 22, 1965:	Merged National Castings Company, by exchange of 299,787 shares of $4.75 cumulative convertible preferred stock on basis of 45/100 share of preferred stock for each share of National Castings common stock. National Castings operated as two divisions.
Fall, 1965:	Acquired Grand Rapids Bright Metal Company.

Exhibit 4

MRC, INC. (B)

U.S. FIBER CONSUMPTION (IN MILLIONS OF POUNDS) AND PRICES
(IN DOLLARS PER POUND)

Year	Natural Fibers				Man-Made Fibers					
	Cotton		Wool		Rayon		Nylon		Polyester	
	Pounds	Staple Price $	Pounds	Staple Price $	Pounds	Staple Price $	Pounds	Staple Price $	Pounds	Staple Price $
1910	n.a.	n.a.	n.a.		*					
1930	2,617		263		119	0.40				
1935	2,755		418		200	0.31				
1940	3,959		408		300	0.25	*			
1945	4,516	0.39	645		420	0.25	25			
1950	4,683	0.57	635	1.41	650	0.36	75	1.65	*	
1955	4,382	0.39	414	1.08	966	0.34	231	1.48	13	1.60
1956		0.33		1.08	870	0.32	246	1.30	20	1.35
1957		0.36		1.22	836	0.31	293	1.30	38	1.41
1958		0.33		0.90	750	0.31	293	1.20	44	1.41
1959		0.30		1.02	848	0.33	356	1.06	79	1.36
1960	4,191	0.31	411	1.07	716	0.28	376	0.92	110	1.36
1961		0.31		1.03	797	0.28	455	0.92	112	1.24
1962	4,188	0.30	429	1.09	884	0.28	551	0.92	162	1.14
1963	4,040	0.29	412	1.18	960	0.28	625	0.92	223	1.14
1964	4,244	0.29	357	1.28	975	0.28	754	0.92	274	0.98
1965	4,477	0.29	387	1.19	1,046	0.28	861	0.82	416	0.84
1966	4,633 est.		370 est.		1,026 est.		978 est.		545 est.	

Fibers compete for shares of the total fiber market principally on the basis of relative prices and relative quality characteristics. Relative prices appear to have been an important consideration in the substitution of rayon for cotton in certain uses. The noncellulose fibers offer serious price competition for apparel wool. However, price advantage has not accounted for the rapid increase in share of the fiber market gain by noncellulose fibers, although sharply reduced prices in recent years have undoubtedly expanded their use.

Synthetic fibers yield a greater amount of fabric from a pound of fiber than does cotton, thus reducing the price of synthetic fiber per unit of product output. The equivalent net weight pounds of cotton staple for each pound of man-made fiber is (a) rayon staple fiber, 1.10; and (b) nylon and polyester staple fiber, 1.37.

* Date of fiber introduction.

Sources: Statistical Abstract of the United States—1967, pp. 642, 760, 761. Textile Organon: December, 1966, p. 199; February, 1967, pp. 28, 29. Modern Textiles Magazine, December, 1965. National Advisory Commission on Food and Fiber, Cotton and Other Fiber Problems and Policies in the United States, Technical Papers, Vol. 2 (Washington, D.C., 1967), pp. 24, 33, 36, 39.

Exhibit 5

MRC, INC. (B)

VARIATION IN UNIT COST OF PRODUCTION WITH SIZE OF PLANT

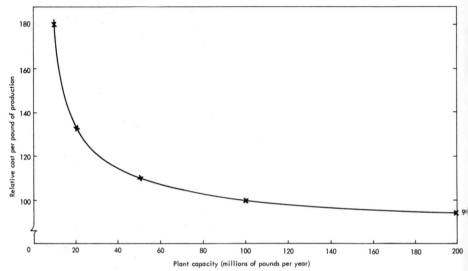

Plant capacity (millions of pounds per year)

Based on a chart in Jesse W. Markham, *Competition in the Rayon Industry* (Cambridge, Mass.: Harvard University Pre 1952), p. 150.

Exhibit 6

MRC, INC. (B)

CAPITAL INVESTMENT IN POLYESTER

(In millions)

	ARI Division
Working capital.....................................	$ 6.5
Production facilities................................	20.3
Total existing investment.......................	$26.8
Between 1/1/67 and 12/31/71, additional investments were to be made as follows:	
Polyester resin and fiber plant.........................	$17.4
Polyester tire cord spinning facility....................	1.8
Other polyester facilities.............................	1.0
Polyester plants...............................	$20.2
Various rayon additions..............................	5.3
Total plant additions............................	$25.5
Additional accounts receivable and inventories...........	5.0
Total additional investment.....................	$30.5
Grand total.................................	$57.3

The timing and size of the cash expenditure for the project would be as follows:

	1967	1968	1969	1970	1971	Five-Year Totals
Additions to plant......	$16.9	$5.7	$0.9	$1.0	$1.0	$25.5
Additions to working capital..............	1.1	3.3	0.6	0	0	5.0
	$18.0	$9.0	$1.5	$1.0	$1.0	$30.5

Exhibit 7

MRC, INC. (B)
CASH FLOWS FROM POLYESTER PROJECT, 1967–81
(In thousands)

Year	Existing	Investment New	Income after Tax	Cash Flow from Operations
1967	$26,800	$18,029	$1,663	$ 3,788
1968		8,995	3,416	6,740
1969		1,480	8,397	12,543
1970		1,000	7,710	11,477
1971		1,000	7,597	11,286
1972			7,427	10,869
1973			7,659	10,611
1974			7,861	10,385
1975			8,034	10,184
1976			8,186	10,009
1977			8,317	9,853
1978			8,431	9,714
1979			8,529	9,590
1980			8,574	9,521
1981			8,574	9,496 14,338 ← return of working capital and plant write-off

Discounted cash flow return on investment = 15.2%
DCF-ROI assuming 10% decline in selling
prices of polyester, 1972–81 = 13.6%

Exhibit 8

MRC, INC. (B)

FIVE-YEAR SALES, PROFIT, CASH FLOW, AND PRICE FORECASTS OF PROJECT

(Dollar figures in millions)

		1967				1968		
	Total	Poly-ester	Hi-Wet Modulus Rayon Staple	Rayon Tire Cord	Total	Poly-ester	Hi-Wet Modulus Rayon Staple	Rayon Tire Cord
Net sales..........................	$50.0	$ 6.4	$4.9	$38.7	$68.3	$21.5	$7.7	$39.1
Cost of sales:								
Normal..........................	40.5							
Extraordinary start-up...............	0.5							
Depreciation........................	2.1	0.1	2.0		2.9	1.0	1.9	
Total cost of sales................	$43.1				$56.2			
Gross income......................	$ 6.9				$12.1			
Nonmanufacturing expense.............	4.0				6.3			
Income before interest and income taxes...	$ 2.9	$(1.2)	$4.1		$ 5.8	$ 0.9	$4.9	
Interest............................	0.0				0.0			
Income before taxes.................	$ 2.9				$ 5.8			
Income taxes @ approx. 50%:								
Current...........................	1.4				2.5			
Deferred...........................	—				0.4			
Total............................	$ 1.4				$ 2.9			
Less investment credit................	0.2				$ 0.5			
Net provision....................	$ 1.2				$ 2.4			
Net income........................	$ 1.7				$ 3.4			
Depreciation and deferred taxes..........	2.1				3.3			
Cash flow..........................	$ 3.8				$ 6.7			

	Product Sold (Millions of Lbs.)	Price ($ per Lb.)		Product Sold (Millions of Lbs.)	Price ($ per Lb.)
Rayon staple (hi-wet modulus)...........	16	$0.310		25	$0.310
Rayon tire cord........................	67	0.578		67.5	0.578
Polyester:					
Tire cord............................	7.5	0.850		10	0.809
Staple fiber.........................	0.0	0.785		18.8	0.725
Resin (or polymer)...................	0.0	0.380		0.0	0.380
Total polyester..................	7.5	$0.850		28.8	$0.754

	1969				1970				1971			
	Total	Poly-ester	Hi-Wet Modulus Rayon Staple	Rayon Tire Cord	Total	Poly-ester	Hi-Wet Modulus Rayon Staple	Rayon Tire Cord	Total	Poly-ester	Hi-Wet Modulus Rayon Staple	Rayon Tire Cord
	79.8	$32.9	$7.7	$39.2	$79.7	$32.8	$7.7	$39.2	$79.5	$32.6	$7.7	$39.2
	3.3	1.7		1.6	3.3	—		—	3.4	—		—
	57.8				$57.8				$57.8			
	22.0				$21.9				$21.7			
	6.5				6.6				6.6			
	15.5	$10.5		$5.0	$15.3	$10.3		$5.0	$15.1	$10.1		$5.0
	0.0				1.5				1.1			
	15.5				$13.8				$14.0			
	6.9				5.7				6.2			
	0.9				0.5				0.3			
	7.8				$ 6.2				$ 6.5			
	0.7				0.1				0.1			
	7.1				$ 6.1				$ 6.4			
	8.4				$ 7.7				$ 7.6			
	4.1				3.8				3.7			
	12.5				$11.5				$11.3			

Product Sold (Millions of Lbs.)	Price ($ per Lb.)	Product Sold (Millions of Lbs.)	Price ($ per Lb.)	Product Sold (Millions of Lbs.)	Price ($ per Lb.)
25	$0.310	25	$0.310	25	$0.310
67.8	0.578	67.8	0.578	67.8	0.578
10	0.795	10	0.795	10	0.795
10	0.705	30	0.705	30	0.705
10	0.380	10	0.372	10	0.350
50	$0.658	50	$0.656	50	$0.652

Exhibit 9

MRC, INC. (B)
CURRENT AND PLANNED CAPACITY OF POLYESTER FIBER COMPETITORS

	Polyester Capacity Feb., 1966 (In Millions of Pounds)	Announced Expansion by End of 1968 (In Millions of Pounds)	Number of Plants End of 1968	Other‡ Fibers Manufactured	Total Sales Volume of Company in 1965 (In Millions)	Average Return on Total Capital (1961–65)
Allied Chemical	0	?	?	N	$1,121	10%
American Enka	0	?	?	N, R	193	11
American Viscose (Div. FMC)	0	?	?	A, R		
Beaunit Fibers (Div. Beaunit Corp.)	0	?	?	R		
Chemstrand (Div. Monsanto)	20	40	1	N	1,468	9
Du Pont	240	360	3	A, N	3,020	19
Fiber Industries*	95	155	2	A, N, R	862	8
Firestone Tire & Rubber	0	?	?	N	1,610	9
Goodyear Tire & Rubber	60	40	1		2,226	10
Hercules	0	30	1		532	13
ARI Fibers (Div. MRC)	0	?	?	R		
Phoenix Works, Inc. (Sub. Bates Mfg. Co.)	0	25	1			
Tennessee Eastman Co. (Div. Eastman Kodak)	50	100	2	A		
U.S. Rubber Company	0	?	?			
Vectra Co.† (Div. Nat. Plastic Products)	0	?	?	N		
	465	750	11			

* Owned 62.5% by Celanese Corp. of America.
† Jointly owned by Enjay Chemical Co. & J. P. Stevens & Co.
‡ A = Acetate; N = Nylon; R = Rayon.

PECHINEY UGINE KUHLMANN—CEBAL
(A Capital Investment Project)

^^

In the fall of 1974, the management of Cebal, one of the two packaging materials manufacturing subsidiaries of the French aluminum giant, Pechiney Ugine Kuhlmann, was studying a proposal to invest FF 97.9 million to build a two-piece aluminum can[1] manufacturing plant in northern Italy. The factory would begin production in 1977 and would be jointly owned with the Wilson Division of the Brown Company. The Brown Company was a U.S. manufacturer of packaging materials with 1974 sales of $340 million. The Wilson Division, with 1974 revenues of $112 million, specialized in the manufacture of two-piece cans (both aluminum and tin) for carbonated drinks and beer.

The managements of Brown and Cebal had already arranged to sell the output of the new plant to the Italian division of Byron, Ltd., the well-known English beer and beverage producer, under a five-year contract. Byron, Ltd. had agreed to buy the cans at a price which would be set initially at 80 lire per can and which would be indexed to the principal cost components of manufacturing. Thus, the Brown/Cebal venture was effectively protected against inflation.

Pechiney Ugine Kuhlmann (PUK)

PUK was the largest French industrial concern, with 1974 revenues of FF 22.2 billion. (See Exhibit 1 for selected financial information about PUK.) The company had been formed in 1971 with the merger of the Pechiney group and the Ugine-Kuhlmann group, and was divided into five major branches as follows:

	1974 Turnover (In billions of francs)	Percent of 1974 Turnover
Aluminum	FF 7.3	33%
Chemicals	4.9	22
Steel and electrometallurgy	3.3	15
Copper mining and nuclear energy	4.9	22
Special products	1.8	8
	FF 22.2	100%

---

[1] Most cans are three-piece—a bottom, a top, and the middle. Two-piece cans are a relatively new phenomenon in Europe.

The Cebal subsidiary was part of the packaging division of the aluminum branch of Pechiney (see Exhibit 2). Turnover had grown dramatically from FF 25 million in 1968 to FF 400 million in 1974. Of the FF 400 million, FF 60.4 million represented non-French sales. The company's product line included aluminum containers, easy-open cans, collapsible tubes, and aluminum caps and closures.

The analysis of capital budgeting proposals at PUK

The analysis of investment projects at PUK was intimately linked to the long-range planning process. Essentially, each business sector was analyzed in terms of its strategic strengths and weaknesses. In this regard, competition, current and potential market share, technological capabilities, as well as numerous other factors were considered. The PUK management then evaluated both the current and expected profitability of each of its principal sectors and subsectors of activity.

The primary measure of profitability used in this analysis was the return on gross assets employed. The return on gross assets was defined as the ratio of the industrial margin (earnings before interest and taxes minus an allowance for straight-line depreciation) of a given sector to the gross assets (fixed assets plus inventory) employed by that sector.[2]

The profitability and strategic analysis outlined above was designed to identify development objectives. Essentially, development objectives were outlines of investment (or disinvestment) projects, all of which would warrant completion if there were no limitation on the availability of investment funds.

After development objectives were identified, the implied total need for funds was calculated. At the same time, the expected total sources of funds were determined. If the implied uses exceeded the estimated sources of funds, as had always been the case at PUK, then it was necessary to modify the development objectives. A long-range plan was completed when the expected uses of funds were equal to the expected sources of funds.

The inclusion of specific development objectives in the PUK long-range plan did not mean that the underlying projects were already approved. Each individual investment project had to be analyzed in great detail before corporate capital would be released for expenditure.

Actually, the analysis of individual investment projects was divided into three related parts. First, each proposal was evaluated on the strategic level. At issue was how the project matched with the strategic strengths and weaknesses of the group.

The second step in the analysis of individual capital expenditure proposals entailed the preparation of detailed operating budgets including funds-flow

---

[2] Generally, gross assets were valued on a historical cost basis. However, in analyzing the return on gross assets of each sector, the ratio was re-computed using both price-level adjusted and replacement values for gross assets.

forecasts, income statements, and balance sheets. It was at this stage that the profitability of the individual project was measured.

The measure of profitability of capital investment proposals used at PUK was the expected internal rate of return. The internal rate of return was that discount rate at which the *net* present value of the project was zero.

Ordinarily, the profitability of the project was measured using several different plausible variations. A variation might entail making a different assumption about the price expectations for a new product or locating the new plant at a different site. Changing the assumptions underlying the project also allowed management to identify the sensitivity of the profitability estimates to certain key variables.

The reason behind using several variations and testing the sensitivity of the project to changes in certain variables was to specify the risk in the project.

The final step in analyzing individual investment projects was to outline a tentative financing plan that specified the probable sources and cost of finance for the project.

The three parts to the analysis of individual projects comprised the "investment file." The completed investment file was submitted to the appropriate manager for approval.

The setting of investment return objectives at PUK

In order to achieve its overall profitability goals, the PUK management believed that each individual investment project had to meet certain profitability criteria, chief among which was a minimum internal rate of return.

The process of determining the minimum required internal rate of return for all projects at PUK involved several steps. First, it was necessary to calculate the cost of equity capital, the cost of debt capital, and, therefore, the overall cost of capital for the entire PUK group. The cost of equity capital for PUK was estimated to be roughly 11%. The aftertax cost of debt for PUK was estimated at approximately 4.5%.

The overall cost of capital was calculated as a weighted average of the cost of equity and the cost of debt capital.[3] PUK used the current relative book values of shareholders' equity and long- and medium-term debt to weight the cost of each. The overall cost of capital for PUK was estimated to be roughly 9.0% after taxes.

The minimum required internal rate of return for individual projects was initially set equal to the estimated overall cost of capital. However, the PUK management noted three reasons why this rule was not optimal. First, there were a number of investment projects which were absolutely necessary but which would not earn a positive return for the company (e.g., pollution-control equipment). Second, despite the best efforts of the management groups submit-

---

[3] See Appendix A for a more complete description of the method used by PUK to compute the cost of capital for the group.

ting the projects for approval, the PUK staff believed it was inevitable that all the costs of the projects would not be taken into consideration.

Finally, in order to take into account the riskiness of the new project, the PUK staff believed that the minimum required rate of return should be higher than the estimated cost of capital. The risks envisioned in this regard included uncertainty about the general economic and political situation as well as uncertainty about the particular market for which the new product was being produced.

Thus, in order to take into account these three items, the minimum required rate of return was set at a level of 15% as compared to the estimated cost of capital of 9%.

The Brown/Cebal project

Under the terms of the proposed venture, Cebal would own 51% of the project and Brown, 49%. Essentially, Brown would provide the expertise necessary to build and put into operation the can plant. For this contribution, Brown would be paid a royalty by the newly formed company.

The new plant would be managed by Cebal which would receive a management fee equal to one half of the royalties paid to Brown.

The cans produced by the new plant would be sold to the Italian division of Byron, Ltd. Under the terms of the proposed contract with Byron, Ltd., Byron-Italy would agree to purchase virtually the entire output of the new plant for the first five years of production beginning in 1977. The price to be paid by Byron, Ltd. would be linked to an index of the cost elements of production. (See Exhibit 3 for a resume of the contract with Byron, Ltd.)

Canned beer was first introduced by Byron, Ltd. in Italy in 1973, having been sold only in bottled form prior to that time. Byron, Ltd. was just finishing the construction of its first canning plant, located at Varese near Milano in the north of Italy. It was to this new plant that Brown/Cebal would sell its production. Byron-Italy, which had been importing its cans from Austria and Belgium, was primarily interested in having its can requirements met by a plant near the canning facilities.

Byron-Italy had been the first European subsidiary to substitute the two-piece can for bottles. Should the new venture be successful, Brown/Cebal would be in an excellent position to win further can-supply contracts from Byron, Ltd.'s other European subsidiaries. Similarly, Brown/Cebal might also win contracts from other beverage producers who might switch from one-way bottles to two-piece cans.

One important aspect of the proposed new venture was the expected sources of supply of the aluminum necessary to manufacture the cans. Essentially, Brown/Cebal would purchase its aluminum requirements from the market supplier offering the most advantageous terms, which might or might not be PUK's aluminum division, Cégédur Pechiney. However, if Cégédur Pechiney's price was competitive, then Brown/Cebal would purchase as much of its aluminum needs as Cégédur Pechiney wished to provide. At current and predicted prices, it was expected that Cégédur Pechiney would supply roughly 75% of Brown/Cebal's raw material requirements.[4]

In return for the preferential treatment of Cégédur Pechiney, the Brown Company had required that Cégédur Pechiney act as a supplier of last resort to the Brown/Cebal project. Thus, if a worldwide shortage of aluminum developed or if other suppliers refused to supply aluminum to Brown/Cebal, Cégédur Pechiney would have to supply the aluminum. On the other hand, if there occurred a world glut of aluminum, the price to be paid by Brown/Cebal for the aluminum purchased from Pechiney was subject to certain minimums.

The expected total investment in the Brown/Cebal project was FF 86 million for the first production line and FF 106 million for a second production line, assuming an 8.4% per year increase in plant and equipment costs due to inflation. (See Exhibit 4 for a schedule showing the timing of investment outlays for the Brown/Cebal project). The second line would begin production in 1980 should Byron, Ltd.'s requirements exceed the capacity of the first line and/or should new markets open up for the Brown/Cebal product. Indeed, both events were expected to take place.

The proposed financing plan for this investment relied on six primary sources of funds:

1. *Equity capital:* FF 24.0 million in 1975–76 (51% to be provided by Cebal).

2. *Stockholder loans:* FF 22.4 million from 1976 to 1979, then FF 24.8 million in 1979; terms—interest rate of 12% and repayable in 1980–81 (51% to be provided by Cebal).

3. *Long-term loans:* FF 8.0 million at 12.0% interest in 1975–76 for the building of the factory; FF 20.8 million in 1978–79 for the equipment for the second production line, assuming it is not leased.

4. *Leasing:* FF 53.9 million worth of equipment beginning in 1976 from a leasing company that would be formed by Cebal and Brown and that would purchase the equipment and then lease it to the Italian operation. The purchase would be financed completely by parent company guaranteed long-term debt. The ownership of the separate leasing company would be divided between Brown and Cebal in the same proportions as the project (i.e., 49%–51%). Payments to the leasing company would be denominated in U.S. dollars.

5. *Local borrowing:* The working capital needs of the company would be met with short-term debt in Italy at an interest rate of 20%. It was forecast that local bank borrowing would reach FF 19 million by year-end 1977.

---

[4] Cégédur Pechiney would make a reasonable profit at the current and expected prices and costs. Cégédur Pechiney had adequate capacity to meet the needs of the Brown/Cebal project.

6. *Internally generated funds:* Beginning in 1978, the project was expected to show a positive and increasing cash flow.

(See Exhibit 4 for a table showing the financing plan for the project.)

In presenting the Brown/Cebal project for approval, the Cebal financial analysis staff had stressed the low amount of investment required by Cebal. The investment proposal included the following statement:

Cebal, as a 51% shareholder, must invest FF 43.9 million for the first production line and FF 97.9 million total for the two lines.

However, given the proposed financing plan, the actual funds put in by Cebal will be much smaller than that. Recourse will be made to long-term debt and to leasing.

Therefore, Cebal's actual investment in the first production line will be only FF 5.71 million in 1975, FF 9.79 million in 1976, and FF 4.90 million in 1977. The total investment for these three years will be roughly FF 20.8 million, comprised of FF 12.24 million equity, and FF 8.56 million in shareholders' loans to be repaid starting in 1980. The second production line will only require a FF 15.9 million investment in 1978 and 1979.

Thus, it is only for FF 20.8 million that we are making a capital appropriation request.

In making forecasts of the income statements and funds flows for the can manufacturing plant, the Cebal management had evaluated three alternative projects. The first was the most likely and involved manufacturing two-piece aluminum cans in Italy as described previously.

The second project evaluated was different only in that the cans were to be made of tin rather than aluminum. This was a feasible alternative in that tin could be substituted for aluminum on the same machines and Byron, Ltd. was willing to accept tin cans. However, this alternative was not as attractive because the added benefit of purchasing aluminum from Cégédur Pechiney would be lost.

The final option studied by the Cebal management entailed building the plant in France, some 500 kilometers from the proposed Italian location. This alternative had the advantage of avoiding an investment in Italy but, concurrently, had the disadvantage of removing the plant from its primary market. The potential market for cans in France was considered to be less than in Italy. Further, Byron-Italy was hesitant to have its can requirements met by a plant so far away. Finally, transportation costs were high relative to the value of the product.

The first and most attractive option of manufacturing aluminum cans in Italy was expected to show accounting profits beginning in 1978. (See Exhibit 5 for the projected income statement for Brown/Cebal and an outline of the major assumptions underlying the forecasts.) The alternative projects were also expected to show profits in 1978, though initial losses were higher and subsequent profits lower.

The return on the total funds actually invested by the 51% shareholder,

Cebal, was estimated at 33% for the proposed Italian aluminum-can option. The funds flows projections upon which this calculation was based included as cash outflows the subscriptions to equity and debt by Cebal, which financed the initial losses and the investment. The management fee, the interest on the loans and the expected dividends comprised the inflows to Cebal. (See Exhibit 6 for a table showing the forecasted inflows and outflows and the underlying assumptions upon which this calculation was based. Exhibit 7 shows pro forma balance sheets for the subsidiary.)

The estimated return of 33% resulted in part from the significant extent to which the subsidiary would raise its own finance from sources other than the parent. If the return was calculated on the basis of the total cash flows of the project before any financing arrangements, the return would be 22%. (See Exhibit 8.)

Finally, the profitability of the project at the level of the entire aluminum sector was analyzed. This calculation was based on a marketing study recently completed within the aluminum sector which found that the expected, integrated internal rate of return on new investment projects for manufacturing aluminum beverage cans was on the order of 17%.[5] The integrated return was calculated for the complete investment project, starting with the supply of raw aluminum and ending with the sale of the final product, aluminum cans. The marketing study referred to predicted a decline in profitability over time due to product-pricing pressures. These pressures would be absent from the specific Brown/Cebal project for the first five years due to the contract with Byron, Ltd.

All of the measures of profitability for the Brown/Cebal project exceeded minimum investment return objectives set by the PUK management.

The analysis of the project extended beyond the numerical calculations of expected profitability. The Cebal management had identified three major sources of risk in the project. First, there was the risk that the price of tin would decline relative to aluminum. This possibility was believed to be unlikely, and the project showed a reasonable return even if it was to occur and tin was substituted for aluminum.

The second risk identified by the Cebal management was the possibility of some form of prohibitive legislation on no-deposit packaging (i.e., cans, one-way bottles). Management believed that prohibition of such containers would not occur in the near future, though some form of tax or deposit might be imposed. By agreement, Cebal would be able to pass on any producer tax to Byron, Ltd.

The final and most important risk was potential deterioration in the economic and political situation in Italy. This concern was addressed by the Cebal management:

With the political instability, lack of government, deteriorated economic and social situation, the deficit in the balance of payments and the commercial trade

---

[5] This figure refers not to this project in particular, but to other, similar projects facing the aluminum sector.

balance, heavy foreign debt, high union demands present at the end of 1974, Italy gives all indication of being a country and an economy which should not attract investments.

However, are Italy and its 50 million people irretrievably destined to anarchy, and is the proposed Brown/Cebal investment destined to failure? Let's be straight-forward. The risk cannot be eliminated, but the concrete risks can be analyzed and reduced.

The most serious risk is without a doubt the strike risk. But for our project, assuming three shift operations, salaries represent only 10% of sales, and the number of workers is only 88 for each line; a policy of "high salary" should reduce the strike risk without penalizing the profits too much. Byron, Ltd. has been subject to only one day of strike in Italy since January 1974 (the national strike).

The projected operating results have been established by including, in addition to paid vacation, an allowance for one week of strike per year.

The risk of devaluation is also serious. The contract with Byron, Ltd. substantially reduces the risk by indexing raw-materials costs which are paid for in foreign exchange by Brown/Cebal.

This risk remains, however, for the leasing contract made in dollars; a 10% devaluation of the lire would reduce the annual profit FF 800,000 during the life of this contract.

The risk of nationalization does not appear very big for a factory of 100 to 150 people.

Are the risks resulting from the Italian environment so much higher than the risks that would be run with the same investment in France?

By 1977, the date of the starting up of the factory (located, moreover, in an industrial region in the northeast of Italy, considered as socially calm), won't Italy have found again an acceptable financial and economic appearance? Can one think that a situation such as that of 1974 will prolong itself another three years, while Italy belongs to the European community, while its interests are not isolated from those of Germany, France, and the United States?

The assured sale of the production for five years to a customer with a solid international reputation and position counterbalances, in our opinion, the risk of locating in Italy.

Furthermore, the opportunity to earn a 33% return on the funds supplied by Cebal on this project as well as on future possible projects with Byron, Ltd., seems highly attractive; and does not even include the benefits to Cégédur Pechiney.

Exhibit 1

PECHINEY UGINE KUHLMANN-CEBAL
FINANCIAL REVIEW
(In millions of francs except per share data)

	1971	1972	1973	1974
Balance sheet:				
Current assets.................FF	8,115	FF 9,625	FF 10,608	FF 13,545
Net fixed assets................	7,951	8,128	8,386	8,726
Other fixed assets..............	2,531	2,220	2,346	2,567
Total assets...............FF	18,597	FF 19,973	FF 21,340	FF 24,838
Current liabilities...............	5,041	6,252	7,203	9,711
Medium- and long-term debt......	5,168	5,181	5,294	5,281
Deferred taxes..................	1,059	1,145	1,227	1,461
Minority interest...............	1,286	1,279	1,341	1,626
Shareholders' equity, reserves and profits for the year.........FF	6,043	FF 6,116	FF 6,275	FF 6,759
Income statement:				
Net revenues..................FF	13,581	FF 13,425	FF 16,027	FF 22,221
Net income....................	308	273	365	744
Earnings per share.............FF	12.25	FF 10.85	FF 14.50	FF 29.55
Dividends per share............	12.00	12.00	13.20	13.50
Ratios:				
Current assets to current liabilities....................	1.61	1.54	1.47	1.39
Debt to total capitalization (equity plus debt)............	0.42	0.42	0.41	0.39
Sales to total assets.............	0.73	0.67	0.75	0.89
Net income to sales.............	2.27%	2.03%	2.28%	3.35%
Total assets to shareholders' equity*....................	2.62	2.75	2.84	3.02
Net income to shareholders' equity*....................	4.34%	3.74%	4.86%	9.00%
Stock price per share				
High........................	n.a.	FF 172	FF 167	FF 144
Low.........................	n.a.	130	118	99
Last........................	n.a.	133	127	118

n.a. = not available.
*Equals shareholders' equity plus minority interests.

Exhibit 2

PECHINEY UGINE KUHLMANN-CEBAL
ORGANIZATION CHART SHOWING POSITION OF CEBAL

General Direction P U K
Functional Staff
International Service Staff

Chemical Branch

Steel and Electrometallurgy

Aluminum Branch

Copper Mines Branch and Nuclear

Special Products

Pechiney Aluminum

Bauxite Division

Aluminum Div. Fluoride Prod.

Aluminum Division

Sales Group for Pechiney Aluminum

Marketing Division

Sales Division and Foundries

R & D

Transformation Division

Packaging Division

Precision Foundries *

Affimet *

Copper and Alloys *

Crans Forges *

Cégédur Pechiney *

Cebal *

Scal *

*Principal Subsidiaries

Exhibit 3

PECHINEY UGINE KUHLMANN-CEBAL
Summary of the Principal Clauses of the Proposed Contract
between Brown (Wilson)/Cebal and Byron, Ltd.

1. *Duration of the contract:* five years (then annual renewal by tacit agreement).
2. *Minimum and maximum quantities:* to be sold by the supplier and purchased by the
    customer:
    First year....................   50–110 million units
    Second year..................   120–180 million units
    Third year and following........   150–200 million units
3. *Sales forecasts:* they will be established by Byron, Ltd. three months in advance and
    revised each month.
4. *Sales price* (delivered to the customer's factory): 80 lire
5. *Sales price indexing:*
    a.   The standards for materials consumed by each physical unit (metal, ink, energy,
         etc...) and the standard costs per unit will be communicated to Price Water-
         house by Brown/Cebal as soon as the contract is signed (for aluminum cans
         or for tin cans).
         Category 1.............Basic raw materials: metal, paint, ink, etc.
         Category 2.............Salaries and social charges
         Category 3.............Other cost elements: packaging, energy, tooling,
                                             maintenance, taxes,
                                             royalties
    b.   All changes in unit consumption of materials and all changes in standard unit
         costs (in lire) will bring about, after verification by Price Waterhouse, a change
         in the sales price (for the cost components listed in categories 1, 2, and 3).
         The sales price is subject to revision every two months.
    c.   Each increase in the standard costs for categories 1 and 2 will be increased an
         additional 25% to cover the costs, such as depreciation, leasing, research and
         development, profits, and their eventual modification, these cost factors being
         considered as fixed in the framework of the contract.
6. *Payment terms:* thirty days from the billing date; a discount of 1% for payment in
    the week following the billing day. All payments will be made in lire.
7. *Inventory:* three weeks of finished products at the Brown/Cebal factory.
8. *Sales to third parties:* Brown/Cebal will be able to sell to other customers, even com-
    petitors of Byron, Ltd., after having satisfied the contract.
9. *Responsibility:* the seller and the buyer will be "excused" for not satisfying their
    respective obligations in case of extreme outside conditions. Such conditions are
    fire, floods, strikes, acts of God, and so forth.
10. *Arbitration:* all litigation will be submitted to an international commercial court
    and to arbitrators following the laws in practice.

Exhibit 4

PECHINEY UGINE KUHLMANN-CEBAL

Sources and Uses of Funds by Italian Aluminum Can Subsidiary
(In millions of francs)

	1975	1976	1977	1978	1979	1980	1981	1982	1983	1984	Total
Sources											
Equity from parents	FF 11.2	FF 12.8	FF 0	FF 0	FF 0	FF 0	FF 0	FF 0	FF 0	FF 0	FF 24.0
Loans from parents	0	6.4	9.6	6.4	24.8	0	0	0	0	0	47.2
Lease agreement	0	53.9	0	0	0	0	0	0	0	0	53.9
Other long-term loans	3.2	4.8	4.8	4.8	16.0	0	0	0	0	0	28.8
Bank loans	0	14.4	4.8	0	0	0	0	0	0	0	19.2
Credit from suppliers	0	0.8	4.8	4.0	2.4	6.4	6.4	3.2	2.2	2.4	32.6
Accrued taxes	0	0	0	0	0	7.3	21.1	9.6	5.3	10.8	54.1
Cash flow from operations	(0.3)	(4.8)	(11.2)	12.5	22.3	37.0	65.5	81.0	91.3	99.8	393.1
Total sources	FF 14.1	FF 88.3	FF 8.0	FF 27.7	FF 65.5	FF 50.7	FF 93.0	FF 93.8	FF 98.8	FF 113.0	FF 652.9
Uses											
Investment in fixed assets	FF 10.8	FF 73.8	FF 1.1	FF 23.1	FF 59.9	FF 2.7	FF 2.8	FF 4.5	FF 6.5	FF 6.9	FF 192.1
Start-up costs	2.7	8.3	0	0	0	0	0	0	0	0	11.0
Increase in inventories	0	1.6	4.0	4.8	2.9	6.4	9.0	4.5	2.1	2.4	37.7
Increase in accounts receivable	0	0	2.4	2.4	1.4	3.2	4.0	2.2	1.1	1.2	17.9
Repayment of borrowings:											
Shareholder loans	0	0	0	0	0	28.8	18.4	0	0	0	47.2
Other medium- and long-term	0	0	0.3	0.8	0.8	1.3	2.9	2.9	2.9	16.9	28.8
Supplier loan	0	0	0	0	0	1.1	19.3	2.5	2.5	2.5	27.9
Bank loan	0	0	0	0	0	0	19.2	0	0	0	19.2
Dividends to parents	0	0	0	0	0	9.7	17.4	77.2	83.7	83.1	271.1
	FF 13.5	FF 83.7	FF 7.8	FF 31.1	FF 65.0	FF 53.2	FF 93.0	FF 93.8	FF 98.8	FF 113.0	FF 652.9
Investment in liquid assets	0.6	4.6	0.2	(3.4)	0.5	(2.5)	0	0	0	0	0
Total uses	FF 14.1	FF 88.3	FF 8.0	FF 27.7	FF 65.5	FF 50.7	FF 93.0	FF 93.8	FF 98.8	FF 113.0	FF 652.9

Exhibit 5

PECHINEY UGINE KUHLMANN-CEBAL
Operating Forecasts for Italian Aluminum Can Project

	1975	1976	1977	1978	1979	1980	1981	1982	1983	1984
Millions of units	0	0	60	140	170	245	330	360	360	360
Number of production lines	0	0	1	1	1	2	2	2	2	2
	In Millions of Francs									
Net sales	FF 0	FF 0	FF 45.3	FF 113.6	FF 147.6	FF 227.6	FF 328.1	FF 383.1	FF 409.9	FF 438.6
Cash manufacturing costs	0	0	31.2	68.4	88.2	138.0	193.6	226.7	242.6	259.5
Other cash costs	0	0	4.1	4.8	6.0	7.0	8.2	9.6	10.2	11.0
Industrial margin before leasing	FF 0	FF 0	FF 10.0	FF 40.4	FF 53.4	FF 82.6	FF 126.3	FF 146.8	FF 157.1	FF 168.1
Leasing expense		2.6	12.3	12.3	12.3	12.3	12.3	12.3	12.3	0
Industrial margin	FF 0	FF (2.6)	FF (2.3)	FF 28.1	FF 41.1	FF 70.4	FF 114.0	FF 134.5	FF 144.8	FF 168.1
Brown royalties		0	2.3	5.7	5.9	9.1	9.8	11.5	8.2	8.8
Cebal management fee		0	1.1	2.8	3.0	4.6	4.9	5.7	4.1	4.4
Interest costs:										
Stockholder loans	0	0.2	1.3	1.9	2.3	5.3	2.1	0	0	0
Other loans	0.3	2.0	4.2	5.1	7.6	7.0	7.8	2.6	2.2	1.0
Profit before depreciation and taxes	FF (0.3)	FF (4.8)	FF (11.2)	FF 12.6	FF 22.3	FF 44.3	FF 89.4	FF 114.7	FF 130.3	FF 153.9
Depreciation expense	0	0	3.6	5.2	10.4	13.9	18.5	18.4	19.0	18.6
Amortization of start-up expense	0	0	2.2	2.2	2.2	2.2	2.2	0	0	0
Profit before taxes	FF (0.3)	FF (4.8)	FF (17.0)	FF 5.2	FF 9.7	FF 28.2	FF 68.7	FF 96.3	FF 111.3	FF 135.3
Taxes*	0	0	0	0	0	7.3	24.0	33.7	39.0	54.1
Profit after taxes	FF (0.3)	FF (4.8)	FF (17.0)	FF 5.2	FF 9.7	FF 20.9	FF 44.7	FF 62.6	FF 72.3	FF 81.2
Noncash charges	0	0	5.8	7.3	12.6	16.1	20.8	18.4	19.0	18.6
Cash flow from operations	FF (0.3)	FF (4.8)	FF (11.2)	FF 12.5	FF 22.3	FF 37.0	FF 65.5	FF 81.0	FF 91.3	FF 99.8

*Tax rate, 35% until 1984 when it increases to 40%.

(See major assumptions on next page.)

Exhibit 5—Continued

Major Assumptions Underlying Income Statement Projections

1. *Inflation:* all items leading up to the industrial margin have been adjusted to take into account the expected inflation of 8.4% per year over the period in question. All other items are set by contract or by accounting principles and will not be impacted by inflation.

2. *Reference money:* $1 = FF4.75 and 100 lire = FF0.71. The line items for each year have been converted from lire to francs on the basis of the 100 lire/FF0.71 exchange rate.

3. *Sales price estimates:* the initial price is 80 lire per can (79.20 lire after deducting the 1% discount given for payment within ten days). In constant prices, the price per can has been assumed to fall 10% in 1982 when the contract with Byron, Ltd. is up for renewal. The revenues have been converted to current francs as per item 1, above.

4. *Sales volume estimates:* it is assumed that, beginning in 1980, sales will begin to be made outside Italy: 1980 (10%); 1981 (20%); 1982 to 1984 (25%).

5. *Materials costs and scrap:* these figures are based on current prices and assume that Cégédur Pechiney supplies 75% of the aluminum for the can frames and 100% for the can tops. Alcoa will supply the remaining 25% for the can frames.

6. *Transportation cost:* estimated at FF0.29 per 100 cans in Italy and FF3.92 per 100 cans for sales outside of Italy.

7. *Direct manufacturing costs:* the assumed operating efficiencies are as follows:

1977, June................	40%
1977, December...........	55%
1978, May................	65%
1978, October............	70%
1979, September..........	75%

8. *Financial costs:* 12% for medium-term loans in Italy and 20% for short-term loans in Italy.

9. *Leasing costs:* the contract duration is seven years with an interest rate of 15% and is denominated in U.S. dollars.

10. *Depreciation schedules:* all straight-line.

Buildings.................	20 years
Installation..............	7 years
Tools and replacement parts.....	3 years
Start-up costs............	5 years

Exhibit 6

PECHINEY UGINE KUHLMANN-CEBAL
CASH FLOW ANALYSIS OF ITALIAN ALUMINUM CAN PROJECT
(In millions of francs)

	1975	1976	1977	1978	1979	1980	1981	1982	1983	1984	Total
Investment in form of:											
Loan..................	FF 0	FF (3.2)	FF (4.9)	FF (3.3)	FF (12.6)	FF 0	FF 0	FF 0	FF 0	FF 0	FF (24.2)
Equity.................	(5.6)	(6.6)	0	0	0	0	0	0	0	0	(12.2)
Interest income on loan....	0	0.1	0.7	1.0	1.2	2.7	1.0	0	0	0	6.7
Management fee..........	0	0	1.1	2.8	3.0	4.6	4.9	5.7	4.1	4.4	30.6
French tax on interest and management fee*	0	0	(.9)	(1.9)	(2.1)	(3.7)	(2.9)	(2.9)	(2.0)	(2.2)	(18.6)
Dividends from sub........	0	0	0	0	0	4.9	8.9	39.4	42.7	42.4	138.3
French tax on dividends†....	0	0	0	0	0	(1.7)	(3.1)	(13.8)	(14.9)	(14.8)	(48.3)
Loan repayment by sub.....	0	0	0	0	0	15.0	9.0	0	0	0	24.0
Residual value‡..........	0	0	0	0	0	0	0	0	0	15.0	15.0
Annual aftertax cash flows to Cebal ..	FF (5.6)	FF (9.7)	FF (4.0)	FF (1.4)	FF (10.5)	FF 21.8	FF 17.8	FF 28.4	FF 29.9	FF 44.8	FF 111.5

internal rate of return = 33%
net present value at 15% = FF27.7 million
payback = period 6

* Interest and the management fee would be taxed at a 50% rate.
† Dividends would be taxed at a 35% rate.
‡ Residual value was estimated equal to Cebal's share of the book value at year-end 1984, adjusted for any taxes on liquidation dividends [.51 x FF27.3 million − .35 (.51 x FF27.3 million − FF24 million)]. Exhibit 7 shows a pro forma balance sheet for year-end 1984, with book value of FF27.3 million.

Exhibit 7

PECHINEY UGINE KUHLMANN-CEBAL

PROJECTED BALANCE SHEETS FOR ITALIAN ALUMINUM CAN SUBSIDIARY

(In millions of francs)

ASSETS	1975	1979	1984
Cash and marketable securities.............	FF 0.6	FF 2.5	FF 0
Accounts receivable......................	0	6.2	17.9
Inventory..............................	0	13.3	37.7
Total current assets....................	FF 0.6	FF 22.1	FF 55.6
Gross fixed assets........................	FF 10.8	FF 114.8	FF 138.2
Less: accumulated depreciation............	0	19.2	107.7
Net fixed assets..........................	10.8	95.6	30.5
Capitalized start-up costs..................	2.7	4.4	0
	FF 14.1	FF 122.1	FF 86.1
LIABILITIES AND NET WORTH			
Accounts payable........................	0	12.0	4.7
Accrued taxes...........................	0	0	54.1
Bank loan..............................	0	19.2	0
Total current liabilities.................	FF 0	FF 31.2	FF 58.8
Shareholder loan.........................	0	47.2	0
Other medium- and long-term loans.........	3.2	26.9	0
Shareholders' equity......................	10.9	16.8	27.3
	FF 14.1	FF 122.1	FF 86.1

PECHINEY UGINE KUHLMANN-CEBAL

ANALYSIS OF TOTAL CASH FLOWS BEFORE ANY FINANCING ARRANGEMENTS—ITALIAN ALUMINUM CAN PROJECT
(In millions of francs)

	1975	1976	1977	1978	1979	1980	1981	1982	1983	1984	Total
Industrial margin before leasing*	FF 0	FF 0	FF 10.0	FF 40.4	FF 53.4	FF 82.6	FF 126.3	FF 146.8	FF 157.1	FF 168.1	FF 168.1
Brown royalties*	0	0	2.3	5.7	5.9	9.1	9.8	11.5	8.2	8.8	8.8
Cebal management fee*	0	0	1.1	2.8	3.0	4.6	4.9	5.7	4.1	4.4	4.4
Depreciation expense*	0	0	3.6	5.2	10.4	13.9	18.6	18.4	19.0	18.6	18.6
Imputed depreciation leased equipment	0	0	7.7	7.7	7.7	7.7	7.7	7.7	7.7	0	
Amortization of start-up expense*	0	0	2.2	2.1	2.2	2.2	2.2	0	0	0	0
Profit before taxes	FF 0	FF 0	FF (6.9)	FF 16.9	FF 24.2	FF 45.1	FF 83.1	FF 103.5	FF 118.1	FF 136.3	FF 136.3
Italian taxes	0	0	0	3.5	8.5	15.8	29.1	36.2	41.3	54.5	54.5
French taxes on dividends	0	0	0	0	0	3.4	6.1	27.0	29.3	29.1	29.1
Profit after taxes	FF 0	FF 0	FF (6.9)	FF 13.4	FF 15.7	FF 25.9	FF 47.9	FF 40.3	FF 47.5	FF 52.7	FF 52.7
Noncash charges	0	0	13.5	15.0	20.3	23.8	28.5	26.1	26.7	18.6	18.6
Cash flow from operations	FF 0	FF 0	FF 6.6	FF 28.4	FF 36.0	FF 49.7	FF 76.4	FF 66.4	FF 74.2	FF 71.3	FF 71.3
Investment in fixed assets	FF (10.8)	FF (73.8)	FF (1.1)	FF (23.1)	FF (59.9)	FF (2.7)	FF (2.8)	FF (4.5)	FF (6.5)	FF (6.9)	FF (192.1)
Start-up costs	(2.7)	(8.3)	0	0	0	0	0	0	0	0	(11.0)
Increase in inventories	0	(1.6)	(4.0)	(4.8)	(2.9)	(6.4)	(9.0)	(4.5)	(2.1)	(2.4)	(37.7)
Increase in accounts receivable	0	0	(2.4)	(2.4)	(1.4)	(3.2)	(4.0)	(2.2)	(1.1)	(1.2)	(17.9)
Increase in accounts payable	0	0.8	4.8	4.0	2.4	5.3	(12.9)	0.7	(0.3)	(0.1)	4.7
Increase in accrued taxes	0	0	0	7.7	3.9	9.0	13.6	8.0	3.4	14.6	60.2
Cash flow from operations	0	0	6.6	28.4	36.0	49.7	76.4	66.4	74.2	71.3	
Total cash flow	FF (13.5)	FF (82.9)	FF 3.9	FF 9.8	FF (21.9)	FF 51.7	FF 61.3	FF 63.9	FF 67.6	FF 75.3	FF 75.3

Note:
Internal rate of return, ignoring any terminal value = 21%.
Internal rate of return, assuming terminal value equals net book value in 1985 = 22%.
Payback period = year 6.
*See Exhibit 5.

APPENDIX

COST OF CAPITAL

1. Cost of capital

PUK obtains funds from borrowing and from increasing its stockholders' equity. This money has a cost. It is not difficult to determine the cost for debt; it is the rate of interest. Concerning equity funds, we will indicate the different possible approaches for realistically estimating their cost, that is the "interest" for the stockholders.

The cost of capital for PUK is the weighted average of these two rates of interest (on debt and on equity). It is the average interest rate which must be obtained on long-term capital available to us.

1.1 Cost of debt

The correct cost to take into account is that of future debt and not the average cost of current debt.

The gross cost of future debt can be estimated at 9% (that is 4.5% after taxes at a 50% tax rate).

1.2 Cost of equity

Method 1. The only serious studies of the cost of equity funds over a long period were made for the financial market in the United States. These studies established that, on average, the return on an investment in the stock market (dividends and capital gains) was between 7% and 8% before inflation. These statistics have led to the following formula:

$$\frac{\text{current interest rate of}}{\text{the common stock market}} = 7\% \text{ to } 8\% + \text{the rate of inflation}$$

The current rate of inflation being exceptionally high, the inflation rate to be used in the formula is around 4% to 5%. Thus, the cost of equity funds runs from 11% to 13% for the average company.

Method 2. One can use a discounting formula by assuming that the stockholder discounts a series of dividends and the resale price (terminal value) of his shares. However, the resale price will depend on the series of future dividends.

In this way one reaches the conclusion that the price of a share today is equal to the discounted value of an infinite series of dividends, these dividends increasing at the same rate as reinvested profits. This reasoning leads to the following mathematical formula:

$$\text{rate of interest of equity funds} = D/P + g, \text{ where:}$$

$D =$ dividend per share
$P =$ price of the share
$g =$ rate of increase of the dividend per share to infinity

This formula verifies the hypotheses that the stockholder expects, on the one hand, a certain annual return from his investment (dividend) and, on the other hand, an increase in this return due to the future return on retained earnings. (This formula is however not valid for "growth stocks.")

1.3   Cost of equity for PUK

The relationship (in percent) of the dividend/price of the stock has moved from less than 3% in 1963 (2.8% for the Pechiney shares and 1.8% for the Ugine Kuhlmann shares) to 5.7% in 1973 (taking 140 francs as the average price). This evolution is without a doubt due, on the one hand, to the acceleration of inflation and, on the other hand, to anticipation of smaller dividend increases today than ten years ago.

The average increase of the dividend over the 1963–70 period was 7% per year (for Pechiney as well as for Ugine Kuhlmann). In 1972 and 1973, the dividend was not changed because of the particularly difficult economic situation.

One can presume that the stockholder expects a renewed annual progression of the dividend from 5% to 6%, this increase being lower than that experienced in the past but slightly higher than the long-term rate of inflation (4% to 5%).

Application of the formula gives an interest rate for equity funds of between *11% and 12%* after taxes. We use the lowest estimate (11%) as the cost of equity funds because it seems the most realistic over the long term, even if the probable actual cost is around 13%, given the level of the stock price and inflation.

1.4   Cost of capital

The cost of capital is the weighted average of the interest rates for debt and for equity funds. For the weighting coefficients two approaches can be used:

Method 1.   The respective weighting of the debt and the equity can be taken from the 1972 PUK consolidated balance sheet.

$$\text{Cost of capital} = \frac{re \times SE + i\,(1-t)\,D}{SE + D}$$

re = cost of equity funds   =   11%

SE = shareholders' equity + minority interest   = 7 261 MF

i = gross cost of debt   =   9%

t = tax rate for the totality of the consolidated companies   =   0.40

D = consolidated medium- and long-term debt = 5 181 MF

One obtains a cost of capital equal to 8.7%.

Method 2.   Instead of using the consolidated net shareholders' equity as the weighting coefficient for equity funds, one can use current stockmarket value and the current cost of equity funds (13%).

$$\text{Cost of capital} = \frac{re \times mv + i\,(1-t)\,D}{mv + D}$$

re = current rate of interest on equity funds   =   13%

mv = stockmarket value (on the basis of an average
stockmarket price ex-dividend of FF 140) + minority
interest and annual dividends   = 4 845 MF

The other factors remain unchanged.

The cost of capital evaluated by this method is equal to 9.1%.

We retain 9% as the cost of the capital. The stockmarket capitalization is lower than the consolidated net position, which reflects the current poor return on equity funds. This shows that improving the stockmarket price of the shares depends closely on an improvement in profits. Therefore, it is necessary to establish return on investment objectives which are as ambitious as possible.

BACKGROUND NOTE ON
THE SULPHUR INDUSTRY

∧∧

Sulphur is one of nature's most abundant resources. However, the mineral rarely occurs in a form which is sufficiently concentrated to justify mining operations. Sulphur is produced throughout the world by three very different but fairly simple processes. In the United States and Mexico, most sulphur is produced via the Frasch process (lines 1, 2, and 6, Exhibit 1).

The Frasch process

The Frasch process is useful for mining natural deposits of elemental sulphur found in geological formations known as "salt domes"; these domes dot the coastal area around the Gulf of Mexico. In Frasch mining, a well four to eight inches in diameter is drilled with rotary rigs similar to those used in the petroleum industry. A nest of three concentric pipes is then inserted into the outer drill casing. Superheated water and compressed air are injected into the well through two of the inner pipes; liquid sulphur (which melts at 116°C) rises to the surface through the third pipe as shown below.

The Frasch process is fairly simple. However, the economics of this process are more complicated. Unit production costs are a function of the volume of hot water required to produce a ton of sulphur and the size of the water-boiling plant needed for the specific sulphur deposit.

A fairly rich sulphur deposit may require only 1,600 gallons of hot water to produce one ton of sulphur. If the deposit is large enough, it is most economical to build a boiler plant with a capacity of 8 million gallons per day. As shown in column 1, Exhibit 2, such a facility can produce sulphur for about $4.80 per ton. However, if the deposit is only large enough to justify a boiler plant with a capacity of 1 million gallons per day, production costs rise to about $7.69 per ton (column 3, Exhibit 2).

While boiler plant size is an important variable in determining overall production economics, the "water-ratio" for a deposit is even more important. A sulphur deposit requiring a boiler plant of 4 million gallons per day capacity needs from 1,600 to 9,000 gallons of water to produce a ton of sulphur. As shown in the right half of Exhibit 2, high water-ratios dramatically increase costs. Large, low water-ratio plants are ideal from the standpoint of production

UNDERGROUND PIPING ARRANGEMENT FOR FRASCH SULPHUR PRODUCTION*

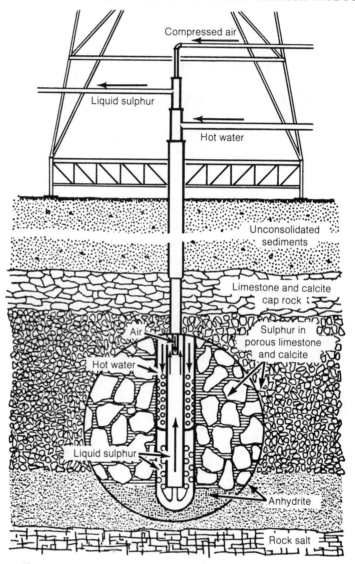

*Jared E. Hazleton, *The Economics of the Sulphur Industry*, (Washington, D.C.: Resources or the Future, Inc., 1970), p. 13.

economics. Unfortunately, nature has not supplied sulphur producers with many deposits which permit the use of such plants.

A record number of sulphur deposits were being mined in the United States in 1966, a year in which the industry was straining to meet demand. This record, however, represented only 11 deposits. While capacity and hot-water-ratio data (and, by implication, cost data) were not available for most sulphur deposits, it is clear from Exhibit 3 that a number of them had production costs in excess of $20 per ton.

Pyrites as a sulphur source

Pyrite ores represent the second major world source of sulphur. Elemental sulphur is not produced directly from pyrites; they are roasted to produce sulphuric acid, the major intermediate sulphur product. The primary sources of pyrite ores are Japan, Spain, and Italy. Pyrites have never been a significant competitive factor in the North-American sulphur market. The high costs of shipping pyrite ores (which contain only about 46% sulphur) make this ore competitive primarily in markets close to production sites.

Recovered sulphur from natural gas

The third but fastest growing process for the production of sulphur involves the separation of hydrogen sulfide from natural gas and the subsequent conversion of hydrogen sulfide to elemental sulphur. Natural gas found in some fields is "polluted" with hydrogen sulfide in amounts ranging from trace quantities to as much as 85%. Before natural gas can be used as a fuel, any hydrogen sulfide contamination must be removed. The "sour" gas fields of Lacq, France and Alberta, Canada thus represent a major source of recovered sulphur (lines 4 and 5, Exhibit 1).

The U.S. sulphur industry

The post-World War II history of the sulphur industry in the United States is essentially the history of two companies, Freeport Sulphur and Texas Gulf Sulphur. In 1966, these two firms produced 95% of the Frasch sulphur mined in the United States (column 3, Exhibit 3). While these firms *produced* most of the U.S. Frasch sulphur, they did not originally *discover* the sulphur they produced.[1] Sulphur discoveries are almost always made by disappointed oil companies. These oil companies generally turn their discoveries over to Freeport or Texas Gulf in return for royalties. Royalties usually equal 50% of the profits before royalty payments and income taxes generated by the production of sulphur from these properties.

The sulphur industry had been profitable until the late 1950s and early 1960s (column 7, Exhibit 4). At that time, prices were eroded by new production from Canada and France (lines 4 and 5, Exhibit 1; columns 8 and 9, Exhibit 4). By 1963, however, a slowdown in the growth of new supplies, combined with a rapid growth in fertilizer sales[2] (Exhibit 5) resulted in a firming of prices. In 1964, the industry began a return to its former level of profitability. Indeed,

---

[1] The two largest sulphur producers had historically carried out modest exploratory drilling programs. In 1965, a growing world sulphur shortage induced these firms to bid $15 million for offshore leases which contained the salt dome formations characteristic of sulphur deposits. The exploration programs were unsuccessful, however, and the lease investments were later written off.

[2] Fertilizer represented the largest use of sulphur in the United States (Exhibit 5).

by late 1967, the market for sulphur was so tight that contract[3] prices had jumped to $38 per ton. Both Freeport and Texas Gulf had voluntarily cut back their exports by 1966 (column 3, Exhibit 6) and were allocating supplies at reduced levels to regular domestic contract customers. Spot buyers of Canadian and Mexican sulphur were paying $50 per ton when and where supplies were available. Sulphur producers everywhere were scrambling for new sources of supply.

---

[3] Contracts were generally written for a minimum of one year and sometimes extended for as long as five or ten years. The seller was often allowed to increase price 30 days after notifying the buyer so long as the buyer chose not to exercise his right to cancel the contract. The buyer could also cancel the contract if he received a bona fide offer from another seller at a lower price and if the original seller chose not to meet the new price.

Exhibit 1

BACKGROUND NOTE ON THE SULPHUR INDUSTRY

FREE-WORLD SULPHUR PRODUCTION

(000s of long tons)

	1958	1959	1960	1961	1962	1963	1964	1965	1966	1967 Est.
Free-world sulphur production										
Frasch production										
1 U.S.	4,200	4,500	4,900	5,400	4,975	4,875	5,225	6,125	7,025	7,000
2 Mexico	1,600	1,300	1,300	1,200	1,350	1,475	1,625	1,475	1,600	1,800
3 Total Frasch production	5,800	5,800	6,200	6,600	6,325	6,350	6,850	7,600	8,625	8,800
Recovered sulphur production										
4 W. Canada	200	300	400	500	1,025	1,275	1,475	1,600	1,725	2,175
5 France	100	400	800	1,100	1,325	1,375	1,475	1,500	1,500	1,600
6 U.S.	600	800	800	900	975	1,000	1,075	1,225	1,250	1,300
7 Other	1,100	1,100	1,100	1,200	1,075	1,025	1,025	1,100	525	650
8 Total recovered sulphur production	2,000	2,600	3,100	3,700	4,400	4,675	5,050	5,425	5,000	5,725
9 Other brimstone	—	—	—	—	—	—	—	—	625	725
10 Total brimstone	7,800	8,400	9,300	10,300	10,725	11,025	11,900	13,025	14,250	15,250
11 Pyrites	5,900	5,700	6,100	6,000	5,950	5,675	5,800	6,125	6,275	6,450
12 Smelter gases and other	2,400	2,500	2,700	2,800	2,825	3,025	3,175	3,350	3,700	3,775
13 Total free-world sulphur production	16,100	16,600	18,100	19,100	19,500	19,725	20,875	22,500	24,225	25,475

* Included in "other" recovered sulphur production prior to 1966.

Source: Engineering and Mining Journal, Sulphur Industry Annual Reviews.

Exhibit 2

BACKGROUND NOTE ON THE SULPHUR INDUSTRY

ESTIMATED PRODUCTION COSTS FOR FRASCH SULPHUR PLANTS OF VARYING SIZES

	(1)	(2)	(3)	(4)	(5)	(6)
	Plants with Different Hot-Water Capacities at Similar Water Ratios			Plants with Similar Hot-Water Capacities at Different Water Ratios		
Capacity (gallons of water per day)	8,000,000	4,000,000	1,000,000	4,000,000	4,000,000	4,000,000
Water ratio (gallons per ton produced)	1,600	1,600	1,600	1,600	4,000	9,000
Capacity (tons of sulphur per year)	1,750,000	875,000	218,750	875,000	350,000	155,400
			$ per ton			
Variable costs						
Production wells	$ 1.12	$ 1.12	$ 1.12	$ 1.12	$ 2.80	$ 6.31
Fuel	1.00	1.01	1.02	1.01	2.53	5.69
Severance tax	1.03	1.03	1.03	1.03	1.03	1.03
Other	.69	.69	.69	.69	.88	1.25
Total variable costs	$ 3.84	$ 3.85	$ 3.86	$ 3.85	$ 7.24	$14.28
Fixed costs						
Wages and salaries	.50	.76	3.04	.76	1.90	4.19
Depreciation	.27	.36	.46	.36	.90	2.02
Other	.19	.25	.33	.25	.64	1.44
Total fixed costs	$ .96	$ 1.37	$ 3.83	$ 1.37	$ 3.44	$ 7.65
Total unit production costs	$ 4.80	$ 5.22	$ 7.69	$ 5.22	$10.68	$21.93

Source: Jared E. Hazleton, *The Economics of the Sulphur Industry* (Washington, D.C.: Resources for the Future, Inc., 1970), p. 40.

Exhibit 3

BACKGROUND NOTE ON THE SULPHUR INDUSTRY

Data Pertaining to the 11 Frasch Sulphur Production Sites in Operation during 1966

Name of Dome	(1) Location	(2) Date Opened	(3) 1966 Production (000s of long tons)	(4) Cumulative Production	(5) Capacity (million gallons of water per day)	(6) Hot Water Ratio (gallons of water per ton of sulphur produced)	Mine Operator
Grand Isle	Louisiana	1960	1,424	6,500	n.a.	n.a.	Freeport Sulphur
Grand Ecaille	Louisiana	1933	1,317	33,000	n.a.	900	
Garden Island Bay	Louisiana	1953	804	8,200	n.a.	n.a.	
Lake Pelto	Louisiana	1960	604	3,300	n.a.	n.a.	
			4,149				
Boling	Texas	1929	1,388	62,500	n.a.	2,500	Texas Gulf Sulphur
Spindletop	Texas	1952	672	7,500	n.a.	n.a.	
Moss Bluff	Texas	1949	255	5,500	n.a.	n.a.	
Fannett	Texas	1958	137	2,000	n.a.	n.a.	
Gulf	Texas	1919	96	12,700	n.a.	n.a.	
			2,548				
Long Point	Texas	1946	250	4,551	3.5	4,500	Jefferson Lake
Orchard	Texas	1938	78	5,149	n.a.	n.a.	Duval
Total U.S. Frasch sulphur produced			7,025				

n.a. = not available.

Source: First Manhattan Co., "Sulphur—A Basic Industry Study," May 26, 1968, pp. 9, 10; and Jared E. Hazleton, *The Economics of the Sulphur Industry* (Washington, D.C.; Resources for the Future, Inc., 1970), pp. 17, 41.

Exhibit 4

BACKGROUND NOTE ON THE SULPHUR INDUSTRY

AVERAGE INVESTMENT, AFTERTAX PROFITS, RATE OF RETURN, PRICE REALIZED PER TON, AND POSTED PRICES FOR THE U.S. FRASCH SULPHUR INDUSTRY, 1940–1967

| Year | Rate of Return after Taxes on Invested Capital (Percent) | | | | Frasch Sulphur Industry | | | Average Price Realized on Domestic Shipments f.o.b. mine ($ per long ton) | Year-End Posted Price for Domestic Shipments f.o.b. mine† ($ per long ton) |
	Texas Gulf	Freeport	Jefferson Lake	Duval	Invested Capital ($ millions)	Income after Taxes ($ millions)	Rate of Return (Percent)		
1940	15.4%	12.4%	28.7%	20.6%	$ 82.6	$ 12.7	15.4%	$15.40	$16.00
1941	15.3	13.6	10.5	25.1	83.2	12.6	15.1	15.70	16.00
1942	15.0	10.6	(13.8)	29.0	83.4	11.3	13.6	15.30	16.00
1943	13.6	12.5	6.5	30.9	82.9	11.3	13.7	15.10	16.00
1944	16.4	11.6	16.2	31.1	82.6	13.0	15.7	15.40	16.00
1945	16.9	14.4	13.2	30.0	84.5	13.7	16.2	15.30	16.00
1946	24.8	15.5	11.5	35.7	89.2	20.0	22.3	15.10	16.00
1947	32.9	9.1	11.4	25.7	103.4	25.8	25.0	17.00	18.00
1948	42.1	12.8	11.6	19.5	97.1	29.5	30.4	17.00	18.00
1949	47.5	17.0	13.6	21.6	92.3	31.0	33.6	16.60	18.00
1950	45.1	19.3	28.7	18.3	104.3	35.3	33.8	18.00	18.00
1951	39.4	16.3	26.1	14.0	117.4	34.4	29.3	20.40	21.00
1952	36.5	17.8	21.7	25.6	126.6	36.5	28.8	20.20	21.00
1953	33.4	19.4	23.6	24.8	124.6	37.8	30.3	26.70	25.50
1954	36.6	21.0	30.2	*	139.5	42.9	30.8	24.90	26.50
1955	33.8	21.8	21.0		161.7	46.7	28.9	27.00	26.50
1956	26.5	19.9	18.5		182.4	43.2	23.7	25.40	26.50
1957	15.9	17.9	13.2		193.0	31.9	16.5	22.90	23.50
1958	12.0	13.0	(6.0)		235.4	27.3	11.6	22.80	23.50
1959	11.6	10.0	(11.7)		278.2	27.3	9.8	22.70	23.50
1960	10.6	9.5	1.7		277.6	25.5	9.2	23.10	23.50
1961	10.1	9.2	10.2		277.5	26.7	9.6	23.60	23.50
1962	9.2	8.8	10.8		288.8	26.0	9.0	21.20	23.50
1963	6.6	8.4	*		295.1	22.2	7.5	19.30	23.50
1964	7.6	9.6			312.9	27.0	8.6	19.70	23.50
1965	11.0	12.7			337.3	40.1	11.9	21.70	25.50
1966	14.1	17.2			389.9	60.8	15.6	22.70	28.50
1967								30.20 est.	38.00 est.

*Jefferson Lake was acquired by Occidental Petroleum in 1964; data not available in 1964. Data for Duval after 1953, due to diversification, no longer reflect results from sulphur mining.

†"Posted" prices were often higher than "realized" prices since discounts and freight absorption were often used to retain customers when market demand was insufficient to maintain prices at the posted level.

Source: Jared E. Hazleton, *The Economics of the Sulphur Industry* (Washington, D.C.: Resources for the Future, Inc., 1970), pp. 114, 156–157.

Exhibit 5

BACKGROUND NOTE ON THE SULPHUR INDUSTRY
U.S. DOMESTIC SULPHUR CONSUMPTION BY SOURCE
(000s of long tons)

	1962	1963	1964	1965	1966	1967 Est.
Fertilizers	2,410	2,675	3,090	3,610	4,425	4,735
Plastic and synthetic products	465	475	505	555	560	500
Paper products	490	500	515	535	565	525
Paints	515	480	505	510	520	510
Nonferrous metals	255	230	235	265	310	260
Explosives	195	205	215	230	260	265
Petroleum refining	140	150	155	165	190	195
Iron and steel production	260	270	330	295	275	225
Other	1,537	1,759	1,652	1,860	2,072	2,117
Total U.S. primary demand	6,267	6,744	7,202	8,025	9,177	9,332

Source: U.S. Department of the Interior.

Exhibit 6
BACKGROUND NOTE ON THE SULPHUR INDUSTRY
U.S. Sulphur Supply, Demand, and Inventory Statistics, 1953–1967
(000s of long tons)

	(1) U.S. Sulphur Production	(2) Imports	(3) Exports	(4) Producers' Inventory Increase	(5) U.S. Domestic Consumption	(6) Producers' Jan. 1 Inventory	(7) Producers' Inventory Increase	(8) Producers' Dec. 31 Inventory	(9) Weeks Sales in Inventory on Jan. 1
1953	6,248	92	1,271	(34)	5,069	3,164	(34)	3,130	32
1954	6,675	135	1,675	207	4,928	3,130	207	3,337	35
1955	7,026	206	1,636	(36)	5,632	3,337	(36)	3,301	30
1956	7,818	387	1,675	755	5,775	3,301	755	4,056	37
1957	7,004	669	1,593	524	5,556	4,056	524	4,580	43
1958	6,141	755	1,602	39	5,254	4,580	39	4,619	46
1959	6,168	777	1,636	(669)	5,978	4,619	(669)	3,950	34
1960	6,660	885	1,787	(172)	5,930	3,950	(172)	3,778	33
1961	7,172	966	1,596	1,035	5,507	3,778	1,035	4,813	45
1962	6,757	1,185	1,554	121	6,267	4,813	121	4,934	41
1963	6,644	1,461	1,613	(252)	6,744	4,934	(252)	4,682	36
1964	7,093	1,582	1,928	(455)	7,202	4,682	(455)	4,227	31
1965	8,212	1,646	2,635	(802)	8,025	4,227	(802)	3,425	22
1966	9,155	1,674	2,373	(721)	9,177	3,425	(721)	2,704	15
1967 est.	9,136	1,639	2,193	(750)	9,332	2,704	(750)	1,954	

Source: U.S. Department of the Interior, *Minerals Yearbook*, 1953–1967.

KELOR CHEMICAL CORPORATION

^^

In mid-1967, the Kelor Chemical Corporation consisted of three divisions which operated in four different businesses: (1) the production of sulphur from sour natural gas; (2) the manufacture of fertilizer; (3) the extraction and processing of liquefied petroleum gas and natural gasoline from natural gas; and (4) the design, engineering, and construction of chemical processing plants. Kelor was not a large competitor in any of these businesses. Kelor's sales in each of its four businesses in fiscal 1967 amounted to less than $4 million.

In the fall of 1967, Kelor was planning to construct and operate a sulphur recovery plant which would greatly expand the company's output and importance in the sulphur industry. The size and speed of its expansion promised to increase the firm's sulphur production tenfold and to triple its assets in only two years. The proposed plant, designed to produce 350,000 tons of sulphur per year, would make Kelor the fourth largest sulphur producer in the United States. (See "Background Note on the Sulphur Industry," Exhibit 3.) Clearly Kelor's growth objective represented a quantum leap forward for the company. Arranging the financing for the new facility which would make this growth plan a reality was a critical management problem.

The sulphur recovery plant

Kelor's proposed plant was to exploit a new method by which sulphur was recovered from gypsum,[1] a rock-like substance. The gypsum was reduced with heat to yield calcium sulfide, which was converted into hydrogen sulfide and slaked lime. The hydrogen sulfide was converted into sulphur. The new process had been developed and tested by Kelor on a pilot-plant basis at a cost of almost $1 million. The process was thought to be unique, and Kelor had a patent application pending on it. Kelor had also taken steps to assure that its unpatentable know-how would be preserved for the company's sole use.

According to the company's plans, the new plant could be operational one year after the start of construction, (i.e., by the end of calendar 1968). The plant would use large amounts of gypsum, natural gas, electricity, and water.

---

[1] The chemical formula of gypsum is $CaSO_4 \cdot 2H_2O$. It contains 18% sulphur by weight.

Kelor had committed for 20-year supplies of natural gas and water;[2] company-owned reserves of gypsum at the proposed site in West Texas were sufficient to support operations for 80 years at the 350,000-ton-per-year operating level. The economics of sulphur recovery at the new facility were believed to be comparable to, and competitive with, most of the other primary sources of sulphur recovery which were being placed in operation during 1967. However, the Kelor process promised higher production costs than some Frasch deposits which had been placed in operation in earlier years. (See "Background Note on the Sulphur Industry," Exhibit 3.)

Capital requirements and investment returns

Kelor concluded that the minimum amount of capital needed to bring its plant on line would be $24.6 million, allocated as outlined in the top half of Exhibit 1. An additional $2.0 million of working capital would be needed to support normal operations at the 350,000-ton-per-year production level. Finally, Kelor's management projected a need for an additional $4.2 million to meet possible contingencies such as construction cost overruns and start-up problems. In all, as much as $30.8 million of new financing would be required. When this amount was compared to Kelor's total assets and earning power (bottom of Exhibit 1), it was clear that Kelor was proposing a quantum leap in corporate size.

This leap promised to be profitable, however. At projected future sulphur price levels ranging from $35.50 to $41.50 per ton (versus a price of $38.00 per ton in September 1967, Exhibit 2), Kelor's sulphur recovery facility offered the following returns over the period 1969–88:

Sulphur Price per Ton	Discounted Cash Flow Internal Rate of Return	Net Present Value of Project at 10% Discount Rate
$35.50	12.5%	$ 5.6 million
38.50	14.9	11.4
41.50	17.2	16.7

Given Kelor's existing financial resources, the projected profitability of the new facility was problematical, however, unless some method could be found for financing the project.

Financing the new facility

Kelor had identified two very different programs for financing its sulphur recovery facility. Both presented problems of implementation.

---

[2] As shown in line 4, Exhibit 3, Kelor was committed to purchase $3.3 million of natural gas, water, and electricity each year. By making these commitments, Kelor assured future supplies at contractually fixed prices somewhat more favorable than current "noncontract" prices. Kelor was also able to escape the initial cash outlay for items such as a 76-mile gas pipeline and electrical transmission lines to the sulphur recovery plant; the cost of these items was included in the prices which Kelor would pay for gas and electricity over 20 years.

The first alternative offered both greater risks and a higher level of return on equity. It was made possible partly because of the way Kelor planned to sell its new sulphur output. Because sulphur was in short supply worldwide, Kelor had been able to induce a number of sulphur buyers to commit to purchase contracts running through June 1974. Under the terms of these contracts, the buyers were obligated to pay the posted price for sulphur f.o.b. Kelor's plant, subject to a minimum price of $35.50 per ton.[3] Kelor had signed up customers for 55% of its output under these terms[4] and anticipated little difficulty in committing 85% of planned production. The remaining uncommitted 15% of total production would be sold in the "spot" market, where prices ranged from 5% to 20% higher in 1967.

The first financing alternative

Kelor's sales contracts promised to reduce the risk for those who financed the sulphur recovery project. This reduced risk would make it possible for the company to sell 100,000 shares of common stock and $12.5 million face amount of convertible subordinated debentures. This would net Kelor approximately $5.3 million and $12.2 million, respectively, after underwriting expenses.[5]

The shortfall between the $17.5 million so raised and the $24.6 million anticipated construction cost (or the $30.8 million total need) would be financed in two steps. First, a commercial bank would provide an $8.0 million short-term construction loan secured by all of the new plant assets. Second, this loan would then be "taken out" from the proceeds of an $18.0 million 15-year loan from two insurance companies. The insurance-company commitment would be arranged concurrently with the other financing. It would be available for takedown after Kelor had committed 70% of its sulphur production under the five-year contract terms outlined earlier and after the recovery facility was completed and operating successfully.[6] The $18.0 million proceeds would be used to retire the $8.0 million bank loan, provide $5.3 million of added working capital for the new plant, and retire $4.7 million of Kelor debt outstanding on June 30, 1967, which was unrelated to the new project.

The second financing alternative

A second possible financing alternative for the sulphur recovery plant was to raise $30.8 million of straight equity capital. Kelor's stock price had risen dramatically since the company's stock had first been sold to the public in

---

[3] The terms of Kelor's contracts differed from those which were common in the industry in that the buyer could not cancel if offered a lower price elsewhere.

[4] Kelor's principal customers under these contracts were Du Pont, Allied Chemical, American Cyanamid, and Stauffer.

[5] Stock would be sold at a net price of $53½ per share. The convertible debentures would be convertible at $65 per share, carry an interest rate of 5½%, and be payable in 20 years with no sinking fund for the first 10 years.

[6] Successful operation for purposes of the loan agreement meant production of 3,500 tons of sulphur in a consecutive seven-day period by the end of April 1969.

December 1966. Part of the reason for this rise was increased investor interest in the securities of sulphur companies as sulphur prices and industry profits rose. (See "Background Note on the Sulphur Industry," Exhibit 4.)

The common stock prices of Kelor, Freeport, and Texas Gulf were all rising throughout this period (Exhibit 2). Perhaps more important in Kelor's case, however, was the degree of investor interest in the company's new process for sulphur production. Kelor was believed to have created a competitive advantage in the future production of gypsum-derived sulphur as a result of possible patent protection, strong technical capability, and the availability of cheap raw materials. Kelor's new facility was thus seen as only the first of a number of similar facilities which the company might build. Kelor's high price-earnings ratio was thus thought to be as much a reflection of the future earnings potential of the new *process* as it was the reflection of profit anticipations from the *specific plant* being built. Kelor had only 300,000 shares of common stock trading in public hands;[7] nonetheless the volume of trading was substantial for a stock of this size, and institutional interest was fairly high.

It was believed that Kelor might be able to raise $30.8 million by selling 680,000 shares at a net price (after underwriting expenses) of $45 per share. This represented a significant reduction from the $53½ net price expected under the other financing alternative (where only 100,000 shares would be sold); however, the larger discount was believed necessary to successfully place an issue of this size.

Comparing the financing alternatives

The earnings contribution and cash flows of the new plant, assuming the project was financed primarily via debt (Alternative 1), are presented in lines 13 and 15 of Exhibit 3. This exhibit also includes earnings growth projections for Kelor's other lines of business (line 16) thus making it possible to project earnings per share (EPS) data for the total firm. As shown in line 19, at the contractually agreed minimum price of $35.50 per ton, the company would earn over $2.50 per share by 1970 if debt-oriented financing were chosen. While this result came as no surprise, Exhibit 4 shows significantly lower EPS projections for the all-equity financing (Alternative 2) over the expected range of future sulphur prices.

Kelor's future EPS position was clearly more attractive under debt-oriented

---

[7] The ownership of Kelor's stock on June 30, 1967, was as follows:

4 Principals............................	577, 392 (in equal amounts)
Other officers and directors..............	62,778
Relatives of officers and directors.........	112,104
Other private investors..................	101,657
Public...............................	300,000
Total...........................	1,153,931

financing. Unfortunately, this alternative placed a fairly heavy burden on the company's total earnings and cash flow in the form of interest and principal repayments (Exhibit 5). It also left Kelor in a less flexible position regarding the financing of additional sulphur recovery facilities in the future.

Exhibit 1

KELOR CHEMICAL CORPORATION
FINANCING NEED FOR THE KELOR SULPHUR RECOVERY FACILITY
VERSUS KELOR'S FINANCIAL STRENGTH

Financing Need for Sulphur Recovery Facility
($ millions)

Design, engineering, and piloting	$ 1.3
Mining and beneficiation equipment	18.6
Rail cars and sulphur storage	2.4
Railroad spur	1.8
Start-up and interest costs	1.5
Total project cost	$25.6
Less: expended to date	1.0
Project cost to be financed	$24.6
Plus: normal working capital	2.0
Plus: contingency working capital	4.2
Total financing need	$30.8

Kelor Historical Financial Data
($ 000s except per share data)

	6/30/64	6/30/65	6/30/66	6/30/67
Profit after taxes	$ 140	$ 324	$ 625	$ 1,028
Average shares outstanding (000s)	853	853	853	1,029*
Earnings per share	$ 0.16	$ 0.38	$ 0.73	$ 1.00
Net worth	$ 1,813	$ 2,287	$ 2,913	$ 6,609
Total assets	10,942	13,302	15,010	16,712

* The "actual" rather than the "average" number of shares outstanding was 1,153,931 on June 30, 1967. The average was lower than the actual since 300,000 shares were sold to the public in late 1966.

Exhibit 2

KELOR CHEMICAL CORPORATION

COMMON STOCK PRICE AND TRADING VOLUME DATA FOR SULPHUR PRODUCERS VERSUS POSTED PRICE DATA FOR DOMESTIC SULPHUR SHIPMENTS, 12/31/66 to 9/30/67

	Kelor Chemical		*Freeport Sulphur*		*Texas Gulf Sulphur*		*Posted Price for Domestic Sulphur Shipments*
Month/Year	*Price per Share*	*Trading Volume (000s)*	*Price per Share*	*Trading Volume (000s)*	*Price per Share*	*Trading Volume (000s)*	*($ per ton)*
12/66	10¾	38	38⅜	146	105¾	687	28.50
1/67	15¾	53	38½	315	118⅞	1,049	28.50
2/67	16	69	42⅜	201	110	672	28.50
3/67	16¾	83	52½	188	107⅜	743	28.50
4/67	21¼	76	55⅛	141	116⅜	370	32.50
5/67	25⅞	39	54¾	148	114⅞	710	32.50
6/67	35⅜	80	55⅜	125	122⅜	282	38.00
7/67	35	63	68	195	153	481	38.00
8/67	48	67	66	175	146	348	38.00
9/67	60¾	84	74⅞	165	148¾	367	38.00

Note: On December 31, 1966, the total number of shares outstanding for Kelor, Freeport, and Texas Gulf was 1.2 million, 15.4 million, and 10.0 million, respectively.

Exhibit 3

KELOR CHEMICAL CORPORATION

ECONOMIC ANALYSIS OF KELOR'S NEW SULPHUR RECOVERY FACILITY AND THE IMPACT OF THIS FACILITY ON KELOR'S FUTURE EARNINGS PER SHARE, 1968–1975

($000s except per ton and per share data)

		6/30/68	6/30/69	6/30/70	6/30/71	6/30/72	6/30/73	6/30/74	6/30/75
	NEW PROJECT ONLY								
1	Volume of sulphur sold (000 tons)*		88	350	350	350	350	350	350
2	Price per ton ($)		$35.50	$35.50	$35.50	$35.50	$35.50	$35.50	$35.50
3	Total revenue		$3,106	$12,425	$12,425	$12,425	$12,425	$12,425	$12,425
4	Natural gas, electricity, water†		$ 825	$3,300	$3,300	$3,300	$3,300	$3,300	$3,300
5	Interest on debt		482	1,926	1,926	1,830	1,735	1,640	1,545
6	Depreciation and amortization‡		376	1,505	1,505	1,505	1,505	1,429	1,201
7	Severance tax§		90	361	361	361	361	361	361
8	Other expenses		750	3,000	3,000	3,000	3,000	3,000	3,000
9	Profit before depletion and taxes		$ 583	$2,333	$2,333	$2,429	$2,524	$2,695	$3,018
10	Depletion‖		291	1,166	1,166	1,215	1,262	1,347	1,509
11	Profit before taxes		$ 292	$1,167	$1,167	$1,214	$1,262	$1,348	$1,509
12	Taxes		146	584	584	607	631	674	755
13	Profit after taxes#		$ 437	$1,749	$1,749	$1,822	$1,893	$2,021	$2,263
14	Depreciation and amortization		376	1,505	1,505	1,505	1,505	1,429	1,201
15	Cash flow		$ 813	$3,254	$3,254	$3,327	$3,398	$3,450	$3,464
	EXISTING LINES OF BUSINESS								
16	Profit after taxes**	$1,149	$1,287	$1,414	$1,614	$1,808	$2,025	$2,268	$2,540
	KELOR TOTAL CORPORATION DATA								
17	Profit after taxes	$1,149	$1,724	$3,163	$3,363	$3,630	$3,918	$4,289	$4,803
18	Average shares outstanding (000s)	1,254	1,254	1,254	1,254	1,254	1,254	1,254	1,254
19	Earnings per share ($)	$ 0.92	$ 1.37	$ 2.54	$ 2.68	$ 2.89	$ 3.12	$ 3.42	$ 3.83

* The facility was projected to be operational by December 31, 1968. Capacity operations would not commence until March 31, 1969, so fiscal 1969 benefited from only one quarter of a year of operations. Losses from prior operations were capitalized as start-up costs.

† These amounts represented firm obligations incurred by Kelor under long-term contracts which guaranteed the supply of natural gas, electricity, and water.

‡ $1.5 million of start-up and interest costs were amortized over five years. Other depreciable assets were depreciated over 20 years.

§ State taxes of $1.03 per ton were levied on each ton of sulphur extracted.

‖ Depletion was a noncash expense which was allowed for purposes of reducing income taxes. The deduction was permitted in order to stimulate mining activity. Depletion was limited in size to the lesser of (a) 50% of project profit before depletion and taxes or (b) 15% of project revenues.

As noted above, since depletion was a noncash expense used only in the calculation of Kelor's tax liability, this amount was added back to Kelor's profit after taxes as reported to shareholders.

** Profits from Kelor's other operations were assumed to grow at 12% per year.

Exhibit 4

KELOR CHEMICAL CORPORATION

TOTAL KELOR EPS UNDER THE TWO FINANCING ALTERNATIVES FOR THE SULPHUR RECOVERY FACILITY
ASSUMING THREE DIFFERENT PRICE LEVELS FOR SULPHUR SHIPMENTS, 1969–1975

($ per share)

	6/30/69	6/30/70	6/30/71	6/30/72	6/30/73	6/30/74	6/30/75	
Financing Alternative 1—debt*	1.37	2.54	2.68	2.89	3.12	3.42	3.83	} Sulphur price = $35.50/ton
" 2—equity	1.11	2.45	2.54	2.65	2.77	2.92	3.13	
Financing Alternative 1—debt	1.53	3.17	3.31	3.52	3.75	4.05	4.45	} Sulphur price = $38.50/ton
" 2—equity	1.20	2.78	2.87	2.98	3.10	3.25	3.46	
Financing Alternative 1—debt	1.69	3.79	3.92	4.12	4.33	4.59	4.94	} Sulphur price = $41.50/ton
" 2—equity	1.28	3.11	3.20	3.31	3.42	3.58	3.78	

* Because of (a) Kelor's high price-earnings ratio at the time the convertible debentures were sold and (b) the low effective tax rate resulting from depletion allowances, Kelor's EPS was not significantly reduced by conversion of the convertible debentures. For the year ending June 30, 1975, for example, at a $35.50 per ton sulphur price, EPS on a fully diluted basis would have been $3.68 as opposed to $3.83 on an undiluted basis.

Exhibit 5

KELOR CHEMICAL CORPORATION

PROJECTION OF EARNINGS AND CASH FLOWS AVAILABLE TO MEET FIXED FINANCIAL CHARGES AND THE CALCULATION OF THE FIXED FINANCIAL CHARGES ASSOCIATED WITH FINANCING ALTERNATIVE 1 FOR THE KELOR SULPHUR RECOVERY FACILITY, 1969–1979

(Sulphur recovery project only; $000s)

	6/30/69	6/30/70	6/30/71	6/30/72	6/30/73	6/30/74	6/30/75	6/30/76	6/30/77	6/30/78	6/30/79
Earnings before interest, depletion and taxes (lines 5 + 9, Exhibit 3)	$1,065	$4,259	$4,259	$4,259	$4,259	$4,335	$4,563	$4,563	$4,563	$4,563	$4,563
Interest											
6⅞% senior debt	$ 310*	$1,238	$1,238	$1,142	$1,047	$ 952	$ 857	$ 761	$ 666	$ 571	$ 476
5½% convertible subordinated debt	172*	688	688	688	688	688	688	688	688	688	688
Total interest	$ 482	$1,926	$1,926	$1,830	$1,735	$1,640	$1,545	$1,449	$1,354	$1,259	$1,164
Cash flow (line 15, Exhibit 3)	$ 813	$3,254	$3,254	$3,327	$3,398	$3,450	$3,464	$3,536	$3,607	$3,679	$3,756
Debt principal repayments											
Senior debt	$ 0	$ 0	$1,385	$1,385	$1,385	$1,385	$1,385	$1,385	$1,385	$1,385	$1,385
Convertible subordinated debt	0	0	0	0	0	0	0	0	0	0	1,250†
Total debt	$ 0	$ 0	$1,385	$1,385	$1,385	$1,385	$1,385	$1,385	$1,385	$1,385	$2,635

* Interest incurred prior to the start of production was capitalized and written off over the five years following the start of full-scale operations.
† Principal repayments on the convertible subordinated debt were not scheduled to start until 1979.

Exhibit 6

KELOR CHEMICAL CORPORATION

SUMMARY BALANCE SHEET DATA FOR KELOR UNDER THE ALTERNATIVE PROPOSALS FOR FINANCING THE SULPHUR RECOVERY FACILITY, 1967–1975

($ millions)

	6/30/67	6/30/68	6/30/69	6/30/70	6/30/71	6/30/72	6/30/73	6/30/74	6/30/75
	Financing Alternative 1								
BALANCE SHEET DATA									
1 Net working capital*	$ 2.4	$ 7.7	$ 6.8	$10.0	$11.7	$13.4	$15.3	$17.2	$19.0
2 Plant and equipment (sulphur recovery)†	—	12.5	26.9	25.4	23.9	22.4	20.9	19.5	18.3
3 Plant and equipment (other)†	10.4	11.6	13.1	14.6	16.4	18.4	20.6	23.0	25.8
4 Other	0.2	0.2	0.2	0.2	0.2	0.2	0.2	0.2	0.2
5 *Total assets‡*	$13.0	$32.0	$47.0	$50.2	$52.2	$54.4	$57.0	$59.9	$63.3
6 Senior debt	$ 0	$ 0	$18.0	$18.0	$16.6	$15.2	$13.9	$ 12.5	$ 11.1
7 Convertible subordinated debt	0	12.5	12.5	12.5	12.5	12.5	12.5	12.5	12.5
8 Other long-term debt	5.9	5.9	1.2	1.2	1.2	1.2	1.2	1.2	1.2
9 Total debt	$ 5.9	$18.4	$31.7	$31.7	$30.3	$28.9	$27.6	$26.2	$24.8
10 Deferred taxes	0.5	0.5	0.5	0.5	0.5	0.5	0.5	0.5	0.5
11 Shareholders' equity§	6.6	13.1	14.8	18.0	21.4	25.0	28.9	33.2	38.0
12 *Total liabilities*	$13.0	$32.0	$47.0	$50.2	$52.2	$54.4	$57.0	$59.9	$63.3
	Financing Alternative 2								
BALANCE SHEET DATA									
13 Net working capital*	$ 2.4	$20.6	$ 6.8	$11.4	$15.7	$20.1	$24.5	$28.8	$33.0
14 Plant and equipment (sulphur recovery)†	—	12.5	26.9	25.4	23.9	22.4	20.9	19.5	18.3
15 Plant and equipment (other)†	10.4	11.6	13.1	14.6	16.4	18.4	20.6	23.0	25.8
16 Other	0.2	0.2	0.2	0.2	0.2	0.2	0.2	0.2	0.2
17 *Total assets‡*	$13.0	$45.0	$47.0	$51.5	$56.2	$61.1	$66.2	$71.5	$77.3
18 Total long-term debt	$ 5.9	$ 5.9	$ 5.9	$ 5.9	$ 5.9	$ 5.9	$ 5.9	$ 5.9	$ 5.9
19 Deferred taxes	0.5	0.5	0.5	0.5	0.5	0.5	0.5	0.5	0.5
20 Shareholders' equity§	6.6	38.6	40.6	45.1	49.8	54.7	59.8	65.1	70.9
21 *Total liabilities*	$13.0	$45.0	$47.0	$51.1	$56.2	$61.1	$66.2	$71.5	$77.3

*Net working capital was calculated as a "plug" figure.

†Plant and equipment for the sulphur recovery facility was assumed to decline with annual depreciation charges. Plant and equipment utilized in Kelor's other lines of business was assumed to grow 12% year, in line with sales growth.

‡The total-asset figure for June 30, 1967 differs from that shown in Exhibit 1 since for convenience Exhibit 6 figures net out current liabilities from current assets.

KELLOGG COMPANY

∧∧

Company background

On December 31, 1972, the Kellogg Company of Battle Creek, Michigan completed its 21st year of uninterrupted growth in sales and earnings per share (columns 1 and 5 of Exhibit 1). Kellogg, the leader in the manufacture of RTE[1] cereals, was one of the most profitable companies in the United States. The firm's return on equity had consistently exceeded 20% for two decades (column 6, Exhibit 2).

Kellogg's success in the U.S. securities markets was comparable to its success in the cereal business. Investors had historically given the company a more generous stock price measured against both book value and earnings per share, for example, than they had given to the 30 companies comprising the Dow Jones Industrial Average (columns 8–11, Exhibit 2).

By traditional U.S. standards, Kellogg was very conservatively financed. A small amount of funds was borrowed overseas, and these foreign loans represented the only borrowed money on the company's balance sheet. In addition to its large reserve of borrowing power, historically the company had maintained cash and marketable securities equal to about 20% of total assets.

The RTE cereal industry

Kellogg was the leading RTE cereal manufacturer in the United States by a wide margin. Indeed, Kellogg's cereal sales were more than twice as large as the cereal sales of the company's nearest competitor, General Mills (Exhibit 3). In 1972, Kellogg produced 12 different brands of RTE cereals with individual national market shares exceeding 1%.

The introduction of new products was particularly important in the RTE cereal business (Exhibit 3). Between 1954 and 1964, for example, the number of RTE cereals carried in a typical grocery chain more than doubled (Exhibit 4). During this period, the number of old cereals which *disappeared* from supermarket shelves was almost as large as the total number of items *carried* in 1954. In 1964, RTE cereals introduced since 1954 accounted for more than 23% of total cereal sales.

---

[1] Ready-to-eat (RTE) cereals require no heating before they are eaten.

While the introduction of new cereals was fairly common, these introductions were nevertheless expensive. As indicated in Exhibit 5, expenditures on research and development (R&D), marketing research, and test marketing amounted to $1.1 million before a typical new RTE cereal product was introduced. During the first year following the start of national distribution, marketing expenditures for a new RTE cereal averaged 51% of sales.

New RTE cereals were expensive to launch; they also had a high mortality rate and took a long time to break even (if they ever did break even). New cereals also took a long time to move from the R&D stage to the marketplace (Exhibit 5). Only 40% of the new RTE cereals introduced between 1954 and 1964 had reached breakeven[2] within four years after they were first introduced nationally. The average new RTE cereal took roughly 55 months to move from R&D to national distribution. By way of contrast, most other manufactured food products had lower introduction costs, higher rates of success, and shorter product-introduction cycles (Exhibit 5).

Battle Creek under siege—1972

Kellogg's preeminent position in the cereal business was the source of the company's great strength; however, this position had also created problems. One of these was with the U.S. Federal Trade Commission (FTC). During the late 1960's, a major policy debate had gone on internally at the FTC. This debate centered around first "whether" and second "how" the FTC ought to try to restructure some of the nation's most concentrated[3] industries in an effort to make them more competitive. The essence of the debate was captured in June 1969 by the chief of the FTC's Division of General Trade Restraints:

To put the matter rather bluntly, this country's laws against monopolization and the various forms of consumer exploitation that it implies have not, at least until the last few years, kept pace with the changes that have come about in our various industrial organizations. Markets are being "restructured" almost daily by private business firms, while the public itself is frequently assumed, without much discussion, to have no right, save in the case of mergers, to undo what business has done. The so-called "anticompetitive practices" that were so popular with the industrial barons of the late 19th and early 20th century years have, for the most part, gone the way of the "horizontal" merger, being replaced by something more subtle and elusive. Much of what the law forbids today, the modern would-be monopolist doesn't *need* to practice anyway. And what he *does* need in order to ply his trade, the law often allows. The point, of course, is that, in many areas, the law has seized the shadow and missed the substance of the problem at hand. While it chases a menagerie of relatively insignificant business "practices," new oligopolies are being perfected and more consumers are being compelled to pay prices that are higher

---

[2] "Breakeven" is defined here in a cumulative sense. That is, all R&D, market-research, and product-introduction expenses had been recovered before a product was deemed to have reached breakeven.

[3] The degree of "concentration" in an industry is generally measured in terms of the value of shipments of the top producers (usually four) to the value of shipments of all producers in the total industry.

and higher above the level that would have prevailed had competition remained effective in those industries.

The question, of course, is whether the law can and should be directed away from the relatively superficial features of business "conduct" that have preoccupied it in the past and begin to assess the genuinely significant (from the consumer's standpoint) questions of *structure* (concentration, product differentiation, and entry barriers) and *performance* (particularly prices). Legally, the issue is whether it either is or should be considered a violation of the Sherman Act and/or the Federal Trade Commission Act for, say, three or four firms to "concentrate" 70% or 80% of an industry in their hands and then exercise the power that market share gives them to charge a price that exceeds by say 20% the price that would have prevailed had that market remained less concentrated. As we indicated above, the precedent in this area is thin indeed, and a careful and comprehensive development of the law and economics of the monopoly/oligopoly phenomenon would no doubt be necessary in order to convince the courts that the substance of the problem—noncompetitive structure and performance characteristics, particularly the unnecessarily concentrated markets and supercompetitive prices characteristic of many of these industries—can and should be reached directly, rather than attempting to reach it indirectly, by challenging only one of its many, and often elusive, symptoms.[4]

As the internal struggle within the FTC progressed, a target industry was needed for the Commission staff's deconcentration efforts. Of those highly concentrated industries shown in Exhibit 6, the RTE cereal industry was selected. The FTC then undertook a series of economic studies aimed at buttressing its proposed complaint against the major companies in the RTE cereal industry.

In 1969, the FTC issued an economic report which attempted to statistically link the profitability of food-manufacturing firms to levels of concentration and advertising/sales ratios in the specific product markets served by these firms. The FTC based its report upon a lengthy study of the cereal industry completed in 1966 by the National Commission on Food Marketing.

A second FTC report (also issued in 1969) suggested the possibility of a reduction in cereal prices of 20% to 25% if the RTE cereal industry were made more competitive.[5]

The FTC made no public mention of the fact that the RTE cereal industry would be the target of a major new investigation. However, press reports made it apparent outside the FTC by 1971 that the RTE cereal industry could expect a regulatory challenge based on previously "untested" legal theory. Observers following the FTC's progress in initiating the case suggested that:

If such a case is in fact filed by the FTC, it would easily be the most important antitrust action in the nation's history, one that, by its mere filing, would amount to nothing less than a challenge to the legality of perhaps a third of the country's

---

[4] Rufus E. Wilson, "The FTC's Deconcentration Case Against the Breakfast Cereal Industry: A New 'Ballgame' in Antitrust?" *Antitrust Law and Economics Review*, Summer, 1971, pp. 70–71.

[5] Given the data of Exhibit 7, it is unclear how reductions of this magnitude might occur if reasonable profits were still to be earned.

manufacturing sector, the third that, in Professor Galbraith's phrase, constitutes the country's "industrial heartland."[6]

Complaint is filed

On April 26, 1972, the U.S. Federal Trade Commission filed a complaint against Kellogg, General Mills, General Foods, and Quaker Oats (the respondents), alleging violations of the U.S. Federal Trade Commission Act.[7] The Commission alleged that the top four U.S. cereal manufacturers had engaged in four specific anticompetitive practices.[8] The following text is quoted directly from the FTC complaint:

A. Brand Proliferation, Product Differentiation and Trademark Promotion. Respondents have introduced to the market a profusion of RTE cereal brands. During the period 1950 through 1970 approximately 150 brands, mostly trademarked, were marketed by respondents. Over half of these brands were introduced after 1960. . . .

Respondents artificially differentiate their RTE cereals. Respondents produce basically similar RTE cereals, and then emphasize and exaggerate trivial variations, such as color and shape. . . .

Respondents have steadily increased the level of advertising expenditures for RTE cereals. During the period 1950 through 1970, respondents' aggregate annual advertising expenditures for RTE cereals tripled from $26 million to $81 million. In 1970, respondents' advertising to sales ratio for RTE cereals averaged 13 percent.

These practices of proliferating brands, differentiating similar products and promoting trademarks through intensive advertising result in high barriers to entry into the RTE cereal market.

B. Unfair Methods of Competition in Advertising and Product Promotion. (1) By means of statements and representations contained in their advertisements, respondents:

In advertisements aimed at children, represent directly or by implication, that their RTE cereals enable children to perform the physical activities depicted or described in their advertisements.

. . . . .

C. Control of Shelf Space. Kellogg is the principal supplier of shelf space services for the RTE cereal sections of retail grocery outlets. Such services include

---

[6] "The FTC's Deconcentration Case," p. 58.

[7] The companies were specifically charged with violating Section 5(a)(1) of the Federal Trade Commission Act which reads as follows: "Unfair methods of competition in commerce, and unfair or deceptive acts or practices in commerce, are hereby declared unlawful."

[8] Note by editors: The respondent companies vigorously denied and labeled as false many of the assertions and conclusions stated in the FTC complaint. The allegations against Quaker Oats were dismissed by the Administrative Law Judge of the FTC following the completion of the FTC's affirmative case. As of June 1980, the proceedings before the Administrative Law Judge were still in process. No opinion by the Administrative Law Judge on the merits of the allegations against the other three respondents is anticipated until mid-1981 or later. Regardless of what the Administrative Law Judge finds, it is entirely possible that a considerable number of years may pass before the case is finally decided. Any opinion adverse to the respondents is almost certain to be appealed all the way to the Supreme Court both on issues of due process and on substantive grounds.

the selection, placement and removal of RTE cereals and allocation of shelf space for RTE cereals to each respondent and to other RTE cereal producers.

Through such services respondents have interfered with and now interfere with the marketing efforts of other producers of RTE and other breakfast cereals and producers of other breakfast foods. Through such services respondents restrict the shelf positions and the number of facings for Nabisco and Ralston RTE cereals and remove the RTE cereals of small regional producers.

All respondents acquiesce in and benefit from the Kellogg shelf space program which protects and perpetuates their respective market shares through the removal or controlled exposure of other breakfast food products including but not limited to RTE cereal products.

D. *Acquisition of Competitors.* During the past 70 years numerous acquisitions have occurred in the breakfast cereal industry. One of the effects of these acquisitions was the elimination of significant sources of private label RTE cereal. Among them are the following:

In 1943, General Foods acquired Jersey Cereal Company, a Pennsylvania corporation. Before acquisition by General Foods, Jersey Cereal Company was a substantial competitor in the sale of private-label and other RTE cereal.

In 1943, Kellogg leased and controlled the manufacturing facilities of Miller Cereal Company, Omaha, Nebraska, a substantial competitor in the sale of private label and other RTE cereal. In 1958, upon termination of the said leasing agreement, Kellogg purchased the assets of Miller.

In 1946, General Foods acquired the RTE manufacturing facilities of Campbell Cereal Company, Minneapolis, Minnesota, a substantial competitor in the sale of RTE cereal. Following this acquisition, General Foods dismantled the RTE facilities of Campbell and shipped said facilities to South Africa.

The aforesaid acquisitions have enhanced the shared monopoly structure of the RTE cereal industry.[9]

The practices cited above were alleged by the Commission to have had the following effects, among others:

a. Respondents have, individually and collectively, established and maintained artificially inflated prices for RTE cereals.

b. Respondents have obtained profits and returns on investment substantially in excess of those that they would have obtained in a competitively structured market.

. . . . .

[c.] Meaningful price competition does not exist in the RTE cereal market.

[d.] American consumers have been forced to pay substantially higher prices for RTE cereals than they would have had to pay in a competitively structured market.[10]

The Commission further alleged that by means of the previously mentioned acts and practices:

---

[9] "In the Matter of Kellogg Company et al.," U.S. Federal Trade Commission, April 26, 1972, pp. 5–9.

[10] Ibid., pp. 9–10.

a. Respondents individually and in combination have maintained, and now maintain, a highly concentrated, noncompetitive market structure in the production and sale of RTE cereal, in violation of Section 5 of the Federal Trade Commission Act.

b. Respondents, individually and collectively, have obtained, shared and exercised, and now share and exercise, monopoly power in, and have monopolized, the production and sale of RTE cereal, in violation of Section 5 of the Federal Trade Commission Act.

c. Respondents, and each of them, have erected, maintained and raised barriers to entry to the RTE cereal market through unfair methods of competition, in violation of Section 5 of the Federal Trade Commission Act.[11]

Finally, in filing its complaint the Commission stated that if, following adjudicative proceedings, it were to find the respondents guilty, the Commission could "order such relief as . . . is deemed necessary and appropriate including, but not limited to":

1. Divestiture of assets, including plants and other facilities, for the formation of new corporate entities to engage in the manufacture, distribution, and sale of RTE cereals, and such trademarks, brand names, and know-how as may be required for, or useful in, such manufacture, distribution, and sale;

2. Licensing of existing brands or trademarks and future brands or trademarks on a royalty-free basis for a specified period of time;

3. Prohibition of acquisition of stock or assets of firms engaged in the business of manufacturing or selling RTE cereals for a specified period of time;

4. Prohibition of any practices found to be anticompetitive, including but not limited to shelf space services or use of particular methods of selling or advertising acts or practices, and other provisions appropriate to correct or remedy the effects of such anticompetitive practices.[12]

Regulatory problems outside the United States

The highly attractive investment returns earned by Kellogg on its domestic U.S. cereal business were under attack as a result of the FTC complaint. Fortunately for Kellogg, not all of the company's business was in the United States. Indeed, in 1972, Kellogg's sales outside of North America had exceeded $165 million (Exhibit 8). While this represented less than 25% of Kellogg's total sales, the firm had been able to capture a major share of the RTE cereal business in at least one other important area. That area was the United Kingdom, where Kellogg controlled an even larger market share than in the United States (Exhibit 9). Unfortunately for Kellogg, the company's regulatory problems in the United Kingdom were even more serious than in the United States. The added seriousness of the company's U.K. problems resulted from the fact that whereas the U.S. regulatory challenge had only been *initiated* at

---

[11] Ibid., p. 10.
[12] Ibid., p. 12.

the close of 1972, a similar challenge in the United Kingdom had already been *concluded.*

Indeed, after completing a 14-month study of the breakfast-cereal industry requested by the Department of Trade and Industry,[13] the U.K. Monopolies Commission in August 1972 recommended (a) that Kellogg's U.K. subsidiary be indefinitely forbidden from raising its prices for breakfast cereals without specific government approval, and (b) that the company's profit rates be kept under review. These recommendations were given the force of law when accepted by the U.K. government, which hinted that Kellogg would find future price increases very difficult to obtain.[14]

The Monopolies Commission's contention was that Kellogg's predominant market share (Exhibit 9) and its large advertising expenditures (column 2, Exhibit 10) would allow the company to price its product so as to achieve excessive returns (column 6, Exhibit 10; Exhibit 11). Some excerpts from the Monopolies Commission's 40-page report on the breakfast cereals industry follow:

Kellogg told us [the Monopolies Commission] as did Nabisco and Weetabix, that prices were not determined by the structure of the industry or by the fact that Kellogg held a substantial share of the market or by the number of competing firms, but by the nature of the product and of the market. In Nabisco's view the level of prices reflected the manufacturing and marketing efficiency of the producers. Kellogg submitted that neither the small number of producers nor their share of the market had "any real bearing upon the part price competition plays in this industry." The effective factor in this regard was, in Kellogg's view, the limited extent of price sensitivity of the various products, bearing in mind that they were not in the nature of a commodity, but were branded products, each offering to the consumer a different bargain comprised of product type, product base, taste and presentation, as well as price.

· · · · ·

In describing its pricing policy Kellogg said:

The level of prices charged by the Company bears upon the Company's share of the market, and the maintenance of its share, in two ways which are interconnected. In the first place, the Company's share of the market depends upon its ability to continue to persuade the consumer that its products for what they offer, represent a good bargain relative to other competing products in favour of which

[13] Under U.K. law, the Secretary of State for Trade and Industry has the authority to order the Monopolies Commission to (a) investigate, (b) render a report, and (c) recommend possible remedies for competitive situations in which a dominant firm accounts for at least one third of the supply of a specific product or service. After receiving the Monopolies Commission report, the Department of Trade and Industry may, at its discretion, negotiate remedies with the companies involved. Remedies are sought only if the competitive situation "operates or may be expected to operate against the public interest." While some sort of negotiated settlement is almost always arrived at, the Department of Trade and Industry can issue compulsory orders. These orders are subject to appeal in the courts.

[14] "Britain: A Chill on Kellogg's Pricing Policies," *Business Week*, March 3, 1973.

an alternative choice might be exercised. Second, it depends upon not setting its prices at levels which are such as to encourage new entry or such as to give existing competitors a real opportunity of increasing the volume of their sales by selling at significantly lower prices. Unless the level of prices charged by the Company had met these requirements it would not have achieved its present position, and unless the requirements continue to be met, the Company's market share cannot be maintained. In particular, if the level of prices were such as to encourage new entry, a permanent loss of market share could be expected, since only a price war, with all that entails, can drive out someone who has established himself as a producer in the market.

· · · · ·

Kellogg expressed the view that price competition as a principal marketing weapon was only to be expected where there was a sufficient degree of price sensitivity. The Company saw that degree existing where the consumer is offered a choice between two products, one of which is a copy of the other, as for instance Kellogg's Corn Flakes and retailers' own brands of cornflakes, and Kellogg stressed its need, in setting the prices for its Corn Flakes, to pay regard to the prospective prices of own brand cornflakes. The view of Viota,[15] as the producer of the own-brand cornflakes, was that producers did compete fully with one another in price and that the level of prices charged by Kellogg for Corn Flakes was extremely competitive.

· · · · ·

In summary, Kellogg accepted that, subject to the competition offered by retailers' own brands, the industry is fairly described as one in which, because there has been competition only in a limited sense between differentiated products and because these have been products of vigorously advertised and promoted convenience appeal, the public has, within limits, been willing to pay for them what the manufacturers have chosen to ask it to pay.[16]

The Monopolies Commission was "not prepared to conclude that Kellogg's profits are excessive at present" (mid-1972). However, the Commission did conclude that in the past "these profits have . . . been excessive."[17] Control over any upward revision in Kellogg's pricing was seen as a remedy against the possibility of Kellogg's return to excess profitability in the future.

---

[15] Viota Limited began producing private-label (own-brand) cornflakes in 1963. Viota's business began to grow rapidly in 1966 (Exhibit 9). By the end of 1971, Viota had as customers 25 different retail chains in the United Kingdom which accounted for nearly 50% of total cornflakes sales. Viota's private-label cornflakes generally sold at retail for 9.5 pence for a 12-ounce box (Exhibit 12). Kellogg's Corn Flakes generally sold for 10.5 pence for a box of similar size.

[16] "Breakfast Cereals, A Report on the Supply of Ready Cooked Breakfast Cereal Foods," U. K. Monopolies Commission, February 20, 1973, pp. 19–21.

[17] Ibid., p. 28.

Exhibit 1

KELLOGG COMPANY

GROWTH OF SALES AND EARNINGS PER SHARE OF THE KELLOGG COMPANY VERSUS THE U.S. GROSS NATIONAL PRODUCT AND THE FIRMS COMPRISING THE DOW JONES INDUSTRIAL AVERAGE, 1951–1972

	Kellogg Sales ($ millions)	U.S. GNP ($ billions)	Kellogg Growth in Sales (Percent)	Growth in GNP (Percent)	Kellogg EPS ($)	Earnings of DJIA Stocks ($)	Kellogg Growth in EPS (Percent)	Growth in Earnings of DJIA Stocks (Percent)
1972	$704.5	$1,151.8	3.5%	9.7%	$1.66	$67.11	9.9%	21.8%
1971	680.8	1,050.4	10.1	7.6	1.51	55.09	11.0	8.0
1970	618.5	976.4	13.3	4.8	1.36	51.02	9.7	(10.5)
1969	545.9	931.4	15.5	7.7	1.24	57.02	5.5	(1.5)
1968	472.5	865.0	4.8	9.0	1.18	57.89	3.5	7.5
1967	450.9	793.9	4.9	5.9	1.14	53.87	6.1	(6.6)
1966	429.7	749.9	16.5	10.1	1.07	57.68	9.2	7.5
1965	368.7	681.2	5.0	7.8	.98	53.67	8.3	15.6
1964	351.3	631.7	8.8	7.0	.91	46.43	16.0	12.7
1963	322.8	590.5	11.3	5.4	.78	41.21	15.5	13.1
1962	290.1	560.3	6.5	7.7	.68	36.43	10.6	14.2
1961	272.5	520.1	5.9	3.3	.61	31.91	3.4	(1.0)
1960	257.2	503.7	5.8	4.1	.59	32.21	11.8	(6.1)
1959	243.1	483.7	10.2	8.1	.53	34.31	3.9	22.8
1958	220.6	447.3	3.1	1.4	.51	27.94	8.5	(22.6)
1957	213.9	441.1	6.0	5.2	.47	36.08	13.6	8.2
1956	201.8	419.2	10.7	5.3	.41	33.34	10.0	(6.8)
1955	182.3	398.0	7.6	9.1	.38	35.78	9.1	27.0
1954	169.5	364.8	5.7	0	.35	28.18	34.6	3.5
1953	160.3	364.6	5.0	5.5	.26	27.23	6.8	9.9
1952	152.7	345.5	14.2	5.2	.24	24.78	5.4	(6.8)
1951	133.7	328.4			.22	26.59		

Sources: Kellogg annual reports; U.S. Department of Commerce, *Survey of Current Business*; *Barron's*, April 23, 1973.

Exhibit 2

KELLOGG COMPANY

HISTORICAL FINANCIAL DATA OF THE KELLOGG COMPANY PLUS COMPARISONS OF PROFITABILITY, VALUATION, AND EARNINGS RETENTION DATA OF KELLOGG VERSUS THE FIRMS COMPRISING THE DOW JONES INDUSTRIAL AVERAGE, 1951–1972

	Kellogg Data					Profit/Equity†		Market Value/Book Value of Common Stock		Common Stock P/E Ratio‡		Earnings Retention§/Profit	
	Cost of Sales/Sales	S, G, and A/Sales	Sales/Assets	Profit*/Sales	Assets/Equity†	Kellogg	DJIA	Kellogg	DJIA	Kellogg	DJIA	Kellogg	DJIA
1972	.624	.212	1.75	.086	1.39	.209	.104	4.0	1.6	18.9	15.2	.37	.52
1971	.620	.218	1.80	.081	1.43	.207	.091	3.5	1.5	16.9	16.2	.34	.44
1970	.610	.231	1.78	.080	1.41	.202	.089	3.6	1.5	17.6	16.4	.34	.38
1969	.605	.233	1.72	.082	1.43	.201	.105	3.3	1.5	16.6	14.0	.35	.41
1968	.605	.225	1.65	.089	1.39	.205	.111	3.6	1.8	17.7	16.3	.36	.46
1967	.592	.230	1.80	.090	1.32	.214	.113	4.0	1.9	18.8	16.8	.43	.44
1966	.600	.224	1.83	.089	1.36	.222	.121	3.8	1.7	17.1	13.6	.44	.45
1965	.610	.229	1.78	.095	1.41	.239	.118	5.1	2.1	21.2	18.1	.44	.47
1964	.609	.228	1.77	.092	1.51	.247	.111	6.6	2.1	26.6	18.8	.45	.33
1963	.593	.233	1.85	.087	1.47	.236	.097	6.5	1.8	27.5	18.5	.45	.43
1962	.596	.232	1.85	.084	1.45	.225	.091	4.7	1.6	20.8	17.9	.45	.36
1961	.605	.231	1.89	.080	1.47	.223	.083	6.8	1.9	30.3	22.9	.45	.29
1960	.603	.231	1.94	.082	1.51	.240	.087	5.2	1.7	21.6	19.1	.47	.34
1959	.604	.238	2.01	.078	1.54	.240	.101	4.4	2.0	18.4	19.8	.48	.40
1958	.584	.229	1.94	.082	1.65	.263	.090	4.8	1.9	18.1	20.9	.51	.28
1957	.607	.214	2.06	.078	1.76	.282	.121	2.9	1.5	10.2	12.1	.53	.40
1956	‖	‖	2.20	.072	1.84	.293	.117	2.9	1.8	9.9	15.0	.55	.31
1955			2.22	.073	1.98	.321	.132	4.1	1.8	12.9	13.7	.50	.40
1954			2.25	.072	2.17	.350	.113	4.2	1.6	11.9	14.4	.55	.38
1953			2.32	.056	2.37	.310	.122	3.7	1.3	12.1	10.3	.40	.41
1952			2.43	.055	2.44	.328	.116	3.8	1.4	11.5	11.8	.35	.38
1951			2.21	.058	2.72	.351	.131	5.0	1.0	14.1	10.8	.44	.39

* "Profit" is defined as profit after tax and preferred dividends.
† "Equity" refers only to the equity of the common stock shareholders. Preferred stock is not included.
‡ Market value and price-earnings ratio data are based on Dec. 31 price figures.
§ Earnings retentions equal profit after tax less preferred and common stock dividends.
‖ Expense data prior to 1957 were not broken down into these categories.

Sources: Kellogg annual reports; *Barron's*, April 23, 1973; *Barron's*, January 22, 1973; *Bank and Quotation Record*.

Exhibit 3

KELLOGG COMPANY
MARKET SHARE OF THE MAJOR U.S. RTE CEREAL MANUFACTURERS, 1940–1972
(Percent of total pounds sold in the U.S. market)

	1940	1950	...	1963	1964	1965	...	1969	1970	1971	1972
Kellogg Co.											
Corn Flakes...........				13.0	13.0	12.0		10.0	9.1	9.2	8.1
Rice Krispies..........				6.0	6.0	6.0		6.0	6.1	6.2	6.1
Sugar Frosted Flakes....				5.5	5.5	5.5		6.0	6.1	6.2	6.1
Special K.............				4.0	4.0	4.0		4.0	4.2	5.3	4.0
Raisin Bran...........				2.0	2.0	2.0		3.1	3.3	3.3	3.6
Froot Loops...........								1.6	1.6	1.9	2.2
Sugar Pops............								1.5	1.5	1.6	1.8
Product 19............								1.3	1.9	1.8	1.6
Frosted Mini Wheats...								—	—	1.6	1.5
Sugar Smacks..........								1.5	1.6	1.4	1.6
Cocoa Crispies........								1.0	1.3	1.3	1.2
Apple Jacks...........								—	—	—	1.1
Other................								7.5	7.5	5.6	4.6
Total............				43.5	43.5	41.0		43.5	44.2	44.4	43.5
General Mills											
Cheerios..............				7.0	7.5	8.0		7.3	7.0	6.8	6.7
Wheaties..............				6.0	6.5	6.5		4.7	4.2	4.0	3.8
Total................				—	1.5	2.0		2.5	2.7	3.0	2.6
Buc Wheats...........								—	—	0.6	1.5
Lucky Charms.........								1.5	1.4	1.4	1.3
Trix..................								1.5	1.2	1.1	1.3
Cocoa Puffs...........								1.0	1.0	1.0	1.0
Count Chocula and Frankenberry											
Baron Von Redberry and Sir Grapefellow......								—	—	1.0	1.9
Other................								1.9	1.9	1.0	0.6
Total............				20.5	21.0	22.0		20.2	19.4	19.9	20.7
General Foods											
Raisin Bran...........				2.0	2.0			3.0	3.0	2.8	3.0
Grape Nuts...........				1.8	1.5	1.5		2.8	2.4	2.4	2.5
Sugar Crisps..........								2.3	2.4	2.3	2.2
Post Toasties..........				4.5	4.5	4.5		2.4	2.2	2.4	2.5
Alpha-Bits............				2.0	2.0	1.5		1.2	1.3	1.2	1.1
Bran Flakes...........								1.1	1.1	1.1	1.0
Oat Flakes............								1.1	1.0	0.9	0.7
Honeycombs..........								1.2	1.1	0.9	0.9
Pebbles...............								—	—	0.8	0.7
Pink Panther..........								—	—	—	0.8
Other................								2.1	3.4	3.0	1.9
Total............				21.0	19.0	18.5		17.2	18.0	17.8	17.3

Exhibit 3—Continued

Quaker Oats

Cap'n Crunch			—	1.5	3.0	2.5	2.2	2.7	2.9
Life			1.8	2.0	2.0	1.9	1.6	1.6	1.9
Quisp and Quake						1.1	1.2	1.3	1.0
King Vitamin						—	1.0	1.0	0.9
100% Natural						—	—	—	0.5
Vanilly Crunch						—	—	—	0.3
Other						1.5	1.3	0.5	0.4
Total			4.0	5.0	7.0	7.0	7.3	7.1	7.8
Big 4	68.0	84.0	89.0	88.5	88.5	87.9	88.9	89.2	89.3
Nabisco			4.5	5.0	5.0	5.0	4.7	5.0	5.3
Ralston Purina			3.0	3.0	3.5	3.7	3.5	3.2	3.0
Other			3.5	3.5	3.0	3.4	2.9	2.6	2.4
TOTAL			100.0	100.0	100.0	100.0	100.0	100.0	100.0

Sources: *Advertising Age*, March 26, 1973; *Printers Ink*, June 24, 1966, p. 22; "In the Matter of Kellogg Company et al.," U.S. Federal Trade Commission, April 26, 1972, p. 5.

Exhibit 4

KELLOGG COMPANY
Ten-Year Summary of RTE Cereal Products Stocked, Added, and Dropped in a Typical Retail Grocery Chain, 1954–1964

Year	Total Number of RTE Cereals Stocked
1954	32
1956	44
1958	47
1960	53
1962	63
1964	67

RTE cereals stocked in 1954	32
New RTE cereals added 1954–64	62
Old RTE cereals dropped 1954–64	27
Net change in RTE cereals carried	35
RTE cereals stocked in 1964	67

Source: Robert D. Buzzell and Robert E. M. Nourse, *Product Innovation in Food Processing, 1954–1964* (Boston: Division of Research, Harvard Graduate School of Businesss Administration, 1967), pp. 37, 138.

Exhibit 5

KELLOGG COMPANY

NEW FOOD PRODUCT INTRODUCTION DATA INCLUDING (A) INTRODUCTION AND MARKETING COSTS BY CATEGORY AND BY YEAR; (B) PROPORTION OF NEW FOOD PRODUCTS BREAKING EVEN AT VARIOUS POINTS IN TIME, AND (C) THE AVERAGE NUMBER OF MONTHS A TYPICAL NEW FOOD PRODUCT REMAINS IN VARIOUS STAGES OF THE INTRODUCTORY PROCESS

Product Category	Costs of Product R&D	Costs of Mkt. Research	Costs of Test Mktg.	1st Year Avg. Mktg. Expenditure	2nd Year Avg. Mktg. Expenditure	1st Year Average Sales	2nd Year Average Sales	1st Year Mktg. Expend./ Sales	2nd Year Mktg. Expend./ Sales
	($ in 000s)							Percent	
Breakfast cereals—RTE	$122	$60	$921	$3,401	$1,374	$6,605	$4,580	51%	30%
Cake mixes	27	13	61	575	300	938	526	61	57
Frozen dinners and specialties	15	8	47	83	n.a.	416	n.a.	20	n.a.
Pet foods	91	37	531	1,926	n.a.	3,943	n.a.	49	n.a.

PROPORTION OF NEW FOOD PRODUCTS ACHIEVING BREAKEVEN* PROFIT LEVELS AFTER ONE, TWO, THREE, AND FOUR YEARS OF NATIONAL DISTRIBUTION

	Year 1	Year 2	Year 3	Year 4
Breakfast cereals—RTE	18%	23%	36%	40%
Cake mixes	n.a.	n.a.	n.a.	n.a.
Frozen dinners and specialties	8%	33%	60%	67%
Pet foods	22%	33%	40%	75%

AVERAGE NUMBER OF MONTHS A NEW FOOD PRODUCT REMAINS IN EACH STAGE OF DEVELOPMENT†

	R&D Stage	Product Testing Stage	Test Marketing Stage	Limited Distribution	Full Distribution
Breakfast cereals—RTE	32	14	6	5	55
Cake mixes	15	9	6	11	29
Frozen dinners and specialties	18	13	12	12	41
Pet foods	11	9	14	9	40

n.a. = not available.
* Breakeven profit is defined here on a cumulative basis; that is to say that a product "breaks even" when its cumulative contribution has been sufficient to recover its R & D, market research, and test marketing costs.
† Individual stage averages do not include data relating to products which skipped the stage in question.

Source: Robert D. Buzzell, and Robert E. M. Nourse, Product Innovation in Food Processing, 1954–1964 (Boston: Division of Research, Harvard Graduate School of Business Administration, 1967), pp. 107, 112, 117, 129, 132.

Exhibit 6

KELLOGG COMPANY
INDUSTRIES* WHERE THE TOP FOUR FIRMS ACCOUNT
FOR 70% OR MORE OF TOTAL INDUSTRY SHIPMENTS

Product	Value of Shipments ($ billions)	Concentration in 4 Largest Companies (Percent)
Consumer Products		
Motor vehicles	$27.3	92%
Cereal preparations	0.8	88
Chewing gum	0.3	86
Cigarettes	3.0	81
Sewing machines	0.1	81
Household laundry equipment	0.9	78
Chocolate and cocoa products	0.5	77
Household vacuum cleaners	0.3	76
Woven carpets and rugs	0.1	76
Household refrigerators and freezers	1.8	73
Soaps and other detergents	2.6	70
Industrial Products		
Locomotives and parts	$ 0.7	97%
Flat glass	0.6	94
Electron tubes—receiving type	0.3	94
Telephone and telegraph apparatus	1.5	92
Electric lamps	0.8	91
Hard-surface floor coverings	0.2	89
Steam engines and turbines	1.0	88
Reclaimed rubber	0.1	87
Cellulose man-made fibers	0.9	86
Carbon and graphite products	0.3	86
Primary batteries—dry and wet	0.3	85
Organic fibers, noncellulose	2.0	84
Cathode-ray picture tubes	0.8	84
Calculating and accounting machines	0.7	83
Tire cord and fabrics	0.4	83
Typewriters	0.6	81
Gypsum products	0.4	80
Primary copper	0.3	77
Nonferrous forgings	0.3	77
Electrometallurgical products	0.5	74
Medicinals and botanicals	0.4	74
Metal cans	2.9	73
Carbon black	0.2	72
Mineral wool	0.5	71
Pressed and molded pulp goods	0.1	71
Tires and inner tubes	3.7	70
Electron tubes, transmitting	0.4	70
Gum and wood chemicals	0.2	70

* According to the Standard Industrial Classification (SIC) System, there are 422 manufacturing industries and 1,200 manufactured product classes in the U.S. As shown in this exhibit, 39 out of 422 industries (or slightly more than 10%) had top four firm concentration ratios of 70% or more.

Source: "Concentration Ratios in Manufacturing," 1967 *Census of Manufactures*, Part I.

Exhibit 7

KELLOGG COMPANY
SALES, COST, AND PROFIT DATA AS A PERCENTAGE
OF SALE—BREAKFAST CEREAL INDUSTRY, 1940 AND 1964

	1940	1964	
	All Cereal Companies	All Cereal Companies	4 Largest Cereal Companies
Net sales..	100.0%	100.0%	100.0%
Ingredients...................................		20.7	20.0
Packaging.....................................		14.0	14.4
Other materials and supplies....................		.4	.1
Total materials and supplies...............	47.7%	35.1%	34.5%
Total mfg. payroll............................	6.1	10.8	10.9
Other mfg. expenses..........................	10.3	6.8	7.2
Total mfg. costs and expenses.............	64.1%	52.7%	52.6%
Salespersons' compensation.....................		2.1	2.1
Commissions to brokers........................		.3	—
Other selling expenses.........................		1.2	1.1
Distribution and delivery.......................	5.8	5.6	5.4
Advertising-media expenditures..................	13.1	15.2	14.9
Other advertising expenses.....................		1.7	1.9
Sales promotion*..............................		2.3	2.1
Marketing research............................	1.3	.5	.5
Total distribution costs...................	20.2%	28.9%	28.0%
Management and office salaries..................		2.4	2.2
Other administrative and general expenses........		1.9	2.0
Total administrative and general expenses...	3.3%	4.3%	4.2%
Net income before "other income" and taxes......	12.4%	14.1%	15.2%
Other income.................................		.4	.4
Net income before taxes.......................		14.5	15.6
Taxes...		7.2	7.8
Profit after taxes.............................		7.3	7.8

* Includes advertising allowances.

Source: *Studies of Organization and Competition in Grocery Manufacturing, Technical Study No. 6,* National Commission on Food Marketing, June 1966, pp. 142, 206, 207, 214.

Exhibit 8

KELLOGG COMPANY
HISTORICAL FINANCIAL DATA RELATING TO KELLOGG
COMPANY OPERATIONS OUTSIDE NORTH AMERICA

	Net Sales ($ millions)	Revenue/ Assets	Profit/ Revenue	Assets/ Equity	Profit/ Equity
1972	$165.7	1.78	.044	1.76	.137
1971	156.3	1.78	.048	1.85	.157
1970	136.9	1.74	.056	1.73	.169
1969	129.0	1.76	.058	1.83	.188
1968	119.4	1.71	.067	1.84	.210
1967	121.0	1.94	.077	1.73	.259
1966	114.1	1.90	.067	1.99	.252
1965	84.4	1.76	.080	1.63	.230
1964	80.6	1.88	.069	2.15	.278
1963	74.2	2.03	.086	1.71	.299
1962	66.0	2.20	.091	1.63	.326
1961	61.1	2.23	.097	1.59	.346

Source: Form 10K Reports to the U.S. Securities and Exchange Commission.

Exhibit 9

KELLOGG COMPANY
MARKET SHARES OF THE MAJOR U.K. RTE CEREAL MANUFACTURERS, 1955–1972
(Percent of total sales by weight in the U.K. market)

Kellogg's Corn Flakes	36.8	37.7	37.3	36.1	37.3	37.5	37.7	37.9	38.4	38.9	36.7	35.5	36.1	35.0	34.5	32.5	30.5	
All other Kellogg	17.0	17.4	18.2	18.3	18.8	19.3	21.3	21.1	20.3	19.7	20.6	20.7	21.3	22.6	24.0	24.4	24.6	
Weetabix	15.3	14.6	13.4	13.5	13.3	13.9	13.9	16.1	17.0	17.6	18.6	20.5	20.5	20.3	19.9	20.5	22.2	
Nabisco	18.0	17.6	17.7	18.2	16.8	17.5	16.9	15.6	15.0	14.6	14.2	13.2	12.3	11.3	10.5	11.9	12.2	
Quaker Oats	9.6	10.0	10.7	11.5	10.3	8.3	7.0	6.8	7.0	7.2	7.2	7.1	6.3	6.3	6.0	5.7	4.5	
Own brand cornflakes*	-	-	-	-	-	-	-	-	-	-	-	-	0.6	1.2	1.8	2.5	3.1	3.7

%

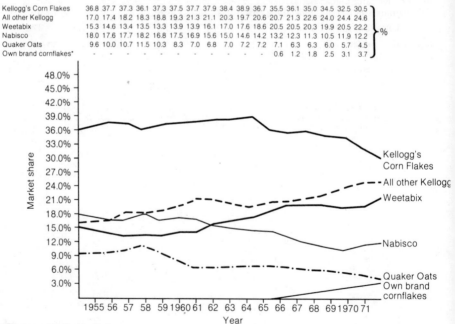

*Figures estimated by Kellogg

Source: "Breakfast Cereals, A Report on the Supply of Ready Cooked Breakfast Cereal Foods," U.K. Monopolies Commission, February 20, 1973, p. 35.

Exhibit 10

KELLOGG COMPANY

Historical Financial Data Relating to the U.K. Subsidiary of the Kellogg Company, 1967–1972

Year	Sales	Advertising	Promotion	Pretax Profit	Aftertax Profit	Profit after Tax/ Capital Employed Total Business	Pretax Profit/Sales		
							Total Business	Corn Flakes	Other Products
		(£ in 000s)							
1972 (1st half)	14,000	n.a.	n.a.	1,428	788	14.3	10.2	n.a.	n.a.
1971 (1st half)	13,900	n.a.	n.a.	1,696	936	17.5	12.2	n.a.	n.a.
1971	27,341	2,500	670	3,665	2,023	20.3	13.4	10.6	16.6
1970	24,651	2,250	640	3,677	2,095	22.2	14.9	13.5	16.2
1969	23,909	2,275	642	4,441	2,558	28.1	18.6	21.1	16.3
1968	21,923	2,189	617	4,286	2,477	27.7	19.6	23.3	18.8
1967	20,521	1,969	555	4,818	2,811	34.1	23.5	24.6	22.6

Year	Sales	Advertising	Promotion	Pretax Profit	Aftertax Profit
					(Percent)
1972 (1st half)	100.0	n.a.	n.a.	10.2	5.6
1971 (1st half)	100.0	n.a.	n.a.	12.2	6.7
1971	100.0	9.1	2.5	13.4	7.4
1970	100.0	9.1	2.6	14.9	8.5
1969	100.0	9.5	2.7	18.6	10.7
1968	100.0	10.0	2.8	19.6	11.3
1967	100.0	9.6	2.7	23.5	13.7

n.a. = not available.

Sources: "Breakfast Cereals, A Report on the Supply of Ready Cooked Breakfast Cereal Foods," U.K. Monopolies Commission, February 20, 1973, pp. 5, 6, 14, 16, 17; and casewriter estimates.

Exhibit 11

KELLOGG COMPANY

HISTORICAL OPERATING PROFIT* TO NET SALES RATIO OF THE U.K. SUBSIDIARY
OF THE KELLOGG COMPANY, 1935–1971

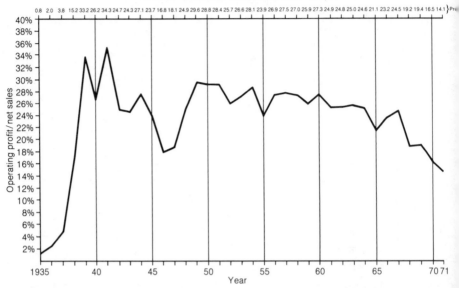

0.8 2.0 3.8 15.2 33.2 26.2 34.3 24.7 24.3 27.1 23.7 16.8 18.1 24.9 29.6 28.8 28.4 25.7 26.6 28.1 23.9 26.9 27.5 27.0 25.9 27.3 24.9 24.8 25.0 24.6 21.1 23.2 24.5 19.2 19.4 16.5 14.1 }Pr

*Operating profit equals profit before taxes and other nonoperating expenses such as interest.
Source: "Breakfast Cereals, A Report on the Supply of Ready Cooked Breakfast Cereal Foods," U.K. Monopolies Co
mission, February 20, 1973, p. 37.

Exhibit 12

KELLOGG COMPANY

COST AND PRICE BREAKDOWN IN THE MANUFACTURE AND SALE OF CORNFLAKES
IN THE UNITED KINGDOM
(12-ounce package—1971)

	Kellogg		*Viota*	
	(Pence)	Percent*	(Pence)	Percent*
Raw material.....................	2.05	24.1		
Packaging.......................	1.54	18.1		
Labor (direct)....................	.26	3.1		
Other manufacturing..............	1.28	15.0		
Total factory...............	5.13	60.3	5.50	73.3
Freight and storage................	.92	10.8	1.00	13.3
Advertising and promotion..........	1.02	12.0	.20	2.7
General overhead..................	.47	5.5	.30	4.0
Operating profit...................	.96	11.4	.50	6.7
Price to retailer..............	8.50	100.0	7.50	100.0
Retail margin.....................	2.00	23.5	2.00	26.7
Retail price to consumer............	10.50	123.5	9.50	126.7
Contribution margin†.............		28.8		

*Percent of selling price to retailer.
† At a price of 8.5 P to the retailer, the margin of Kellogg's contribution to profit was estimated at 28.8%.
Sources: Kellogg Company—"Breakfast Cereals, A Report on the Supply of Ready Cooked Breakfast
Foods," U.K. Monopolies Commission, February 29, 1973, pp. 10, 13; and Viota—casewriter estimates.

NOTE: COMPUTER LEASING INDUSTRY

^^^

The electronic data processing industry can be broken down into five major segments which include (1) main frame hardware[1] manufacturers, (2) peripheral equipment manufacturers, (3) supporting services (programming consultants, etc.), (4) computer utilities (sellers of computer time), and (5) computer leasing companies. This note will focus on the independent computer leasing industry. Since the policies of computer manufacturers play a key role in determining the operating environment of the computer leasing companies, introductory information will also be provided on the producers of main frame hardware.

BACKGROUND—COMPUTER HARDWARE MANUFACTURERS

Structure of industry

Only nine U.S. companies are significantly involved in the manufacture of main frame hardware. Most of these manufacturers decline to release the information necessary to determine market shares within the industry. For this reason, the statistics cited in the financial press relating to competitive positions are based on uncertain estimates. In spite of this uncertainty, it is clear that International Business Machines Corporation (IBM) is far and away the industry leader.

According to an article in *Forbes* magazine, IBM had, through 1965, installed 75% of the dollar value of computer equipment in use within the United States and 67% of the value of such equipment in use throughout the world.[2] Another trade source estimated the value of computers shipped by manufacturers during 1966 as shown in Exhibit 1.

Regarding IBM's share of the total computer market, the *Forbes* article went on to state:

IBM dominates the world computer business in a way no other giant industrial dominates any other major market. General Motors has about 52% of the U.S.

---

[1] "Main frame hardware" refers to the central processing units of a computer where numerical calculations are actually performed. This is distinct from input and output devices (peripheral equipment) such as card readers and tape drives.

[2] "International Business Machines," *Forbes*, September 15, 1966, p. 46.

471

Exhibit 1

COMPUTER LEASING INDUSTRY

ESTIMATED VALUE OF COMPUTERS SHIPPED BY MANUFACTURERS DURING 1966

(Dollar amounts in millions)

	Amount	*% of Total*
IBM	$2,500	68.3%
Honeywell	270	7.4
Control Data	200	5.5
Univac	195	5.3
General Electric	190	5.2
National Cash	95	2.6
Radio Corporation	95	2.6
Burroughs	60	1.6
Scientific Data	30	0.8
Others	25	0.7
Total	$3,660	100.0%

Source: "EDP Industry and Market Report," International Data Publishing Co.

auto business. . . . U.S. Steel has only about 25% of the domestic steel market, . . . [and] Standard Oil (N.J.) . . . [has] about 15% of the Free World crude production.[3]

Market growth

The estimated value of general-purpose computers shipped annually since 1955 and future demand projected through 1970 are shown in Exhibit 2. Between 1960 and 1965 industry shipments grew at a compounded rate of more than 25% annually. With deliveries of IBM's third-generation[4] "System/360" equipment beginning in earnest late in 1965, the 1965–66 annual rate of growth swelled to over 45%.

Computer manufacturers face financial problems similar to those of any industrial company experiencing rapid growth. Accounts receivable and in-process inventories of growing companies often jump sharply in response to rising sales levels. Plant and equipment expenditures may simultaneously increase if capacity must be expanded to bring production into a more reasonable balance with sales demand. In addition to the normal problems accompanying rapid growth, computer manufacturers face one additional financial problem that is *not* characteristic of most companies in fast-growing industries. That problem arises from the fact that computer users have traditionally leased rather than purchased more than 80% of the computer equipment they have accepted for installation.[5]

---

[3] *Ibid.*

[4] The "generation" of computer equipment is determined by the state of advancement in its electronic circuitry. First-generation equipment employed thousands of vacuum tubes in its circuitry. These relatively slow and inefficient machines were superseded in 1960 by second-generation equipment (such as IBM's 1401) employing transistors. The System/360 machines represent a third generation, which relies on integrated circuits (IC's) and hybrids of IC's and transistors.

[5] Barton M. Biggs, "Numbers Game," *Barron's*, July 24, 1967, p. 3.

Exhibit 2

COMPUTER LEASING INDUSTRY

ESTIMATED ANNUAL VALUE OF COMPUTER EQUIPMENT SHIPPED
BY U.S. MANUFACTURERS

(In millions of dollars)

	General-Purpose Digital Computers	Total*
1955	$ 75	$ 339
1960	720	2,225
1965	2,300	4,800
1966	3,660	6,535
1967	4,200–4,400	7,250– 7,640
1968	4,600–4,900	8,010– 8,660
1970	5,300–5,800	9,180–10,360

* Total includes general-purpose digital computers, special-purpose computers, independent peripheral equipment, software service bureau and consultants, and supplies and supporting services.
Source: "EDP Industry and Market Report," International Data Publishing Co.

Cash flow implications of leasing

The practice of leasing rather than selling a rapidly growing product line can place a terrific strain on a corporation's cash resources. A typical computer selling for $1,000,000 has a manufacturing cost of about $400,000. All other corporate operating expenses, such as engineering, selling, and administrative overhead, add another $300,000 to the machine's cost, leaving a pretax profit of $300,000 for the manufacturer if the machine is sold outright.[6,7] The same computer installed under a manufacturer's standard lease contract would produce annual revenues of about $238,000, but the expenses associated with earning this revenue would amount to $460,000 during the first year as shown in Exhibit 3.

Exhibit 3

COMPUTER LEASING INDUSTRY

FIRST-YEAR FINANCIAL STATEMENT RELATING TO THE LEASE OF A
COMPUTER WITH A SALES PRICE EQUAL TO $1,000,000

Revenue		$ 238,000
Depreciation	$160,000	
Other costs	300,000	
Total costs		460,000
Pretax profit (loss)		$(222,000)
Income tax (credit)		(111,000)
After-tax profit (loss)		$(111,000)
Add: Depreciation		160,000
Cash inflow from lease		$ 49,000
Cash outflow to manufacture		400,000
Net cash outflow in first year		$ 351,000

---

[6] *Ibid.*
[7] Annual Report, 1967, Digital Equipment Corp.

If the computer's basic manufacturing cost of $400,000 is depreciated over four years using the sum-of-the-years'-digits method, the depreciation expense for the first year would be $160,000. This depreciation method is reported to be general industry practice for tax accounting.[8] The previously mentioned corporate operating expenses of $300,000 are not capitalized. Instead they are immediately charged off as an expense. This leads to a first year loss on the leased machine amounting to $222,000. If corporate income from other sources is available to offset the loss on this lease transaction, tax savings eliminate half of this loss, or $111,000. Adding depreciation, a noncash expense, to the after-tax loss gives $49,000 as the first year cash inflow from the leased computer. Since the manufacturer incurred an initial cash outflow of $400,000 to produce the machine, the lease transaction during the first year causes a net cash drain of $351,000. From this analysis it is easy to see why a large volume of computer shipments placed out on lease can be very damaging to a manufacturer from a cash standpoint.

Short-term leasing as a competitive weapon

Widespread leasing of equipment has long been a custom in the computer industry. Prior to 1956, this phenomenon could be explained by IBM's refusal to offer its data processing equipment for sale. As a result of a legal action in that year IBM must now "offer for sale all equipment which it offers for lease and must establish a sales price for such equipment which will have a commercially reasonable relationship to its lease charges for the same equipment."[9]

While the Consent Decree made the outright purchase of equipment possible, most users of IBM equipment still favor the one-year lease contract. A short-term lease frees the user from any risk of technological obsolescence and makes "trading-up" a simple matter if the user's data processing needs outgrow the capacity of the machine in question.

Almost through an accident of corporate history the popularity of one-year lease contracts has given IBM a strong competitive advantage within the computer industry. IBM enjoys the unique advantage of cash revenues in excess of a billion dollars annually from rentals of items such as punch card accounting equipment and typewriters placed in the field many years ago.[10] Other manufacturers without this cash flow have considerable difficulty meeting the huge cash drain that necessarily accompanies short-term leases. Cash shortages force manufacturers such as Honeywell to encourage outright sales or long-term leases (three to five years) against which they can immediately borrow almost the total value of future lease payments. Inability to offer one-year leases places a computer manufacturer such as Honeywell at a

---

[8] Biggs, op. cit.

[9] United States v. International Business Machines Corporation, 1956 Trade Cas. 71, 117 (S.D.N.Y. 1956).

[10] "Data Processing Equipment Leasing," Equity Research Associates, August 19, 1966.

competitive disadvantage since many lessees favor the one-year contract in order to avoid obsolescence risk and the necessity of showing a large future lease obligation in a footnote to their balance sheets.

Theoretically IBM assumes the risk of massive annual equipment returns since the company is protected only by one-year leases. In practice, however, a lessee rarely returns a piece of equipment in less than three to four years because of the considerable expense and time lost in converting existing programs to a new system. Lessees simply continue their contracts on a 90-day notification basis once they expire. Returned machines present only minor marketing problems. If the returned computer is new enough so that the model is still in production, IBM's large sales force will usually be able to place it with another lessee at the full rental rate enjoyed by a comparable piece of new equipment.

IBM cash shortage

Although the ability to offer a one-year lease contract represents a strong competitive weapon for IBM, customer acceptance of the System/360 line of computers was so great that in 1966 the company became a victim of its own success. The cash throw-off from operations, which amounted to $1,258,000,000 in 1966,[11] was no longer sufficient to sustain internally IBM's growth rate. Whereas in 1964 the corporation could boast of cash balances totaling nearly one billion dollars, the situation had changed markedly by 1966 and the company found it necessary to raise the money from external sources. Since IBM avoids debt of any consequence in proportion to equity, in 1966 its shareholders were called upon to supply the company with over $350,000,000 in new equity capital. It is clear that IBM's cash shortage in 1966 was unanticipated, since in 1964 the company had *prepaid* $160,000,000 of loans bearing $3\frac{1}{2}\%$ interest to The Prudential Insurance Company. By 1966, however, in addition to raising the new equity capital already mentioned, the company had to establish new bank lines of credit equal to $160,000,000, this time at an interest rate of $5\frac{1}{2}\%$. In light of this fact, the Prudential prepayment decision ". . . stands as one IBM decision about which there is, in retrospect, no controversy—it was a mistake."[12]

The lease-sales ratio

System/360 was dramatically successful for IBM in terms of market acceptance, but the high percentage of shipments placed on a lease basis drained the corporation financially. Exhibit 4 presents estimates of IBM's cash requirements arising *solely* from shipments of System/360 equipment placed on lease.

In September, 1966, IBM moved to bring its lease-sales ratio down to a level consistent with the company's ability to finance its leases through

---

[11] Annual Report, IBM, 1966.

[12] T. A. Wise, "The Rocky Road to the Marketplace," *Fortune*, October, 1966, p. 206.

Exhibit 4

COMPUTER LEASING INDUSTRY

ESTIMATED IBM CASH FLOW ARISING SOLELY FROM SHIPMENTS
OF SYSTEM/360 EQUIPMENT PLACED ON LEASE

($ Millions)

	1966	1967	1968	1969	1970
Total lease revenue..................	$518.3	$1,130.7	$1,800.3	$2,510.7	$3,272.5
Depreciation expense...............	348.4	673.0	933.2	1,108.2	1,198.3
Other costs.......................	653.3	771.9	844.1	895.5	960.1
Pretax income.....................	−483.4	−314.3	23.1	507.1	1,114.0
After-tax net......................	−241.7	−157.1	11.5	253.5	557.0
Total inflow from operation.........	106.7	515.9	944.7	1,361.7	1,755.3
Total equipment investment.........	871.1	1,029.2	1,125.4	1,194.0	1,280.2
Cash inflow-outflow...............	−764.4	−513.3	−180.7	167.7	475.1

	1966	1967	1968	1969	1970

Assumptions:
1. Sales value of total industry computer shipments (billions) from Exhibit 2.
   $3.66 $4.40 $4.90 $5.30 $5.80
2. IBM's share of above from Exhibit 1, plus casewriter's estimates.
   0.70   0.68   0.66   0.64   0.62
3. IBM's lease-sales ratio from page 311, plus casewriter's estimates.
   0.85   0.86   0.87   0.88   0.89
4. According to this exhibit, in 1966 IBM could expect to place out on lease System/360 computer equipment
   with a sales value of $2.18 billion. This figure can be derived by multiplying together three numbers: the
   sales value of industry shipments ($3.66 billion); IBM's share of total industry shipments (0.70); and
   IBM's lease-sales ratio (0.85).
   Exhibit 3 shows the first-year cash flow relating to a leased computer with a sales price equal to $1,000,000.
   To arrive at IBM's 1966 cash flow arising from leasing equipment with a sales value of $2.18 billion, we
   simply multiply the figures in Exhibit 3 by 2,180.
Source: Publicly available estimates and casewriter's projections.

internal cash generation. IBM reduced the sales price of its computers by 3%
and shortly thereafter raised its lease rental rates by 3%. The expectation of
trade sources was that this new pricing schedule would stop and perhaps
reverse the rising trend in IBM's lease-sales ratio. When the new pricing
decision was announced, the value of shipments made on a lease basis was
estimated to exceed the value of shipments sold outright by a very wide
margin. If the new pricing schedule would reduce the lease to sales ratio
significantly from its estimated level of 85%,[13] the immediate cash inflow
would be substantial, and the downward pressure on corporate earnings
implied by Exhibit 3 would be reduced. Since the heavy placements of leased
systems were depressing earnings in 1966, this price change presumably
helped the company maintain its historical uptrend in earnings per share.

INDEPENDENT COMPUTER LEASING INDUSTRY

Enter the financial entrepreneur

The cash squeeze at IBM, coupled with the fact that an entirely new
generation of computers was being introduced, created a clear profit opportunity for financial entrepreneurs. IBM had widened substantially the spread
between the revenues available to computer lessors and the cost of purchasing

---

[13] Biggs, *op. cit.*

computers to be placed on lease. Financial middlemen could purchase computers from IBM at standard prices and place them with lessees at rental rates
ranging from 10% to 20% lower than those charged by IBM. If the machines
were depreciated over 8 or 10 years in contrast to the manufacturer's practice
of using 4 years, reported profits could be substantial even during the first
year that the equipment was placed in service. Since the System/360 represented an entirely new computer generation when it was introduced in late
1965, the economic life of these machines was expected to extend well into the
1970's, limiting an early buyer's risk of premature technological obsolescence.
Experience showed that second-generation equipment such as IBM's 1400
series was actively manufactured and marketed for as long as six years
(1960–66), and the continued rental of existing equipment in this series was
expected to remain profitable for a number of years to come.

Short-term versus long-term leases

While four or five publicly owned computer leasing companies were in
existence prior to 1966 (Exhibit 5), the majority of the companies were
created to take advantage of the profit opportunity afforded by IBM's pricing
decision of September, 1966. With two exceptions the companies concentrate
on writing leases of short duration, the average being about two years.
Pricing policy among the companies is quite uniform, with the lessee usually
paying the leasing company 90% of the standard manufacturer's rental rate
on a two-year lease.

The rental rates charged by computer manufacturers allow them to recover
the full sale price of their computers after about 47 months of continuous
rental receipts. Since the independent computer leasing companies charge at
most 90% of the manufacturer's rental rate, it takes the leasing companies at
least 52 months to recover the full purchase price. With a purchase price
payback of at least 52 months and an average lease term of 24 months, the
computer leasing companies are obviously concerned with future marketability of returned machines. Concern with this problem leads most of the
companies to restrict their computer purchases to models with proved market
acceptance. Machines with large order backlogs or a large number of existing
installations (such as IBM's System/360–30) are favored for purchase by the
leasing companies. This is true because every user renting a System/360–30
from the manufacturer represents a potential future customer should the
leasing company find itself with a returned machine of the same model. The
concern with future marketability has led computer leasing companies to deal
almost exclusively in IBM System/360 equipment.

Leasco Data Processing Equipment Corporation, the one company specializing in non-IBM equipment, writes only noncancellable full payout leases. In
such a lease the entire purchase price plus interest is recovered during the
initial lease term. Because Leasco carries essentially no obsolescence risk, its
business is substantially different from that of the other computer leasing
companies, which specialize in leases with much shorter terms. First, Leasco's

Exhibit 5

COMPUTER LEASING INDUSTRY

COMPARISON OF COMPUTER LEASING COMPANIES

Computer Leasing Companies	Computer Investment[1]	Type of Computers	Type of Leases	Service	Marketing	Principals
GC Computer Corp. (1966)	$73.1 MM gr. $51.1 MM net (12/31/66) 96 leases	IBM's ⅔—1400's 7000's ⅛— 360's	Length: Most 1–3 yrs. Range: 1 mo.—8 yrs. Rental: 90% of IBM's Costs recovery: 70–78 mos. (all costs)	No repair, maintenance, or programming.	Own marketing organization with five sales offices around the U.S.	Owned by Greyhound.
Randolph Computer Corp. (1965)	$35.9 MM gr. (2/10/67) 68 systems 31 lessees	IBM 360's Cost $225 M–$747 M	Length: 2–5 yrs. Rental: 90% of IBM's Cost recovery: 6 yrs. (all costs) 4–5 yrs. (machine cost) Options: Purchase options at 7½% per annum discount (purchase price always slightly above book value)	No repair or maintenance. In April, acquired United Data Processing, Inc., to add software capability.	The eight officers find most leasing opportunities. Work out of NY office.	Randolph (Pres.) from Boothe Leasing. Arbour (EVP) marketing man from IBM.
Levin-Townsend Computer Corp.	$20.5 MM gr. (3/10/67) 35 leases	IBM 360's	Length: Most 1 year Rental: About 90% of IBM	No maintenance or repair. Programming and systems consulting for a fee.	Own marketing force (about five men). Also representatives who find deals for commissions. 67 employees.	Levin (Pres.) is former math professor and founded L-T as consulting firm in data processing.
Data Processing Financial & General Corp. (1961)	$18.2 MM gr. (11/30/66)	IBM's Cost $85 M–$2.3 MM	Length: 1 mo.–5 yrs. About 20% are monthly, about 40% are 1 yr. Rental: n.a. Options: A few leases have options at fair market value—exercisable any time.	No repair, maintenance, or programming.	Uses some brokers on commission basis. Has 10 full-time salesmen. (12/1967).	Harry Goodman (Pres.) data processing expert—formerly in IBM market forecasting.
Leasco Data Processing Equipment Corp. (1961)	$20–25 MM gr. (4/30/67 est.)	CDC and others	Length: 2–8 yrs. *full payout leases* Rentals: About 80% of manufacturers'. Options: A few have purchase option at fair market—end of lease. Most provide for renewal at lower rental.	No repair or maintenance. Plans to acquire Documentation, Inc., to provide software capability.	Has 37 salesmen among its 71 employees. Also trains manufacturer's salesmen in lease techniques. Manufacturer then sells lease package with machine. Has exclusive contract for CDC payout leases.	Steinberg Family controls. They are leasing, not computer experts. VP Sweetbaum is former accounting machine salesman.
Standard Computer Corp.	$8.2 MM gr. (2/28/67)	IBM's Cost $171 M–$3.9 MM	Length: 1 mo.–8 yrs. most 2 yrs. Cost recovery: 5–7 yrs. Options: None except in the case of an 8-yr. lease	No repair, maintenance, or programming.	Uses brokers and Lease Finance Co. (parent) to find deals.	Formed by: Auerbach (Tech. consulting firm which evaluates deals); Lease Finance Co. (management consultant which puts together deals); Blair & Co.; Pres. Affel is an engineer from Auerbach.

(1) Amounts shown are gross. "Net" amount is nearly as large in all cases. Most machines are less than 2 years old and are depreciated over an 8- to 10-year life.

sharply limited risk allows it to command a 4 to 1 debt to equity ratio, to be compared with about a 2 to 1 debt to equity ratio for its "short-term" counterparts. Second, Leasco has arranged its pricing policy to insulate the company from possible future increases in the cost of maintaining its computer equipment. Leasco accomplishes this by offering its lessees the standard 10% discount and adding to this amount a second deduction equal to the cost of the equipment manufacturer's full service maintenance contract at the time the lease is signed. The lessee must then assume the cost of a separate maintenance contract, which normally amounts to about 10% of the cost of renting the machine from its manufacturer. The companies specializing in short-term leases almost always assume the cost of maintenance contracts. While their higher rental charges offset this cost, the short-term leasing companies shoulder all the risk involved in future cost increases for the maintenance service.

Leasco enjoys the advantages of reduced risk and increased financial leverage, but these benefits do not come without cost. Leasco must give up a substantial part of the residual value in the equipment it leases in order to induce lessees to accept a longer term. "At the end of the initial lease term . . . , lessees may then renew the term at a negotiated rental rate which frequently ranges between 30% and 50% of the rental . . . originally charged."[14]

Importance of remarketing

Leasco's approach to computer leasing leaves the company practically immune from the problem of remarketing returned equipment. In contrast, the companies writing shorter leases face problems in two areas: (1) that of avoiding equipment inventories and (2) that of providing programming assistance to "second users."

1. It is of critical importance to these companies to keep all machines productively utilized since the average lease contract involves over $500,000 worth of computer equipment. Because the System/360 line of computers is so new, through 1967 no leasing company has yet had to remarket a returned machine in this series. Levin-Townsend Computer Corporation, a leasing company that occasionally purchases second generation equipment (at a considerable discount from its original purchase price), has had some experience with returns of this older equipment. Regarding the importance of rapidly remarketing equipment returns the company's president, Howard S. Levin, has said, "We hold sales contests with the salesman who places the computer keeping his job."[15] Presumably the comment was not made entirely with tongue in cheek. Leasing companies never purchase equipment for inventory: a lease agreement is always simultaneously executed. In fact, two simultaneous transactions generally occur in closing a deal. The leasing

---

[14] "Leasco—A Study for Institutional Investors," Goodbody and Co., February 1967.
[15] "Computer Leasing Stocks," *Fortune*, July, 1967, p. 171.

company signs a purchase agreement with the equipment manufacturer for a computer already chosen by company A. Company A simultaneously signs a contract with the leasing company to rent the machine for a period of from one to five years.

2. At present, it is IBM's policy to provide education, systems assistance, and other services to customers who are "first users" of its equipment but not necessarily to subsequent users. Through 1967 all System/360 lessees renting through leasing companies have been first users, but in future years as equipment is returned and remarketed, this will not continue to be the case. At some future time, therefore, computer leasing companies may be forced to furnish software support. Otherwise they might face a serious competitive disadvantage in the remarketing of equipment to second and later users.

Ease of growth

The growth rate of a manufacturing company is often constrained by the need for comparable expansion of such factors as capital resources, physical facilities, top-management talent, and a trained force of production employees. For the computer leasing business, available capital is the principal factor restricting growth. The "people" and "facilities" factors are far less critical. Indeed, Data Processing Financial & General Corporation was purchasing equipment at an annual rate of $50 million in September, 1967, with a staff of 10 people including the office secretaries.[16]

The computer leasing companies have purchased equipment at a spectacular rate since the end of 1965. Probably the only factor restraining even faster growth is the companies' limited cash resources. Yet even in the area of raising equity capital the companies have had few problems. Rapid price appreciation and growth in earnings per share have given the stocks in this industry a large market following. If we ignore the sharp general market setback between February and October, 1966, prices of the companies' common stocks have risen as dramatically as their equipment holdings, as shown in Exhibits 6 and 7. Almost everyone buying the securities of computer leasing companies has made money, a factor that greatly contributes to the ability of these corporations to keep coming to the market for additional financing.

Exhibit 7 shows the public financing pattern of three companies in the computer leasing industry. Each new security issue has been larger in absolute terms, and in many cases successive issues have grown larger and larger as a percentage of total computer equipment previously owned.

Accounting policies boost earnings

Corporate growth depends on the availability of funds and the availability of funds for computer leasing companies depends in large measure on a rising stock price. Price appreciation is the only return a common shareholder can

---

[16] *Preliminary Prospectus*, Data Processing Financial & General Corp., August 22, 1967.

Exhibit 6

LEVIN-TOWNSEND COMPUTER CORPORATION

STOCK PRICES AND VALUE OF EQUIPMENT OWNED

DECEMBER, 1965–SEPTEMBER, 1967

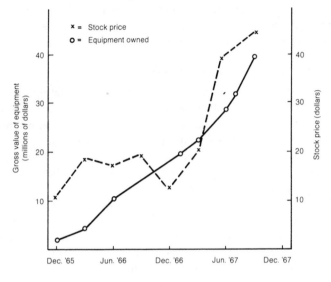

Exhibit 7

COMPUTER LEASING INDUSTRY

AMOUNTS AND PRICES OF PUBLIC SECURITY ISSUES OF SELECTED COMPANIES

Company	Date of Public Security Issue	Amount of Security Issue	Computer Equipment Owned	Elapsed Time Since Previous Security Issue	Common Stock Price $
		In Thousands of Dollars			
Standard	April, 1966	2,500	6,000	....	5
Computer	March, 1967	4,000	12,143	11 mos.	15¾
Corporation	June, 1967	8,000	14,476	3 mos.	19½
Randolph	April, 1966	1,800	3,057	....	20
Computer	March, 1967	5,000	35,945	11 mos.	41¼
Corporation	July, 1967	10,000	44,913	4 mos.	46
Data Processing	December, 1965	3,300	6,000	....	11
Financial &	March, 1967	12,000	18,183	15 mos.	41⅛
General Corporation	September, 1967	50,000	38,941	6 mos.	73¼

expect for a number of years since loan covenants accepted by these companies severely restrict and generally prevent dividend payments.

Perhaps in an effort to provide the rising stock price necessary for growth in computer leasing, the companies in this industry have adopted accounting policies allowing them to report the highest possible current earnings. Thus, even though IBM depreciates a System/360–40 computer over 4 years using accelerated depreciation in its financial statements to its shareholders, most of the leasing companies depreciate the identical machine over 10 years using straight-line depreciation for shareholder reporting. To reduce their income tax liability, however, the companies use sum-of-the-years'-digits depreciation and an eight-year life for tax reporting. In a similar vein, leasing companies "flow through" the 7% investment tax credit as rapidly as possible rather than spreading the credit evenly over the life of the asset in question.

Automatic growth in reported earnings

Exhibit 8 shows pro forma financial statements relating to a typical short-term lease for a $1,000,000 computer system placed in service on January 1, 1966. The upper half of the page, lines 1–21, shows pro forma income statements as reported for purposes of calculating the annual federal income tax liability. The lower half of the page, lines 22–32, shows how the income statements would appear in a leasing company's shareholder reports.

Although the complexity of Exhibit 8 may at first appear overwhelming, detailed study of the numbers presented is unnecessary. Careful examination of a very few lines (those relating to depreciation expense and after-tax income) will provide most of the information needed for a thorough understanding of the importance of management accounting choices in the earnings reports of companies operating in this industry.

Lines 9 and 27 project the annual pretax profit for tax and shareholder reports, respectively. It is important to note that except for the depreciation charge, all the revenue and expense items used to calculate pretax profit in the tax and shareholder reports are exactly the same each year. Although tax loss carryforwards and the investment tax credit play a major role in determining after-tax income (lines 12 and 30), the striking numerical differences found in these two lines result entirely from the variation in depreciation charges.

While the importance of accounting policy in determining earnings is highlighted by Exhibit 8, two other key factors can be gleaned from the figures. First, net income for shareholder purposes (line 30) has a built-in increase of at least 15% per year during the first four years of the computer's life. This is caused by decreasing interest payments as the debt outstanding is reduced. Second, the first-year return on equity equals 10% ($32,799/$334,000). So long as equity for new equipment purchases is sold at a price exceeding 10 times current earnings, future earnings per share will be enhanced by simply buying and leasing additional equipment with the proceeds from new common stock issues. With leasing company equities selling at well above 20 times current earnings, the enhancement in earnings arising from simply selling additional stock to purchase and lease more computer equipment is dramatic.

The industry's future

While reported profits are currently moving even higher, a number of factors weigh heavily on the future prospects of the computer leasing indus-

Exhibit 8

COMPUTER LEASING INDUSTRY

FINANCIAL STATEMENTS RELATING TO A $1,000,000 COMPUTER PLACED UNDER A TWO-YEAR LEASE CONTRACT

BOOK VERSUS TAX ACCOUNTING FOR A TYPICAL COMPUTER LEASING COMPANY

Leasing Company Tax Reports

#		1966	1967	1968	1969	1970	1971	1972	1973	1974	1975
1	IBM rental rate	256,000	256,000	256,000	256,000	256,000	256,000	256,000	256,000	256,000	256,000
2	(1) Discount allowed	25,600	25,600	30,720	35,840	40,960	46,080	51,200	56,320	61,440	66,560
3	Overtime premium	7,680	7,680	7,680	7,680	7,680	7,680	7,680	7,680	7,680	7,680
4	Gross rentals	238,080	238,080	232,960	227,840	222,720	217,600	212,480	207,360	202,240	197,120
5	Maintenance expense (10% of line 1)	25,600	25,600	25,600	25,600	25,600	25,600	25,600	25,600	25,600	25,600
6	(2) Depreciation expense	188,889	165,278	141,667	118,056	94,444	70,833	47,222	23,611	.....	.....
7	(3) Interest (9% of line 18)	59,940	48,354	35,726	22,375	8,238	.....	.....	.....	.....	.....
8	Selling, general, and administrative	23,808	23,808	23,296	22,784	22,272	21,760	21,248	20,736	20,224	19,712
9	Pretax profit (loss)	(60,157)	(24,960)	6,672	39,025	72,166	99,407	118,410	137,413	156,416	151,808
10	Taxes (before investment credit)	.....	.....	.....	.....	16,373	49,703	59,204	68,706	78,208	75,904
11	(4) Investment credit used	.....	.....	.....	.....	8,186	24,851	29,602	7,359	.....	.....
12	Net profit	(60,157)	(24,960)	6,672	39,025	63,979	74,555	88,807	76,066	78,208	75,904
13	Add depreciation	188,889	165,278	141,667	118,056	94,444	70,833	47,222	23,611	.....	.....
14	Total cash inflow	128,732	140,318	148,338	157,081	158,424	145,388	136,030	99,677	78,208	75,904
15	Debt repayment	128,732	140,318	148,338	157,081	91,531	.....	.....	.....	.....	.....
16	Available for equity holders	.....	.....	.....	.....	66,893	145,388	136,030	99,677	78,208	75,904
17	(5) After-tax cash flow from liquidation	.....	.....	.....	.....	.....	.....	.....	.....	.....	275,000
18	Debt outstanding (start of yr.)	666,000	537,268	396,950	248,612	91,531	.....	.....	.....	.....	.....
19	Equity invested (start of yr.)	334,000	334,000	334,000	334,000	334,000	267,107	121,719	(14,311)	(113,988)	(192,196)
20	Remaining investment credit	70,000	70,000	70,000	70,000	61,813	36,962	7,359	.....	.....	.....
21	Tax loss carry-forward	60,157	85,117	78,445	39,420	.....	.....	.....	.....	.....	.....

Leasing Company Shareholder Reports

#		1966	1967	1968	1969	1970	1971	1972	1973	1974	1975
22	Gross rentals	238,080	238,080	232,960	227,840	222,720	217,600	212,480	207,360	202,240	197,120
23	(2) Depreciation	85,000	85,000	85,000	85,000	85,000	85,000	85,000	85,000	85,000	85,000
24	Maintenance	25,600	25,600	25,600	25,600	25,600	25,600	25,600	25,600	25,600	25,600
25	(3) Interest	59,940	48,354	35,726	22,375	8,238	.....	.....	.....	.....	.....
26	Selling, general, and administrative	23,808	23,808	23,296	22,784	22,272	21,760	21,248	20,736	20,224	19,712
27	Pretax profit	43,732	55,318	63,338	72,081	81,610	85,240	80,632	76,024	71,416	66,808
28	Taxes (before investment credit)	21,866	27,659	31,669	36,040	40,805	42,620	40,316	38,012	35,708	33,404
29	(4) Investment credit used	10,933	13,829	15,834	18,020	11,384	.....	.....	.....	.....	.....
30	Net profit	32,799	41,488	47,503	54,061	52,189	42,620	40,316	38,012	35,708	33,404
31	(5) After-tax cash flow from liquidation	.....	.....	.....	.....	.....	.....	.....	.....	.....	275,000
32	Remaining investment credit	59,067	45,238	29,404	11,384	.....	.....	.....	.....	.....	.....

Assumptions:

(1) Discount: 10% of the IBM rate through 1967; increasing by 2 percentage points per year thereafter to 26% in 1975.

(2) Depreciation: 8 yrs. sum of years' digits, 15% residual value for tax purposes; 10 yrs., straight line, 15% residual for shareholders.

(3) Interest: 9% rate on outstanding balance which is reduced each year by the full cash flow.

(4) Investment credit: 7% investment credit deducted from tax liability as fast as possible rather than evenly amortized over the life of asset.

(5) Cash flow from liquidation: The computer is sold for 40% of original cost at the end of 1975; taxes paid at the corporate rate (0.50).

try. In the short run, the industry is threatened by the fact that it is dependent on the pricing strategy adopted by computer manufacturers. Should these manufacturers find their cash positions improving substantially in the next few years, they might wish to finance a higher proportion of computer shipments themselves. Higher computer sale prices relative to lease rental charges would tend to raise the manufacturers' lease to sales ratio. Higher computer maintenance fees would also tend to reduce the leasing companies' profit margins, thus slowing their growth and raising the manufacturers' lease to sales ratio.

Over the longer term, computer leasing companies are threatened by the obsolescence of their third-generation System/360 machines in less than the anticipated 10 years. Second-generation computers were manufactured and marketed for six full years from 1959 to 1965. Machines of this vintage dropped in used value from over 70% of the original purchase price to around 40% of the purchase price within a year after System/360 was introduced. With sales prices so sharply reduced, rental rates of the second generation machines were under considerable pressure. Whether this price pattern will be repeated with third-generation equipment remains a question for the future.

COMPULEASE CORPORATION

∧∧

Late in December, 1967, Mr. James A. Kralik, president of Compulease Corporation, was considering whether his company should continue to purchase third-generation computer equipment.

Corporate history

Compulease Corporation had shown dramatic growth in the area of short-term leasing since its inception in 1965. The company had been closely held during its first year. During this period the original investor group put together by the management banking firm of Bachman, Dillard and Hanover (BD&H) had participated in three rounds of private financing. In the first round, which occurred in January, 1966, the BD&H group had purchased 77,777 shares of Compulease common stock at $12.34 for a total commitment of $960,000. The Compulease co-founders, James Kralik, Philip Jameson, and John Bailey, had received 22,223 shares for a total consideration of $40,000. In two later rounds of private financing during 1966, the BD&H group had purchased, for $10 a share, an additional 233,333 shares of the company's common stock. Since the Compulease co-founders had exhausted their personal resources in the first round of financing, they were not able to purchase additional shares in later financing.

As originally planned, Compulease went public early in January, 1967, by offering 317,144 shares at a price of $20 a share. By the end of 1967, the company's common stock price had risen to $46, giving handsome paper profits to the original investors in Compulease and the purchasers of shares in the initial public offering.

Compulease expected to report earnings per share of $1.63 for 1967, a figure up nearly 70% from the $0.97 earned in 1966. Based on the 1967 earnings estimate, the company's common stock was selling at over 28 times earnings, a conservative figure by industry standards, as Exhibit 1 indicates.

The company's return on equity

When his company had started purchasing third-generation computer equipment two years earlier, Mr. Kralik had been well aware that the useful life of these machines would *not* be determined by any physical deterioration. Since the obsolescence would be technological rather than physical, the

485

remaining life of a third-generation computer purchased in 1965 would be the same as the remaining life of a similar machine purchased two years later, in December, 1967. The fact that similar equipment became obsolete at a specific *point* in time (shortly after the introduction of a new computer generation) rather than after an elapsed *period* of time made the continued purchase of third-generation machines a somewhat hazardous undertaking. This was true because those machines purchased earliest in the life cycle of the third generation were all but certain to earn the highest returns. Were Mr. Kralik to continue purchasing third-generation equipment for many more years, he could be certain of sustaining losses on those computers purchased too late in the product's life cycle to allow an economic return.

In his original 1965 projections (which were based on Exhibit 8, "Note: Computer Leasing Industry") Mr. Kralik estimated that the life cycle of third-generation computer equipment would extend through 1975. The passage of two years had not caused him to significantly revise these estimates. Thus, in calculating the return on equity invested in third-generation equipment purchased during 1968, he felt safe in assuming a remaining life of only eight years. Exhibit 2 shows that a two-year decline in life would cause the expected return on equity invested in third-generation equipment to drop from 12.9% to 11.7%.

Mr. Kralik was a little perturbed at the prospect of investing greater and greater sums of money at successively lower returns, and he wondered how the shareholders of Compulease would fare if the company continued its buying activity for at least another year. He was somewhat puzzled as to how he should go about evaluating the financial impact on shareholders of an additional year of purchasing third-generation equipment, but he decided to approach the problem from two different viewpoints, with an eye toward finally comparing the results of the two approaches.

First approach to shareholders' return on investment

Mr. Kralik's first attempt at estimating the impact of continuing computer purchases was based on valuing the cash flows generated through operations. Exhibit 3 shows Compulease's actual earnings reports through 1967 and estimated financial statements through 1975, assuming a halt in computer purchasing activity by the end of 1967. All future cash flows would be used first to retire outstanding debt, as was required in the company's agreement with its bank lenders. The cash flow remaining after debt amortization could then be returned to the shareholders, along with the cash realized from ultimately selling the computer equipment at the end of 1975.

At lines 25 and 26 of Exhibit 3, the company's cash flow is expressed on a per share basis to make possible a calculation of the rate of return to shareholders who bought the company's common stock at different prices.

According to Mr. Kralik's calculations (assuming all computer purchases were halted at the end of 1967), the original investors, who purchased their shares at an average cost of $10, would realize a rate of return equal to 17% on their investment if (1) they ignored all price gyrations in the stock market and held their shares through 1975, and (2) the company paid out its entire cash flow after debt amortization. Those investors who purchased their stock a year later at the initial public offering price of $20 a share would receive a return of only 8.8% under similar assumptions (line 28, Exhibit 3).

Mr. Kralik was a little unhappy about the return to the second group of investors. He wondered how a third group would fare under the same type of analysis if Compulease sold a new issue of common stock in 1968, thus allowing the company to continue purchasing third-generation computers for at least another year.

Mr. Kralik was advised by his investment banker that Compulease could easily raise enough equity through a common stock offering at $40 a share to enable the company to purchase some $40 million worth of third-generation computers in 1968. The sale of 306,000 shares of common stock would raise approximately $12,250,000. This amount, added to the earnings of $1,050,000 retained in 1967, would enlarge the company's equity base by $13,300,000. Compulease could borrow $26,700,000 (at a 2 to 1 debt-equity ratio) on this base, achieving a total potential cash infusion of nearly $40 million in 1968.

Exhibit 4 is Mr. Kralik's revision of the pro forma financial statements for Compulease Corporation for 1968–75, assuming a third round of external financing in 1968 and the purchase in that year of some $40 million worth of third-generation computer equipment. Mr. Kralik noted that under the continued buying assumption, the rate of return to the first two sets of investors rose from 17% to 21% and from 8.8% to 13.5% respectively (lines 27 and 28, Exhibits 3 and 4). Continued equipment purchases for at least another year would clearly be advantageous to these investors.

While the first two groups of investors profited substantially from a third year of purchasing activity, Mr. Kralik was startled to see that the last group of investors, who would purchase their shares at $40, could expect a return of only 4.4% (line 29, Exhibit 4) if they held their shares through 1975.

Second approach to shareholders' return on investment

Since no investor would knowingly place his capital at 4.4% in a situation as risky as computer leasing, Mr. Kralik felt that his valuation model based on discounting the cash flows from operations might be inappropriate. Investors were probably not looking to Compulease's future operating cash flows in making their stock purchase decisions. They were far more likely to count on getting their return through selling their shares in the open market at higher future prices. Their return might thus be entirely independent of Compulease's estimated future operating cash flows. The fact that the trading volume in Compulease's common stock was averaging 6% of the outstanding shares per week tended to give support to the idea that many investors were looking for profits from this security in the short run rather than through 1975. If investors were looking to a higher future stock price for their return on investment, Mr. Kralik felt they probably paid close attention to two factors contributing to future stock prices: (1) estimates of future earnings per share and (2) computer leasing industry price-earnings ratios.

Since Mr. Kralik was fairly confident of the earnings projections in Exhibits 3 and 4 (lines 38 and 39), he computed the price-earnings ratios necessary to keep the price of Compulease stock high enough to assure a 15% compound annual rate of return on his investment to an investor who purchased stock near the current price and held the stock over the next one to three years.

This analysis, presented in Exhibit 5, indicated clearly that investors in Compulease would be far less vulnerable to a downward reevaluation of price-earnings ratios in the computer leasing industry if equipment purchases were continued another year. Indeed, Mr. Kralik feared that the high price-earnings ratios characteristic of this industry might be a direct result of investors' expectations that the high rate of earnings growth from 1966 to 1967 would be repeated in the future. If Compulease failed to purchase computers through 1968, the projected growth in its per share earnings in the period 1967–68 promised to drop from 52% to 15%. A decline of this magnitude in the growth rate might be the very factor to precipitate the drop that Mr. Kralik feared in the company's price-earnings ratio.

Comparing the models

From the analysis of both valuation models, Mr. Kralik saw strong arguments for continuing computer purchases through 1968 in spite of the increased hazards inherent in pursuing such a policy. On the other hand, he felt that similar arguments might lead him to continue equipment purchases right into the 1970's.

Looking to the future

Although the decision regarding a cutoff date for purchases of third-generation computer equipment was the most immediate corporate problem, Mr. Kralik recognized a second problem of equal significance looming in the future. When Compulease did finally stop purchasing third-generation computers, Mr. Kralik was counting on the lapse of a number of years before the company could begin buying fourth-generation machines. Similarly, because of debt repayment terms, it would be four years before the company could use any significant portion of its cash flow for reinvestment or return to the shareholders. During this "dead" period between the third and fourth generation, Compulease would have no growth in its existing business and no cash to get into a new business. Fortunately, reported earnings would still rise about 15% a year for three years after new purchases ceased (Exhibits 3 and 4, lines 38 and 39), but even so Mr. Kralik thought that investors would probably take an unfavorable view of any company that remained inactive for a long period of time and drastically reduced its price-earnings multiple.

Mr. Kralik currently felt boxed into a situation where to maintain the price of his company's stock, he might have to commit increasing sums of money in situations offering decreasing expected returns. To avoid this problem, he felt that Compulease would have to diversify into some new business area in the near future. He wondered whether this diversification move should be into the area of commercial finance or some area outside of finance within the computer industry. Exhibit 1 provides financial data on possible fields within the computer industry, and Exhibit 6 contains data on two commercial finance companies.

Exhibit 1

COMPULEASE CORPORATION

FINANCIAL FACTS ON COMPANIES OPERATING IN THE DATA PROCESSING INDUSTRY

Company	Sales (Thousands) Latest 12 Months	Principal Activity	Five-Year Earnings per Share					Recent Price	P-E Ratio ('67 Earns)
			1963	1964	1965	1966	1967E		
Applied Data Research	$ 1,386	Software	$ 0.35D	$0.30	$ 0.21	$0.04	$0.30	17	57
ARIES Corp.	3,198	Software	0.09	0.25	0.13	0.50	0.50	23½	47
Automatic Data Proc.	8,900E	Svc. Bur.	0.03	0.09	0.19	0.50	c.80	43⅜	54
C-E-I-R	21,862	Svc. Bur.	(a −0.45D) (b −1.20D)	0.65 / 0.98	0.79 / 1.12	(0.13) (0.88)	0.25	17⅞	69
Calif. Computer Prod.	11,318	Hardware	0.18	0.58	0.55	0.67	c1.22	85¾	70
Computer Applications	24,542	Software	0.31	0.58	0.18	0.46	0.55	21¼	39
Computer Sciences	38,860	Software	0.12	0.07	(a −0.04D) (b −0.07)	0.17 (0.66)	c.40	26⅜	65
Computer Usage	12,000E	Software	0.20	0.37	0.53	0.64	0.90	43½	48
Comp. & Software(f)	12,045	Svc. Bur.	0.09	0.19	0.33	0.44	0.75	33½	45
Data Proc. Fin. & Gen.	3,500	Leasing	0.02	0.04	0.17	0.60	1.50	71⅜	48
Data Products Corp.	12,500E	Hardware	0.40D	0.22	0.05D	0.04	c.21	14⅜	68
Decision Systems(g)	780	Software	0.35	0.41	0.03	0.79D	0.82D	2½	::
Digitek Corp.	825E	Software	0.03	0.07	0.15	0.28	1.35D	5¾	::
Elec. Comp. Prog. Inst.	2,406	Schools	0.13	0.18	0.34	0.54	0.85	42¼	50
Gerber Scientific Inst.	6,751	Hardware	0.24	0.14	0.56	0.62	0.95	39½	42
Informatics Inc.(h)	6,428	Software	0.14D	0.15	0.19	0.37	c.51	31¾	62
Leasco Data Proc.	3,250	Leasing	0.24	0.35	0.54	0.88	1.40	76⅞	55
Levin-Townsend Comp.	3,938	Leasing	0.01	0.27	0.32	0.41	c1.14	41⅝	37
Planning Research	16,021	Software	0.49	0.56	1.10	0.96	c1.29	47⅜	37
Programming & Syst.	1,283	Schools	0.01D	0.05D	0.11	0.12	c.30	16½	55
Randolph Computer	2,958	Leasing	n.a.	n.a.	0.12D	0.77	1.25	36⅞	30
Scientific Comp.(i)	2,000E	Svc. Bur.	0.42D	0.17D	0.12	(i)	0.25	6½	26
TBS Comp. Centers (j)	2,509	Svc. Bur.	0.15	0.35	0.37	0.43	c.33	11½	35
University Computing	9,000E	Svc. Bur.	0.04	0.21	0.40	0.93	2.00	113	57

D—Deficit. E—Estimated. n.a.—Not applicable.
a—Actual, from operations. b—As reported, after special credits and/or charges (later restated). c—Actual, as reported, for FY 1967. f—Formerly Telecomputing Corp.; now 61%—held by Whittaker Corp. g—Formerly Computronics, Inc. h—70%—held by Data Products Corp. i—23%—held by Control Data Corp.; changed to fiscal year basis in 1966; earnings for six months ended 6/30/66 reported as $0.09 per share. j—Formerly Tabulating & Business Services Inc.

Source: "THINKing Big," Barron's, September 18, 1967.

Exhibit 2

COMPULEASE CORPORATION

DISCOUNTED CASH FLOW RATE OF RETURN ON THE
CORPORATION'S INVESTMENT IN THIRD-GENERATION
COMPUTER EQUIPMENT

Life of Equipment (Years)	*Rate of Return*
4	Loss
5	7.0%
6	10.3
7	11.3
8	11.7
10	12.9

Source: Calculated from Exhibit 8, "Note: Computer Leasing Industry."

Exhibit 3

COMPULEASE CORPORATION

ACTUAL FINANCIAL STATEMENTS, 1966–67, AND PRO FORMA STATEMENTS, 1968–75 ASSUMING PURCHASING ACTIVITY CEASES BY THE CLOSE OF 1967

Report groups (brace labels at right): rows 2–28 = **Tax Reports**; rows 29–39 = **Shareholder Reports**.

#	Item	1966	1967	1968	1969	1970	1971	1972	1973	1974	1975
1	Year	1966	1967	1968	1969	1970	1971	1972	1973	1974	1975
2	Gross equipment purchases	10,000,000	20,000,000	0	0	0	0	0	0	0	0
3	Gross equipment owned	10,000,000	30,000,000	30,000,000	30,000,000	30,000,000	30,000,000	30,000,000	30,000,000	30,000,000	30,000,000
4	IBM rental rate	2,553,191	7,659,574	7,659,574	7,659,574	7,659,574	7,659,574	7,659,574	7,659,574	7,659,574	7,659,574
5	Discount allowed	255,319	765,957	919,149	1,072,340	1,225,532	1,378,723	1,531,915	1,685,106	1,838,298	1,991,489
6	Overtime premium	76,596	229,787	229,787	229,787	229,787	229,787	229,787	229,787	229,787	229,787
7	Net rent received	2,374,468	7,123,404	6,970,213	6,817,021	6,663,830	6,510,638	6,357,447	6,204,255	6,051,064	5,897,872
8	Maintenance expense	255,319	765,957	765,957	765,957	765,957	765,957	765,957	765,957	765,957	765,957
9	Depreciation expense	1,888,889	5,430,555	4,722,222	4,013,889	3,305,555	2,597,222	1,888,889	1,180,556	472,222	0
10	Interest expense	600,000	1,684,647	1,328,205	952,093	554,539	133,613	0	0	0	0
11	General, selling, and administrative	237,447	712,340	697,021	681,702	666,383	651,064	635,745	620,426	605,106	589,787
12	Pretax profit	−607,187	−1,470,096	−543,194	403,380	1,371,395	2,362,782	3,066,856	3,637,317	4,207,778	4,542,128
13	Taxes	0	0	0	0	0	758,540	1,533,428	1,818,658	2,103,889	2,271,064
14	After-tax profit	−607,187	−1,470,096	−543,194	403,380	1,371,395	1,983,511	2,300,142	2,727,987	2,148,576	2,271,064
15	Depreciation expense	1,888,889	5,430,555	4,722,222	4,013,889	3,305,555	2,597,222	1,888,889	1,180,556	472,222	0
16	Investment credit used	0	0	0	0	0	379,270	766,714	909,329	44,687	0
17	Total cash inflow	1,281,702	3,960,460	4,179,028	4,417,269	4,676,951	4,580,734	4,189,031	3,908,543	2,620,798	2,271,064
18	Liquidation inflow in 1976	8,250,000									
19	Debt outstanding	6,666,667	18,718,298	14,757,838	10,578,810	6,161,541	1,484,591	0	0	0	0
20	Capital from investors	3,333,333	10,000,000	10,000,000	10,000,000	10,000,000	10,000,000	6,903,857	2,714,826	−1,193,717	−3,814,515
21	Unused investment credit	700,000	2,100,000	2,100,000	2,100,000	2,100,000	1,720,730	954,016	44,687	0	0
22	Tax loss carryover	607,187	2,077,283	2,620,476	2,217,096	845,701	0	0	0	0	0
23	Shares sold in year	333,333	317,144	0	0	0	0	0	0	0	0
24	Total shares outstanding	333,333	650,478	650,478	650,478	650,478	650,478	650,478	650,478	650,478	650,478
25	Cash return per share	0	0	0	0	0	4.76	6.44	6.01	4.03	3.49
26	Liquidation return per share in 1976	12.68									
27	ROR 1st investor	0.171									
28	ROR 2nd investor	0.088									
29	Net rent received	2,374,468	7,123,404	6,970,213	6,817,021	6,663,830	6,510,638	6,357,447	6,204,255	6,051,064	5,897,872
30	Depreciation expense	850,000	2,550,000	2,550,000	2,550,000	2,550,000	2,550,000	2,550,000	2,550,000	2,550,000	2,550,000
31	Maintenance expense	255,319	765,957	765,957	765,957	765,957	765,957	765,957	765,957	765,957	765,957
32	Interest expense	600,000	1,684,647	1,328,205	952,093	554,539	133,613	0	0	0	0
33	General, selling, and administrative	237,447	712,340	697,021	681,702	666,383	651,064	635,745	620,426	605,106	589,787
34	Pretax profit	431,702	1,410,460	1,629,029	1,867,269	2,126,951	2,410,004	2,405,745	2,267,872	2,130,000	1,992,128
35	Taxes	215,851	705,230	814,514	933,634	1,063,475	1,205,002	1,202,872	1,133,936	1,065,000	996,064
36	Investment credit used	107,926	352,615	407,257	466,817	531,738	233,648	0	0	0	0
37	After-tax profit	323,777	1,057,845	1,221,771	1,400,452	1,595,213	1,438,649	1,202,872	1,133,936	1,065,000	996,064
38	Earnings per share	0.97	1.63	1.88	2.15	2.45	2.21	1.85	1.74	1.64	1.53
39	Unused investment credit	592,074	1,639,460	1,232,202	765,385	233,648	0	0	0	0	0

Assumptions: Investor No. 1 purchases @ $10 per share in January, 1966; Investor No. 2 purchases @ $20 per share in January, 1967.

Exhibit 4

COMPULEASE CORPORATION

ACTUAL FINANCIAL STATEMENTS, 1966–67, AND PRO FORMA STATEMENTS, 1968–75, ASSUMING PURCHASING ACTIVITY CEASES BY THE CLOSE OF 1968

	1966	1967	1968	1969	1970	1971	1972	1973	1974	1975	
1 Year	1966	1967	1968	1969	1970	1971	1972	1973	1974	1975	
2 Gross equipment purchases	10,000,000	20,000,000	40,000,000	0	0	0	0	0	0	0	
3 Gross equipment owned	10,000,000	30,000,000	70,000,000	70,000,000	70,000,000	70,000,000	70,000,000	70,000,000	70,000,000	70,000,000	
4 IBM rental rate	2,553,191	7,659,574	17,872,340	17,872,340	17,872,340	17,872,340	17,872,340	17,872,340	17,872,340	17,872,340	
5 Discount allowed	255,319	765,957	2,144,681	2,502,128	2,859,574	3,217,021	3,574,468	3,931,915	4,289,362	4,646,808	
6 Overtime premium	76,596	229,787	536,170	536,170	536,170	536,170	536,170	536,170	536,170	536,170	
7 Net rent received	2,374,468	7,123,404	16,263,830	15,906,383	15,548,936	15,191,489	14,834,042	14,476,596	14,119,149	13,761,702	
8 Maintenance expense	255,319	765,957	1,787,234	1,787,234	1,787,234	1,787,234	1,787,234	1,787,234	1,787,234	1,787,234	
9 Depreciation expense	1,888,889	5,430,555	12,277,777	10,625,000	8,972,222	7,319,444	5,666,667	4,013,889	2,361,111	944,444	
10 Interest expense	600,000	1,684,647	3,728,205	2,907,225	2,041,309	1,126,414	158,132	0	0	0	
11 General, selling, and administrative	237,447	712,340	1,626,383	1,590,638	1,554,894	1,519,149	1,483,404	1,447,660	1,411,915	1,376,170	Tax Reports
12 Pretax profit	−607,187	−1,470,096	−3,155,770	−1,003,714	1,193,277	3,439,248	5,738,606	7,227,813	8,558,889	9,653,853	
13 Taxes	0	0	0	0	0	0	2,067,182	3,613,907	4,279,444	4,826,927	
14 After-tax profit	−607,187	−1,470,096	−3,155,770	−1,003,714	1,193,277	3,439,248	4,705,015	5,420,860	6,338,900	4,826,927	
15 Depreciation expense	1,888,889	5,430,555	12,277,777	10,625,000	8,972,222	7,319,444	5,666,667	4,013,889	2,361,111	944,444	
16 Investment credit used	0	0	0	0	0	0	1,033,591	1,806,953	2,059,456	0	
17 Total cash inflow	1,281,702	3,960,460	9,122,007	9,621,286	10,165,499	10,758,692	10,371,681	9,434,749	8,700,011	5,771,371	
18 Liquidation inflow in 1976	19,250,000										
19 Debt outstanding	6,666,667	18,718,298	41,424,505	32,302,498	22,681,212	12,515,713	1,757,021	0	0	0	
20 Capital from investors	3,333,333	10,000,000	23,333,333	23,333,333	23,333,333	23,333,333	23,333,333	14,718,673	5,283,925	−3,416,087	
21 Unused investment credit	700,000	2,100,000	4,900,000	4,900,000	4,900,000	4,900,000	3,866,409	2,059,456	0	0	
22 Tax loss carryover	607,187	2,077,283	5,233,053	6,236,767	5,043,490	1,604,242	0	0	0	0	
23 Shares sold in year	333,333	317,144	306,887	0	0	0	0	0	0	0	
24 Total shares outstanding	333,333	650,478	957,365	957,365	957,365	957,365	957,365	957,365	957,365	957,365	
25 Cash return per share in 1976							9.00	9.85	9.09	6.03	
26 Liquidation return per share in 1976	20.10										
27 ROR 1st investor	0.211										
28 ROR 2nd investor	0.135										
29 ROR 3rd investor	0.044										
30 Net rent received	2,374,468	7,123,404	16,263,830	15,906,383	15,548,936	15,191,489	14,834,042	14,476,596	14,119,149	13,761,702	
31 Depreciation expense	850,000	2,550,000	5,950,000	5,950,000	5,950,000	5,950,000	5,950,000	5,950,000	5,950,000	5,950,000	
32 Maintenance expense	255,319	765,957	1,787,234	1,787,234	1,787,234	1,787,234	1,787,234	1,787,234	1,787,234	1,787,234	Shareholder Reports
33 Interest expense	600,000	1,684,647	3,728,205	2,907,225	2,041,309	1,126,414	158,132	0	0	0	
34 General, selling, and administrative	237,447	712,340	1,626,383	1,590,638	1,554,894	1,519,149	1,483,404	1,447,660	1,411,915	1,376,170	
35 Pretax profit	431,702	1,410,460	3,172,007	3,671,286	4,215,499	4,808,692	5,455,272	5,291,702	4,970,000	4,648,298	
36 Taxes	215,851	705,230	1,586,004	1,835,643	2,107,750	2,404,346	2,727,636	2,645,851	2,485,000	2,324,149	
37 Investment credit used	107,926	352,615	793,002	917,821	1,053,875	1,202,173	472,588	0	0	0	
38 After-tax profit	323,777	1,057,845	2,379,005	2,753,464	3,161,624	3,606,519	3,200,225	2,645,851	2,485,000	2,324,149	
39 Earnings per share	0.97	1.63	2.48	2.88	3.30	3.77	3.34	2.76	2.60	2.43	
40 Unused investment credit	592,074	1,639,460	3,646,458	2,728,636	1,674,761	472,588	0	0	0	0	

Assumptions: Investor No. 1 purchases @ $10 per share in January, 1966; investor No. 2 purchases @ $20 per share in January, 1967; investor No. 3 purchases @ $40 per share in January, 1968.

Exhibit 5

COMPULEASE CORPORATION

MARKET PRICES OF COMPULEASE CORPORATION COMMON STOCK NECESSARY TO SUSTAIN VARIOUS RATES OF RETURN TO INVESTORS

Year	Projected Earnings per Share*	Market Price Necessary for Compound Annual Rate of Return of			Price-Earnings Ratio Required for Compound Annual Rate of Return of		
		5%	15%	25%	5%	15%	25%
Assumes computer purchases cease after 1967							
1968	$1.88	$42.00	$46.00	$50.00	22.3	24.5	26.6
1969	2.15	44.20	53.00	62.50	20.6	24.7	29.0
1970	2.45	46.40	61.00	78.30	18.9	24.9	32.0
Assumes computer purchases cease after 1968							
1968	2.48	42.00	46.00	50.00	16.9	18.5	20.2
1969	2.88	44.20	53.00	62.50	15.3	18.4	21.7
1970	3.30	46.40	61.00	78.30	14.1	18.5	23.7

* Lines 38 and 39, Exhibits 3 and 4.
† Assumes initial purchase at $40 a share.

Exhibit 6

COMPULEASE CORPORATION

FINANCIAL DATA—COMMERCIAL FINANCE COMPANIES

Year	Earnings per share	Average P-E Ratio	Return on Equity*
Commercial Credit Corporation			
1966	$2.24	12.5	7.6%
1965	2.26	16.5	7.8
1964	3.07	13	11.2
1963	2.98	14.5	11.4
1962	2.97	15	11.9
C.I.T. Financial Corporation			
1966	2.74	10.5	12.5
1965	2.63	12.5	12.7
1964	2.54	14.5	12.7
1963	2.47	17.0	12.8
1962	2.43	16.5	13.0

* Defined as net profit/net worth.

COOPER INDUSTRIES, INC.

In May, 1972, Robert Cizik, executive vice president of Cooper Industries, Inc., was reviewing acquisition candidates for his company's diversification program. One of the companies, Nicholson File Company, had been approached by Cooper Industries three years earlier but had rejected all overtures. Now, however, Nicholson was in the middle of a takeover fight that might provide Cooper with a chance to gain control.

Cooper Industries

Cooper Industries was organized in 1919 as a manufacturer of heavy machinery and equipment. By the mid-1950's, the company was a leading producer of engines and massive compressors used to force natural gas through pipelines and oil out of wells. Management was concerned, however, over its heavy dependence on sales to the oil and gas industries and the violent fluctuation of earnings caused by the cyclical nature of heavy machinery and equipment sales. Although the company's long-term sales and earnings growth had been above average, its cyclicality had dampened Wall Street's interest in the stock substantially. (Cooper's historical operating results and financial condition are summarized in Exhibits 1 and 2.)

Initial efforts to lessen the earnings volatility were not successful. Between 1959 and 1966, Cooper acquired (1) a supplier of portable industrial power tools, (2) a manufacturer of small industrial air and process compressors, (3) a maker of small pumps and compressors for oil field applications, and (4) a producer of tire changing tools for the automotive market. The acquisitions broadened Cooper's markets but left it still highly sensitive to general economic conditions.

A full review of Cooper's acquisition strategy was initiated in 1966 by the company. After several months of study, three criteria were established for all acquisitions. First, the industry should be one in which Cooper could become a major factor. This requirement was in line with management's goal of leadership within a few distinct areas of business. Second, the industry should be fairly stable with a broad market for the products and a product line of largely "small ticket" items. This product definition was intended to eliminate any company that had undue profit dependence upon a single customer or several large sales per year. Finally, it was decided to acquire only leading companies in their respective market segments.

The new strategy was initially implemented with the acquisition in 1967 of the Lufkin Rule Company, the world's largest manufacturer of measuring rules and tapes. Cooper acquired a quality product line, an established distribution system of 35,000 retail hardware stores throughout the United States, and plants in the United States, Canada, and Mexico. It also gained the services of William Rector, president of Lufkin, and Hal Stevens, vice president of sales. Both were extremely knowledgeable in the hand tool business and had worked together effectively for years. Their goal was to build through acquisition a hand tool company with a full product line that would use a common sales and distribution system and joint advertising. To do this they needed Cooper's financial strength.

Lufkin provided a solid base to which two other companies were added. In 1969, the Crescent Niagara Corporation was acquired. The company had been highly profitable in the early 1960's, but had suffered in recent years under the mismanagement of some investor–entrepreneurs who gained control in 1963. A series of acquisitions of weak companies with poor product lines eroded the company's overall profitability until, in 1967, a small loss was reported. Discouraged, the investors wanted to get out and Cooper—eager to add Crescent's well-known and high-quality wrenches, pliers, and screwdrivers to its line—was interested. It was clear that some of Crescent's lines would have to be dropped and inefficient plants would have to be closed, but the wrenches, pliers, and screwdrivers were an important part of Cooper's product policy.

In 1970, Cooper further expanded into hand tools with the acquisition of the Weller Electric Corporation. Weller was the world's leading supplier of soldering tools to the industrial, electronic, and consumer markets. It provided Cooper with a new, high-quality product line and production capacity in England, West Germany, and Mexico. (Information on the three acquisitions is provided in Exhibit 3.)

Cooper was less successful in its approach to a fourth company in the hand tool business, the Nicholson File Company. Nicholson was on the original "shopping list" of acceptable acquisition candidates which Mr. Cizik and Mr. Rector had developed, but several attempts to interest Nicholson in exploring merger possibilities had failed. The Nicholson family had controlled and managed the company since its founding in 1864 and Paul Nicholson, chairman of the board, had no interest in joining forces with anyone.

Nicholson File Company

But Nicholson was too inviting a takeover target to be overlooked or ignored for long. A relatively poor sales and profit performance in recent years, conservative accounting and financial policies, and a low percentage of outstanding stock held by the Nicholson family and management all contributed to its vulnerability. Annual sales growth of 2% was far behind the industry growth rate of 6% per year, and profit margins had slipped to only one third those of other hand tool manufacturers. In 1971, the Nicholson common stock was trading near its lowest point in many years and well below its book value of $51.25. Lack of investor interest in the stock was reflected in its low price–earnings ratio of 10–14, which compared with 14–17 times earnings for other leading hand tool companies. The stock was clearly selling on the basis of its dividend yield, with only limited hopes for capital appreciation. (Exhibits 4 and 5 show Nicholson's operating results and balance sheets.)

What made Nicholson so attractive was its basic competitive strength—strengths that the family-dominated management had not translated into earnings. The company was one of the largest domestic manufacturers of hand tools and was a leader in its two main product areas. Nicholson held a 50% share of the $50 million market for files and rasps, where it offered a broad, high-quality line with a very strong brand name. Its second product line, hand saws and saw blades, also had an excellent reputation for quality and held a 9% share of this $200 million market. Only Sears, Roebuck and Company and Disston, Inc. had larger market shares.

Nicholson's greatest asset, however, was its distribution system. Forty-eight direct salesmen and 28 file and saw engineers marketed its file, rasp, and saw products to 2,100 hardware wholesalers in the United States and Canada. These wholesalers in turn sold to 53,000 retail outlets. Their efforts were supported by heavy advertising and promotional programs. Overseas the company's products were sold in 137 countries through 140 local sales representatives. The company seemed to have all the necessary strengths to share fully in the 6–7% annual sales growth forecast for the industry.

The raid by H. K. Porter Company

Cooper was not alone in its interest in Nicholson. H. K. Porter Company, a conglomerate with wide ranging interests in electrical equipment, tools, nonferrous metals, and rubber products, had acquired 44,000 shares of Nicholson stock in 1967 and had been an attentive stockholder ever since. On March 3, 1972, Porter informed Nicholson management of its plan to tender immediately for 437,000 of Nicholson's 584,000 outstanding shares at $42 per share in cash. The offer would terminate on April 4, unless extended by Porter; and the company was unwilling to acquire less than enough shares to constitute a majority.

Nicholson management was alarmed by both the proposal and the proposer. The company would contribute less than one sixth of the combined sales and would clearly be just another operating division of Porter. It was feared that Porter's quest for higher profits might lead to aggressive cost cutting and the elimination of marginal product lines. Nicholson's Atkins Saw Division seemed especially vulnerable in view of its low profitability.

Loss of control seemed both painful and likely. The $42 cash offer represented a $12 premium over the most recent price of the stock and threatened to create considerable stockholder interest. The disappointing performance of the stock in recent years would undoubtedly increase the attractiveness of the $42 offer to Nicholson's 4,000 stockholders. And the Nicholson family and management owned only 20% of the outstanding shares—too little to assure continued control.

Immediately after learning of the Porter tender offer, Mr. Cizik and Mr. Rector approached the Nicholson management with an offer of help. It was clear that Nicholson had to move immediately and forcefully; the first ten days of a tender offer are critical. Cizik and Rector stressed that Nicholson must find a better offer and find it fast. Indeed, Cooper would be willing to make such an offer if Nicholson's management and directors would commit themselves to it—now.

Nicholson was not ready for such decisive action, however, and three days passed without any decision. With each day the odds of a successful counter-offer diminished. Finally, the Cooper officers decided the risks were too great and that Porter would learn of Cooper's offer of help and might retaliate. Cooper's stock was depressed and it was possible that an angry Porter management might strike for control of Cooper. The offer was withdrawn.

By late March, the situation was increasing in seriousness. Management of Nicholson moved to block the raid. It personally talked with the large shareholders and it made a strong public statement recommending against the offer. But announcements by Porter indicated that a substantial number of Nicholson shares were being tendered. It was no longer a matter of whether or not to be acquired. The issue was, by whom!

Management sought to find an alternative merger that would ensure continuity of Nicholson management and operating independence. Several companies had communicated with Nicholson in the wake of the Porter announcement, but no one other than Cooper had made a specific proposal. This was largely due to their reluctance to compete at the price levels being discussed or to enter into a fight with Porter.

Finally, on April 3, agreement was reached with VLN Corporation on the terms of a merger with VLN. VLN was a broadly diversified company with major interests in original and replacement automotive equipment and in publishing. Under the VLN merger terms, one share of new VLN cumulative convertible preferred stock would be exchanged for each share of Nicholson common stock. The VLN preferred stock would pay an annual dividend of $1.60 and would be convertible into five shares of VLN common stock during the first year following the merger, scaling down to four shares after the fourth year. The preferred stock would be callable at $50 a share after the fifth year and would have liquidating rights of $50 per share. (See Exhibit 6 for a financial summary of VLN.)

Nicholson management, assured of continued operating independence, supported the VLN offer actively. In a letter to the stockholders, Paul Nicholson pointed out that (1) the exchange would be a tax-free transaction, (2) the $1.60 preferred dividend equalled the current rate on the Nicholson common stock, and (3) a preferred share was worth a minimum of $53.10 (VLN common stock had closed at $10.62 on the day prior to the offer). He felt confident that the necessary majority of the outstanding common stock would be voted in favor of the proposed merger when it was brought to a vote in the fall. (Under Rhode Island law, a simple majority was sufficient to authorize the merger.)

Porter quickly counterattacked by pointing out to Nicholson stockholders that VLN common stock had recently sold for as low as $4⅝, which would put a value in the first year of only $23.12 on the VLN preferred stock. Furthermore, anyone who converted into VLN common stock would suffer a sharp income loss since VLN had paid no common dividends since 1970.

Nicholson's stockholders were thus presented with two very contradictory appraisals of the VLN offer. Each company based its argument on some stock price, either the highest or the lowest, that would make the converted preferred stock compare favorably or not with the $42 cash offer.

Opportunity for Cooper?

Mr. Cizik and his staff were still attracted by the potential profits to be realized from Nicholson. It was felt that Nicholson's efforts to sell to every market segment resulted in an excessive number of products, which held down manufacturing efficiency and ballooned inventories. Cooper estimated that Nicholson's cost of goods sold could be reduced from 69% of sales to 65%.

The other major area of cost reduction was Nicholson's selling expenses. There was a substantial overlap of Nicholson's sales force and that established by Cooper for its Lufkin-Weller-Crescent hand tool lines. Elimination of the sales and advertising duplications would lower selling, general and administrative expenses from 22% of sales to 19%.

There were other possible sources of earnings, but they were more difficult to quantify. For instance, 75% of Nicholson's sales were to the industrial market and only 25% to the consumer market. In contrast, sales by Cooper's hand tool group were distributed between the two markets in virtually the exact opposite proportions. Thus, sales increases could be expected from Nicholson's "pulling" more Cooper products into the industrial markets and vice versa for the consumer market. Also, Cooper was eager to use Nicholson's strong European distribution system to sell its other hand tool lines.

The battle between Porter and VLN seemed to provide Cooper with an unexpected, second opportunity to gain control of Nicholson. Porter had ended up with just 133,000 shares tendered in response to its offer—far short of the 249,000 shares needed to give it majority control.[1] Its slate of directors had been defeated by Nicholson management at the Nicholson annual meeting on April 21. T. M. Evans, president of Porter, now feared that Nicholson might consummate the merger with VLN and that Porter would be faced with the unhappy prospect of receiving VLN preferred stock for its 177,000 shares of Nicholson stock. Mr. Evans knew that the VLN stock had been a lackluster

---

[1] Porter needed 292,584 shares to hold 50.1% majority control. It already owned 43,806 shares and needed, therefore, an additional 248,778 shares.

performer and might not show any significant growth in the near term. Furthermore, the $1.60 dividend rate seemed low in relation to current market yields on straight preferred stocks of 7%. Finally, he feared that it would be difficult to sell a large holding of VLN stock, which traded in small volume on the American Stock Exchange.

On the other hand, a merger of Cooper and Nicholson would allow Mr. Evans to convert his Nicholson shares into either common stock or convertible preferred stock of Cooper. This was a much more attractive alternative, assuming that an acceptable exchange rate could be set. Mr. Evans anticipated that earnings should rebound sharply from the cyclical downturn in 1971, and felt that Cooper stock would show significant price appreciation. Furthermore, Cooper stock was traded on the New York Exchange, which provided substantial liquidity. At a private meeting in late April, Mr. Evans tentatively agreed to support a Cooper-Nicholson merger on the condition that he receive Cooper common or convertible securities in a tax-free exchange worth at least $50 for each Nicholson share he held.

Mr. Cizik was now faced with the critical decision of whether or not to move for control. Cooper had acquired 29,000 shares of Nicholson stock during the preceding month in the open market—in part to build some bargaining power but largely to keep the loose shares out of the hands of Porter. Still uncommitted, however, were an estimated 50,000–100,000 shares that had been bought by speculators in the hope of an escalation of acquisition offers. Another 150,000–200,000 shares were unaccounted for, although Mr. Cizik suspected that a considerable number would go with the recommendation of Nicholson management. (Exhibit 7 shows Mr. Cizik's best estimate of the distribution of Nicholson stock in early May.) His hopes for gaining 50.1% of the Nicholson shares outstanding[2] depended upon his gaining support of at least 86,000 of the shares still either uncommitted or unaccounted for.

If he decided to seek control, it would be necessary to establish both the price and the form of the offer. Clearly, the terms would have to be sufficiently attractive to secure the shares needed to gain majority control.

Mr. Cizik also felt that the terms should be acceptable to the Nicholson management. Once the merger was complete, Cooper would need to work with the Nicholson family and management. He did not want them to feel that they and other Nicholson stockholders were cheated by the merger. As a matter of policy Cooper had never made an "unfriendly" acquisition and this one was to be no exception. The offer should be one that would be supported by the great majority of the stockholders.

However, the price and the form of the payment had to be consistent with

---

[2] Nicholson File was incorporated in Rhode Island. Under Rhode Island corporation law, a merger can be voted by shareholders holding a majority of the common stock outstanding. For reasons specific both to the laws of Rhode Island and to the Nicholson situation, dissenting stockholders of Nicholson would not be entitled to exercise the rights of dissent and would be forced to accept the exchange offer.

Cooper's concern that the acquisition earn a satisfactory long-term return and improve the trend of Cooper's earnings per share over the next five years. (A forecast of Cooper's earnings per share is shown in Exhibit 8.) The company anticipated making additional acquisitions, possibly on an exchange of stock basis, and maintenance of a strong earnings pattern and stock price was therefore important. On May 3, the common stock of Cooper and Nicholson closed at $24 and $44 respectively.

Exhibit 1

COOPER INDUSTRIES, INC.

CONDENSED OPERATING AND STOCKHOLDER INFORMATION

	1967	1968	1969	1970	1971
Operations (In millions):					
Net sales..............................	$ 198	$ 206	$ 212	$ 226	$ 208
Cost of goods sold.......................	141	145	154	164	161
Depreciation...........................	4	5	4	4	4
Selling and administrative expenses.........	23	25	29	29	29
Interest expense........................	1	2	3	4	3
Income before taxes and extraordinary items................................	$ 29	$ 29	$ 22	$24	$ 11
Income taxes...........................	14	15	11	12	5
Income before extraordinary items..........	$ 15.2	$ 13.9	$ 10.6	$ 12.4	$ 5.6
Preferred dividend.......................	1.0	.9	.9	.9	.9
Net income applicable to common stock.....	$ 14.2	$ 13.0	$ 9.7	$ 11.5	$ 4.7
Per Share of Common Stock:					
Earnings before extraordinary items.........	$ 3.34	$ 3.07	$ 2.33	$ 2.75	$ 1.12
Dividends..............................	1.20	1.25	1.40	1.40	1.40
Book value.............................	16.43	17.26	18.28	19.68	18.72
Market price............................	23–59	36–57	22–50	22–35	18–38
Price-earnings ratio......................	7–18	12–19	9–22	8–13	16–34

Exhibit 2

COOPER INDUSTRIES, INC.

BALANCE SHEET AS OF DECEMBER 31, 1971

(In millions)

ASSETS		LIABILITIES AND NET WORTH	
Cash.................................	$ 9	Accounts payable....................	$ 30
Accounts receivable..................	49	Accrued taxes.......................	3
Inventories.........................	57	Long-term debt due..................	5
Other...............................	2	*Total current liabilities*...........	$ 38
Total current assets...............	$117	Long-term debt*.....................	34
Net plant and equipment.............	47	Deferred taxes......................	4
Other...............................	8	Preferred stock.....................	11
Total assets..................	$172	Common equity (4,218,691 shares outstanding)......................	85
		Total liabilities and net worth.....	$172

* Maturities of long-term debt are $5.5 million, $6.0 million, $4.0 million, $2.0 million, and $2.0 million in the years 1972 through 1976 respectively.

Exhibit 3

COOPER INDUSTRIES, INC.

SUMMARY OF RECENT ACQUISITIONS

(In millions)

	Year Preceding Acquisition by Cooper				
	Sales	Net Income	Book Value	Acquisition Price Paid	Form of Transaction
Lufkin Rule Company.................	$22	$1.4	$15	$20.6	Convertible preferred
Crescent Niagara Corporation..........	16	0.04	4.9	12.5	Cash
Weller Electric Corporation............	10	0.9	4.4	14.6	Common stock

Exhibit 4

COOPER INDUSTRIES, INC.

CONDENSED OPERATING AND STOCKHOLDER INFORMATION
FOR NICHOLSON FILE COMPANY

	1967	1968	1969	1970	1971
Operations (In millions):					
Net sales..........................	$48.5	$49.1	$53.7	$54.8	$55.3
Cost of goods sold...................	32.6	33.1	35.9	37.2	37.9
Selling, general, and administrative					
expenses..........................	10.7	11.1	11.5	11.9	12.3
Depreciation expense................	2.0	2.3	2.4	2.3	2.1
Interest expense.....................	0.4	0.7	0.8	0.8	0.8
Other deductions....................	0.3	0.1	0.2	0.2	0.2
Income before taxes.................	$ 2.53	$ 1.85	$ 2.97	$ 2.42	$ 2.02
Taxes*............................	0.60	0.84	1.31	0.88	0.67
Net income........................	$ 1.93	$ 1.01	$ 1.66	$ 1.54	$ 1.35
Percentage of Sales:					
Cost of goods sold...................	67%	67%	67%	68%	69%
Selling, general, and administrative					
expenses..........................	22%	23%	21%	22%	22%
Income before taxes.................	5.2%	3.8%	5.5%	4.4%	3.7%
Stockholder Information:					
Earnings per share...................	$ 3.19	$ 1.65	$ 2.88	$ 2.64	$ 2.32
Dividends per share.................	1.60	1.60	1.60	1.60	1.60
Book value per share...............	45.66	48.03	49.31	50.20	51.25
Market price.......................	33–46	35–48	29–41	25–33	23–32
Price-earnings ratio.................	10–14	21–30	10–14	9–13	10–14

* The ratio of income taxes to income before taxes has been reduced primarily by the investment tax credit and by the inclusion in income of equity in net income of partially-owned foreign companies, the taxes for which are provided for in the accounts of such companies and not in the tax provision of Nicholson. It was estimated that the average tax rate would be 40% in future years.

Exhibit 5

COOPER INDUSTRIES, INC.

BALANCE SHEET OF NICHOLSON FILE COMPANY AS OF DECEMBER 31, 1971

(In millions)

ASSETS		LIABILITIES AND NET WORTH	
Cash	$ 1	Accounts payable	$ 2
Accounts receivable	8	Other	2
Inventories*	18	*Total current liabilities*	$ 4
Other	1	Long-term debt	12
Total current assets	$28	Common stock	31
Investment in subsidiaries	3	*Total liabilities and net worth*	$47
Net plant and equipment	16		
Total assets	$47		

* Inventories in the amount of $11.8 million are priced at cost on the last-in, first-out method. The estimated replacement cost exceeds the carrying amounts by $9.2 million. The remaining inventories are priced at the lower of cost on the first-in, first-out method or market.

Exhibit 6

COOPER INDUSTRIES, INC.

CONDENSED OPERATING AND STOCKHOLDER INFORMATION FOR VLN CORPORATION

	1967	1968	1969	1970	1971
Operations (In millions):					
Net sales	$45	$97	$99	$98	$100
Net income	1.97	3.20	3.20	1.13	2.98
Financial Position (In millions):					
Current assets	$25	$46	$49	$41	$ 46
Current liabilities	6	11	15	10	13
Net working capital	19	35	34	31	33
Long-term debt	10	18	16	15	17
Shareholders' equity	21	36	40	39	41
Stockholder Information:					
Earnings per share	$ 0.78	$ 0.61	$ 0.53	$ 0.27	$ 0.54
Dividends per share	—	—	—	.20	—
Shareholders' equity per share	8.23	9.64	10.00	9.24	9.69
Market price range	6–17	10–18	7–18	4–10	5–8
Price-earnings ratio	8–22	16–30	13–34	15–37	9–15

Exhibit 7

COOPER INDUSTRIES, INC.

ESTIMATED DISTRIBUTION OF NICHOLSON FILE COMPANY STOCK

Shares supporting Cooper:
H. K. Porter....................................	177,000	
Cooper Industries...............................	29,000	206,000

Shares supporting VLN:
Nicholson family and management................	117,000	
Owned by VLN................................	14,000	131,000

Shares owned by speculators.................................	50–100,000
Shares unaccounted for......................................	197–147,000
Total Nicholson shares outstanding.....................	584,000

Exhibit 8

COOPER INDUSTRIES, INC.

FIVE-YEAR FORECAST OF EARNINGS, EXCLUDING
NICHOLSON FILE COMPANY*

	1972	1973	1974	1975	1976
Net income available to common stockholders (in millions)................................	$11.0	$11.9	$12.8	$13.8	$15.0
Number of shares outstanding (in millions)......	4.21	4.21	4.21	4.21	4.21
Primary earnings per share....................	$ 2.61	$ 2.83	$ 3.04	$ 3.27	$ 3.56

* Casewriter's estimates

KENNECOTT COPPER CORPORATION

On March 29, 1968, Kennecott Copper Corporation purchased the assets and business of Peabody Coal Company for $285 million in cash, the assumption of $36.5 million of liabilities, and a reserved production payment of $300 million.[1] The transaction was designed to give Peabody's shareholders $47.50 per share for their stock. Immediately prior to the public announcement that acquisition discussions were underway between Kennecott and Peabody, Peabody's stock sold at about $30 per share. The acquisition represented a major diversification for Kennecott. At the time of the acquisition, Kennecott was the largest domestic producer of copper and copper products. Peabody was the largest domestic producer of coal.

The acquisition of Peabody promised two major benefits to Kennecott. First, Peabody's profits were expected to moderate the wide swings in Kennecott's profitability. This profit volatility was produced, in large measure, by sharp changes in copper prices and copper sales (columns 4 and 6, Exhibit 1). Second, the acquisition was expected to provide Kennecott with significant future investment opportunities outside of the copper industry.

In the years following the Peabody acquisition, the firm did little to moderate the swings in Kennecott's profitability (columns 1 and 7, Exhibit 1). In fact, Kennecott's profits were more erratic in the 1970s than they had been in the 1960s. The 1971 expropriation of Kennecott's extensive copper operations in Chile, the huge capital expenditures in the United States to meet environmental standards, and excess world copper production all put pressure on Kennecott's profits which Peabody's unexpectedly poor earnings were unable to offset. Peabody was, however, Kennecott's major investment outlet throughout the 1970s. Between 1968 and 1976, Kennecott contributed $532 million to Peabody's capital and allowed Peabody to retain essentially all of its earnings (columns 7–10, Exhibit 1).

---

[1] A third party, Green River Coal Company, paid Peabody this $300 million. Green River was to receive a specified percentage of the net mine revenue from Peabody's coal production until the $300 million, plus interest thereon, was repaid. Full repayment was expected by 1975. Neither Kennecott nor Peabody had any liability to pay the production payment, which was payable solely out of the proceeds from the production of coal. The obligations of Peabody under the production payment with respect to the production and sale of coal were, however, guaranteed by Kennecott.

Kennecott's approach to the financing of Peabody's growth was extremely conservative. At December 31, 1976, Peabody had almost no debt but enjoyed a net worth of over $900 million. Over 65% of Kennecott's net worth was represented by its investment in Peabody (Exhibit 2).

When the proposed Peabody acquisition was first announced in March 1967, Kennecott encountered considerable resistance from both the U.S. Department of Justice and the U.S. Federal Trade Commission (FTC). Kennecott was able to overcome the opposition of the Department of Justice in October 1967 by agreeing to divest within two years three Illinois mines capable of producing 6 million tons of coal annually for 20 years. The FTC was more difficult to satisfy. Prior to the completion of the Peabody acquisition, the FTC announced that it would challenge the acquisition under Section 7 of the Clayton Act. The FTC alleged that the acquisition of Peabody would tend to lessen competition in the coal industry. The FTC complaint was filed in August 1968. Kennecott's *1967 Annual Report* noted that:

> Our outside counsel, Messrs. Sullivan and Cromwell, is of the opinion that this acquisition does not violate any of the federal antitrust laws as so far construed by the courts or the Federal Trade Commission, and that an action seeking divestiture would not be successful.[2]

As luck would have it, the key phrase in the Sullivan and Cromwell opinion turned out to be ". . . as so far construed. . . ." In March 1970, the hearing examiner in the FTC case ruled in favor of Kennecott. FTC counsel then appealed to the Commission itself. In May 1970, the Commission ruled against Kennecott. The company then appealed this decision to the United States Court of Appeals. In October 1972, the Court of Appeals affirmed the FTC's decision and Kennecott appealed to the United States Supreme Court. In 1974, the United States Supreme Court declined to hear the company's appeal. Kennecott then began the task of divesting Peabody.

The Peabody Coal Company divestiture

In its effort to comply with the FTC's order to divest Peabody, Kennecott retained the services of two investment-banking firms. Kuhn, Loeb & Co. and The First Boston Corporation were asked to examine every feasible form of divestiture.

Kennecott's shareholders were assured in the firm's *1975 Annual Report* that ". . . the sole criterion by which alternative means of divestiture have been measured . . . will . . . be the best interests of shareholders."[3] Regardless of the method of divestiture chosen, Kennecott indicated that to avoid leaving Kennecott in a highly leveraged condition, and to assure its access to the capital markets, a substantial portion of the $532 million capital contribution made by Kennecott to Peabody would have to be retained in Kennecott.

---

[2] Kennecott Copper Corporation, *1967 Annual Report*, p. 3.

[3] Kennecott Copper Corporation, *1975 Annual Report*, p. 2.

The principal forms of divestiture considered by Kennecott were:

1. A public offering of Peabody shares.
2. A rights offering of Peabody shares to Kennecott's shareholders at a significant discount from the anticipated market value of these shares.
3. A spin-off of Peabody's shares to Kennecott's shareholders.[4]
4. A private sale of Peabody.

The first three alternatives were ruled out because in the opinion of the investment bankers and Kennecott's board, Peabody's shares in the public market would be valued:

. . . principally on the basis of historic earnings as well as current and immediate future earnings—and in Peabody's case the past earnings record has been poor. The initial public market price for Peabody's shares would not reflect adequately the value of Peabody based on its extensive coal reserves and its potential earnings capacity over the long term.[5]

The investment bankers and Kennecott's board judged that the total market value of Kennecott and Peabody as independent, publicly held firms would be significantly less than the market value of Kennecott alone after Kennecott had received the proceeds from a privately negotiated sale of Peabody.

On October 14, 1976, Kennecott reached agreement to sell Peabody (subject to FTC approval) to a holding company formed specifically for the purpose of acquiring Peabody. Ownership of the holding company was as follows:

Firm	Ownership Percentage
Newmont Mining Corp.	27.5%
The Williams Companies	27.5
Bechtel Corp.	15.0
Boeing Co.	15.0
Fluor Corp.	10.0
Equitable Life Assurance	5.0
	100.0%

In early June 1977, the FTC approved the transaction, and the sale was closed on June 30, 1977. Kennecott received the following package of securities in exchange for Peabody (see top of page 510).

Assuming a 90-day Treasury bill rate of 4.75% and a prime rate of 6.75% at June 30, 1977, the cash and notes received from the Peabody sale could be expected to produce about $75 million in annual interest income.

---

[4] If Peabody borrowed money to pay a large dividend to Kennecott or to repurchase some of its shares from Kennecott, then Peabody could be spun off and Kennecott could still capture a large fraction of the $532 million capital contribution it had made to Peabody. Alternatively, Kennecott could sell a portion of its Peabody shares publicly for cash and spin off the remainder of the Peabody shares to Kennecott shareholders.

[5] Kennecott Copper Corporation, *Letter to Shareholders*, October 14, 1976, p. 2.

	Face Value ($ millions)	Market Value ($ millions)
Cash................................	$ 235	$235.0
Notes due 1/3/78 at prime rate........	365	365.0
Notes due 6/30/98 at 9½% interest*....	200	200.0
Subordinated income notes due 6/30/08 at 5% interest.............	400	162.5
Total......................	$1,200	$962.5

*These notes could be prepaid without penalty at any time after January 1, 1978. Required prepayments of $20 million were due annually on March 1 from 1988 to 1996, inclusive.

Kennecott's problem in mid-1977

As the Peabody sale drew to a close, Kennecott faced three problems. First, copper prices were down sharply,[6] and both consumer and producer inventories were at all-time highs. Little relief was in sight since world copper production was heavily concentrated in Chile, Zambia, Peru, and Zaire, all LDCs where copper exports represented a major source of foreign exchange earnings. The foreign exchange needs of these countries meant that, to some extent, the expansion of copper production in these countries would be dictated by considerations other than the expectation of an adequate financial return on investment. Copper product prices and industry profitability might be expected to suffer as a result. Second, Kennecott also had problems which related to the price of its common shares. During the second quarter of 1977, Kennecott's stock price had averaged under $28 per share. This was less than two thirds of Kennecott's $42.50 book value per share.[7] Indeed, it was even less than the $29 per Kennecott share (in cash and market value of securities) received from the Peabody sale. Not surprisingly, some of Kennecott's shareholders hoped for a direct cash participation in the proceeds of the Peabody sale.

One Kennecott shareholder[8] brought suit against Kennecott and its directors in an attempt to force this result. The suit sought to compel Kennecott to submit the Peabody sale proposal to a shareholder vote and to direct Kennecott to submit to its shareholders an alternative proposal under which surplus proceeds from any sale of Peabody would be distributed to Kennecott's shareholders. The suit was unsuccessful, but for a time it threatened to delay the Peabody divestiture. The suit was not dismissed until mid-June 1977.

While some Kennecott shareholders were anxious to participate in the pro-

---

[6] During the third quarter of 1977, Kennecott's average domestic copper price was 57¢ per pound. In 1960 constant dollars (column 5, Exhibit 1), this was equal to 27.8¢ per pound, the lowest level in 40 years.

[7] The value of Kennecott to a firm interested in establishing a position in the copper business was estimated at over $80 per share based on the cost of replacing Kennecott's integrated copper mine, milling, smelting, and refining operations. (Source: L. F. Rothschild, Unterberg, Towbin, "Tax Switch Recommendation," December 7, 1977, p. 3.)

[8] This suit was brought on behalf of David T. Greene and Company. This firm was noted for its interest in firms whose break-up value was believed to be greater than the value of the firm as a single entity.

ceeds of the Peabody sale via dividends or a Kennecott share-repurchase program, still other shareholders were hoping that the Peabody sale proceeds would make Kennecott an attractive candidate for a cash tender offer. Kennecott's 33.2 million common shares had a market value of about $900 million at the end of May 1977. Since Kennecott would receive cash or near cash of $600 million from the Peabody sale, a takeover of Kennecott could probably be financed in large measure from Kennecott's own funds. The Peabody sale proceeds made Kennecott a potential target for any acquisition-minded firm with roughly $500 million or more of available funds. Considering only cash-in-hand and neglecting borrowing power, at December 31, 1976, 26 U.S. nonfinancial firms could have fairly easily financed a Kennecott takeover. Some financial details relating to U.S. firms with significant cash holdings are presented in Exhibit 3. While numerous firms had the resources to finance a Kennecott takeover, capacity could hardly be equated with interest. Nonetheless, rumors circulated among stock traders that Kennecott might be a takeover target of any one of four oil companies including Mobil, Occidental, Royal Dutch/Shell, and Standard Oil Company of Indiana.[9]

In the face of these divergent hopes regarding the disposition of the Peabody sale proceeds and Kennecott's future as an independent company, one industry analyst commented as follows:

"If Kennecott just sits there fat, dumb and happy with the proceeds from the Peabody sale, they'll be a sitting duck takeover target themselves, so there'll be some pressure on them to lay off at least a good chunk of the proceeds through an investment before anybody out there gets too tempted."[10]

Third and finally, Kennecott was under additional pressure since copper industry labor contracts expired on June 30, 1977. "The industry was prepared to take at least a three to four month strike. . . . Worldwide copper stocks [stood] at more than 2 million tons, or nearly double normal levels."[11]

A long strike left open the prospect that Kennecott might suffer both large operating losses and a further reduced stock price at a most unattractive time. Fortunately, Kennecott was able to reach a settlement within a few hours after the firm was struck. The Kennecott settlement, which set the pattern for the industry, was not greeted warmly by Kennecott's competition:

"The (Kennecott) settlement is appallingly generous. I'm so mad that when I spit, nothing hits the floor," said Myles Jacobs, Chairman of Inspiration. "It just means we'll face still more competition from lower-cost foreign copper producers," said an executive at another major U.S. copper producer.

. . . . .

"Kennecott's settlement just isn't explainable in terms of copper industry eco-

---

[9] *The Wall Street Journal*, July 15, 1977.

[10] Ibid., June 28, 1977.

[11] Ibid., July 5, 1977.

nomics," said a puzzled official at one competitor. . . . "Maybe there is something in the financial arrangements of the Peabody deal that could explain this," he said.[12]

By early July 1977, some of the uncertainties facing Kennecott had been resolved. The shareholder suit had been dismissed and the strike threat was averted. Kennecott's management and board of directors could turn their full attention to the issue of the utilization of the Peabody sale proceeds.

Kennecott's July 15 board of directors' meeting

Kennecott's first board meeting following the sale of Peabody occurred on July 15, 1977. At this meeting, Kennecott's president, Mr. Frank R. Milliken, noted that the firm had undertaken a number of analyses focusing on the capital requirements of the copper business, the need for diversification of the firm's assets and earnings base, and the feasibility of a special dividend to shareholders, or a tender for the corporation's own shares. A number of hypothetical alternatives involving the use of the Peabody sale proceeds were presented at the meeting. These were a "no acquisition" case, a "$300 million" acquisition case, and a "$500 million" acquisition case. Anticipated overall financial results for Kennecott were summarized for each of these cases. The summary favored the acquisition of a going business of significant size that possessed certain minimum current earnings to which Kennecott could apply accumulated tax credits, as well as relatively predictable earnings growth.

In addition to performing its own internal analysis of the best use of the Peabody sale proceeds, Kennecott had also retained Morgan Stanley & Co. Incorporated in May 1977 to analyze its options.

A managing director of Morgan Stanley & Co. Incorporated, Mr. David B. Strickler, presented his observations to Kennecott's board members:

Mr. Strickler then advised the Board of the results of Morgan Stanley's independent survey of the attitude of the financial community and investors toward the copper business, toward Kennecott, and toward significant new investment in the copper business. The survey found that there exists a deep pessimism among investors about the prospects for copper under present and anticipated world economic and political conditions, and accompanying concern that price recovery and consumption growth may be both modest and too distant in time, and that due to low grades and increasing costs the U.S. copper producers may become marginal competitors. As to Kennecott, the Morgan Stanley survey found concern over the possibility that [Kennecott] may become over-committed to copper, that sound diversification would be welcome, and that investors are looking for a well-articulated corporate plan.[13]

Morgan Stanley's recommendations were summarized as:

(1) Favoring a significant diversification, with the amount open but preferably in the $400–$600 million range, which Morgan Stanley believes to be well within Kennecott's financial capability;

---

[12] *The Wall Street Journal,* July 5, 1977.

[13] Minutes of the regular meeting of the board of directors of Kennecott Copper Corporation, July 15, 1977, p. 4626.

(2)   Trimming down to the extent feasible further significant capital investment in copper;

(3)   Disfavoring a special cash distribution to shareholders, by a tender offer for shares, or otherwise, because the cash is otherwise required for investment which must be given priority in pursuing the proper management of the shareholder's equity interests.

. . . . .

At the conclusion of the discussion, it was the unanimous consensus of the Board to adopt a corporate strategy which gives priority to a significant diversification by acquisition.[14]

The search for a replacement for Peabody Coal Company

In the months following the July 15 board meeting, Kennecott began a search for attractive acquisition candidates. There was a sense of urgency to this search. Kennecott explained this urgency as follows:

Inasmuch as Kennecott's copper business is presently operating at substantial and continuing losses, it is important for the stability and the credit rating of Kennecott that it promptly move to acquire a reliable source of earnings. It would not be good corporate management to use available cash simply to cover operating losses and thus inevitably impair the corporation's asset base and its ability to effect a major acquisition which is (and has been for many years) an essential component in its long-term planning.[15]

Kennecott's search for acquisition candidates initially was focused on oil and gas and forest-products areas. The search later broadened to include the industrial sector. By October 1977, several good prospects had been developed. Management had been nearly ready to present one candidate to the board for its consideration when another, more attractive candidate suddenly emerged. The more attractive candidate was The Carborundum Company, one of the world's principal producers of a complete line of abrasive products.

The Carborundum Company acquisition opportunity

On October 31, 1977, The Carborundum Company announced that it had received an acquisition offer. The identity of the proposed acquirer and the price offered were not disclosed. One day later, Carborundum's board of directors announced that they had received and rejected as inadequate an offer from Eaton Corporation to acquire Carborundum at $47 per share. Prior to the announcement that the firm had received an acquisition offer, Carborundum's shares were trading at $33¼ per share. The historic high for Carborundum's shares was $40⅝. For the year ending December 31, 1976, Carborundum's earnings per share and book value per share were $4.14 and $34.63, respectively. If Carborundum's cost of goods sold, inventories, and fixed assets (other than

---

[14] Ibid., pp. 4628–29.

[15] *Frederick S. Danziger et al.* v. *Kennecott Copper Corporation et al.*, Supreme Court of the State of New York, County of New York, Index Number 21941–77, Affidavit of Milton Stern, November 27, 1977, pp. 20–21.

land) had been valued at *replacement cost*[16] rather than *historic cost* as of December 31, 1976, then Carborundum's earnings per share and book value per share would have been $3.20 and $53.55, respectively (Exhibit 4).

Immediately after receiving the offer from Eaton, Carborundum retained the investment banking firm of Morgan Stanley & Co. Incorporated as advisers with respect to the tender offer, and Morgan Stanley, in turn, advised Kennecott about the availability of Carborundum on October 31. Morgan Stanley contacted 23 firms seeking alternative offers for Carborundum. These 23 firms were offered confidential financial information provided by Carborundum and the opportunity to meet and question Carborundum's management if (a) they signed a confidentiality agreement with Carborundum and (b) they advised Morgan Stanley that, based on public information, they were prepared to consider the acquisition at a price of more than $55 per share.[17]

Several firms, including Kennecott, agreed to these terms and received confidential financial data from Carborundum. On November 3, Kennecott retained The First Boston Corporation as advisers relating to the Carborundum acquisition. On November 5, Kennecott supplied First Boston with the internal Carborundum projections, which are summarized in Exhibit 5. First Boston at one point had 12 professionals involved in the Carborundum analysis. On November 8, First Boston advised Kennecott that Carborundum appeared to be an attractive acquisition candidate for Kennecott. The following day, First Boston recommended that Kennecott offer $60 per share to acquire Carborundum. The firm then began to prepare a detailed report for presentation to Kennecott's board of directors.

After November 5, representatives of Kennecott and First Boston held numerous meetings with Carborundum personnel in an effort to place a valuation on Carborundum's shares. Kennecott's internal group determined that at a 10.5% discount rate, a figure they believed to be the weighted average cost of capital for a corporation of Kennecott's standing, the value of Carborundum based on Carborundum's projections would justify a price of $85 per share. Under more conservative assumptions, they concluded that a price of $70 was reasonable. Kennecott's management was impressed with Carborundum's ability to forecast its earnings. Prior forecasts of Carborundum's management for earlier years compared well, in the view of Kennecott's management, with the actual results achieved in those years. Since Carborundum's

---

[16] Securities and Exchange Commission Accounting Series Release No. 190 required large firms such as Carborundum to disclose the estimated current replacement cost of inventories and productive capacity at the end of each fiscal year (after December 25, 1976) for which a balance sheet was required and the approximate cost of sales and depreciation based on replacement cost.

[17] Morgan Stanley's advice to Carborundum regarding the Eaton offer may well have been influenced by an earlier tender offer battle over The Babcock & Wilcox Company, a firm which had been pursued by both United Technologies and J. Ray McDermott & Co., Inc. In this situation, United offered $42 per share for the stock of Babcock & Wilcox in March 1977 at a time when Babcock & Wilcox's stock was selling for $34¾ per share. After a lengthy series of publicly announced bids and counter bids, J. Ray McDermott ultimately acquired Babcock & Wilcox at a price of $65 per share.

projections for 1978–82 (Exhibit 5) had been prepared as a normal part of that company's planning process before the threat of the Eaton tender offer was apparent, Kennecott's management evidently felt reasonably comfortable with these forecasts.

On the evening of November 14, Kennecott's chief executive and his advisers from First Boston met with Carborundum's chief executive and his advisers from Morgan Stanley. At the meeting, Kennecott's chief executive indicated his intention to recommend to the Kennecott board a purchase offer of $60 per share for Carborundum's stock. The meeting adjourned, and later that evening, a representative of Morgan Stanley telephoned to advise Kennecott that another substantial company was prepared to pay about $60 per share. The meeting with Morgan Stanley was reconvened, and it was indicated at this meeting that a Kennecott offer of $62 per share would also be unsuccessful. This meeting then adjourned with the understanding that if Kennecott wished to make a final bid, the bid would have to be received prior to 10:00 A.M. of the following morning.

On the morning of November 15, Kennecott advised Morgan Stanley that its management was prepared to recommend an offer of $66 per share to Kennecott's board the following day. This offer was accepted, and a joint Kennecott-Carborundum press release was issued that day. Also on November 15, Kennecott notified its board of directors of a special board meeting scheduled for 9:00 A.M. the following day. Only 11 of Kennecott's 17 board members (five inside directors and six outside directors) were able to attend the meeting on short notice.[18]

Kennecott's November 16 board of directors' meeting

Kennecott's board meeting on November 16 lasted nearly four hours. The meeting was taken up largely by the discussion of the financial aspects and implications of the proposed Carborundum acquisition. An 88-page review of the proposed acquisition prepared by First Boston represented the focal point of the meeting. The First Boston report suggested three net-income scenarios for Carborundum over the decade 1978–87 assuming that the firm remained independent (Exhibit 6). If these data were adjusted to reflect (a) Kennecott's acquisition of Carborundum at $66 per share, (b) Kennecott's subsequent write-up of Carborundum's assets to fair value, (c) Kennecott's leverage of Carborundum's capital structure via a $100 million loan which would be followed immediately by a $140 million dividend to Kennecott, (d) Kennecott's realization of tax benefits associated with the write-up of Carborundum's assets, and (e) Kennecott's utilization of $40 million of tax-loss carryforwards available from the firm's other operations, then First Boston concluded that the Carborun-

---

[18] Two of the attending inside directors and five of the attending outside directors first learned of the Carborundum offer on the morning of the board meeting. One other outside director learned of the offer the previous day. (Source: Affidavit of Richard F. Danziger in Opposition to Defendant's Motion for Summary Judgment, December 5, 1977, p. 4.)

dum acquisition would produce the discounted cash flow ROIs to Kennecott indicated in Exhibit 7.

Detailed calculations that produce an ROI result similar to that indicated in Scenario A, Case 1 (with the appropriate assumptions indicated) are shown in Exhibit 8.[19]

The First Boston report noted that the $66 price negotiated for Carborundum was quite consistent with the price paid by the acquiring firms in the other major contested offers in 1977 (Exhibit 9).

Finally, Sullivan and Cromwell, legal counsel to Kennecott's board, informed the directors:

... that the Board's legal responsibility was to exercise reasonable business judgment in the best interests of the Corporation and its continuing body of shareholders and that the Board was not required to act in accordance with the special interests of particular shareholders, such as those seeking short-term market profits, i.e., those who might prefer the partial liquidation of the Corporation's earnings base or its takeover by another. Counsel said that the Board had before it the careful analysis and judgment of its management and the careful analysis of financial advisors of the highest standing, and that its legal obligation was to exercise its own deliberative business judgment, taking such analyses, judgments and recommendations into account. [Counsel] further stated that the basic decision to make a major acquisition had been taken months earlier [at the July 15 meeting] after thorough deliberation and the need for prompt action on this opportunity to implement that decision was created by factors beyond the Board's control. In view of these and other factors [Counsel] believed that there was an adequate basis for the Board to exercise reasonable and prudent business judgment as required by law.[20]

A call for a vote on the Carborundum acquisition

At 12:55 P.M., the following resolution was moved, seconded, and put to a vote:

RESOLVED, that the Corporation make a cash tender offer to shareholders of the Carborundum Company for any and all of the outstanding shares of the common stock of said Company at a price of $66 per share.[21]

---

[19] The First Boston forecast of the cash flows to Kennecott that produce the Scenario A, Case 1 return-on-investment calculation of 17.4% which appears in Exhibit 7 were not publicly available. The detailed cash flows indicated in Exhibit 8 were thus developed by the casewriter from publicly available information.

[20] Minutes of a special meeting of the board of directors of Kennecott Copper Corporation, November 16, 1977, p. 17.

[21] Ibid., p. 18.

Exhibit 1

KENNECOTT COPPER CORPORATION

FINANCIAL DATA FOR THE KENNECOTT COPPER CORPORATION AND ITS WHOLLY OWNED SUBSIDIARY, PEABODY COAL COMPANY, 1960–1977

	(1)	(2)	(3)	(4)	(5)	(6)	(7)	(8)	(9)	(10)
			Kennecott Copper Corporation				Peabody Coal Company ($ millions)			
	Profit After Taxes* ($ millions)	Depreciation and Depletion ($ millions)	Cash Flow From Operations ($ millions)	Current Dollar Average Domestic† Copper Price (¢/lb)	1960 Constant Dollar Average Domestic Copper Price (¢/lb)	Copper Sales Domestic and Foreign (000 tons)	Profit after Taxes	Kennecott Capital Contributions Less Dividends Received‖	Acquisition Cost and Sale Realization	Book Value of Kennecott's Investment in Peabody
Pre-Peabody acquisition:										
1960.	$ 77.4	$ 17.2	$ 94.6	31.0¢	31.0¢	540.6	$ 12.5			
1961.	61.9	18.6	80.5	29.3	29.0	591.7	13.5			
1962.	65.6	20.6	86.2	30.0	29.4	555.3	14.7			
1963.	57.0	20.8	77.8	30.1	29.1	555.9	17.2			
1964.	66.1	22.5	88.6	31.5	30.1	569.8	21.3			
1965.	102.0	25.1	127.1	35.2	33.1	619.0	22.5			
1966.	126.7	28.1	154.8	37.0	33.8	616.7	26.3			
1967.	111.1	32.5	143.6	38.6	34.3	489.5	19.5‡			
Post-Peabody acquisition:										
1968.	111.2	50.9	162.1	42.5	36.2	551.9	16.8‡	$73.2	$306.5	$396.5
1969.	165.4	72.7	238.1	49.1	39.7	697.4	13.9	73.2		483.6
1970.	150.9	73.3	224.2	57.9	44.2	679.6	(15.2)	73.2		541.6
1971.	87.2	72.5	159.7	51.2	37.5	488.3§	(13.8)	73.2		601.0
1972.	47.4	77.7	125.1	50.7	35.9	464.8	7.9	73.2		682.1
1973.	159.4	80.6	240.0	60.7	40.4	474.1	(3.1)	73.3		752.3
1974.	210.9	91.3	302.2	76.7	46.1	387.5	3.9	79.0		835.2
1975.	21.7	49.0	70.7	61.2	33.7	269.4	40.8	29.0		905.0
1976.	8.8	50.5	59.3	66.8	34.8	356.0	30.8	(7.4)		928.4
1977.									925.8#	

* Data are as originally reported to shareholders and after 1967, include the Peabody results.

† Prior to 1966, data are reported as the average price for both domestic and foreign sales.

† 1967 profit data for Peabody are for the nine months ended 9/30/67; 1968 profit data for Peabody are for the nine-month period 3/29/68–12/31/68. Since Peabody was acquired ʻore 3/31/68, Peabody was never required to report data for the year ended 12/31/68 or for the subperiod 1/1/68–3/29/68.

§ In 1971, Kennecott's copper operations in Chile were nationalized; after 1970 all of Kennecott's copper production was domestic.

‖ Data for 1968–73 are *estimated* as to the annual amount, but *actual* as to the six-year cumulative total.

Estimated market value of sale proceeds after income taxes.

Sources: Kennecott annual reports to shareholders and quarterly reports to shareholders; and casewriter estimates.

Exhibit 2

KENNECOTT COPPER CORPORATION

BALANCE SHEET DATA FOR KENNECOTT COPPER CORPORATION AND SUBSIDIARIES, AND PEABODY COAL COMPANY AND SUBSIDIARIES, DECEMBER, 31, 1976
($ millions)

	Kennecott Copper Corp. and Subsidiaries	Peabody Coal Company and Subsidiaries
ASSETS		
Cash and marketable securities..............	$ 38.6	$ 26.3
Other current assets......................	398.1	208.4
Total current assets.....................	$ 436.7	$ 234.7
Investment in Peabody Coal..................	928.4*	—
Property, plant, and equipment..............	131.5	99.3
Other assets.............................	823.3	813.9
Total assets...........................	$2,319.9	$1,147.9
LIABILITIES AND NET WORTH		
Short-term debt...........................	$ 44.7	$ 16.0
Other current liabilities......................	159.2	125.9
Total current liabilities..................	$ 203.9	$ 141.9
Long-term debt...........................	540.2†	12.0
Other liabilities...........................	165.2	65.6
Net worth................................	1,410.6	928.4*
Total liabilities and net worth............	$2,319.9	$1,147.9

* It should be noted that Kennecott accounted for its ownership of Peabody in 1976 by the equity method. Kennecott's investment in Peabody was thus equal to Peabody's net worth.

† Kennecott's long-term debt included:

7⅞% debenture due 5/1/01.................	$200.0
Term loan due 6/30/82...................	250.0
Revolving credit/term loan due 12/31/85....	51.0
Other loans less current maturities..........	39.2
	$540.2

Source: Kennecott Copper Corporation, *1976 Annual Report.*

Exhibit 3

KENNECOTT COPPER CORPORATION

U.S. NONFINANCIAL CORPORATIONS WITH CASH AND EQUIVALENTS
EXCEEDING $500 MILLION AT DECEMBER 31, 1976

Firm	*Cash and Equivalents*	*Cash and Equivalents Less Borrowed Money*	*(Cash and Equivalents Less Borrowed Money) Divided by Net Worth*
Halliburton Co.	$ 512	$ 187	.14
Getty Oil Co.	539	332	.16
McDermott (J. Ray) & Co.	542	373	.54
Boeing Co.	550	411	.38
U.S. Steel Corp.	561	(1,595)	(.31)
Chrysler Corp.	572	(717)	(.26)
Westinghouse Electric	586	(31)	(.02)
United Air Lines	611	(373)	(.47)
Raytheon Co.	619	514	.96
Atlantic Richfield Co.	663	(1,945)	(.48)
Shell Oil Co.	671	(585)	(.13)
Xerox Corp.	672	(471)	(.22)
Phillips Petroleum Co.	702	(182)	(.07)
Texaco, Inc.	763	(2,403)	(.27)
Eastman Kodak Co.	780	606	.15
Procter & Gamble Co.	795	153	.07
Standard Oil Co. (Indiana)	957	(918)	(.15)
Standard Oil Co. (California)	975	(714)	(.10)
Continental Oil Co.	1,055	(171)	(.07)
Mobil Corp.	1,280	(2,354)	(.31)
General Electric Co.	1,613	(320)	(.06)
Ford Motor Co.	1,664	(367)	(.05)
Gulf Oil Corp.	1,989	682	.10
General Motors Corp.	4,625	2,940	.21
Exxon Corp.	5,074	(483)	(.03)
IBM Corp.	6,156	5,765	.45

Source: Standard & Poor's Corporation, Compustat tapes.

Exhibit 4

KENNECOTT COPPER CORPORATION

The Carborundum Company Financial Data Based on Historical Cost, 1968–1976, and Replacement Cost, 1976
($ millions except per share and ratio data)

	1968	1969	1970	1971	1972	1973	1974	1975	1976	Data Based on Replacement Cost 1976
Income statement										
Sales	$255.1	$290.4	$302.0	$311.4	$339.9	$415.1	$556.8	$563.1	$613.9	$613.9
Net income	14.0	14.7	14.2	12.5	16.3	20.6	26.7	27.2	32.8	25.4
Income per share	1.92	2.02	1.94	1.71	2.21	2.79	3.44	3.50	4.14	3.20
Dividends per share	0.68	0.70	0.73	0.75	0.78	0.80	0.83	0.85	0.95	0.95
Average shares outstanding (millions)	7.4	7.4	7.4	7.4	7.4	7.5	7.8	7.9	8.0	8.0
Balance sheet										
Cash + Marketable securities − Short-term debt	$ 10.4	$ 1.8	$ (8.1)	$ (5.4)	$ 24.6	$ 30.9	$ 1.9	$ 71.5	$ 69.0	$ 69.0
Net working capital	83.8	86.5	80.5	89.8	99.6	118.8	125.1	170.7	186.7	222.7
Properties, plant, and equipment (net)	100.9	108.9	116.5	122.9	120.4	120.6	137.9	151.8	164.6	278.6
Total assets	253.0	270.1	282.9	298.6	307.7	356.5	416.4	470.7	532.2	682.6
Long-term debt	51.8	49.6	43.9	41.2	35.5	39.3	37.0	74.2	75.8	75.8
Shareholders' equity	149.0	158.8	168.0	176.4	187.8	202.8	224.5	248.1	274.4	424.4
Total capital	200.8	208.4	211.9	217.6	223.3	242.1	261.5	322.3	350.2	500.2
Book value per share	20.41	21.72	22.92	24.01	25.45	27.44	28.93	31.46	34.63	53.55
Market value per share	27.50	23.75	24.38	29.31	34.19	20.50	24.00	24.25	35.63	

Capital sources								
Profit retentions	$ 9.6	$ 8.8	$ 7.1	$ 10.6	$ 14.7	$ 20.4	$ 20.6	$ 25.3
External equity financing	0.2	0.4	0.3	0.8	0.3	1.3	3.0	1.0
Debt financing (net)	(2.2)	(5.7)	(2.7)	(5.7)	3.8	(2.3)	37.2	1.6
Total capital added	$ 7.6	$ 3.5	$ 4.6	$ 5.7	$ 18.8	$ 19.4	$ 60.8	$ 27.9

Key financial ratios									
Growth rate in sales (%)		13.8	4.0	3.1	9.2	22.1	34.1	1.1	9.0
Sales/assets	1.01	1.08	1.07	1.04	1.10	1.16	1.34	1.20	1.15
Profit/sales	0.055	0.051	0.047	0.040	0.048	0.050	0.048	0.048	0.053
Assets/net worth	1.70	1.70	1.68	1.69	1.64	1.76	1.86	1.90	1.94
Profit/net worth	0.094	0.093	0.085	0.071	0.087	0.102	0.119	0.110	0.120
β	1.22	1.39	1.19	1.13	0.97	1.79	1.25	1.32	1.07
Treasury bill rate (90-day)	0.055	0.075	0.052	0.043	0.049	0.073	0.074	0.055	0.045

Note: Replacement cost data used are the midpoint of ranges reported in Carborundum's 1976 10K report to the SEC. Also, under standard accounting conventions, no tax benefits would be associated with the increased level of costs resulting from the application of replacement cost accounting to existing assets since such benefits would not, in fact, be received for tax purposes. On new investments, however, such benefits would be realized. Since the profitability of new investments is an important issue in valuing any security, tax benefits are assumed to exist where existing assets are valued at replacement cost in Exhibit 4.

Sources: Carborundum annual reports and 1976 10K Report to the SEC; Salomon Brothers, "An Analytical Record of Yields and Yield Spreads," November 1977; Investors Management Sciences, Inc. "Financial Dynamics," May 27, 1977.

Exhibit 5

KENNECOTT COPPER CORPORATION

The Carborundum Company Financial Forecasts Assuming Carborundum Continued to Operate as an Independent Public Company, 1977–1982

($ millions except per share and ratio data)

| | 1977* | Pro Forma | | | | |
		1978	1979	1980	1981	1982
Income statement						
Sales	$717.6	$790.1	$885.9	$1,005.2	$1,129.9	$1,265.5
Net income	38.4	43.1	50.7	60.1	70.6	84.7
Income per share	4.70	5.27	6.14	7.23	8.44	10.05
Dividends per share	1.18	1.32	1.54	1.81	2.15	2.46
Average shares outstanding (millions)	8.2	8.2	8.3	8.3	8.4	8.4
Balance sheet						
Cash + Marketable securities — Short-term debt	n.a.	n.a.	n.a.	n.a.	n.a.	n.a.
Net working capital	$198.8	$213.4	$214.2	$247.6	$290.6	$349.6
Properties, plant, and equipment (net)	181.8	215.8	254.7	277.5	298.7	315.8
Total assets	584.3	647.5	712.6	785.9	879.6	986.8
Long-term debt	86.2	91.7	83.4	83.4	83.5	83.5
Shareholders' equity	309.0	343.7	384.3	432.2	488.0	555.5
Total capital	395.2	435.4	467.7	515.6	571.5	639.0
Book value per share	37.90	41.92	46.58	52.01	58.31	65.90
Capital sources						
Profit retentions	$ 28.7	$ 32.3	$ 37.9	$ 45.1	$ 52.5	$ 64.0
External equity financing	5.9	2.4	2.7	2.8	3.3	3.5
Debt financing (net)	10.4	5.5	(8.3)	0	0.1	0
Total capital added	$ 45.0	$ 40.2	$ 32.2	$ 47.9	$ 55.9	$ 67.5
Key financial ratios						
Growth rate in sales (%)	16.9	10.1	12.1	13.5	12.4	12.0
Sales/assets	1.23	1.22	1.24	1.28	1.28	1.28
Profit/sales	0.054	0.055	0.057	0.060	0.062	0.067
Assets/net worth	1.89	1.88	1.85	1.82	1.80	1.78
Profit/net worth	0.124	0.125	0.132	0.139	0.145	0.152
β*†	1.16					
Treasury bill rate (90-day)†	0.056					

n.a. = not available.

* The year 1977 was almost complete as of the date of this forecast.

† The β and Treasury bill rate information are as of 9/30/77 and were not presented as part of the First Boston Corporation report. These data have been added by the casewriter. For the period February 1972 through September 1977, Carborundum's β value based on month-end data for 60 months ranged from a low of 1.04 to a high of 1.26.

Sources: (1) Frederick S. Danziger et al. v. Kennecott Copper Corporation et al., Supreme Court of the State of New York, County of New York, Index 21941-77, Affidavit of Frederick S. Danziger, Exhibit B, November 29, 1977, p. 375; (2) Salomon Brothers, "An Analytical Record of Yields and Yield Spreads," November 1977; (3) Merrill Lynch, Pierce, Fenner & Smith, Inc., "Security Risk Evaluation," October 1977; (4) casewriter estimates.

Exhibit 6

KENNECOTT COPPER CORPORATION
PROJECTED NET INCOME OF THE CARBORUNDUM COMPANY
UNDER VARIOUS ASSUMPTIONS

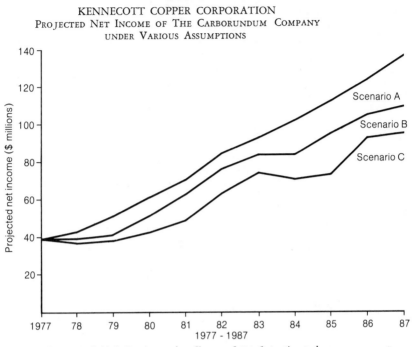

Source: *Frederick S. Danziger et al.* v. *Kennecott Copper Corporation et al.*,
Supreme Court of the State of New York, County of New York, Index 21941-
77, Affidavit of Milton Stern, Exhibit A, November 27, 1977, p. 263.

Exhibit 7

KENNECOTT COPPER CORPORATION
KENNECOTT'S ESTIMATED ROI FROM THE ACQUISITION OF THE
CARBORUNDUM COMPANY AT $66 PER SHARE UNDER
VARIOUS ASSUMPTIONS AS CALCULATED BY
THE FIRST BOSTON CORPORATION

	Net Income Scenario		
	A	B	C
Case 1*	17.4%	15.2%	12.7%
Case 2*	15.6%	13.4%	11.0%
Case 3*	13.5%	11.3%	8.9%

*Cases 1, 2, and 3 assume terminal values in 1987 equal to 10, 8, and 6
times 1987 earnings, respectively.

Source: *Frederick S. Danziger et al.* v. *Kennecott Copper Corporation et al.*,
Supreme Court of the State of New York, County of New York, Index 21941-
77, Affidavit of Milton Stern, Exhibit A, November 27, 1977, p. 266.

Exhibit 8

KENNECOTT COPPER CORPORATION

PROJECTED CARBORUNDUM COMPANY FINANCIAL DATA ADJUSTED TO REFLECT THE ACQUISITION OF CARBORUNDUM BY KENNECOTT AT A PRICE OF $66 PER SHARE, 1977–1987
($ millions except for per share and ratio data)

	1977 Unadjusted	Adjustments[1]	1977 Adjusted	1978	1979	1980	1981	1982	1983	1984	1985	1986	1987
Income statement													
Sales	$717.6			$790.1	$885.9	$1,005.2	$1,129.9	$1,265.5	$1,392.1	$1,531.3	$1,684.4	$1,852.8	$2,038.1
Net income (before adjustments)	38.4			43.1	50.7	60.1	70.6	84.7	93.2	102.5	112.7	124.0	136.4
Interest adjustment[2]	0			6.5	7.8	8.5	9.2	9.8	10.7	11.7	12.8	14.0	15.4
Goodwill adjustment[3]	0			2.0	2.0	2.0	2.0	2.0	2.0	2.0	2.0	2.0	2.0
Plant write-up adjustment[4]	0			2.8	2.8	2.8	2.8	2.8	2.8	2.8	2.8	2.8	2.8
Net income (after adjustments)	$38.4			$31.8	$38.1	$46.8	$56.6	$70.1	$77.7	$86.0	$95.1	$105.2	$116.2
Balance sheet													
Working capital	$198.8	+ 37.0 / + 100.0 / − 140.0	$195.8	$202.9	$223.0	$248.1	$274.2	$302.8	$329.3	$358.6	$390.7	$426.1	$465.0
Property, plant, and equipment	181.8	+ 124.0	305.8	334.2	367.4	384.6	400.1	411.6	437.5	466.6	499.1	535.6	576.1
Goodwill	0	+ 80.0	80.0	78.0	76.0	74.0	72.0	70.0	68.0	66.0	64.0	62.0	60.0
Total assets	584.3	+ 201.0	785.3	824.0	889.9	948.4	1,007.0	1,065.8	1,135.5	1,213.1	1,299.0	1,394.6	1,500.3
Long-term debt	86.2	+ 100.0	186.2	220.9	238.8	252.9	266.8	280.1	297.7	317.5	339.4	363.9	391.0
Shareholders' equity	309.0	+ 101.0	410.0	410.1	443.5	469.7	495.4	520.2	553.0	589.6	630.3	675.7	726.0
Total capital	395.2	+ 201.0	596.2	631.0	682.3	722.6	762.2	800.3	850.7	907.1	969.7	1,039.6	1,117.0
Capital sources													
Profit retentions				$ 0.1	$33.4	$26.2	$25.7	$24.8	$32.8	$36.6	$40.7	$45.4	$50.3
Capital contributed by Kennecott													
Debt financing (net)				34.7	17.9	14.1	13.9	13.3	17.6	19.8	21.9	24.5	27.1
Total capital added	$34.8			$34.8	$51.3	$40.3	$39.6	$38.1	$50.4	$56.4	$62.6	$69.9	$77.4
Key financial ratios													
Growth rate in sales (%)	16.9			10.1	12.1	13.5	12.4	12.0	10.0	10.0	10.0	10.0	10.0
Sales/assets	1.23			0.96	1.00	1.06	1.12	1.19	1.23	1.26	1.30	1.33	1.36
Profit/sales	.054			0.040	0.043	0.047	0.050	0.055	0.056	0.056	0.056	0.057	0.057
Assets/net worth	1.89			2.01	2.01	2.02	2.03	2.05	2.05	2.06	2.06	2.06	2.07
Profit/net worth	.124			0.078	0.086	0.100	0.114	0.135	0.141	0.146	0.151	0.156	0.160

Cash flow to Kennecott

Acquisition of Carborundum[1]	$(550.0)										
Dividends to Kennecott[3]	140.0	$31.7	$ 4.7	$20.6	$30.9	$45.3	$44.9	$49.4	$54.4	$59.8	$ 65.9
Utilization of Kennecott tax loss carryforwards[6]	—	20.0	20.0	—	—	—	—	—	—	—	—
Tax shelter from plant write-up adj.[4]		2.8	2.8	2.8	2.8	2.8	2.8	2.8	2.8	2.8	2.8
Terminal value at 10 times earnings[7]											1,044.9
Net cash flow	$(410.0)	$54.5	$27.5	$23.4	$33.7	$48.1	$47.7	$52.2	$57.2	$62.6	$1,113.6

Assumptions:

[1]Kennecott would pay $550 million to acquire Carborundum's equity which had a book value of $309 million. The $241 million in excess of purchase price over book value of assets acquired would be allocated as follows: (a) $37.0 million would be added to inventory to reflect the replacement cost of inventories; (b) $11.0 million would be added to land to reflect the market value of land; (c) $113 million would be added to net plant and equipment to reflect the depreciated replacement cost of plant and equipment; and (d) $80 million would be added to goodwill. Immediately following the acquisition of Carborundum, Carborundum borrows $100 million and then pays a $140 million dividend to Kennecott. This dividend is financed with the $100 million plus $40 million of Carborundum's excess cash.

[2]Interest at the rate of 10% (5% after taxes) is paid on the difference between the amount of Carborundum debt outstanding in Exhibit 8 and the amount of debt assumed to be outstanding in Exhibit 5. In Exhibit 8, it is assumed that Carborundum will have 35% debt in its total capital structure after 1977.

[3]The $80 million of goodwill created as a result of the acquisition is amortized over 40 years. This expense is not tax-deductible.

[4]The $113 million write-up of plant and equipment is depreciated over a 20-year life, providing a reduction in profit after taxes and an increase in cash flow equal to ($113/20) x .5. It is assumed that this added cash flow is paid to Kennecott as dividends.

[5]Dividends to Kennecott equal the difference between Carborundum's net profit (after adjustment) and the profit retention requirements needed to support Carborundum's growth.

[6]The utilization of $40 million of tax loss carry-forwards and investment tax credit carryforwards available to Kennecott are assumed to be utilized as a result of the Carborundum acquisition and that these would expire unutilized without the acquisition.

[7]Carborundum is assumed to be sold at the end of ten years at a price equal to ten times earnings. The proceeds from this sale, $1,162 million, are reduced by $117.1 million as a result of taxes on the capital gain of $1,162−$726. Carborundum's net worth at 12/31/87 is assumed to be $726 million.

Sources: Exhibit 5 and casewriter projections.

Exhibit 9

KENNECOTT COPPER CORPORATION

COMPARISON OF THE PROPOSED $66 PER SHARE TENDER OFFER FOR CARBORUNDUM'S COMMON STOCK WITH THE AVERAGE OF SEVEN OTHER LARGE CONTESTED TENDER OFFERS OF 1977

	Milgo Electronics	Babcock & Wilcox	Avis	Chemetron	Coca Cola Bottling of L.A.	Imperial American Energy	Floyd Enterprises	7 Firms Average	Carborundum
Premium over market price four weeks prior to announcement...	125.0%	113.1%	67.6%	62.7%	76.8%	50.5%	96.9%	84.7%	89.9%
Premium over market price one day prior to announcement......	88.2%	87.1%	57.1%	57.4%	83.9%	63.3%	75.0%	73.1%	98.5%
Tender offer price as a multiple of net income.............	27.8	15.3	9.4	26.4	16.7	N.M.F.	13.8	13.7	14.0
Tender offer price as a multiple of book value............	2.8	1.9	1.5	.9	2.6	2.5	1.3	1.9	1.9

N.M.F. = not meaningful figure.

Source: *Frederick S. Danziger et al. v. Kennecott Copper Corporation al.,* Supreme Court of the State of New York, County of New York, Index 21941-77, Affidavit of Milton Stern, Exhibit A, November 27, 1977, p. 274.

HARRINGTON CORPORATION

^^

In March, 1971, Paul Brooks was working on a proposal to purchase his employer, the Harrington Corporation. The Harrington Corporation, with corporate headquarters in Boston, Massachusetts, was a leading manufacturer of commercial desk calendars. Mr. Brooks, vice president of finance and administration, considered the company an excellent acquisition opportunity, provided he should conclude that the owner's asking price was acceptable, and provided he could arrange satisfactory financing for the transaction.

BACKGROUND

A few weeks earlier, Thaddeus Baring, board chairman, president, and sole owner of Harrington Corporation, had informed his senior management group that he intended to retire from business and was about to initiate a campaign to sell the company. For several years, his physician had been urging him to avoid all stress and strain; now Mr. Baring had decided to sever his business connections and devote his time to travel and a developing interest in art history and collection.

On the basis of previous offers for the company, Mr. Baring had decided to ask for $10 million, with a minimum of $8 million immediately payable in cash. He thought acquisitive corporations should find this price attractive, and he believed it would be easy to dispose of the corporation.

Mr. Baring had assured the management group that their jobs and benefits would be well protected by the terms of any sale contract that he might negotiate. Despite his faith in Mr. Baring's good intentions, Mr. Brooks had been quite apprehensive about the prospect of having his career placed in the hands of an unknown outsider. However, after some reflection, Mr. Brooks had concluded that the sale decision should be viewed as an opportunity to acquire control of a highly profitable enterprise. Purchase of Harrington would not only assure career continuity but also provide a chance to turn a profit in the company's equity. Mr. Brooks had realized that his personal financial resources were far too limited to allow him to bid alone for control of Harrington. Consequently, he had persuaded Kim Darby, vice president–marketing, Keith Jackson, vice president–manufacturing, and Waldo Sloane, the controller, to join him in trying to buy the corporation, rather than standing by while control passed to an outsider. In response to Mr. Brooks' request,

Mr. Baring had agreed to defer all steps to merchandise the company until he should have accepted or rejected a purchase proposal from the management group, provided this proposal was submitted within six weeks.

Because of his background in finance and his role in initiating the project, Mr. Brooks had assumed primary responsibility for assessing the profit potential of the opportunity and for structuring a workable financial plan for the acquisition. Since Mr. Baring had not yet solicited bids from other potential purchasers, Mr. Brooks believed that it would be most realistic to regard Mr. Baring's stated sale terms as fixed and nonnegotiable.

Mr. Brooks, then, needed to determine whether he could meet the asking price and still realize a profit commensurate with the risk in this purchase. Moreover, he needed to figure out how the management group, with roughly a quarter of a million dollars between them, could finance the purchase and at the same time obtain voting control of the corporation.

Thus far Mr. Brooks had managed to obtain a tentative commitment for a $3,000,000 unsecured bank term loan, and he had persuaded Mr. Baring to accept unsecured notes for the noncash portion of the purchase price. He was still faced with the problem of raising close to $5,000,000 on an equity base of $250,000 without giving up control to outsiders.

Mr. Brooks now had three weeks in which to come up with a workable financial plan or lose the deal. He was acutely aware that the life savings of his associates and himself would ride on his judgment and ingenuity.

THE COMPANY

The Harrington Corporation was the leading producer of business calendars in the United States. The company was established in 1920 by Joshua Harrington (Mr. Baring's maternal grandfather) to do contract printing of commercial calendars. Mr. Baring had joined the organization in 1932 upon graduation from college, and in 1937, he had inherited the company.

Under Mr. Baring's leadership primary emphasis was placed on controlled expansion in the established line of business. By 1971, Harrington, with an estimated 60–65% share of its market, had been for over a decade the largest company in a small but lucrative industry. Operations had been profitable in every year since 1932, and sales had increased in every year since 1955. In 1970, the most recently completed fiscal year, earnings had amounted to $983,000 on sales of approximately $7.6 million. The return on average invested capital in 1970 was over 20%. Over the past five years, sales had increased at a 7% compound rate, while earnings, benefiting from substantial cost reductions, had more than doubled. Exhibits 1 through 3 present recent financial figures for the company.

Products

As noted above, Harrington's principal products were commercial desk calendars. The company designed and manufactured disposable page and flipover page desk calendar pads in a variety of sizes. The company also sold desk calendar bases which were purchased from outside suppliers who manufactured to Harrington's specifications. In 1970, standard desk calendar pads had contributed approximately 80% of net sales and 90% of earnings before taxes. Bases accounted for 10% of sales, and miscellaneous merchandise, chiefly wall calendars, accounted for the rest.

Sales were highly seasonal. Most final consumers did not start using calendars for the forthcoming year until November or December of the current year. In consequence about 90% of Harrington's total shipments typically took place between June and December, with about 60% of shipments concentrated in the third quarter and 25% in the fourth quarter. Since calendar pads were dated, any merchandise remaining in stock at the end of the selling season was subject to rapid obsolescence.

Manufacturing

The production process was relatively simple, employing widely available skills and technology. Highspeed offset presses were used to print appropriate dates on paper purchased in bulk from outside suppliers; the printed sheets were then trimmed to the required sizes and stored for shipment. The entire process was highly automated and was characterized by high fixed costs, high set-up costs, and low variable costs.

In spite of highly seasonal sales, Harrington operated on level production schedules. Since the product lines were for all practical purposes undifferentiated from competing lines and the relevant production technology was well known, the capacity to sell on the basis of price, while achieving a good return on invested capital, was regarded by management as a critical success factor in the industry. Minimum production costs were therefore imperative.

Level production enabled the company to take advantage of extremely long production runs and thus to minimize down time, the investment in equipment, expensive set ups, and the use of transient labor. Level production in conjunction with the company's dominant market share provided scale economies well beyond the reach of any competitor.

The combination of seasonal sales and level production resulted in the accumulation of large seasonal stocks. However, by concentrating the sales effort in the middle six months of the year, Harrington was able to circumvent most of the risk usually connected with level production in a seasonal company in return for modest purchase discounts. Since they could easily predict their needs for Harrington products as their budgets for the forthcoming year took shape, customers were willing to place their orders well in advance of shipment. As a result, Harrington could manufacture against a firm backlog in the last few months of the year and thus circumvent the risk of overproducing and ending the year with large stocks of outdated finished goods.

Harrington maintained production facilities in western Massachusetts and, through a wholly owned subsidiary, in Puerto Rico. Earnings of the Puerto Rican subsidiary, which sold all its output to the U.S. parent, were entirely exempt from U.S. taxes and until 1982 would be exempt from all Puerto Rican taxes. The tax exemption on Puerto Rican production accounted for Harrington's unusually low income tax rate. All Harrington plants and equipment were modern and excellently maintained. A major capital expenditures program, completed in 1966, had resulted in Harrington's having the most modern facilities in the industry. At the predicted rate of future sales growth, Mr. Jackson, the chief production officer, did not anticipate any need for substantial capital expenditures for at least 5 or 6 years.

None of the company's work force was represented by labor unions.

Marketing

As its products were nondifferentiable, Harrington's marketing program concentrated on providing high quality customer service and a uniformly high quality product. Harrington products were sold nationwide to about 1,800 accounts. Geographically the company was strongest in the Northeast, the Southwest, and the far West. Large accounts were handled by the company's five-man sales force, and smaller accounts were serviced by office supply wholesalers. Roughly 10% of sales had gone to the federal government in 1970. The company's six largest customers generally accounted for about 20% of sales.

Even though the product was undifferentiated, Mr. Darby, the marketing vice president, believed that it did have some significant advantages from a marketing viewpoint. Selling costs were extremely low, as consumption of the product over the course of a year automatically generated a large replacement demand without any effort on the part of Harrington. About 95% of total sales generally consisted of reorders from the existing customer base, with only 5% of sales going to new customers. Historically over 98% of the customer base annually reordered Harrington pads and, as needed, additional Harrington bases. By dealing with only one source of supply, the customer was able to take maximum advantage of discounts for volume purchases. As the product was virtually immune to malfunction and the resultant customer dissatisfaction, once Harrington bases had been installed the typical buyer never received any incentive to spend time and money on a search for alternative sources. Consumption of Harrington products was, in addition, extremely insensitive to budget cuts, economy drives, consumer whims, and the like. The desk calendar was a small ticket but high priority item. It was an essential in the work routines of most of its end users, and it was not expensive enough to yield a meaningful reward in savings to would-be cutters. As a dated product, the desk calendar, unlike many other office products, represented a nondeferrable purchase.

Finances

The dominant influence on Harrington's financial policy was Mr. Baring's still vivid memory of the Great Depression. Mr. Baring steadfastly refused to consider levering his equity in the company. Accordingly, Harrington operated with an all equity capitalization. The size of the capital budget was determined by the volume of internally generated funds in conjunction with Mr.

Baring's decision on how much to withdraw in the form of dividends. Dividend payments had sometimes been sharply contracted to accommodate capital investment opportunities. Over the past three years, however, internally generated funds had been plentiful, and dividends had averaged 70% of net earnings.

Like the capital budget, the seasonal accumulation of inventories and receivables was financed from internal sources. To minimize warehousing expenses for finished goods, Harrington provided generous credit terms to customers who accepted early shipments. Payments for June through October shipments were not due until the end of November, although substantial discounts were offered for earlier payment. The collection period averaged 60 days. Credit experience was excellent, and generous credit terms were considered a key factor in the company's competitive success.

Although the company had not resorted to seasonal borrowing in close on ten years, it maintained for emergency purposes two $1 million lines of credit at Boston banks. Exhibit 4 shows 1970 working capital balances by month.

Harrington's credit with suppliers was excellent. All trade obligations were promptly paid when due.

Management

The senior management team consisted of Mr. Baring plus the four individuals interested in buying the corporation. Transfer of ownership to the latter would not occasion much change in the de facto management of the organization. Although Mr. Baring continued to exercise the final authority on all major issues of policy and strategy, over the past few years he had gradually withdrawn from day-to-day affairs and now spent much of his time in Europe and Puerto Rico. As Mr. Baring had relaxed his grip on Harrington's affairs, he had increasingly delegated the general management of the firm to Mr. Brooks.

Compensation was extremely lush at the senior executive level. Mr. Baring drew an annual salary of $200,000; his four key subordinates received an average salary of $45,000. In addition, the four senior executives received annual bonuses which aggregated 10% of earnings before taxes and bonuses.

Apart from Mr. Brooks, the members of the purchasing group were all in their early 50's and between them represented close to 90 years experience in the business. After being graduated from a leading graduate school of business administration, Mr. Brooks, age 40, had worked for five years in the venture capital department of a large Boston bank and for two years in his own management consulting firm before joining Harrington.

COMPANY PROSPECTS

The overall prospect was for continued growth at a steady, though unspectacular, pace. The rate of Harrington sales growth, management believed, was closely correlated with the rate of growth in the size of the domestic white collar work force. Given expectations of a continuing shift of labor out of agricultural and blue collar occupations and into white collar positions, this suggested that the company should grow somewhat faster than the economy as a whole. Assuming no material changes in product lines or market share, management thought sales growth would average about 5–6% per annum in the foreseeable future. Profit margins were expected to improve somewhat over the next few years, as volume expanded and an increasing proportion of new production was directed to the tax-exempt Puerto Rican facility.

Competition

Although the commercial desk calendar industry was profitable indeed for its leading participant, it was not, in the opinion of Harrington management, an attractive area for potential new competitors. At present the industry was divided between Harrington with roughly a 60–65% share of market and Algonquin Industries, a privately held company, with an estimated 20–25% share. Algonquin's strength was concentrated in the Midwest and Southeast. The remainder of industry sales was fragmented among a host of small, financially weak printing shops. Harrington management found it difficult to imagine how a potential competitor could arrive at an economically justifiable decision to enter their market. Price was the only conceivable basis on which a new entrant could compete, but, lacking the scale economies available to Harrington, a new entrant would necessarily be a high cost competitor. Mr. Darby estimated that it would take a new entrant at least 3–5 years to reach breakeven, assuming no retaliatory price cuts by Harrington. Furthermore, entering this market would necessitate a minimum capital investment of $1.5–2 million plus the working capital needed to support seasonal sales. On balance, it seemed unlikely that a potential competitor would brave these obstacles in the hope of grabbing a share of a $13–14 million industry with mediocre growth prospects.

Mr. Baring judged that Harrington's financial strength, relative cost advantages, and entrenched distribution system had served to deter Algonquin from trying to invade any of Harrington's prime market areas. Likewise, he thought Harrington could not take away a substantial market share from Algonquin without risking a price war that might seriously impair margins for a protracted period.

Unexploited opportunities

The business plan finally approved by Mr. Baring had not incorporated a diversification scheme vigorously advanced by the other members of senior management. The vice presidents had contended that Harrington could significantly boost both the rate of growth and level of earnings by using its cash flow and its production and distribution strengths to expand into related product lines. The proposal had called for expansion into other dated products, such as appointment books, planning books, and the like, imprinted with the name, logo, or other message of the customer, and into desk calendars similarly imprinted. Mr. Brooks had estimated that this project would require an initial capital investment of $100,000 and special product development and merchandising expenses of $450,000 spread over the first two years of the undertaking. It had been estimated that the new line should yield sales of approximately $500,000 in the first full year of operation with a growth rate of about 40% per annum in years 2 through 4, as the line achieved nationwide distribution and recognition. A 12–15% growth rate was anticipated in subsequent years. It was thought that this type of product line would have a profit margin before taxes of about 6%. The management group believed that the proposed line could serve as a profitable first step toward developing a full line of desk top products for commercial, industrial, and government markets.

Mr. Baring had rejected the proposal on several grounds. He had observed that the proposal advocated entering a riskier line of business in which none of the management group had experience. In the proposed line of business the customer could choose among a variety of competing designs, and manufacturers had to actively generate repeat sales. He had also pointed out that the project would require a substantial investment in working capital for seasonal sales, if the new line grew as predicted. Finally he had stated that he was quite content with his present income and, at his age, unwilling to reinvest earnings in the hope of achieving a strong position in a more competitive and less profitable business than the present one.

With Mr. Baring out of the picture, the management group would have the freedom to pursue its growth program. Mr. Brooks believed that over a period of years Harrington's growth rate could be improved significantly if earnings were reinvested in related businesses rather than disbursed as dividends. The higher growth rate would be translated into profits for management, if the faster growth allowed them to take the company public at a higher price-earnings ratio.

THE PURCHASE PROPOSAL

Mr. Brooks recognized that a successful proposal would have to blend and reconcile the interests and goals of all parties to the transaction: the seller, the buyers, and external suppliers of finance.

The management group had determined that between them they could raise at most about $250,000 for investment in Harrington. Raising this amount would necessitate drawing down savings accounts, refinancing home mortgages, and liquidating positions in the stock market. Mr. Brooks was prepared to commit $80,000, Mr. Jackson $70,000, and Messrs. Darby and Sloane $50,000 apiece. It had been tentatively agreed that all members of the management group would buy stock at the same price. It had also been tentatively concluded that the group would not accept a proposal that left them with less than 51% of the shares. With less than 51% of the stock the management group might not achieve the autonomy to establish corporate policy or to dispose of the company where and as they chose.

Valuation

As pointed out above, Mr. Brooks believed that Mr. Baring's asking terms of $10 million with a minimum of $8 million in cash would remain fixed, at least until the company had been shown to a number of prospective buyers. In the past year, Mr. Baring had held discussions with two companies that had made unsolicited bids to purchase Harrington. The first offer, $7.5 million in cash, had come from a medium-sized firm with a diversified line of office products. It had been rejected by Mr. Baring on the basis of price. The second offer had come from a highly diversified medium-sized company sporting a price–earnings ratio of 40 and seeking to establish a position in office products through a series of acquisitions. The final offer had come to $18 million in letter stock[1] of the acquirer. Mr. Baring had found this bid extremely tempting, but had been unwilling to tie up his wealth in unmarketable shares of a company with which he was not intimately familiar. The acquirer, lacking excess debt capacity and unwilling to float new stock, had backed out of the discussions.

Mr. Brooks had, in addition, assembled financial figures on the publicly traded companies he thought most comparable to Harrington. These data are presented in Exhibit 5.

Financing

In terms of the mechanics of the transaction, Mr. Brooks planned to effect the purchase through a new corporation in which the management group would buy 250,000 common shares at $1.00 a share. Given the management group's $250,000 versus the $10 million asking price, the biggest problem facing Mr. Brooks was how to fund the new company at all, not to mention the objective of keeping control in the management group. Mr. Brooks had managed to obtain tentative commitments for $5.25 million, including the management group's $250,000. Prior to submitting a purchase proposal to Mr. Baring, however, he would have to line up commitments for the entire $10 million funds needed.

It was clear that the noncash component of the purchase price would have to be met by issuing notes with a market value of $2 million to Mr. Baring. In order to maintain the maximum amount of flexibility and borrowing capacity for raising financing from outsiders, Mr. Brooks had proposed that Mr. Baring take 4%, junior subordinated, non-amortizing notes. After some negotiation, Mr. Baring had expressed his willingness to accept a $3,000,000 non-amortizing, 4% five-year note which would be junior to all other debt

---

[1] Letter stock is unregistered stock. Such stock may not be sold to the public without registration under the Securities Act of 1933, a costly and time-consuming process. Because letter stock is restricted in its transferability, it represents a relatively illiquid investment and generally sells at a discount below the price that registered stock would command in the public securities markets. When letter stock is issued in an acquisition, the acquirer generally specifies that the stock cannot be registered for a certain period of time.

obligations of the newly formed corporation. The members of the management group as well as the corporate acquirer would have to endorse the note. It was agreed that covenants on the note would include: (1) no additional debt or leases except debt incurred in the acquisition of Harrington, short-term seasonal borrowings, or debt incurred to retire the five-year note; (2) no dividends and maintenance of at least $1.5 million in working capital; (3) no changes in management or increase in management compensation; (4) no sale of Harrington shares by Messrs. Brooks, Darby, Jackson, or Sloane so long as the five-year note was outstanding. If the borrower should default on any terms of this note or of any other indebtedness, the junior subordinated notes would become immediately due and payable. If not promptly paid, ownership of the shares held by the management group would revert to Mr. Baring. The note could be retired before maturity in whole or in part in accord with the following schedule of discounts:

Year	% of Face Value
1	58 %
2	71
3	81
4	96
5	100

In his efforts to line up financing from outside sources, Mr. Brooks had succeeded in obtaining a tentative commitment for a $3,000,000 term loan from a large New York City bank known for its aggressive lending policies. This loan would be amortized over a maximum period of six years through annual installments. The rate would be two points above floating prime, and the borrower would have to maintain average compensating balances of 20% of the outstanding principal amount of the loan. The amount of $3 million was the maximum the bank would commit for on a term basis. Lending officers of the bank had emphasized that any additional term indebtedness incurred in the acquisition of Harrington would have to be effectively subordinated to this loan. Exhibit 6 presents an abstract of the provisions that the bank term loan would bear. Exhibit 7 presents Mr. Brooks' forecast of Harrington's cash flows over the next six years.

Having negotiated the bank commitment, Mr. Brooks was still left with the problem of raising an additional $4.75 million. He thought that he would have to turn to venture capital sources to raise the rest of the funds needed. Based on his experience in venture finance, Mr. Brooks knew that a venture capitalist would expect to earn about 20–25% on his funds. He also knew that most venture capitalists preferred to place their funds in the form of debt securities rather than common stock. The venture capitalist could generally exercise more effective control over his investment through the covenants on a debt obligation than through the voting power on stock. Principal on debt also provided a mechanism for a tax-free recovery of capital; this might not be possible with stock until the company had gone public. Mr. Brooks expected to have to pay an 8–9% coupon rate on any debt funds obtained from a venture capital source. The venture capitalist would probably attempt to realize the rest of his return by taking warrants to buy shares in the new corporation at $1.00, the same price initially paid by the management group. The venture capitalist would probably insist on having the option of exercising the warrants in either cash or Harrington debentures.

Exhibit 1

HARRINGTON CORPORATION

CONSOLIDATED INCOME STATEMENTS
(In thousands)

	1966	1967	1968	1969	1970
Net sales	$4,870	$5,022	$5,974	$6,985	$7,630
Cost of sales	2,918	2,824	3,497	4,152	4,649
Gross profit on sales	$1,952	$2,198	$2,476	$2,833	$2,981
Selling and administrative expenses	1,108	1,036	1,235	1,511	1,637
Other income and (expense)—net	20	54	36	64	60
Profit before income taxes	$ 864	$1,216	$1,277	$1,386	$1,404
Federal income taxes	408	486	460	471	421
Net profit	$ 456	$ 730	$ 817	$ 915	$ 983

Exhibit 2

HARRINGTON CORPORATION

CONSOLIDATED BALANCE SHEET AS OF DECEMBER 31, 1970
(In thousands)

ASSETS		LIABILITIES AND SHAREHOLDERS' EQUITY	
Current assets:		Current liabilities:	
Cash and marketable securities	$2,881	Accounts payable	$ 327
		Accrued expenses	183
Accounts receivable	1,270	Accrued income taxes	123
Inventories at lower of cost or market	294		
Prepaid expenses	54		
Total current assets	$4,499	Total current liabilities	$ 633
Property, plant, and equipment—net	1,055	Shareholders' equity:	
Miscellaneous assets	37	Common stock ($1.00 par value)	100
Total assets	$5,591	Retained profits	4,858
		Total liabilities and shareholders' equity	$5,591

Exhibit 3

HARRINGTON CORPORATION

TEN-YEAR SUMMARY OF OPERATIONS

(In thousands except per share data)

	1961	1962	1963	1964	1965	1966	1967	1968	1969	1970
Net sales	$3,844	$4,178	$4,263	$4,395	$4,675	$4,870	$5,022	$5,974	$6,985	$7,630
Net profit	319	334	371	374	379	456	730	817	915	983
Dividends	300	100	140	140	220	220	240	610	687	740
Earnings per share	3.19	3.34	3.71	3.74	3.79	4.56	7.30	8.17	9.15	9.83
Net profit margin	8.3%	8.0%	8.7%	8.5%	8.1%	9.4%	14.5%	13.7%	13.1%	12.9%

Exhibit 4

HARRINGTON CORPORATION

MONTHLY WORKING CAPITAL BALANCES, 1970

(In thousands)

	Jan.	Feb.	Mar.	Apr.	May	Jun.	Jul.	Aug.	Sep.	Oct.	Nov.	Dec.
Cash	$2,768	$2,857	$2,698	$2,392	$2,164	$2,049	$1,177	$ 383	$1,025	$1,915	$2,867	$2,881
Accounts receivable	740	380	367	402	359	302	1,716	3,052	3,082	2,161	1,199	1,270
Inventories	562	833	1,105	1,376	1,647	1,919	1,377	835	263	294	304	294
Current liabilities	(593)	(610)	(621)	(573)	(711)	(672)	(536)	(608)	(587)	(692)	(670)	(633)
Net working capital	$3,477	$3,460	$3,549	$3,597	$3,459	$3,598	$3,734	$3,662	$3,783	$3,678	$3,700	$3,812

Exhibit 5

HARRINGTON CORPORATION

COMPARATIVE DATA ON SELECTED COMPANIES IN RELATED LINES OF BUSINESS

	Dow Jones Industrial Average	*Standard & Poor's 425 Industrial Stocks*	*Linden-Johns, Inc.**		*Kane Co.†*		*Granger, Inc.‡*		*Harrington Corp.*	
Trading market			OTC		OTC		OTC		—	
Current market price			$22¼		$14¾		$29¼		—	
Indicated dividend yield			5.5%		8.7%		3.7%		—	
Price-earnings ratio										
1970	14.6	16.4	8.7		7.2		10.5		—	
1969	14.0	15.7	6.4		5.0		10.2		—	
1968	16.3	18.6	10.8		11.9		13.8		—	
Price range										
1970			24⅝–16¼		14⅞–8⅛		33⅛–26½		—	
1969			18½–12⅛		11½–5⅛		19¾–12⅞		—	
Earnings per share (E) and index (I)			(E)	(I)	(E)	(I)	(E)	(I)	(E)	(I)
1970			$2.48	110	$1.62	82	$2.98	177	$9.83	216
1966			2.26	100	1.97	100	1.68	100	4.56	100
Sales (S) (in thousands) and index (I)			(S)	(I)	(S)	(I)	(S)	(I)	(S)	(I)
1970			$16,427	142	$12,223	108	$18,608	160	$7,630	157
1966			11,568	100	11,317	100	11,630	100	4,870	100
Net earnings (N) (in thousands) and index (I)			(N)	(I)	(N)	(I)	(N)	(I)	(N)	(I)
1970			$1,051	117	$501	84	$1,656	178	$983	216
1966			902	100	600	100	930	100	456	100
Net profit margins										
1970			6.4%		4.1%		8.9%		12.9%	
1966			7.8		5.3		8.0		9.4	
Profit/net worth										
1970			16.6%		6.0%		16.9%		19.8%	
1969			14.2		5.7		15.0		19.0	
1968			15.4		8.8		14.7		19.2	

Exhibit 5—Continued

	Dow Jones Industrial Average	Standard & Poor's 425 Industrial Stocks	Linden-Johns, Inc.* 12/31/70		Kane Co.† 12/31/70		Granger, Inc.‡ 12/31/70		Harrington Corp. 12/31/70	
Book capitalization (dollar figures in thousands)										
Long-term debt................			$3,995	38.7%	$1,822	18.0%	$4,173	29.9%	$ —	— %
Common stock and surplus.......			6,318	61.3	8,298	82.0	9,783	70.1	4,958	100.0
Total..................			$10,313	100.0%	$10,120	100.0%	$13,956	100.0%	$4,958	100.0%
Total market value (in thousands)......			$9,456		$4,573		$16,234		$ —	
Shares outstanding (in thousands).......			425		310		555		100	

* Producer of desk top accessories, advertising specialty calendars, office stationery.
† Producer of advertising specialty calendars.
‡ Producer of broad line of office paper products and desk accessories.

Exhibit 6

HARRINGTON CORPORATION

EXCERPTS FROM SUMMARY OF LOAN AGREEMENT FOR BANK TERM LOAN

Description of the Loan

Amount: $3,000,000

Rate: Prime rate plus 2%, floating.*

Term: 6 years.

Repayment: Annual payments equal to the greater of $500,000 or the sum of net profit plus amortization of goodwill and debt discounts less $100,000.

Prepayment: Permitted in whole or in part at any time without penalty. All prepayments to be applied to the outstanding principal balance of the loan in inverse order of maturity.

Compensating Balances: Borrower must maintain average annual deposit balances equal to at least 20% of the outstanding principal amount of the loan.

Conditions Precedent

Prior to the making of the loan described above, borrower must have satisfied the following terms and conditions:

Incorporation: Borrower must be a duly incorporated corporation authorized to undertake this borrowing and all other transactions associated with this borrowing.

Purchase Agreement: Borrower must have entered a contract to purchase 100% of the Harrington Corporation.

Financing: Borrower must have arranged firm commitments for the financing of this transaction in a manner consistent with the terms of this loan agreement.

Equity Purchase: Messrs. Brooks, Darby, Jackson, and Sloane must have committed not less than $250,000 to the purchase of common stock in the newly formed corporation which will purchase Harrington.

Affirmative Covenants

During the life of this loan, borrower will adhere to the following terms and conditions:

Financial Statements: Quarterly financial statements must be provided within 60 days of the end of the first three quarters. Audited financial statements bearing an unqualified opinion from a public accounting firm must be provided within 90 days of the end of borrower's fiscal year.

Accounting Changes: Borrower will make no changes in its method of accounting.

Negative Covenants

During the life of this loan, borrower will not do any of the following without written consent of the lender:

Continuation of Management: No changes in management. Aggregate compensation to Messrs. Brooks, Darby, Jackson, and Sloane not to be increased by more than 5% in any year, present compensation to serve as a base for this computation.

Negative Pledge: No assets to be pledged or otherwise used as collateral for any indebtedness.

Sale of Assets: No sale of a substantial portion of the assets of the borrower. Borrower will not merge with or be acquired by any other entity.

Acquisitions: Borrower will not acquire any other entity.

Capital Expenditures: Not to exceed $150,000 in any one year.

Dividends: In any one year restricted to after-tax profits minus all principal repayments on outstanding indebtedness.

Working Capital: Not to decline below $1,500,000.

Additional Indebtedness: No additional debt (including leases) with a term exceeding one year, unless subordinated to this loan. Any short-term debt must be retired for a period of at least 30 consecutive days in every year.

Senior Debt: Senior debt, including all short-term indebtedness, may not exceed $5 million plus all earnings retained in the business after Dec. 30, 1971.

Exhibit 6—Continued

Events of Default

In the event of default, this loan plus accrued interest will become immediately due and payable. The following will constitute events of default:

—Failure to pay interest or principal when due.
—Violation of any affirmative or negative covenant on this loan.
—Bankruptcy, reorganization, receivership, liquidation.
—Commission of an event of default on any other indebtedness.

* At present the prime rate is 5¼%.

Exhibit 7

HARRINGTON CORPORATION

CASH FLOW FORECASTS

(In thousands)

	1971	1972	1973	1974	1975	1976
sales	$8,012	$8,422	$8,843	$9,285	$9,749	$10,236
nings before interest and taxes*...	1,516	1,636	1,717	1,804	1,894	1,988
erest expense†	637	585	523	454	400	400
fit before tax	$ 879	$1,051	$1,194	$1,350	$1,494	$ 1,588
:es	137	182	220	278	330	357
fit after tax	$ 742	$ 869	$ 974	$1,072	$1,164	$ 1,231
d back noncash charges	120	130	142	150	155	170
h flow from operations	$ 862	$ 999	$1,116	$1,222	$1,319	$ 1,401
s: Increase in working capital....	78	81	85	90	95	100
s: Capital expenditures	60	67	71	75	233	300
ailable for debt retirement	$ 724	$ 851	$ 960	$1,057	$ 991	$ 1,001
nned debt retirement:						
Bank loan	$ 724	$ 851	$ 960	$ 465	$ 0	$1,001
Baring's note	0	0	0	592	2,383‡	0
Subordinated loan	0	0	0	0	0	0
t as % of total capital	89%	80%	70%	58%	47%	35%

*Reflects elimination of Baring's salary.
†9% coupon on subordinated loan of $3 million; 4% coupon on seller's note of $3 million; 7¼% rate on bank term loan; rate on seasonal loan.
‡Baring's note is retired from cash flow and a $1.4 million new bank term loan in 1975.

Part IV

comprehensive overview

VERENIGDE MACHINEFABRIEKEN
STORK N.V. (A) (Abridged)

∧∧∧

In early November 1975, Mr. J. L. M. van Rhijn, director of planning and management information at Verenigde Machinefabrieken Stork (VMF-Stork), was faced with a difficult choice. Said Mr. van Rhijn:

> According to our forecasts, we will need to raise roughly Fl 140 million in 1976. We think it would be best to raise Fl 75 million in early 1976 and the rest in mid-1976. We don't need the entire Fl 140 million at the beginning of 1976. Also, Fl 75 million is about the largest sum we could raise easily on the Dutch capital markets.
>
> My problem is deciding which of several alternative financing methods should be used. The options range from borrowing short-term funds to issuing equity. Of course, the financing choice we make in 1976 will necessarily influence our later financing decisions.

VMF-Stork background information

VMF-Stork, headquartered in Amsterdam, the Netherlands was a large, widely diversified company with 1974 turnover of approximately Fl 1.5 billion.[1] The company was divided into eight divisions, each division comprised of several independent operating companies.

VMF-Stork had been formed in 1954 when two well-established Dutch heavy machinery manufacturers (Machinefabrieken Stork and Werkspoor N.V.) merged. The merger had been consumated in order to take advantage of the considerable overlap between the two companies—approximately 80% of their product lines were similar. However, by the late 1960s, the desired integration and rationalization of the two companies had not taken place. Each company, for example, had retained the same board of directors as before. Also, operating companies, which had competed before the merger, continued to compete after the merger.

The lack of integration and the internal competition were two important contributing factors to a financial crisis at VMF-Stork in the late 1960s. In

---

[1] VMF-Stork's reported turnover was a three-year moving average of actual revenues. The Dutch currency is guilders and is abbreviated Fl.

1969, the company recorded a trading loss of almost Fl 29 million and found it necessary to suspend the payment of a dividend. The difficulties had a severe impact on the price of the common stock, which fell from a high of Fl 152 in early 1969 to Fl 58 by late 1970. With working capital at unexpectedly high levels and very limited access to the capital markets, VMF-Stork was faced with a severe liquidity crisis.

Response to the 1969–1970 crisis

The immediate response to the liquidity problem was to institute a program to improve cash flow. A concerted drive to collect overdue accounts receivable, to drive down levels of inventories and work in process, and to improve advance payments by customers, yielded nearly 80 million guilders within a 15-month period. The VMF-Stork management also had to make some very difficult decisions about which businesses to retain and which to sell or liquidate. Each existing product line was analyzed in light of VMF-Stork's strengths and weaknesses and also in terms of market potential. Corporate management believed that at least two related factors were crucial to make a business profitable in the long run and thus warrant its inclusion in VMF-Stork's portfolio. First, VMF-Stork should have the technological capabilities to compete in the market. Second, VMF-Stork should be able to attain a level of market penetration which would enable it to achieve economies of scale. Corporate management believed strongly that too low a market share, even if profits could be made, significantly increased the riskiness of the business. Alternatively, a high market share in an economically undesirable market was also to be avoided.

After extensive management surveys, it was decided to eliminate unprofitable activities representing 30% of turnover. Implementing this plan of action was complicated by the fact that the Dutch government and the relevant labor unions were opposed to closing plants. In 1969, VMF-Stork employed almost 26,000 men and women. In 1970, this figure was reduced to 24,361 and was targeted to decline eventually to 20,000. The Dutch government was also opposed to VMF-Stork closing its railroad rolling-stock division (which employed 1,200 people) because it was viewed by the government as an important strategic industry. However, the long-run economics of the business for VMF-Stork dictated that the plant be closed and the government finally concurred.

The restructuring programs implemented by VMF-Stork had a beneficial impact on the liquidity and profitability of the company. By 1974, turnover reached 1.5 billion guilders, up 50% from 1969, and net profit was almost 25 million guilders. The common stock had risen from the 1970 low of Fl 58 per share to a 1974 high of Fl 180, aided by the restoration of the dividend in 1972. Total employment, which had declined from 26,000 in 1969 to under 20,000 in 1973, rose to 21,863 in 1974. (See Exhibit 1 for a history of the earnings, dividends, and price of VMF-Stork's common stock.)

The impact of the 1969–1970 financial crisis

One result of the 1969–70 difficulties and subsequent resolution was that

VMF-Stork's management became convinced of the need for a formal long-range strategic planning system. VMF-Stork had been neither rationally organized nor well-positioned in a number of its product markets. It was decided that strategic planning at VMF-Stork would be designed to insure that the company would be correctly situated to take advantage of economically attractive markets.

From this perspective, management viewed its evolving role as one of a portfolio manager more concerned with strategic decisions than with operating decisions. Each division and each operating company was viewed as an independent investment. The objective of the portfolio manager was to maximize return on investment for a given level of risk.[2] New investments were only to be made in those old or new businesses which were consistent with the overall corporate strategy. Divestitures would occur in those businesses offering no prospect of profitably fitting into the strategy.

Finally, as a direct result of its 1969–70 difficulties, VMF-Stork was very concerned with maintaining financial flexibility. That is, management was averse to finding itself short of cash as had happened in 1969 and 1970. One implication of this aversion was that businesses which required continuing large net cash investments were to be avoided wherever possible.

The nature of VMF-Stork's business

VMF-Stork was in a wide variety of businesses ranging from the manufacture of diesel engines to the construction of sugar refineries. The characteristics of each business varied significantly. For example, the diesel-engine business operated at a relatively low rate of return on investment and required large continuing capital investments. On the other hand, the engineering-services division was characterized by a high return on investment, primarily due to the low amount of capital required. (See Exhibit 2 for a description of the investment characteristics and turnover of each of VMF-Stork's operating divisions.)

Another aspect of VMF-Stork's business was that a significant portion of the company's revenues were derived from very large contracts. For example, the company was in the midst of completing the manufacture of a Fl 400 million sugar factory in Iran. Under VMF-Stork's accounting system, the revenues and profits on such a contract were not recognized until the contract was completed.[3]

It was normal in VMF-Stork's contract business to receive a significant downpayment from its customers, perhaps as much as 15% of the total value of the contract. These downpayments had a beneficial impact on the company's

---

[2] A concurrent objective, as stated by the VMF-Stork management, was to fulfill the social obligations of the company. For example, if economic considerations dictated the closing of a plant, VMF-Stork management viewed aiding in the resettlement of displaced workers as one of its responsibilities.

[3] One impact of this contract business was that VMF-Stork's actual revenues were uneven and depended on the timing of the completion of major contracts. This is the reason why VMF-Stork reported its turover as a three-year moving average. See Exhibit 2 for the actual historical revenues (booked-off orders) of VMF-Stork from 1968 to 1974.

liquidity. On the other hand, VMF-Stork had to guarantee to complete the contract. VMF-Stork's guarantee took the form of a performance bond which was issued by a consortium of banks to VMF-Stork's customers.

Finally, virtually all of the contracts signed by VMF-Stork were indexed to inflation. Thus, the company was not vulnerable to inflation-caused cost overruns, though it was vulnerable to overruns not related to inflation.

Financial planning at VMF-Stork

VMF-Stork's financial planning system was comprised of several parts. First, each operating company was required to submit a one-year operating plan to the major product division management.[4] After a process of negotiation and consolidation, each division was required to submit a detailed one-year plan to corporate management. Once again, a process of negotiation occurred before a final one-year plan was determined.

One of the most important outputs of this operating plan was the expected financial needs of each operating company, each division, and the entire company.

A quite similar planning process was used by VMF-Stork to make longer-term projections. Each year, the company developed a five-year strategic plan of which the first year was the operating plan described above.

One aspect of the financial forecasting system was somewhat unusual. Each year, the corporate financial staff "adjusted" the forecasts made in the operating company strategic and operating plans in order to obtain more realistic forecasts. The adjustments were based on the historical forecasting ability of the operating companies and the divisions. In the past, the strategic plan had always been too optimistic; thus, the reason for the adjustments. The end result of this adjustment process was labeled the "most-likely" plan.

VMF's expected financial needs

In late 1975, VMF-Stork estimated that it would need on the order of Fl 133 million in 1976 and a total of Fl 403 million by 1980. These were cumulative totals in that if the company raised money at any point in time, the financial gap declined by the amount of financing. (See Exhibit 3 for the most-likely balance sheets.)

The difference between this estimate of the financial gap and that derived from using the nonadjusted operating company and division forecasts was dramatic. In the latter projection, the company was expected to have a small financial surplus in 1980 instead of a *gap* of Fl 403 million. There were three main reasons for this discrepancy. First, in the strategic plan, invested capital in 1980 was expected to total Fl 969 million whereas in the most-likely (adjusted) projections, the comparable figure was Fl 1,141 million. Since revenue projections were the same, the underlying difference was in the assumed rate of turn-

---

[4] The major economic assumptions underlying the plans were determined by the headquarters staff and were the basis for all planning at VMF-Stork.

over of invested capital. (See Exhibit 4 for a chart demonstrating the impact of changes in the assumed rate of turnover of invested capital.)

The second major source of the discrepancy was in the profit forecasts. The strategic plan projection called for a net profit in 1980 of Fl 190 million versus the most-likely estimate of Fl 86 million. (See Exhibit 5.)

Finally, the impact of the projected rate of growth of turnover was dramatic. The inflation estimate embodied in the forecasts was 8.4% per year implying a total growth rate of turnover of roughly 19%. If inflation were to decline, the need for invested capital would also decline dramatically. (See Exhibit 6.)

The financing alternatives

There were several major alternatives available to VMF-Stork in late 1975. Mr. van Rhijn, director of planning and information, described these choices:

The basic choice we have to make is whether to issue equity or some form of debt. Of course, there are several alternatives within each of these two categories. With regard to debt, we could issue either short-, medium-, or long-term obligations or some combination thereof.

With regard to equity, there are two possibilities: issuing new shares or issuing a convertible subordinated debenture. In Holland, a convertible subordinated bond is treated as equity by the major financial institutions.

Another alternative which would provide us with at least part of the necessary funds would be to sell one of our less attractive operating companies or perhaps even a division. Unfortunately, we would probably have to report a large loss on such a sale which would penalize our earnings per share (EPS). Given the debacle of 1969–70, we have a stated policy to maintain a steady EPS growth rate of 15%. It is especially important that EPS not decline.

Thus, we would be hesitant to jeopardize our earnings by selling part of our business. Also, given that the timing of such a sale is unpredictable, we have not made any allowance for it in our funds needs projections.

In considering the alternative of financing our needs with some form of debt, several factors are important. First, in the covenants of our existing loans, we are constrained in the amount and type of debt we can issue. The ratio of shareholders' equity to long-term debt has to be greater than two to one. The ratio of stockholders' equity to the total of medium- and long-term debt must exceed three to two. These covenants were originally negotiated with the huge Dutch insurance company, Nationale Nederlanden, and several other Dutch financial institutions. Nationale Nederlanden is the largest single holder of our debt securities.[5]

In late 1974, we made a private placement of Fl 70 million long-term debt. Only Fl 18.7 million was taken down in 1974 and the rest in 1975. The coupon rate on this issue was, with hindsight, a disastrously high 12%, but we needed the money. This debt issue pushed us to the limits under our current covenants on long-term debt. Thus, we are effectively precluded from issuing long-term debt in early 1976,

---

[5] VMF-Stork had discussed the possibility of changing the loan covenants to remove the ratio constraints and replacing them with some form of interest-coverage constraint. Negotiations were still in process.

though it is certainly a viable option in mid-1976 if we sell some form of equity first. In early 1976, we project a cost of long-term debt of 9.75%, and in mid-1976, a range of between 9.75% and 9.25%.

With regard to medium-term debt, we could conceivably issue Fl 50 million or so. We could supplement this with Fl 25 million of short-term debt. The rate of interest on the medium-term debt would be roughly 8.0% and perhaps 5.25% on the short-term debt. However, I have several problems with this option. In the first place, issuing that much debt first would significantly diminish our flexibility.

We have been actively pursuing a number of acquisition possibilities. With our stock selling at six times earnings, and given our stated policy against diluting earnings per share, it would be extremely difficult to use stock to make an acquisition. Thus, we can only make acquisitions using cash.

Further, I am not enthusiastic about adding very much short-term debt. We have run into liquidity problems before, and I think short-term debt is very risky. We used some in 1974 and 1975 to a degree which I would be reluctant to see increased.

Finally, there is a possibility that it will be far more difficult to issue long-term securities in mid-1976. The Dutch National Bank can control the timing of issues of long-term debt. I am afraid that there will be a long queue by mid-1976, in part aggravated by the deficit financing of the government. Last year, the budgeted deficit of the government was Fl 5.8 billion, and the actual deficit was Fl 9.4 billion. In 1976, the budgeted deficit is Fl 16.2 billion, all of which has to be financed. It's possible that rates will rise as a result of these financing needs.

Thus, at least with respect to the financing in early-1976, the options seem limited to some form of equity. We could sell straight equity at a price of about Fl 135 to Fl 140, compared to our recent stock price range of Fl 165 to Fl 170. We would offer these shares to our existing shareholders. Preemptive rights are not required in Dutch law, but are normal.

The problem with the option of selling shares is that our earnings per share would be diluted and would certainly show a decline in 1976. We are just now restoring investor credibility in VMF-Stork after our 1969–70 debacle, and showing an earnings per share decline would not be advisable.

Also, I think our stock price is going to increase from current levels. The outlook for the company is excellent, and the world economy is fast recovering from the recession. I believe that the price will reflect these trends and will be perhaps 10% higher within several months.

Early next month, we are going to list our shares on the stock exchanges of Dusseldorf and Frankfurt. Price-earnings ratios are generally higher in Germany than in Holland for our industry, and I hope this will have a beneficial impact on our stock price in the longer run.

In Holland, it is difficult to make large issues of stock. Most of the financial institutions, including the insurance companies, have limitations on the amount of stock they can purchase. In general, they prefer to purchase bonds.[6]

The only viable option seems to be issuing a convertible debenture. We have discussed this with Nationale Nederlanden and with some of the large institutions who

---

[6] See Exhibit 7 for some background information on the Dutch capital markets.

own our shares. They generally agree that a convertible would be best as it would not dilute earnings per share.[7] Also, it would be less expensive than straight debt, and we could sell our shares at a premium of approximately 12% to 15% over our recent share price of Fl 170. The debenture would have a maturity of 15 to 18 years, could be converted after two or three years, and we would be able to call it at a very small premium beginning a couple of years after issue. The coupon would probably be on the order of 8.75%.

Issuing a convertible also makes sense from another perspective. The money we raise will be invested in projects which won't begin to make profits for some time. The lower interest cost and the deferred sale of equity features of a convertible make it especially appropriate given our investment plans.

Thus, I think selling a convertible is the best alternative, but I wouldn't preclude any of the several other options I have mentioned. We could, for example, renegotiate the covenants on our outstanding loans so that we could issue long-term debt in early-1976. Anyway, in the long run, I would like to see those covenants change from an equity-to-debt-ratio basis to an interest-coverage basis.

Before making our decision, I want to think through all the implications of our decision for early-1976 for our financing in mid-1976. It is also important that our decisions in 1976 be consistent with our notions as to an appropriate long-term financing mix.

---

[7] It was the customary practice of security analysts in Holland to calculate and evaluate earnings per share on a preconversion (nondiluted) basis. Also, a convertible debenture would be considered as equity by Nationale Nederlanden in testing for compliance with the existing loan covenants.

Exhibit 1

VERENIGDE MACHINEFABRIEKEN STORK N.V. (A) (Abridged)
PRICE, DIVIDEND, AND EARNINGS HISTORY FOR VMF-STORK;
DUTCH STOCK-MARKET INDEX

Through October 31, 1975

Capital International Index—Netherlands: Market value = $13.9 billion; P/BV^* = 0.62; $P/CE\dagger$ = 3.3; $P/E\ddagger$ = 10.1; yield = 7.2%.

Through October 31, 1975

Verenigde Machinefabrieken — Netherlands: Market value = $54 million; P/BV^* = .46; $P/CE\dagger$ = 2.4; $P/E\ddagger$ = 5.8; yield = 8.0%.

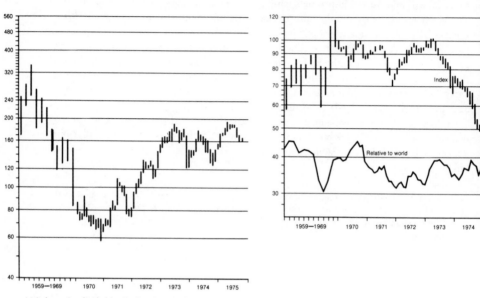

* Market price divided by book value per share.
† Market price divided by cash earnings per share.
‡ Market price divided by earnings per share.

	1966	1967	1968	1969	1970	1971	1972	1973	1974	Forecast 1975
Earnings per share.........	22.1	20.1	19.4	(39.4)	(5.1)	4.3	18.4	24.8	28.5	27.8
Dividends per share.......	12.0	12.0	12.0	0.0	0.0	0.0	8.0	12.0	13.5	14.0
Earnings plus depreciation per share..............	62.0	65.5	61.8	4.7	40.4	49.3	60.2	65.1	71.7	n.a.
Shares outstanding, end of year (000s).......	567.1	596.8	626.7	728.1	728.1	728.1	728.1	742.2	872.5	900.0

n.a. = not available.
Source: *Capital International*, various issues.

Exhibit 2

VERENIGDE MACHINEFABRIEKEN STORK N.V. (A) (Abridged)
DIVISIONAL INVESTMENT CHARACTERISTICS

Division	Current ROI*	Expected ROI†	Risk	Funds Needs	1974 Turnover‡,§ (Fl millions)	Total 1974 Turnover (%)
Light processing industry	Low	Medium	High	Medium	Fl 137	9
Paper and textile industry	High	High	Low	Medium	182	12
Heat and air technology	Low	Low	Medium	High	122	8
Energy	High	Medium	High	Low	197	13
Engineering and construction	High	High	High	Low	106	4
Materials handling and industrial equipment	Medium	Medium	Low	Medium	243	16
Diesel engines, foundries	Low	Medium	High	High	258	17
Miscellaneous	Low	Medium	High	High	61	6

* ROI = Return on investment.
† Five years out.
‡ Three-year moving average of actual revenues. (See bottom of page for actual revenues)
§ In 1975, the guilder/dollar exchange rate varied from 2.45 to 2.75.

Actual Revenues for VMF-Stork (Fl millions)

1968	1969	1970	1971	1972	1973	1974
Fl 794	Fl 1,110	Fl 1,095	Fl 1,255	Fl 1,350	Fl 1,315	Fl 1,439

Source: VMF-Stork.

Exhibit 3

VERENIGDE MACHINEFABRIEKEN STORK N.V. (A) (Abridged)
Most-Likely Balance Sheet
(Fl in millions)

ASSETS	Actual 1974	Forecast 1975	1976	... 1980
Cash................................	Fl 42	Fl 70	Fl 75	Fl 80
Debtors (30% sales)..............	460	527	696	1,225
Stocks (50% sales)...............	810	875	1,166	2,043
Total current assets..........	Fl 1,312	Fl 1,472	Fl 1,937	Fl 3,348
Other................................	39	60	55	60
Net fixed assets.................	238	258	312	511
Total assets.................	Fl 1,589	Fl 1,790	Fl 2,304	Fl 3,919
LIABILITIES AND EQUITY				
Creditors (13% sales).............	Fl 220	Fl 229	Fl 301	Fl 531
Amounts payable and taxes (19% sales)..................	280	334	441	776
Customer advances (36% sales)....	582	633	807	1,471
Total current liabilities.......	Fl 1,082	Fl 1,196	Fl 1,549	Fl 2,778
Medium-term loans..............	41	70	70	70
Long-term loans.................	112	155	150	109
Other.............................	30	33	45	81
Equity...........................	324	336	350	478
Financing need.................	—	0	140	403
Total liabilities and equity....	Fl 1,589	Fl 1,790	Fl 2,304	Fl 3,919

HISTORICAL RELATIONSHIPS	Percent of Sales 1971	1972	1973	1974
Debtors........................	28%	32%	29%	32%
Stocks.........................	60	45	44	56
Creditors......................	14	11	12	15
Amounts payable and taxes.......	19	19	21	19
Customer advances..............	43	33	30	40
Stocks (−) customer advances....	17	12	14	16

Exhibit 4

VERENIGDE MACHINEFABRIEKEN STORK N.V. (A) (Abridged)
INFLUENCE OF THE RATE OF TURNOVER OF INVESTED CAPITAL ON THE
LEVEL OF INVESTED CAPITAL, WHERE TURNOVER IS DEFINED AS SALES DIVIDED
BY THE SUM OF NET WORKING CAPITAL PLUS NET FIXED ASSETS

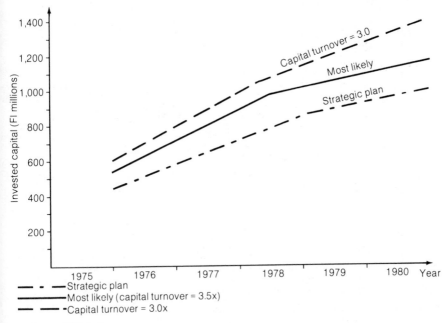

— · —Strategic plan
————Most likely (capital turnover = 3.5x)
— — -Capital turnover = 3.0x

Source: VMF-Stork.

Exhibit 5

VERENIGDE MACHINEFABRIEKEN STORK N.V. (A) (Abridged)
MOST-LIKELY PROFIT AND LOSS STATEMENT
(Fl in millions except per share data)

	1975	1976	1977	1978	1979	1980
Turnover	Fl 1,758	Fl 2,319	Fl 2,835	Fl 3,324	Fl 3,705	Fl 4,085
Earnings before interest and taxes	Fl 51	Fl 70	Fl 101	Fl 149	Fl 170	Fl 189
Interest on debt outstanding as of year-end 1975:						
medium-term	3	5	5	5	5	5
long-term	13	13	12	12	11	11
Interest on new debt	0	10	0†	0†	0†	0†
Income before taxes	Fl 35	Fl 42				
Taxes	10	13				
Net income	Fl 25	Fl 29				
Shares outstanding (000s)	873	873*				
Earnings per share	Fl 28.6	Fl 33.22				
Dividends per share	14.0	16.0				

* Based on sale of Fl 75 million of convertible debentures and Fl 65 million of long-term debt in 1976.
† The amount of interest will depend on the future financing decisions.

Exhibit 6

VERENIGDE MACHINEFABRIEKEN STORK N.V. (A) (Abridged)
INFLUENCE OF THE RATE OF GROWTH OF TURNOVER
ON THE LEVEL OF INVESTED CAPITAL*

Invested capital
(Fl millions)

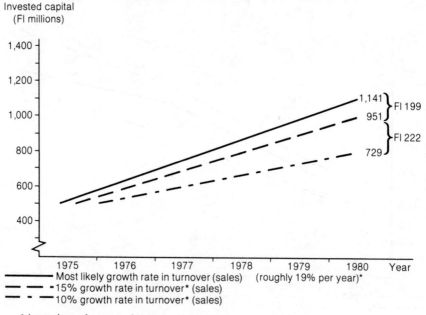

————— Most likely growth rate in turnover (sales)   (roughly 19% per year)*
— — —15% growth rate in turnover* (sales)
— — - 10% growth rate in turnover* (sales)

* Assumed rate of turnover of invested capital is 3.5X.

Exhibit 7

VERENIGDE MACHINEFABRIEKEN STORK N.V. (A) (Abridged)
SOME INFORMATION ON THE DUTCH CAPITAL MARKETS
(Fl in millions)

| | 1973 | 1974 | 1975 | | | | | | | | | | Jan.–Oct. 1975 Total |
			Jan.	Feb.	Mar.	Apr.	May	June	July	Aug.	Sept.	Oct.	
Net security issues	Fl 1,334	Fl 2,221	Fl 312	Fl 715	Fl 134	Fl 188	Fl 611	Fl 208	Fl 446	Fl 446	Fl 87	Fl 416	Fl 3,563
Net share issues	90	74	77	0	7	67	74	44	0	17	30	0	315
Net public loan issues	500	1,134	(50)	621	57	(27)	235	87	268	299	(47)	325	1,768
Net private bond issues	743	1,013	(3)	252	94	70	148	302	81	178	131	104	1,355
Market value of quoted shares	40,678	28,776	34,664	36,010	36,168	37,563	35,591	36,621	37,302	36,832	n.a.	n.a.	36,344*
Total stock exchange turnover	25,660	16,402	2,298	2,265	2,040	2,255	2,171	2,057	1,943	1,735	n.a.	n.a.	16,762
Shares	19,045	10,444	1,480	1,262	1,355	1,312	1,231	1,060	1,023	939	n.a.	n.a.	9,663
Fixed interest securities	6,615	5,959	819	1,003	684	943	939	996	919	795	n.a.	n.a.	7,099

* Average for the eight months.
Source: *Eurostat* (general statistics), various issues.

BIO-TECH, INC.

∧∧

In November 1974, Mr. William Montgomery, vice president of finance of Bio-Tech, Inc., faced two financial decisions. One concerned the amount and timing of investment to be made in new production facilities for the rapidly expanding Laboratory Products Group (LPG). The second concerned a possible sale of Bio-Tech's more slowly growing Consumer Products Group (CPG). An unsolicited offer to buy the group for $25 million had recently been received from General Drug, Inc., a well-known proprietary drug manufacturer. The offer was believed to have been motivated by the latter's desire to make more profitable use of its strong national distribution organization.

The need for an early decision on both matters had fortuitously thrown their analysis into the context of Mr. Montgomery's long-range financial planning. Bio-Tech's internally stated goal was to double sales and income in approximate five-year periods, and long-range planning had come to be accepted as a necessary and valuable activity in furthering that objective. Each product group was expected to review and update its current five-year plan at yearly intervals as part of the company's regular budgeting routine. The plans were then sent to the headquarters' financial staff to be consolidated and reviewed, and it was Mr. Montgomery's responsibility to prepare a matching financial plan for the company as a whole.

The plans which had been submitted for 1975–79 showed that new financing would be required each year in large and ever-growing amounts. The plans did not take account, however, of the questions which only recently had been raised concerning the investment to be made in LPG's production facilities and the possible sale of the Consumer Products Group. Each of these decisions involved amounts which were large enough to cause substantial adjustment of the first estimates of external financing needs and thus, perhaps, of the types of financing to be recommended. In that sense, each decision had a direct bearing on the financial plan which Mr. Montgomery was expected to present to Bio-Tech's president in the coming week.

The company

Bio-Tech began business as the Ferguson Supply Company in 1921 in Bridgeport, Connecticut. Initially, the company specialized in the manufacture and sale of rubber surgical gloves. Business was profitable, and the company soon began to diversify into other fields of medical and laboratory supplies. Product lines were added through acquisitions and, more importantly as time went on, through the development of a respectable in-house research and development capability. In 1958, the firm's name was changed to Bio-Tech to better identify the nature of its business and the fact that internally developed products were beginning to contribute to the rapid development of the fields which the company was supplying. Two years later, the company had its first (and so far its only) public offering of common stock.

In the mid-1960s, Bio-Tech was formally divided into operating divisions or "groups" so that management responsibilities could be more effectively defined in terms of markets served and distribution channels used. Three groups were established: medical products, laboratory products, and consumer products. This organization was continued, and some indication of the variety of products sold by each group in 1974 is indicated by the listings in Exhibit 1. All of the lines together included several thousand individual products.

The product lines which contributed most to Bio-Tech's rapid growth over the past five years had grown out of the research and development (R&D) group's persistent interest in the disposable-item concept. The group was successful in developing new manufacturing and sterilizing and packaging techniques, for example, which permitted plastic to be substituted for many of the staple glass and metal items in use in every laboratory and hospital and doctor's office in the country. Disposable plastic products had the advantage of lower user cost, convenience, and prepackaged sterility.

Research and development had also been supported to make sure that the company's products were not made obsolete by the rapid progress of medical technology. Old products were continuously being replaced by new ones in the industry, and Bio-Tech's officers had little confidence in the protection which patents could provide against innovators and determined imitators. Lead time and efficient manufacturing and skilled marketing were far more important in their view, and Bio-Tech had gained a respected reputation for its capabilities in each field. Financial statements showing Bio-Tech's asset and sales and income growth over the past three years are presented in Exhibits 3 and 4. A ten-year review of selected financial data is shown in Exhibit 2.

The growth of demand for medical and laboratory supplies had created intense competition among established manufacturers in those fields. Many were financially stronger and larger than Bio-Tech. Additional competition had been created by the backward integration of a number of medical distributors and by the entry of aggressive foreign companies into some product fields. Bio-Tech's success, therefore, was probably best measured by the fact that market share had been gained in its principal medical and laboratory products fields. Furthermore, this trend was expected to continue. The operating plans of the Medical and Laboratory Products Groups projected 10% and 12% growth in real terms for the 1975–79 period (19% and 21% in nominal terms with 8% inflation [Exhibit 5]).

Capital expenditures in the Laboratory Products Group

The rapid growth in sales achieved by LPG had exhausted plant capacity in some major product lines (disposable culture dishes, disposable laboratory ware), and a proposal to expand production facilities for those lines had been approved some months earlier, apart from the year's regular budget. Bio-Tech owned a suitable site for the plant in West Haven, Connecticut, and it was anticipated, therefore, that plant construction and equipment installation could be completed in 1975. The planned building was expected to cost $5 million and provide space for projected production requirements through 1979. The specialized machinery needed to provide such production capacity was estimated to cost $10 million. Approval of the project had therefore been viewed as a commitment to spend $15 million in 1975.

The decision to rethink that plan had been prompted by some questioning of the reality of the 8% inflation assumption built into all of the company's investment and purchase planning and some questioning as a result of the wisdom of building excess capacity so far in advance of its probable utilization. Deferral of part of the expenditure would have the further advantage of easing Bio-Tech's immediate financing problem.

Upon additional investigation, LPG's general manager found that the required specialized equipment could be purchased and installed in two steps. The first step would cost a total of $10 million, of which $5 million would be the cost of the building itself, and would provide for projected capacity production needs through 1977. Additional machinery needed to satisfy the projected growth of demand in 1978 and 1979 was estimated to cost $6 million (in 1974 prices). The equipment manufacturers were not willing to speculate on their own products' future price increases, and they were not willing to contract for future equipment sales without fully escalating cost- and profit-covering price contracts. The decision therefore concerned both the timing and amount of future outlays.[1]

In both cases, there was acknowledged risk in building capacity ahead of market growth because the economic life of the equipment was most likely to be set by the pace of product technology not by the physical durability of the equipment. Mr. Montgomery was well aware that the Laboratory Products Group had consistently had more difficulty in predicting future demand than had the company's other two groups.

Sale of the Consumer Products Group

Mr. Montgomery's second decision, as noted, concerned the possible sale of

---

[1] For simplicity, assume that the equipment in both cases would be depreciated by the straight-line method over ten years with no net salvage value at the end of year ten. An investment tax credit of 10% seemed certain to be available for equipment purchased in 1975. Its availability for equipment purchased in 1978 was clearly uncertain, but again for simplicity, assume that the 10% investment tax credit would be available indefinitely for future equipment purchases.

CPG to General Drugs, Inc. The group manufactured and sold such products as reusable and disposable insulin syringes and needles, thermometers, and elastic bandages. Although the sale of CPG had not been under consideration prior to General's offer, Bio-Tech's president was somewhat dissatisfied with CPG's performance in recent years. Unit sales had grown only marginally over the past five years. Disposable products had demonstrated steady sales growth, but that had been offset by falling sales in other product lines. In addition, CPG's profit margin was not only smaller than the margins of the other divisions but also smaller than the margins achieved by firms competing in CPG's product markets.

While the Medical Products and Laboratory Products Groups achieved economies through shared distribution channels, CPG's products were marketed through separate channels. When Mr. Montgomery had questioned CPG's ability to utilize these channels as efficiently as its larger competitors, CPG's general manager had replied that he did not think that his group's marketing was ineffective nor did he believe that it was fair to judge CPG by comparison with the other two divisions which competed in markets characterized by much greater profit and growth potential and much higher risk. CPG's lower margins could be justified by the stability of its operations. Unlike the other groups which depended on a continuous stream of new products, CPG was relatively immune from the effects of an unproductive year or two in R&D. The uncertainty created by increasingly stringent federal standards for new products was also absent in CPG.

The general manager of CPG also believed that the company's internal accounting practices unfairly penalized the operating results of his division. Bio-Tech's research and development activities, costing almost $11 million per year, were centralized in a major facility in Virginia. While CPG clearly benefited from these expenditures, the general manager felt that many of the group's products were by-products of Bio-Tech's basic R&D effort. He questioned the reasonableness of allocating corporate expenditures for R&D to each of the three groups according to their relative sales volume. For CPG, the $2.1 million charge in 1974 was substantial in relation to profits.

Mr. Montgomery believed that General's strategy was to use its excess cash to purchase complementary product lines which could be marketed immediately by General's strong distribution organization. Since CPG seemed to fit that description, Mr. Montgomery had hoped initially to persuade General to raise its $25 million offer. That had proved impossible, however, in the prevailing climate of low stock market price-earnings ratios.

Consideration at the last board meeting of the possible sale of CPG had sparked a spirited discussion. Some board members questioned the liquidation of such a large portion of Bio-Tech. Years of work had been directed toward building the company. Was it now to be dismantled? And what were the action's longer-term policy implications? Other members reopened the question of CPG's role in the future of Bio-Tech. All members expressed concern about the effect of a sale on Bio-Tech's financial statements and stock price. For one thing, it was pointed out that the sale of CPG for $25 million would create a book loss of more than $13.8 million.

Nevertheless, Mr. Montgomery felt that General's offer merited very serious consideration as it would provide funds needed to finance the strong growth of the Medical and Laboratory Products Groups. The meeting was finally closed on the promise that Mr. Montgomery would present his evaluation of the pros and cons of a sale at the next board meeting.

Financing alternatives

Mr. Montgomery and his staff, with the help of the firm's investment banker, had been investigating a variety of financing sources. Unfortunately, the financial markets appeared in November to be in a state of considerable turmoil. The bank prime rate had hit a peak of 12% in late September while AAA corporate bonds appeared to have topped out in early October. On the other hand, Baa corporate rates had not yet shown a downturn. (See Exhibit 10 for graphs of various market rates.) Conditions in the stock market were also confused. As of November, the Standard & Poor's Index of 500 Stocks was down to about 70, which was 35% under its 1972 peak of 109. Although the stock market had risen slightly in November, it was again demonstrating signs of weakness.

In this environment of very tight bank credit, historically high long-term interest rates, lack of market access for low-rated firms, and a depressed stock market, Mr. Montgomery was forced to choose among a limited set of feasible financing options. Although he knew of firms which had been forced out of the market in recent months by unforeseen adverse conditions, his best estimate was that *at the current time* the following financing options would be open to Bio-Tech:

1. Up to $40 million on a two-year bank credit agreement at the prime rate (just lowered to 11% on November 4). The balance outstanding at the end of two years then would become payable in full at the end of the third year. This option would require: (a) a compensating balance of 10% of the line; (b) a minimum current ratio of 2.0; (c) a minimum working capital position (current assets less current liabilities) of $80 million; (d) a maximum ratio of total debt (short- and long-term) to net worth of 0.5; and (e) a limit on cumulative post-1974 dividends to 25% of cumulative post-1974 profit after taxes (excluding any loss on sale of CPG).

2. A $30 million to $60 million issue of 25-year debentures at a coupon rate of 9.5%, noncallable except for sinking fund purposes for 10 years, with fully amortizing sinking fund payments running from the 6th through the 25th year. Restrictions would be the same as under the bank credit agreement, with minor variations.

3. A $30 million to $45 million common stock issue at an estimated price

of $30 per share with net proceeds to the company of $27 per share (current stock price, $32).

In addition to the three above, Mr. Montgomery had considered the possibility of a convertible debenture. However, a quick investigation revealed almost no market for such securities as of late 1974. Furthermore, he was interested in the financing terms he might be able to obtain on one or more of the financing options in subsequent years. Although no one could forecast the exact terms in the future, he did have some assurance at least that these three options would be available to Bio-Tech in a future round of financing in 1976.

Bio-Tech's last major long-term financing had taken place in 1968. In that year the company had sold $45 million of 15-year 6% debentures to a group of three insurance companies. Sinking fund payments of $5 million per year were scheduled to begin in 1975 (Exhibit 7). The company's only other financing arrangement of importance was a $15 million line of credit with its banks. The line had not been drawn upon until mid-1974, when $12.3 million was taken down to finance increased working capital requirements. That amount remained outstanding in November (Exhibit 4).

Any final financing plan would have to be consistent with management's strong concern over its year-to-year pattern of earnings per share. The family of one of the company's founders was intent on selling a substantial portion of its holdings, and a strong stock price would be an important facilitating condition.

*   *   *   *   *

The material which Mr. Montgomery had obtained from his staff for use in preparing his report included the following:

Exhibits 1–4: Bio-Tech's financial statements for recent years.
Exhibit 5:   Past and projected financial data, by groups.
Exhibits 6–7: Projected financial statements for Bio-Tech—including Consumer Products Group
Exhibit 8:   Consumer Products Group's assets.
Exhibit 9:   Information on other medical products companies.
Exhibit 10:   Interest rates—charts.
Appendix: Research report—outlook for medical products industry

Exhibit 1

BIO-TECH, INC.
COMPANY PRODUCTS

Medical Products Group. Reusable and disposable hypodermic syringes and needles, blood collecting equipment, surgical blades, plastic medical tubing, medical examination gloves, diagnostic instruments, electronic thermometers, inhalation-therapy and anesthesia products.

Laboratory Products Group. Bacteriological culture media, antimicrobial sensitivity discs, tissue culture media and plastic laboratory ware, syphilis and brucellosis detection kits, injectable diagnostics, disposable pipettes, blood typing sera, cross-matching reagents, blood cell reagents.

Consumer Products Group. Reusable and disposable insulin syringes and needles, thermometers, elastic bandages, household and recreational gloves, athletic training-room supplies.

Exhibit 2

BIO-TECH, INC.
TEN-YEAR FINANCIAL REVIEW

	1965	1966	1967	1968	1969	1970	1971	1972	1973	1974 (Est.)	Nov. 22, 1974
Sales ($ millions)	80.9	99.0	110.8	122.8	145.3	157.7	172.8	192.7	228.8	275.4	
Net income ($ millions)	5.3	7.2	8.1	9.2	10.9	11.7	11.1	12.8	16.5	18.1	
Earnings per share ($)	.69	.88	.97	1.09	1.27	1.39	1.31	1.52	1.95	2.13	
Dividends per share ($)	.13	.20	.27	.27	.33	.40	.40	.40	.47	.47	
Market price of common stock ($)											
High	23	35	53	60	69	78	62	65	57	62	32
Low	13	21	31	48	53	44	44	35	41	26	15
Midpoint	18	28	42	54	61	61	53	50	49	44	
Midpoint P/E	26	32	43	50	48	44	40	33	25	21	

Exhibit 3

BIO-TECH, INC.
INCOME STATEMENTS FOR YEARS 1971–1974
($ thousands except per share data)

	1971	1972	1973	1974 (Est.)
Net sales	$172,803	$192,665	$228,781	$275,437
Cost of sales	98,225	108,939	127,118	159,613
Selling, general, administrative	43,375	48,324	57,444	66,266
Research and development expense	6,438	7,549	8,902	10,857
Interest expense	2,700	2,700	2,700	3,317
Other	754	502	812	563
Income before taxes	$21,311	$24,651	$31,805	$34,821
Federal income taxes	10,229	11,832	15,266	16,714
Net income after tax	$11,082	$12,819	$16,539	$18,107
Common dividends	$ 3,380	$3,384	$3,961	$3,965
Addition to retained earnings	7,702	9,435	12,578	14,142
Common shares outstanding (000s)	8,447	8,457	8,488	8,492
Earnings per share	$ 1.31	$ 1.52	$ 1.95	$ 2.13
Dividends per share	$ .40	$ .40	$ .47	$ .47
Capital expenditures	$10,782	$ 9,598	$16,801	$25,455
Depreciation	5,219	6,853	7,915	8,774

Exhibit 4

BIO-TECH, INC.
BALANCE SHEETS AS OF DECEMBER 31
($ thousands)

	1972	1973	1974 (Est.)
ASSETS			
Cash and marketable securities	$ 32,212	$ 18,935	$ 3,251
Accounts receivable	30,892	39,117	50,019
Inventory	44,376	58,545	78,730
Other	4,551	4,476	4,091
Total current assets	$112,031	$121,073	$136,091
Net fixed assets	59,835	68,721	85,402
Other	3,980	3,176	2,561
Total assets	$175,846	$192,970	$224,054
LIABILITIES AND NET WORTH			
Bank loans	$ 0	$ 0	$ 12,258
Accounts payable	12,698	15,114	17,525
Accrued expenses	9,651	11,445	13,678
Current maturities, long-term debt	0	0	5,000
Total current liabilities	$ 22,349	$ 26,559	$ 48,461
Long-term debt	45,000	45,000	40,000
Net worth	108,497	121,411	135,593
Total liabilities and net worth	$175,846	$192,970	$224,054

Exhibit 5

BIO-TECH, INC.
SELECTED FINANCIAL DATA BY GROUPS
($ millions)

SALES AND PROFIT PERFORMANCE:

	1971	1972	1973	1974
Medical Products Group				
Sales	$ 92.7	$102.1	$122.3	$148.5
EBIT*	15.5	17.1	21.3	24.0
EBIT as a percentage of sales	16.7%	16.8%	17.4%	16.2%
Laboratory Products Group				
Sales	$ 39.8	$ 46.6	$ 57.3	$ 73.3
EBIT*	4.6	5.8	8.1	9.0
EBIT as a percentage of sales	11.7%	12.4%	14.1%	12.3%
Consumer Products Group				
Sales	$ 40.3	$ 44.0	$ 49.2	$ 53.6
EBIT*	3.9	4.4	5.1	5.1
EBIT as a percentage of sales	9.6%	10.1%	10.4%	9.5%

FIVE-YEAR PLAN PROJECTIONS:†

	1975	1976	1977	1978	1979
Medical Products Group					
Sales	$176.5	$209.6	$249.0	$295.8	$351.4
EBIT (.17 × sales)*	30.0	35.6	42.3	50.3	59.8
Capital expenditures	8.6	17.0	12.0	17.0	15.6
Depreciation	5.7	5.8	6.6	6.9	7.6
Investment in working capital	13.0	10.8	14.5	16.7	21.6
Laboratory Products Group‡					
Sales	$ 88.7	$107.2	$129.7	$156.9	$189.8
EBIT (.13 × sales)*	11.5	13.9	16.9	20.4	24.7
Capital expenditures	16.0	10.7	9.0	14.0	12.7
Depreciation	3.1	3.6	4.7	5.2	6.3
Investment in working capital	7.8	7.8	8.0	8.9	10.5
Consumer Products Group					
Sales	$ 59.0	$ 65.0	$ 71.7	$ 78.9	$ 87.0
EBIT (.10 × sales)*	5.9	6.5	7.2	7.9	8.7
Capital expenditures	0.7	1.0	1.5	2.0	2.7
Depreciation	1.4	1.7	2.1	2.5	3.1
Investment in working capital	2.5	2.7	3.0	3.4	3.7

* After allocation of total corporate research and development expenditures to each of the three groups according to sales volume.
† Assumes annual inflation rate of 8%.
‡ Projected capital expenditures for the group assume that the estimated $15 million expenditures for the West Haven plant are made in 1975.

Exhibit 6

BIO-TECH, INC.

PRO FORMA INCOME STATEMENTS FOR BIO-TECH 1975–1979,
ASSUMING CONSUMER PRODUCTS GROUP IS RETAINED
($ millions)

	1974	1975	1976	1977	1978	1979
Sales.	$275.4	$324.1	$381.8	$450.4	$531.6	$628.2
EBIT.	$ 38.1	$ 47.4	$ 56.0	$ 66.4	$ 78.6	$ 93.2
Interest expense*.	3.3	3.6	3.3	3.0	2.7	2.4
Income before taxes.	$ 34.8	$ 43.8	$ 52.7	$ 63.4	$ 75.9	$ 90.8
Net income after tax.	18.1	22.8	27.4	33.0	39.5	47.2
Dividends (.25 × net income). . . .	$ 4.0	$ 5.7	$ 6.8	$ 8.2	$ 9.9	$ 11.8
Addition to retained earnings.	14.1	17.1	20.6	24.8	29.6	35.4

*Does not include the interest expense on any new debt issues.

Exhibit 7

BIO-TECH, INC.

PRO FORMA BALANCE SHEETS, 1975–1979,
ASSUMING CONSUMER PRODUCTS GROUP IS RETAINED
($ millions)

	1974	1975	1976	1977	1978	1979
ASSETS						
Cash and marketable securities. . . .	$ 3.3	$ 3.3	$ 3.3	$ 3.3	$ 3.3	$ 3.3
Accounts receivable and inventory (.48 × change in sales).	128.7	155.6	183.2	216.2	255.2	301.6
Other.	4.1	5.0	5.0	5.0	5.0	5.0
Total current assets.	$136.1	$163.9	$191.5	$224.5	$263.5	$309.9
Net fixed assets*.	85.4	100.5	118.1	127.2	145.6	159.6
Other.	2.6	3.0	3.0	3.0	3.0	3.0
Total assets.	$224.1	$267.4	$312.6	$354.7	$412.1	$472.5
LIABILITIES AND NET WORTH						
Bank debt.	$ 12.3	$ 12.3	$ 12.3	$ 12.3	$ 12.3	$ 12.3
Accounts payable and accrued expenses (.11 × change in sales).	31.2	35.7	42.0	49.5	58.5	69.1
Current portion, long-term debt. . .	5.0	5.0	5.0	5.0	5.0	5.0
Total current liabilities.	$ 48.5	$ 53.0	$ 59.3	$ 66.8	$ 75.8	$ 86.4
Long-term debt.	40.0	35.0	30.0	25.0	20.0	15.0
Net worth.	135.6	152.7	173.3	198.1	227.7	263.1
External financing required.	0	26.7	50.0	64.8	88.6	108.0
Total liabilities and net worth.	$224.1	$267.4	$312.6	$354.7	$412.1	$472.5

*Assumes that the estimated $15 million expenditures for the West Haven plant are made in 1975.

Exhibit 8

BIO-TECH, INC.
ASSET POSITION, CONSUMER PRODUCTS GROUP
($ thousands)

ASSETS

Cash*	$ 0
Net working capital†	24,136
Other	1,000
Total	$25,136
Net fixed assets	12,800
Other	800
Total assets (net)	$38,736

*Bio-Tech employs a centralized cash-management system administered by corporate headquarters.

† Consists of:

Accounts receivable	$12,486
Inventory	17,547
Accounts payable	3,217
Accrued expenses	2,680

Exhibit 9

BIO-TECH, INC.
INFORMATION ON SELECTED MEDICAL PRODUCTS COMPANIES

	Abbott Labs				American Hospital Supply				Baxter Labs			
	1970	1971	1972	1973	1970	1971	1972	1973	1970	1971	1972	1973
Sales ($ millions)	457	458	521	620	510	576	688	829	187	242	278	355
Earnings per share ($)	2.92	1.71	2.88	3.35	.76	.85	.99	1.13	.52	.68	.77	.95
Dividends per share ($)	1.10	1.10	1.10	1.20	.24	.26	.27	.28	.10	.11	.13	.15
Average market price/EPS	23	41	26	19	48	41	47	39	52	48	60	54
Common stock price range ($)												
High	78	85	88	80	47	40	55	52	35	39	56	61
Low	56	54	64	47	26	30	37	36	19	25	35	41
Beta (1973 year-end estimate)				.92				1.26				1.10
Aftertax return on equity	15.5%	8.7%	13.4%	14.1%	9.0%	9.4%	10.1%	10.7%	11.8%	11.4%	11.5%	12.4%
Capitalization ($ thousands)												
Short debt	40,577	19,248	32,852	93,216	5,037	9,491	7,785	24,335	9,597	8,177	23,650	40,490
Long debt	47,169	90,244	91,693	98,825	17,610	14,916	14,114	18,893	95,802	148,726	147,992	186,609
Equity	258,842	267,521	293,396	325,807	286,234	307,320	335,735	372,157	121,333	168,252	193,374	224,771
Bond ratings (1973)	Debentures Aa				Not available				Conv. subord. debs. Ba			
Interest coverage	12.3	4.8	7.4	6.0	41.2	41.0	48.6	27.4	5.8	5.8	7.2	6.4
Shares outstanding (1973)	13,625,275				35,302,493				29,350,000			

	Becton-Dickinson				Johnson & Johnson				Bio-Tech			
	1970	1971	1972	1973	1970	1971	1972	1973	1970	1971	1972	1973
Sales ($ millions)	222	255	289	340	1,002	1,140	1,317	1,611	158	173	193	229
Earnings per share ($)	1.08	1.03	1.24	1.45	1.51	1.82	2.15	2.59	1.39	1.31	1.52	1.95
Dividends per share ($)	.30	.30	.30	.35	.34	.43	.45	.52	.40	.40	.40	.47
Average market price/EPS	42	35	34	26	32	43	53	45	44	40	33	25
Common stock price range ($)												
High	62	47	50	45	60	100	133	132	78	62	65	57
Low	27	25	33	33	37	56	94	101	44	44	35	41
Beta (1973 year-end estimates)				1.39				.94				1.28
Aftertax return on equity	13.1%	11.3%	12.6%	13.1%	15.7%	16.4%	16.5%	16.2%	12.9%	11.2%	11.9%	13.6%
Capitalization ($ thousands)												
Short debt	1,603	6,168	6,002	15,239	0	0	0	15,339	0	0	0	17,258
Long debt	77,715	78,463	81,100	76,464	25,494	20,153	31,475	40,569	45,000	45,000	45,000	40,000
Equity	133,024	145,788	165,732	186,558	533,829	622,324	732,878	868,372	91,360	99,062	108,497	121,411
Bond ratings (1973)	Conv. subord. debs. Baa				Not rated				Not rated			
Interest coverage	10.0	7.8	9.1	10.2	102.2	74.7	75.6	53.0	8.4	8.9	10.1	12.8
Shares outstanding (1973)	16,014,052				57,523,443				8,492,000			

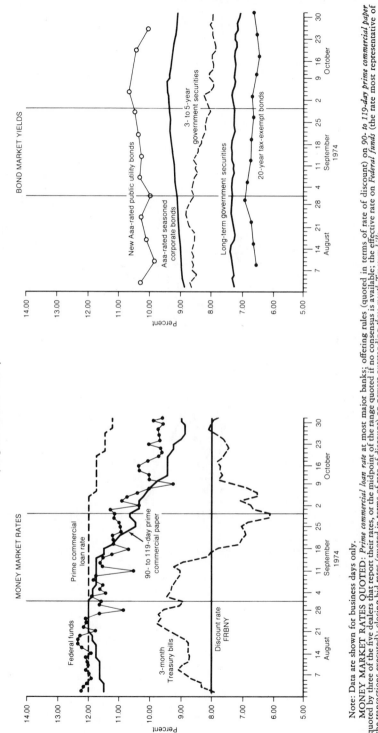

Exhibit 10

BIO-TECH, INC.
SELECTED INTEREST RATES,
(August–October 1974)

Note: Data are shown for business days only.

MONEY MARKET RATES QUOTED: *Prime commercial loan rate* at most major banks; offering rules (quoted in terms of rate of discount) on *90- to 119-day prime commercial paper* quoted by three of the five dealers that report their rates, or the midpoint of the range quoted if no consensus is available; the effective rate on *Federal funds* (the rate most representative of the transactions executed); closing bid rates (quoted in terms of rate of discount) on newest outstanding *three-month Treasury bills.*

BOND MARKET YIELDS QUOTED: Yields on *new Aaa-rated public utility bonds* are based on prices asked by underwriting syndicates, adjusted to make them equivalent to a standard Aaa-rated bond of at least twenty years' maturity; daily averages of yields on *seasoned Aaa-rated corporate bonds;* daily averages of yields on *long-term Government securities* (bonds due or callable in ten years or more) and on *Government securities due in three to five years,* computed on the basis of closing bid prices; Thursday averages of yields on twenty seasoned *twenty-year tax-exempt bonds* (carrying Moody's ratings of Aaa, Aa, A, and Baa).

Sources: Federal Reserve Bank of New York, Board of Governors of the Federal Reserve System, Moody's Investors Service, Inc., and The Bond Buyer.

Exhibit 10—Continued

SELECTED INTEREST RATES

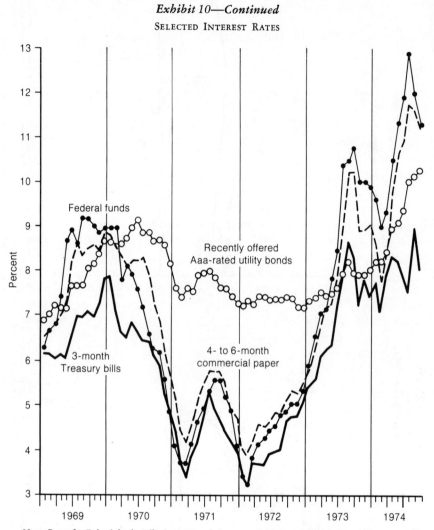

Note: Rates for Federal funds (effective rate) and three-month Treasury bills (market yield) are monthly averages of daily figures. Yields on recently offered Aaa-rated utility and four- to six-month commercial paper are monthly averages of weekly figures.

Source: Board of Governors of the Federal Reserve System.

APPENDIX

OUTLOOK FOR THE MEDICAL PRODUCTS INDUSTRY; RESEARCH UPDATE

by

Grim, Turcotte, Rotz and Shoemaker, Inc.

The recent reports from some firms in the medical products industry that orders have slowed recently do not call for a revision of our optimistic outlook for the industry over the next five years. We expect a very modest slowdown in sales growth for 1975. This is primarily, due to cash-short hospitals attempting to cut back inventories to the lowest possible levels. Hospital admissions continue their increase in 1975; the problem is not a shortage of patients but their ability to pay their bills. The proposal, now being considered in the U.S. Senate, to appropriate funds to continue expiring health care benefits for laid-off workers should help ameliorate some of the potential cash flow crises.

Earnings prospects for the medical products industry are excellent. We continue to project an average growth in earnings of 15% for the next five years—which compares favorably with the average growth rate of 12% experienced by the industry in the 1965 to 1974 period. Continued strength in overseas earnings will contribute to this growth, as will continued extensions of private and public insurance programs in the United States, especially Medicare and Medicaid.

Table 1 (below) presents the five year earnings outlook for the five major medical products companies which were reviewed in our research report of last month.

Table 1

MEDICAL PRODUCTS INDUSTRY OUTLOOK

Company	Projected 1975–1980 EPS Growth Rate	Actual 1965–1974 EPS Growth Rate	Recent P/E Ratio
American Hospital Supply	14.0%	15.5%	19
Abbott Laboratories	13.5	9.0	12
Baxter Laboratories	19.0	19.0	24
Becton-Dickinson	13.5	14.5	16
Johnson & Johnson	15.5	20.5	28
Industry average	15.1%	12.1%	20

CHRYSLER U.K. (A)

∧∧∧

John Riccardo, the newly appointed chairman of the board of Chrysler Corporation, was preparing for his first board of directors meeting in October 1975. Foremost on the list of topics for the meeting was the deteriorating situation of Chrysler's subsidiary in the United Kingdom. Riccardo had visited the U.K. government several times to discuss Chrysler's position in that country. The seriousness of the situation now called for action. Riccardo had recently reviewed a major plan to revitalize Chrysler U.K., but the investment needed would be enormous. Furthermore, it was clear that Chrysler U.K. would continue to lose a substantial amount in 1975 and that additional finance would not be available from British banks. The situation in the United Kingdom was aggravated by the poor operating performance of Chrysler worldwide. Consolidated losses of Chrysler Corporation amounting to $232 million in the first nine months of 1975 would be announced in three days, and Riccardo was under pressure to halt the bleeding.

History of Chrysler U.K.

Chrysler experienced serious problems in the United States between 1958 and 1962. Its share of U.S. automobile production fell from 20% in 1957 to a low of just over 10% in 1962. The corporation's profitability suffered substantially and was less than half that of its two main competitors, General Motors and Ford Motor Company. The responsibility of planning Chrysler's recovery fell to Lynn Townsend, who was appointed president in 1961. Townsend pursued a development package based on aggressive marketing in the United States and the expansion of Chrysler in Europe.

The European expansion required the choice of either establishing a new plant and facilities as part of a program of designing and manufacturing vehicles for the Western European market or, alternatively, pursuing the more immediate policy of purchasing an existing producer. At the time, Chrysler's only manufacturing investments in Europe were represented by a minority interest in Simca in France and a small-scale commercial vehicle operation in the United Kingdom.

Chrysler decided that the expense and delay of constructing a new manufacturing plant and distribution system were too great and, therefore, chose a strategy of entry by acquisition. Its first moves were to gain majority control of Simca and to purchase 40% interest in Barreiros Diesel S.A., a Spanish vehicle manufacturer. (Chrysler increased its ownership to 77% in 1967.) It then turned its attention to the United Kingdom market.

In August 1964, Chrysler established a manufacturing foothold in the United Kingdom by acquiring a majority holding in Rootes Motors Limited. Rootes was available possibly due to its poor financial performance. During 1955–63, Rootes was at the lower end of the United Kingdom's "big five" automobile manufacturers. The formation and consolidation of British Motors Corporation (BMC) and the expansion of Ford in the United Kingdom had made BMC and Ford the two dominant influences in the U.K. market. Management at Rootes had been concerned as to whether their company could compete effectively and profitably in the 1960s.

Chrysler U.K.'s share of total U.K. car production fared well during the 1966–73 period as the result of a substantial increase in exports:

U.K. PRODUCTION OF CARS
(In thousands of units)

	1966	1967	1968	1969	1970	1971	1972	1973	1974
Total U.K. industry production....	1,604	1,552	1,816	1,717	1,641	1,742	1,921	1,747	1,534
Total U.K. production by Chrysler U.K...	174	181	187	213	217	282	264	265	262
For home market......	123	132	121	82	117	138	165	153	118
For export.....	51	49	66	131	100	143	99	112	144
Percent of industry total	10.8%	11.7%	10.3%	12.4%	13.2%	16.2%	13.7%	15.2%	17.1%

Chrysler U.K.'s primary sources of export sales were non-European markets. The company had an important contract with Iran to supply completely knocked-down cars (CKDs) for assembly in Iran by one of Iran's largest privately owned companies, Iran National Industrial Manufacturing Company (INIM). A plant designed by Rootes engineers for the assembly and progressive manufacture of Rootes cars had been opened in Teheran in 1967. The new contract for the supply of CKDs was signed by Chrysler U.K. and Iran in 1970. In 1974, Chrysler U.K. delivered 78,000 CKDs to the assembly plant in Teheran, and 125,000 CKDs were forecast for 1975. This accounted for a very large part of the company's estimated net exports of $300 million in 1975.

However, within the U.K. market, Chrysler U.K. had suffered from a narrow model range, a shortage of new models, lack of economies of scale, and, in 1974–75, a general recession in the European automobile industry.

Chrysler U.K. produced a narrow model range consisting of only three basic models.[1] British Leyland produced 18 basic models; Ford produced 6; and

---

[1] Chrysler U.K. supplemented its line with Simca models, selling 20,000 to 30,000 Simcas a year in the United Kingdom.

Vauxhall produced 5. Of the three basic models, the Imp was introduced in 1963, the Hunter in 1967, and the Avenger in 1970. Chrysler's share of the U.K. market suffered as a result:

U.K. MARKET PENETRATION
(In thousands of units)

	1965	1966	1967	1968	1969	1970	1971	1972	1973	1974
Total new industry registrations	1,099	1,048	1,110	1,104	965	1,077	1,286	1,638	1,661	1,269
Chrysler new registrations	131	123	135	113	93	113	135	154	159	114
Percent of industry	12%	12%	12%	10%	10%	11%	11%	9%	10%	9%

Chrysler U.K. also found itself in a difficult labor situation along with the other domestic U.K. auto manufacturers. The company had to negotiate with 53 separate unions every year and each union often tried to outdo the others in their negotiations. A long history of disagreement between workers and management throughout the industry had led to a serious lack of faith between the two sides. Workers at Chrysler U.K. were especially nervous about the company's aging product line and their own future with the company. Over-manning and a slow average work-pace in the British automobile industry as a whole resulted in a low output per worker in relation to continental European plants. Lower wages in Britain did not make up for the lower productivity per worker.

Chrysler had also failed to gain the economies of scale which were important in automobile manufacturing. One industry expert estimated that the minimum efficient size for various levels of car manufacturing would be as follows:

MINIMUM EFFICIENT SIZE
(Identical units per plant per year)

Final assembly.................... 250–300,000 units/year
Engine and transmission
  machining and assembly.......... 500,000 units/year
Casting of engine block............ 100,000 units/year

There were also scale requirements in design and die-making. Export sales had helped Chrysler increase production and reduce per unit costs. Nonetheless the company was not producing enough cars to fully benefit from economies of scale.

The combination of low market share, difficult labor conditions, and an inability to secure scale economies had resulted in an erratic financial performance for Chrysler U.K., culminating in a sharp deterioration during the recent industrywide recession. In the ten years between 1966 and mid-1975, Chrysler U.K. incurred losses in poor years aggregating £ 58 million, while in good years profits only totaled £ 10 million. Even in 1973, the British car market's last boom year, Chrysler could only manage a pretax profit of £ 3.1 million. The performance of Chrysler U.K. was significantly worse than that of almost all of its major European or Japanese competitors in the areas of return on shareholders' funds, return on capital invested, and return on trading assets.

The 1974–1975 recession

Chrysler U.K. was not alone in its difficulties. Europe's auto industry for the past 18 months had been floundering through its worst setback in three decades. A number of large manufacturers were producing at little more than half of their capacity as they struggled to unload a glut of completed new cars. It seemed likely that the industry would build only about 7.2 million autos in 1975, 36% fewer than the 11.3 million it turned out in 1973, when production was at an all-time high.

The deepening worldwide recession was the main reason for the automobile producers' troubles, but several special pressures complicated and increased the difficulties for European countries. Job security was paramount in the minds of European workers, union officials, and governments. Mass layoffs were regarded as politically impossible, and auto makers had been forced to resort to three-day weeks and other inefficient forms of "short-time" work schedules in an effort to pace output to match their shrinking sales. Work forces could be only slightly reduced, and pay increases had pushed up total labor costs for some companies even though production had declined.

By the beginning of 1975, having curtailed production too little and too late, the manufacturers had filled lots with some 1.7 million unsold cars costing an estimated half a million dollars a day to finance. Only five of the 14 major auto companies reported substantial profits in 1974, while at least six suffered large losses. The industry's net loss exceeded $500 million and 1975 seemed likely to be worse.

U.K. car manufacturers were hit by both a sharp contraction in the passenger car market and severe foreign competition. New registrations fell 28% between 1973 and 1975.

DEVELOPMENT OF PASSENGER CAR DEMANDS IN THE UNITED KINGDOM

Year	(000s cars)	Year	(000s cars)
1966	1,048	1972	1,638
1968	1,104	1973	1,662
1970	1,077	1974	1,269
1971	1,286	1975	1,194

Equally serious was the increase in imports' share of the U.K. market from 6% in 1966 to 24% in 1972 and 33% in 1975. The trend toward imports had been aided by Britain's entry into the Common Market in 1973 and the resultant gradual reduction in tariff barriers between member countries. It also reflected the unbalanced product ranges of U.K. manufacturers and poor records of quality, reliability, and delivery. Manufacturing costs in the United Kingdom were also higher than those of other countries, and a growing number of consumers felt that British manufacturers provided less car for the money than that of imports.

IMPORTS SHARE OF MARKET IN THE UNITED KINGDOM
(Percent of total new registrations)

	1966	1968	1970	1971	1972	1973	1974	1975
All imports	6	8	14	19	24	27	28	33
Chrysler France			.7	1.9	2.0	1.9	1.9	1.4

The situation at Chrysler U.K. deteriorated substantially during 1974 and the first nine months of 1975. (See Exhibit 1.) The company's share of market declined from 10% in 1973 to 9% in 1974 and only 6.6% in August–September 1975. United Kingdom registrations of Chrysler fell from 159,000 in 1973 to an estimated 80,000 to 90,000 for all of 1975. Some of the U.K. sales decline was offset by an increase in export sales. Nevertheless, total production was forecast to decline from 265,000 in 1973 to approximately 225,000 to 235,000 in 1975. The company's pretax losses were $41 million in 1974 and an additional $35 million in the first six months of 1975.

Chrysler U.K.'s performance during the two years had also suffered considerably from labor disputes. In 1974 and at the rate of travel in 1975, a total of 1,640,609 man-hours was lost as a result of internal disputes within Chrysler U.K. operations (excluding commercial vehicle operations). This was equivalent to a total vehicle loss of 47,929.

The outlook for U.K. automobile manufacturers

As of 1975, the outlook for the automobile industry in the United Kingdom and Western Europe was fairly uncertain. There was substantial uncertainty concerning new-car registrations in Western Europe. Various sources estimated that new-car registrations would fall somewhere in the range of 9.6 to 13.0 million in 1980 and 11.5 to 14.7 million in 1985, compared to 9.8 million in 1973 and 8.0 in 1974. (See Exhibit 2.) Forecasts for new-car registrations in the United Kingdom varied widely as well. (See Exhibit 3.) Major car manufacturers in Western Europe had all suffered overcapacity in 1974. (See Exhibit 4.) Although 1975 was thought to be the bottom of the slump, overcapacity within the industry was expected to continue to be a major problem.

The United Kingdom, as well as the rest of Western Europe, was almost certain to come under more competitive pressure from imports from Eastern Europe and Japan.[2] Japan was currently making 45% of its car sales in the North American market but was coming under more pressure as the U.S. domestic car industry began to compete directly with the Japanese imports by launching a series of new, subcompact cars. In the last few years, Japan had been expanding in Western Europe. During the first six months of 1975, Japanese imports accounted for 9.3% of the U.K. market.

[2] Iran, Turkey, and South America were developing automobile industries and could be a longer-term threat.

Western Europe's automobile exports were also threatened. In 1974, European imports accounted for 15% of the U.S. market, or 1.37 million cars. European exports to the United States, however, were coming under the same pressure as the Japanese imports. Also, European exports to developing nations would likely decrease as these nations established or expanded their own car industries.

Without a change in cost structure, the U.K. automobile industry faced substantial losses through 1980, as the chart below depicts.

U.K. MOTOR INDUSTRY COMPOSITE BREAK-EVEN CHART

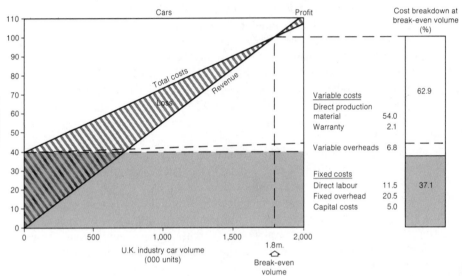

Source: Central Policy Review Staff, *The Future of the British Car Industry* (London: Her Majesty's Stationery Office, 1975).

Only the most optimistic sources believed that the break-even level of 1.8 million cars could be reached by the year 1980. (See Exhibit 5.)

Outlook for Chrysler U.K.

Despite Chrysler U.K.'s performance over the past several years, management believed that the company still had several things going for it. Chrysler U.K. had a strong distribution network of 700 dealers in the United Kingdom; and a very successful new model, the Alpine, manufactured by Chrysler France, had been named "European Car of the Year." It was scheduled for introduction in the United Kingdom in 1976. Also, Chrysler had a large number of owners of Chrysler products in the United Kingdom. Assuming successful development of new models, these owners represented an important source of repeat business.

Chrysler U.K.'s contract with Iran was also an advantage for the company. Chrysler U.K. had sold 46,000 CKD kits to Iran in 1973, 78,000 in 1974, and projected 125,000 in 1975. At the end of 1975, 50,000 kits were projected either in transit or in stock in Iran for use in 1976. Therefore, Chrysler U.K. was only planning to ship 70,000 kits in 1976. Shipments were expected to increase to 220,000 kits in 1977, however. Some forecasts predicted that Chrysler U.K. would be shipping as many as 500,000 CKD kits by 1980, but there was considerable uncertainty attached to these estimates.[3] The Iranian market was expanding rapidly, and INIM, which produced two thirds of all passenger cars in Iran, had an overwhelming market advantage in terms of price, spare parts, and dealerships. However, it was difficult to predict how much Iranian domestic content would increase as a percentage of the total kit. There would also be competition from Renault, Peugeot, Toyota, and Volkswagen, all of which were believed to be planning to build assembly plants in Iran. Fortunately for Chrysler, there was a strong, mutual dependence, in terms of engineering and capital equipment, between plants assembling CKD vehicles and the supplier of their CKD kits. Chrysler U.K. was also providing INIM with technical assistance in the form of product planning, engineering skills, and detailed model improvement and modernization. The earliest that the INIM contract could be terminated was May 1981. A shift to a supplier other than Chrysler would create major difficulties for INIM.

Management at Chrysler U.K. planned to improve profits by three means: (1) the introduction of new car models, (2) greater integration with Chrysler France, and (3) the rationalization of plant operations.

Chrysler U.K. considered the introduction of new models to be necessary for increasing sales and market share. In order to offer a competitive product range, Chrysler U.K. needed to accurately assess future market requirements. It was critical that the assessment be accurate for two reasons. First, the investment in new dies, special tools, and machines was large. It could require additional cash of about $150 million over the next few years to introduce a range of new models to provide a strong, competitive product lineup. Second, the time required to develop a new model was also great. Management needed to decide upon a model concept and specifications four to five years before the consumer saw the car. The appearance of the vehicle could not be significantly altered once production of the dies for the pressing had begun (i.e., perhaps two years before the first vehicle was produced).

As a second means of improving profitability, Chrysler U.K. was planning to integrate its manufacturing and assembly operations with the Chrysler operations on the Continent.[4] Ford and General Motors had already integrated car production between their British and continental subsidiaries. At the moment, there was a limited amount of integration between the two Chrysler U.K. and Chrysler France operations, resulting in low-volume production and high unit costs. The Chrysler companies in France and Spain had been largely integrated,

---

[3] The INIM had announced its intention to increase production.

[4] Chrysler had seven plants in France. The cumulative four-year sales for Chrysler France (1971–74) were FF16.2 billion with a cumulative net profit of FF354 million. In the third quarter of 1975, the FF exchange rate equaled $0.22.

but there was clearly opportunity to improve Chrysler's entire European operations by integrating Chrysler U.K. with Chrysler's operations in France and thereby securing scale economies in design, manufacturing, and marketing. Vehicle production for the two subsidiaries, including both private and commercial vehicles, in 1973 amounted to 569,962 vehicles in France and 319,308 in the United Kingdom. It would also allow more efficient utilization of capacity by allowing a product manufactured in one country to be sold in a second. For example, the French subsidiary was rapidly approaching full capacity operations and would need additional plant and equipment in 1976 based on market forecasts. Integration of operations would allow it to use U.K. capacity, if available.

In order to take advantage of scale economies in Europe, Chrysler would need car designs which provided sufficient variety for consumers but with a minimum number of different component parts. Chrysler could then use common parts and engines in many different models.

By 1979, Chrysler U.K.'s product line was to consist of only models made on a European-wide basis. By concentrating on four basic models and perhaps only three engines, Chrysler Europe could achieve efficient low-cost production runs.[5] Although Chrysler was likely to remain the smallest of the European automobile mass producers, its integration and rationalization would offset some of its size disadvantages.

If Chrysler U.K. continued to operate, it would need to integrate with Chrysler France and to rationalize its own plants within Britain, resulting in the laying off of 8,000 workers. (See Exhibit 6.) Chrysler U.K. would also have to sustain heavy losses in 1976 and 1977 while accomplishing the change. By 1978, Chrysler U.K.'s sales and market share were expected to have increased enough to render the company profitable.

The financing of the Chrysler program

In addition to the long-term financing requirements, the company was likely to need $25 million to $35 million on hand to finance the early stages of any possible future downturns when lags in cutting back production resulted in inventory accumulation. However, in light of Chrysler U.K.'s poor operating results in 1974 and 1975 and its forecast for even poorer results in 1976, management believed that the company could not raise the funds it needed on its own. All of Chrysler U.K.'s bank debt was already guaranteed by the parent company. Furthermore, Chrysler Corporation had found it necessary to invest additional funds of its own into its U.K. subsidiary to meet the worsening situation of the last two years (i.e., $12 million in December 1974; $13 million in January 1975; and $13 million in February 1975). This investment had been against Chrysler Corporation's philosophy that after initial equity funds from the parent, a subsidiary should be self-financing.

---

[5] Individual firms with annual production below 750,000 vehicles could not adequately make use of economies of scale.

Chrysler U.K. had tried to secure a $75 million loan from Finance for Industry, but its effort had been unproductive.[6] Banks in London were also unwilling to supply additional finance to Chrysler U.K., reflecting concern over the weak Chrysler U.K. balance sheet on September 30, 1975 and the subsidiary's poor profitability. (See Exhibit 7.) The company was forced to rely on the loans from Chrysler Corporation plus U.S. and Canadian bank financing which was almost entirely utilized throughout all of 1975.

Chrysler Corporation had substantial problems of its own. (See Exhibit 8 for Chrysler Corporation's financial performance, 1968–74.) Chrysler had been caught at the time of the oil embargo in the midst of a $250 million revision of their automobile line. Chrysler's specific market segment—lower income, blue-collar workers—were the first to drop out of the market in the recession. The high earnings of 1973 were quickly replaced by losses in 1974. In October 1974, Chrysler's finance company, Chrysler Financial Corporation (CFC), had difficulties selling its commercial paper due to bad news concerning car inventories, plant closings, and profits. Moody's downgraded CFC's rating of commercial paper to P-2, the second highest rating, and then dropped the rating in December 1974. In December 1974, Moody's dropped the rating of Chrysler's senior debt one category from A to BBB and its rating for subordinated debt one category to BB. At the end of 1974, CFC's paper outstanding had fallen from $1.5 billion earlier in the year to only $740 million. (See Exhibit 9 for Chrysler Corporation's balance sheet at the end of 1974.) In January 1975, the company had 120 days of unsold cars in inventory compared to a normal of 60 days. Chrysler Corporation's share of market in the United States had fallen from 16% in 1973 to 15% in 1975.

With a $52 million loss projected in 1974, Chrysler Corporation had spent December 1974 improving its credit facilities in the United States. More than $455 million in U.S. lines of credits were converted to a three-year revolving credit agreement. This was in addition to about $100 million in existing credit with U.S. banks, and $175 million of medium-term revolving credit agreements with foreign banks. In January 1975, more than half of the company's 153,000 workers were out of work, and in February, Chrysler stopped paying quarterly dividends for the first time since the Great Depression, due to losses and the restrictive covenants in the bank revolving credit agreements. The layoffs in the work force continued in March, despite management's belief that the company would recover in late 1975. During the six months ending in May 1975, Chrysler Corporation had reduced its U.S. salaried and nonproduction worker manpower levels by 30%, reduced its capital spending by $100 million, and put stringent limits on all expenditures. Despite these actions, the consolidated loss for the first nine months of 1975 was $255 million before taxes, or $232 million after tax.

---

[6] Finance for Industry had been established after World War II to supply intermediate-term funds on a commercial basis to companies located in the United Kingdom for the purpose of productive investment and the development of exports. Its major shareholders were the clearing banks, although the Bank of England held 15%.

The October decision

As Riccardo prepared for the meeting of the board of directors, he saw only two alternatives for Chrysler U.K. in order to stop incurring further losses and in light of the financing required: liquidate Chrysler U.K., or, preferably, convince the British government to take over the company. Chrysler might retain a small minority interest (less than 20%) of the company if further investment was not required.

The liquidation of Chrysler U.K. would involve additional losses over and above the $74 million operating loss forecasted for 1975. Chrysler could attempt to relocate production of the CKD kits going to Iran, but the disruptions would be so great that Iran could decide to terminate the contract. Termination costs incurred by Chrysler U.K. including employee separation payments, dealership terminations, warranty costs, and other phase-out costs might total $50 million to $70 million. Additionally, it was not clear exactly how much could be realized for the assets. Upon liquidation of its subsidiary, Chrysler Corporation would be legally able to deduct against U.S. income tax all investments and operating losses on Chrysler U.K. totaling $175 million, plus any losses incurred in liquidation. As long as the subsidiary was in operation, however, Chrysler Corporation could not deduct losses for U.S. tax purposes.

Exhibit 1

CHRYSLER U.K. (A)

OPERATING DATA 1965–1974

(£ in thousands)

	1965	1966	1967	1968	1969	1970	1971*	1972	1973†	1974
Sales	£175,000	£178,000	£171,000	£176,000	£165,000	£179,000	£320,000	£281,000	£322,000	£313,000
Income before taxes	(2,226)	(3,291)	(10,716)	3,804	707	(10,613)	405	1,641	3,724	(17,734)
Depreciation and amortization of special tools	4,117	5,013	6,740	6,916	4,745	5,553	6,851	4,971	5,187	4,176
Cash flow from operations	2,025	1,426	3,775	9,974	5,352	(5,331)	7,365	6,571	8,937	(13,558)
U.S. $/£ sterling (period average)					$2.39	$2.40	$2.44	$2.50	$2.45	$2.34

* For 16 months ended November 30, 1971.
† For 13 months ended December 31, 1973.

Exhibit 2

CHRYSLER U.K. (A)
MARKET PROSPECTS FOR WESTERN EUROPEAN CAR INDUSTRY
(In millions of units)

	1974	1980	1985
Sales of new cars in Western Europe...............	8.0	9.6–10.9	11.3–12.6
Imports of new cars in Western Europe.............	0.4	1.0–0.6	1.1–0.7
Exports of new cars from Western Europe..........	2.1	1.1–1.7	1.1–2.0
Production of new cars in Western Europe.........	9.6	9.7–12.0	11.3–13.9
Capacity in Western Europe.....................	14.1	14.8	14.8
Spare capacity (percent).........................	32%	19%–34%	6%–24%

Exhibit 3

CHRYSLER U.K. (A)
UNITED KINGDOM
NEW CAR REGISTRATIONS

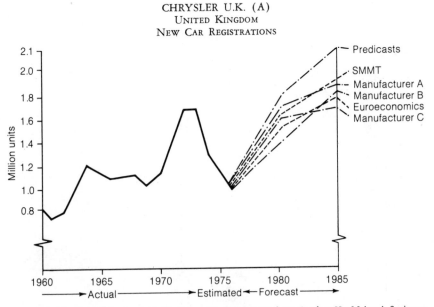

Source: Central Policy Review Staff, *The Future of the British Car Industry* (London: Her Majesty's Stationery Office, 1975), p. 39.

Exhibit 4

CHRYSLER U.K. (A)

MAJOR CAR MANUFACTURERS UTILIZATION OF EUROPEAN ASSEMBLY CAPACITY
(In thousands of units except percent figures)

	Two-Shift Capacity	*Production in Best Year*	*Percent Capacity Utilization*	*1974 Actual Production*	*Percent Utilization*
British Leyland.............	1,190	916	77%	738	62%
Chrysler U.K. and France....	900	780	86	647	72
Fiat......................	1,850	1,514	82	1,206	65
Ford U.K. and Germany.....	1,450	1,428	98	807	56
G.M. Opel and Vauxhall....	1,400	1,116	80	715	51
Peugeot-Citroen...........	1,570	1,263	80	1,127	72
Volkswagen...............	1,800	2,032	113%	1,436	80%

Source: Central Policy Review Staff, *The Future of the British Car Industry* (London: Her Majesty's Stationery Office, 1975).

Exhibit 5

CHRYSLER U.K. (A)
(Without a change in cost structure, the U.K. motor industry faces
substantial losses through 1980)
PRETAX PROFIT* VERSUS U.K. CAR INDUSTRY VOLUME

* Excludes commercial vehicles.
Sources: Estimates from published sources.

Exhibit 6

CHRYSLER U.K. (A)

PLANNED RATIONALIZATION OF CHRYSLER PLANTS IN THE UNITED KINGDOM

	Linwood (Glasgow)	Ryton (Coventry)	Stoke (Coventry)	Dunstable (Luton)	Maidstone	Other
1975 situation						
Operating rates						
Assembly	39.3%	57.1%		41.7%		
Machining	59.9%		56.5%	43.0%	37.2%	
Stamping	49.4%					
1975 employment	6,700	4,012	5,493	2,350	505	6,001
Type of operation	Power train, stamping, paint and trim, assembly of Arrow and Imp	Paint and final assembly of Avenger	Power train and foundry	Machinery and van/truck assembly	Miscellaneous machinery	Staff and diecasting and plastics
Plan						
Type of operation	Power train, stamping, paint and trim, final assembly of Avenger and Hunter	Paint and final assembly of Alpine	Power train and foundry	Machinery and van/truck assembly	Closed	Staff and diecasting and plastics
1976 employment	3,700	2,961*	3,383	2,391	—	4,537

* Employment at Ryton was expected to quickly increase from the 1976 low. Chrysler France was approaching full-capacity operations due to the strong market acceptance of the Alpine. Ryton, therefore, would likely be able to produce Alpines for the export market.

Exhibit 7

CHRYSLER U.K. (A)

CHRYSLER U.K. BALANCE SHEET, SEPTEMBER 30, 1975

($ in millions)

ASSETS			LIABILITIES AND SHAREHOLDERS' EQUITY		
Cash........................		$ 0.2			
Accounts receivable:			Bank debt................		$ 71.5
Trade and other........	$38.8		Current portion of		
Intercompany...........	18.0	56.8	long-term debt:		
Inventories:			Bank..................	$ 1.0	
Raw..................	$ 3.8		Public and government...	5.4	6.4
In-process..............	60.6		Accounts payable:		
Finished goods..........	42.4		Trade and other.........	$69.9	
Nonproductive..........	6.3		Intercompany...........	29.0	98.9
Service parts............	33.2		Accrued expenses..........		54.8
Other (mainly			Intercompany notes and		
revaluation)...........	22.6	168.9	advances..............		13.0
Prepaid insurance,			Provision for taxes........		0.5
taxes, and other........		1.2	*Total current liabilities.*		$245.1
Total current assets....		$227.1	Other liabilities............		3.5
Investments..............		11.5	Long-term debt:		
Property, plant, and			Bank..................	$24.6	
equipment:			Public and government...	15.4	
Net buildings...........	$56.1		Intercompany...........	28.6	68.6
Net machinery and			*Total liabilities.......*		$317.2
equipment.............	20.1		Shareholders' equity........		17.0
Net special tools........	16.1		*Total liabilities and*		
Other.................	0.7	93.0	*shareholders' equity..*		$334.2
Other assets.............		2.6			
Total assets.........		$334.2			

NOTES TO THE ACCOUNTS OF CHRYSLER U.K.

1. At December 31, 1974, there were unutilized losses for the purposes of U.K. corporation tax amounting to $81 million which are available to be carried forward and set against profits arising in future years.

2. All of the borrowings from banks and other long-term debt is guaranteed by Chrysler Corporation.

3. Chrysler U.K. is committed to buying back all unsold stocks of spare parts and new vehicles at cost from dealers. Dealer inventories totaled $61 million at December 31, 1974.

4. In addition to the accounts receivable of $56.8 million at September 30, 1975, an additional $39.5 million (secured by new-vehicle inventories at dealers) was owed by Chrysler U.K. dealers to Chrysler Wholesale Limited, a subsidiary of Chrysler Financial Corporation which in turn is a subsidiary of Chrysler Corporation.

Exhibit 8

CHRYSLER U.K. (A)

CHRYSLER CORPORATION FINANCIAL PERFORMANCE, 1968–1974

($ in millions except per share data)

	1968	*1969*	*1970*	*1971*	*1972*	*1973*	*1974*
Sales	$ 7,445.3	$ 7,052.2	$ 6,999.7	$ 7,999.3	$ 9,759.1	$11,774.4	$10,971.4
Net income	303	9.9	(0.8)	8.4	220	255	(52)
Earnings per share	6.23	2.09	(0.16)	1.67	4.27	4.80	(0.92)
Dividends per share	2.00	2.00	.06	0.60	0.90	1.30	1.40
Price range	72¾–48	57⅛–31⅜	35¾–16⅛	33⅜–24½	41⅝–28	44¼–14¾	20⅛–7
Book value per share	42.81	43.84	42.40	43.82	46.87	49.74	44.47
Long-term debt	535.3	587.0	791.1	818.4	789.6	955.9	995.4
Interest coverage, defined as $\frac{EBIT}{i}$	15.3	3.4	—	1.5	4.3	4.0	—

Exhibit 9

CHRYSLER U.K. (A)

CHRYSLER CORPORATION AND CONSOLIDATED SUBSIDIARIES
CONSOLIDATED BALANCE SHEET, DECEMBER 31, 1974
($ in millions)

ASSETS		LIABILITIES AND STOCKHOLDERS' EQUITY	
Cash	$ 138		
Marketable securities	130	Accounts payable	$1,282
Accounts receivable	707	Accrued expenses	611
Inventories	2,453	Short-term debt	620
Other	269	Current maturities—	
Total current assets	$3,697	long-term debt	184
		Other	12
Investment in and advances		*Total current liabilities*	$2,709
to associated companies and			
unconsolidated subsidiaries	876	Other liabilities	368
Other assets	49	Long-term debt	995
Net property, plant, and equipment	2,063	Stockholders' equity	2,661
Goodwill	48	*Total liabilities and*	
Total assets	$6,733	*stockholders' equity*	$6,733

NOTES TO THE CONSOLIDATED BALANCE SHEET OF CHRYSLER CORPORATION

1. In December 1974, Chrysler Corporation entered into a revolving credit agreement with a group of banks in the United States, extending through March 31, 1978 unless sooner terminated by the Corporation. Under the agreement, the Corporation agrees that it will:
   a. pay and discharge, and cause its significant subsidiaries (those with total assets exceeding 5% of total consolidated assets) to pay and discharge, at or before their maturity, all their respective obligations and liabilities except where the same may be contested in good faith.
   b. maintain consolidated working capital (defined as the excess of current assets over current liabilities) of at least $500 million plus any unpaid principal amount of the notes not classified as a current liability on a consolidated balance sheet.
   c. maintain a ratio of consolidated current assets to consolidated current liabilities plus any unpaid principal amount of the notes not classified as a current liability on a consolidated balance sheet, of at least 1.2 to 1.
   d. not allow the aggregate outstanding short-term and long-term debt (excluding normal credit from suppliers, accrued taxes, and accrued liabilities) to exceed 80% of consolidated net worth.

2. As of December 31, 1974, the actually computed value of "vested" benefits exceeded the total of the pension funds (at market value) by approximately $1,201 million.

3. The U.S. tax loss in 1974 reduced the Corporation's potential loss carryback income tax benefits to approximately $13 million.

4. Summary balance sheets at 12/31/74 of unconsolidated subsidiaries (millions of dollars):

Exhibit 9—Continued

ASSETS	Chrysler Financial	Chrysler Realty
Cash and equivalent	$ 295	$ 1
Accounts receivable	2,831	7
Net properties	14	489
Other	271	53
Total assets	$3,411	$ 550

LIABILITIES AND STOCKHOLDERS' EQUITY

	Chrysler Financial	Chrysler Realty
Notes payable	$2,559	$ 296
Long-term debt	195	
Other liabilities	163	61
Stockholders' equity	494	193
Total	$3,411	$ 550

WINCO DISTRIBUTION COMPANY

^^^

In early June, 1965, the directors of Winco Distribution Company were faced with two major financial decisions that would have a long-run impact on the future of the firm. The first was the possible acquisition of Taylor Markets, Inc. The second was a major overhaul of the long-term capital structure of the company.

The first part of this case will present in summary form background information about Winco Distribution Company, stressing its growth and financing in the years immediately preceding 1965. Thereafter the information relevant to the acquisition of Taylor Markets and to alternative methods of reconstructing Winco's long-term capital structure will be summarized.

Growth of Winco Distribution Company

Winco was founded in 1907 to sell supplies to cotton plantations in the vicinity of Memphis, Tennessee. Through the years it expanded and underwent several changes in the nature of its business. By the end of World War II it had evolved into a grocery wholesaler with headquarters in Memphis servicing grocery stores in 10 states; it also owned and operated a chain of 18 retail food stores in Nashville, Tennessee.

Winco grew steadily from 1945 until 1965. The number of affiliated stores increased from 300 in 1945 to 1,350 in 1965 (Exhibit 1). This growth was also reflected in its operating statements and balance sheets for recent years (Exhibits 2 and 3). By 1965 the company's distribution system had expanded from the original single warehouse to a network of eight distribution points and three marine terminals from which it supplied ships calling in port.

In 1965 Winco was by far the larger of the two independent wholesale grocers in Memphis. It provided a wide range of ancillary services for affiliated retail stores. Stores could operate under their own names with standard brands or under a wide variety of advertising groups sponsored by Winco. Winco's staff was available to help plan all aspects of store operations from advertising to insurance and renovations. Financial support was also available to its retail associates. This support was given in the form of direct loans to 180 stores; of guarantees by Winco of liabilities of affiliates or suppliers; and of leases for prime store space signed by Winco and then sublet at cost to its retail affiliates. Management believed that these arrangements were basically quite secure and that they did not expose Winco to major financial risks.

Despite heavy competition from national chains such as A&P, Kroger, and National Tea, Winco's management believed that the sales volume of its own stores and its affiliates was equal to or larger than that of any chain or similar wholesale group in its area of operation. Independent studies by brokerage houses confirmed the ability of Winco and several large grocery wholesalers in other parts of the country to compete effectively with the national chains.

Background information on acquisitions prior to 1965

Part of the rapid expansion of Winco during the 1961–65 period was accounted for by acquisitions rather than by internal growth.

Certain assets of the Henstock Company, a wholesale grocery business operating in southeastern Texas and southwestern Louisiana, were acquired in July, 1962, for $700,000 in cash and common stock of Winco valued at $1.4 million (108,655 shares with a market price at the time of acquisition of about $13). Henstock's after-tax earnings were about $175,000 in the most recent year before acquisition. The book value of the assets acquired, after the deduction of certain liabilities assumed, was $1.7 million. The financial statements for Winco shown in Exhibits 2 and 3 have not been adjusted for the years prior to fiscal year 1963 to show the operations of the combined companies because the transaction was a purchase of assets rather than a merger.

In May, 1964, Winco acquired the principal operating assets of the Warrilow Corporation, a closely held wholesale grocery business and retail store chain operating in Nashville, Tennessee, and nearby areas. Winco paid the owners of Warrilow slightly over $12 million. Payment was made in three parts: (1) $4.8 million in cash; (2) $5 million of 6% cumulative preferred stock (described in more detail in the next section); and (3) the assumption by Winco of $2.4 million of the liabilities of Warrilow. The price paid was estimated by Winco's management at approximately 13 times Warrilow's earnings after taxes. The assets purchased had been carried on Warrilow's books at about $2 million less than the net price Winco paid for them. Most of this amount was assigned to individual asset accounts on Winco's books on the basis of an independent professional appraisal of the acquired assets. The remainder was carried as goodwill.

Financing in connection with the Warrilow acquisition

As previously indicated, Winco issued $5 million of 6% cumulative preferred stock to the owners of the Warrilow Corporation as partial payment for this acquisition. The terms of the preferred stock provided for the retirement of the entire issue in May, 1968, although Winco was given the right to call at par part or all of the issue for retirement prior to that date. If the preferred stock were not retired by May, 1968, the preferred stockholders would be entitled to elect a majority of the board of directors. Furthermore, the holders of the preferred stock could require redemption of their shares on 30 days' notice if the paid-in surplus and retained earnings of Winco should fall below $5.5 million.

The management of Winco did not expect to be able to generate funds from its own working capital position to cover all the $4.8 million cash payment and the $2.4 million in increased liabilities assumed in the Warrilow Corporation purchase. It did anticipate, however, that a smaller amount of current assets would be required to operate the combined businesses than the sum of their current assets before the acquisition. Inventory duplications could be eliminated, and other efficiencies were expected to reduce somewhat the need for working capital. Because the Winco management was uncertain about the exact amount of funds required to finance the expanded scale of operations, it decided to seek interim financing rather than longer term debt.

The cash required for the Warrilow acquisition was therefore raised mainly through an intermediate-term loan negotiated in June, 1964, with banks in Memphis and Nashville. The banks gave Winco a revolving line of credit at $5\frac{1}{4}\%$ in addition to the balance outstanding on a $5\frac{1}{4}\%$ loan previously made to Winco in 1963. The new loan was granted with the understanding that it would be paid off or replaced by longer term debt when a more precise estimate of the company's financial requirements could be made. On June 27, 1964, the end of Winco's 1964 fiscal year, $5 million of the new line of credit had been drawn down. By the end of fiscal year 1965, Winco was only borrowing $1.9 million under this arrangement.

Future plans

Except for the possible acquisition of Taylor Markets, Inc., which will be discussed below, the management of Winco knew of no future possible acquisitions of retail or wholesale grocery firms. Moreover, in the foreseeable future the management did not expect to commit funds to integrate operations backward into processing, packaging, and manufacturing. No major additions were planned for Winco's physical plant; funds generated from depreciation charges would be sufficient to cover construction of whatever new fixed assets might be required. Growth was expected to come primarily from an increased volume of business in existing market areas. The region served by Winco was attracting industry at a significant rate; standards of living were rising and population was increasing. Moreover, as previously noted, the management of Winco was confident of its ability to compete effectively with the national chains. It anticipated a probable growth rate of sales of about 13% for the foreseeable future and set the likely boundaries on the range of this growth rate as 10% and 16%. The existing physical plant, with relatively minor additions, was more than adequate to accommodate this rate of growth for some years to come.

Taylor Markets, Inc.

The management of Winco knew of only one prospect for expansion by acquisition in the foreseeable future. It had recently learned that the owners of Taylor Markets, an aggressive retail chain of 10 stores in Memphis, were willing to sell their chain to Winco if suitable terms could be negotiated. The Taylor chain had grown from a single store opened in 1947 to its current size. An independent market survey conducted early in 1964 indicated that Taylor had 18% of the Memphis food store business.

Winco had maintained a long and close relationship with Taylor Markets, which had been a member of Winco's voluntary plan since the first Taylor store was opened. The Taylor management had been very impressive, generating sufficient profits to open new stores with a minimum of financial assistance from Winco. Taylor Markets paid approximately $261,000 annually for the properties it leased. Many of these properties had been subleased from Winco and thus were already contingent liabilities of Winco.

The only severe difficulty Taylor Markets had encountered was caused by a labor dispute growing out of an acquisition the chain had made in 1961. As a consequence the company had shown losses for several years, but the issue had been completely resolved by 1965. The management of Winco regarded Taylor Markets' earnings of $220,000 in fiscal year 1965 as reasonably reflecting its true earning power. This figure was also considered a reasonable estimate of Taylor Markets' earning capacity on its existing stores over the next several years. (Recent earning statements of Taylor Markets are shown in Exhibit 4. Its estimated balance sheet for June 26, 1965, is given in Exhibit 5).

The owners of Taylor Markets wished to continue operating the business after its sale. For tax reasons they preferred to sell by means of an exchange of stock rather than for cash. A sale for cash would involve immediate heavy capital gains taxes whereas an exchange of stock would qualify as a taxfree transaction.

A merger with Taylor Markets might be considered as containing seeds of conflict with the independent retail affiliates of Winco. The Winco management, however, had found no ill will generated from its acquisition of the Warrilow stores in Nashville. All retailers, including wholly owned stores, were given the same terms and treatment. Management had concluded that under these circumstances there was little difference between supplying, on the one hand, a wholly owned store and its independent competitor and, on the other hand, two independent retailers who were competing with each other.

Long-term financing

Winco's long-term debt structure as of June 26, 1965, can be summarized as follows:

Current maturities on long-term debt.................................$ 300,000
Balloon maturity due in 1968 on 5¼% note of 1963...................... 2,000,000
Amount outstanding on revolving 5¼% loan in connection with Warrilow
  acquisition.. 1,900,000
Other long-term debt (about half of which was scheduled to mature during or
  prior to 1968)... 1,400,000
                                    $5,600,000

In addition to the long-term debt owed by Winco, Taylor Markets had $650,000 outstanding in short-term notes payable. If Taylor was acquired, $650,000 would be required to pay off these notes.[1]

In reviewing its debt position the management of Winco had definitely decided to refinance $5.0 million of its existing debt ($5.65 million if Taylor was acquired). An insurance company had expressed a willingness to share a loan of this size with Winco's banks. The interest rate on the outstanding balance would be between 5% and 5¼%. The principal of the loan would be amortized at an even rate over a 20-year period. If the loan was for $5.0 million, the banks would loan $1.25 million and the insurance company $3.75 million. The loan would be paid off at the rate of $250,000 a year, with the full amount going to the banks for the first five years and the remainder to the insurance company for the last 15 years. The covenants on the new loan would be less restrictive than those on the company's existing indebtedness.

Refinancing the $5 million of preferred stock along with the outstanding debt was also under consideration. The lending institutions had indicated that they would be willing to increase the size of the new 20-year loan to a maximum of $7.5 to $8.0 million on the same terms except for a proportionate increase in the annual payments needed to retire the principal of the loan in 20 years. An $8.0 million loan, however, was the maximum amount that they would grant at this time.

In addition to these needs for long-term or equity funds, Winco required seasonal financing each year. Peak needs occurred during the fall months and had amounted to about $1 million in recent years. These funds were borrowed through Winco's Memphis bank, where a 90-day line of credit of $3.5 million was maintained for seasonal financing. No change was expected in this arrangement for seasonal financing.

In its consideration of the restructuring of its long-run financing, Winco's management was considering two other sources of funds to refinance part or all of its needs above the amount that it expected to borrow on a 20-year basis.

Possible issue of common stock

The first was a public issue of common stock. Winco stock, which was traded over the counter, had recently reached an all time high of $28⅞ a share, bid. (Exhibit 6 shows the range of Winco stock prices to June 10, 1965.) The bid price had only declined to about $28 during the recent softening of the stock market in the second quarter of 1965. During the same period the Dow-Jones average of 30 industrial stocks had declined from 920 to 875.

The company's investment banker had indicated that a new issue of up to $5 million of common stock could probably be sold at a price of about $25 a

---

[1] Winco also had contingent liabilities and lease obligations for its affiliates and suppliers amounting to $900,000, and it leased property in its own name involving annual rental payments of $850,000. Neither of these items was shown on its balance sheet.

share to the public provided that the price of Winco common stock did not decline any further. The management of Winco did not want to price the stock so high as to "crowd the market" for fear that the stock might perform unfavorably thereafter. Fees and expenses were estimated at about 7% of the gross receipts of a $5 million issue and, because of the fixed costs involved, at a somewhat higher percentage of a smaller issue.

Winco common stock had first been made available to the public in July, 1961. At that time the company had sold 115,500 shares to raise funds to retire debt and for general purposes; members of the founder's family had sold 201,000 shares of their personal holdings at the same time. In order to minimize the cash drain from dividends during the first years of public ownership, the family had converted some of the shares they retained into a Class A common stock. The Class A stock was identical with the regular common stock except that it did not participate in dividends. It was convertible share for share into regular common stock according to a fixed schedule. After converting the remaining 109,638 shares of Class A stock on July 1, 1965, the founder's family would own about 437,000 shares of common stock. Other officers and directors owned about 90,000 regular common shares.

Management considered the public stock issue in 1961 a success. It was priced at $12 a share and subsequently rose to a high of $18½ before the stock market decline in April, 1962. At that time the price fell back to about $12.

By 1965 Winco had 1,373 registered stockholders located in 37 states. Some of the stock was held in "street names," the ultimate owner having left the stock in the name of his bank or brokerage house. Some mutual and pension funds had taken positions in the stock. Nevertheless, the number of round lots (100-share lots) held by the public was still small.

An investment banking firm with a special interest in the leading wholesale grocers had noted the limited marketability, the relatively small capitalization, and the lack of listing of these stocks as drawbacks. It expected, though, that these problems would diminish in intensity during the next several years for the larger wholesale grocers such as Winco. Exhibit 7 includes some financial statistics for several large wholesale grocers.

Possible issue of convertible debentures

The management of Winco had also discussed the possibility of issuing a subordinated convertible debenture to the public. Its investment banker had indicated that a company like Winco could raise roughly $5 million by issuing a 15-year or 20-year subordinated convertible debenture bearing interest at a rate of between 4% and 4½%. This rate was lower than Winco could obtain on a straight debt issue because of the potential value of the convertible feature to the lender. The conversion price would be set about 20% above the market price of the common stock at the time the debenture was sold, or at about $34 a share on the basis of the $28 market price. In other words, each $1,000 bond would be convertible into 29.41 shares of common stock. Fees and expenses would be 3½% to 4% of gross funds raised. The banks and insurance company that had offered to lend up to $8 million on a 20-year amortization basis had indicated that they would not object to an issue of convertible debentures provided that these debentures were subordinated to the 20-year loan.

It was normally expected that the price of the common stock of a growing company would rise sufficiently within a few years to make a conversion privilege attractive, thereby enabling the company to force conversion by calling the debenture issue for redemption. Consequently, it was not customary to require a sinking fund for the first few years of a convertible debenture's life. If Winco should issue a 20-year convertible debenture, for example, the repayments on principal would be scheduled to begin after five years and to be sufficient to retire the debt over the remaining 15 years, assuming that it had not been converted in the meantime.

Timing of issue of common stock or convertible debentures

Although an issue of stock or debt could be canceled at the last minute if the market proved extremely unfavorable, a public issue had to be planned several months in advance so that the necessary registration information could be compiled and filed with appropriate authorities. The nature of the information would differ depending on whether management had decided tentatively to issue stock or debt. A decision to shift from one type of issue to the other after planning was well under way would require a substantial revision of the preparatory paper work. The date of issue would be delayed, and an additional investment in management time and in legal and accounting fees would be necessary. For this reason, if a public issue of Winco securities was selected, management was anxious to choose a form of security that would not have to be changed because of moderate changes in stock market conditions during the next several months.

*   *   *   *   *

With the preceding facts in mind, the management of Winco had to decide (1) what action to take with respect to the merger with Taylor Markets; (2) whether to raise more than the $5 million it had already decided to secure by an issue of bonds; and (3) if so, the amount and the source of these additional funds. Management had prepared the forecasts shown in Exhibit 8 as background information for these decisions.

Exhibit 1
WINCO DISTRIBUTION COMPANY
NUMBER OF CLIENT STORES

			Fiscal Year		
	1961	*1962*	*1963*	*1964*	*1965*
Number of stores, beginning of year	747	767	774	797	1,197
Number of stores added	53	64	41	418*	161*
Number of stores dropped	33	57	18	18	8
Number of stores at year-end	767	774	797	1,197	1,350

* Of the 418 stores added in fiscal year 1964 and the 161 stores added in 1965, 376 and 128 respectively were formerly served by the Warrilow Corporation and became affiliated stores of Winco as a result of the acquisition of Warrilow or by affiliation with Winco after the acquisition.

Exhibit 2

WINCO DISTRIBUTION COMPANY

Income Statements for the Fiscal Years 1961–65

(Dollar figures in millions)

Fiscal year ended	June 24, 1961		June 30, 1962		June 29, 1963		June 27, 1964		(Preliminary) June 26, 1965	
Net sales and service fees*	$ 74.4	100.0%	$ 86.3	100.0%	$121.4	100.0%	$138.7	100.0%	$211.8	100.0%
Cost of sales less discounts	69.5	93.4	80.6	93.4	112.6	92.8	128.1	92.3	192.0	90.7
Gross profit on sales and service fees	$ 4.9	6.6%	$ 5.7	6.6%	$ 8.8	7.2%	$ 10.6	7.7%	$ 19.8	9.3%
Operating expenses:										
Warehouse and delivery	$ 1.7		$ 1.9		$ 2.8		$ 3.1		$ 4.9	
Selling, general, and administrative	1.9		2.3		3.9		5.2		10.6	
Total operating expenses	$ 3.6	4.8	$ 4.2	4.9	$ 6.7	5.5	$ 8.3	6.0	$ 15.5	7.3
Income from operations	$ 1.3	1.8%	$ 1.5	1.7%	$ 2.1	1.7%	$ 2.3	1.7%	$ 4.3	2.0%
Add: Other income (expenses) net	0.1		0.1		0.1		0.1		(0.2)‡	
Less: Interest	0.1		0.1		0.2		0.2		0.4	
Income before taxes	$ 1.3	1.8%	$ 1.5	1.7%	$ 2.0	1.6%	$ 2.2	1.6%	$ 3.7	1.8%
Provision for income taxes	0.7	1.0	0.8	0.9	1.0	0.8	1.1	0.8	1.8	0.9
Net income after tax	$ 0.6	0.8%	$ 0.7	0.8%	$ 1.0	0.8%	$ 1.1	0.8%	$ 1.9	0.9%
Preferred dividends	...		...		...		...		$ 0.3	
Net income applicable to common shares	$ 0.6		$ 0.7		$ 1.0		$ 1.1		$ 1.6	
Number of shares of common stock outstanding at end of each period†	704,411		819,911		928,566		932,901		938,393	
Net income per share†	$ 0.85		$ 0.86		$ 1.07		$ 1.21		$ 1.66	
Dividends per share paid on common shares only	$ 0.04		$ 0.26		$ 0.34		$ 0.41		$ 0.50	
Depreciation (millions)	n.a.		n.a.		$ 0.4		$ 0.5		$ 0.9	

* In fiscal year 1964 includes $10.3 million in sales and a negligible amount in net profits from Warrilow for the period May 4, 1964–June 27, 1964. For the full fiscal year 1965, Warrilow contributed sales of $70.0 million and income from operations of $1.5 million.

† Includes both classes of common stock.

‡ Includes $0.3 million loss on abandonment of equipment in the Warrilow operation.

Exhibit 3

WINCO DISTRIBUTION COMPANY

BALANCE SHEETS AS OF END OF FISCAL YEARS 1961–65

(Dollar figures in millions)

ASSETS	June 24, 1961*	June 30, 1962	June 29, 1963	June 27, 1964	(Preliminary) June 26, 1965
Current assets:					
Cash	$1.0	$ 1.6	$ 2.4	$ 4.2	$ 2.5
Receivables (net)	1.8	3.3	4.7	8.5	10.2
Inventories of merchandise and supplies	4.3	4.5	7.0	12.7	13.0
Total current assets	$7.1	$ 9.4	$14.1	$25.4	$25.7
Investments, advances to affiliates, and other assets	$1.2	$ 0.5	$ 1.8	$ 1.7	$ 1.8
Property and equipment:					
Property and equipment	$2.2	$ 2.5	$ 3.5	$ 7.0	$ 6.9
Less: Accumulated depreciation	0.7	1.0	1.3	2.1	2.4
Net property and equipment	$1.5	$ 1.5	$ 2.2	$ 4.9	$ 4.5
Goodwill, deferred charges, and other assets	...	...	0.1	0.8	0.8
Total assets	$9.8	$11.4	$18.2	$32.8	$32.8
LIABILITIES					
Current liabilities:					
Notes payable, bank	$1.5	$ 0.5	$ ...	$ 0.1	$ 0.4
Current maturities, long-term debt	0.1	0.1	0.3	0.3	0.3
Trade accounts payable and other accruals	2.2	2.8	4.7	8.6	10.0
Income taxes payable	0.6	0.6	0.8	0.9	1.4
Total current liabilities	$4.4	$ 4.0	$ 5.8	$ 9.9	$12.1
Long-term debt	$0.9	$ 0.8	$ 4.1	$ 8.8	$ 5.3
Stockholders' equity:					
4% preferred stock, noncumulative	$0.4	$ 0.4	$ ...	$ ...	$ ...
6% preferred stock, cumulative, due 1968	...	...	...	5.0	5.0
Common stock, $1 par value†	0.4	0.5	0.6	0.7	0.8
Common stock Class A, $1 par value†	0.3	0.3	0.3	0.2	0.1
Paid-in surplus	0.5	1.8	3.1	3.1	3.2
Retained earnings	2.9	3.6	4.3	5.1	6.3
Total stockholders' equity	$4.5	$ 6.6	$ 8.3	$14.1	$15.4
Total liabilities and stockholders' equity	$9.8	$11.4	$18.2	$32.8	$32.8

* The statement as of June 24, 1961, has not been restated to allow for certain subsidiaries consolidated in 1962 and subsequent years. The assets of these subsidiaries totalled about $350,000.
† Total number of shares outstanding in each period shown in Exhibit 2.

Exhibit 4

TAYLOR MARKETS, INC.

INCOME STATEMENTS

(Dollar figures in thousands)

Fiscal year ended	June 29, 1963		June 27, 1964		(Preliminary) June 26, 1965	
Net sales	$16,463	100.0%	$18,504	100.0%	$18,162	100.0%
Cost of sales	13,270	80.6	14,833	80.2	14,379	79.2
Gross profit on sales	$ 3,193	19.4%	$ 3,671	19.8%	$ 3,783	20.8%
Operating expenses:						
Direct store expenses	$ 2,041	12.4%	$ 2,203	11.9%	$ 2,176	12.0%
Selling, general, and administrative	1,112	6.8	1,238	6.7	1,100	6.0
Total operating expenses	$ 3,153	19.2%	$ 3,441	18.6%	$ 3,276	18.0%
Income from operations	$ 40	0.2%	$ 230	1.2%	$ 507	2.8%
Other income	19	0.1	46	0.3	3	...
	$ 59	0.3%	$ 276	1.5%	$ 510	2.8%
Other expenses:						
Interest	$ 70		$ 71		$ 66	
Other	15		2		5	
Total other expenses	$ 85	0.5%	$ 73	0.4%	$ 71	0.4%
Net income (loss) before taxes	$ (26)	(0.2%)	$ 203	1.1%	$ 439	2.4%
Provision for state and federal income taxes	...	...	95	0.5	219	1.2
Net income (loss)	$ (26)	(0.2%)	$ 108	0.6%	$ 220	1.2%

Exhibit 5

TAYLOR MARKETS, INC.

PRELIMINARY BALANCE SHEET AS OF JUNE 26, 1965
(Dollar figures in thousands)

ASSETS

Current assets:

Cash..		$ 884
Accounts receivable.......................................		10
Inventory...		600
Prepaid expenses..		116
Total current assets....................................		$1,610
Cash value of life insurance..............................		16
Total property and equipment............................	$1,659	
Less: Depreciation..	808	
Net property and equipment...........................		851
Deferred charges...		1
Total assets..		$2,478

LIABILITIES

Current liabilities:

Note payable..	$ 650
Current maturities, long-term debt.......................	125
Accounts payable and miscellaneous accruals..............	501
Accrued state and federal taxes.........................	219
Total current liabilities.............................	$1,495

Long-term debt:

4% note payable.......................................	$ 42
5% note payable.......................................	130
	$ 172

Stockholders' equity:

Common stock, $100 par, 536 shares outstanding...........	$ 54
Paid-in surplus..	71
Retained earnings	686
Total stockholders' equity	$ 811
Total liabilities......................................	$2,478

Exhibit 6

WINCO DISTRIBUTION COMPANY

MARKET PRICE OF COMMON STOCK*

Calendar Years	High	Low
1962:		
First quarter	$18½	$16½
Second	15¾	12¼
Third	14¼	12½
Fourth	13½	13
1963:		
First	14	13⅜
Second	17⅝	14¾
Third	17⅛	17
Fourth	17⅜	16⅜
1964:		
First	17	16½
Second	21⅝	19
Third	21½	21⅜
Fourth	24	21½
1965:		
First	25	24
Second (to June 10)	28⅞	24

* Bid price in over-the-counter market.

Exhibit 7

WINCO DISTRIBUTION COMPANY

FINANCIAL STATISTICS, FOUR GROCERY WHOLESALERS

	Winco Distribution Company	Fleming Company	Scot Lad Foods	Super Value Stores
Most recent fiscal year ended	June, 1964	Dec., 1964	June, 1964	Dec., 1964
Most recent fiscal year:				
Sales (millions)	$139	$313	$183	$466
Profit after taxes (millions)	$ 1.1	$ 2.6	$ 1.4	$ 3.2
Gross margin (%)	7.7%	6.6%	11.8%	6.2%
Common dividends as a percentage of profit after taxes	25.5%*	47.5%	21%	43.8%
Stock price, fiscal 1964 range	16⅜–21⅝	22¼–28½	19⅝–27¼	27⅛–35½
Price-earnings ratio (based on average price for fiscal year 1964)	15.7	18.5	12.3	18.3
Yield (fiscal 1964 figures)	2.2%	2.6%	1.7%	2.4%
Quoted bid price, June 11, 1965	$ 28¼	$ 29¾	$ 24¾	$ 33½
Capitalization:				
Long-term debt	38.3%	25.6%	38.5%	22.3%
Preferred stock	21.8	3.4	...	8.6
Common stock and surplus	39.9	71.0	61.5	69.1
	100.0%	100.0%	100.0%	100.0%
Five-year compound growth rate:				
Sales	15.0%	11.6%	21%	17.2%
Profits after taxes	13.3	12.6	28	15.5
Earnings per share	8.4	8.8	18	9.8

* Based on dividends actually paid on the common stock. If dividends at the same rate had been paid on both the regular common and the Class A common stock, dividends would have been 34.8% of profit after taxes.

Exhibit 8

WINCO DISTRIBUTION COMPANY

PRO FORMA PROJECTIONS, FISCAL YEARS 1966 THROUGH 1968*

(Dollar figures in millions)

	Actual 1965	┌──*Projected, 1966–68*──┐		
		1966	1967	1968
1. Sales and Earnings:				
Sales—13% annual growth............................	$211.8	$239.3	$270.4	$305.6
Earnings before interest and taxes...................	4.1	4.4	4.9	5.6
2. Projected balance sheet data†				
Current assets and advances to affiliates:				
Cash..	$ 2.5	$ 3.6	$ 4.0	$ 4.6
Receivables (net)................................	10.2	11.0	12.4	13.9
Inventories.......................................	13.0	14.6	16.4	18.5
Advances to affiliates...........................	1.8	1.9	2.0	2.1
Total...	$ 27.5	$ 31.1	$ 34.8	$ 39.1
Current liabilities:				
Accounts payable................................	$ 10.0	$ 10.8	$ 12.2	$ 13.7
Income taxes payable............................	1.4	1.5	1.7	2.0
Other..	0.7	0.7	0.7	0.7
Total...	$ 12.1	$ 13.0	$ 14.6	$ 16.4
Net working capital and advances to affiliates.........	$ 15.4	$ 18.1	$ 20.2	$ 22.7
Incremental funds required for NWC and advances to affiliates...	...	2.7	2.1	2.5
Cumulative increase in funds required for NWC and advances to affiliates....................................	...	2.7	4.8	7.3
3. Minimum financial charges following the proposed $5 million refinancing‡:				
Interest on the $5 million of long-term debt.........	...	$ 0.25	$ 0.24	$ 0.22
Interest on other remaining long-term debt.........	...	0.04	0.03	0.03
Debt repayment—$5 million of long-term debt.....	...	0.25	0.25	0.25
Debt repayment—other remaining long-term debt...	...	0.09	0.09	0.09

* Note: The projections in this exhibit do *not* include any adjustments to reflect the possible acquisition of Taylor Markets currently under consideration by the management of Winco.

† The balance sheet data in this section include only current assets and current liabilities with the single exception that "advances to affiliates" is classified here with current assets. As stated in the text, expenditures on fixed assets were expected to be about equal to depreciation expenses.

‡ These charges are computed on the assumption that $5 million of new long-term debt is borrowed at an interest rate of 5% with repayments of principal of $250,000 per annum. If more than $5 million of long-term debt were borrowed, then charges related to long-term borrowings would have to be increased proportionately.

Appendixes

A. TAX TABLE[1]

∧∧

FEDERAL TAX RATES ON CORPORATE INCOME
AND PAYMENT DATES

Income Years	Rate‡	Income Years	Rate‡
1940*.	24%	1954–63.	52%
1941*.	31	1964.	50
1942–45*.	40	1965–67.	48
1946–49.	38	1968–69†.	52.8
1950.	47	1970†.	49.2
1951–53*.	52	1971–78.	48
		1979–80.	46

* Excess profits tax also in effect for part or all of year.
† Includes special surcharge.
‡ Rate applicable to top bracket of tax, excluding the excess profits tax, when in effect.

The 52% rate in effect from 1951 through 1963 consisted of a normal tax of 30% of taxable income and a surtax of 22% of taxable income in excess of $25,000. The 50% rate in effect in 1964 consisted of a normal tax of 22% and a surtax of 28%; and the 48% rate in effect from 1965 through 1974 consisted of a normal tax of 22% and a surtax of 26% on taxable income in excess of $25,000.

In addition, in 1968 a special surcharge of 10% was imposed making the effective rate for that year 52.8%. This rate held for 1969, but the special surcharge was phased out gradually by quarters during 1970 so that the overall effective rate for that year was 49.2%, and by 1971 the rate was again 48%.

For tax years ending after 1974 and before 1979 the normal tax rates were 20% on the first $25,000 of taxable income and 22% on taxable income over $25,000. The surtax rate was 26% on taxable income over $50,000. For tax

---

[1] This table has been prepared for use in connection with cases in this book. It is not a complete statement of applicable rates, and it should not be used as a reference for general purposes.

years beginning after 1978 the taxable income of corporations was subject to graduated tax rates as follows:

Amount of Taxable Income	Applicable Tax Rate
Zero–$25,000	17%
over $25,000–$50,000	20
over $50,000–$75,000	30
over $75,000–$100,000	40
over $100,000	46

Since 1967 corporate income tax payments have moved close to current payment. Beginning in 1950, payments were gradually accelerated until in 1954 they were brought entirely within the first half of the year following the tax liability. The Revenue Acts of 1954 and 1964 and the Tax Adjustment Act of 1966 set up even more accelerated schedules. Through 1967, all tax liabilities up to $100,000 were payable in equal amounts on March 15 and June 15 of the year following the tax liability. The Revenue Act of 1968 provided for a gradual acceleration of tax payments for corporations with tax liabilities of less than $100,000 as well as for corporations with tax liabilities of more than $100,000. Tax liabilities over $100,000, for companies on a calendar year, were payable according to the following schedule. For 1967 and subsequent years, if the actual tax liability for the year exceeded the amount of estimated tax payments made on this liability during the year, the balance had to be paid in equal installments on March 15 and June 15 of the following year.

Year	Percentage Paid in Income Year*				Percentage Paid in Following Year†			
	Apr. 15	June 15	Sept. 15	Dec. 15	Mar. 15	June 15	Sept. 15	Dec. 15
1949	—	—	—	—	25	25	25	25
1950	—	—	—	—	30	30	20	20
1951	—	—	—	—	35	35	15	15
1952	—	—	—	—	40	40	10	10
1953	—	—	—	—	45	45	5	5
1954	—	—	—	—	50	50	—	—
1955	—	—	5	5	45	45	—	—
1956	—	—	10	10	40	40	—	—
1957	—	—	15	15	35	35	—	—
1958	—	—	20	20	30	30	—	—
1959–1963	—	—	25	25	25	25	—	—
1964	1	1	25	25	24	24	—	—
1965	4	4	25	25	21	21	—	—
1966	12	12	25	25	13	13	—	—
1967 and subsequent years	25	25	25	25	—	—	—	—

*These are percentages of the estimated tax liability on income of the current year.
†These are percentages of the tax liability on income of the previous year.

B. NOTE ON INVESTMENT TAX CREDIT[1]

A tax credit subsidy for business purchases of capital goods was first enacted by the U.S. Congress in 1962. Its purpose was twofold. First, the United States was emerging from a small economic recession in 1961, and it was hoped that the credit would encourage business spending for new plants and equipment. While the prime goal of the credit probably was to bolster a sagging economy, it also promised a substantial secondary benefit. For a number of years trade groups from numerous basic American industries had complained that European producers with lower labor costs and more modern physical facilities were slowly exporting more and more of their production to the United States. It was hoped that a tax subsidy encouraging new investment in capital goods would allow American producers to modernize their facilities and reduce their costs enough to be more competitive in the U.S. market with European producers.

Between 1962 and 1968, the investment credit underwent several revisions. It was "permanently" repealed (there had been a temporary suspension in 1966) by the Tax Reform Act of 1969. Because of a continuing business recession and rising unemployment in 1971, the investment tax credit was reenacted in the Revenue Act of 1971 under the name "job-development credit." As the law stood after reenactment, a purchaser of "Sec. 38"[2] property could deduct from his federal income tax liability 7% of the cost of new "Sec. 38" property in the year it was purchased, so long as the property had an expected useful life of seven years or more. For property with a life of from five to seven years the credit was equal to two thirds of this 7%, and for property with a useful life of three to five years the credit was equal to one third of 7%. Property with a useful life of less than three years did not qualify for the credit. (Under the old investment tax credit repealed in 1969, the required lives were one year longer; that is, the upper limit was eight years and the lower limit was four years.)

The investment credit was increased from 7% to 10% for qualified business property acquired and placed in service after January 21, 1975. Corporate tax-

---

1 This statement has been prepared for use in connection with cases in this book. It is not a definitive statement, and it should not be used as a reference for general purposes.

2 For purposes of the credit, "Sec. 38" property is defined as all depreciable property (not including buildings) used as an integral part of (a) manufacturing, (b) mining, (c) production, and (d) furnishings of services such as transportation, energy, water, and sewage disposal.

payers were allowed an additional 1% credit for qualified investment if an amount equal to the 1% credit were contributed to an employee stock ownership plan (ESOP). Starting in 1977, an additional 0.5% credit could be claimed if the employer contributed this extra amount to the ESOP and it was matched by employee contributions to the ESOP. Starting after September 30, 1978, an additional 10% investment credit was available for designated "energy property" (see p. 364 of the Pressco, Inc. [Abridged] case). The definition of "useful life" remained unchanged. Various changes, too specialized to describe here, were made in the definition of qualified property eligible for the investment credit. Under the current law, subject to certain limitations, up to $100,000 of the cost of used property may be taken into account in calculating the credit for any one year.

The investment tax credit does not act to reduce the basis for depreciation of equipment; however, the same time span of useful life must be used for calculating the investment tax credit as is used for taking depreciation deductions.

The investment tax credit represents a direct credit against the total income tax liability. For a company in the 46% tax bracket, a tax credit of $100,000 can save as much in income taxes as a $217,391 deduction from pretax income. Taxpayers who have a total tax liability of $25,000 or less are allowed to credit up to 100% of the liability. For those whose tax liability exceeds $25,000, the limit on the credit is $25,000 plus the following percentage of the liability in excess of $25,000.

1979	60%
1980	70
1981	80
1982 or thereafter	90

Any credit that cannot be used currently may be carried back for three years and forward for seven years.

TAX VERSUS BOOK ACCOUNTING

Internal revenue regulations require corporations to take the investment tax credit in their tax accounting to the maximum allowable amount in the year it arises. In reports of earnings to shareholders, however, public accounting firms permit the credit to be handled by either of two methods. The entire credit can be taken in a single year, as it is for tax purposes, or it can be spread out and taken over the productive lives of the assets giving rise to the credit. The American Institute of Certified Public Accountants, in a survey of 600 major companies, found that over 86% of these companies adopted the former, the "flow-through," treatment.[3] This method results immediately in higher reported earnings.

---

[3] AICPA, *Accounting Trends and Techniques*, 33d ed. (New York: 1979), p. 261.

Exhibit 1 shows how the accounting convention chosen can affect the after-tax income reported by a corporation to its shareholders.

Exhibit 1

ACME CORPORATION

	Tax Accounts	Shareholder Reports One-Year *Lump Sum*	Shareholder Reports *Spread Over Eight Years*
Purchases of new "Sec. 38" property......	$2,000,000	$2,000,000	$2,000,000
Profit before federal income tax..........	800,000	800,000	800,000
Federal income tax before credit*.........	400,000	400,000	400,000
Less: Investment tax credit............	200,000	200,000	25,000
Federal income tax after credit...........	200,000	200,000	375,000
Profit after taxes.................	$ 600,000	$ 600,000	$ 425,000

* For convenience, a 50% tax rate is assumed.

In 1967, the Accounting Principles Board (APB) of the American Institute of Certified Public Accountants proposed to eliminate the "flow-through" option allowing corporations to take the entire amount of the credit in a single year in reports of earnings to shareholders. Instead, corporations would be required to adopt the "deferral" approach and spread the tax saving over the lives of the assets giving rise to the credit. The APB argued that a corporation's after-tax profit as reported to shareholders was subject to great distortion if the entire credit was taken in a single year.

Permitting the investment credit to flow through to net income in the period when the benefit is used to reduce income taxes payable may result in increasing or decreasing reported net income solely by reason of the timing of acquisition, rather than the use, of property. The result is inconsistent with the accepted concept that income results from the use and not from the acquisition of assets. Allocation of the investment credit to those periods in which the property that gives rise to the credit is utilized associates the income effects of the credit with the use of the property, not its acquisition.[4]

In response to the proposed change, the APB was deluged with nearly 1,000 letters concerning the proposal from corporate financial officers, a large portion of whom were critical of the APB's investment tax credit proposal. The officers of those companies whose reported earnings would be affected most (for example, airlines and equipment leasing companies) were the most vocal opponents, but many other businessmen and even government representatives jumped into the fray. The Assistant Secretary for Tax Policy of the U.S. Treasury Department charged that the board's proposed treatment of the investment tax credit could well blunt its effectiveness as an incentive to modernization and expansion.

---

[4] "Exposure Draft, Proposed APB Opinion: Accounting for Income Taxes," *Accounting Principles Board*, September 14, 1967, paragraph 58b.

Again, when the investment tax credit was reenacted in 1971, the accounting profession made an attempt to tighten the rules governing the financial reporting of the 7% investment tax credit. The APB had the support of the SEC for its ruling that companies would have to report tax savings in income statements over the useful life of the property involved, and the ruling would have specifically disallowed the flow-through accounting method. However, the Senate, with the formal approval of the Nixon administration, vetoed the attempt and in fact inserted into the law a provision that "no taxpayer shall be required to use for the purposes of financial reports . . . any particular method of accounting for the credit allowed by such Section 38." The taxpayer must disclose in his reports the method he uses in accounting for the credit and must use the same method in all financial reports.

C. PRESENT VALUE TABLES

Table C-1

PRESENT VALUE OF $1

Periods until Payment	1%	2%	2½%	3%	4%	5%	6%	8%	10%	12%	14%	15%	16%	18%	20%	22%	24%	25%	26%	30%	40%	50%
1	0.990	0.980	0.976	0.971	0.962	0.952	0.943	0.926	0.909	0.893	0.877	0.870	0.862	0.847	0.833	0.820	0.806	0.800	0.794	0.769	0.714	0.667
2	0.980	0.961	0.952	0.943	0.925	0.907	0.890	0.857	0.826	0.797	0.769	0.756	0.743	0.718	0.694	0.672	0.650	0.640	0.630	0.592	0.510	0.444
3	0.971	0.942	0.929	0.915	0.889	0.864	0.840	0.794	0.751	0.712	0.675	0.658	0.641	0.609	0.579	0.551	0.524	0.512	0.500	0.455	0.364	0.296
4	0.961	0.924	0.906	0.888	0.855	0.823	0.792	0.735	0.683	0.636	0.592	0.572	0.552	0.516	0.482	0.451	0.423	0.410	0.397	0.350	0.260	0.198
5	0.951	0.906	0.884	0.863	0.822	0.784	0.747	0.681	0.621	0.567	0.519	0.497	0.476	0.437	0.402	0.370	0.341	0.328	0.315	0.269	0.186	0.132
6	0.942	0.888	0.862	0.837	0.790	0.746	0.705	0.630	0.564	0.507	0.456	0.432	0.410	0.370	0.335	0.303	0.275	0.262	0.250	0.207	0.133	0.088
7	0.933	0.871	0.841	0.813	0.760	0.711	0.665	0.583	0.513	0.452	0.400	0.376	0.354	0.314	0.279	0.249	0.222	0.210	0.198	0.159	0.095	0.059
8	0.923	0.853	0.821	0.789	0.731	0.677	0.627	0.540	0.467	0.404	0.351	0.327	0.305	0.266	0.233	0.204	0.179	0.168	0.157	0.123	0.068	0.039
9	0.914	0.837	0.801	0.766	0.703	0.645	0.592	0.500	0.424	0.361	0.308	0.284	0.263	0.225	0.194	0.167	0.144	0.134	0.125	0.094	0.048	0.026
10	0.905	0.820	0.781	0.744	0.676	0.614	0.558	0.463	0.386	0.322	0.270	0.247	0.227	0.191	0.162	0.137	0.116	0.107	0.099	0.073	0.035	0.017
11	0.896	0.804	0.762	0.722	0.650	0.585	0.527	0.429	0.350	0.287	0.237	0.215	0.195	0.162	0.135	0.112	0.094	0.086	0.079	0.056	0.025	0.012
12	0.887	0.788	0.744	0.701	0.625	0.557	0.497	0.397	0.319	0.257	0.208	0.187	0.168	0.137	0.112	0.092	0.076	0.069	0.062	0.043	0.018	0.008
13	0.879	0.773	0.725	0.681	0.601	0.530	0.469	0.368	0.290	0.229	0.182	0.163	0.145	0.116	0.093	0.075	0.061	0.055	0.050	0.033	0.013	0.005
14	0.870	0.758	0.708	0.661	0.577	0.505	0.442	0.340	0.263	0.205	0.160	0.141	0.125	0.099	0.078	0.062	0.049	0.044	0.039	0.025	0.009	0.003
15	0.861	0.743	0.690	0.642	0.555	0.481	0.417	0.315	0.239	0.183	0.140	0.123	0.108	0.084	0.065	0.051	0.040	0.035	0.031	0.020	0.006	0.002
16	0.853	0.728	0.674	0.623	0.534	0.458	0.394	0.292	0.218	0.163	0.123	0.107	0.093	0.071	0.054	0.042	0.032	0.028	0.025	0.015	0.005	0.002
17	0.844	0.714	0.657	0.605	0.513	0.436	0.371	0.270	0.198	0.146	0.108	0.093	0.080	0.060	0.045	0.034	0.026	0.023	0.020	0.012	0.003	0.001
18	0.836	0.700	0.641	0.587	0.494	0.416	0.350	0.250	0.180	0.130	0.095	0.081	0.069	0.051	0.038	0.028	0.021	0.018	0.016	0.009	0.002	0.001
19	0.828	0.686	0.626	0.570	0.475	0.396	0.331	0.232	0.164	0.116	0.083	0.070	0.060	0.043	0.031	0.023	0.017	0.014	0.012	0.007	0.002	0.001
20	0.820	0.673	0.610	0.554	0.456	0.377	0.312	0.215	0.149	0.104	0.073	0.061	0.051	0.037	0.026	0.019	0.014	0.012	0.010	0.005	0.001	
21	0.811	0.660	0.595	0.538	0.439	0.359	0.294	0.199	0.135	0.093	0.064	0.053	0.044	0.031	0.022	0.015	0.011	0.009	0.008	0.004	0.001	
22	0.803	0.647	0.581	0.522	0.422	0.342	0.278	0.184	0.123	0.083	0.056	0.046	0.038	0.026	0.018	0.013	0.009	0.007	0.006	0.003	0.001	
23	0.795	0.634	0.567	0.507	0.406	0.326	0.262	0.170	0.112	0.074	0.049	0.040	0.033	0.022	0.015	0.010	0.007	0.006	0.005	0.002		
24	0.788	0.622	0.553	0.492	0.390	0.310	0.247	0.158	0.102	0.066	0.043	0.035	0.028	0.019	0.013	0.008	0.006	0.005	0.004	0.002		
25	0.780	0.610	0.539	0.478	0.375	0.295	0.233	0.146	0.092	0.059	0.038	0.030	0.024	0.016	0.010	0.007	0.005	0.004	0.003	0.001		
26	0.772	0.598	0.526	0.464	0.361	0.281	0.220	0.135	0.084	0.053	0.033	0.026	0.021	0.014	0.009	0.006	0.004	0.003	0.002	0.001		
27	0.764	0.586	0.513	0.450	0.347	0.268	0.207	0.125	0.076	0.047	0.029	0.023	0.018	0.011	0.007	0.005	0.003	0.002	0.002	0.001		
28	0.757	0.574	0.501	0.437	0.333	0.255	0.196	0.116	0.069	0.042	0.026	0.020	0.016	0.010	0.006	0.004	0.002	0.002	0.002	0.001		
29	0.749	0.563	0.489	0.424	0.321	0.243	0.185	0.107	0.063	0.037	0.022	0.017	0.014	0.008	0.005	0.003	0.002	0.002	0.001			
30	0.742	0.552	0.477	0.412	0.308	0.231	0.174	0.099	0.057	0.033	0.020	0.015	0.012	0.007	0.004	0.003	0.002	0.001	0.001			
40	0.672	0.453	0.372	0.307	0.208	0.142	0.097	0.046	0.022	0.011	0.005	0.004	0.003	0.001	0.001							
50	0.608	0.372	0.291	0.228	0.141	0.087	0.054	0.021	0.009	0.003	0.001	0.001	0.001									

Source: Jerome Bracken and Charles J. Christenson, Tables for Use in Analyzing Business Decisions (Homewood, Ill.: Richard D. Irwin, Inc., 1965), except for the data on 2½%, the source for which is Mathematical Tables from Handbook of Chemistry and Physics (6th ed.) ...

PRESENT VALUE OF $1 RECEIVED ANNUALLY

Periods to Be Paid	1%	2%	2½%	3%	4%	5%	6%	8%	10%	12%	14%	15%	16%	18%	20%	22%	24%	25%	26%	30%	40%	50%
1	0.990	0.980	0.976	0.971	0.962	0.952	0.943	0.926	0.909	0.893	0.877	0.870	0.862	0.847	0.833	0.820	0.806	0.800	0.794	0.769	0.714	0.667
2	1.970	1.942	1.927	1.914	1.886	1.859	1.833	1.783	1.736	1.690	1.647	1.626	1.605	1.566	1.528	1.492	1.457	1.440	1.424	1.361	1.224	1.111
3	2.941	2.884	2.856	2.829	2.775	2.723	2.673	2.577	2.487	2.402	2.322	2.283	2.246	2.174	2.106	2.042	1.981	1.952	1.923	1.816	1.589	1.407
4	3.902	3.808	3.762	3.717	3.630	3.546	3.465	3.312	3.170	3.037	2.914	2.855	2.798	2.690	2.589	2.494	2.404	2.362	2.320	2.166	1.849	1.605
5	4.853	4.713	4.646	4.580	4.452	4.330	4.212	3.993	3.791	3.605	3.433	3.352	3.274	3.127	2.991	2.864	2.745	2.689	2.635	2.436	2.035	1.737
6	5.795	5.601	5.508	5.417	5.242	5.076	4.917	4.623	4.355	4.111	3.889	3.784	3.685	3.498	3.326	3.167	3.020	2.951	2.885	2.643	2.168	1.824
7	6.728	6.472	6.349	6.230	6.002	5.786	5.582	5.206	4.868	4.564	4.288	4.160	4.039	3.812	3.605	3.416	3.242	3.161	3.083	2.802	2.263	1.883
8	7.652	7.325	7.170	7.020	6.733	6.463	6.210	5.747	5.335	4.968	4.639	4.487	4.344	4.078	3.837	3.619	3.421	3.329	3.241	2.925	2.331	1.922
9	8.566	8.162	7.971	7.786	7.435	7.108	6.802	6.247	5.759	5.328	4.946	4.772	4.607	4.303	4.031	3.786	3.566	3.463	3.366	3.019	2.379	1.948
10	9.471	8.983	8.752	8.530	8.111	7.722	7.360	6.710	6.145	5.650	5.216	5.019	4.833	4.494	4.192	3.923	3.682	3.571	3.465	3.092	2.414	1.965
11	10.368	9.787	9.514	9.253	8.760	8.306	7.887	7.139	6.495	5.938	5.453	5.234	5.029	4.656	4.327	4.035	3.776	3.656	3.544	3.147	2.438	1.977
12	11.255	10.575	10.258	9.954	9.385	8.863	8.384	7.536	6.814	6.194	5.660	5.421	5.197	4.793	4.439	4.127	3.851	3.725	3.606	3.190	2.456	1.985
13	12.134	11.348	10.983	10.635	9.986	9.394	8.853	7.904	7.103	6.424	5.842	5.583	5.342	4.910	4.533	4.203	3.912	3.780	3.656	3.223	2.468	1.990
14	13.004	12.106	11.691	11.296	10.563	9.899	9.295	8.244	7.367	6.628	6.002	5.724	5.468	5.008	4.611	4.265	3.962	3.824	3.695	3.249	2.478	1.993
15	13.865	12.849	12.381	11.938	11.118	10.380	9.712	8.559	7.606	6.811	6.142	5.847	5.576	5.092	4.676	4.315	4.001	3.859	3.726	3.268	2.484	1.995
16	14.718	13.578	13.055	12.561	11.652	10.838	10.106	8.851	7.824	6.974	6.265	5.954	5.668	5.162	4.730	4.357	4.033	3.887	3.751	3.283	2.488	1.997
17	15.562	14.292	13.712	13.166	12.166	11.274	10.477	9.122	8.022	7.120	6.373	6.047	5.749	5.222	4.775	4.391	4.059	3.910	3.771	3.295	2.492	1.998
18	16.398	14.992	14.353	13.754	12.659	11.690	10.828	9.372	8.201	7.250	6.467	6.128	5.818	5.273	4.812	4.419	4.080	3.928	3.786	3.304	2.494	1.999
19	17.226	15.678	14.979	14.324	13.134	12.085	11.158	9.604	8.365	7.366	6.550	6.198	5.878	5.316	4.844	4.442	4.097	3.942	3.799	3.311	2.496	1.999
20	18.046	16.351	15.589	14.877	13.590	12.462	11.470	9.818	8.514	7.469	6.623	6.259	5.929	5.353	4.870	4.460	4.110	3.954	3.808	3.316	2.497	1.999
21	18.857	17.011	16.185	15.415	14.029	12.821	11.764	10.017	8.649	7.562	6.687	6.312	5.973	5.384	4.891	4.476	4.121	3.963	3.816	3.320	2.498	2.000
22	19.660	17.658	16.765	15.937	14.451	13.163	12.042	10.201	8.772	7.645	6.743	6.359	6.011	5.410	4.909	4.488	4.130	3.970	3.822	3.323	2.498	2.000
23	20.456	18.292	17.332	16.444	14.857	13.489	12.303	10.371	8.883	7.718	6.792	6.399	6.044	5.432	4.924	4.499	4.137	3.976	3.827	3.325	2.499	2.000
24	21.243	18.914	17.885	16.936	15.247	13.799	12.550	10.529	8.985	7.784	6.835	6.434	6.073	5.451	4.937	4.507	4.143	3.981	3.831	3.327	2.499	2.000
25	22.023	19.523	18.424	17.413	15.622	14.094	12.783	10.675	9.077	7.843	6.873	6.464	6.097	5.467	4.948	4.514	4.147	3.985	3.834	3.329	2.499	2.000
26	22.795	20.121	18.951	17.877	15.983	14.375	13.003	10.810	9.161	7.896	6.906	6.491	6.118	5.480	4.956	4.520	4.151	3.988	3.837	3.330	2.500	2.000
27	23.560	20.707	19.464	18.327	16.330	14.643	13.211	10.935	9.237	7.943	6.935	6.514	6.136	5.492	4.964	4.524	4.154	3.990	3.839	3.331	2.500	2.000
28	24.316	21.281	19.965	18.764	16.663	14.898	13.406	11.051	9.307	7.984	6.961	6.534	6.152	5.502	4.970	4.528	4.157	3.992	3.840	3.331	2.500	2.000
29	25.066	21.844	20.454	19.188	16.984	15.141	13.591	11.158	9.370	8.022	6.983	6.551	6.166	5.510	4.975	4.531	4.159	3.994	3.841	3.332	2.500	2.000
30	25.808	22.396	20.930	19.600	17.292	15.372	13.765	11.258	9.427	8.055	7.003	6.566	6.177	5.517	4.979	4.534	4.160	3.995	3.842	3.332	2.500	2.000
40	32.835	27.355	25.103	23.115	19.793	17.159	15.046	11.925	9.779	8.244	7.105	6.642	6.234	5.548	4.997	4.544	4.166	3.999	3.846	3.333	2.500	2.000
50	39.196	31.424	28.362	25.730	21.482	18.256	15.762	12.233	9.915	8.304	7.133	6.660	6.246	5.554	4.999	4.545	4.167	4.000	3.846	3.333	2.500	2.000

SOURCE: Jerome Bracken and Charles J. Christenson, *Tables for Use in Analyzing Business Decisions* (Homewood, Ill.: Richard D. Irwin, Inc., 1965), except for the data on 2½%, the source for which is *Mathematical Tables from Handbook of Chemistry and Physics* (6th ed.; Cleveland: Chemical Rubber Publishing Co., 1938).

YEAR-END ACCUMULATIONS

Table C–3 shows the year-end accumulation at various effective annual interest rates[1] of $1 received in periodic installments during the year. Observe that fractional interest rates appear at the bottom of the table.

Each period's installment is assumed to be received at the *end* of the period. For example, the entries in the column for a one-half-year period show the accumulation one year from now of two $0.50 payments the first of which is received one-half-year from now, the second one year from now.

The entries in the column for a 0 period show the year-end accumulation of $1 received "continuously" during the year. More accurately, they show the limit approached by the accumulation of $1 received in periodic installments as the period between installments approaches 0.

Example. At 10 percent effective annual interest, $1 received in installments of $0.25 each at the end of each quarter of a year will accumulate to $1.037 at the end of the year.

---

[1] If a single payment of $1 accumulates in one year to $(1 + i)$, the "effective annual" rate of interest is i or $100i$ percent.

Table C-3. YEAR-END ACCUMULATION OF $1

Interest Rate	Period						
	1 year	½ year	¼ year	1 month	1 week	1 day	0
.01	1.000	1.002	1.004	1.005	1.005	1.005	1.005
.02	1.000	1.005	1.007	1.009	1.010	1.010	1.010
.03	1.000	1.007	1.011	1.014	1.015	1.015	1.015
.04	1.000	1.010	1.015	1.018	1.019	1.020	1.020
.05	1.000	1.012	1.019	1.023	1.024	1.025	1.025
.06	1.000	1.015	1.022	1.027	1.029	1.030	1.030
.07	1.000	1.017	1.026	1.032	1.034	1.035	1.035
.08	1.000	1.020	1.030	1.036	1.039	1.039	1.039
.09	1.000	1.022	1.033	1.041	1.043	1.044	1.044
.10	1.000	1.024	1.037	1.045	1.048	1.049	1.049
.11	1.000	1.027	1.040	1.049	1.053	1.054	1.054
.12	1.000	1.029	1.044	1.054	1.058	1.059	1.059
.13	1.000	1.032	1.048	1.058	1.062	1.063	1.064
.14	1.000	1.034	1.051	1.063	1.067	1.068	1.068
.15	1.000	1.036	1.055	1.067	1.072	1.073	1.073
.16	1.000	1.039	1.058	1.071	1.076	1.078	1.078
.17	1.000	1.041	1.062	1.076	1.081	1.083	1.083
.18	1.000	1.043	1.065	1.080	1.086	1.087	1.088
.19	1.000	1.045	1.069	1.084	1.090	1.092	1.092
.20	1.000	1.048	1.072	1.089	1.095	1.097	1.097
.21	1.000	1.050	1.076	1.093	1.100	1.101	1.102
.22	1.000	1.052	1.079	1.097	1.104	1.106	1.106
.23	1.000	1.055	1.083	1.101	1.109	1.111	1.111
.24	1.000	1.057	1.086	1.106	1.113	1.115	1.116
.25	1.000	1.059	1.089	1.110	1.118	1.120	1.120
.26	1.000	1.061	1.093	1.114	1.122	1.125	1.125
.27	1.000	1.063	1.096	1.118	1.127	1.129	1.130
.28	1.000	1.066	1.100	1.123	1.132	1.134	1.134
.29	1.000	1.068	1.103	1.127	1.136	1.138	1.139
.30	1.000	1.070	1.106	1.131	1.141	1.143	1.143
.35	1.000	1.081	1.123	1.152	1.163	1.166	1.166
.40	1.000	1.092	1.140	1.172	1.185	1.188	1.189
.45	1.000	1.102	1.156	1.192	1.207	1.210	1.211
.50	1.000	1.112	1.172	1.212	1.228	1.232	1.233
.55	1.000	1.122	1.187	1.232	1.250	1.254	1.255
.60	1.000	1.132	1.203	1.252	1.271	1.276	1.277
.70	1.000	1.152	1.234	1.290	1.312	1.318	1.319
.80	1.000	1.171	1.263	1.328	1.353	1.360	1.361
.90	1.000	1.189	1.293	1.365	1.394	1.401	1.402
1.00	1.000	1.207	1.321	1.401	1.433	1.441	1.443
.0250	1.000	1.006	1.009	1.011	1.012	1.012	1.012
.0275	1.000	1.007	1.010	1.013	1.013	1.014	1.014
.0300	1.000	1.007	1.011	1.014	1.015	1.015	1.015
.0325	1.000	1.008	1.012	1.015	1.016	1.016	1.016
.0350	1.000	1.009	1.013	1.016	1.017	1.017	1.017
.0375	1.000	1.009	1.014	1.017	1.018	1.019	1.019
.0400	1.000	1.010	1.015	1.018	1.019	1.020	1.020
.0425	1.000	1.011	1.016	1.019	1.021	1.021	1.021
.0450	1.000	1.011	1.017	1.020	1.022	1.022	1.022
.0475	1.000	1.012	1.018	1.022	1.023	1.024	1.024
.0500	1.000	1.012	1.019	1.023	1.024	1.025	1.025
.0525	1.000	1.013	1.019	1.024	1.026	1.026	1.026
.0550	1.000	1.014	1.020	1.025	1.027	1.027	1.027
.0575	1.000	1.014	1.021	1.026	1.028	1.028	1.028
.0600	1.000	1.015	1.022	1.027	1.029	1.030	1.030

Copyright 1966 by the President and Fellows of Harvard College.

Index of cases

This book has been set hot metal in 10 and 9 point Bodoni Book, leaded 2 points. Part numbers and part titles are set in 24 and 18 point Bodoni No. 175 respectively. Case titles are set in 14 point Bodoni No. 275. The size of the type page is 27 by 46½ picas.